# ROUTLEDGE HANDBOOK OF COACHING CHILDREN IN SPORT

"Beyond other resources, the *Routledge Handbook of Coaching Children in Sport* provides a contemporary overview of a wide-range of key topic areas associated with coaching children in sport. This book provides a breadth and depth of child-specific coaching content like no other, and is therefore important reading for students, researchers and practitioners interested (or working) in child and youth sport."

– Ed Cope, *Loughborough University, UK*

The *Routledge Handbook of Coaching Children* in Sport provides a comprehensive and extensive range of critical reflections of key areas impacting on children's sport and coaching up to the age of 16. With coaching related chapters authored by academic across various disciplines, including nutrition, psychology, pedagogy, medicine, youth development and sociology, the text provides detailed reviews of the existing state of research and consideration of the implications of these particular factors upon parents, coaches, administrators and clearly the young people themselves as well as recommendations for future research.

This new volume provides in-depth investigation to key topics of coaching topics such as Learning and Child Development, Protecting Young Athletes, Talent Identification and Development and Inclusive Coaching and finally introduce a broad array of contextual considerations for coaches from considering professional learning through to coaching in particular contexts.

This book is more than simply an academic text and it offers insights that will further inform practice in children's sport coaching. The handbook is relevant for students (UG, PG), researchers, academics, parents, coaches and administrators, as well as those interested in children's sport coaching and the related topics therein.

**Martin Toms, PhD** is a senior lecturer (associate professor) in the School of Sport, Exercise and Rehabilitation Sciences at the University of Birmingham, UK. A former professional sports coach with an MPhil and PhD exploring the sociological issues of young people in junior sport, Martin has been heavily involved in juniors sport all of his adult life. He has published widely and presented extensively around the world on youth sport, including working on international projects and for NBGs/Federations and National Governmental organisations. He has gained European and SCUK funding for youth and coaching related projects as well as being involved in international consultancy. He is a co-editor of the European Journal for Sport and Society as well as the current Editor in Chief of the International Journal of Golf Science.

**Ruth Jeanes, PhD** is an associate professor in the Faculty of Education at Monash University, Australia. Ruth's research examines inclusion and exclusion within youth sport, particularly examining how sport can be used to achieve broader social policy objectives targeted at young people. Within this, she is particularly interested in the role of coaches in facilitating broader social outcomes for young people. Ruth has published extensively in these areas with over 100 publications across journal articles, book chapters and books. She is widely cited and has been successful in securing extensive funding for her research including two highly competitive Australian Research Council grants.

# ROUTLEDGE RESEARCH IN SPORTS COACHING

The *Routledge Research in Sports Coaching* series provides a platform for leading experts and emerging academics in this important discipline to present ground-breaking work on the history, theory, practice and contemporary issues of sports coaching. The series sets a new benchmark for research in sports coaching, and offers a valuable contribution to the wider sphere of sports studies.

Available in this series:

**Professional Advances in Sport Coaching**
*Research and Practice*
Edited by Richard Thelwell and Matt Dicks

**Athlete Learning in Elite Sport**
*A Cultural Framework*
Edited by Natalie Barker-Ruchti

**Sport Coaching with Diverse Populations**
*Theory and Practice*
Edited by James Wallis and John Lambert

**Birth Advantages and Relative Age Effects in Sport**
*Exploring Organizational Structures and Creating Appropriate Settings*
Edited by Adam L. Kelly, Jean Côté, Mark Jeffreys, and Jennifer Turnnidge

**Complexity in Games Teaching and Coaching**
*A Multi-Disciplinary Perspective*
Felix Lebed

**Coach Education in Football**
*Contemporary Issues and Global Perspectives*
Edited by Thomas M. Leeder

For more information about this series, please visit: https://www.routledge.com/Routledge-Research-in-Sports-Coaching/book-series/RRSC

# ROUTLEDGE HANDBOOK OF COACHING CHILDREN IN SPORT

*Edited by Martin Toms and Ruth Jeanes*

Routledge
Taylor & Francis Group
NEW YORK AND LONDON

Cover image: FatCamera

First published 2023
by Routledge
605 Third Avenue, New York, NY 10158

and by Routledge
4 Park Square, Milton Park, Abingdon, Oxon, OX14 4RN

*Routledge is an imprint of the Taylor & Francis Group, an informa business*



ISBN: 978-1-032-05819-1 (hbk)
ISBN: 978-1-032-05820-7 (pbk)
ISBN: 978-1-003-19935-9 (ebk)

DOI: 10.4324/9781003199359

Typeset in Bembo
by MPS Limited, Dehradun

# CONTENTS

# FIGURES

# TABLES

# ACKNOWLEDGEMENTS

It is important to note our sincere thanks to the chapter authors of this book, and to those involved in the process of editing, reviewing and supporting the production process. In particular to Michael Butson for his detailed editing and reviewing.

More specifically we cannot forget those who are involved in children's sport at every level. It is for them this that book was put together and it is dedicated to those who make a positive difference with and through sport on the lives of young people.

# CONTRIBUTORS

**Martin Toms** is an associate professor in the School of Sport, Exercise and Rehabilitation Science at the University of Birmingham, England. Martin is a sociologist who focuses upon grass roots children's sport, talent identification and sports participation. A former PE teacher and professional coach, he explores the socio-cultural factors that impact upon participation across multiple contexts and cultures. He has edited and contributed to multiple sources as well as funded projects in sport. He works at an international level across a number of countries to support their development. Recent contributions aim to make a difference in children's sport – hence the idea for this book. Currently he is involved in a range of volunteering activities in children's contexts within the community.

**Ruth Jeanes** is a professor in sport, physical activity and social inclusion and Head of the School of Curriculum, Teaching and Inclusive Education at Monash University, Australia. Ruth is a sociologist whose research interests focus on the use of sport and active recreation as a community development and education resource, particularly to address social exclusion amongst acutely marginalised groups. Within this she is interested in the ways in which critical pedagogies can be utilised within sporting context to address exclusion and contribute to wider social change. Recent publications include a co-edited volume with associate professor Dawn Trussell, Families, Sport, Leisure and Social Justice (Routledge, 2021).

**Deborah Agnew** is an associate professor in the College of Education, Psychology and Social Work at Flinders University, Adelaide, Australia. She teaches sport, sport coaching and sport sociology in the Bachelor of Sport, Health and Physical Activity. Her primary research interest is athlete welfare and retirement from elite sport. Other research interests include junior sport, Australian football, masculinity and men's health.

**Matthew Atencio** is a professor in the Department of Kinesiology at California State University, East Bay, USA. He is a Co-Director of the "Center for Sport and Social Justice" which is a multi-disciplinary faculty and community leadership organisation that aims to use sport as a vehicle for positive social change. He has researched social justice and equity issues in global contexts such as France, Australia, Singapore, Japan, Vietnam, Turkey, and the United Kingdom. He has recently co-authored two books, *Moving Boarders: Skateboarding and the*

*Changing Landscape of Urban Youth Sports* (University of Arkansas Press, 2018) and *Adventure and Society* (Palgrave MacMillan, 2019).

**Duke W. Austin** is an associate professor and the Chair of the Department of Sociology at Cal State East Bay, USA. His teaching and research focus on race, gender, immigration, environmental justice, community engagement and social justice pedagogy. He is most interested in addressing racial and ethnic inequality in various settings, including childhood sports. He co-edited the book Impacts of Racism on White Americans in the Age of Trump (Palgrave MacMillan, 2021) and the ANNALS volume Bringing Fieldwork Back In: Contemporary Urban Ethnographic Research (Sage, 2012).

**Joseph Baker** is a professor in the School of Kinesiology and Health Science at York University, Canada. His research considers the varying influences on optimal human development, ranging from issues affecting athlete development and skill acquisition to barriers and facilitators of optimal aging.

**Michael Barth** is a postdoctoral researcher at the Department of Sport Science at the University of Innsbruck, Austria. Michael is an economist and sports scientist whose research focuses on sports promotion. Michael's recent interests include the application of advanced data analysis methods, i.e. machine learning, to problems related to the development of sporting excellence. A second major focus of his research is the analysis of injuries in alpine ski racing. He has published extensively in these areas.

**Haley Baxter** is a PhD candidate in the Department of Recreation and Leisure Studies at the University of Waterloo, Canada. Her research focuses on volunteer management in nonprofit community sport organisations. She is a former varsity women's ice hockey player and currently coaches children in the Waterloo Ravens Girls Hockey Club and the Woolwich Thrashers Sledge Hockey Club.

**Andrew Bennie** works on the traditional lands of the Darug Peoples as an associate professor in Health and Physical Education (HPE) and Sport Development at Western Sydney University, Australia. Dr Bennie is an interdisciplinary researcher with interests in sports coaching; Indigenous Peoples' sport participation; and teaching and learning in HPE. He is also the co-founder of Coaching Unlimited – a sport specific coach education program designed with, and for, Aboriginal & Torres Strait Islander coaches.

**John Anders Bjørkøy** is the head of research and development at the Olympic Sport Centre in Norway. John Anders is a practitioner within coach education and talent development and is particularly interested in the process of coaching in elite sport.

**Craig Brown** is a research assistant with the University of Manitoba (UofM), and also provides sport psychology services to the UofM's women's soccer team as well as through the Canadian Sport Centre Manitoba. His research has primarily focused on the lived acculturation experiences of newcomer athletes, as well as those who work with newcomers in the sport setting, in Manitoba. He has also contributed to projects exploring anti-racism in sport in Winnipeg, and an organisational equity, diversity, and inclusion review.

**Mark W Bruner** is a Canada Research Chair in Youth Development through Sport and Physical Activity and a professor in the School of Physical and Health Education. His research program is funded by Social Sciences and Humanities Research Council of Canada (SSHRC) and investigates group dynamics and psychosocial development in youth sport and physical activity. Dr. Bruner has published over 70 academic journal articles, 9 chapters, and co-edited a book, *The Power of Groups in Youth Sport.* He has been a mental performance consultant for 21 years and worked with elite youth and university sport teams, the Canadian Armed Forces, and businesses.

**Tim Buszard** is a research fellow within the Institute of Health and Sport at Victoria University, Australia, and the Game Insight Group at Tennis Australia. He specialises in skill acquisition, with a particular interest in how the constraints of sport can be scaled to match the physical capabilities of children. Tim also works as an applied skill acquisition specialist across several sports where the primary aim is to improve the daily training environment.

**Tania Cassidy** is an associate professor in the School of Physical Education, Sport and Exercise Sciences at the University of Otago, Dunedin, New Zealand. Her research focuses on sport pedagogy, investigating topics such as coach and athlete development, politics and policies of coach development/education and talent identification/development. She is the lead author of *Understanding Sports Coaching: The Pedagogical, Social, and Cultural Foundations of Coaching Practice* (Cassidy *et al.*, 2004, 2009, 2016) and *Understanding Strength and Conditioning as Sport Coaching: Bridging the Biophysical, Pedagogical and Sociocultural Foundations of Practice* (Cassidy *et al.*, 2020).

**Stephen Cobley** is an associate professor in the Discipline of Exercise & Sport Science within The Faculty of Medicine & Health at The University of Sydney. Steve's research interests examine the developmental factors inhibiting or facilitating athlete development from a bio-ecological and multi-disciplinary perspective. Steve is co-editor of *Talent identification and development: International perspectives* (Routledge, 2012); *The Routledge handbook of talent identification and development in sport* (Routledge, 2017) and *Talent identification and development: International perspectives* (2nd Ed; Routledge, 2020). Steve's research and applied work has informed the evaluation and modification of athlete development policy, programming and practice within several sporting organisations.

**Jean Côté** is a professor in the School of Kinesiology and Health Studies at Queen's University where he served as the director of the School from 2006 to 2019. He is a Fellow of the Canadian Society for Psychomotor Learning and Sport Psychology (SCAPPS) and the International Society of Sport Psychology (ISSP). Dr. Côté's research interests include the examination of (a) the interaction between youth, their social dynamics (coaches, parents, peers), and the environment for the development of personal assets and excellence in sport and (b) the factors that affect personal development, participation and performance in sport.

**Ian Cowburn** is a senior lecturer in Sport Coaching within the Carnegie School of Sport at Leeds Beckett University, UK. His research focuses on enhancing youth sport environments and experiences by understanding the influence of all stakeholders. Dr Cowburn is particularly interested in how we develop the whole-person, and the role coaches and parents have in contributing to that holistic development. He has undertaken research for the FA, UK Coaching, UK Sport and the United States Tennis Association in the areas of effective and ethical coaching and sport parenting.

**Emma Cronk** is currently a PGY-3 in family medicine at Emory University. Emma will be completing her fellowship in sports medicine starting July 2022 at Maine Medical Center. She is particularly interested in women's health and mental health in regard to the student athlete and will be continuing this research throughout her fellowship. She has been a member of AMSSM for the past six years and is the only member to win both the inaugural medical student scholarship award and resident scholarship award.

**Sean Cumming** is a professor of Paediatric Exercise Science at the University of Bath, England. He is recognised internationally as a leading expert in the study and assessment of growth and maturation in sport and exercise. Adopting a biocultural perspective, his research examines how individual differences in growth and maturity impact children's experiences and participation in sport and exercise. He has worked in research and consultancy roles for numerous leading national governing bodies and professional sports teams including the Premier League, Football Association, Lawn Tennis Association, and British Gymnastics.

**Keith Davids** is a professor of Motor Learning in the Sport and Human Performance Research Group at Sheffield Hallam University, UK. His research programme in ecological dynamics investigates constraints on coordination tendencies in athletes and sports teams, conceptualised as complex adaptive systems. He integrates ideas from ecological psychology and nonlinear dynamics to study skill adaptation in pedagogical frameworks like Constraints-led Coaching, Nonlinear Pedagogy and the Athletic Skills Model. He investigates practice, skill acquisition and talent development at many skill levels, publishing widely in sports pedagogy, psychology, movement science and sport science.

**Peter Donnelly** is a professor Emeritus in the Faculty of Kinesiology and Physical Education and founding Director of the Centre for Sport Policy Studies at the University of Toronto. His research interests include sport policy and politics, with emphases on sport for all, children in high performance sport and safe sport.

**James H. Dugdale** is a lecturer in Sport Science and Coaching within the School of Applied Sciences at Edinburgh Napier University, Scotland. James' research examines talent identification and development processes with a particular emphasis on youth soccer players. He is particularly interested in how selection and deselection decisions are made across childhood and adolescence, and factors related to youth-to-professional transition. He has published several peer-reviewed articles on this topic and has worked in research and applied roles with several professional soccer teams.

**Rochelle Eime** is a professor of Sport Participation and Director of Physical Activity and Sport Insights research group (PASIglobal.com). Rochelle is a behavioural epidemiologist with over 20 years of research experience. Her research investigates sport and physical activity participation for evidence-based decision making for the sport, physical activity, health and wellbeing sector. She has strong industry networks within the sport and health sector including state and national, government agencies as well as sport and recreation organisations. Rochelle has published extensively in sport management and public health and has received over $6 million AUD in research grants.

**Sam Elliott** is a senior lecturer in sport psychology and coaching at Flinders University, Australia. Sam adopts both sociological and psychological perspectives to examine parental involvement in youth sport. He is particularly interested in how sporting club environments set up parents' involvement at the beginning of the sporting journey. He has published extensively in the field and has presented his work internationally in Australia, China, the UK, Canada and the US. Sam is a Chief Investigator on three youth sport and parenting projects funded by the South Australian state government and a leading youth sport authority of national repute.

**Damian Farrow** is the coaching & innovation manager for the Australian Football League. He is also a professor of Skill Acquisition in the Institute of Health and Sport, Victoria University, Australia. His current roles are typical of Damian's career, being situated both in the high-performance sport industry and academia. His research and practical interests centre on the development of sport expertise with a particular focus on practice methodology and decision-making skill. He is the author/editor of 7 books and over 150 peer reviewed articles and book chapters.

**Jessica Fraser-Thomas** is an associate professor in the School of Kinesiology and Health Science at York University. She is a member of LaMarsh Centre for Child and Youth Research and PYD SportNET. Her research focuses on children and youths' development through sport with particular interest in how psychosocial and contextual factors (e.g. coaches, family, culture) influence sport trajectories and outcomes (e.g. positive youth development, participation, performance). She is a recipient of the Canadian Society for Psychomotor Learning and Sport Psychology Young Scientist Award, and the Province of Ontario Volunteer Service Award.

**Matheus Galdino** is a PhD candidate, lecturer and researcher in Sports Science within the Faculty of Psychology and Sports Science at Bielefeld University, Germany. He holds a M.Sc. in Sport Management from the German Sport University Cologne, has worked with athlete management at Red Bull, media acquisitions at ESPN, and as a strategic consultant supporting elite athletes and professional football players. He is now pursuing his UEFA coaching licenses with the Portuguese Football Federation, and his research interests revolve around football coaching, talent development and performance management.

**Brian T. Gearity** is an associate Professor, founder, and director of online graduate degrees in sport and an undergraduate minor in Kinesiology and Sport Studies at the University of Denver. He co-edited the book, *Coach Education and Development in Sport: Instructional Strategies* and co-authored, *Understanding Strength and Conditioning as Sport Coaching: Bridging the Biophysical, Pedagogical and Sociocultural Foundations of Practice*. He is Editor-in-Chief for the National Strength and Conditioning Association's practitioner journal *NSCA Coach* and serves on the editorial board of *International Sport Coaching Journal*, *Sport Coaching Review*, *Qualitative Research in Sport, Exercise, and Health*, and *Strength & Conditioning Journal*.

**Sebastian Gehrmann** is a lecturer and post-doc researcher for Sport Sociology and Sport and Education at the Department of Sports Science within Faculty of Psychology and Sports Science at Bielefeld University, Germany. He is an educational scientist whose research examines sport participation and inequality, grading in physical education, and aspirations in sport and education.

**Audrey R. Giles** is a professor in the School of Human Kinetics in the Faculty of Health Sciences at the University of Ottawa, Canada. Audrey is an applied anthropologist whose research examines the intersections of culture, gender, ethnicity, and place. Audrey conducts most of her research with Indigenous peoples in the Arctic and Sub-Arctic. She is particularly interested in ensuring that programs and policies reflect Indigenous northerners' lived experiences. She has received numerous grants from the Social Sciences and Humanities Research Council of Canada.

**Victoria Goodyear** is an associate professor in Pedagogy in Sport, Physical Activity and Health in the School of Sport, Exercise and Rehabilitation Sciences, University of Birmingham, UK. Her research focuses on understanding and enhancing young people's health and wellbeing through research on pedagogy and digital technologies. Her research is interdisciplinary, and has been supported by research councils, trusts and industry, and published in education, public health, psychology and qualitative journals. She has given keynotes and invited talks in numerous countries around the world, as well as communicating her research to policy and the media.

**Kenny Greenough** is the programme leader of all coaching degrees and a senior lecturer in Sports Coaching in the Department of Sport and Physical Activity at Edge Hill University, UK. He is an Institutional Teaching Fellow and a Senior Fellow of HEA. He holds a UEFA 'A' Licence as a Coach and is a former NGB Coach Educator whose interests lie in applied coaching practice, coaching performance, and coach learning in elite and community sport, and in educational environments. He is particularly interested in pedagogical practice within sports coaching.

**Mark Griffiths** is an associate professor of Sport Pedagogy, and head of Postgraduate Taught Programmes in the School of Sport, Exercise and Rehabilitation Sciences, University of Birmingham, UK. His research and teaching in Sport Pedagogy focuses on understanding and improving theory and practice in sport and physical education by supporting practitioner learning (teachers/coaches). He is currently evaluating the impact of several professional development programmes with UK sport organisations, and has previously secured funding from the Arts and Humanities Research Council (UK) to examine the role of community sport coaches to facilitate a wide range of individual and social benefits.

**Arne Güllich** is a professor and head of Department of Sports Science at the University of Technology Kaiserslautern, Germany. Until 2008, he served as the head of various departments in the German Olympic Sports Confederation. Arne has also been a coach for 30 years, working with athletes ranging from youth to Olympians. His major research interests concern talent identification and development, sport organisations, and evaluation research. Arne has conducted his research in domestic and international teams, cooperating with the NBA, UK Sport, and numerous national sport federations.

**David Z. Hambrick** is a professor in the Department of Psychology at Michigan State University. He is the author of more than 100 scientific articles, chapters and reviews on the origins and underpinnings of expertise. His work has been funded by the Office of Naval Research. Dr. Hambrick is co-founding editor of the Journal of Expertise – the first journal devoted to expertise – and was lead editor of the book *The Science of Expertise: Behavioral, Neural, and Genetic Perspectives on Complex Skill.* He has written about expertise and related topics for the New York Times, Scientific American, and Slate.

**Jennifer Hamer** is an emerging researcher within the School of Health Sciences at Griffith University on the Gold Coast in Australia. Her research focuses on supporting coaches to create environments that are conducive to long-term athlete health. Jennifer is particularly interested in developing strategies to encourage changes to coach language, behaviours and everyday practices to mitigate the risks of low energy availability and/or eating disorders in developing athletes. She is engaged with key stakeholders and national sporting organisations to translate research into practical evidence informed educational interventions for coaches, aiming to optimise athlete health and wellbeing.

**Jeremy Hapeta** is a senior lecturer in Māori physical education at the University of Otago. Previously, Dr Hapeta spent almost 15 years at Massey University in various roles, including as lecturer as well as their research development advisor – Māori, in the Office of Research and Enterprise. Jeremy has a rugby background, playing professionally in New Zealand and Internationally (Japan, France) and coaching in Italy. He is also passionate about teaching. Jeremy is currently the Co-Director of Te Koronga: an Indigenous Science Research Theme and Graduate Research Excellence programme. His research interests include Indigenous Sport for Development (SFD) and Sport for Reconciliation.

**Meghan Harlow** is an assistant professor (LTA) teaching in the Department of Recreation and Leisure Studies at Brock University (Ontario, Canada). She is also a research associate at York University (Toronto, Canada), and trainee member of their LaMarsh Centre for Child and Youth Research. Her research interests include organised physical activity and sport participation among children during early childhood, as well as the supporting roles of parents and coaches towards the optimal delivery of preschooler sport programs. She also works with a number of community partners to integrate experiential education opportunities into the classroom.

**Chris Harwood** is a professor of Sport Psychology in the School of Sport, Exercise and Health Sciences at Loughborough University, England. As a scientist-practitioner, he has published extensively in the area of psychosocial aspects of athlete development and performance including the roles of the coach, parents, and the wider organisational culture. As a registered sport psychologist he has worked with several national governing bodies and professional youth academies in providing services for young athletes and promoting the importance of coaching to facilitate health and well-being in youth sport.

**John Hayton** is a senior lecturer in the Department of Sport, Exercise, and Rehabilitation within the Faculty of Health and Life Sciences at Northumbria University, UK. John's research examines aspects of management and policy in and across the nonprofit and voluntary sector in respect of those organisations that facilitate and deliver community sport and physical recreation, as well as the personnel that sustain them. John has published extensively in the areas of sport development, management, policy and sociology.

**Dan Henhawk** is Kanien'kehá:ka (Mohawk) person from the Six Nations of the Grand River community in southern Ontario. Dr Henhawk is currently an assistant professor in the Faculty of Kinesiology and Recreation Management at the University of Manitoba. His research interests revolve around Western conceptualisations, and practices, of leisure and Indigenous ways of knowing and being. His current research is focussed on the tensions and intersections of leisure with Indigenous ways of knowing and being, specifically within the area of outdoor education and Indigenous land-based education.

**Oliver Hooper** is a lecturer in Physical Education and Sport Coaching in the School of Sport, Exercise and Health Sciences at Loughborough University, UK. Dr Hooper's research explores young people's experiences within physical education, health and youth sport contexts with a specific focus on the experiences of marginalised youth. He is particularly interested in 'youth voice' and the use of participatory methods to facilitate young people's meaningful involvement within research. Oliver has published various articles, papers and book chapters in these areas and his current research – on care-experienced youths' engagements with sport/physical activity – is funded by the British Academy.

**Christopher Hudson** is an established educational leader and teacher in Melbourne, Australia. He is a Doctor of Education candidate at The University of Melbourne. His research interests include rural school leadership and the intersectionality of social justice and sports pedagogy.

**Andreas Ivarsson** is an associate professor and director of Research in the School of Health and Welfare at Halmstad University, Sweden. His research is focused on strategies to promote sustainable participation in sport and physical activity. He is particularly interested in implementing strategies to facilitate self-determinate motivation as well as health and well-being within both youth as well as professional sports. He has ongoing collaborations with several sport associations, such as the Swedish Ice Hockey Association and Swedish Soccer Association. He is also a sport psychology practitioner currently working with the Norwegian female national soccer team.

**Neeru Jayanthi** leads Emory's Tennis Medicine program, is the director of Emory Sports Medicine Research and Education, and co-directs Emory's Youth Sports Medicine program. Dr. Jayanthi has been a course director over 30 times and has been an invited speaker over 170 times to local, regional conferences as well as at national academy conferences, international sports medicine, international Olympic committee (IOC) congresses and also at numerous Tennis Medicine, USTA, USPTA and PTR conferences. She has won multiple AMSSM Foundation Research Grants for his collaborative research on early sports specialised training and overuse injury in young athletes.

**Kathryn Johnston** works in the department of Athletics & Recreation at York University. Her role consists of supporting student athletes from an academic, developmental, and wellness perspective. She also holds research and consulting positions with multiple high-performance sport teams, with an emphasis on enhancing talent identification, selection and developmental practices.

**Adam L. Kelly** is a senior lecturer and course leader for Sports Coaching and Physical Education at Birmingham City University, UK. Alongside attaining his PhD from the University of Exeter, Adam is a senior fellow of the HEA, BASES CSci and UEFA A Licenced Coach. Broadly, his research interests explore organisational structures in youth sport to better understand the athlete development process and create more appropriate settings. He is currently collaborating with a number of regional, national and international organisations across a range of sports including cricket, football, rugby union, squash and swimming.

**Gretchen Kerr** is a professor and dean of the Faculty of Kinesiology and Physical Education at the University of Toronto. She is also a co-Director of E-Alliance, the Canadian Gender Equity in Sport Research Hub. Gretchen's research addresses gender-based violence in sport with a specific focus on maltreatment and the promotion of safe, healthy and equitable sport opportunities.

**Camilla J. Knight** is a professor of Sport Psychology and Youth Sport at Swansea University and University of Agder. She is also a BASES accredited Sport Scientist (psychology) and the Youth Sport Lead for the Welsh Institute of Performance Science. Utilising a psychosocial lens, her research broadly explores the area of parental involvement in youth sport with a particular focus on the experience of parents. She has published broadly extensively in the area of youth sport and parental involvement, collaborating with international teams of researchers. She also works with numerous national and international sports organisations to translate sport parenting research into practice.

**Nickolas Kosmenko** is a sessional instructor within the Faculty of Kinesiology and Recreation Management at the University of Manitoba, Canada. His research examines factors influencing First Nations athletes' sport participation, especially at high performance levels. He is particularly interested in creating more inclusive, healthier sport environments through encouraging cultural awareness among sport participants.

**Sara Kramers** is a PhD Candidate within the School of Human Kinetics at the University of Ottawa, Canada. Within the sports psychology and pedagogy stream, her doctoral research explores how competitive youth sport can become safer, more inclusive, and meaningful for all athletes. Specifically, her research focuses on supporting coaches' reflection and learning as they facilitate inclusive sport spaces and intentionally support the positive development of their athletes. Beyond her studies, she coaches a recreational running program in Ottawa, where she aims to foster young girls' positive developmental experiences through sport.

**Clayton R. Kuklick** is a clinical associate professor in the Master of Arts in Sport Coaching program at the University of Denver. He authored the book chapter entitled "Coaching Baseball with Positive Pedagogy" (2020) and co-authored the chapter "Reflective Practice to Enhance Coach Development and Practice" (2020). He serves as an editorial board member for the *International Sport Coaching Journal* and a reviewer for *Sport Coaching Review*, *Sport Education and Society*, and *Strength and Conditioning Journal*.

**Melanie Lang** is a Reader in Child Protection in Sport and director of the Centre for Child Protection and Safeguarding in Sport in the Department of Social Sciences at Edge Hill University, UK. Her work centres on violence and abuse in sport and children's rights and agency. She has trained safeguarding in sport officers as part of the International Olympic Committee's certification course, is a member of the Council of Europe Pool of European Experts on Safe Sport and works closely with national and international organisations to realise safe sport.

**Sergio Lara-Bercial** is a professor of Sport Coaching at Leeds Beckett University and the vice-president for Strategy and Development for the International Council for Coaching Excellence. He has published widely on variety of topics including youth sport and coach development. He is the co-founder of ICOACHKIDS, a global movement helping coaches put kids first in sport. He also consults for multiple high-level organisations such as Nike, UEFA and FIBA. He is a former international basketball coach for Great Britain and has coached club and community basketball for over 25 years.

**Jordyn L. Learner** is a master's student in the Graduate School of Professional Psychology pursuing a degree in sport and performance psychology at the University of Denver, USA. She is interested in the impact of sport on athletes' mental health and well-being. As a research assistant, she is involved in projects focused on the study of fun in youth sport and barriers to having fun. Recently, as a co-author, she published a systematic review of coaches' role in athletes' eating pathology. She also serves as a teaching assistant for research methods and psychology of sport injury courses at The George Washington University.

**Iain Lindsey** is an Associate Professor in the Department of Sports and Exercise Sciences at Durham University, UK. Iain's research has primarily examined sport policy and development, especially youth and community sport policy in the UK and the use of sport for development in Africa. He has published widely in sport, development and politics journals and he has co-authored two monographs: *Sport Policy in Britain* (with Professor Barrie Houlihan, Loughborough University) and *Localizing Global Sport for Development* (with Tess Kay, Ruth Jeanes and Davies Banda).

**Rhodri S. Lloyd** is a professor of Paediatric Strength and Conditioning and Chair and co-founder of the Youth Physical Development Centre at Cardiff Metropolitan University, which provides after-school strength and conditioning to ~140 young athletes. His research interests surround the impact of growth and maturation on long-term athletic development and the neuromuscular mechanisms underpinning training responsiveness and injury risk in young athletes. To date, he has published in excess of 135 peer-reviewed manuscripts, 28 book chapters and three textbooks on the topics of paediatric strength and conditioning and long-term athletic development, including the *ACSM Essentials of Youth Fitness.*

**Carla Luguetti's** overarching research and teaching focus on topics of sport pedagogy and social justice. Collaboratively and in partnership with communities, Carla's line of research aims at co-designing curriculum and/or programmes with diverse youth (from socially vulnerable backgrounds, CALD, and refugee-backgrounds).

**Brooke N. Macnamara** is an associate professor of Psychology within the College of Arts and Sciences at Case Western Reserve University, USA. She is a psychologist whose research examines individual differences in skill acquisition and expertise. She is particularly interested in when predictors of complex performance differ, such as depending on the cognitive demands of the task, the ability level and development of the performer, and the amount of training received. She has published extensively in these areas.

**Luc J Martin** is an Associate Professor in the School of Kinesiology and Health Studies at Queen's University. His research interests generally involve group dynamics in sport, with specific topics such as social identity, cohesion, team building, and subgroups/cliques. Dr Martin is on the editorial board with the *Journal of Applied Sport Psychology* and a section editor with the *International Journal of Sport and Exercise Psychology.* His research is predominantly funded by the Social Sciences and Humanities Research Council of Canada (SSHRC).

**James Maurice** is a PhD candidate in the Faculty of Education, Health and Wellbeing, at Wolverhampton University researching the workings of the coach, player, parent triad within elite academy football in the United Kingdom. He is a chartered sport and exercise psychologist and has provided support across several category one football academies in the United Kingdom and currently provides support for coaches, players and parents across the foundation phase (U9s to U12s) at a football academy in the English Premier League.

**Brent McDonald** is an associate professor and researcher in the Institute for Health and Sport at Victoria University, Australia. His research is grounded in sociology and focuses on social inclusion and social change, especially in community level sport settings. He utilises action research frameworks to engage directly with community sport practitioners to understand the issues faced in achieving sustained and equitable inclusive practice especially regarding diversity and intersectionality. His work looks to use sociological thinking as a tool to improve coaching practices and experiential outcomes for young people.

**Jonathon McKeever** is a PhD candidate in the School of Sport, Exercise, and Rehabilitation Sciences, University of Birmingham, UK. His PhD focusses on young people's engagement with social media, and the design of school-based social media practices to support young people's engagement with physical activity. Jon is an experienced PE teacher and Middle School Coordinator in Sweden.

**Colin D. McLaren** is a Postdoctoral Fellow in the School of Physical and Health Education at Nipissing University. Dr McLaren is a sport psychologist whose research examines group dynamics in youth sport teams and focuses on how various perceptions of the group environment and group processes relate to important individual and team outcomes. In particular, his research examines social identity, leadership, and positive youth development through sport. His work is published in leading journals in the areas of sport psychology and group dynamics, and his research has been funded by the Social Science and Humanities Research Council of Canada.

**Brandon Mines** is an assistant professor in the department of orthopedics and sports medicine. He works closely with athletes of all ages and is intimately involved with the diagnosis and treatment of sports related concussion. He serves on a consulting committee of the National Football League that is tasked with setting the rules and protocols for concussion diagnosis, management and return to play in the players of that league. He treats sport related concussion in the youth athletes as a part of his clinical practice.

**Katie E Misener** is an associate professor in the Department of Recreation and Leisure Studies within the Faculty of Health at the University of Waterloo, Canada. Her primary research focuses on the capacity and social impact of nonprofit community sport organisations, with a particular focus on how capacity can be enhanced to support sport service delivery and foster social engagement through sport. She has published extensively in these areas and secured a range of external research income including three research grants from the Social Sciences and Humanities Research Council of Canada.

**Tom Mitchell** is a senior lecturer in Sport Coaching, within the Carnegie School of Sport, Leeds Beckett University. Dr Mitchell has an interest in the lived experience of youth academy soccer players, the transitions they make and the role their environment plays. He is particularly interested in how coaches seek to support the development of psychosocial skills and characteristics in academy soccer players and what informs such strategies. He has published peer reviewed papers in these areas and undertaken consultancy work within professional and academy settings.

**Frode Moen** is an associate professor at the department of education and lifelong learning at the University, and Head of the Olympic sport center in Middle Norway, and is responsible for coaching and sport psychology in elite sport. Dr Moen is both a sport scientist and practitioner whose research examines sport psychology, coach athlete-relationships, coach education, sleep and recovery and executive brain functions. Frode is particularly interested in mental processes and the development of strong alliances between coaches and their athletes. He has published extensively in these areas with both books and scientific papers, educational lectures, as well as extensively practical work in these areas.

**Sylvia Moeskops** is a lecturer in Strength and Conditioning at Cardiff Metropolitan University, and a strength and conditioning coach within the Youth Physical Development Centre. She is passionate about developing young athletes' athletic performance and reducing their injury risk. Her research interests centre around the effects of growth, maturation and neuromuscular training on young gymnasts' performance. She has published numerous international peer-reviewed articles, contributed to book chapters and has provided CPD workshops for professional sporting organisations.

**Kylie Moulds** is a PhD candidate in Exercise & Sport Science in The Faculty of Medicine & Health Science. Kylie is a former tennis player and coach at the Australian Institute of Sport and has been involved with athlete identification and development programs for several national sporting bodies. Kylie's research interests examine athlete development issues from a psycho-social perspective.

**Michelle Mullins** is a primary care sports medicine physician with Rothman Orthopaedics Institute based in Florida, USA. Her clinical interests include sideline sports coverage, overuse injuries, concussion, tennis medicine, and bone stress injury management. She has authored peer-reviewed journal articles and book chapters on a range of sports medicine topics including the prevention of sport-related injury in youth athletes, concussion management, exercise prescription and exercise physiology.

**Alex Murata** is a doctoral student studying at Queen's University in Kingston, Ontario Canada. Alex completed a master's degree in Kinesiology at Queen's following time spent at The University of British Columbia (B.A. Psychology) and the University of Ottawa (Hons. B.A. Communications). Broadly, his research interests lie in the examination of how adult stakeholder behaviour (i.e. sport parents, sport coaches, sport administrators) can affect athlete experiences, athlete development, and the youth sport environment overall. Outside of his studies, Alex coaches' youth ice hockey at a variety of levels and tries to sample as many different sports as possible.

**Kacey C. Neely** is a lecturer in Sport Psychology in the Faculty of Health Sciences and Sport at the University of Stirling in Scotland. Dr Neely's research examines psychosocial aspects of youth sport, with a specific focus on stress, coping and emotion. She has a particular interest in examining issues related to selection and deselection processes in sport and the impact of deselection on athlete wellbeing. She is also interested in positive youth development through sport and how positive youth development can be integrated into grassroot sport programs. She has published several peer-reviewed papers in both of these areas and works with various sport organisations in the UK and Canada.

**Rachael A. Newport** has recently been awarded a PhD from Swansea University, where she undertook research to understand the parent journey within youth academy football and developed a parent support programme. She has a particular interest in how parents can be better supported within youth sport and has presented at a number of international conferences. She is a BPS Chartered and HCPC Registered Sport and Exercise Psychologist running her own business providing support to parents and athletes. She currently works for Disability Sport Wales undertaking research to provide insight and develop learning opportunities to improve the experiences of disabled people within sport.

**Justen P O'Connor** is an associate professor in the school of Teaching and Inclusive Education within the Faculty of Education at Monash University, Australia. Dr O'Connor's research focuses on transforming existing community sport towards more inclusive practice and progressing alternative informal forms of participation in both community and education settings. Justen has an interest in coaching and teaching practices within sport and educational settings. Justen has published extensively in related areas and secured a range of external research income including an Australian Research Council project focused on community sport engagement.

**Jimmy O'Gorman** is a senior lecturer in Sports Development, Management and Coaching in the Department of Sport and Physical Activity where he teaches on the undergraduate Sports Development, Management and Coaching, and the MSc Sport, Physical Activity and Mental Health programmes. Dr O'Gorman is also a member of the Centre for Child Protection and Safeguarding in Sport (CPSS). His research is underpinned by sociological and political science perspectives and focuses on the welfare and well-being of sports workers, coach education, and the development, implementation, and enactment of sport policy and programmes, ranging from community/grassroots to participation and performance contexts.

**Jon L. Oliver** is a professor of Applied Paediatric Exercise Science at Cardiff Metropolitan University, where he co-founded the Youth Physical Development Centre. Dr Oliver is also an adjunct professor at the Sports Performance Research Institute New Zealand. His research interests focus on three interlinking themes of long-term athlete development; physical performance, injury risk and health and wellbeing of young athletes. Jon has published over 150 international peer-review articles, contributed to numerous consensus and position statements and worked with a host of sports and professional organisations.

**Anthony Papathomas** is a senior Lecturer in Sport and Exercise Psychology within the School of Sport, Exercise, and Health Sciences at Loughborough University. Dr Papathomas has written extensively on mental health issues across a variety of sport and exercise contexts. Anthony's principal research focus addresses athlete experiences of body dissatisfaction and disordered eating in sport. His work has been funded by organisations such as the English Institute of Sport and the International Olympic Committee. As a prominent science communicator, he has advanced thinking on how sport psychologists and other practitioners should manage athlete disordered eating in an ethical way.

**Maria Luisa Fernanda Pereira Vargas** is a doctoral researcher in the School of Sport, Exercise and Health Sciences at Loughborough University, UK. Luisa's research focuses on athlete experiences of mental illness within sport using a range of qualitative methods. She has published in the areas of disordered eating and mental illness in sport.

**David Piggott** is a senior lecturer in Sport Coaching and leads the MSc programmes in coaching and coach development at Leeds Beckett University. Dr Piggott has a diverse range of research interests, from coach development to the psychology of peak performance and the philosophy of knowledge. He has undertaken large funded research and consultancy projects for Uefa, the ECB, the FA and UK Sport.

**Shane Pill**, is an associate professor in the College of Education, Psychology and Social Work at Flinders University, Adelaide, Australia. A former HPE teacher of 18 years, since 2016 he now teaches and researches in physical education, sport coaching and development, pedagogy and curriculum studies. Dr Pill has published extensively, and has collaborated and consulted widely with state and national sport and education organisations. He is author of the popular Play with Purpose series of resources, as well as books published by Routledge on Athlete-Centred Coaching, Game-based Coaching, and The Spectrum of Teaching and Coaching Styles.

**Gary Priest** is a PhD Candidate in the School of Sport, Exercise and Rehabilitation Sciences, University of Birmingham, UK. His research seeks to bridge the complex research/practice gap in coach education by focusing on innovative digital training tools from which to facilitate the translation of research driven evidence.

**Erin Prior** is a doctoral researcher and University Teacher in Sport and Exercise Psychology within the School of Sport, Exercise, and Health Sciences at Loughborough University. Erin's current research focuses on athlete mental health within elite sport. Previous research explores areas such as athletes' experiences of performance blocks, and expertise in sports parenting. Alongside her research, she is a chartered Sport and Exercise Psychologist who works with a range of organisations, teams and individuals. Erin uses this applied experience to inform her research within sport.

**Laura G Purdy** research focuses on the careers and lives of sports workers in professional sport. Her recent projects have examined the welfare, representation and advocacy of sport workers in European contexts.

**Gary Putt** is a research engagement manager at Auckland University of Technology, New Zealand. His recent research, associated with a Master of Business in Sport Leadership and Management at Auckland University of Technology, explored fun in New Zealand youth rugby from players' perspectives. As a youth sport coach and researcher, his interests are in understanding factors that influence fun for youth rugby players that can be used to inform policy, administration and coaching practices that improve the sporting experience and motivate players of all skill levels to continue their involvement.

**Thomas Quarmby** is a reader in Physical Education and Sport Pedagogy in the Carnegie School of Sport at Leeds Beckett University, UK. Dr Quarmby's research centres around the role and value of physical education, physical activity and sport for children and young people from socially vulnerable backgrounds (including those who are care-experienced). Tom's current work explores how those working with/for vulnerable youth can integrate trauma-aware pedagogies into their practice.

**Jake Quinton** is a master's student in the Department of Recreation and Leisure Studies at Brock University, Canada. Jake's research focuses on exploring and understanding the experiences of gay men in sporting environments. Jake is particularly interested in exploring how gay men, who willingly choose to participate in organised sports, navigate potentially stressful environments to derive experiences of well-being from sports.

**Ludvig Johan Torp Rasmussen** is an assistant professor, lecturer, and supervisor at the Sport Science education at Aalborg University, Denmark, where he is part the research group Sport and Social Issues. Ludvig primarily conducts applied research in the intersection between sport psychology and sport pedagogy, focusing on the topic of creativity from a socio-cultural perspective. He has published extensively on the role of creativity in enriching sport experiences, sustaining sport participation and supporting personal development. His recent research on athletes' perspectives on creativity is funded by the Danish Ministry of Culture.

**Machar Reid** is the head of Innovation for Tennis Australia and General Partner at Wildcard Ventures. In his time in tennis, Machar has trained Grand Slam winners and top 10 professional players, held senior management posts in high performance and in the media. He holds a PhD in biomechanics and has published widely in the design of junior sport.

**Kyle A. Rich** is an assistant professor in the Department of Recreation and Leisure Studies at Brock University, Canada. Dr Rich's research looks at the impact of policy, community, and inclusion/exclusion on experiences in sport, recreation and physical activity programming. Kyle is particularly interested in using community-based and participatory research methodologies in order to help community organisers understand and address local issues in efforts to improve community health.

**Sam Robertson** is a professor within the Institute for Health & Sport at Victoria University, Australia. Dr Robertson's research focuses predominantly on improving the decision-making of athletes, coaches and sports organisations. This work brings together expertise from complexity science, machine learning, technology, evaluation and human performance. Sam works with more than 10 major organisations globally in sports including football, tennis, Australian football, basketball and baseball.

**Christina Rodriguez** is an undergraduate student in Kinesiology at California State University East Bay. She is interested in community interventions that support low-income youth of colour in local communities. She has participated in research studies focused on youth in sports, and specifically seeks to understand gender inclusion issues facing youth in their sporting endeavours.

**Fieke Rongen** is a senior lecturer in Sport Coaching, within the Carnegie school of Sport, Leeds Beckett University. Dr Rongen's research predominantly focuses on whether and how involvement with (intensified) youth sport contexts can be healthy. She has a particular interest in understanding how the sporting environment and specifically program staff may facilitate the holistic, whole-person development of their athletes alongside pursuing performance outcomes. She has undertaken funded research for Uefa, the FA, UK Sport, UK Coaching and Active Communities Network. She is also a TASS lifestyle advisor, supporting student-athletes in balancing the multiple demands placed upon them.

**Niels Nygaard Rossing** is an assistant professor, lecturer and supervisor at the Sport Science education at Aalborg University, Denmark, where he is part the research group Sport and Social Issues. Dr Rossing is also a part-time mental trainer in Elitesport Aalborg. Niels' primary area of interest is sport psychology and his research examines talent development and identification, inclusion within community and disability sport, and applied sport psychology for youth athletes. He is particularly interested in how community and disability sport can be organised to ensure they are successful in developing and retaining athletes.

**Martyn Rothwell** is a senior lecturer and researcher in the Sport and Human Performance Research Group. Dr Rothwell conducts field-based research that identifies key constraints on skill acquisition, sport expertise and talent development. More recently this has included adopting ethnographic and case study research methods to explore the challenges of applying contemporary methodologies to support athlete development and preparation in applied settings. He is developing a growing research profile in this area.

**Olivier Y. Rouquette** holds a PhD, double degree in Sport Sciences and Psychology from Swansea University and Université Grenoble Alpes. He is also a charted clinical psychologist (Belgium) and sport psychologist working with athletes, coaches and federations. Dr Rouquette's research in sport is aiming at providing a better understanding of how athletes' relationships with significant others could influence their performance and wellbeing. Olivier is currently a researcher and data scientist at Swansea University Medical School working with population data aiming at providing a better understanding of young people's mental health.

**James R. Rudd** is a professor in Motor Learning and Pedagogy within the Department of Teacher Education & Outdoor Studies at the Norwegian School of Sport Sciences, Norway. Dr Rudd's research explores how motor learning principles can inform pedagogical design and then evaluates the impact on learning using a combination of realist and complexity science methodologies. His theoretical grounding is situated at the intersection between ecological psychology and dynamical systems theory. He has published extensively on these topics.

**Stig Arve Sæther** is an associate professor and head of the research group Skill and Performance Development in Sports and School, at the department of Sociology and Political science, Norway. Dr Sæther is a sport scientist whose research examines talent development, sport psychology and youth sports. Stig Arve is particularly interested in the processes of talent development from a system, environment and individual approach. He has published both books and a range of papers on this topic.

**Rachel Sandford** is a senior lecturer in Young People and Sport in the School of Sport, Exercise and Health Sciences at Loughborough University, UK. Dr Sandford's research centres on issues related to young people's development in/through sport and physical activity and she has a particular interest in notions of popular culture, embodied identity and positive youth development in this respect. Rachel's current work has been funded by successive British Academy grants and focuses on care experienced young people's engagements with sport/physical activity.

**Pooja Sharma** is a physician within the Department of Family Medicine at Emory University. Dr Sharma will continue her training in a sports medicine fellowship. She has a strong interest in basketball medicine and throughout her career she hopes to create a basketball medicine program which would entail on-court evaluation and research focusing on basketball injuries, treatment, and prevention strategies. She has presented various case presentations at the American Medical Society for Sports Medicine conferences and enjoys mentoring people interested in pursuing a family and sports medicine career.

**Andy Smith** is a professor of Sport and Physical Activity in the Department of Sport and Physical Activity at Edge Hill University, UK. Dr Smith is a sociologist whose research interest focus on sport, physical activity and mental health in community and professional sport. He works with various organisations in these fields, and is Chair of the national Sport, Mental Health and Wellbeing group led by the Sport for Development Coalition. He is the Managing Editor of Leisure Studies and a former co-editor of the International Journal of Sport Policy and Politics.

**Ramón Spaaij** is a sociologist at Victoria University and also the School of Governance, Utrecht University, Utrecht, Netherlands whose interests focus on questions of social cohesion, conflict and social change. Dr Spaaij has two established fields of research that address these questions: the sociology of sport and the sociology of terrorism. He has published widely on these topics in refereed journals, books and book collections.

**Carl Stempel** is a professor of Sociology at California State University East Bay. Dr Stempel is a sociologist whose research on sport focuses on sport and class boundaries; sport, race, masculinity and militarism; and adult sport participation as constitutive of neoliberal culture. He also studies refugee migration and resettlement processes, focusing on how gender relations, discrimination, status loss and intergenerational relations influence well-being and economic integration. He is currently studying recently arrived Afghan evacuees. He is also currently studying white identity politics in the US, focusing on the intersection of racial resentment and economic egalitarianism.

**Leisha Strachan** is a professor in the Faculty of Kinesiology and Recreation Management at the University of Manitoba. She is one of the co-creators of Project SCORE (www.projectscore.ca) and also a member of PYDSportNet. Her research is focused on positive youth development through sport and how the 4 Cs (competence, confidence, connection, character) could be incorporated to promote positive youth sport spaces through coaching delivery and parent behaviours. Further, she was part of a research team exploring anti-racism policies and practices in Winnipeg and the sport experiences of newcomers in the community.

**Anna-Maria Strittmatter** is associate professors in Sport Management at the Norwegian School of Sport Sciences in Oslo and visiting associate professor at the Inland Norway University of Applied Sciences in Lillehammer. Dr Strittmatter's research focuses on sport governance and sport political processes within and outside organised sports, as well as sport event management. A special focus is on youth sport and self-organised sport.

**Brendan SueSee** is a senior lecturer within the Faculty of Education at University of Southern Queensland. Dr SueSee is a former PE teacher (20 years) who is passionate about pedagogy, The Spectrum of teaching styles, coaching styles, game based approaches, syllabus alignment and fidelity and community sport. Brendan is particularly interested in teacher's use of teaching styles to effect quality PE/learning and reducing the difficulties teachers face in implementing syllabus documents. He has published extensively on these topics and recently edited and authored *The Spectrum of Teaching Styles in Physical Education* and *The Spectrum of Sport Coaching Styles*.

**Sam Thrower** is a senior lecturer in Sport and Exercise Psychology within the School of Life and Health Sciences at the University of Roehampton, England. Dr Thrower is also a British Psychological Society Chartered Psychologist. He is predominantly a qualitative researcher, although he has conducted research as part of interdisciplinary teams using both quantitative and mixed-method designs. His main research interests lie in the area of youth sport and specifically the psychosocial development of young athletes.

**Robert C. Townsend** is a senior lecturer in Sport Coaching and Pedagogy at the University of Waikato, New Zealand. Dr Townsend's research interests span qualitative research, social science and disability studies, with an established publication record in disability sport and sport coaching. He leads several research projects developed in partnership with the disability sport sector and has secured external research income from the New Zealand Health Research Council and Marsden Fund on projects focused on ableism and community sport.

**Dawn E. Trussell** is an associate professor in the Department of Sport Management at Brock University, Canada. Dr Trussell was awarded Brock University's Chancellor's Chair for Research Excellence (2021–2024) for her work on allyship and activism in sport. Her research focuses on sport and leisure culture in the lives of individuals, families and communities and is funded by the Social Sciences and Humanities Research Council of Canada and Sport Canada. She is the President of the Canadian Association for Leisure Studies and serves on the scientific committee for the Canadian Gender+ Equity in Sport Research Hub.

**Jennifer Turnnidge** is currently a Health Education Research Associate with the Office of Professional Development and Educational Scholarship in the Faculty of Health Sciences at Queen's University. Dr Turnnidge completed her master's and doctoral degrees in Kinesiology and Health Studies. Using both quantitative and qualitative methods, her work focuses on developing, implementing, and evaluating evidence-informed resources to promote high-quality interpersonal relationships and positive developmental outcomes.

**Amanda J. Visek** is an associate professor in the Milken Institute School of Public Health at The George Washington University, USA. Dr Visek's research is focused on translational science methods to improve the quality of athletes' sport experiences to promote sustained participation. She is particularly interested in the role of fun in athletic development and motivation. Her research includes funding from federal agencies including the National Institutes of Health and Ministry of Sport, and research partnerships with the Swedish Ice Hockey Association and U.S. Tennis Association. She serves as the sport psychology practitioner for the Washington Spirit, D.C.'s women's professional soccer team.

**Casey Wagner** is a non-operative sports medicine physician and assistant professor of Orthopaedics and Sports Medicine at Emory University. Here Dr Wagner serves as the director of the golf medicine program, Oglethorpe University team physician and team physician to local high schools. Prior to joining Emory University Orthopaedics, he was the team physician for University of Arkansas, New York Jets (NFL), and Seton Hall University as well as other teams. His clinical interests include injury prevention, safe return to sports and joint preservation.

**Catherine Waite** is a senior lecturer in the Department of Environmental and Geographical Sciences, within the Faculty of Arts, Science and Technology at the University of Northampton, UK. Dr Waite is a geographer whose research examines migration, young people and career development. She uses sport to explore these topics and draw parallels and identify differences to other global industries. She has published her research on these topics in both geography-specific journals as well as journals that are more focused on sport.

**Nick Wattie** is an associate professor in the Faculty of Health Sciences at Ontario Tech University, Canada. Dr Wattie's research examines how constraints interact to influence talent identification and development in sport, expertise development and applied skill acquisition.

**Jeffrey Webb** is a primary care sports medicine physician and an assistant professor of Orthopaedics at Emory University. Dr Webb completed a residency in pediatrics at the University of Virginia and a fellowship in primary care sports medicine at the American Sports Medicine Institute. He is a team physician for the National Football League's Atlanta Falcons and Major League Baseball's Atlanta Braves as well as several local high schools in Georgia. His clinical and research interests include youth sports medicine, injury prevention, ultrasound guided procedures and sports concussions.

**Belinda Wheaton** is a professor in the School of Health teaching Sport Development and Coaching and Community Health. Dr Wheaton is best known for her research on informal and lifestyle sport cultures, social inclusion and policy, including monographs *The Cultural Politics of Lifestyle Sports, Action Sports* and the *Olympic Games: Past, Present, Future'* (Wheaton and Thorpe, 2022) and 3 edited collections. This research has been funded by UK research councils (ESRC, AHRC), an IOC research grant and Sport England. Belinda is Co-editor of The Palgrave *Handbook of Feminism and Sport, Leisure and Physical Education* and Managing Editor of *Annals of Leisure Research.*

**Pamela Wicker** is a professor for Sport Management and Sport Sociology within the Faculty of Psychology and Sports Science at Bielefeld University, Germany. Dr Wicker is a social sports scientist whose research examines sport organisations including gender diversity; the societal relevance of sport; sport participation and public health; and environmental sustainability of sport. She is particularly interested in providing empirical evidence for how sport at all levels can be better supported and managed. She has published over 150 peer-reviewed articles and secured external research income from academic funding agencies, sport governing bodies and governmental organisations.

**Carl T. Woods** is a senior research fellow within the Institute for Health & Sport at Victoria University, Australia. Dr Woods is a sport scientist whose research explores concepts of skill, knowing, learning and education in sport, with his theoretical grounding situated at the intersection of social anthropology and ecological psychology. He has published extensively on these concepts and has consulted to many national sporting teams and coaching staff in Australia and abroad.

**E. Missy Wright is** an associate professor in the Department of Kinesiology at California State University East Bay. She is a Co-Director of the Center for Sport and Social Justice and teaches courses in sport sociology, sport psychology, and research methods. Her's research and service centre around social justice and sport projects

**Paul Wylleman is a** full-professor at the faculty of Physical Education and Physiotherapy and faculty of Psychology and Educational Sciences teaching sport psychology, high performance management and mental support for talented and elite athletes. Dr Wylleman's research and publications focus on athletic transitions, (dual) career management and sport psychology support services. He is head of the university department Topsport and Study and the research group Sport Psychology and Mental Support. He is past-President of the European Federation of Sport Psychology (FEPSAC) and lead psychologist at TeamnNL of the Olympic Committee of the Netherlands.

# INTRODUCTION

*Martin Toms and Ruth Jeanes*

The study of children in sport is an area that has historically grown out of a number of separate and broader fields of study (in particular education), however one of the key issues it faces is the problem of definitions in the research, As chapters in this text reflect, both the issues of research evidence and the definition of "children" are somewhat challenging. In this book we have chosen to define children as *those under the age of 16*, however, the research evidence is more varied and studies engage with a range of ages and definitions which include: children, youth, adolescents, juniors, young people and teenagers – meaning that a clear understanding of this age group is hard to both explore and define. In turn, that means much of the research covers a broad span of ages, developmental stages and experiences. In this text we have requested authors attempt to focus their reviews on the Under 16 age groups but must acknowledge that this is more difficult than it seems in many areas and this will be visible within the sections here. The complexities of these definitions are often grounded in the socio-historic, political and cultural context of the education systems within those countries. This in itself suggests that the definitions used in research on ages below 18 need more consideration and more careful nuanced investigation. We hope in some way that this book will add to this discussion.

One of the significant aspects of research on children in sport is that, often like coaching, both funding and focus tend to be at a higher level of performance than grass roots. As such the notion that doing research on children in sport will often give high moral but low social status in terms of value and perception. However, as this book attempts to show, there are significant contributions that can be made across the multi and interdisciplinary field by work undertaken in this area.

The aim of the *Routledge Handbook of Coaching Children in Sport* is to bring in key academics in the field to produce summaries of the existing research (i.e. not simply provide an inclusion of empirical papers) in such a way that it can be used by parents, coaches, students, teachers, researchers and practitioners (e.g. those involved in coaching young people) to help understand and develop the area of coaching children in both an applied and theoretical level. The chapters herein provide a flavour of the key topics currently under examination in children's sport. The chapters are by no means exhaustive and do not claim to cover all areas that are being investigated at the moment. Rather, they provide the reader with an idea of the current breadth of research and topics under investigation at the time of publication. We certainly welcome future proposals for reviews of literature for the next edition of the book from those involved in the academic study of children's sport and coaching.

DOI: 10.4324/9781003199359-1

It has been a pleasure to have been able to work with so many colleagues to put this book together and to see the breadth of work being undertaken in this field. In particular, the chance to produce an inter- and multi-disciplinary text with so many experts providing a review of the current research within their areas of expertise. We suspect that over the next decade research will become even more focussed upon particular areas of children's sport and coaching, and will reflect the national and international policies, practice, education and agendas that continually change and develop. We hope that those of you reading this book will find answers, but also raise additional questions that can challenge researchers, academics, policymakers, coaches, parents and teachers alike. Most importantly, we hope that this book will contribute to the field and ultimately make a difference to the lives of children in sport.

# SECTION I

# Learning and Skill Development

## Introduction: Learning and Skill Development

*Martin Toms and Ruth Jeanes*

There is no doubt that one of the greatest areas of focus on children's sport is around the creation of environments, practices and engagement opportunities to allow them to learn new skills as well as develop as individuals. The use of sport (away from educational contexts) is often one influenced by social and cultural opportunities, and within this the complex nature of coach and child relationships. Whilst it is often considered that sport has many health, social and educative benefits for young people, it is the nature of the activities and the environment created for them that is so important. Without a well-considered and contextual environment for coaching to take place, then the level of learning and thus skill development will be compromised – as will the long-term participation of the children themselves. So, whilst the importance of supporting children to learn, improve and succeed in their chosen activities is important, this itself must be underpinned by the way that these activities are experienced by them, for without a positive experience then participation is compromised. The chapters in this section thus explore a number of key areas that have both a direct and indirect impact on all of these factors.

This section explores some of the broad contexts of both coaching and learning that directly influence coaching behaviour and the importance of understanding how this can impact children's experiences. Further, the exploration of the context if 'creativity' and aspects of learning that can be used to support skill development are also considered. Again, the context here is important to consider to better understand this whole process.

This section engages with a number of areas that are directly relevant to children's coaching – none more so than the growing awareness of pre-schooler sport, itself a growing area of participation and focus and probably the 'earliest' period of direct organised sports involvement. Related to this the broader discussions around the vital notion of fun are also explored, since fun in children's sport (in fact in sport at all ages) is essential for continued participation. Thus, we cannot underestimate the first engagement children have with sport and the importance of the environment we create to help them engage – skills that are directly related to our own understanding of coaching and how we as adults practice it.

The section also considers the role that psychology has on participation and learning – areas that are key to engagement – even with children. The focus around being able to coach life skills through sport and also positive youth development are important ones that need to

DOI: 10.4324/9781003199359-2

be considered carefully and contextually. Related to this the further areas of transitions within child and youth sport (and other leisure activities) are inextricably linked, as is the role of the coach on player retention and attrition. The section considers many inter-related areas that impact learning in several ways, all of which underpin engagement, which itself underpins future participation and all are areas that need consideration and adaptation in the 21st Century.

# 1

# COACHING CHILDREN IN SPORT: A FOCUS ON LEARNING

*Justen P. O'Connor*

## Introduction

As a core part of their role, coaches are tasked with providing an effective learning environment. Indeed, learning sits at the heart of children's sport coaching, yet despite its conceptual prevalence, how we come to understand learning in sport coaching contexts remains opaque. Because we cannot observe learning directly, we cannot know what precisely has been learned or indeed how it came to be learned. In the absence of a highly testable unified or unifying theory that clearly explains learning and its relationship to coaching or teaching (Anson *et al.*, 2005), there remains uncertainty as to the most effective approaches coaches can adopt to support learning. This chapter attempts to explore a sample of the literature over the past decade focused on aspects of learning in movement related to sports coaching, and where it can traverse boundaries to glean insights into theoretically informed but quite practical implications for coaches who want to support player learning.

There are many important things that can be learned in and around sport, such as interpersonal skills, socio-cultural understandings, fitness knowledge, drivers of personal motivation and embodied meaning-making. This chapter limits itself to exploring learning in relation to the development of skilfull players, particularly in relation to the playing of sports. Skill here, refers to a learned motoric ability that is relatively error-free (accurate) and performed with efficiency. Improving expertise in sport can be thought of as improving the capacity of participants to produce consistent performances in changing contexts. Skill is taken in the context of the wider game/activity, and consequently encompasses strategy and tactics. To retain a focus on learning, the chapter targets literature that ties itself to key theoretical perspectives that attempt to account for learning. The following provides brief overview of common theoretical perspectives associated with learning in sport.

## Review of Current Research

Debate abounds around learning in and across different disciplines. Within education settings there is a strong assertion that long-term memory is central to understanding human learning (Kirschner *et al.*, 2006; Sweller 2011). Here, scholars advocate for direct and explicit instruction by teachers to minimise the impact on cognitive load and aid the formation of representations

DOI: 10.4324/9781003199359-3

or memories. Others suggest memory storage and retrieval offers an incomplete explanation of learning (Jonassen, 2009). On the back of this, non-representational frameworks for explaining how individuals learn to move with skill and efficiency have become increasingly popular. That debate exists is in itself not surprising as "the acquisition of skilled movement, like the origin of the universe is associated with more than one possible explanation" (Anson *et al.*, 2005, p. 220).

Two major frameworks to understand learning in sport can be summed up as (1) an internal or computational approach and (2) an external dynamic ecological approach that comprises a direct connection (coupling) between an individual and their environment (Shaw, 2003). With the computational approach, acquiring a new skill involves the learner (re)producing and refining an ideal technique, often, but not necessarily supported through direct instruction and specific corrective feedback (Gray, 2020). Variability is progressively introduced as the learner moves through stages. Here, learning typically involves the refinement of a set of rules, mediated by symbols (representations stored in memory) and the requirement for information processing (a chain of cognitive events that produces a response, much like a computer analogy) (Shaw, 2003). This position aligns with Fitts and Posner's skill acquisition model (Fitts and Posner, 1967), Schema Theory (Schmidt, 1975) and Cognitive Load theory found in education (Kirschner *et al.*, 2006).

Two, an alternative ecological dynamics approach (Davids *et al.*, 2013b), suggests a much more direct coupling between an individual and their environment as a natural (embodied) process. In this perspective, perception and action are coupled together (Gibson, 1979). Acquiring skill involves self-organisation through exploration, often in varied environments, in order to yield individual technique('s) that offer solutions to movement tasks (Shaw, 2003; Gray, 2020). Here, the coach's role is to design variable practice activities, representative of performance contexts (i.e. match-play), that allow for the exploration of a range of movement solutions (Gray, 2020; Davids *et al.*, 2013b; Renshaw *et al.*, 2016; Renshaw and Chow, 2019). Constraints refer to those things (task, body, environment) that shape the emergence of coordinated behaviours, or that drive the self-organisation of functional movement solutions Davids *et al.* (2008). The coach manipulates constraints to facilitate exploration and the self-organisation of movement solutions. This perspective has origins in disciplines and sub-disciplines like ecological psychology, dynamic systems, complexity sciences, evolutionary biology and non-linear physics (Davids *et al.*, 2013b; Renshaw *et al.*, 2016) with ties to prominent theories that include the Constraints Led Approach (CLA) (Newell, 1986; Davids *et al.*, 2008).

Despite attempts to find common ground, these approaches are generally considered to offer alternate explanations of skilled learning (Anson *et al.*, 2005). For a detailed overview of ecological dynamics see Davids *et al.* (2013b). A third perspective, arguably more aligned with an education context (as opposed to motor learning science), can be added to the mix that sits somewhere between (or alongside) the two. Games-centred approaches (GCA's), such as teaching games for understanding (TGfU), have, according to Harvey *et al.* (2018), strong ties to discovery learning (at least guided discovery) and alignment with constructivism. Harvey *et al.* (2018), along with Light (2003), suggest constructivist approaches consider "both the psychological (individual) and social (interactionist) aspects of learning … [and involve] … conversation at both the non-conscious (action) and conscious (speech) levels" (Harvey *et al.*, 2018, p. 175). For coaches, this theoretical position proposes that representative games and activities are punctuated with more explicit questioning/reflecting moments, in order to develop cognitive understandings and game intelligence. On the basis that GCA and CLA share key features such as a holistic view of the learner; the role of the coach and design characteristics of learning tasks, arguments for merging GCA and CLA have been put forward (Tan *et al.*, 2012; Storey and Butler, 2013). Despite common ground (i.e. the modification of game constraints, coach as facilitator, and the use of game simulation), this idea has been theoretically challenged (Renshaw *et al.*, 2016; Harvey *et al.*, 2018). Harvey et al. (2012) point to epistemological differences and argue that in relying solely on the game as teacher, CLA may miss opportunities for learning. That is, learning is enhanced when it involves a degree of conscious (for example through questioning) and non-conscious (embodied interaction) interaction (Light and Fawns, 2003). Renshaw *et al.* (2016) note the strong links in CLA between theory and practice, and the emphasis on the interaction between perception and action in movement over the development of declarative or procedural knowledge about a performance.

To better understand where the field is at in relation to the learning of skills, an informal review of the literature was conducted that attempted to tie coaching to any of the above learning theories. A final set of 154 papers published between 2011 and 2021 were read, themed and broadly summarised to give some insights about contemporary considerations for coaching (elite, adult, youth, children), with considerations for implications for learning in children's sport.

## *The Manipulation of Constraints*

A significant portion of the contemporary literature that had as its focus the learning of motor skills, centres in some way on the manipulation of task, environment or individual constraints to elicit opportunities for learners to develop functional responses. This sits firmly with the second approach outlined earlier, non-linear pedagogy using a CLA. Manipulating pitch dimensions and game format was a particular focus for researchers. Carvalho *et al.* (2021) found that increasing pitch dimensions during small-sided football (soccer – U17 level) games promoted greater dispersion of players (width and length) for both offensive and defensive play, yet teams retained patterns of exploiting space in offensive and increasing player concentration in defence. Caso and van der Kamp (2020) demonstrated that players undertook more individual actions (i.e. passes) in smaller, small-sided conditioned game (SSCG) format compared to a larger SSCG format and an 11-aside match. They noted creative actions emerged most often in the smaller SSCG, concluding that SSCG stimulates variability and creativity of individual actions in football (Caso and van der Kamp, 2020).

Nunes *et al.* (2021) also explored pitch size and game formats in football (i.e. 4v3, 4v4, 4v5) and noted larger areas were associated with more running and sprinting, an increase in repetitions and in combination with a fewer number of players, fostered more tactical individual actions. Vilar *et al.* (2014c) found fewer opportunities to maintain ball possession on smaller pitches but no impact on opportunities to shoot at goal, or pass the ball. Fleay *et al.* (2018) explored SSCG in Australian football and noted smaller playing fields generated more turnovers, more ineffective handballs, more tackles, fewer bounces, lower velocities and less distance covered, compared with larger game spaces, with implications for planning training to emphasise different elements. Overall the research supports coach manipulation of playing areas to achieve particular foci. The use of small-sided games can allow for greater player involvement (i.e. practice attempts), without compromising the learning of play principles. Manipulating player spaces can produce opportunities to reinforce concepts such as defensive concentration (smaller pitches) or offensive use of space (wider pitches).

Other research that manipulated constraints explored how children's kicking (Mally *et al.*, 2011) and throwing patterns (Southard, 2011) change with a focus on increasing distance or velocity, along with external or internal cues (Southard, 2011). Increasing the focus on force/distance was effective for supporting children to explore and therefore learn to throw or kick, while an external focus produced the most accurate conditions. Constraints-based research was also concerned with how training accurately represented performance or match-play contexts as noted below.

## Representative Learning Designs

Within research focused upon constraints, was research concerned with representational design. Representational design refers to the extent to which designed practice activities accurately represent the types of experiences players are immersed in when playing the actual performative game/sport. In keeping with both the CLA and GCA approaches, practice tasks that align closely with the demands of the performance setting are believed to augment both transfer and skill learning. In tennis, Krause *et al.* (2019b) found common tennis practice tasks were not representative of movement and shot characteristics typically found in match-play. The same team found a non-linear relationship between the representativeness of the practice task related to serving and skill acquisition (Krause *et al.*, 2019c) and that improving the simulation of specific practice conditions leads to greater success and alignment with match-play (Krause *et al.*, 2019a). In football, (soccer) Oppici *et al.* (2019) presented research to suggest Futsal provided an appropriate representative practice environment for learning the passing skill, beyond what football practice alone provides. This research supports the notion that practice conditions should represent the play experience.

Headrick *et al.* (2015), presented a conceptual piece that argued for the inclusion of emotion (affect) in learning experiences that reflect the demands of performance environments whilst considering individual emotional/behavioural tendencies of their athletes (e.g. by narrating a scenario, using a vignette). For example, in the sport of long jump, McCosker *et al.* (2019) identified how athletes considered the consequences of a foul jump in round one and the implications this had on distance attained across subsequent rounds. Considering how coaches represent psychological and emotional demands in training can add to the representative training experience (Headrick *et al.*, 2015). To do this well, may require input from athletes. For example Woods *et al.* (2021) argue for the co-design of practice learning tasks to better simulate interacting constraints of competition and enrich learning environments. Representative co-design might ask a player or players, at different time points, about how well the practice task resembles game play and how alterations might improve it. In GCA's, participants are often invited to consider changes to the task constraints (rules, space, equipment). This approach in more formal coaching settings may lead to greater ownership, motivation and responsibility for learning and performance development.

## Synergies in Team Performance

Shifting the relevant scale of analysis from inside the individual (as has been the focus in computational type theoretical frames), to a level of analysis that considers the individual-environment relationship as the relevant scale (as in CLA, GCA frames) (Davids, 2015), has led to a body of research that is now exploring collective team tendencies at the sporting team level. As part of the representational design, practice task design is now being considered for how it reproduces tendencies for synergy to form between players in different phases of performance (attack, transition, defence) and understanding how collective behaviours in sports teams emerge from groups of players that coordinate as a sub-group within games (Ramos *et al.*, 2020). This research to date has primarily focused on experienced males in team sports such as futsal (Travassos *et al.*, 2011), basketball (Lamas *et al.*, 2011; Bourbousson *et al.*, 2014), football (Gonçalves *et al.*, 2014; Silva *et al.*, 2016; Memmert *et al.*, 2017; Low *et al.*, 2020) and team sports generally (Vilar *et al.*, 2012a; Vilar *et al.*, 2012b; Correia *et al.*, 2013; López-Felip *et al.*, 2018; Low *et al.*, 2020). More recently, net games like volleyball (Paulo *et al.*, 2018) and tennis (Pereira *et al.*, 2018; van Meurs *et al.*, 2021) have been explored to see relations between, for example serve receiver dyads/phases. Combat sports are also being explored as interpersonal synergies (Krabben *et al.*, 2019).

How patterns of play appear and disappear may have future implications for how training is structured. For example increasing understanding as to how different defence structures work (Frias and Duarte, 2014), how space is created in team games (Lamas *et al.*, 2011), how numbers of players impact representativeness (Aguiar *et al.*, 2015), the impact of experience on team structure (Olthof *et al.*, 2015; Menuchi *et al.*, 2018), types of passes that give a competitive edge (Paulo *et al.*, 2018), the effects of increasing pitch dimensions (Carvalho *et al.*, 2021) and positional advantage in net games (van Meurs *et al.*, 2021). In Futsal, attackers in team games showed more variability than defenders and that player behaviour was tied to game structures and intentions (Travassos *et al.*, 2011). Ball location is not as important as location of the goal (Vilar *et al.*, 2012b) and scoring was tied to changing the angular and distance relationships with defender relative to the goal (Vilar *et al.*, 2012b; Vilar *et al.*, 2014a; Vilar *et al.*, 2014b). Ramos *et al.*'s (2020) meta-analysis revealed inconsistent findings, suggesting variability promotes flexible behaviours. Another systematic review in football found higher movement regularity, wider dispersion and a shorter readjustment delay between teammates and opponents was indicative of greater tactical expertise amongst youth athletes (Low *et al.*, 2020).

In time, this work may be utilised to inform the design of practice structures for younger players by understanding how a 'knowledge of the environment' leads to the emergence of coordinated behaviours in team sports, based upon interpersonal synergies in game play (Silva *et al.*, 2013).

The data to date supports the notion that learning is likely to be helped when individuals are provided with repeated opportunities to adjust their actions relative to others and a goal in game-play conditions (Davids *et al.*, 2013a). Within children's sport, research in this area should lead to greater guidance around optimising constraints in practice and effective representative learning design.

## *Variability across Groupings*

A significant body of the literature has explored how emergent patterns of movement (individual or team) differ across different categorisations of groups (i.e. over time, ability, or experience level). This body of research has explored changes in coordination variability from beginner to intermediate gymnasts (Busquets *et al.*, 2016; Vicinanza *et al.*, 2018), differences in coordination variability in running gait between trained runners and non-runners (Floría *et al.*, 2018), in-game decision making changes across age groups in football (González-Víllora *et al.*, 2015), on-field tactical behaviour of teams with talented soccer players, differences in teams tactical behaviour during small-sided games across two age categories (Olthof *et al.*, 2015), differences in interpersonal coordination in match-play for players of different skill levels (Pereira *et al.*, 2018), variability in behaviours between elite and national volleyball teams (Ramos *et al.*, 2017), how structures and tactics have evolved over time in soccer and Australian rules football (Wallace and Norton, 2014; Woods *et al.*, 2017), how different movement solutions emerge for different groups of swimmers (Bideault *et al.*, 2013), how elite cricketers failed to exploit tactics suited to different country conditions (Crowther *et al.*, 2018) and, how kicking performances differ across competition tiers in Australian rules football (Browne *et al.*, 2019). This research focus suggests that understanding variability across levels of experience, expertise and time can help to inform playing structures and coaching with implications for younger participants.

Participants with less experience tended to show more exploration and variability in their movement patterns (Busquets *et al.*, 2016; Vicinanza *et al.*, 2018), with the exception of running where there was no difference (Floría *et al.*, 2018). In football, inexperienced players were more likely to carry the ball and miss opportunities to pass whilst exhibiting more advanced attacking capabilities than defending capabilities (González-Víllora *et al.*, 2015). More experienced players were also more likely to exploit pitch width (Olthof *et al.*, 2015). Looking at football over time, shows a progressive increase in ball speed, congestion and passing rates as players exploit stoppage times to operate at higher speed. Inexperienced tennis players spent more time moving around the court following a serve compared to the more skilled players (Pereira *et al.*, 2018). Experienced volleyballers were more likely to exploit stable conditions in setting and blocking to show greater unpredictability in attacking actions (faster tempos, diversifying attack zones) at critical moments (Ramos *et al.*, 2017). This body of research has the potential to signal ongoing trends and help develop priorities for learning (Wallace and Norton, 2014).

## *Approaches to Teaching and Learning*

Tied to non-linear pedagogy and the CLA, Clark *et al.* (2018) suggested there was a lack of sufficient evidence to advocate CLA over other approaches. Their meta-analysis came out in support of CLA approaches, yet yielded concern over potential bias in the selection of studies and adherence to foundations of CLA (Newcombe *et al.*, 2019). Other examples of efficacy for CLA as an approach include Buszard *et al.* (2014) who found improvements as a result of young children playing with scaled racquets and low-compression balls; Lee *et al.* (2014) who manipulated task constraints (equipment and rules) to learn a tennis forehand stroke; Fitzpatrick *et al.* (2018) who found improvements by scaling key features like space and equipment to enhance young tennis player movement patterns; improvements in baseball abilities using CLA (Gray, 2018, 2020) and; Moy *et al.* (2020) who provided empirical evidence to support the efficacy of the CLA in improving university students' motor performance in the hurdles. Newcombe *et al.* (2019) suggest there is more work to be done in building the efficacy base for CLA, particularly in relation to experimental design and adhering to CLA features, in particular, a constraints focus and representative learning design. Given the focus on performance and formal sport within the research, what may also be needed is an understanding of how CLA (or GCA approaches) consider the context of the child, particularly around their motives for participation and the end-goals to be achieved.

A body of work involving Moy, Brendan and Renshaw has explored how CLA gets introduced and taken up by pre-service PE teachers. Whilst not focused on coaching settings, similarities between physical education and coaching suggest this has implications for coach education approaches. Pre-service physical education teachers arrive with pre-conceived idea that a traditional, transmissive and reproductive approach is best. Following training in a CLA model, researchers were able to overcome acculturation into that approach and transition them towards viewing CLA more positively (Moy *et al.*, 2014). They found participants who used CLA were more motivated with higher levels of self-determination compared to traditional approaches (Moy *et al.*, 2016a). Participants learning about CLA felt that an underpinning theory, efficacy from a learning point of view and a way to achieve greater inclusion were significant features for pursuing CLA (Moy *et al.*, 2016b).

According to Renshaw and Chow (2019), whilst teachers and coaches are adopting the ideas of CLA, they hold concerns that the difficult concepts associated with the approach act as a key barrier to its take up and will potentially lead to poor implementation. As an example, for pre-service physical education teachers, implementing the approach presented significant challenges (Moy *et al.*, 2019). The complex nature of student learning within a non-linear informed approach meant students went unaware of multiple pupil responses that emerged from modified learning environments and they had difficulty manipulating constraints to facilitate learners' tactical problem-solving behaviour (Moy *et al.*, 2019). When considered in relation to coaching children's sport, this body of work suggests that if novice volunteer coaches are to adopt CLA and use non-linear pedagogy effectively, a professional development process will likely be needed comprising efficacy, theory and practical application.

Novice coaches may need ongoing support to progressively develop their knowledge and conceptual understandings of non-linear approaches if they are to be effective. Yet this story is not limited to CLA. Following a shift to GCA and in particular TGfU as part of the United Kingdom Coaching Certificate, Roberts (2011) was able to demonstrate how coaches struggled to use a questioning strategy, felt they had insufficient pedagogic content knowledge, and found it difficult to access appropriate support material needed to maintain a theory-informed constructivist focus. Coaches are seeking practical examples of TGfU and felt it was not part of a shared philosophy amongst coach educators. GCA's (TGfU), like CLA, present a challenging and demanding approach for coaches with a need for ongoing professional development.

## Implications for Coaches

The bulk of the contemporary literature tied to a targeted review of learning theory in sport coaching appears to be centred on creating practice opportunities that simulate performance conditions whilst allowing learners ample opportunities to explore (self-organise) varied and functional movement solutions. The bulk of the research reviewed was conducted with experienced participants, playing predominantly traditional invasion or net games leaving a significant gap in the sports coaching literature that focuses on young, novice, diverse participants with varied interests across a range of sporting forms.

This body of literature suggests coaches should spend time considering how the design of practice tasks take into consideration the learners' specific needs and current capabilities in setting up constraints that represent performance conditions, in order to facilitate opportunities for practice and learning (Orth *et al.*, 2019). The research appears far less concerned about what is happening inside the learner, rather it adopts an external focus on the relation between individual/team and context (task, body and environmental constraints). There was a lack of research in the sport coaching literature that explored the extent to which more explicit practices, such as how coach questioning or player reflection aimed at developing cognitive understandings or game intelligence impacts learning.

The complexity underpinning CLA and even GCA approaches suggests support for coaches is needed in the form of ongoing professional development. For team sports, SSCGs are being deployed to facilitate the discovery of 'skilled' functional movement. Coaches of children wanting to apply CLA, are being asked to consider how they design game simulations in practice (manipulate the constraints of task and environment) to allow learners to optimise movement solutions. Smaller playing spaces yield more passes, under greater pressure but produce less overall running. In invasion games, positioning changes when a goal is added and instability and creativity happens when attack and defence compress. Simulating phases within team games (1v1, 2v2, 4v2), presents particular information to learners that afford (suggest) action solutions as well as providing more opportunities for actions to occur between attackers and defenders. Rather than operate static drills, moving around cones, repetitive tasks, line-based drills or relay type activities, coaches are being encouraged to consider how the activities provide for variability, whilst retaining authenticity. In sports like tennis, coaches are encouraged to move away from traditional repetitive skill/drill approaches, to utilise specific practice conditions and scaled equipment in a way that more closely simulates match-play. In the teaching of skills like throwing, jumping and kicking, coaches might emphasise external requirements of the task such as varying distances to emphasise force and focus attention on the goal/outcome rather than how a particular limb might need to be positioned.

Results also suggest that movement patterns and tactical decision making differ across contexts and time in ways that suit individual, team, task or environmental constraints (for example Bideault *et al.*, 2013). In exploring differences across contexts, coaches can consider how learning might progress or differ based upon experience, with this guiding the structure and focus for practice. For example, less experienced learners tend to ignore opportunities to pass, focus more on attack and make less use of space in football type games.

## Summary and Future Directions

Through exploring team synergies, researchers are attempting to identify key points in sport that yield instability and opportunities for learning. The extent to which practice environments consider affective elements needs further exploration, particularly in relation to younger learners and how their intentions operate as constraints. The role of cognition and in particular, approaches that incorporate explicit modelling/demonstration, feedback, reflection or player questioning to develop understandings (common in CGA (TGfU) approaches), needs more research in the sport coaching context. Coaches need to be confident, particularly in working with children, that the manipulation of constraints alone is sufficient for optimal learning, or if indeed more explicit instruction, guidance and cognitively expressed understandings augment learning (Anson *et al.*, 2005; Kirschner *et al.*, 2006; Ericsson, 2008; Mayer, 2009; Tobias and Duffy, 2009; Renshaw *et al.*, 2016; Harvey *et al.*, 2018). It is quite likely, at least in the short-term, we need more than one theory to explain learning in sport coaching contexts.

## References

Aguiar, M., *et al.*, 2015. Footballers' movement behaviour during 2-, 3-, 4- and 5-a-side small-sided games. *Journal of Sports Sciences*, 33 (12), 1259–1266.

Anson, G., Elliott, D., and Davids, K., 2005. Information processing and constraints-based views of skill acquisition: Divergent or complementary? *Motor Control*, 9 (3), 217.

Bideault, G., Herault, R., and Seifert, L., 2013. Data modelling reveals inter-individual variability of front crawl swimming. *Journal of Science and Medicine in Sport*, 16 (3), 281–285.

Bourbousson, J., Deschamps, T., and Travassos, B., 2014. From players to teams: Towards a multi-level approach of game constraints in team sports. *International Journal of Sports Science and Coaching*, 9 (6), 1393–1406.

Browne, P.R., *et al.*, 2019. Prevalence of interactions and influence of performance constraints on kick outcomes across Australian Football tiers: Implications for representative practice designs. *Human Movement Science*, 66, 621–630.

Busquets, A., *et al.*, 2016. Differing roles of functional movement variability as experience increases in gymnastics. *Journal of Sports Science and Medicine*, 15 (2), 268–276.

Buszard, T., *et al.*, 2014. Modifying equipment in early skill development: A tennis perspective. *Research Quarterly for Exercise and Sport*, 85 (2), 218–225.

Carvalho, T., *et al.*, 2021. Effects of pitch dimension and skilllevel on the application of space and concentration principles in football small-sided and conditioned games. *Journal of Physical Education and Sport*, 21 (3), 1587–1593.

Caso, S. and van der Kamp, J., 2020. Variability and creativity in small-sided conditioned games among elite soccer players. *Psychology of Sport and Exercise*, 48, N.PAG–N.PAG.

Clark, M.E., McEwan, K., and Christie, C.J., 2018. The effectiveness of constraints-led training on skill development in interceptive sports: A systematic review. *International Journal of Sports Science and Coaching*, 14 (2), 229–240.

Correia, V., *et al.*, 2013. From recording discrete actions to studying continuous goal-directed behaviours in team sports. *Journal of Sports Sciences*, 31 (5), 546–553.

Crowther, R.H., *et al.*, 2018. Ecological dynamics of spin bowling in test match cricket: A longitudinal analysis of delivery speed between Australia and India. *International Journal of Sports Science and Coaching*, 13 (6), 1048–1056.

Davids, K., 2015. Athletes and sports teams as complex adaptive system: A review of implications for learning design. / Atletas y equipos deportivos como sistemas adaptativos complejos: Una revision de las Implicaciones para el diseño del aprendizaje. *RICYDE. Revista Internacional de Ciencias del Deporte*, 11 (39), 48–61.

Davids, K., Button, C. and Bennett, S.J., 2008. *Dynamics of skill acquisition. A constraints-led approach.* Champaign Illinois: Human Kinetics.

Davids, K., *et al.*, 2013a. How small-sided and conditioned games enhance acquisition of movement and decision-making skills. *Exercise and Sport Sciences Reviews*, 41 (3), 154–161.

Davids, K., *et al.*, 2013b. An ecological dynamics approach to skill acquisition: Implications for development of talent in sport. *Talent Development and Excellence*, 5 (1), 21–34.

Ericsson, A.K., 2008. Deliberate practice and acquisition of expert performance: A general overview. *Academic Emergency Medicine*, 15 (11), 988–994.

Fitts, P.M. and Posner, M.I., 1967. *Human performance.* Brooks/Cole.

Fitzpatrick, A., Davids, K., and Stone, J.A., 2018. Effects of scaling task constraints on emergent behaviours in children's racquet sports performance. *Human Movement Science*, 58, 80–87.

Fleay, B., *et al.*, 2018. Manipulating field dimensions during smallsided games impacts the technical and physical profiles of australian footballers. *Journal of Strength and Conditioning Research (Lippincott Williams and Wilkins)*, 32 (7), 2039–2044.

Floría, P., *et al.*, 2018. Effects of running experience on coordination and its variability in runners. *Journal of Sports Sciences*, 36 (3), 272–278.

Frias, T. and Duarte, R., 2014. Man-to-man or zone defense? Measuring team dispersion behaviors in small-sided soccer games. *Trends in Sport Sciences*, 21 (3), 135–144.

Gibson, J. (1979). The ecological approach to visual perception. London: Hughton Mifflin.

Gonçalves, B.V., *et al.*, 2014. Effect of player position on movement behaviour, physical and physiological performances during an 11-a-side football game. *Journal of Sports Sciences*, 32 (2), 191–199.

González-Víllora, S., García-López, L.M., and Contreras-Jordán, O.R., 2015. Decision making and skill development in youth football players. / Evolución de la toma de decisiones y la habilidad técnica en fútbol. *Revista Internacional de Medicina y Ciencias de la Actividad Física y del Deporte*, 15 (59), 467–487.

Gray, R., 2018. Comparing cueing and constraints interventions for increasing launch angle in baseball batting. *Sport, Exercise, and Performance Psychology*, 7 (3), 318–332.

Gray, R., 2020. Comparing the constraints led approach, differential learning and prescriptive instruction for training opposite-field hitting in baseball. *Psychology of Sport and Exercise*, 51, N.PAG–N.PAG.

Harvey, S. et al., 2012. Sport education as a pedagogy for promoting sport as ethical practice. In S. Harvey & Light (Eds.). Ethics in Youth Sport.Routledge: London, 107–121.

Harvey, S., Pill, S., and Almond, L., 2018. Old wine in new bottles: A response to claims that teaching games for understanding was not developed as a theoretically based pedagogical framework. *Physical Education and Sport Pedagogy*, 23 (2), 166–180.

Headrick, J., *et al.*, 2015. The dynamics of expertise acquisition in sport: The role of affective learning design. *Psychology of Sport and Exercise*, 16, 83–90.

Jonassen, D., 2009. Reconciling a human cognitive architecture. In S. Tobias & T. M. Duffy (Eds.). *Constructivist instruction.* Routledge, 25–45.

Kirschner, P.A., Sweller, J., and Clark, R.E., 2006. Why minimal guidance during instruction does not work: An analysis of the failure of constructivist, discovery, problem-based, experiential, and inquiry-based teaching. *Educational Psychologist*, 41 (2), 75–86.

Krabben, K., Orth, D., and van der Kamp, J., 2019. Combat as an interpersonal synergy: An ecological dynamics approach to combat sports. *Sports Medicine*, 49 (12), 1825–1836.

Krause, L., *et al.*, 2019a. Assessment of elite junior tennis serve and return practice: A cross-sectional observation. *Journal of Sports Sciences*, 37 (24), 2818–2825.

Krause, L., *et al.*, 2019b. Application of representative learning design for assessment of common practice tasks in tennis. *Psychology of Sport and Exercise*, 41, 36–45.

Krause, L., *et al.*, 2019c. Enhancing skill transfer in tennis using representative learning design. *Journal of Sports Sciences*, 37 (22), 2560–2568.

Lamas, L., et al, 2011. Space creation dynamics in basketball offence: Validation and evaluation of elite teams. *International Journal of Performance Analysis in Sport*, 11 (1), 71–84.

Lee, M., *et al.*, 2014. Nonlinear pedagogy: An effective approach to cater for individual differences in learning a sports skill. *PloS one*, 9(8).

Light, R. (2003). Integrating speech and action in games teaching through TGfU.*Quest*, 55(2), 161–176.

López-Felip, M.A., *et al.*, 2018. A cluster phase analysis for collective behavior in team sports. *Human Movement Science*, 59, 96–111.

Low, B., *et al.*, 2020. A systematic review of collective tactical behaviours in football using positional data. *Sports Medicine*, 50 (2), 343–385.

Mally, K.K., Battista, R.A., and Roberton, M.A., 2011. Distance as a control parameter for place kicking. *Journal of Human Sport and Exercise*, 6 (1), 112–134.

Mayer, R., 2009. Constructivism as a theory of learning versus constructivism as a prescription for instruction. *In*: S. Tobias and T.M. Duffy, eds. *Constructivist instruction: Success or failure?* New York: Routledge, 184–200.

McCosker, C., *et al.*, 2019. How performance analysis of elite long jumping can inform representative training design through identification of key constraints on competitive behaviours. *European Journal of Sport Science*, 19 (7), 913–921.

Memmert, D., Lemmink, K., and Sampaio, J., 2017. Current approaches to tactical performance analyses in soccer using position data. *Sports Medicine*, 47 (1), 1–10.

Menuchi, M.R.T.P., *et al.*, 2018. Effects of spatiotemporal constraints and age on the interactions of soccer players when competing for ball possession. *Journal of Sports Science and Medicine*, 17 (3), 379–391.

Moy, B., Renshaw, I., and Davids, K., 2014. Variations in acculturation and Australian physical education teacher education students' receptiveness to an alternative pedagogical approach to games teaching. *Physical Education and Sport Pedagogy*, 19 (4), 349–369.

Moy, B., Renshaw, I., and Davids, K., 2016a. The impact of nonlinear pedagogy on physical education teacher education students' intrinsic motivation. *Physical Education and Sport Pedagogy*, 21 (5), 517–538.

Moy, B., Renshaw, I.A.N., and Pavey, T., 2020. Impact of the constraints-led approach on students' motor performance. *Journal of Physical Education and Sport*, 20 (6), 3345–3353.

Moy, B., *et al.*, 2016b. Overcoming acculturation: Physical education recruits' experiences of an alternative pedagogical approach to games teaching. *Physical Education and Sport Pedagogy*, 21 (4), 386–406.

Moy, B., *et al.*, 2019. Preservice teachers implementing a nonlinear physical education pedagogy. *Physical Education and Sport Pedagogy*, 24 (6), 565–581.

Newcombe, D.J., *et al.*, 2019. The effectiveness of constraint-led training on skill development in interceptive sports: A systematic review (Clark, McEwan and Christie) – A commentary. *International Journal of Sports Science and Coaching*, 14 (2), 241–254.

Newell, K.M., 1986. Constraints on the development of coordination. *In*: M.G. Wade and H.T.A. Whiting, eds. *Motor development in children: Aspects of coordination and control.* The Netherlands, Dordrecht: Martinus Nijhoff Publishers, 341–360.

Nunes, N.A., *et al.*, 2021. How playing area dimension and number of players constrain football performance during unbalanced ball possession games. *International Journal of Sports Science and Coaching*, 16 (2), 334–343.

Olthof, S.B.H., Frencken, W.G.P., and Lemmink, K.A.P.M., 2015. The older, the wider: On-field tactical behavior of elite-standard youth soccer players in small-sided games. *Human Movement Science*, 41, 92–102.

Oppici, L., *et al.*, 2019. Futsal task constraints promote the development of soccer passing skill: Evidence and implications for talent development research and practice. *Science and Medicine in Football*, 3 (3), 259–262.

Orth, D., van der Kamp, J., and Button, C., 2019. Learning to be adaptive as a distributed process across the coach-athlete system: Situating the coach in the constraints-led approach. *Physical Education and Sport Pedagogy*, 24 (2), 146–161.

Paulo, A., Davids, K., and Araújo, D., 2018. Co-adaptation of ball reception to the serve constrains outcomes in elite competitive volleyball. *International Journal of Sports Science and Coaching*, 13 (2), 253–261.

Pereira, T.J.C., *et al.*, 2018. Interpersonal coordination analysis of tennis players from different levels during official matches. *Journal of Biomechanics*, 67, 106–113.

Ramos, A., *et al.*, 2020. The constraint-led approach to enhancing team synergies in sport - What do we currently know and how can we move forward? A systematic review and meta-analyses. *Psychology of Sport and Exercise*, 50, N.PAG–N.PAG.

Ramos, A., *et al.*, 2017. How players exploit variability and regularity of game actions in female volleyball teams. *European Journal of Sport Science*, 17 (4), 473–481.
Renshaw, I. and Chow, J.Y., 2019. A constraint-led approach to sport and physical education pedagogy. *Physical Education and Sport Pedagogy*, 24 (2), 103–116.
Renshaw, I., *et al.*, 2016. Why the constraints-led approach is not teaching games for understanding: A clarification. *Physical Education and Sport Pedagogy*, 21 (5), 459–480.
Roberts, S., 2011. Teaching games for understanding: The difficulties and challenges experienced by participation cricket coaches. *Physical Education and Sport Pedagogy*, 16 (1), 33–48.
Schmidt, R.A., 1975. A schema theory of discrete motor skill learning. *Psychological review*, 82 (4), 225.
Shaw, R., 2003. The agent-environment interface: Simon's indirect or gibson's direct coupling? *Ecological Psychology*, 15 (1), 37–106.
Silva, P., *et al.*, 2016. Practice effects on intra-team synergies in football teams. *Human Movement Science*, 46, 39–51.
Silva, P., *et al.*, 2013. Shared knowledge or shared affordances? Insights from an ecological dynamics approach to team coordination in sports. *Sports Medicine*, 43 (9), 765–772.
Southard, D., 2011. Attentional focus and control parameter: Effect on throwing pattern and performance. *Research Quarterly for Exercise and Sport*, 82 (4), 652–666.
Storey, B. and Butler, J., 2013. Complexity thinking in PE: Game-centred approaches, games as complex adaptive systems, and ecological values. *Physical Education & Sport Pedagogy*, 18 (2), 133–149.
Sweller, J., 2011. Cognitive load theory. *Psychology of learning and motivation*. New York: Elsevier, 37–76.
Tan, C.K., Chow, J. and Davids, K., 2012. 'How does TGfU work?': Examining the relationship between learning design in TGfU and a nonlinear pedagogy. *Physical Education & Sport Pedagogy*, 17(4), 331–348.
Tobias, S. and Duffy, T.M., 2009. *Constructivist instruction: Success or failure?* Routledge.
Travassos, B., *et al.*, 2011. Interpersonal coordination and ball dynamics in futsal (indoor football). *Human Movement Science*, 30(6), 1245–1259.
van Meurs, E., *et al.*, 2021. Interpersonal coordination in tennis: Assessing the positional advantage index with Australian Open Hawkeye data. *International Journal of Performance Analysis in Sport*, 21(1), 22–32.
Vicinanza, D., *et al.*, 2018. Limit cycle dynamics of the gymnastics longswing. *Human Movement Science*, 217–226.
Vilar, L., *et al.*, 2012a. The role of ecological dynamics in analysing performance in team sports. *Sports Medicine*, 42 (1), 1–10.
Vilar, L., *et al.*, 2012b. Constraints on competitive performance of attacker – Defender dyads in team sports. *Journal of Sports Sciences*, 30 (5), 459–469.
Vilar, L., *et al.*, 2014a. Interpersonal coordination tendencies supporting the creation/prevention of goal scoring opportunities in futsal. *European Journal of Sport Science*, 14 (1), 28–35.
Vilar, L., *et al.*, 2014b. Coordination tendencies are shaped by attacker and defender interactions with the goal and the ball in futsal. *Human Movement Science*, 33, 14–24.
Vilar, L., *et al.*, 2014c. The influence of pitch dimensions on performance during small-sided and conditioned soccer games. *Journal of Sports Sciences*, 32 (19), 1751–1759.
Wallace, J.L. and Norton, K.I., 2014. Evolution of World Cup soccer final games 1966–2010: Game structure, speed and play patterns. *Journal of Science and Medicine in Sport*, 17 (2), 223–228.
Woods, C.T., Robertson, S. and Collier, N.F., 2017. Evolution of game-play in the Australian Football League from 2001 to 2015. *Journal of Sports Sciences*, 35 (19), 1879–1887.
Woods, C.T., *et al.*, 2021. Representative co-design: Utilising a source of experiential knowledge for athlete development and performance preparation. *Psychology of Sport and Exercise*, 52, N.PAG–N.PAG.

# 2

# COACHING PEDAGOGY

*Shane Pill and Brendan SueSee*

## Introduction

This chapter identifies key pedagogical concepts informing coaching practice and subsequently player effective learning in junior and youth sport. Sport coaching is framed as an educative endeavour (Jones, 2006a) as it is centrally concerned with enhancing player education in movement, the technical, tactical and physical performance aspects of a sport. As a form of teaching (Jones *et al.*, 2004), pedagogy needs to be a focus for junior and youth sport coaching. The first section of the chapter considers learning theories that inform approaches to coaching: behavourist, constructivist and ecological. Stemming from the latter two theories, contemporary pedagogical models subject to much of the recent research and scholarship in sport coaching will be reviewed, and the implications for children and youth sport coaching considered with respect to their motivation to continue in sport: perceived competence, enjoyment, learning and friendships (Bailey *et al.*, 2013). The common refrain of coaches that 'modern' models of sport coaching are often explained differently but look the same in practice is addressed. This is achieved by connecting the Game Sense coaching approach and the constraints-led coaching perspective through an epistemology of representation. That is, they share the idea of purposeful manipulation of determining factors to shape and focus player's game development by specifying the information load on players. This is done to facilitate and stimulate learning through and from the 'realistic context' of game form play (Pill, 2021a). Although both approaches are sometimes referred to as 'discovery' orientated, use of a pedagogical lens provided by The Spectrum of Teaching Styles (Mosston, 1966; Mosston and Ashworth, 2008) shows that frequently they are more likely a practice style of coaching (SueSee *et al.*, 2020). Finally, the chapter introduced a "non-versus" philosophy to emphasise that no one coaching method can achieve all things and encourage coaches to view the methods they choose to enact in this way to achieve the best outcomes with their players.

## Review of Literature: Sport Coaching as an Educative Endeavour

### *Pedagogy*

The mechanism by which sport coaching is an educative endeavour is pedagogy. Pedagogy is the term for activity producing planned learning (Capel, 2005). Sport pedagogy, as a sub-discipline of


DOI: 10.4324/9781003199359-4

pedagogy, is concerned with the educational aspects of sport coaching. As an area of study, sport pedagogy encompasses teaching and learning processes associated with sport as a codified and institutionalised form of movement. Pedagogy as an endeavour is often associated with a curriculum. A curriculum is a program of practice and its related sport pedagogy that directs coaches in understanding how to construct the purpose of their coaching, the subject content of their sport teaching, the impact or execution of their sport coaching and the reflection and evaluation of that impact (Pill, 2012). Many sports have developed curriculum for junior coaches to follow. Examples include USA Soccer (2011), England Cricket Board (ECB, 2018), Football Federation Australia (FFA, 2013) and the Australian Football League (AFL, 2021).

The term pedagogy "draws attention to the process through which knowledge is produced" (Lusted, 1986 p. 2) and "under what conditions and through what means we 'come to know'" (Lusted, 1986, p. 3). "Pedagogy often refers to a practice or set of practices, the purpose of which is to pass on or produce knowledge" (Tinning, 2008, p. 416). There must be an explicit intention to 'pass on' knowledge by someone for pedagogical work to be done. It is a practice with intentionality (Tinning, 2008). However, it is acknowledged that at times the terms didactics, instruction, teaching and pedagogy may be used interchangeably (Tinning, 2008).

In consideration of how sport pedagogy is framed to this point, adapting The European Educational Research Association (EERA, 2011) definition of pedagogy, sport pedagogy has three dimensions to its construct:

1 Knowledge in context (the game being coached);
2 Players and their learning;
3 Coaches providing sport outcomes for participants with diverse needs.

Pedagogy needs to be a central concern of the sport coach as mediators of children's participation in sport include learning new skills and the perception of competence (Bailey *et al.*, 2013). Coaching practice not aligned with the mediators of children's participation is likely to be ineffective and potentially harmful to their continued involvement in the sport (Bailey, 2012). The coach and their pedagogy are factors in children's choice to continue playing a sport (Agnew *et al.*, 2016). Poor organisation of practice and sport programs have long been recognised as a major reason for children's attrition from sport (Robertson, 1989).

## Pedagogical Models and Approaches

Similar to what Rink (2001) found in physical education, literature and research in sport coaching sees debate, activism and zealous argument in methods, models and approaches. Advocates of methods, models and approaches seek to provide research, scholarship and postulating that the method they align with is better than what gets labelled 'traditional', as well as better than other ways of pedagogical expression competing for attention (Harvey *et al.*, 2018). What gets labelled as a 'traditional' coaching approach infers a dominance of command and practice style coaching, with coach instructional voice dominating the practice session. This approach to coaching is often aligned with a behavourist paradigm because of an emphasis on reproducing behaviours via direct coach instruction (Light, 2012), which Kirk (2010) called sport as sport techniques. Research in sport settings suggested time allocated to practicing contextually in games was low, and children spent large amounts of time in non-functional activities like waiting in a line for 'a turn' at doing something, with the result that often only a relatively small amount of time was invested in the performance of relevant to learning to play the game movement tasks. This meant that the practice design of coaches was not congruent with the motivations of children to join sport teams: learn new skills and to play the game (Watt *et al.*, 1993).

Beginning in the 1960s, approaches and models of pedagogical behaviour emerged that were explained by a constructivist paradigm. These came to be called game-based or game-centred approaches, and they had in common recognition of purposeful play using deliberately designed games as the core and focus of practice sessions, and a shift in the language of coaches from mostly prescriptive and direct instruction towards more inquiry oriented pedagogical using methods of questioning players (Pill, 2021b). Purposefully conditioned (Worthington, 1974), modified and designer games (Charlesworth, 1994) were encouraged. The Game Sense cards (Australian Sports Commission: ASC, 1999) illustrating and explaining conditioned game play are an example of what became advocated for children's sport. The 'play-based' (but not play only: Pill, 2021c) nature of practice sessions that stem from game-based coaching approaches were also explained by complex learning theory, as the representative nature of the game children were being coached to play was retained in the games used as practice tasks so the tasks held the logic of the play while the complexity of the game was simplified to meet the challenge point of the players. This notion of complex learning was contrasted to the historically common practice of deconstruction of game play into constituent techniques and coaching the techniques before children were allowed to play a game, which was referred to as complicated learning (Light, 2008).

Decades ago, it was recognised that game design dictates children's success in participation, enjoyment and learning (Morris, 1976) and that in addition to modifying conditions of a game such as the dimensions of play space and the number of players, equipment also needed to be modified to cater for the physical readiness of children (Evans, 1980; Haywood, 1984). This recognition led to modified game forms being encouraged for children's sport. In Australia, that resulted in the Aussie Sport Program (1985, 1990a, 1990b) which contained modified age-appropriate sport forms developed by national sport organisation, and later the Active After-School Communities (AASC) program (ASC, 2005) which used the Game Sense approach (ASC, 1996) as its pedagogical model. Many sports developed entry level sport programs for coaching children using the 'game sense games' from the AASC program.

## *Learning Theories that Inform Pedagogy as an Approach to Coaching: Behavourist, Constructivist and Ecological*

Much of the early writing on player learning in sport learning contexts is explained using education theory. Hence the contrast between behaviourist and constructivist learning theories as a way of explaining the difference between a historically common 'coach-centred' pedagogy residing in the pedagogical styles of command and practice and contemporary 'athlete-centred' (also called 'player-centred') approaches which are game-based (Hewitt *et al.*, 2018). From a behavourist explanation, sport coaching as directive instruction and practice style coaching is concerned with the operant conditioning of the control of prescriptive movements, commonly called techniques. Coaching can become focussed on eliminating unwanted movement responses and facilitating 'correct' movement responses (Allison and Aylon, 1980). This 'restrictive' view of sport coaching assumes that the role of the coach in coaching children is instructing, direction and modelling (Light, 2008; Bennett and Culpan, 2014). Cognitive dimensions of learning to play, such as playing as a team (systems thinking often referred to as team strategy) and player tactics (player in the moment problem solving) are ignored or marginalised in the coaching process. Whereas, from a constructivist perspective, learning to play is an interactive and reflective process between the player and the activity. A constructivist perspective rejects the notion that there is 'one way' to play the game (a single reality) (Roberts and Potrac, 2014). It suggests that a child makes individual meaning of their sport encounters by building on or altering previous understanding (i.e. constructing their understanding). This 'meaning making' has two elements, a personal cognitive element, and a socially situated element as the child's experience of sport coaching is in an interactive social arrangement with the coach, the player's parent/s, and if in a team sport environment then other players and their parents. A constructivist perspective points away from prescription to coaching children as a pedagogical encounter where the coach must discern what is to be learnt, how it is to be learnt, and how the coach facilitates each child's learning (Bennett and Culpan, 2014). From a constructivist perspective, the game as an educative context becomes an 'advanced organiser' of information, deliberately conditioned to assist the players to retrieve what they already know, and then to further their game development (advanced organiser is the term for a pedagogical technique that connects what a learner already knows and what is planned for the learner to know: Ausubel, 2000, Pill, 2021b). Conditioned, modified and designer games are constructed for the contextual emergence of a cognising moment – an insight like a comprehension that solves a problem or a re-interpretation or extension of understanding. The coach looks to capture the meaning of that moment, and then to insert that meaning back into the context of the play (Pill, 2021b).

As sport science has developed as a field of research and scholarship, literature on coaching and approaches to pedagogical enactment have emerged an already 'crowded' space. The term crowded alludes to the many game-based explanations of coaching practice that exist in scholarship globally. For example, Game Intelligence (Wein, 2004), Teaching Games for Understanding (Bunker and Thorpe, 1982), Tactical Games (Griffith *et al.*, 1997), Game Sense (Australian Sports Commission [ASC], 1996), Play Practice (Launder, 2001) Play with Purpose (Pill, 2007), the Grammar of Games (Forrest, 2015) and MASTER (Eather *et al.*, 2020). Emerging from sport science, the development with perhaps the most scholarship, advocacy, and research endeavour is the constraints-led approach explained by the theory of ecological dynamics. The concept of affordances is central in ecological modelling of perception and action in sport that leads to a constraints-led approach (Rankin *et al.*, 2018). A player is assumed to be a set of capabilities which provides possibilities to engage with properties in the environment that indicate possibilities for action – that is, affordances (Turvey, 1992). The implication for coaching children is for the coach to design practice settings that prepare players to perform in the game seen as an environment-player capability dynamic (Pill, 2014, 2021b). In this model, children must practice in an environment that represents the same affordances and therefore the same information as the game the children are being developed to play (Rankin *et al.*, 2018; Pill, 2021b). Constraints organise the practice activity information-perception relationship between the player and the task by directing their attentional focus (Pill, 2021c)

In common with game-based coaching approaches, a constraints-led approach includes purposeful modification and design of games (called constraints-manipulation) to guide players game-related learning, and the purposeful use of questions to guide player development of game understanding. The Game Sense coaching approach and the constraints-led coaching perspective have a connection through an epistemology of representation in that practice activities are designed to capture action fidelity between the context of practice and one or all the performance contexts of the game children are being coached to play (Pill, 2014, 2021a).

## Implication for Children's Sport Coaching

Two game-based coaching approaches that place an emphasis on discovery as part of (and a result of) the coaching process are a constraints-led approach (CLA) and Game Sense approach

(GSA: ASC, 1996). For example, CLA advocates specify that the purpose of implementing relevant constraints in a practice environment is to assist students 'search' for successful movement solutions – a 'discovery approach' (Renshaw *et al.*, 2010). The emphasis of game-based approaches such as the GSA on the use of problem-solving, reflection and inquiry processes has been described as a guided discovery (Pill, 2006; Breed and Spittle, 2011; Light, 2014). Pill and SueSee (2021) argued as the GSA (ASC, 1996) focusses on developing 'thinking players' it is foregrounded in guided discovery. Whilst both these approaches share this common element of discovery, when The Spectrum of Teaching styles is used as a lens to view a coaching episode, the decisions being made by the coach and the player more closely resemble practice. A GSA approach to a basketball session will be examined through The Spectrum and focus on the cognitive processes that the coach is asking the players to draw upon and the decisions the players are being asked to make.

## The Spectrum

The Spectrum (Mosston and Ashworth, 2008) of teaching styles (from this point referred to as The Spectrum) is underpinned by the central premise that every deliberate act of teaching is a result of a previous decision. Mosston ordered these many possible decisions into three main sets that comprise the Anatomy of any Style. These sets are identified as: (1) pre-impact set; (2) impact set; and (3) post-impact set. The pre-impact set involves making decisions in relation to the planning of the teacher-learner interaction, or in this case, the coach-player interaction. The impact set refers to the implementation of the decisions that occur during the coach-player face-to-face interaction. The post- impact set refers to assessment decisions that can occur at any point during the face-to-face interaction by either the teacher or the learner (Mosston and Ashworth, 2008). By identifying who (i.e. the teacher or learner) makes which decisions, the 11 teaching styles emerge (Figure 2.1). One of the key aspects relating to the use of various teaching styles is matching the appropriate style to the intended learning outcome(s) of the session. Each teaching style has limitations and strengths that can make it more or less beneficial

*Teaching Styles*

Command (A)

Practice (B)

Reciprocal (C)

Self-Check (D)

Inclusion (E)

Guided Discovery (F)

Convergent Discovery (G)

Divergent Discovery (H)

Learner-Designed Individual Program (I)

Learner-Initiated (J)

Self-Teaching (K)

*Figure 2.1* The 11 teaching styles on The Spectrum

to pupil learning. As Mosston (1992, p. 28). summarised: "the fundamental issue in teaching is not which style is better or best, but rather which style is appropriate for reaching the objectives of a given episode. Every style has a place in the multiple realities of teaching and learning",

An assumption of The Spectrum is that humans have the capacity for the production and reproduction of knowledge and the two processes should be viewed as complementary rather than mutually exclusive. The Spectrum further breaks this down positing that during learning experiences, players will be asked to use memory, discovery or creativity and that these cognitive behaviours form the three bases of conscious thinking. If coaches are using styles from A to E the dominant thought process the coach is engaging with player's is memory as the player will be reproducing knowledge. Hence, these styles are known as the Reproduction cluster. If a coach is using styles from F to K the players will be asked to use either discovery or creativity and produce knowledge or understanding that is new to them. These styles form the Production cluster.

The Spectrum views all teaching styles as valuable for what they can achieve, or a NON-VERSUS notion. Each style has its place reaching a specific set of learning objectives; "hence, no style, by itself, is better or best" (Mosston, 1981, p. viii). Therefore, while it is acknowledged that The Spectrum does not identify a teaching style called a Game Sense Approach, or Constraints Led Approach, The Spectrum provides a lens to recognise and identify all teaching, coaching and learning behaviour to enable a coach to see if their teaching aligns with the 'style' of coach they intend to be, or if their pedagogy aligns with the theoretical assumptions they associate with their practice. Our assertion here is based on The Spectrum's premise that all teaching behaviour is about pedagogical decision-making. The following table (Table 2.1) is an example of a GSA being used in basketball (Jarrett and Harvey, 2016).

Jarrett and Harvey (2016) suggested that after the observation and reflection on the game played an aspect of team play is decided for subsequent games, such as: What were the offensive and defensive challenges present in the 3 vs. 3 game?, When in possession of the ball what are your options? Can you demonstrate them in this scenario? When deciding whether to shoot what are you looking for in your opponent? Ensuing games would focus on development of team play to enable better shot selection. For example, 3 vs. 2, 4 vs. 3, 5 vs. 4 small-sided games (i.e. 5 vs. 4 progressing to the inclusion of fifth defender from base line after five offensive passes). Jarrett and Harvey indicated that in this GSA, pedagogy such as pausing play allows the coach to question specific aspects of team play and stimulate critical reflection and team discussion with players.

This session will now be examined through The Spectrum lens. The initial game form seems to be explaining how a 3 vs. 3 game will be played in terms of rules, playing area and how to begin. It does not state the objective, so it is assumed that it is to score under the conditions described. It will also be presumed that the questions come either after the game or during a

*Table 2.1* Game sense basketball session – coaching outline

| |
|---|
| **Initial game form** |
| 3 vs. 3 small-sided game |
| **Space:** Key area out to 3-point line |
| **Rules:** No dribble, start from top of 3-point arc or sideline, teams swap when ball out of bounds or offensive infraction or defensive team gains possession, defensive foul resets play |
| **Questions:** 'What do you need to consider when deciding whether or not to shoot?', 'Where could you move to on the court to maximise your scoring threat?' |

*Table 2.2* Pre-impact, impact and post-impact decision making

- Pre-impact: Teacher chooses subject matter (3 vs. 3 inside the 3-point line. Attempt to stop the other team from scoring).
- Impact set: Students practice passing or dribbling a ball the way they have before. They were not instructed by the teacher to 'discover' or 'create' a way to score which they have not done before.

They were most likely told: "The aim of this game is to beat your opponent by scoring points."

- The subject matter is dribbling, passing, running and defending.
- Students may be stopped during the impact set and asked questions using a Guided Discovery approach to help students identify problems experienced.
- Post impact: Teacher may give feedback about answers to questions, or may ask questions related to the task manipulation

pause in the game. Using The Spectrum to analyse the decisions in the three places allows consideration of the coaching styles used in this example (Table 2.2).

During the pre-impact set, the coach chose the subject matter (3 vs. 3 games considering when to shoot and the rules/playing area). During the impact-set the game constraints or conditions are explained by the coach. No goal has been explained to the players, so it is presumed the coach told the players to score as much as possible, decide when to shoot and stop the other team from scoring. As the players have not been directed to discover or create a way to beat their opponent, it is presumed that the players will most likely choose known ways of dribbling, passing and defending. Further to this, as The Spectrum defines teaching as deliberate behaviour, and the coach has not directed the players to discover/create, the coach could not take credit for the behaviour if it were to occur. The questions came after the playing of the game (or a pause in the play). The coach is asking the players questions that require them to reflect on what has happened during the game. This would mean they are recalling (from memory) events of success or failure to answer the questions. Jarrett and Harvey (2016, p. 104) provided context for the players level of experience when they say the "group has previous experience of being taught basketball in their primary schooling with some playing at the club longer than others". The review questions are not examples of the teaching-learning structure that represents guided discovery. Guided-discovery episodes require a series of questions involving convergent thinking that leads the learner to a predetermined target, that is guided-discovery episodes "require more than one question" (Mosston and Ashworth, 2008 p. 214). In the post-impact set the coach would give feedback about the correctness of the answer provided by the player/s. Based on the decisions that the coach and players have made and the places where they have been made in this episode, this coaching episode has the hallmarks of Practice Style coaching (Mosston and Ashworth, 2008).

However, if the players level of knowledge or experience around when to shoot was not well developed and a question requiring them to focus on a principle to discover was asked before the game was played, then this episode can be viewed as a Divergent Discovery style, as the players are being directed to discover two or more principles (i.e. What do you need to consider when deciding to shoot or not?). Divergent Discovery is when the coach asks players "to discover divergent (multiple) responses to a single question/situation, within a specific cognitive operation" (Mosston and Ashworth, 2008, p. 247). Further to this, if the players had limited knowledge about this principle, then they could discover it. If the players are already aware of when to shoot, then it is impossible to discover something that is already known

(Mosston and Ashworth, 2008). Many game-based approaches (GBA's) are not discovery episodes as they frequently ask questions at the end of the experience. When doing this, the players can only reflect on what has happened, rather than discover. This is not to suggest that asking questions at this time of the practice and in this fashion is not worth doing – it is. It is for the purpose of elaboration and consolidation of understanding, not discovery.

The Spectrum lens has allowed this episode to be viewed in two ways that reveal two important considerations. The first view of the episode shows the characteristics of the decisions made during a Practice Style episode (Mosston and Ashworth, 2008). The episode allowed the players to not only practice the physical skills of dribbling, passing, defending and shooting, but also practice the skill of identifying relevant perceptual cues in a game like environment. These perceptual skills are known as perceptual attunement. Perceptual attunement is an individual's learned ability to detect key information for a given task that has the potential to influence emergent decision-making behaviours (Araújo *et al.*, 2006; Weast *et al.*, 2011; Headrick *et al.*, 2012). The GSA episode in the 3 vs. 3 game provides the opportunity for these perceptual attunement skills to be observed, developed and practised. The second view of the episode suggests that it is Divergent Discovery Style if the coach directs the player/s to discover a principle before they play the game and they attempt to discover it during the game. However, for those that may already know the principle, discovery will be unlikely. This point highlights the importance of the coach being aware of the cognitive history of their players and choosing an appropriate coaching style given this knowledge.

## Summary, Future Directions and Future Research

There are a multitude of different ways coaches of children's sport can cluster pedagogy in a practice session to teach players to learn and develop in the sport (Jones, 2006b). One GBA has been placed on The Spectrum in this chapter. It has been done from a non-versus perspective, meaning that no argument has been made that the episode is 'good' or bad', more so it has been done to identify the decisions that the coach and players have made. The analysis has also highlighted the cognitive processes that have most likely been used by the players during the episode to practice the recall of skills (both physical and perceptual) through a game like environment. Viewing this GBA through The Spectrum lens has highlighted that whilst GBA may seem at times to be discovery learning, it may also have the hallmarks of Practice style coaching.

The reason children participate in sport must be considered with any coaching philosophy if coaches want to retain and develop the participants. Without retention there can be no development. Enjoyment is a major contributing factor for continuing sport participation, derived from a range of factors (Weiss, 2000; Agnew *et al.*, 2016). Viewing GBA's as a cluster of styles and using teaching styles from The Spectrum to implement GBA's may allow for many of these mentioned factors (social interaction from questioning, social recognition for both physical and cognitive competence and mastery through appropriate levels of practice or challenge) to be taught through the pedagogy described here. Research needs to be completed to identify the effect that Spectrum knowledge has on coaches' abilities to implement GBA's and if the outcomes which result for both coach and participants contribute to enjoyment and subsequently player retention. Coaches may need to be supported in developing this knowledge (given The Spectrum's numerous teaching styles) through professional development and opportunities to be supported whilst they practice coaching using different styles. Some (Joyce *et al.*, 1992) suggested that teachers need to use a teaching style ten or more times before they feel comfortable, and no doubt coaches may feel the same, especially if left unsupported.

## References

Agnew, D., Pill, S., and Drummond, M., 2016. Investigating the elements that encourage or inhibit the participation of children and youth in Australian Football. *Annals of Leisure Research*, 19 (1), 27–46.
Allison, M.G. and Aylon, T., 1980. Behavioural coaching in the development of skills in football, gymnastics and tennis. *Journal of Applied Behaviour Analysis*, 13 (2), 297–314.
Araújo, D., Davids, K., and Hristovski, R., 2006. The ecological dynamics of decision making in sport. *Psychology of Sport and Exercise*, 7, 653–676.
Australian Football League., 2021. *National junior coaching curriculum*. Melbourne: Coach AFL.
Australian Sports Commission., 1985. *Aussie sport program*. ACT: Australian Sports Commission.
Australian Sports Commission., 1990a. *Aussie sportsfun resource manual*. ACT: Australian Sports Commission.
Australian Sports Commission., 1990b. *Aussie sport: 14 modified sports*. ACT: Australian Sports Commission
Australian Sports Commission., 1996. *Game sense: Perceptions and actions research report*. ACT: Australian Sports Commission.
Australian Sports Commission., 1999. *Game sense cards*. ACT: Australian Sports Commission.
Australian Sports Commission., 2005. *Active after-school communities playing for life program*. ACT: Australian Sports Commission.
Ausubel, D.P., 2000. *The acquisition and retention of knowledge: A cognitive view*. Dordresht: Kluwer Academic Publishers.
Bailey, R., 2012. So what is developmentally appropriate sport? *Active and Healthy*, 19 (2), 21–24.
Bailey, R., Cope, E., and Pearce, G., 2013. Why do children take part in, and remain involved in sport? A literature review and discussion of implications for sports coaches. *International Journal of Sports Science and Coaching*, 7 (1), 55–74.
Bennett, B. and Culpan, I., 2014. The coach as educator: Content and pedagogical frameworks. *Journal of Physical Education & Health*, 3 (5), 5–18.
Breed, R. and Spittle, M., 2011. *Developing game sense through tactical learning: A resource for teachers and coaches*. Melbourne: Cambridge University Press.
Bunker, D. and Thorpe, R., 1982. A model for the teaching of games in secondary schools. *Bulletin of Physical Education*, 18 (1), 5–8.
Capel, S., 2005. Teachers, teaching and pedagogy in physical education. *In*: K. Green and K. Hardman, eds. *Physical education: Essential issues*. London: Sage, 111–127.
Charlesworth, R., 1994. Designer games. *Sport Coach*, 17 (4), 30–33.
Eather, N., *et al.*, 2020. Evaluating the impact of a coach development intervention for improving coaching practices in junior football (soccer): The "MASTER" pilot study. *Journal of Sports Sciences*, 38 (11–12), 1441–1453.
England Cricket Board., 2018. *Recommended junior formats*. https://www.ecb.co.uk/play/junior/junior-formats/junior-pathway
European Education Research Association., 2011. *Research in sport pedagogy: Core dimensions [online]*. Retrieved from: http://www.eera.ecer.eu/networks/network18/ [Accessed 29 March 2022]
Evans, J., 1980. Objectivity and game modifications – The next step. *Australian Journal of Health, Physical Education and Recreation*, 89, 11–17.
Fajen, B.R., Diaz, G., and Cramer, C., 2011. Reconsidering the role of movement in perceiving action-scaled affordances. *Human Movement Science*, 30 (3), 504–533.
Football Federation Australia., 2013. *The national football curriculum: the roadmap to international success*. Football Federation Australia.
Forrest, G., 2015. New approach for games and sports teaching. *Research and Innovation*, 1, 29.
Griffith, L.L., Mitchell, S.A., and Oslin, J.L., 1997. *Teaching sport concepts and skills: A tactical games approach*. Champaign, Illinois: Human Kinetics
Harvey, S., Pill, S., and Almond, L., 2018. Old wine in new bottles: A response to claims that teaching games for understanding was not developed as a theoretically based pedagogical framework. *Physical Education and Sport Pedagogy*, 23 (2), 166–180.
Haywood, K.M., 1984. Modification of youth sport: a rationale and some examples in youth basketball. *In*: M.R. Weiss and D. Gould, eds. *Sport for children and youths: 1984 olympic scientific congress proceedings*. Human Kinetics, 179–185.
Headrick, J., *et al.*, 2012. Attunement to haptic information helps skilled performers select implements for striking a ball in cricket. *Attention, Perception, and Psychophysics*, 74 (8), 1782–1791.

Hewitt, M., *et al.*, 2018. Applying the game sense approach and Mosston and Ashworth's inclusion style-E to promote athlete-centred tennis coaching with junior novice players. *In*: S. Pill, ed. *Perspectives on athlete-centred coaching*. New York: Routledge, 193–205.

Jarrett, K. and Harvey, S., 2016. Similar, but not the same: Comparing the game based approaches of Teaching games for understanding (TGfU) and game sense. *eJournal de la Recherche sur l'Intervention en Education Physique et Sportive*, 38, 92–113.

Jones, R., 2006a. The sports coach as educator: Reconceptualising sports coaching. *International Journal of Sports Science and Coaching*, 1 (4), 405–412.

Jones, R., 2006b. How can educational concepts inform sports coaching? *In*: R.L. Jones, ed. *The sports coach as educator*. New York: Routledge, 3–13.

Jones, R.L., Armour, K.M., and Potrac, P., 2004. *Sports coaching cultures from practice to theory*. New York: Routledge.

Joyce, B., Weil, M., and Showers, B., 1992. *Models of teaching*. 4th ed. Massachusetts: Allyn and Bacon.

Kirk, D., 2010. *Physical education futures*. New York: Routledge.

Launder, A., 2001. *Play practice: The games approach to teaching and coaching sports*. Illinois: Human Kinetics.

Light, R., 2008. Complex learning theory—Its epistemology and its assumptions about learning: implications for physical education. *Journal of Teaching in Physical Education*, 27 (1), 21–37.

Light, R., 2012. *Game sense: Pedagogy for performance, participation and enjoyment*. New York: Routledge.

Light, R., 2014. Quality teaching beyond games through game sense pedagogy. *University of Sydney Papers in HMHCE – Special Game Sense Edition*, 1–13.

Lusted, D., 1986. Why pedagogy? *Screen*, 27 (5), 2–14.

Morris, D., 1976. Effects ball and background colour have upon the catching performance of elementary school children. *The Research Quarterly*, 47 (3), 409–415.

Mosston, M., 1966. *Teaching physical education*. Ohio: Merrill.

Mosston, M., 1981. *Teaching physical education*. 2nd ed. Ohio: Merrill.

Mosston, M., 1992. Tug-o-war, no more: Meeting teaching-learning objectives using the Spectrum of teaching styles. *Journal of Physical Education, Recreation, and Dance*, 63 (1), 27–31, 56.

Mosston, M. and Ashworth, S., 2008. *Teaching physical education: First online edition*. United States: Spectrum Institute for Teaching and Learning.

Pill, S., 2006. Teaching games for understanding. *Sports Coach*, 29 (2), 21–23.

Pill, S., 2007. *Play with purpose*. Hindmarsh: ACHPER Publications.

Pill, S., 2012. *Rethinking sport teaching in physical education*. PhD thesis, University of Tasmania.

Pill, S., 2014. Informing game sense pedagogy with constraints led theory for coaching in Australian football. *Sport Coaching Review*, 3 (1), 46–62.

Pill, S., 2021a. Reconciling approaches: informing game sense pedagogy with a constraints-led perspective. *In*: R. Light and C. Curry, eds. *Game Sense for teaching and coaching: International perspectives*. New York: Routledge, 25–34.

Pill, S., 2021b. Introduction: Game-based coaching. *In*: S. Pill, ed. *Perspectives on game-based coaching*. New York: Routledge, xvii–xxviii.

Pill, S., 2021c. Reconciling approaches: Informing game sense coaching pedagogy with a constraints-led perspective. *In*: R. Light and C. Curry, eds. *Game sense for coaching and teaching: international perspectives*. New York: Routledge, 25–34.

Pill, S. and SueSee, B., 2021. The game sense approach as play with purpose. *In*: S. Pill, ed. *Perspectives on game-based coaching*. New York: Routledge, 1–10.

Rankin, J., Pill, S., and Magias, T., 2018. Informing the coaching pedagogy of game modification in a game sense approach with affordance theory. *Ágora para la Educación Física y el Deporte*, 20 (1), 68–89.

Renshaw, I., *et al.*, 2010. A constraints-led perspective to understanding skill acquisition and game play: A basis for integration of motor learning theory and physical education praxis? *Physical Education and Sport Pedagogy*, 15 (2), 117–137.

Rink, J., 2001. Investigating the assumptions of pedagogy. *Journal of Teaching in Physical Education*, 20 (2), 112–128.

Roberts, S.J. and Potrac, P., 2014. Behaviourism, constructivism and sports coaching pedagogy: Aconversational narrative in the facilitation of player learning. *International Sport Coaching Journal*, 1, 180–187.

Robertson, I., 1989. The coach and the drop out. *Sports Coach*, 12 (2), 8–14.

SueSee, B., Pill, S., and Hewitt, M., 2020. Reconciling approaches. *In*: B. SueSee, M. Hewitt, and S. Pill, eds. *The spectrum of teaching styles in physical education*. New York: Routledge, 73–84.

Tinning, R., 2008. Pedagogy, sport pedagogy, and the field of kinesiology. *Quest*, 60 (3), 405–424.
Turvey, M., 1992. Affordances and prospective control: An outline of the ontology. *Ecological Psychology*, 4 (3), 173–187.
USA Soccer., 2011. *U.S. soccer curriculum*. Illinois: USA Soccer.
Watt, A., 1993. *A descriptive process analysis and comparison of game modifications in junior netball and basketball*. Unpublished thesis. Edith Cowan University.
Weast, J.A., Shockley, K., and Riley, M.A., 2011. The influence of athletic experience and kinematic information on skill - relevant affordance perception. *The Quarterly Journal of Experimental Psychology*, 64 (4), 689–706.
Wein, H., 2004. *Developing game intelligence in soccer*. Pennsylvania: Reedswain.
Weiss, M., 2000. Motivating kids in physical activity. *The President's Council on Physical Fitness and Sports Research Digest Series*, 3 (11), 1–8.
Worthington, E., 1974. *Teaching soccer skills*. Great Britain: Lepus Books.

# 3
# DEVELOPMENTAL CONSIDERATIONS FOR COACHING PRESCHOOLER SPORT

*Jessica Fraser-Thomas and Meghan Harlow*

## Introduction

Current trends indicate children are participating in organised sport at increasingly earlier ages (American Academy of Pediatrics [AAP], 2001, 2019), with studies suggesting engagement among approximately 50% of preschool-aged children (~3–5 years) in Western nations (ParticipACTION, 2018; Chen *et al.*, 2020). Despite growth in the uptake of preschooler sport programs, limited research has explored participation within this demographic. In fact, a recent scoping review (Harlow *et al.*, 2018) found only nine peer-reviewed studies examining developmental outcomes associated with preschooler-aged sport – with nearly half of these studies being conducted in North America. Relatedly, research frameworks, such as the Developmental Model of Sport Participation ([DMSP]; Côté and Fraser-Thomas, 2016) have largely overlooked preschoolers' participation, suggesting children enter sport around 6 years of age – a milestone which may no longer reflect current trends or realities.

Given evolving social patterns (e.g. concerns for children's safety, decreases in unstructured physical activity [PA]; Jarvis *et al.*, 2014), widespread parental beliefs that sport is a positive pastime with extensive benefits (e.g. Neely and Holt, 2014), coupled with the popularised assumption that early sport specialisation is required to reach elite performance (despite a lack of empirical evidence supporting this notion; LaPrade *et al.*, 2016) – interest and enrolment in preschooler sport will undoubtedly continue to grow. As such, consideration must be given to creating optimal contexts for young children's positive development through sport. Research among children and youth consistently emphasises coaches' key roles in fostering quality sport experiences (e.g. Holt *et al.*, 2017); coaches are believed to play a similar role in facilitating development among preschoolers. This chapter provides an overview of current research to date across four sub-sections: (a) why preschooler sport? (b) coaches' supporting roles, (c) preschoolers' development and (d) program delivery. Given the limited research available, this review focuses largely on preschooler sport patterns and coaching practices through a North American lens. The chapter concludes with implications, a summary, and future research directions.

DOI: 10.4324/9781003199359-5

## Review of Current Research

### *Why Preschooler Sport?*

The growth of organised sport for preschoolers across Western nations is a relatively recent phenomenon. Although the benefits of children engaging in regular PA are well established (Janssen and LeBlanc, 2010), little research has focused on exactly 'how much and how' PA is appropriate or beneficial for preschool-aged children (Timmons *et al.*, 2007). Simultaneously, concern is growing surrounding young children's physical literacy (PL) – described as "the motivation, confidence, physical competence, knowledge, and understanding, to value and take responsibility for engagement in physical activities for life" (Tremblay *et al.*, 2018, p. 16). PL is believed to be critical in laying the foundation for lifelong enjoyment of PA, gaining the confidence to try new things (such as organised sport), and optimising overall health and well-being – thus, should be encouraged from a young age (Whitehead *et al.*, 2018).

Extensive social and cultural changes in Western society over the past half century have resulted in decreased opportunities for children to engage in PA and become PL. While Jarvis *et al.* (2014) outlined the critical role of free play (a form of unstructured PA) in the developmental processes of discovery and learning in early childhood, they argued that time for free play has been engineered *out* of the school day in exchange for performance-based activities, while outdoor play at home has concurrently decreased due to perceived safety concerns, perceptions that play must be supervised, and decreased green space. As such, a paradoxical relationship has developed, whereby organised sport has become relied upon for PA and the promotion PL – in the absence of naturally occurring free play opportunities for young children in their homes or school enviroments (Jarvis *et al.*, 2014).

While only a handful of studies have examined specific outcomes associated with PA and organised sport in early childhood, a review by Timmons *et al.* (2007) highlighted 'exercise play' – a key form of PA for preschoolers (Pellegrini and Smith, 1998) – to be important for motor skill, aerobic fitness and self-esteem development; although they offered little guidance regarding optimal amounts and forms. Similarly, Pienaar *et al.* (2011) advocated the value of 'kinderkinetics' programs in South Africa, given their focus on perceptual-motor skills and abilities. While not formally referred to as 'sport', kinderkinetics programs involve many of the same elements as sport, including that they take place weekly over a seven-month period, consist of a number of activities designed to improve body awareness and fine motor skills, and are led by trained professionals in the field of motor development (i.e. 'kinderkineticists').

More recently, Harlow *et al.* (2018) conducted a scoping review focused on non-physical outcomes of preschooler sport, with findings demonstrating some evidence of positive outcomes related to *social skills* (e.g. building relationships, empathising, complying with rules) and *psychological outcomes* (e.g. responsibility, self-discipline, independence), coupled with decreased emotional problems and hyperactivity (e.g. worry, interpersonal issues). Additionally, small *cognitive benefits* were noted related to enhanced mathematical and linguistic skills. However, Harlow *et al.*'s review found organised sport may also be a context for *negative experiences and outcomes* – most notably related to social maladjustment (e.g. fighting, being disruptive). Although these findings should be interpreted with some caution given the limited number (of low to moderate quality) existing studies, conducted in narrowly specified contexts, findings nonetheless begin to shed light on developmental outcomes associated with preschooler sport participation. Further, while there could be many reasons underlying preschoolers' negative sport experiences (e.g. emotions of frustration/failure, cognitive misunderstandings of competition, short attention spans), coaches likely play a key role in mitigating these potential challenges, to in turn optimise preschoolers' positive experiences and outcomes through sport.

## *Coaches' Roles within Preschooler Sport*

Although extensive research highlights coaches' roles in shaping children and youths' sport experiences and enhancing (or impeding) a range of participant outcomes (e.g. Holt *et al.*, 2017), Muir *et al.* (2011) caution that simply modifying coaching approaches used with youth towards younger children could be problematic. Instead, 'effective' coaches must consider and gain in-depth understanding of the specific context in which they are coaching (Côté and Gilbert, 2009). In the case of preschoolers, coaches must recognise participants' unique needs due to their age and developmental abilities.

Effective coaching is defined as the "consistent application of integrated professional, interpersonal, and intrapersonal knowledge to improve athletes' competence, confidence, connection, and character in specific coaching contexts" (Côté and Gilbert, 2009, p. 316), whereby professional knowledge concerns sport-specific technical and tactical skills, interpersonal knowledge refers to coaches' ability to communicate and effectively interact with athletes, and intrapersonal knowledge refers to coaches' openness towards on-going learning and self-reflection. They assert that these forms of knowledge may contribute to positive athlete outcomes, conceptualised as the '4Cs' (i.e. competence, confidence, connection and character; Côté *et al.*, 2010). Interestingly, however, neither the concept of effective coaching, nor the 4Cs framework have emerged in research with children under 6 years of age in sport.

Exploration of effective coaching may be particularly essential among preschoolers, given coaches are among the first non-parental adult relationships that children form, and they work with children at a critical stage of development (i.e. when lifelong learning, behaviour and PA habits are formed) (Mustard, 2006). It follows that to be effective, preschooler sport coaches should focus on developmentally appropriate (i.e. context specific) program delivery (i.e. drawing upon professional and interpersonal knowledge), to in turn optimise children's positive outcomes (i.e. 4Cs) (Côté and Gilbert, 2009). The question that follows is – what exactly does delivery of such programs look like?

## ***Considering Preschoolers' Development across Key Domains***

For coaches to effectively deliver preschooler programming, children's developmental 'readiness' to participate must be considered – ensuring children are able to meet the demands of a particular sport (e.g. score a goal, practice good sportspersonship, pass to a teammate) (Purcell, 2005; Patel *et al.*, 2017). The preschooler years are a period rapid brain development and growth (Mustard, 2006), with extensive individual differences. Nonetheless, children typically meet certain 'milestones' in similar patterns across key developmental domains (Best Start Expert Panel on Early Learning, 2006). Consideration of these patterns, and in turn, what children are capable of learning in organised sport at this stage of development is important in ensuring realistic age-appropriate expectations (Petty, 2016; Kahn *et al.*, 2019). An overview of preschool-aged children's (3–5 years) typical developmental milestones across physical, social-emotional, language-communication and cognitive domains, *most relevant* to organised sport participation is outlined in the section that follows; summaries draw primarily upon key North American sources (e.g. AAP, 2004; Best Start Expert Panel on Early Learning, 2006; Dosman *et al.*, 2012; Centers for Disease Control [CDC], 2021; Ministry of Ontario, 2021).

*Table 3.1* Physical child development milestones between 3 and 5 years of age

<table>
<tr><th></th><th>3 years</th><th>4 years</th><th>5 years</th></tr>
<tr><td rowspan="8">Physical</td><td>Climbs well</td><td rowspan="4">Catches a bounced ball most of the time</td><td>Stands on one foot for 10 seconds or longer</td></tr>
<tr><td>Runs easily</td><td>May be able to skip</td></tr>
<tr><td>Pedals a tricycle</td><td>Can do a somersault</td></tr>
<tr><td>Walks up and down stairs - one foot on each step</td><td>Swings and climbs</td></tr>
<tr><td colspan="2">Hops and stands on one foot for up to five seconds</td><td rowspan="2">Stands on one foot for 10 seconds or longer</td></tr>
<tr><td colspan="2">Kicks ball forward</td></tr>
<tr><td colspan="2">Throws ball overhand</td><td rowspan="2">Swings</td></tr>
<tr><td colspan="2">Moves forward and backwards with agility</td></tr>
</table>

*Source*: Adapted from AAP (2004) and CDC (2021).

## *Physical Development*

Preschool aged children's motor skills develop considerably through the acquisition of various fundamental movement skills (FMS) – "basic learnt movement patterns that do not occur naturally and are suggested to be foundational for more complex physical and sporting activities" (Barnett *et al.*, 2016, p. 2). FMS are commonly classified into three sub-categories: (a) locomotor movement (e.g. running, hopping), (b) object control (e.g. catching a ball) and (c) stability (e.g. balancing) (Lubans *et al.*, 2010; Gallahue *et al.*, 2012). Table 3.1 offers a summary of key FMS achieved in typically developing preschool aged children. Purcell (2005) argued that "by preschool age, most children have acquired some of these skills, but it is not until they reach the age of 6 years that sufficient combinations of fundamental skills are attained to allow them to begin participating in organised sports" (p. 343).

## *Social-Emotional Development*

Children's social-emotional development also evolves during the first five years of life. The social-emotional domain refers to understanding the emotional experiences of the self and others, and expressing and regulating one's emotions in an age-appropriate way (Malti and Noam, 2016). Much like motor skill development, researchers suggest certain socio-emotional skills act as building blocks for more complex skills that emerge later in life (Jones and Kahn, 2017). For instance, in a sporting context, the ability to practice good sportspersonship (e.g. supress anger after a loss) requires an individual to regulate their emotions, which some researchers believe children are not capable of doing before six years of age (Patel *et al.*, 2017). Some of the key social-emotional skills relevant for preschool-aged children's organised sport involvement are summarised in Table 3.2.

## *Language/Communication Development*

Language and communication are also critical skills that facilitate children's ability to interact within organised sports. Language development refers to the comprehension and

*Table 3.2* Summary of key social-emotional development milestones between 3 and 5 years of age

<table>
<tr><th></th><th>3 years</th><th>4 years</th><th>5 years</th></tr>
<tr><td rowspan="14">Social-Emotional</td><td>Copies adults and friends</td><td>Enjoys doing new things</td><td>Wants to please friends</td></tr>
<tr><td>Shows affection for friends</td><td>Is creative with make-believe play</td><td>Wants to be like friends</td></tr>
<tr><td>Takes turns in games</td><td>Enjoys playing with others as opposed to independently</td><td>Is more likely to agree with rules</td></tr>
<tr><td>Shows concern for a crying friend</td><td>Cooperates with other children</td><td>Likes to sing, dance, and act</td></tr>
<tr><td>Understands 'mine' versus 'theirs'</td><td rowspan="3">Often cannot distinguish between fantasy and reality</td><td rowspan="2">Can tell what's real and what's make-believe</td></tr>
<tr><td>Shows a wide range of emotions</td></tr>
<tr><td>Separates easily from mom or dad</td><td>Shows more independence</td></tr>
<tr><td>May get upset with changes in routine</td><td rowspan="3">Shows increasing emotional regulation over anger, aggression</td><td>Can be sometimes cooperative and sometimes demanding</td></tr>
<tr><td>Engages in social role play – (e.g., doll as playmate, imaginary friend)</td><td>Initiates separations from parents, plays away for several hours</td></tr>
<tr><td>Initiates interactions with peers, plays cooperatively, shares toys</td><td>Noncompliance rare, follows group rules, understands games with rules</td></tr>
<tr><td>Understands rules (tells friends)</td><td>Can resolve conflicts with discussion and negotiation</td><td>Develops sense of conscience, is strict about rules, insists on them with peers</td></tr>
<tr><td>Is able to talk about emotions and situations that elicit them</td><td>Might offer comfort and sympathy to peers, listen to others</td><td>Understands another's perspective, brings aggression under control</td></tr>
<tr><td rowspan="2">Feels guilt for hurting another child and may try to make things better</td><td>Understands moral themes (right and wrong) in stories</td><td rowspan="2">Can display emotions other than the ones felt underneath</td></tr>
<tr><td>Is usually compliant, shows shame and guilt if misbehaves</td></tr>
</table>

*Source*: Adapted from AAP (2004), Dosman *et al.*, (2012), and CDC (2021).

production of words, sentences and ideas (i.e. engagement in speech), while communication involves the exchange of this information during interactions with others (Visser-Bochane *et al.*, 2020). Prechooler aged children must learn to take directions from coaches and interact with other children, both of which necessitate basic language/communication skills. A summary of key language/communication skills adopted by preschool-aged children is offered in Table 3.3.

*Table 3.3* Summary of key language/communication development milestones between 3 and 5 years of age

<table>
<tr><th></th><th>3 years</th><th>4 years</th><th>5 years</th></tr>
<tr><td rowspan="16">Language/Communication</td><td>Follows instructions with 2–3 steps</td><td>Knows basic rules of grammar such as pronouns</td><td>Speaks very clearly in sentences of more than 5 words</td></tr>
<tr><td>Can name familiar things</td><td>Can sing a song from memory</td><td>Tells and recalls simple story using full sentences</td></tr>
<tr><td>Understands words like 'in' 'on' and 'under'</td><td>Can tell stories</td><td>Uses future tense</td></tr>
<tr><td>Can say first name, age, and sex</td><td rowspan="4">Understands the concepts of 'same' and 'different'</td><td rowspan="4">Can say name and address</td></tr>
<tr><td>Can name a friend</td></tr>
<tr><td>Says words like "I" "me" "we"</td></tr>
<tr><td>Can speak using 2–3 sentences</td></tr>
<tr><td>Is understood by people outside of the family, most of the time</td><td>Follows directions involving 3 or more steps</td><td>Describes present, future, and past in detail</td></tr>
<tr><td>Understands the function of print</td><td rowspan="2">Tells stories with a clear beginning, middle, and end</td><td>Knows almost all the sounds of their language without error</td></tr>
<tr><td rowspan="4">Has an awareness of rhyming</td><td>Know all the letters of the alphabet</td></tr>
<tr><td>Speaks in sentences of 5–6 words</td><td rowspan="3">Can identify the sounds at the beginning of some words</td></tr>
<tr><td>Is able to generate simple rhymes</td></tr>
<tr><td>Can match some letters with their sounds</td></tr>
</table>

*Source*: Adapted from AAP (2004), CDC (2021), and Ministry of Ontario (2021).

## Cognitive Development

Finally, children's cognitive development concerns their ability to think, reason and process information and knowledge (Piaget, 1964), which changes dramatically from early childhood through to early school years (Kahn *et al.*, 2019). Cognition also entails the ability to control one's impulses and direct attention and focus toward a task (Jones and Kahn, 2017) – a skill that is arguably crucial in determining whether a child can meaningfully engage in organised sport (i.e. take direction from a coach/adult leader, wait their turn). Table 3.4 offers a summary of key cognitive developmental milestones for children aged 3–5.

## Program Delivery: Being an Effective Preschooler Coach

Understanding preschoolers' abilities within their unique stages of development (outlined above) can offer coaches foundational insight for effective sport programming delivery (Côté and Gilbert, 2009). Additionally, coaches' professional (sport-specific technical skills) and interpersonal knowledge (communication and rapport with athletes) must be considered. Given the modest body of literature specifically exploring coaches' engagement with and support of

*Table 3.4* Summary of key cognitive (thinking/learning) development milestones between 3 and 5 years of age

<table>
<tr><th></th><th>3 years</th><th>4 years</th><th>5 years</th></tr>
<tr><td rowspan="9">Cognitive (thinking, learning)</td><td>Can work toys with buttons, levers, and moving parts</td><td>Can name some colours and numbers</td><td rowspan="2">Can count ten or more things</td></tr>
<tr><td>Plays make-believe</td><td>Understands the idea of counting</td></tr>
<tr><td rowspan="3">Understands what 'two' means</td><td>Starts to understand time</td><td rowspan="2">Can print some letters and numbers</td></tr>
<tr><td>Remembers parts of a story</td></tr>
<tr><td>Can predict what will happen next in a book</td><td>Knows about everyday items like food and money</td></tr>
<tr><td>Understands who, what, where, when, and why questions</td><td rowspan="2">Can understand increasingly complex imaginative play</td><td>Follows group directions</td></tr>
<tr><td>Names one colour, counts two objects, sorts shapes, compares two items</td><td>Understand directions involving "If, then …"</td></tr>
<tr><td>Tells simple stories</td><td>Follows three-part commands</td><td>Correctly names at least four colours</td></tr>
<tr><td>Engages in multi-step pretend play</td><td>Generalises rules from one situation to another</td><td>Better understands the concept of time</td></tr>
</table>

*Source*: Adapted from AAP (2004), Dosman *et al.*, (2012), CDC (2021), and Ministry of Ontario (2021).

very young children in sport, this section highights works primarily from North American child interest groups (e.g. pediatric societies), sport researchers, sport policy models/frameworks and coach education programs, where much of the research to date has been focused.

## *Coaches' Professional Knowledge: Structuring Sessions*

Preschooler coaches' professional knowledge includes their ability to teach, structure and deliver sport sessions aligning with young children's developmental stages. Recommendations emerging from pediatric societies (i.e. Canadian Paediatric Society, 2005; AAP, 2001, 2019) suggest sport activities be tailored to preschoolers through simple modifications, such as holding shorter practice sessions (e.g. 15–20 minutes of structured activities; 30 minutes of free play), using smaller/modified equipment, and focusing sessions around play, experimentation, exploration-based movement and fun, while generally avoiding competition. These recommendations align with Timmons *et al.*'s (2007) suggestions that preschooler PA focus on gross motor play and locomotor activities that children find fun, with consideration of children's natural activity patterns (i.e. spontaneous and intermittent).

A limited number of sport development frameworks and formal coach education programs provide guidance for preschooler coaches. In Canada, the Canadian Long-term Development in Sport and Physical Activity Model ([LTD]; Sport for Life, 2019) suggests an optimal PA and sport journey across the lifespan, with the first '*Active Start*' stage capturing ages 0–6 years. Recommendations for this stage include children engaging in daily active play and PA, to in turn develop FMS. While optimal timing for introducing organised sport is not explicitly stated, the *Active Start* stage promotes swimming, 'well-structured' gymnastics programs, and other (not named) 'developmentally appropriate' activities. Coach education programs in Canada are designed in tandem with the LTD (i.e. National Coaching Certification Program [NCCP]; Coaching Association of Canada [CAC], n. d.), leading to aligning 'Introduction to Coaching' accreditation courses for each unique sport, intended to equip coaches with the skills to support young children's FMS and create positive learning environments (e.g. Hockey Canada, n.d., and Gymnastics Canada, n.d.).

Two recent Canadian empirical studies offer additional insight into preschooler coaches' professional knowledge. Harlow and Fraser-Thomas (in revision) explored coaches' delivery of diverse programs, finding coaches typically introduced children to FMS (i.e. running, jumping) and sport-specific skills (e.g. stick handling, somersaulting). Children engaged in 'deliberate play' (i.e. inherently enjoyable play, governed by flexible rules, standards and expectations; DMSP; Côté and Fraser-Thomas, 2016) for the majority of their session time, yet as such, engaged in very little free play. Timmons *et al.* (2007) have suggested preschooler PA can be enhanced through adult facilitation and appropriate feedback, in turn leading to mastery; however, most programs in Harlow and Fraser-Thomas' study also yielded some form of competition (e.g. races, relays, scrimmages). A subsequent study (Harlow and Fraser-Thomas, 2019) found a key strategy used by effective preschooler coaches included being flexible and adaptive in their program delivery (i.e. changing activities if children appeared disinterested). Collectively, these findings suggest many coaches are drawing upon foundational professional knowledge; however, their delivery of programming may exist within a system that does not always align with developmentally recommended approaches to preschooler sport.

## *Coaches' Interpersonal Knowledge: Interacting with Preschoolers*

Given coaches' interpersonal skills have consistently been highlighted as essential to fostering positive developmental outcomes among youth (Falcao *et al.*, 2020), it follows that preschooler coaches must effectively communicate, interact and build rapport with young children. However, research examining coach education/training programs for youth sport show content is focused primarily on professional rather than interpersonal knowledge (Lefebvre *et al.*, 2016). Although limited, courses targeting preschooler coaches (e.g. *Active Start* or *Introduction to Coaching*) appear to align with this finding, showing a greater focus on sport-specific tactics and skill development, than communication approaches and strategies unique to the preschooler age-group (Hockey Canada, n.d.; Gymnastics Canada, n.d.).

While empirical research exploring preschooler coaching strategies is sparce, literature and resources within early childhood education offer guidance that may be transferable to coaching. For example, the Center on the Social and Emotional Foundations for Early Learning (Ostrosky and Jung, 2010) suggests several means for adult leaders to build connections with young children, including: (a) following children's lead/interest during play, (b) providing clear simple explanations to help children understand expectations, (c) modeling and encouraging listening, (d) genuinely and specifically acknowledging children's accomplishments and efforts, (e) engaging children in the conflict management and problem resolution processes, (f) being at children's level for face-to-face interactions and (g) communicating in a pleasant calm voice, using simple language, while making eye contact. In line with these recommendations, Patel *et al.* (2017) suggest coaches/leaders should rely heavily on repetition and redirection in organised sport environments, particularly given preschoolers' short attention spans. Further, simple sentences combined with visual cues (e.g. videos, pictures), while modeling slow, exaggerated movements when teaching sport skills, are suggested.

Finally, preliminary work exploring preschooler coaches' interpersonal approaches reinforces the value of coaches developing context-specific adaptions (Harlow and Fraser-Thomas, 2019). Specifically, effective coaches ensured programming was age-appropriate by using storytelling to teach skills – evoking children's imaginations based on current popular topics/themes (e.g. "imagine you're a member of Paw Patrol, and you have to *run* from A to B to save a friend!"). Further, coaches described managing behavior by setting visual spatial boundaries, asking children simple reinforcement questions for clarity (e.g. "where should I kick the ball?"), and reframing disruptive behaviour using pro-social approaches (e.g. assigning children as coaches' 'helpers'). However, as this study drew upon a small sample of preschooler coaches from one urban region in Canada, more empirical research is needed to further explore best practices across other regions, nations, and sports.

## Implications for Children's Sport Coaching

A prominent theme throughout this chapter relates to the dearth of empirical research exploring coaching within preschooler sport, despite growth in availability and enrolment in programs in many Western nations (ParticipACTION, 2018; Chen *et al.*, 2020). As previously noted, a scoping review by Harlow *et al.* (2018) found only nine studies exploring developmental outcomes of preschooler sport, with only a few studies emerging since (e.g. McNeill et al., 2018; Chen *et al.*, 2020; Bryant *et al.*, 2021). Interestingly, of these twelve studies, eight were conducted in Canada, the United States, Australia, and the United Kingdom; the remaining four were conducted in Sweden, Turkey, Greece and Egypt. This highlights an important first area for future research – considering *where* research is taking place, whether widespread organised preschooler sport is a phenomenon around the world, and relatedly, if and how it may 'look' different across differing nations or cultures.

In considering how programs may 'look' worldwide, future research must consider what constitutes 'organised' or 'structured' sport among preschoolers. Jarvis *et al.* (2014) highlight the critical developmental value of collaborative free play within this demographic (e.g. process of discovery, learning to share, being social), yet suggest free play has been contemporaneously reduced and replaced by adult directed pursuits. From one lens, organised sport appears to offer a context to artificially (re-)create opportunities for "free" play. However, as an out-of-home adult-directed activity, organised sport may actually limit or occur *instead* of free play. In line with this concern, coaches have suggested children are entering programs with lower FMS levels than in the past, which may be partially due to decreased free play at home (Harlow and Fraser-Thomas, 2019).

Another question when considering how programs 'look' relates to what constitutes 'sport' within the preschooler context. As competition is a key component of most sport definitions, it follows that preschooler sport should include competition; however, as noted, non-competitive sport is often recommended as a more developmentally appropriate form of PA among this demographic (AAP, 1992; 2001; Canadian Paediatric Society, 2005). Given varying interpretations of 'sport' and 'PA' among preschool-aged children (e.g. Kinderkinetics; Pienaar *et al.*, 2011), it is challenging to glean meaningful research on specific outcomes associated with organised sport within this age group. Alongside advancing clarity of these concepts, it may be beneficial to develop a context-specific definition of organised sport for preschoolers – and subsequently, a context-specific definition of preschooler coaching. Similarly, there is value in considering: (a) How is a preschooler coach different than an educator/instructor? (b) What are the parameters of a preschooler coach's role? and (c) What should preschooler coach training look like?

Finally, this review highlights potential misalignment between preschooler sport pedagogy, and preschoolers' developmental abilities/milestones. Patel *et al.* (2017) emphasized the importance of considering children's developmental abilities when appraising their readiness for sport, in addition to giving coaches tools to support developmentally appropriate activities. To date, program delivery and coach training appear to draw primarily upon youth sport models, with adaptions for younger children. Sport stakeholders could likely benefit from utilising early childhood education materials/resources to further optimally engage preschoolers. Many sources underscore the value of *play-based learning*, and *connecting* with preschoolers (e.g. Early Learning for Every Child Today [Best Start Expert Panel on Early Learning, 2007]; Early Years Physical Literacy Planning Model [Clark *et al.*, 2017]; Triple-P Positive Parenting Program [Sanders, 2008]). While sport stakeholders may offer the best insights on physical sport skill progressions, other experts may inform best practices related to preschoolers' social-emotional, language-communication and cognitive development within sport. Contributions by diverse experts may ensure more positive experiences and outcomes, with preschoolers only being asked to do what they are developmentally capable of (e.g. in terms of skills, progressions, competition, length of program, etc.).

## Summary, Future Directions and Future Research

As research in this area expands, sport participation and development models must be adapted to reflect evolving understanding and best practices, given many existing models do not align with common/current pathways (e.g. DMSP, Côté and Fraser-Thomas, 2016), and/or offer direction informed by limited empirical studies (e.g. LTD, Sport for Life, 2019). This is particularly important given new parents' eagerness to seek guidance relating to their young child's optimal development, coupled with the existence of extensive sources of popular/social media that may be ill-informed and could mis-guide parents. In addition to considering developmental milestones (i.e. physical, social-emotional, language/communication and cognitive), models should also shed light on context-specific implementation (e.g. sessions' structure, coaches' interactions) and roles of parents (e.g. optimal age for enrolment, 'good' program fit, balancing organised and unstructured activities). Models may also benefit from further subdividing this demographic (often grouped as *under 6* or *0–6*; DMSP, Côté and Fraser-Thomas, 2016; LTD, Sport for Life, 2019) into smaller chronological increments, given tremendous variation and diversity within each chronological age-grouping at this stage of development. Without more explicit age groupings, a program for children ages 3 to 5 years could include children from 36 months of age up to 72 months of age, invariably placing programmers and coaches in the near impossible position of having to teach children FMS and sport skills that do not match their developmental levels (Harlow *et al.*, 2021).

Collectively, this review highlights the need to better understand what coaching effectiveness should 'look like' in preschooler sport. In line with Côté and Gilbert's (2009) definition of effective coaching, preschooler coaches should focus on developmentally appropriate (i.e. context-specific) program delivery (i.e. drawing upon professional, interpersonal and intrapersonal knowledge), to in turn optimise children's positive outcomes. However, more research is needed to determine what professional, interpersonal and intrapersonal knowledge is most conducive to preschooler sport, as well as what outcomes or experiences are most important for children to gain through preschooler sport. Given preschooler sport participation rates will undoubtedly remain high, it is essential that prioritisation be given to ensure children's earliest sport experiences are positive and developmentally appropriate, to in turn increase the likelihood that children remain engaged in sport over time (Kirk, 2005).

## References

American Academy of Pediatrics, 1992. Fitness, activity, and sports participation in the preschool child. *Pediatrics*, 90 (6), 1002–1004.

American Academy of Pediatrics, 2001. Organised sports for children and preadolescents. *Pediatrics*, 107 (6), 1459–1462.

American Academy of Pediatrics, 2004. *Caring for your baby and young child: birth to age five*. New York: Bantam Books.

American Academy of Pediatrics, 2019. Organised sports for children, preadolescents, and adolescents. *Pediatrics*, 143 (6), 1–22.

Barnett, L.M., *et al.*, 2016. Fundamental movement skills: An important focus. *Journal of Teaching in Physical Education*, 35 (3), 219–225.

Best Start Expert Panel on Early Learning, 2006. *Early learning for every child today: a framework for ontario early childhood settings* [Online]. http://www.cfcollaborative.ca/wp-content/uploads/2010/10/ELECT.pdf [Accessed 30 April 2022].

Bryant, L.M., Duncan, R.J., and Schmitt, S.A., 2021. The cognitive benefits of participating in structured sports for preschoolers. *Early Education and Development*, 32 (5), 729–740.

Canadian Paediatric Society, 2005. Sport readiness in children and youth. *Paediatrics and Child Health*, 10 (6), 343–344.

Centers for Disease Control, July 27, 2021. *CDC's developmental milestones* [online]. https://www.cdc.gov/ncbddd/actearly/milestones/index.html [Accessed 30 April 2022].

Chen, C., *et al.*, 2020. Associations of participation in organised sports and physical activity in preschool children: A cross-sectional study. *BMC pediatrics*, 20 (1), 1–9.

Clark, D., Jewitt, K., and Bruce, P., 2017. *Early years physical literacy planning manual: For child care centres* [online]. https://afdb32fd-877e-4e25-828f-3b88265b25d2.filesusr.com/ugd/05c80a_352ba432de8b41f99fa0cd80e5198ffc.pdf [Accessed 30 April 2022].

Coaching Association of Canada, n.d. *National coaching certification program* [online]. https://coach.ca/national-coaching-certification-program [Accessed 30 April 2022].

Côté, J. and Fraser-Thomas, J., 2016. Youth involvement and positive development in sport. *In*: P.R.E. Crocker, ed. *Sport psychology: A Canadian perspective*, 3rd ed. Canada: Pearson Prentice Hall, 256–287.

Côté, J. and Gilbert, W., 2009. An integrative definition of coaching effectiveness and expertise. *International Journal of Sports Science and Coaching*, 4 (3), 307–323.

Côté, J., *et al.*, 2010. Athlete development and coaching. *In*: J. Lyle and C. Cushion, eds. *Sports coaching: Professionalisation and practice*. China: Elsevier, 63–84.

Dosman, C.F., Andrews, D., and Goulden, K.J., 2012. Evidence-based milestone ages as a framework for developmental surveillance. *Paediatrics and Child Health*, 17 (10), 561–568.

Falcao, W.R., Bloom, G.A., and Sabiston, C.M., 2020. The impact of humanistic coach training on youth athletes' development through sport. *International Journal of Sports Science and Coaching*, 15 (5–6), 610–620.

Gallahue, D.L., Ozmun, J.C., and Goodway, J.D., 2012. *Understanding motor development: Infants, children, adolescents, adults*, 7th ed. New York: McGraw-Hill.

Gymnastics Canada, n.d. *Recreational coaches: Non-competitive community sport stream, focusing on having fun, developing fitness, and acquiring fundamental skills* [online]. http://www.gymcan.org/programs/coaching/recreational-coaches [Accessed 30 April 2022].

Harlow, M., Bassett-Gunter, R., and Fraser-Thomas, J., 2021. Exploring parents', coaches', and children's experiences and perceived outcomes in preschooler sport. *Qualitative Research in Sport, Exercise and Health*, 14(4),1–18.

Harlow, M., and Fraser-Thomas, J., in-revision. Exploring early years sport: Take-up, pathways, and engagement patterns. *Sport in Society*, 1–38.

Harlow, M., and Fraser-Thomas, J., 2019. *Coaching preschoolers and toddlers: Challenges and strategies*. Invited poster presented at the 13th Annual Sport Participation Research Initiative (SPRI) Conference, Ottawa, Canada.

Harlow, M., Wolman, L., and Fraser-Thomas, J., 2018. Should toddlers and preschoolers participate in organised sport? A scoping review of developmental outcomes associated with young children's sport participation. *International Review of Sport and Exercise* Psychology, 13 (1), 40–64.

Hockey Canada, n.d. *Coaching requirements and resources for Timbits U7 hockey* [online]. https://www.hockeycanada.ca/en-ca/hockey-programs/coaching/under-7/coaches/resources [Accessed 30 April 2022].

Holt, N.L., *et al.*, 2017. A grounded theory of positive youth development through sport based on results from a qualitative meta-study. *International Review of Sport and Exercise Psychology*, 10 (1), 1–49.

Janssen, I. and LeBlanc, A.G., 2010. Systematic review of the health benefits of physical'activity and fitness in school-aged children and youth. *International Journal of Behavioral Nutrition and Physical Activity*, 7 (1), 1–16.

Jarvis, P., Newman, S., and Swiniarski, L., 2014. On 'becoming social': The importance of collaborative free play in childhood. *International Journal of Play*, 3 (1), 53–68.

Jones, S.M., and Kahn, J., 2017. *The evidence base for how we learn: Supporting students' social, emotional, and academic development. Consensus statements of evidence from the council of distinguished scientists* [online]. https://files.eric.ed.gov/fulltext/ED577039.pdf [Accessed 30 April 2022].

Kahn, J., Bailey, R., and Jones, S., 2019. *Coaching social and emotional skills in youth sports* [online]. https://assets.aspeninstitute.org/content/uploads/2019/02/CallsForCoaches_Final_Web.pdf [Accessed 30 April 2022].

Kirk, D., 2005. Physical education, youth sport and lifelong participation: The importance of early learning experiences. *European Physical Education Review*, 11 (3), 239–255.

LaPrade, R.F., *et al.*, 2016. AOSSM early sport specialisation consensus statement. *Orthopaedic Journal of Sports Medicine*, 4 (4), 1–8.

Lefebvre, J.S., *et al.*, 2016. Describing and classifying coach development programmes: A synthesis of empirical research and applied practice. *International Journal of Sports Science and Coaching*, 11 (6), 887–899.

Lubans, D.R., *et al.*, 2010. Fundamental movement skills in children and adolescents. *Sports Medicine*, 40 (12), 1019–1035.

Malti, T. and Noam, G.G., 2016. Social-emotional development: From theory to practice. *European Journal of Developmental Psychology*, 13 (6), 652–665.

McNeill, J., *et al.*, 2018. Physical activity and modified organised sport among preschool children: Associations with cognitive and psychosocial health. *Mental Health and Physical Activity*, 15, 45–52.

Ministry of Ontario, May 26, 2021. *Early child development: Learn about programs that can support your child's growth and development from the time they're born until they start school* [online]. https://www.ontario.ca/page/early-child-development [Accessed 30 April 2022].

Muir, B., *et al.*, 2011. Developmentally appropriate approaches to coaching children. *In*: I. Stafford, ed. *Coaching children in sport*. New York: Routledge, 39–59.

Mustard, J.F., 2006. Experience-based brain development: Scientific underpinnings of the importance of early child development in a global world. *Paediatrics and Child Health*, 11 (9), 571–572.

Neely, K.C. and Holt, N.L., 2014. Parents' perspectives on the benefits of sport participation for young children. *The Sport Psychologist*, 28 (3), 255–268.

Ostrosky, M.M. and Jung, E.Y., 2010. *What works briefs: Building positive teacher-child relationships*. http://csefel.vanderbilt.edu/briefs/wwb12.pdf

ParticipACTION, 2018. *Canadian kids need to move more to boost their brain health* [online]. https://www.participaction.com/sites/default/files/downloads/2018_participaction_report_card_-_highlight_report_0.pdf [Accessed 30 April 2022].

Patel, D.R., Soares, N., and Wells, K., 2017. Neurodevelopmental readiness of children for participation in sports. *Translational Pediatrics*, 6 (3), 167–173.

Pellegrini, A.D. and Smith, P.K., 1998. The development of play during childhood: Forms and possible functions. *Child Psychology and Psychiatry Review*, 3 (2), 51–57.

Petty, K., 2016. *Developmental milestones of young children* (revised edition). St Paul, MN: Redleaf Press.

Piaget, J., 1964. Part I: Cognitive development in children: Piaget development and learning. *Journal of Research in Science Teaching*, 2 (3), 176–186.

Pienaar, A.E., Van Rensburg, E., and Smit, A., 2011. Effect of a Kinderkinetics programme on components of children's perceptual-motor and cognitive functioning. *South African Journal for Research in Sport, Physical Education and Recreation*, 33 (3), 113–128.

Purcell, L., 2005. Sport readiness in children and youth. *Paediatrics and Child Health*, 10 (6), 343–344.

Sanders, M.R., 2008. Triple P-Positive Parenting Program as a public health approach to strengthening parenting. *Journal of Family Psychology*, 22 (4), 506–517.

Sport for Life, 2019. *Long-term development in sport and physical activity 3.0* [online]. https://sportforlife.ca/wpcontent/uploads/2019/12/LTD_Framework_December_2019-scaled.png [Accessed 30 April 2022].

Timmons, B.W., Naylor, P.J., and Pfeiffer, K.A., 2007. Physical activity for preschool children—how much and how?. *Applied Physiology, Nutrition, and Metabolism*, 32 (S2E), 122–134.

Tremblay, M.S., *et al.*, 2018. Canada's physical literacy consensus statement: Process and outcome. *BMC Public Health*, 18 (2), 1–18.

Visser-Bochane, M.I., *et al.*, 2020. Identifying milestones in language development for young children ages 1 to 6 years. *Academic Pediatrics*, 20 (3), 421–429.

Whitehead, M.E., Durden-Myers, E.J., and Pot, N., 2018. The value of fostering physical literacy. *Journal of Teaching in Physical Education*, 37 (3), 252–261.

# 4

# SUPPORTING THE DEVELOPMENT OF SPORTING CREATIVITY IN CHILDREN THROUGH AN ENSKILMENT APPROACH

*Carl T. Woods, James Rudd, and Sam Robertson*

## Introduction

This chapter discusses the development of sporting creativity in children, framed through a contemporary ecological-anthropological account of skill, learning and education. It starts by reviewing sporting creativity; a construct which is conceptualised and defined here in a relational way; that is, as an exceptional, adaptive motor solution that functionally achieves a task goal (Orth *et al.*, 2017). This leads to a review of its development through an appropriately scaled theoretical lens; one which situates behaviour as an emergent, embedded and embodied phenomenon. Thus, weaving in key ideas from an ecological dynamics rationale (Button *et al.*, 2021), the development of creativity is reviewed through an *enskilment approach* (Pálsson, 1994; Ingold, 2000; Prins and Wattchow, 2020; Woods *et al.*, 2021).

At its core, an enskilment approach views learning as inseparable from 'doing' in 'place' (Lave, 1990; Ingold, 2000), thereby emphasising the importance of both contextuality and the environment in supporting the development of creativity (inclusive of its sociocultural aspects – Glăveanu, 2020). To highlight the relational foundations of this contemporary approach when applied to sport, it is contrasted with a more traditional account of motor skill learning. Following this, the chapter reviews the key, entangled threads of enskilment, showing how each can contribute to the development of sporting creativity in children. Practical implications are brought to life in this chapter through their alignment with key ideas of an ecological dynamics rationale. Lastly, a brief summary of the chapter is presented, emphasising four key practical takeaways for coaches of children in sport, while highlighting areas for future research.

## Review of Current Research

### *Creativity: A Relational Perspective*

Creativity has been a notoriously hard construct to define in the behavioural sciences (see Simonton, 2012; Glăveanu and Tanggaard, 2014; Glăveanu, 2020 for various examples). In sport,


DOI: 10.4324/9781003199359-6

it has been proposed as consisting of four constructs; traditions, tactics, creativity *in* sport as opposed to *about* sport, and creativity as an emergent property of the organism-environment system (de sa Fardila and Allen, 2020). Viewed through a cognitive lens, creativity has been conceptualised as an idea that results independent of action, in which behaviour is merely the enactment of a creative thought preceding it. A critique of this perspective is that it drives a divide between the mind and body and body and environment (Orth *et al.*, 2017; de sa Fardila and Allen, 2020). This risks a Cartesian dualism, potentially manifesting in *organismic asymmetries* (Davids and Araújo, 2010). Specifically, the internal mechanics or processes of an organism (i.e. child, athlete, coach) are positioned hierarchically to, and studied detached from, the environment (inclusive of historical contexts) in which they inhabit. The risk here for a coach, in their interactions with a child in sport, is that they miss the important role that the environment plays in the development of creativity. For example, due to the separation between the body and environment, there could be a tendency to focus on instilling creative ideas into the mind of the child, to be stored in their long-term memory, and then implemented in practice when the time is right. What this approach risks disregarding is the action capabilities of the child in the environment they are placed, and how these action capabilities implicate the functionality of creative behaviour. In other words, what may be a functionally creative movement solution for one child may not be for another child (or an adolescent or adult), even if in the same environment, given differences in their action capabilities.

In working toward a holistic view of creativity, which acknowledges the interaction between the performer (child) and the environment, a more relational definition has been proposed – situating it not as a mental construct, but as a functionally adaptable motor action:

> Motor creativity reflects an individual's *adaptability*, but is *exceptional* in its level of originality relative to other adaptive solutions (i.e. within and/or between individuals). Motor creativity can be defined as *new ways* of acting adaptive, or acting adaptive in *new solutions* (Hristovski *et al.*, 2011). In both instances, this implies that creative actions are *functional.*
>
> *(Orth et al., 2017, p. 2, emphasis added)*

Accordingly, this chapter defines creativity through this same relational lens – thereby moving away from the dualistic undertones of a more cognitively focused account. However, doing so means that its development needs to be supported by an appropriately scaled theoretical perspective – one which situates learning as a contextual, embedded and embodied, phenomenon.

## Enskilment: A Contemporary Perspective to a Traditional View of Motor Skill

Enskilment is defined as: "'Understanding *in* practice' [...], in which *learning* is inseparable from *doing*, and in which both are *embedded* in the context of a practical engagement in the world" (Ingold, 2000, p. 416, emphasis added). This definition immediately cuts the divide of mind and body and body and environment that traditional, cognitively oriented worldviews of behaviour and learning tend to create (Pálsson, 1994). For example, traditional motor skill learning theories typically focus their scale of analysis on the performer, directing little, if any, focus on the environment in which the performer inhabits, or the context in which a certain behaviour emerges (Anson *et al.*, 2005). The assumption is that changes in a performer's movement capabilities are resultant from computational processes occurring in the mind, which function to process inputted information from the environment to construct a response to then be enacted by the passive body (Anson *et al.*, 2004). This is driven by the view that the environment is not sufficient on its own to directly regulate behaviour – it is informationally *impoverished* (Gibson, 1979) – offering only cues for performers who are then required to integrate them with previously constructed mental representations to control and coordinate movement (Davids and Araújo, 2010). Experts, then, would be understood as performers who are better able to internally represent the environment they occupy, using these representations to act accordingly (Ingold, 2018). From this more traditional view, creativity in children would be understood as a mental or cognitive process, in which a child *thinks* more divergently than their less creative counterparts, with this 'creative thought' then being rolled off by the body when the time is 'right' (Orth *et al.*, 2017; de sa Fardila and Allen, 2020). Teaching a child to be creative then, would be understood as an *indirect* process of instilling, or transmitting creative thoughts into the minds of the performer, to be integrated with their stored knowledge about a task and environment (Ingold, 2000, 2018).

In contrast, an enskilment approach emphasises that learning cannot occur separate from place, as it develops in the messiness of 'doing' in context (Ingold, 2000). This contemporary notion, recently applied to the sport sciences (Woods *et al.*, 2021), aligns with key ideas from an ecological dynamics rationale, which views skilled actions not as contextless repetitions, but as dynamic, body-environment interactions that performers learn to actively self-regulate by directly perceiving opportunities for action toward the achievement of a task goal (Button *et al.*, 2021). What is acquired as one enskils into their environment, then, is a *functionally adaptable fit* between action capabilities and the possibilities for action within an environment (Gibson, 1979; Jacobs and Michaels, 2007). The emergence of this fit is dynamic (Jacobs and Michaels, 2007), in that it continuously changes as the action capabilities of a performer change, along with the possibilities to act within the environment. This means that performers are required to maintain a sensitive perceptual *attunement* to the surrounding sources of information that directly specifies an environments' affordances (i.e. opportunities for action) (Gibson, 1979).

## Enskilment and Creativity

The relational foundations of enskilment, reviewed above, are of importance in supporting the development of sporting creativity in children. For example, although a child's intentionality in sport is often shaped by the governing rules of a game they are playing – like not being allowed to double dribble in basketball, or an outfield player not being able to handle the ball in football – there is a difference between knowing about a games rules, and creatively exploiting them to (en) skilfully 'play' it (Woods *et al.*, 2021). For example, to creatively find a novel, functional and exceptionally adaptable motor solution:

- To achieve an open three point shot, a young basketballer would be continually attuning and adapting to the dynamics of the game environment, such as the ball position, movements and expertise of opponents, defenders and their position on the court.
- To score six runs off the last two deliveries to win a game of cricket, a young batter would need to consider the position of fielders, the arm and wrist position of the bowler, and the balls pitch and bounce off the wicket to hit the ball to an appropriate field location.
- To return a wide forehand in tennis, a young player would need to attune to key information about the balls flight, court location, its bounce and the movement of their opponent.

As is noted, each example is rooted in context, emphasising that creativity emerges in the entanglement of the child's action capabilities, the task requirements, and the opportunities to act within the environment. This means that creativity, developed and supported through an enskilment approach, is not pre-programmed as a thought to be enacted by the body or transmitted by a coach as a 'way of doing'. Rather, it emerges *as* the child interacts with key regulatory sources of information to solve the dynamic, contextual problems experienced during competition (Hsu and Lim, 2016; Woods *et al.*, 2021).

A creatively enskiled child, then, would not be one who just thinks more divergently than their less creative counterpart, but one who is better able to perceive and then exploit opportunities for action in their environment that others may not pick up – thereby solving problems in functional, exceptional and adaptive ways. From an ecological dynamics rationale, such creative performers would likely have established, and continue to develop, an evolving fit between their action capabilities and the opportunities for action perceived within their performance environment (Davids *et al.*, 2012; Orth *et al.*, 2017). The role of a coach in supporting the development of creativity in children, then – viewed through an enskilment lens – would not be instil creative ideas into their minds, but to support them in developing their own creative ways of solving performance-related problems by perceiving unique opportunities to act. This proposition is congruent with the work of Ribeiro *et al.* (2019), who suggested that by harnessing principles of dynamic systems theory, sports coaches could facilitate opportunities in training to support sports performers in self-organising synergised, *innovative* behaviour in a *local-to-global* direction (performer-performer-environment; bottom up), as opposed to just relying on synergy driven in a *global-to-local* direction (performer-performer; top down). As an aside, it is important to note here that the perception of these unique opportunities to act are entangled within the capabilities of the child, and the broader sociocultural contexts in which they are situated. Meaning, enskilfully learning to be creative is not a process that can occur separate to the place and context it is to be developed.

So, *how* would a coach actually go about supporting a child in the development of creativity through an enskilment approach? In answering this question, three related threads of enskilment – *taskscapes*, *guided attention*, and *wayfinding* – are reviewed (Woods *et al.*, 2021). Below, these are each conceptualised and applied at various levels in the development of creativity – the taskscape, viewed as the performance environment; guided attention, viewed as the primary role of the sports coach; and wayfinding, viewed as the growth of an actively self-regulating, creative child.

## The Taskscape as the Performance Environment

At the core of an enskilment approach is the notion that learning not only emerges through doing, but it is inseparable from the place in which it is done (Ingold, 2000). This is because people progressively become familiar with a place's features – what it looks, sounds, smells and feels like, manifest in the movements and tasks of others – understanding how such features impact the task they are taking up with. A task, when viewed through an enskilment approach, is best understood as a practical, goal-directed activity undertaken by an individual interacting with an environment (Ingold, 2000). Thus, the taskscape can be understood as the "entire ensemble of tasks in their *mutual interlocking*" (Ingold, 2000, p. 195, emphasis added). The added emphasis here highlights that tasks are rarely (if ever) completed in isolation of interactions with both people and environment (Woods *et al.*, 2021). This alludes to a self-organisation and temporality of the taskscape – meaning that as children grow and develop, along with their environment, so do task dynamics (Woods *et al.*, 2021). The enskiled performer, then, must be *sensitive*, *responsive* and *adaptive* to the changing dynamics of the taskscape to preserve the functionality of their goal-directed behaviours within it. This means that what constitutes a creative movement solution for a child at one point in their development may not necessarily be so at a later stage of life – demonstrating the dynamism of supporting the development of creativity.

Aligned with an ecological dynamics rationale, these ideas resonate with those of *representative learning design* (Araújo *et al.*, 2005). Fundamentally, representative learning design advocates for practice tasks to consist of key regulatory information sources that are representative of those experienced by performers during competition or play (Pinder *et al.*, 2011). Tasks designed as such preserve the coupling between perception and action, thereby helping children learn to attune to information that directly specifies opportunities for action. In football, this concept could support children in learning to creativity dribble and deceive opponents – skills important in competition – through the design of practice tasks that invite opportunities to perform such actions. For example, Uehara *et al.* (2018) emphasised the importance of unstructured play, and of preserving informationally rich,authentic environments, for Brazilian children learning to play football creatively. While in youth Tennis, Buszard *et al.* (2014) demonstrated that by scaling the size of a racquet to be matched to the action capabilities of the child using it, and modifying a balls compression such that it is easier to be hit, children were able to make better ball-racquet contact in practice, thereby better preserving key – representative – information-movement couplings. As alluded to within the conceptualisation of the taskscape, representative learning design emphasises that what performers learn is not the action *per se*, but how to adaptively *fit* this action within the constraints of the performance environment to functionally achieve a task goal. This idea is captured within the neurobiological concept of *degeneracy* (Edelman and Gally, 2001), which proposes that different structural elements can reorganise to achieve the same (or highly similar) task outcome. So, threading the anthropological ideas of the taskscape with the ecological ideas of representative learning design – what would the taskscape actually 'look' like in a sporting context to support the development of creativity?

## The Taskscape: Implications for the Development of Creativity in Children

When applied to children, the idea of the taskscape emphasises that creativity is far more than the simple enactment of an idea by the body, established prior to and out of context. In learning to snowboard, for example, a child would be required to learn to perform a range of different, but interlocking tasks if they are to:

i *Creatively* find novel movement solutions to optimise point scoring potential during competition,

ii *Creatively* stay 'up' on their snowboard when attempting new routes, tricks or manoeuvrers, or

iii *Creatively* avoid colliding with obstacles on a less familiar slope (like trees, shrubs and/or other snowboarders).

To exemplify, a child snowboarder would need to learn to detect key information sources that specify properties of a slopes surface – perceiving its textural properties, like its hardness or softness – to help them adapt their line while moving toward a jump or traversing down a route. They would need to learn how to concurrently read varying weather conditions, learning how wind, recent snow, or ice could implicate how they interact with the slope's properties during a run. They may learn to customise or manipulate features of their board, changing its design to fit their action capabilities so they feel more 'in tune' with properties of the slope – thereby optimising their functionality while snowboarding. It may also see them learn the sociocultural rules and norms of their local slope by interacting with other, older snowboarders also dwelling in the performance environment – perhaps coming to *know of*

(Gibson, 1966, 1979) certain tricks, routes or manoeuvres that are viewed favourably by their older peers. The key point here, though, is that from an enskilment approach, learning to creatively perform a sporting task, like snowboarding, cannot be achieved in isolation. It is contextual, embedded, emergent, and embodied, influencing (and being influenced by) various other interlocking tasks that make up the taskscape. In other words, the task shapes the child, while their interactions shape the taskscape. Viewed in such a relational way, a child would progressively enter into a type of 'poetic involvement' with their taskscape (Ingold, 2000) – learning to attend to various sights, sounds and feelings, as they creatively find their own way through the task (see Woods *et al.*, 2021).

Having established that the taskscape is *where* and *what* a child learns, the focus now shifts toward *how* a sports coach can support them in learning how to creatively solve emergent performance-related problems encountered within the taskscape. Thus, the next section reviews the coach's role within an enskilment approach to support the development creativity in children.

## Guided Attention as the Primary Role of the Sports Coach

Within an enskilment approach, education is viewed etymologically as *e-ducere* – meaning 'to lead out' (Masschelein, 2010; Rudd *et al.*, 2021; Woods *et al.*, 2021). This view encourages sports practitioners to take on a different role to one that is rooted in teaching via the impartment of knowledge by way of rules or conventions. Rather, it should focus on them working with sports performers to guide their attention toward key features of the taskscape used to help them navigate through it (Woods *et al.*, 2020):

> [with an enskilment approach] The task of the educator, then, is not to explicate knowledge for the benefit of those who are assumed, by default, to be ignorant, but to provide inspiration, guidance and criticism in the exemplary pursuit of truth.
>
> *(Ingold, 2018, p. ix)*

This educative process is critical, with the coach required to help the child become attentive to subtle features of the taskscape through inspiration, patience, guidance and support, while maintaining a deep understanding of the child's action capabilities relative to the task they are undertaking (Rudd *et al.*, 2021; Woods *et al.*, 2021). This can be understood as a type of *active self-discovery* – 'active', which reflects the interaction between the coach and child; 'self-discovery', in that the coach encourages the child to discover, attend to, and interact with the taskscapes key features as they are, where they occur (Ingold, 2013). Given this, the process can be conceived as being both 'hands on' and 'hands off' – hands on in the sense of showing one where to look (guiding one's attention), but hands off by not telling them what to see (Woods *et al.*, 2020; McKay *et al.*, 2021). It is important, here, to briefly elaborate on the etymology of 'attend' given its centrality to the educative process within an enskilment approach – *ad-tendere* – meaning 'to stretch toward' (Ingold, 2018). Thus, in *leading* individuals *out* into the taskscape, the sports coach can support the child in *stretching toward* its key features – like the the sight of an emergent gap between defenders in a football game, the feeling of the waters current while kayaking through rapids or the sound of a ball hitting 'the middle' of a cricket bat.

Guiding a child's attention toward creative movement solutions can take shape in a variety of ways. For example, leaning on key ideas of ecological dynamics (Button *et al.*, 2021), sports coaches could *design* information-rich practice tasks that channel or *constrain* a child's attention toward the exploration of various features of the environment (Chow *et al.*, 2015). The goal of such practice task designs would be to encourage children to search, discover and exploit various opportunities for action (Davids *et al.*, 2008), helping develop their *knowledge of* (Gibson, 1966, 1979) the taskscape. The key aspect here, is that the role of a coach in supporting the development of a creatively enskiled sports performer is one of *guidance*. While this guidance may take shape in forms of showing, nudging or modelling, it rarely takes shape in the pedagogical act of telling or instructing about 'how to do' (Rudd *et al.*, 2021). Relatively softer pedagogical approaches, captured within the guidance of attention, are intended to support the key aspect of education viewed within an enskilment approach (that of active self-discovery). Telling, instructing and informing on what to do risks these educational foundations by encouraging the child to simply conform to conventional standards – 'defined ways of doing' – moving them away from developing and exploring their own, creative ways of achieving a task goal. An analogy that may be of use for this distinction is that of a recipe – a recipe can indeed assist a cook about to make a dish by narrowing the scope of behavioural possibilities (i.e. a coach offering informational task constraints prior to a practice task). However, while cooking, information that directly specifies various smells, tastes and feelings is what regulates, or constrains, behaviour, not the instructions of a recipe (i.e. continued coach instruction and feedback about 'what' to do or 'how' it should look). Though, careful consideration is required on behalf of the coach here, as the pedagogical actions used – while being rooted in the notion of guidance – would likely need to be tailored to the specific needs, action capabilities and perhaps ages of the children they are working with to ensure they are placed in safe, but still uncertain environments.

From a dynamical systems perspective, the 'softer pedagogical approaches' of enskilment supports the child to self-organise and synergise interactions with the environment in a *local-to-global* direction, encouraging them to engage deeply, through which, global patterns of (self-organised) behaviour emerge (Ribeiro *et al.*, 2019). Comparatively, 'hard pedagogical approaches' could be associated with a top-down, coach driven approach, where behaviour is organised by an external agent and synergy is formed in a *global-to-local* direction (Ribeiro *et al.*, 2019). While appreciating its bidirectionality, it should be noted that the former would not likely leave as much room for the emergence of creative, synergised behaviour, as children would simply be following prescribed 'plays', not exploring novel, adaptive solutions. In appreciating this, what could a softer pedagogical approach of guiding attention look like in the design of practice tasks to support the development of creativity in children?

## *Guided Attention: Implications for the Development of Creativity in Children*

In this example, an experienced football coach is working with a youth team who are learning how to creatively find and exploit space during a game. To assist with this, the coach could firstly design a practice task that consists of two opposing teams – both tasked with the goal of outscoring their opponent. To promote the emergence of functionally creative movements during the practice task, the coach could then manipulate the pitch dimensions – doing so in such a way that funnels the pitch out at one end, and narrows it in at the other. This is intended to simulate the type of football (soccer) pitches typically found in urbanised, highly dense areas known for supporting the development of creative footballers (see Uehara *et al.*, 2018). By manipulating the pitch dimensions in such a way, the team shooting toward the wider end, for example, may explore different ways of exploiting their defenders by using the increasing width of the field advantageously – stretching their defenders apart through longer, lofted passes. Comparatively, the team scoring toward the narrowing end may explore ways of performing shorter, faster passes – trying to avoid or minimise the risk of interception from their opponent.

Additionally, a coach could encourage children to explore flare and cheekiness in deceiving their opponents when in possession of the ball, awarding 'bonus' points to players who are able to functionally 'nut-meg' or 'wrong foot' (Uehara *et al.*, 2018) their opponent. The integration of 'functionally' is important here, as part of this deceptive exploration would likely help children learn to contextualise creative actions – learning when actions such as the 'nut-meg' would indeed be an appropriate, *functional*, movement solution based on the interaction of constraints (i.e. perceiving the position of a defender that invites passing between their legs relative to a teammate and time of game). The key point here is that carefully designed practice tasks, informed by skilfully manipulating constraints, can offer one way of engaging in a softer pedagogical approach that *guides* the *attention* of children toward the exploration of functionally creative movement solutions. What these creative solutions 'are', then, are functional behaviours that emerge in the messiness of the child's action capabilities, coupled with the task dynamics, and the environments opportunities to act.

### *Wayfinding: The Actively Self-Regulating Child*

The last thread of an enskilment approach reviewed here encourages coaches to re-conceptualise how children learn and interact with their surrounds. That is, viewed not as passengers who follow conventions, templates or idealised 'techniques', but as wayfinders who rely on perceptions, cognitions, emotions and actions to successfully find their way through the emergent problems of the taskscape (Woods *et al.*, 2020). Wayfinding, then, is a narrative way of coming to 'know' the taskscape – narrative, meaning that people learn of a taskscapes features (i.e. its surfaces, layout, objects, climate and sociocultural norms), by asking questions, listening to stories, and gaining practical, embedded, first-hand experience (Raubal, 2008). This means that wayfinding is far more than simply navigating *across* a taskscape – manifest in sport, for example, by the breaking up of a skill into components to be mastered separately, out of context, prior to being reassembled with the intent of being rolled out in competition. Rather, a creatively enskiled wayfinder is not interested in following pre-specified and de-contextualised routes to 'destinations' (i.e. rehearsing orchestrated and unopposed patterns of play in football), but is more interested in learning to attend to environmental features of the taskscape that emerge along the journey. That is, the outcome of a task, for a wayfinder, is subsequent to the attentiveness grown in its participation.

Wayfinding, as a means of conceptualising the sports performer, has recently been proposed through the framework of ecological dynamics (Woods *et al.*, 2020). In doing so, sports performers have been conceptualised as active self-regulators, who learn to wayfind through dynamic, complex taskscapes by relying on their perceptions, cognitions, emotions and actions – not just the instructions provided by a coach. Threading this back into the design of carefully constrained practice tasks, sport coaches could progressively integrate appropriately scaled challenges and problems into practice tasks that help children develop their self-regulating capacities to creatively solve them. As we go onto exemplify, 'open-ended' questioning could be a soft pedagogical approach that sports coaches could lean on here (Renshaw and Chow, 2019).

## Implications for Children's Sport Coaching

### *Wayfinding: Implications for the Development of Creativity in Children*

In this example, an experienced coach of a baseball team is helping a child learn to perceive and then creatively exploit gaps in the field to score runs while batting. In sticking with the key theme of questioning to support them in wayfinding through the taskscape that is the baseball game, the coach asks carefully designed questions that guides the child's attention toward:

- *Where* the fielders are located,
- *How* their placement may implicate the child's likelihood of hitting a home run or sneaking a quick base,
- *How* the fielding positions may indicate the type of pitch, and
- *How* the child could manipulate different batting strategies to creatively exploit perceived opportunities to score runs or get on base.

The key point of these questions is that they are intended to be answered through the child's creative exploratory actions – not necessarily verbalised in responses provided out of the game. By responding with actions in context, the child is subsequently developing their knowledge of the taskscape, learning of its mutually interlocking features, and how such features could be exploited to support them in creatively wayfinding through it. Moreover, the questioning could prompt the child – when on the pitch – to creatively discover information that supports them to actively self-regulate in performance. For example, the coach could carefully place fielders in front of the child batting. Then they could then ask them: *"where is space on the field without fielders?"* This could encourage the child batting to visually explore that taskscape – picking up information that specifies that there are no fielders located in certain regions of the field. Then, the coach could ask: *"what shots could you play to get the ball to the positions where there are no fielders?"* Following this, the coach then simply observes the type of shots that emerge as the child wayfinds through the taskscape – that is, score runs by hitting the ball to the various field locations without fielders. After a while, the coach may start to manipulate the fielders' positions, asking the child again where the fielders are and what shots they could explore to avoid them. The key point here, is that when performers are viewed as wayfinders, sports coaches are encouraged to lean on softer pedagogical approaches – such as questioning – to help performers learn to actively self-regulate their perceptions, emotions, cognitions and actions by creatively solving the dynamic and complex problems experienced in practice and competition.

## Summary, Future Directions and Future Research

This chapter reviewed key literature surrounding an ecological-anthropological account of creativity, demonstrating what it could mean for coaches supporting its development in children. In doing so, creativity was first conceptualised from an ecologically dynamic worldview, then its development was reviewed through an enskilment approach. Four key components of an enskilment approach can now be summarised following this review to support the development of sporting creativity in children:

1. *Creativity is inseparable from doing in place – filled with contextual information,*
2. *Creativity emerges as a child entangles with the taskscape,*
3. *Creativity is supported by coaches through softer pedagogical channels that guides the attention of children toward key features of the taskscape,*
4. *Viewed as wayfinders, children are encouraged to learn to actively self-regulate their perceptions, emotions, cognitions and actions towards the creative solving of performance-related problems experienced within training and competition.*

Future research into this ecological-anthropological approach could explore the more nuanced details of each thread of enskilment with a specific emphasis on its application in youth sport. For example, the temporality of the performance environment – which we reviewed here as the taskscape – could be explored, understanding how subtle changes to the performance environment changes the emergent, creative opportunities for action picked up and acted upon by children, who are also growing and developing. This would encourage practitioners to conceptualise the performance environment as a dynamic, ever-changing landscape, which shapes, and is shaped by, children over varying timescales of performance, learning and development. Moreover, it would be of interest for future work to explore what guidance from coaches could look like in children of differing ages and action capabilities when learning to be creative in sport.

## References

Araújo, D., Davids, K., and Serpa, S., 2005. An ecological approach to expertise effects in decision-making in a simulated sailing regatta. *Psychology for Sport and Exercise*, 6 (6), 671–692.

Buszard, T. *et al.*, 2014. Modifying equipment in early skill development: A tennis perspective. *Research Quarterly for Exercise and Sport*, 85 (2), 218–225.

Button, C., *et al.*, 2021. *Dynamics of skill acquisition: An ecological dynamics approach*. 2nd ed. Champaign, IL: Human Kinetics.

Chow, J.Y. *et al.*, 2015. *Nonlinear pedagogy in skill acquisition: An introduction*. Abingdon: Routledge.

Davids, K., and Araújo, D., 2010. The concept of 'Organismic Asymmetry' in sport science. *Journal of Science and Medicine in Sport*, 13(6), 633–640.

Davids, K. *et al.*, 2012. Ecological dynamics and motor learning design in sport. *In*: M. Williams, and N. Hodges, eds. *Skill Acquisition in Sport: Research, theory and practice*, 2nd ed. New York and London: Routledge, 112–130.

Davids, K., Button, C., and Bennett, S., 2008. *Dynamics of skill acquisition. A constraints-led approach*. Champaign, IL: Human Kinetics.

de sa Fardila, F., and Allen, J.B., 2020. Defining, assessing, and developing creativity in sport: a systematic narrative review. *International Review of Sport and Exercise Psychology*, 12 (1), 104–127.

Edelman, G.M., and Gally, J.A., 2001. Degeneracy and complexity in biological systems. *Proceedings of the National Academy of Sciences of the United States of America*, 98 (24), 13763–13768.

Gibson, J.J., 1966. *The senses considered as perceptual systems*. London: Houghton, Mifflin and Company.

Gibson, J.J., 1979. *The ecological approach to visual perception*. London: Houghton, Mifflin and Company.

Glăveanu V.P., and Tanggaard, 2014. Creativity, identity, and representation: Towards a socio-cultural theory of creative identity. *New Ideas in Psychology*, 34 (1), 12–21.

Glăveanu, V.P., 2020. A sociological theory of creativity: Bridging the social, the material, and the psychological. *Review of General Psychology*, 24 (4), 335–354.

Hristovski, R., *et al.*, 2011. Constraints-induced emergence of functional novelty in complex neurobiological systems: A basis for creativity in sport. *Nonlinear Dynamics, Psychology, and Life Sciences*, 15 (2), 175–206.

Hsu, E., and Han Lim, C., 2016. Enskilment into the environment: The *Yijin jing* worlds of *Jin* and *Qi*. *Max Planck Institute for the History of Science*, preprint 486.

Ingold, T., 2000. *The perception of the environment: Essays on livelihood, dwelling and skill*. New York and London: Routledge.

Ingold, T., 2013. *Making: Anthropology, archaeology, art and architecture*. New York and London: Routledge.

Ingold, T., 2018. *Anthropology and/as education*. New York and London: Routledge.

Jacobs, D.M., and Michaels, C.F., 2007. Direct learning. *Ecological Psychology*, 19 (4), 321–349.

Lave, J., 1990. The culture of acquisition and the practice of understanding. *In*: J.W. Stigler, R.A. Schweder, and G. Herdt, eds. *Cultural psychology: Essays on comparative human development*. UK: Cambridge University Press, pp 309–327.

Masschelein, J., 2010. E-ducating the gaze: The idea of a poor pedagogy. *Ethics and Education*, 5 (1), 43–53.

McKay, J., *et al.*, 2021. An ecological insight into the design and integration of attacking principles of play in professional rugby union: A case example. *International Sport Coaching Journal*, 8 (3), 394–399.

Orth, D., *et al.*, 2017. Creative motor actions as emerging from movement variability. *Frontiers in Psychology*, 8, 1903.

Pálsson, G., 1994. Enskilment at sea. *Man*, 29 (4), 901–927.

Pinder, R., *et al.*, 2011. Representative learning design and functionality of research and practice in sport. *Journal of Sport and Exercise Psychology*, 33 (1), 146–155.

Prins, A., and Wattchow, B., 2020. The pedagogic moment: Enskilment as another way of being in outdoor education. *Journal of Adventure Education and Outdoor Learning*, 20 (1), 81–91.

Raubal, M., 2008. Wayfinding: Affordances and agent simulation. *In*: S. Shekhar, H. Xiong, and X. Zhou, eds. *Encyclopedia of GIS*. Boston, MA: Springer.

Renshaw, I., and Chow, J.Y., 2019. A constraint-led approach to sport and physical education pedagogy. *Physical Education and Sport Pedagogy*, 24 (2), 103–116.

Ribeiro, J. *et al.*, 2019. Exploiting bi-directional self-organizing tendencies in team sports: The role of the game model and tactical principles of play. *Frontiers in Psychology*, 10, 2213.

Rudd, J.R., *et al.*, 2021. An ecological dynamics conceptualisation of physical 'education': Where we have been and where we could go next. *Physical Education and Sport Pedagogy*, 26 (3), 293–306.

Simonton, D.K., 2012. Creativity, problem solving, and solution set sightedness: Radically reformulating BVSR. *Journal of Creative Behaviour*, 46 (1), 48–65.

Uehara, L., *et al.*, 2018. The role of informal, unstructured practice in developing football expertise: The case of Brazilian Pelada. *Journal of Expertise*, 1 (3), 162–180.

Woods, C.T. *et al.*, 2021. Enskilment: An ecological-anthropological worldview of skill, learning and education in sport. *Sports Medicine Open*, 7 (33), 38.

Woods, C.T., *et al.*, 2020. Wayfinding: How ecological perspectives of navigating dynamic environments can enrich our understanding of the learner and the learning process in sport. *Sports Medicine Open*, 6 (51), 51–63.

# 5

# TO HAVE FUN: WHAT IT MEANS AND ITS SIGNIFICANCE IN SPORT

*Amanda J. Visek, Andreas Ivarsson, Gary Putt, and Jordyn L. Learner*

## Introduction

Among children's rights in sport is their right to positive experiences that are fun. This right is reflected in the United Nations International Children's Emergency Fund (UNICEF) *Children's Rights in Sport Principles*, the World Players Association's *Declaration on Safeguarding the Rights of the Child Athlete*, Norway's *Children's Rights in Sport,* and the Aspen Institute Project Play's *Children's Bill of Rights in Sports*, to name a few. They draw on the United Nation's *Convention on the Rights of the Child* (1989) that asserts children's right to play and recreational activities, including children's right to have their views taken seriously in matters affecting them, like youth sport. Whether the goal is to provide children with a health-promoting leisure activity or talent development, their continued, or discontinued, involvement in sport is typically determined by their having fun or not having fun. Importantly too, in sport, positive experiences affect children's immediate and future human capital – benefiting them physically, socially, emotionally, and intellectually (Bailey *et al.*, 2013b). Though "designing play and practice activities that focus on fun" (Côté and Hancock, 2016, p. 60) is among the evidence-based recommendations for coaching children's sport, what it means for children to have fun still begs to be fully understood and appreciated among the adults responsible for delivering children's sport programming and supporting children in their athletic pursuits. In turn, children's right to have fun has not (yet) been fully realised. As such, the objectives of this chapter are to (a) synthesise empirical research that has given rise to the significance of children's enjoyment of sport and what it means to them to have fun, (b) connect current knowledge of fun with evidence-based theories and models that account for children's participation motives in sport, (c) discuss the implications of a rights-based approach to coaching children's sport with an obligation to make it fun, and finally, (d) suggest future research directions for bridging what is known about fun scientifically with the practice of making children's sport fun.

## Review of Current Research

The review of literature herein presents key findings of early research that underscored the benefits and significance of enjoyment and fun in children's sport with contemporary research that unpacked what having fun really means and children's prioritisation of determinants, i.e.

DOI: 10.4324/9781003199359-7

factors that affect the nature or outcome, that make sport fun. To call attention to the criticalness of fun as a focal point in children's sport, the review connects the fun determinants identified by children with prominent and scientifically supported theories commonly applied to understanding their sport participation motives.

## Early Research

Among the first models to propose and test enjoyment as a central element explaining children's motivation to continue in sport was the sport commitment model (i.e. Scanlan *et al.*, 1993a, 1993b, 1993c). Enjoyment (i.e. described as having fun), along with personal investments (e.g. time, effort, money), social constraints (e.g. social pressure to stay involved in sport), and involvement opportunities (e.g. the chance to engage in valued experiences) were found to positively affect sport commitment. A fifth construct, involvement alternatives (e.g. opportunities to engage in non-sporting activities), negatively affected sport commitment. Among the constructs, children's enjoyment and personal investments were the predominant predictors of their sport commitment. Another study (i.e. Carpenter *et al.*, 1993) also found greater sport enjoyment explained greater sport commitment among children.

Additional studies sought to identify precise predictors and sources of children's sport enjoyment. Among them, getting sufficient playing time, exerting greater effort, perceived athletic ability, experiencing mastery and competence along with performance satisfaction, elements of practice and competition design (e.g. balance between skill level and challenge), having family support, the presence of positive social interactions, and having coaching support positively contributed to children's sport enjoyment (Scanlan and Lewthwaite, 1986; Scanlan *et al.*, 1993a). Another study identified having fun was attributed to children's free choice along with their involvement (i.e. physical action, social interaction), sense of competence (i.e. doing well, improvement), and opportunity to play the sport again (Harris *et al.*, 1995). Later studies identified a positive social climate and pinpointed the role of children's social orientation (i.e. affiliation orientation, status orientation, social recognition) in their sport interest (e.g. Allen, 2003), and the association of peer relationships and positive friendships with children's continued participation (e.g. Ullrich-French and Smith, 2009; Bailey *et al.*, 2013b), enjoyment (Gardner *et al.*, 2016), and fun (e.g. Weiss and Amorose, 2008). Finally, studies also pointed to the role coaches have in promoting fun (e.g. Bengoechea *et al.*, 2004; North, 2007) and the significant influence their behaviors and approaches to interacting with children have on children's motivation in sport and their continued participation (e.g. Barnett *et al.*, 1992; Vallerand and Losier, 1999; Bailey *et al.*, 2013a).

## Contemporary Research

Indeed, early research used the terms 'fun' and 'enjoyment', often interchangeably, to describe an affective experience that is satisfying and pleasurable. Children, though, ordinarily describe their sport experiences bimodally, either as 'fun' or 'not fun' rather than 'enjoyable' or 'not enjoyable'. In addition, "Let's have fun!" is commonly said in coaches' pre-game talks and half-time huddles and "Have fun!" is a popular last message from parents as their children step out onto any playing surface. What though does it really mean to children to have fun and how can this experience be carefully curated? To these ends, contemporary research purposely sought to investigate children's sport experiences from their perspective by mapping fun, i.e. the FUN MAPS, with the intention the findings could assist sport national governing bodies (NGBs), and coaches, in their efforts to make fun the center stone of children's practice and competition experiences.

## What Makes Sport Fun

With the rights of the child in mind, and the objective of leveraging children's voices in sport, the FUN MAPS (Visek *et al.*, 2015) are the result of engaging child-athletes (U9–U19, girls and boys) as the experts of what makes sport fun, along with coaches, and sport parents, who collectively mapped fun. The series of interpretable maps visually display 81 determinants of fun arranged in 11 fun factors: *Trying Hard* (10 fun determinants), *Positive Team Dynamics* (6 fun determinants), *Positive Coaching* (12 fun determinants), *Learning and Improving* (9 fun determinants), *Games* (6 fun determinants), *Practices* (7 fun determinants), *Team Friendships* (7 fun determinants), *Mental Bonuses* (4 fun determinants), *Game Time Support* (6 fun determinants), *Team Rituals* (7 fun determinants), and *Swag* (7 fun determinants). These findings included many of the sources of enjoyment proposed by Scanlan *et al.* (1986, 1993a, 1993b) and tested by Wiersma (2001) through construction of a 28-item enjoyment measure. The FUN MAPS, however, offer a more robust 'big picture' overview of fun's integration in all aspects of children's athletic development, whilst serving as the data-driven blueprint for the fun integration theory. This theory posits development is central to children's sport and having fun is derived from four overarching sources. These include (a) contextual sources (*Practices, Games*), (b) internal sources (*Trying Hard, Learning and Improving, Mental Bonuses*), (c) social sources (*Positive Team Dynamics Team Friendships, Team Rituals*), and (d) external sources (*Positive Coaching, Game Time Support, Swag*). The 81 determinants of fun that make up the 4 sources and 11 factors, respectively, offer coaches a nuanced understanding of how to cultivate fun; see Visek *et al.* (2015) for illustrations of the FUN MAPS and the list of the 81 actionable fun determinants that make up the 11-factors. The fun integration theory's FUN MAPS are consistent with research by Vierimaa *et al.* (2017) that immediate, positive experiences described as enjoyable, accumulated over time, have lasting effects on athletes' development.

Notably, the FUN MAPS are evidence that having fun in sport is not synonymous with being silly, smiles and laughter, and goofing around (see Visek and Feiler, 2021 for further reading on the misconceptions of fun). Rather, contrary to popular (adult) belief, fun can broadly be described as a development-driven, task-oriented, multi-modal experience. Coaches can draw on the 81 fun determinants to intentionally source fun for children, across five domains that encompass the whole sport experience: (1) environmentally (e.g. by setting up well-organised practices that include small-sided games and partner-based drills, allowing children a voice, and opportunities to play different positions), (2) physically (e.g. providing children opportunities to compete and try hard, getting them lots of touches on the ball/puck, giving them high-fives/fist-bumps), (3) verbally (e.g. teaching children about the sport; talking to them in ways they can easily understand, providing feedback and encouragement that builds their confidence), (4) emotionally (e.g. actively listening to children, allowing them to make mistakes and handling mistakes as learning opportunities, being fair and approachable), and (5) socially (e.g. encouraging collaboration and sportsmanship among children, creating team routines/rituals, promoting team identity). Note the examples given here across the five domains are fun determinants drawn directly from the FUN MAPS.

## Children's Fun Priorities

When it comes to further understanding fun in children's sport, very often, the immediate questions asked are centered around the ways in which youth sport typically organises children by sex, age, and playing level. For example, how do girls and boys differ when it comes to fun? Does fun evolve as children develop and mature in age? Is what makes playing sport most fun different for children at recreational levels compared to those at highly select elite levels?

*Table 5.1* Fun factors by order of importance

| *Importance* | *Fun factor* | *No. of determinants* |
|---|---|---|
| Primary | 1. Trying Hard | 10 |
| | 2. Positive Team Dynamics | 6 |
| | 3. Positive Coaching | 12 |
| Secondary | 4. Learning and Improving | 9 |
| | 5. Games | 6 |
| | 6. Practices | 7 |
| | 7. Team Friendships | 7 |
| | 8. Mental Bonuses | 4 |
| | 9. Game Time Support | 6 |
| Tertiary | 10. Team Rituals | 7 |
| | 11. Swag | 7 |

Research has indicated, that regardless of whether child-athletes are girls or boys, younger or older in age, or play on recreational or more elite teams, when it comes to what makes playing sport the most fun, their priorities are overwhelming the same (i.e. Visek *et al.*, 2020). Of primary importance are the fun factors *Trying Hard*, *Positive Team Dynamics*, and *Positive Coaching*. Of secondary importance are *Learning and Improving*, *Games*, *Practice*, *Team Friendships*, *Mental Bonuses*, and *Game Time Support*. Of tertiary importance are *Team Rituals* and *Swag*. Of note, *Team Rituals* and *Swag* must not be misconstrued as being absent of value in having fun. Rather, when considered in tandem with the other nine fun factors, *Team Rituals* and *Swag* do not contribute as much to fun as those of primary and secondary importance, though they are certainly additive to having fun, as identified by children, and illustrated by the FUN MAPS.

In addition to examining children's priorities across the 11 fun factors, Visek *et al.* explored children's prioritisation of all 81 fun determinants. Irrespective of children's sex, age, and playing level, children's prioritisation of the fun determinants from utmost to less importance was also extraordinarily the same. In other words, children's fun priorities have been found to be more similar than they are different. Table 5.1 provides a list of the 11 factors, in order of relative importance, and denotes the number of actionable determinants coaches can utilise to construct fun in practice and competition settings. See Visek *et al.* (2020) for a comprehensive list of all 81 determinants, according to importance.

## *Parents and Coaches Understanding*

In addition to exploring children's fun priorities, parents' and coaches' understanding of children's fun priorities was also investigated. This study, by Visek *et al.* (2018a), indicated that overall, parents reported a relatively high understanding of children's prioritisation of the fun factors and fun determinants, as did coaches of younger children (U9–U13). Interestingly though, coaches of older athletes (U14–U19) reported significantly less understanding. This finding was noteworthy considering adolescence is the period during which most will typically leave sport; and, research has consistently found over time that sport being 'not fun' is the often-cited reason for dropping out (e.g. Durant *et al.*, 1991; Ewing and Seefeldt, 1996; Fraser-Thomas *et al.*, 2008; Armentrout and Kamphoff, 2011; Crane and Temple, 2015; Gardner *et al.*, 2017; Sport New Zealand, 2018; Back *et al.*, 2022). The findings of these studies, coupled with that by Visek *et al.* (2018a), would suggest that if coaches better understood what makes sport fun, and could deliver on making practices and game experiences more fun, athletes who ordinarily would leave sport may perhaps be motivated to stay involved.

## *Understanding Determinants of Fun through Prominent Models and Theoretical Frameworks*

Whilst the sport commitment model was pivotal in leveraging the role of children's enjoyment of sport and fun in their continued involvement, the fun integration theory's FUN MAPS have been a very nuanced and actionable advancement in understanding what makes playing organised sport fun. Next, the fun integration theory's factors and determinants are considered within the scope of research that empirically supports other sport participation models and theories explaining psychological constructs for understanding children's motives in sport. These constructs, including competence, motivation, and achievement, are associated with sources of enjoyment for children playing sport (see Weirsma, 2001), and are determinants of fun (see Visek *et al.*, 2015). Finally, a leisure constraints model is considered through the lens of the fun integration theory to offer an understanding of why children may find one sport more fun than another.

### *Competence Motivation Theory*

Competence motivation theory (Weiss and Chaumenton, 1992) asserts individuals are motivated to feel competent and, to satisfy this desire for competence, they must attempt mastery in their sport. For children, perceived control over their learning and performance skills, along with perceptions of self-confidence, competence, mastery, and success generate emotional states such as fun, enjoyment, happiness, and pride (Weinberg and Gould, 2011). Inversely, low perceived control in conjunction with low levels of confidence, competence, mastery, and success lead to anxiety and shame. Klint and Weiss' (1987) study found competence motivation theory explained the relationship between perceptions of competence and motives for children's sport participation. They found high perceived physical competence was associated with greater skill development and greater likelihood to participate than children who perceived themselves as less physically competent. Similarly, for children with high perceived social competence, the social aspects of sport were a stronger reason to take part than for those with low perceived social competence. Hence, children who perceive themselves as competent and successful are more likely to have fun and continue their sport participation, while those with low perceived competence and success are likely to experience negative emotional states and eventually dropout. Correspondingly, nearly 40% of the 81 fun determinants within the fun integration theory's FUN MAPS are competence-based within the fun factors *Trying Hard* (e.g. playing well, playing with confidence, reaching goals) and *Learning and Improving* (e.g. learning from mistakes, learning new skills), as well as competence-building within *Positive Coaching* (e.g. a knowledgeable coach), *Practices* (e.g. well-organised practices), and *Games* (e.g. getting playing time), which foster children's athletic development.

### *Achievement Goal Theory*

To fulfill our need for competence, achievement goal theory (Nicholls, 1984) posits individuals approach tasks with distinct goal orientations (i.e. outcome goal orientation, task goal orientation, social goal orientation) that differentially influence cognitions, emotions, and behavior. Outcome goal orientation, referred to as ego goal orientation as well, is described as setting goals to perform and defeat others (e.g. winning). Task goal orientation is setting goals to improve upon past performances (e.g. personal best). Social goal orientation is setting goals to achieve social connections (e.g. belonging to a group) whereby competence is judged by group affiliation and being liked by others (Weinberg and Gould, 2011; Lavallee *et al.*, 2012). Strong task goal orientation tends to be associated with stronger work ethic, persistence in the face of failure, and optimal performance (Weinberg and Gould, 2011). Further, for those with strong task orientation, perception of their ability is their reference, therefore it is easier for them to feel confident and have fun in sport. Likewise, research has shown a positive correlation between social goal orientation and enjoyment, perceived competence, and intrinsic motivation (Stuntz and Weiss, 2009). Within the scope of the fun integration theory's FUN MAPS, nearly 28% of the 81 fun determinants align with the task and social goal orientations of achievement goal theory (Visek *et al.*, 2015, 2018b). Whereas, high outcome goal orientation, in which children tend to compare their abilities to others with a focus, for example, on winning, has been associated with low perceived competence resulting in reduced effort, excuse-making, and less fun (Weinberg and Gould, 2011). Of the 81 fun determinants within the fun integration theory's FUN MAPS, just 1% was reflective of ego goal orientation; that is, winning (Visek *et al.*, 2015, 2018b). Coalescing achievement goal theory and the fun integration theory would suggest having fun is determined more significantly by the moment-to-moment task and social experiences accumulated within practices and games and less determined by a singular ego-oriented outcome of these events, such as defeating the other squad in a practice scrimmage or winning a game. Befittingly, this inference is supported by research (e.g. Visek *et al.*, 2020) which had found winning ranked #40 in importance among the 81 fun determinants, indicating there are 39 task- and social-oriented fun determinants ranked higher than winning when it comes to having fun; see Petlichkoff (1992) for additional discussion.

## Self-Determination Theory

Self-determination theory (Deci and Ryan, 1985, 2000) is based on the premise individuals are motivated to undertake an activity, or play a sport, based on innate psychological needs for autonomy, competence, and social connectedness. Many of the fun integration theory's 81 fun determinants promote children's autonomy, competence, and social connectedness in sport (Visek *et al.*, 2015, 2018b). Further to understanding motivation, self-determination theory suggests motivation lies along a continuum from amotivation (i.e. lack of desire to do an activity or sport; an absence of motivation) on one end of the continuum, to extrinsic motivation (i.e. doing an activity or sport as a means to an end; outcome driven), to intrinsic motivation on the other end (i.e. doing an activity or sport as a means in and of itself; process driven). These motivations are influenced by behavioral regulations described as autonomous (i.e. integrated regulation [confirming one's identity] and identified regulation [achieving personal goals]) or controlling (i.e. introjected regulation [to satisfy obligations] and external regulation [for reward or to avoid penalty]). Research suggests those who are motivated either intrinsically or extrinsically, and whose behavior is influenced more autonomously through either integrated regulation or identified regulation, tend to persist in their sport participation compared with those whose extrinsic motivation is controlled through introjected regulation or external regulation (Pelletier *et al.*, 2001; Sarrazin *et al.*, 2007; Rottensteiner *et al.*, 2015). Research by Visek *et al.* (2014) found experiences children described as 'not fun' to be controlling, whereas nearly 84% of the 81 fun determinants within the fun integration theory's FUN MAPS are based on fostering children's autonomy, competence, and social connectedness in sport (Visek *et al.*, 2015, 2018b). In other words, determinants of fun drive motivation, and further to this point, research has shown having fun is among the foremost reasons elite and Olympic athletes persist and pursue the highest levels of their sport (e.g. Snyder, 2014; Berntsen and Kristiansen, 2020).

## *Hierarchical Model of Leisure Constraints*

The hierarchical model of leisure constraints (Crawford *et al.*, 1991) helps explain why children find a particular sport more fun than others. This model identifies constraints (barriers) to leisure activities, including sport, into three categories: (a) intrapersonal, (b) interpersonal, and (c) structural, and are theorised to operate hierarchically. To explain, a child's intrapersonal constraints (e.g. beliefs and personal values; psychological attributes and states; perceived physical attributes and self-skills; and perceived competence and mastery) directly affect their preferences, or what they like or dislike, and are considered foundational to influencing their participation in leisure activities (Crawford and Godbey, 1987). Scanlan et al. (1993a) also identified liking, along with enjoyment and fun, as similar terms to describe the emotional appeal of a given sport. According to the hierarchical model of leisure constraints, children must like a sport and find it sufficiently fun for participation to be initiated or continued. As an example, a child who does not value close physical interaction may avoid contact sports or not find them as much fun as other activities. Only when intrapersonal constraints are overcome do interpersonal constraints impact participation. Interpersonal constraints stem from the interpersonal interactions involved in undertaking a sport, such as parents, coaches, teammates, and competitors. While intrapersonal and interpersonal factors can constrain participation, they also positively influence the fun experience children have while participating. Finally, when intrapersonal and interpersonal constraints are overcome, structural constraints may have a role in constraining or preventing participation, which include environmental constraints on participation, such as availability of competitions, facilities, and resources necessary to play.

Relatedly, the hierarchical model of leisure constraints can be viewed through the lens of the fun integration theory's fun factors to identify intrapersonal (*Trying Hard*, e.g. trying one's best, playing with confidence, working hard; *Learning and Improving*, e.g. learning from mistakes, learning new skills), interpersonal (*Positive Team Dynamics*, e.g. being supported by teammates, showing good sportsmanship; *Positive Coaching*, e.g. having a coach who treats children with respect, encourages the team, is friendly and knowledgeable; *Team Friendships*, e.g. getting along with teammates, being around friends; and *Game Time Support*, e.g. parents showing good sportsmanship while cheering and watching games, referees making consistent calls), and structural factors (*Games*, e.g. getting playing time, playing against evenly matched teams, playing on a nice field or surface; *Practices*, e.g. having well organised practices, doing small-sided games and partner drills, having freedom to play creatively; *Team Rituals*, e.g. carpooling with teammates; and *Swag*, e.g. nice sports gear, a special uniform, traveling to play) – that when unconstrained and able to be experienced, result in fun and thus greater likelihood to participate in sport.

## Implications for Children's Sport Coaching

More than any other physical activity, sport participation offers children the best possible pathway for sustained physical activity in childhood, as well as over their life course (Kjønniksen *et al.*, 2009; Lee *et al.*, 2018; Palomäki *et al.*, 2018; Batista *et al.*, 2019), and is associated with a myriad of positive health outcomes throughout their lifespan (Bailey *et al.*, 2013b; World Health Organisation, 2020). Research to date has shown that, for children, having fun in sport, as well as not having fun, has wide-ranging and very significant implications. For example, children's experiences, over time, clearly affect their sport involvement motivations that ultimately influence whether they will continue their sport participation or dropout. Positive sport experiences, namely having fun, is of paramount importance for keeping children involved in sport. Though children's sport experiences should be described by them as none other than fun, achieving this for every child will require more than just efforts by coaches who operate within a larger sport ecological system (see Dorsch *et al.*, 2020). Meaning, coaches must be supported by sport NGBs in their efforts at every level. Empowering coaches with information of what is fun for children in sport is not sufficient. They must also be provided the infrastructure, resources, and opportunities to develop the knowledge, wisdom, and skills (see Zins, 2007 for discussion of these concepts) that enable them to effectively optimise the quality of children's sport. This, however, will require novel approaches to sport that press upon the responsibility sport has to children to be fun.

To move the needle more significantly in ways that ensure sport is fun for children will necessitate shifting from a needs-based paradigm toward a rights-based paradigm. For so long, much of the efforts to improve children's sport has focused on better meeting children's sport needs, particularly through athlete-centered approaches. Simply put, children who are having fun continue to play (needs met), whereas children who are not having fun dropout (needs unmet). Needs, by definition, are synonymous with necessities and requirements, though they are also synonymous with desires and wishes. The latter, consequently, can be interpreted as optional and voluntary, in turn leading to a general acceptance that some sport programming for children will be delivered satisfactorily, i.e. fun, and others unsatisfactorily, i.e. not fun. However, a rights-based approach asserts that children's rights are human rights and, accordingly, are not optional. Therefore, these rights represent an obligation sport has to children, including discussing and respecting their sport objectives, which include having fun (David, 2005, 2020). The research overviewed in this chapter leverages children's voices, providing coaches, parents, sport administrators, and sport policy makers with the empirical science needed to inform and shape children's sport programming in ways that finally realise their rights.

## Summary, Future Directions, and Future Research

If children's sport experiences are positive, safe, and health-promoting, given the immediate and long-term benefits of children's participation in sport (e.g. Bailey *et al.*, 2013a, 2013b; Eime *et al.*, 2013; Harlow *et al.*, 2018), endeavoring to involve as many of them as possible in sport, and keep them playing, is desired. Research has shown that fun is critical in maintaining children's involvement in sport and identified what is fun for children and how it can be thoughtfully sourced. To further advance our understanding of fun and harness improved ways coaches can deliver on children's right to have fun, the science and evidence-based practice in this area must evolve. As an incumbent next step with the rights of the child in mind, it is recommended that sport NGBs and sport scientists, in partnership, collaboratively develop, test, and scale strategies designed to realise children's right to have fun. These approaches must position children as the experts in their lived sport experiences and exercise their right to have a voice in all sport matters that involve them. The research evidence would suggest the future of sport, for children, depends on it.

## References

Allen, J.B., 2003. Social motivation in youth sports. *Journal of Sport and Exercise Psychology*, 25 (4), 551–567.

Armentrout, S.M. and Kamphoft, C.S., 2011. Organisational barriers and factors that contribute to youth hockey attrition. *Journal of Sport Behavior*, 34 (2), 121–136.

Bailey, R., Cope, E.J., and Pearce, G., 2013a. Why do children take part in, and remain involved in sport? A literature review and discussion of implications for sports coaches. *International Journal of Coaching Science*, 7 (1), 56–75.
Bailey, R., *et al.*, 2013b. Physical activity: An underestimated investment in human capital? *Journal of Physical Activity and Health*, 10 (3), 289–308.
Back, J., *et al.*, 2022. Drop-out from team sports among adolescents: A systematic review and meta-analysis of prospective studies. *Psychology of Sport and Exercise*, 61, 102205.
Barnett, N.P., Smoll, F.L., and Smith, R.E., 1992. Effects of enhancing coach-athlete relationships on youth sport attrition. *The Sport Psychologist*, 6 (2), 111–127.
Batista M.B., *et al.*, 2019. Participation in sports in childhood and adolescence and physical activity in adulthood: A systematic review. *Journal of Sports Sciences*, 37 (19), 2253–2262.
Bengoechea, E.G., Strean, W.B., and Williams D.J., 2004. Understanding and promoting fun in youth sport: Coaches' perspectives. *Physical Education and Sport Pedagogy*, 9 (2), 197–214.
Berntsen, H. and Kristiansen, E., 2020. Perceptions of need-support when "having fun" meets "working hard" mentalities in the elite sport school context. *Sports Coaching Review*, 9 (1) 1–23.
Carpenter, P.J., *et al.*, 1993. A test of the sport commitment model using structural equation modeling. *Journal of Sport and Exercise Psychology*, 15 (2), 119–133.
Côté, J. and Hancock, D., 2016. Evidence-based policies for youth sport programmes. *International Journal of Sport Policy and Politics*, 8 (1), 51–65.
Crane, J. and Temple, V., 2015. A systematic review of dropout from organised sport among children and youth. *European Physical Education Review*, 21 (1), 114–131.
Crawford, D.W. and Godbey, G., 1987. Reconceptualising barriers to family leisure. *Leisure Sciences*, 9 (2), 119–127.
Crawford D.W., Jackson, E.L., and Godbey, G., 1991. A hierarchical model of leisure constraints. *Leisure Sciences*, 13 (4), 309–320.
David, P., 2005. *Human rights in youth sport: A critical review of children's rights in competitive sport*. New York: Routledge.
David, P., 2020. Respecting the rights of the child in sports: Not an option. *In*: B.K. Nastasi, S.N. Hart, and S.C. Naser, eds. *International handbook on child rights and school psychology*. Switzerland: Springer, 377–388.
Deci, E.L. and Ryan, R.M., 1985. *Intrinsic motivation and self-determination in human behaviour*. Boston, MA: Plenum Press.
Deci, E.L. and Ryan, R.M., 2000. The "what" and "why" of goal pursuits: Human needs and self-determination of behavior. *Psychology of Inquiry*, 11 (4), 227–268.
Durant, R.H., *et al.*, 1991. Adolescents' attrition from school-sponsored sports. *American Journal of Diseases of Children*, 145 (10), 119–123.
Dorsch, T.E., *et al.*, 2020. Toward an integrated understanding of the youth sport system. *Research Quarterly for Exercise and Sport*, 93 (1), 1–15.
Eime, R.M., *et al.*, 2013. A systematic review of the psychological and social benefits of participation in sport for children and adolescents: Informing development of a conceptual model of health through sport. *International Journal of Behavioral Nutrition and Physical Activity*, 10 (1), 135–148.
Ewing, M.E. and Seefeldt, V., 1996. Patterns of participation and attrition in American agency-sponsored youth sports. *In*: F. Smoll, ed. *Children and youth in sport: a biopsychosocial perspective*. Dubuque, IA: Kendall/Hunt Pub., 31–45.
Fraser-Thomas, J., Côté, J., and Deakin, J., 2008. Examining adolescent sport dropout and prolonged engagement from a developmental perspective. *Journal of Applied Sport Psychology*, 20 (3), 318–333.
Gardner, L.A., Magee, C.A., and Vella, S.A., 2016. Social climate profiles in adolescent sports: Associations with enjoyment and intention to continue. *Journal of Adolescence*, 52, 112–121.
Gardner, L.A., Magee, C.A., and Vella, S.A., 2017. Enjoyment and behavioral intention predict organised youth sport participation and dropout. *Journal of Physical Activity and Health*, 14 (11), 861–865.
Harlow, M., Wolman, L., and Fraser-Thomas, J., 2018. Should toddlers and preschoolers participate in organised sport? A scoping review of developmental outcomes associated with young children's sport participation. *International Review of Sport and Exercise Psychology*, 13 (1), 40–64.
Harris, A.T., Horn, T., and Freysinger, V.J., 1995. Children's perceptions of fun in organised youth sport settings. *Journal of Sport and Exercise Psychology*, 17 (2), 57.
Kjønniksen, L., Anderssen, N., and Wold, B., 2009. Organised youth sport as a predictor of physical activity in adulthood. *Scandinavian Journal of Medicine and Science in Sports*, 19 (5), 646–654.

Klint, K.A. and Weiss, M.R., 1987. Perceived competence and motives for participating in youth sports: A test of Harter's competence motivation theory. *Journal of Sport Psychology*, 9 (1), 55–65.
Lavallee, D., *et al.*, 2012. *Sport psychology contemporary themes*, 2nd ed. New York: Palgrave Macmillan.
Lee, J.E., Pope, Z., and Gao, Z., 2018. The role of youth sports in promoting children's physical activity and preventing pediatric obesity: A systematic review. *Behavioral Medicine*, 44 (1), 62–76.
Nicholls, J.G., 1984. Achievement motivation: Conceptions of ability, subjective experience, task choice, and performance. *Psychological Review*, 91 (3), 328–346.
North, J., 2007. *Research briefing: Increasing participation in sport – The role of the coach*. Sports Coach UK: The National Coaching Foundation.
Palomäki, S., *et al.*, 2018. Does organised sport participation during youth predict healthy habits in adulthood? A 28-year longitudinal study. *Scandinavian Journal of Medicine and Science in Sports*, 28 (8), 1908–1915.
Pelletier, L.G., *et al.*, 2001. Associations among perceived autonomy support, forms of self- regulation, and persistence: A prospective study. *Motivation and Emotion*, 25 (4), 279–306.
Petlichkoff, L.M., 1992. Youth sport participation and withdrawal: Is it simply a matter of fun? *Pediatric Exercise Science*, 4 (2), 105–110.
Rottensteiner, C., *et al.*, 2015. Youth athletes' motivation, perceived competence, and persistence in organised team sports. *Journal of Sport Behavior*, 38 (4), 432–449.
Sarrazin, P., Boiche, J.C.S., and Pelletier, L.G., 2007. A self-determination theory approach to dropout in athletes. *In*: M. Hagger and N. Chatzisarantis, eds. *Intrinsic motivation and self-determination in exercise and sport*. Champaign, IL: Human Kinetics, 229–241.
Scanlan, T.K. and Lewthwaite, R., 1986. Social psychological aspects of competition for male youth sport participants: IV. Predictors of enjoyment. *Journal of Sport Psychology*, 8 (1), 25–35.
Scanlan, T.K., *et al.*, 1993a. Sources of enjoyment for youth sport athletes. *Pediatric Exercise Science*, 5 (3), 275–285.
Scanlan, T.K., *et al.*, 1993b. An introduction to the sport commitment model. *Journal of Sport and Exercise Psychology*, 15 (1), 1–15.
Scanlan, T.K., *et al.*, 1993c. The sport commitment model: Measurement development for the youth-sport domain. *Journal of Sport and Exercise Psychology*, 15 (1), 16–38.
Sport New Zealand, 2018. *Active NZ 2017 participation report*. Wellington, NZ: Sport New Zealand.
Snyder, C., 2014. The path to excellence: A view on the athletic development of U.S. Olympians who competed from 2000–2012. *In*: S. Riewald, ed. *Initial report of the talent identification and development questionnaire to U.S. Olympians*. Colorado Spring, CO: United States Olympic Committee Sport Performance and Coaching Education Divisions, 1–65.
Stuntz, C.P. and Weiss, M.R., 2009. Achievement goal orientations and motivational outcomes in youth sport: The role of social orientations. *Psychology of Sport and Exercise*, 10 (2), 255–262.
Ullrich-French, S. and Smith A.L., 2009. Social and motivational predictors of continued youth sport participation. *Psychology of Sport and Exercise*, 10 (1), 87–95.
Vallerand, R.J. and Losier, G.F., 1999. An integrative analysis of intrinsic and extrinsic motivation in sport. *Journal of Applied Sport Psychology*, 11 (1), 142–169.
Vierimaa, M., *et al.*, 2017. Just for the fun of it: Coaches' perceptions of an exemplary community youth sport program. *Physical Education and Sport Pedagogy*, 22 (6), 603–617.
Visek A.J. and Feiler, A., 2021. The science of fun in sport: Fact over fiction. *In*: A. Whitehead and J. Coe, eds. *Myths of sport coaching*. North Yorkshire, England: Sequoia Books, 14–23.
Visek, A.J., *et al.*, 2014. The NOT FUN MAPS: Navigational blueprints for understanding and overcoming obstacles to fun in youth sport. *Association for applied sport psychology annual conference*. Las Vegas, NV.
Visek, A.J., *et al.*, 2015. The fun integration theory: Toward sustaining children and adolescents sport participation. *Journal of Physical Activity and Health*, 12 (3), 424–433.
Visek, A.J., *et al.*, 2018a. Perceived importance of the fun integration theory's factors and determinants: A comparison among players, parents, and coaches. *International Journal of Sports Science and Coaching*, 13 (6), 849–862.
Visek, A.J., *et al.*, 2018b. Integrating fun in young athletes' sport experiences. *In*: C. Knight, C.G. Harwood, and D. Gould, eds. *Sport psychology for young athletes*. New York: Routledge, 68–80.
Visek, A.J., *et al.*, 2020. Toward understanding youth athletes' fun priorities: An investigation of sex, age, and levels of play. *Women in Sport and Physical Activity Journal*, 28 (1), 34–49.
Weinberg, R.S. and Gould, D., 2011. *Foundations of sport and exercise psychology*, 5th ed. Champaign, IL: Human Kinetics.

Wiersma, L., 2001. Conceptualisation and development of the sources of enjoyment in youth sport questionnaire. *Measurement in Physical Education and Exercise Science*, 5 (3), 153–177.

Weiss, M.R. and Amorose, A.J., 2008. Motivational orientations and sport behavior. *In*: T.S. Horn ed. *Advances in sport psychology*. Champaign, IL: Human Kinetics, 115–155.

Weiss, M.R. and Chaumenton, N., 1992. Motivational orientations in sport. *In*: T.S. Horn ed. *Advances in sport psychology*. Champaign, IL: Human Kinetics, 61–69.

World Health Organisation, 2020. *Guidelines on physical activity and sedentary behaviour*. Geneva: World Health Organisation.

Zins, C., 2007. Conceptual approaches for defining data, information, and knowledge. *Journal of the American Society for Information Science and Technology*, 58 (4), 479–493.

# 6

# CREATIVITY-ENHANCING APPROACHES IN THE COACHING OF CHILDREN IN SPORT: PRESENT AND FUTURE DIRECTIONS

*Ludvig Johan Torp Rasmussen and Niels Nygaard Rossing*

## Introduction

The concept of creativity has drawn attention across research fields related to children's sport, such as psychology and pedagogy. Several position papers have offered a series of intriguing potentials of promoting creativity in or through sport. For example, Campos (2014) argued that sport environments that provide movement challenges to be solved in creative ways, can enhance the quality and enjoyment of the sport experience, and the participants' self-control, self-discipline, and self-mastery. Similarly, Rasmussen *et al.*, 2019 argued that creativity, understood as curious and playful exploration of novel and unusual action possibilities in open-ended tasks, can expand and enrich sport experiences and develop active habits. Opposed to fixed habits, this helps children take initiative, be inventive (e.g. generate new solutions to problems), adapt to new situations, to shape the environment to extant purposes, and to apply their capacities to novel purposes. Ultimately, creativity-nurturing activities may lead to both cultural and personal growth, which is understood as expanded horizons, purposes, and responses.

However exciting these (and many other) potentials may be, most are yet to be exposed by creativity studies in sport. To discuss current and future directions, the purpose of this chapter is to review and critique international empirical research on creativity-enhancing approaches in children sport contexts (CACS). This scrutiny takes point of departure in the *how* (i.e. the activities applied) and *why* (i.e. the potential implications of creativity) questions of creativity, which is key to inspire future policies and projects.

## Review of Current Research

There have been two recent literature reviews examining creativity in sport (Fardilha and Allen, 2020; Zahno and Hossner, 2020). These reviews suggest research in this area draws on quantitative and qualitative methodologies such as coaching interventions, laboratory experiments (e.g. cognitive-perceptual testing), questionnaires (e.g. sport participation histories), observation

 DOI: 10.4324/9781003199359-8

(e.g. tracing positional data), and interviews (e.g. life positioning analysis). This chapter only includes empirical studies which implement and explore evidence-based approaches to enhance creativity in children sport contexts with participants under the age of 16. Since children can experience creative practices in organised settings such as clubs and schools, we include studies from both contexts.

## Analytical Framework

To provide an overview of the current research within and across CACS, the analysis has been structured using a holistic model developed to inform intervention efforts and the design of sport programs. Hence, we utilise the Personal Assets Framework (PAF; Côté *et al.*, 2020). PAF defines three 'dynamic elements' (i.e. personal engagement in activities; appropriate settings; quality social dynamics integral for development in sport). The interaction of these personal, social, and contextual factors influences the quality of the athletes' 'immediate sport experience', which, in turn, influences the 'short- and long-term outcomes' of sport. While short-term effects are conceptualised in terms of assets such as the 4Cs (i.e. connection; character; confidence; competence), long-term outcomes are defined by the 3Ps (i.e. continued participation; personal development; performance).

Rather than systematically appraising the literature, the aim is to present representative examples of studies from club and school contexts that connect to different parts of PAF to highlight avenues for future research that has not been exhaustively considered in the literature. This will provide researchers, students, and practitioners with broad scaffolding upon which to situate future initiatives to design, implement, and explore CACS.

In what follows, we take point of departure in the dynamic elements to display and discuss the nature of the included studies (i.e. the 'how' question). Subsequently the chapter critically discusses what kinds of immediate, short- and long-term outcomes that has currently been examined or suggested (i.e. the 'why' question).

## Dynamic Elements in Creativity-Enhancing Approaches

Guided by PAF, it is vital to reflect upon how the community and club environment, the quality of relationships between actors in that environment, as well as the diversity of activities in and out of their main sport, stimulates immediate interest by offering creative opportunities and experiences and thereby affects the long-term engagement and development in sport (Côté *et al.*, 2020).

## Personal Engagement in Activities

The first dynamic mechanism of PAF examines children's personal engagement in activities. This component is divided into 'sport of interest' (e.g. play or practice activities), 'complimentary sports' (e.g. specialize or sample), and 'complimentary non-sport activities' (e.g. engagement in non-sport activities). Exploring a variety of activities helps children gain a better understanding of their interests and develop a range of competencies that can transfer between different contexts (Côté *et al.*, 2020). Besides enhancing personal development and long-term participation, research shows that diversification (e.g. experiences from diverse sport contexts) and deliberate play (especially in their main sport) and practice, is crucial to develop both general (e.g. Richard *et al.*, 2017) and sport-specific creativity (e.g. Roca *et al.*, 2021). Accordingly, several approaches include diversified and/or play activities in both school (e.g. Memmert, 2007) and club-based initiatives (e.g. Greco *et al.*, 2010). For example, in the Skill4Genius program (Santos *et al.*, 2017), the main disciplines are football, handball, and basketball, but during the program, the children are exposed to activities in several other sports such as ultimate frisbee and volleyball.

In this regard, however, it seems that CACS studies are uniformal when it comes to selecting the sport content. Within school-based studies, creative dance and/or movement are the most typically chosen activity. Similarly, in the sport-based research there is an overweight of studies on team ball sports. Therefore, we have little knowledge on what happens when creativity-enhancing approaches are implemented in sports that are not usually associated with imaginative, spontaneous, or expressive activities (e.g. athletics; swimming).

## *Appropriate Settings*

Our analysis shows that the extant CACS research has the most focus on setting features proximal to the participants, namely 'the playing field', which concerns aspects such as activities, field surface, equipment, rule manipulations, and other parts of the physical micro-environment. Even though some studies do control for community factors such as socio-economic background and participation in other activities (e.g. Bournelli and Mountakis, 2008), most creativity studies in sport (generally, not just CACS studies), do not consider 'community structures' such as club proximity, infrastructure, psychological safety, combining sport and school, or opportunities to engage in (self-) organised sport afforded by the community. Likewise, extant CACS research is mostly deprived of reflections regarding 'organisational structures' that could have an impact on children's creativity, or the effectiveness of applying new approaches. As an exception, Rasmussen *et al.* (2022) highlighted political (e.g. power distribution), cultural (e.g. social expectations), conceptual (e.g. ideologies), and pedagogical (e.g. sport-specific assumptions) dilemmas of implementing creativity-enhancing tasks in elite youth football. Also, some school studies mention opportunities afforded by curriculum goals (e.g. Keun and Hunt, 2006; Zachopoulou *et al.*, 2006). When creativity is explicitly endorsed in national curriculum documents, it may be easier for teachers to deliver creative activities, since they can refer to these learning goals to justify atypical teaching activities.

Informed by key elements listed by Côté *et al.* (2020) in relation to creating appropriate settings, researchers and practitioners alike could turn attention towards 'organisational structures' such as club size (e.g. number of teams/classes) and physical structure, access to resources (e.g. quality coaching/facilities), the club's approach to (de-)selection, efforts to reduce dropout and/or sustain participation, or the club's development philosophy. Although these aspects are specific to sport clubs, similar structures could be explored in school-based studies (e.g. the school's approach to learning and development).

Organisational structures like those listed above influence the competitive environment as well as children's experience of psychological safety. Both aspects may limit children's willingness to be creative. For example, participative safety is seen as a key feature of creative climates (Friedrich *et al.*, 2011). Hence, structural initiatives to ensure as many sport participants for as long as possible, could potentially enhance the success of creativity-enhancing approaches. For example, the Norwegian football club, Bryne BK, made their soccer dome with artificial turf highly accessible for peer-led activities among their youth players (Erikstad *et al.*, 2021). In the short-term, this resulted in immense and enjoyable but still competitive peer-created football activities such as a game called World Cup. In this non-organised setting, players could also perform drills presented by coaches during training. Supported by the organisational principle that no players should ever be de-selected at any stage and coaching activities focusing on individual skill development, enjoyment, and optimal challenges (e.g. questioning), among others, this structural initiative contributed to build strong, positive social connections among all players on the team studied by Erikstad *et al.* (2021), where 35 of 40 players continued playing football until entering adulthood. In similar ways, inspirational coaching activities focusing on creativity could help players design and engage in creative activities in non-organised settings (e.g. open facilities in the club or other recreational contexts).

Another point is that both sport and school studies' descriptions of the implemented activities vary in quality. It is often difficult to grasp what happened during the sessions intended to promote creativity. While some studies provide rich descriptions such as lesson plans (e.g. Zachopoulou *et al.*, 2006), scripted activities (e.g. Chatoupis 2013), instruction points (e.g. Neville and Makopoulou, 2021), and constraints (e.g. Richards *et al.* 2018), several studies only describe the content on a general level (e.g. Bournelli and Mountakis, 2008). For example, the approach of Amado *et al.* (2016) involves questions and premises that require original answers, but no examples are given. Similarly, Theodorakou and Zervas (2003) state that their approach involves learning through discovery, problem-solving, improvisation, and exploration without specifying how such aspects were facilitated.

Unfortunately, CACS research reflect a tendency in sport psychology, where intervention methodologies are often under-reported or presented in an overly complex way (Ely *et al.*, 2020). This lack of transparency limits catalytic authenticity (Smith and Caddick, 2012) and thereby reduces the chance of igniting the readers' curiosity as well as the chance of moving them to implement, adopt or be inspired from the new approaches. The lack of description of creative activities extends to the next dynamic mechanism of PAF, namely quality social dynamics.

## Quality Social Dynamics

This PAF component covers 'interpersonal relationships' between children, adults, peers, and parents. Whereas most CACS studies focus on the role of coaches or teachers, few involve principles for how to establish creative relationships among the children (e.g. Lykesas *et al.*, 2009; Chatoupis, 2013), and none actively include parents. Several CACS studies illustrate coaches' and teachers' influence on general- and sport-specific creativity. These approaches have emerged from perspectives such as theories grounded in pedagogy, learning, motivation, and creativity. For example, several approaches in creative dance and movement studies are based on the divergent discovery, guided discovery, and/or divergent production teaching styles of Mosston and Ashworth (e.g. Bournelli and Mountakis, 2008; Chatoupis, 2013; Theocharidou *et al.*, 2018), and/or build on dance-related models involving movement elements (e.g, those of Rudolf Laban) such as body, space, time, dynamics, and relationships.

In general, the CACS literature advocate coaching or teaching behaviours that (1) maintain a person-centred approach, where learning is facilitated (e.g. asking questions) rather than transmitted (e.g. giving instructions) and (2) encourage participants to discover, invent, and explore personally new solutions or movements. Despite these general points, there are seldomly rigorous descriptions of coach/teacher behaviours during activities, and especially between activities/sessions, which affect relationship formation.

Moreover, no CACS studies consider the impact of more profound behaviours affecting the quality of adult-child relationships such as showing genuine trust in one's coach/teacher or care for one's players/pupils. Recently, Tuan (2020) explored humility (e.g. transcend oneself by appreciating others' contributions) as a vital quality of leaders that affects their relationship with others to foster the need for uniqueness and thereby enhance creativity. Research also indicates that approaches such as transformational leadership may build interpersonal relationships conducive to creativity (Bosselut *et al.*, 2020). However, such aspects have not yet been implemented in children sport or school contexts to nurture creativity.

The component of quality social dynamics also covers 'team dynamics' (e.g. team structures; team processes; and teams' emergent state) and 'the broader social environment' (e.g. cultural norms and values; task- rather than outcome-oriented climate). Due to the relatively low number of studies conducted in sport clubs (eight according to our analysis), only a few scholars consider team processes such as communication (e.g. Santos and Morgan, 2019; Oboeuf *et al.*, 2020). Further, no CACS studies explicitly consider 'team structures' such as normative expectations, adaptive positional competition, or roles (e.g. experiencing different roles; role clarity; and interactions between roles), or emergent states such as social identity and cohesion. For example, competitiveness dynamics make team ball players attune to and utilise different affordances (e.g. invest in different resources) to enhance their ability to compete against others in the performance context (Passos *et al.*, 2016).

In terms of 'the social environment', several studies assume that the development of creativity contributes to the environments' capacity to ensure the mental well-being and flourishing of participants and their groups (e.g. Amado *et al.*, 2016; Theocharidou *et al.*, 2018). Nevertheless, no studies have explored how wider cultural changes may impact creativity (e.g. facilitate collective buy-in of creative procedures). For example, to focus on creativity, cultural values could be adapted to form a task- rather than a performance-oriented climate. As argued by Vaughan *et al.* (2019), training activities are more conducive to creativity if they amplify or dampen cultural socio-cultural constraints. This especially concerns those values overemphasised (e.g. quality) or deprioritised (e.g. aesthetics) in the given sport environment. However, such approaches have not been explored in empirical studies.

## *Immediate Experiences*

As implied by PAF, 'immediate sport experiences' are essential in shaping both short- and long-term outcomes of sport participation. Due to a methodological focus on pre-post-testing, few CACS studies consider the children's immediate experience. Hence, only a few studies include positive immediate experiences when justifying the relevance of studying creativity. For example, Keun and Hunt (2006) believe that cultural conditioning of creativity will enhance children's personal experience, Lykesas *et al.* (2009) state that discovery and creation entails pride, enthusiasm, and satisfaction, and Theodorakou and Zervas (2003) state that creativity help children feel freer and be more open and independent in exploratory processes. Nonetheless, children's immediate experiences of creativity-enhancing approaches are rarely examined empirically. For example, Amado *et al.* (2016) developed a creative dance program to equalise differences in motivation between males and females in artistic-expressive activities. This study showed inconclusive results. However, a few other studies indicate that creativity supports the psychological needs of competence, relatedness, and autonomy (e.g. Rasmussen and Østergaard, 2016).

Several CACS studies introduce approaches that intend to help the children be curious, inventive, and creative during sessions (e.g. in terms of exploratory behaviour). Among more, these include diverse task constraints (e.g. Richard *et al.*, 2018; Santos *et al.*, 2018), imaginary themes (Keun and Hunt, 2006), fantasy stories (Zachopoulou *et al.*, 2006), creation of original choreographies (Neville and Makopoulou, 2021), and blocking usual action possibilities (e.g. Rasmussen *et al.*, 2022). For example, Santos and Morgan (2019) describe how the young volleyball players were asked to construct and discuss different solutions for offensive strategies and challenged to do the opposite of what they would usually do (or what their opponents would expect).

In this regard, some approaches implement more discipline-specific activities (e.g. Memmert, 2007; Memmert and Roth, 2007), where the children do not necessarily engage in creative problem-solving during the sessions (e.g. absence of task constraints that enhance the possibilities for novel (inter)actions to emerge). Although they may leave more room for flexible and rare actions to emerge due to dynamic interactions among the children in the absence of specific instructions and feedback (Memmert and Roth, 2007), the activities are not specifically designed to facilitate exploratory behaviour, or atypical, or unusual actions. For example, the program developed by Oboeuf *et al.* (2020) focuses on training football-specific *praxemes,* which is a directory of signs derived from various in-game behaviours, to facilitate players' nonverbal communication in different game situations to help them decode strategic choices of their opponents and anticipate possibilities for interacting with their teammates.

Conversely, the programs based more directly on creativity components may be more likely to elicit immediate creative experiences in terms of providing unique challenges to be overcome in imaginative and atypical ways. For example, in the *Skills4genius* program (Santos *et al.*, 2017), creativity components such as attempts (e.g. mistakes and inefficient actions) and fluency (e.g. produce as many movements as possible) are incorporated into the training of fundamental (e.g. 'using gaps'), situational (e.g. 'explore and improvise offensive movements'), and collective (e.g. 'position specific behaviour') game principles. Based on differential learning, this program also involved small-sided games with disturbances, or stochastic perturbations, such as odd arm positions (e.g. play with arms raised), obstacles (e.g. robes on the field) and alternative pitch dimensions (e.g. triangle or circle). These are intended to amplify noise, motor variability, and facilitate adaptive behaviour and improvisation.

Similar ideas were explored in the action research conducted by Rasmussen *et al.* (2022), where the researcher and a U17 football coach experimented with a variety of creativity concepts to develop principles for designing creativity-nurturing activities with creative components (e.g. openness and originality) as learning goals. Among more, this led to the principles *play with quantity* (i.e. as trying as many ideas as possible in repeated, technical tasks), *plan and break* (i.e. groups collaborate to create a plan for how to surprise and outplay opponents in any given game or scenario), and *instant problems* (i.e. games where cues such as numbers are provided during the game to elicit spontaneous actions). Further, the study identified six potentials of applying the novel principles. Those most relevant in terms of shaping immediate sport experiences were (1) supporting autonomy and ownership, (2) revitalising curiosity, (3) forming a playful atmosphere, and (4) facilitating extraordinary and rare (inter)actions and 'wow' moments.

## Short-Term Effects

One of the key assumptions in the latest version of PAF is that immediate sport experiences play a crucial role in shaping the development of both short- and long-term outcomes (Côté *et al.*, 2020). In terms of 'short-term effects', the implementation of a creativity-enhancing approach may lead to developing a wide variety of personal and relational competencies that are important within and across disciplines.

Unsurprisingly, the most prominent short-term effect analysed in CACS studies is creativity (e.g. as measured by a variety of constructs). For example, creative behaviour in team ball sports is measured as fails, attempts, fluency, versatility, and originality in the children's passing, dribbling, and shooting during game performance (Santos *et al.*, 2018). Opposed to sport-specific creativity tests, the most school-based studies focus on general kinds of creative behaviour, such as divergent movement ability (e.g. Chatoupis, 2013) and motor creativity (e.g. Richard *et al.*, 2018), and other studies trace changes in divergent thinking (e.g. Neville and Makopoulou, 2021).

As argued by Kaufman (2018), scholars tend to treat creativity as an output rather than an input (as a dependent rather than an independent variable). This issue is reflected in the CACS literature. Only a handful of studies focus on creativity as an input to explore its effect on other outcomes. In this regard, Theodorakou and Zervas (2003) show that it is possible to improve children's perception of social, scholastic, and athletic competencies through creative activities such as exploration, problem-solving, and improvisation. Also, Lobo and Winsler (2006) developed social competences of pre-schoolers through dance improvisation based on poems or stories and creative movement in a 'magic box' (i.e. an imaginary space for creating personal dance moves). Other CACS studies examined whether creative activities underscore aspects such as children's health-related quality of life (Theocharidou *et al.*, 2018), their perception of enjoyment and effort (e.g. Amado *et al.*, 2016), and motor skills (e.g. Lykesas *et al.*, 2009).

As implied above, creativity should not only be evaluated by means of assessing signs of divergent thinking or movement since it involves positive transformations of individuals, communities, and societies. Hence, the scarce amount of qualitative CACS studies provides more rich accounts of the potential outcomes of the programs (e.g. Rasmussen and Østergaard, 2016; Rasmussen *et al.*, 2022). For example, Santos and Morgan (2019) showed that the formation of a culture of collaborative creativity by means of jazz principles such as empathetic attunement (e.g. take risks and stimulate new ideas in fellow players), motifs, verbal cooperation (i.e. creative discussions prior to play), and verbal collaboration (i.e. discussions following play) had a positive impact on young volleyball players match play through improved communication channels and a better understanding of the game's complexity.

As argued by Côté *et al.* (2016), sport programs have the potential to promote a variety of important outcomes, but when focusing on sole objectives, they limit the potential contribution to the overall development of children. In this regard, some studies do measure other variables in connection to measuring effects on creativity variables (e.g. Greco *et al.*, 2010; Santos *et al.*, 2017). For example, Richard *et al.* (2018) developed a non-linear pedagogical program to enhance divergent thinking, creative movement, self-efficacy, and adaptation probability, and reduce the perception of exercise difficulty. Among more, the program covered movement activities with manipulated task constraints (e.g. one limb only), instructional constraints to enhance improvisation (e.g. 'do anything you think of') and variability (e.g. 'show me another way to ...'), tasks with problem-solving (e.g. 'find ways to ... '), fantasy play (e.g. 'imagine you ...'), and creation (e.g. generation of new solutions). Although the results only provided significant differences for original thinking and fluent and flexible movement, the study expose potential outcome-variables that could be considered when implementing creativity-enhancing approaches.

## Long-Term Effects

As suggested by the short-term effects examined in CACS studies and their additional rationales for implementing creativity-enhancing approaches, these may have a positive impact on the children's long-term sport participation (e.g. enhance intrinsic motivation), personal development (e.g. develop creative abilities), and performance (i.e. in main sport, or future work). However, several studies provide inadequate information about why creativity is important for children, sport contexts, wider communities, or even societies. Especially, school-based studies draw on an implicit understanding of its long-term value.

Whereas most school-based studies seem to focus on personal development, the club-based studies (and a list of school-based studies focusing on team ball sports), are characterised by a divide between approaches utilising creativity as a resource for personal development or continued sport participation (e.g. Rasmussen and Østergaard, 2016; Santos and Morgan, 2019), and those focusing on creative performances in terms of enhancing players ability to make fluent, varied and original decisions/actions in matches (e.g. Memmert and Roth, 2007; Orangi *et al.*, 2021). As argued by Rasmussen *et al.* (2019), treating creativity as an end rather than a means may lead to approaches detracted from immediate creative experiences.

CACS approaches are currently being developed to be applied across developmental stages in sport contexts (Santos *et al.*, 2016; Rasmussen *et al., in press*) to support children's long-term participation, personal development, and performance. However, the full span and potentials of these approaches have not yet been explored. Informed by calls for culturally competent and context-driven research (e.g. Schinke and Stambulova, 2017), hosting clubs (or coaches) can adapt these approaches to their cultural and structural makeup (e.g. train own game principles in new ways). This may entail more sustainable organisational learning than intervention content predetermined by researchers (where the changes easily disperse when researchers leave). As discussed by Ely *et al.* (2020), overly structured interventions with rigorous procedures are at risk of widening the research-to-practice gap in sport.

As implied above, there is a lack of knowledge regarding the long-term effects of creativity-enhancing approaches. In the only CACS study investigating long-term effects, Bournelli and Mountakis (2008) completed a nine-year follow-up study using Wyrick's test of motor creativity, where three tasks (i.e. parallel line; ball-wall; hoop) are performed in as many ways as possible. Based on Mosston and Ashworth's styles of 'practice' and 'divergent production', the program covered topics such as becoming aware of movement in space and time. While the creativity scores of the children in a normal physical education program remained stable over a nine-year period after the end of the program, those participating in the special program continued to improve.

These results are intriguing in terms of personal development since the children continued to improve although they received no additional motor creativity interventions. In this regard, Bournelli and Mountakis (2008) argued that the program developed "the creative intellect of the pupils" (p. 79), which led the subsequent development of motor creativity. Informed by PAF, continued development was more likely to occur due to changes in interpersonal relationships, group dynamics, or even the social environment in the classes taking part in the program. However, it is difficult to provide a conclusive answer, since the study did not specify what was said and done by the teacher to encourage the children to engage in activities with motor creativity.

## Implications for Children's Sport Coaching

The previous review of literature points to several implications for coaching children. First, coaches and teachers need to answer two basic questions before choosing and implementing creativity-enhancing approaches. The answers will guide which approach they choose and how the new activities are designed and applied. They should critically reflect and decide upon (1) what creativity is and (2) why this is important in their context in an immediate, short-term, and long-term perspective. In this regard, creativity should not just be seen as an end (e.g. improve creative abilities), but also as a means of developing a range of important skills and competencies. For example, if the aim is to develop creative and social competencies, it makes most sense to utilise an approach covering principles for creative collaboration (e.g. Rasmussen and Østergaard, 2016; Santos and Morgan, 2019).

They also need to consider whether it provides immediate positive and creative experiences, which are crucial for developing creativity-relevant assets in the short term and sustained participation, personal development, and performance in the long term. This requires activities that facilitate creative (inter)actions among the children, for example using various task constraints that challenges the use of ordinary actions and invites children to imagine, explore, attempt, and invent personally new solutions/movements. This does not only develop creative abilities but also provides the joy of discovery and creation.

Answering these questions may also be useful in terms of helping both adults and children understand why they should challenge, adapt, or subvert established practice forms to nurture creativity. Most CACS studies are put forth as undogmatic alternatives to traditional practice forms, which are explicitly or implicitly thought to limit creativity-related components. In this regard, practitioners should be careful in terms of uncritically abandoning established practice, which may involve more children-centred, exploratory, and imaginative activities than those traditional ones (e.g. high amounts of adult-centred activities and specific instructions). Different aspects may be taken from different approaches to supplement established practice forms, and we hope that this review will help practitioners navigate between different kinds of creativity, at different age levels, and for different purposes.

## Summary, Future Directions, and Future Research

This chapter has provided a critical overview of the extant empirical research on creativity-enhancing approaches in children's sport and school contexts. Guided by PAF, the chapter has explored these approaches in terms of the three dynamics elements (e.g. personal engagement in activities; appropriate setting; quality social dynamics) and their potential to lead to immediate, short- and long-term outcomes, not limited to creativity.

In general, the CACS literature underscore that it is possible to develop children's general and sport-specific creative abilities through sport when comparing creativity-enhancing approaches to traditional practice forms (as discussed above). In future studies, more focus could be directed towards what characterises the most efficient programs. This should not only be evaluated in terms of the program's efficiency in developing creative players (e.g. as done by Zahno and Hossner, 2020) but take broader aims of children sport into consideration.

Further, as demonstrated by our review, it is critical that future research consider not only the physical micro-environment (e.g. activities on the playing field), but also central features of the macro-environment (e.g. organisational structures, interpersonal relationships, team dynamics, and social environments) when designing and reporting their creativity-enhancing methodology. Reporting the macro-environmental aspects in future studies, as well as describing the creativity-enhancing activities more transparently, could make it easier for practitioners to understand both the intervention and its potentials, and subsequently inspire them to apply selected parts of these programs in the real world for the benefit of individuals, communities, and societies.

Whereas extant research has advanced our knowledge regarding potential outcomes of nurturing creativity in and through children sport, there are still several unexplored areas, as suggested by several position papers (for an overview, see Rasmussen, 2019). In this regard, future research should focus more on how creativity-enhancing approaches contributes to shaping positive immediate sport experiences.

## References

Amado, D., *et al.*, 2016. Analysis of the impact of creative technique on the motivation of physical education students in dance content: Gender differences. *Journal of Creative Behavior*, 50 (1), 64–79.

Bournelli, P. and Mountakis, C., 2008. The development of motor creativity in elementary school children and its retention. *Creativity Research Journal*, 20 (1), 72–80.

Bosselut, G., Guilbert, L., and Chareyre, L., 2020. Transformational leadership and creativity in sport: Examining the mediating role of support for innovation. *Journal of Sports Sciences*, 38 (23), 2698–2707.
Campos, D.G., 2014. On creativity in sporting activity: With some consequences for Education. *Fair Play. Revista de Filosofia, Ética y Derecho Del Deporte*, 2 (4), 52–80.
Chatoupis, C., 2013. Young children's divergent movement ability: A study revisited. *Early Child Development and Care*, 183 (1), 92–108.
Côté, J., Turnnidge, J., and Vierimaa, M., 2016. A personal assets approach to youth sport. *In*: K. Green and A. Smith, eds. *Routledge handbook of youth sport*. London: Routledge, 243–255.
Côté, J., *et al.*, 2020. Youth sport research: Describing the integrated dynamic elements of the personal assets framework. *International Journal of Sport Psychology*, 51 (6), 562–578.
Ely, F.O., Jenny, O., and Munroe-Chandler, K.J., 2020. How intervention research designs may broaden the research-to-practice gap in sport psychology. *Journal of Sport Psychology in Action*, 12 (2), 101–113.
Erikstad, M.K. and Johansen, B.T., 2021. "As many as possible for as long as possible" – A case study of a soccer team that fosters multiple outcomes. *The Sport Psychologist*, 35 (2), 131–141.
Fardilha, F.S. and Allen, J.B., 2020. Defining, assessing, and developing creativity in sport: A systematic narrative review. *International Review of Sport and Exercise Psychology*, 13 (1), 104–127.
Friedrich, T.L., Stenmark, C.K., and Mumford, M.D., 2011. Climate for creativity. *In*: M.A. Runco and S. Pritzker, eds. *Encyclopedia of creativity* (2nd edition). New York: Academic Press, 208–213.
Greco, P., Memmert, D., and Morales, J.C.P., 2010. The effect of deliberate play on tactical performance in basketball. *Perceptual and Motor Skills*, 110 (3), 849–856.
Kaufman, J.C., 2018. Finding meaning with creativity in the past, present, and future. *Perspectives on Psychological Science*, 13 (6), 734–749.
Keun, L.L. and Hunt, P., 2006. Creative dance: Singapore children's creative thinking and problem-solving responses. *Research in Dance Education*, 7 (1), 35–65.
Lobo, Y.B. and Winsler, A., 2006. The effects of a creative dance and movement program on the social competence of head start preschoolers. *Social Development*, 15 (3), 501–519.
Lykesas, G., Koutsouba, M., and Tyrovola, V., 2009. Creativity as an approach and teaching method of traditional Greek dance in secondary schools. *Studies in Physical Culture and Tourism*, 16 (2), 207–214.
Memmert, D., 2007. Can creativity be improved by an attention-broadening training program? An exploratory study focusing on team sports. *Creativity Research Journal*, 19 (2–3), 281–291.
Memmert, D. and Roth, K., 2007. The effects of non-specific and specific concepts on tactical creativity in team ball sports. *Journal of Sports Sciences*, 25 (12), 1423–1432.
Neville, R.D. and Makopoulou, K., 2021. Effect of a six-week dance-based physical education intervention on primary school children's creativity: A pilot study. *European Physical Education Review*, 27 (1), 203–220.
Oboeuf, A., *et al.*, 2020. Influence of traditional sporting games on the development of creative skills in team sports. The case of football. *Frontiers in Psychology*, 11, 611803.
Orangi, M.B. *et al.*, 2021. The effects of linear, nonlinear, and differential motor learning methods on the emergence of creative action in individual soccer players. *Psychology of Sport and Exercise*, 56, 102009.
Passos, P., Araújo, D., and Davids, K., 2016. Competitiveness and the process of co-adaptation in team sport performance. *Frontiers in Psychology*, 7, 1562.
Rasmussen, L.J.T., 2019. *On the role of creativity in sport*. Phd dissertation, Aalborg University, Det Sundhedsvidenskabelige Fakultet. Phd Serien. Aalborg, Denmark: Aalborg Universitetsforlag.
Rasmussen, L.J.T., Glăveanu, V.P., and Østergaard, L.D., 2022. "The principles are good, but they need to be integrated in the right way": Experimenting with creativity in elite youth soccer. *Journal of Applied Sport Psychology*, 34 (2), 294–316.
Rasmussen, L.J.T. and Østergaard, L.D., 2016. The creative soccer platform: New strategies for stimulating creativity in organised youth soccer practice. *Journal of Physical Education, Recreation and Dance*, 87 (7), 9–19.
Rasmussen, L.J.T., Østergaard, L.D., and Glăveanu, V.P. 2019. Creativity as a developmental resource in sport training activities. *Sport, Education and Society*, 24 (5), 491–506.
Rasmussen, L.J.T. *et al.*, (In press). *Kreativitet som legende udforskning* [Creativity as playful exploration]. Aalborg, Denmark: Aalborg Universitetsforlag.
Richard, V., Abdulla, A.M., and Runco, M., 2017. Influence of skill level, experience, hours of training, and other sport participation on the creativity of elite athletes. *Journal of Genius and Eminence*, 2 (1), 65–76.
Richard, V., *et al.*, 2018. Developing cognitive and motor creativity in children through an exercise program using nonlinear pedagogy principles. *Creativity Research Journal*, 30 (4), 391–401.

Roca, A. and Ford, P.R., 2021. Developmental activities in the acquisition of creativity in soccer players. *Thinking Skills and Creativity*, 41, 100850.
Santos, M. and Morgan, K., 2019. Developing creative team games players: From jazz to sport coaching. *International Journal of Sports Science and Coaching*, 14 (2), 117–125.
Santos, S., *et al.*, 2016. The spawns of creative behavior in team sports: A creativity developmental framework. *Frontiers in Psychology*, 7, 1282.
Santos, S., *et al.*, 2017. Effects of the Skills4Genius sports-based training program in creative behavior. *PLoS ONE*, 12 (2), e0172520.
Santos, S., *et al.*, 2018. Differential learning as a key training approach to improve creative and tactical behavior in soccer. *Research Quarterly for Exercise and Sport*, 89 (1), 11–24.
Schinke, R.J. and Stambulova, N., 2017. Context-driven sport and exercise psychology practice: Widening our lens beyond the athlete, *Journal of Sport Psychology in Action*, 8 (2), 71–75.
Smith, B. and Caddick, N., 2012. Qualitative methods in sport: a concise overview for guiding social scientific sport research. *Asia Pacific Journal of Sport and Social Science*, 1 (1), 60–73.
Theodorakou, K. and Zervas, Y., 2003. The effects of the creative movement teaching method and the traditional teaching method on elementary school children's self-esteem. *Sport, Education and Society*, 8 (1), 91–104.
Theocharidou, O., *et al.*, 2018. The positive effects of a combined program of creative dance and braindance on health-related quality of life as perceived by primary school students. *Physical Culture and Sport*, 79 (1), 42–52.
Tuan, L.T., 2020. Coach humility and player creativity: The roles of knowledge sharing and group diversity. *Sport Management Review*, 23 (2), 284–301.
Vaughan, J., *et al.*, (2019). Developing creativity to enhance human potential in sport: A wicked transdisciplinary challenge. *Frontiers in Psychology*, 10, 2090.
Zachopoulou, E., Trevlas, E., and Konstadinidou, E., 2006. The design and implementation of a physical education program to promote children's creativity in the early years. *International Journal of Early Years Education*, 14 (3), 279–294.
Zahno, S. and Hossner, E.J., 2020. On the issue of developing creative players in team sports: A systematic review and critique from a functional perspective. *Frontiers in Psychology*, 11, 575475.

# 7

# COACHING PSYCHOLOGICAL AND LIFE SKILLS THROUGH SPORT: ADVANCING THE CONTEMPORARY COACHING AGENDA

*Chris Harwood, Sam Thrower, Sara Kramers, and Paul Wylleman*

## Introduction

As scholars working in youth sport settings, the roles and responsibilities of the modern-day coach in such contexts appear to have increased exponentially over the past decade. Coaches are often seen as the 'gatekeepers' to child-athlete development in performance terms (Harwood *et al.*, 2019); yet interest in the value of sport as a vehicle for wider psychosocial outcomes (Weiss, 2008) continues to influence *what sport should be about* and *how sport should be delivered*. In paediatric sport psychology, applied research spans a focus on the psychosocial, environmental, and organisational processes of talent development (Martindale *et al.*, 2005; MacNamara *et al.*, 2010) and the role of psychological skills training through to a recent surge in studies exploring positive youth development (PYD) and life skills interventions through sport (Holt, 2016; Pierce *et al.*, 2017). Such research lies adjacent to more global, public health and well-being concerns over the integrity and safety of organised sport cultures vis-à-vis their duty of care to children and young people and prevention of athlete mental health issues (DCMS, 2017; Rhind *et al.*, 2017).

These avenues of research matter in terms of informing the contemporary coaching agenda, yet there has been variable involvement and engagement of the coach in such empirical work. This chapter reviews the existing literature on young athletes' psychological skills development and life skills development in the context of coaching practice. Furthermore, the chapter considers the implications for coaches and relevant organisations before offering a range of research and applied considerations for advancing how coaches can optimise both the personal and athletic developmental experiences of the children and young people they support.

DOI: 10.4324/9781003199359-9 

## Review of Current Research

### Psychological Skills Development within Youth Sport

Psychological skills (PS) development or training refers to the techniques and strategies designed to teach or enhance basic (e.g. goal setting, imagery, self-talk and/or relaxation) or more complex (e.g. emotional and attentional control) mental skills that facilitate performance and positive approaches to sport competition (Vealey, 1988; Hardy *et al.*, 2010). As such, PS represent an act or task being performed rather than a psychological attribute or outcome per se (e.g. confidence, motivation; Arthur *et al.*, 2019). Although researchers examining PS development and use within the sport psychology literature have primarily focused on studying adult athletes (see Brown and Fletcher, 2017), there is evidence to suggest that child-athletes as young as 10 years of age demonstrate a basic understanding of PS (e.g. goal setting and imagery; McCarthy *et al.*, 2010). Young athletes have also been identified as being more receptive to psychological skills training (PST) than older athletes who may have already internalised dysfunctional or maladaptive responses to sport competitions (Vealey, 1988). Furthermore, PS have been recognised as essential in order to help young athletes cope with the growing demands and expectations associated with increasingly professionalised youth sport environments (i.e. training, competition) and elite athlete developmental pathways.

Given the importance of PS development within youth sport, it is perhaps not surprising that a growing body of literature has developed consulting models to guide PST with children and young athletes (e.g. Visek *et al.*, 2009), provided practitioners with accounts of conducting PST (e.g. Henriksen *et al.*, 2014), and evaluated the effectiveness of a range of different psychological strategies and techniques at enhancing young athletes' performances (see Harwood and Thrower, 2019). Focusing on the latter, studies have highlighted the effectiveness of cognitive-specific imagery (e.g. Post *et al.*, 2010), motivational and instructional self-talk (e.g. Hatzigeorgiadis *et al.*, 2008), relaxation (e.g. Haddad and Tremayne, 2009), and goal setting protocols (e.g. Pierce and Burton, 1998) on a variety of performance or learning-related indices. Furthermore, there is some evidence to suggest that more novel or innovative techniques such as self-modelling (e.g. Ste-Marie *et al.*, 2011), music (e.g. Bishop *et al.*, 2009), and mindfulness (e.g. Bernier *et al.*, 2014) can also help to enhance young athletes' sport performance. Such studies endorse the value of introducing individual psychological strategies and techniques to athletes at a young age.

### The Role of the Coach in the Delivery of Psychological Skills Training

Despite substantial evidence to support the effectiveness of both individual and multimodal PST for performance enhancement in youth sport, intervention studies tend to have been delivered by applied researchers and/or sport psychology practitioners. In doing so, the vast majority of studies have overlooked the role that coaches (and other social agents) play in determining intervention effectiveness. This is somewhat surprising given the potential benefits of integrating coaching knowledge in intervention design (e.g. self-talk instructions or imagery script refinements; Munroe-Chandler *et al.*, 2005), incorporating coach education alongside the delivery of PST programmes (Sharp *et al.*, 2013), and including coaches as part of multidisciplinary intervention delivery teams (Bell *et al.*, 2013). For example, Sharp *et al.* (2013) qualitatively evaluated the effectiveness of a mental skills training program for elite under-16 male rugby players ($n$ = 21) and their coaches ($n$ = 4). Findings from the six-month intervention suggested that the PST program was believed to increase athlete knowledge of PST skills and techniques, aid team cohesion, and increase athlete openness, honesty, and self-regulation. Furthermore, coaches' knowledge and understanding of PST improved following the intervention, resulting in increased coach support and application of PST within their coaching. These findings emphasise the importance of educating coaches of youth athletes to ensure they develop a clear knowledge of how to support and encourage athlete use of PS. Such educational initiatives are also significant in that the introduction, practice, and refinement of certain PS may be more impactful at different developmental stages through childhood and adolescence (see MacNamara *et al.*, 2010).

Alongside studies which have *indirectly* involved coaches within the design or delivery of PST interventions, researchers have also evaluated the effectiveness of interventions *directly* delivered by youth sport coaches (e.g. Mamassis and Doganis, 2004; Fournier *et al.*, 2005; Post *et al.*, 2010; Ste-Marie *et al.*, 2011). These studies have provided initial support for the effectiveness of both a coach-delivered individual strategy (e.g. self-modelling, imagery; Post *et al.*, 2010; Ste-Marie *et al.*, 2011) and multimodal PST interventions (Mamassis and Doganis, 2004; Fournier *et al.*, 2005). For instance, Fournier *et al.* (2005) explored the effects of a season long multimodal PST program delivered by a coach on gymnastic performance and PS development within an elite gymnastics academy. Adopting a multiple baseline single case design, ten national level female gymnasts ($M_{age}$ = 12 years) followed a five step PST program consisting of relaxation (8 sessions), self-talk (5 sessions), goal setting (3 sessions), focusing (4 sessions), and visualisation (5 sessions) for 30 minutes per week. These sessions were integrated into the weekly training schedule, whilst gymnasts training at a similar level academy in a different area formed a control group of participants. From self-reported data on PS development, the intervention was most effective on improving imagery skills, relaxation, activation, focusing, and refocusing. Importantly, the gymnasts' performances in the coach-led intervention group progressed 5% more than a control group of gymnasts on three events (i.e. bars, beam, floor).

These studies provide support for the notion that when delivering interventions, it may be beneficial for practitioners to engage youth sport coaches (*indirectly* or *directly*) to elicit greatest effects. Such findings are consistent with evidence suggesting that coaches are the most effective provider of psychological interventions for adult athletes, potentially as a result of the athlete and their coach possessing a more matured relationship and established rapport (see Brown and Fletcher, 2017). Furthermore, coach engagement and/or provision is likely to be particularly important during adolescence (and emerging adulthood) when coaches become one of the most significant influences on young athletes' psychosocial development (see Wylleman, 2018). Nevertheless, as Arthur *et al.* (2019) suggested, carefully designed coach-delivered interventions are far removed from the reality of everyday coaching in youth sport. The coaching of PS by coaches unfortunately rarely occurs, and research suggests that coaches often report a lack of confidence and knowledge as key barriers in delivering PST (Callow *et al.*, 2010; Arthur *et al.*, 2019; Feddersen *et al.*, 2021).

## *Integrating Psychological Skills Training in Coaching Practices*

In order to navigate the challenges associated with coach-initiated PST in youth sport, and render psychological support more accessible to young athletes, applied researchers have started to explore how to more effectively integrate PS development within coaching practices (e.g. Harwood, 2008; Callow *et al.*, 2010; Camiré and Trudel, 2014; Harwood *et al.*, 2015; Zakrajsek *et al.*, 2017; Lauer *et al.*, 2020). These interventions have typically been delivered via face-to-face workshops, focused on providing coaches with behavioural guidelines (see Harwood, 2008; Harwood *et al.*, 2015), and been evaluated via coach and/or player self-report. Whilst these studies have generated positive outcomes for both coaches (e.g. greater knowledge, understanding, and confidence towards PS) and young athletes (e.g. increases in positive psychosocial responses across the intervention; Harwood *et al.*, 2015), actual coaching behaviour change has either not been formally assessed or has remained relatively unchanged (Arthur *et al.*, 2019). Furthermore, from a methodological perspective, such interventions are not always evidence or theory-based and have lacked rigorous methodological designs to accurately evaluate effectiveness.

To address these limitations, Arthur *et al.* (2019) recently developed a conceptual framework for coaching PST through extended interviews with four elite coaches and five elite athletes. Results highlighted six dimensions which were integrated within fundamental coaching of basic PS (i.e. imagery, goal setting, relaxation, imagery). The fundamental coaching of PS (i.e. CPS-F) included coaches' observations of athlete's PS use (e.g. looking for breaks in pre-performance routines, providing challenges to see how athletes coped), motivating or instructing using targeted PS cues (i.e. verbal instructions of a psychological nature or imagery-based cues), directly instructing athletes to use PS, and reinforcing PS use. Furthermore, participants highlighted the importance of need supportive coaching of PS (i.e. coaches helping the athletes to understand what PS are and how to use them in a way which would be relevant to them).

These recent advances have started to bridge the gap between the delivery of PS based education and the craft of integrating PS in coaching contexts. In so doing, they have illustrated coaches' preference to learn PS in a user-friendly manner (i.e. behavioural guidelines; see Harwood *et al.*, 2015) and the need for greater support and practical training resources to build their confidence in executing this specific role (Harwood, 2008). In addition, the development of a conceptual framework which includes fundamental coaching PS behaviours, as well as validated questionnaires to measure such behaviours (see Arthur *et al.*, 2019), provides the foundations for the effective integration and evaluation of PS development within coaching practice. It is important to note that observational tools also offer an alternative way to enable coaches to identify behaviours specific to the use of PS and/or the consequences of their use. Whilst still in its infancy, such progress paves the way for more evidence-informed coaching and delivery of PS to optimise young athletes' experiences, performance, and development within competitive youth sport settings.

## *Extending Coaching Responsibilities to PYD and Life Skills*

Young athletes and their families can make heavy investments in personal, emotional, and financial terms to 'organised sport', yet few athletes in 'talent development pathways' will maintain the progression and transition to professional, elite sport (see Sweeney *et al.*, 2021). There is strong advocacy for sport organisations and systems to consider their moral and psychosocial duty of care to children and families who specialise and invest early in a sport because of the competitive structure and pathway of a system that may implicitly promote early specialisation. Over the last two decades, scholars within the fields of PYD and life skills have actively encouraged a holistic approach to athlete development, whereby young people are provided with the intrapersonal and interpersonal tools and coping resources to develop as people within and beyond their sport (Weiss, 2008; Larsen *et al.*, 2014; Camiré, 2015). The PYD framework represents a strengths-based, flexible, and relationally centred approach with a focus on supporting children and young people as they develop assets, strengths, and skills through appropriate developmental opportunities (e.g. Lerner *et al.*, 2005; Geldhof *et al.*, 2013). Given that sport participation in and of itself does not automatically lead to the learning of life skills (e.g. Coakley, 2016), researchers have focused on how the youth sport coach is a key external asset to intentionally foster PYD and life skills through sport (e.g. Bean *et al.*, 2018).

The discussion on coaches teaching life skills through sport has evolved over the last two decades, and the research literature is more well developed around the challenges of this specific 'coaching role' compared to coaching psychological skills (PS) for performance enhancement. Gould and Carson (2008) first suggested that coaches use *indirect* (e.g. demands of the sport, social reinforcement from peers, positive social norms) and *direct* strategies (e.g. use of clear and consistent rules, providing leadership opportunities) to teach life skills. Turnnidge *et al.* (2014) then defined two approaches to life skills transfer in sport, including the *implicit* approach (i.e. fostering positive coach-athlete relationships and sport-specific physical and personal development outcomes without deliberate attention paid to transfer) and *explicit* approach (i.e. satisfying elements of the implicit approach in conjunction with deliberate attention paid to the transfer of life skills). Recently, Bean *et al.* (2018) postulated that there are varying levels of implicitness and explicitness at which coaches can facilitate life skills development and transfer, rather than through dichotomous approaches. As such, Bean *et al.* created a continuum of life skills development and transfer, with six levels of intentionality that moved from implicit coaching behaviours (i.e. structuring the sport context and facilitating a positive climate) to explicit coaching behaviours (i.e. discussing life skills, practicing life skills, discussing transfer, and practicing transfer).

Researchers have championed the need for coaches to apply more explicit coaching practices as this is believed to directly heighten young athletes' awareness around the importance of life skills within and beyond sport (Holt *et al.*, 2017; Bean *et al.*, 2018). Nevertheless, our knowledge derived from studies where coaches have been involved in life skills development within youth sport contexts suggests that the marriage between 'coaching practice' and 'life skill outcomes' is not an easy one.

## Coaching Practice and Life Skills Development

Only a handful of studies have investigated athletes' developmental outcomes from direct and intentional coach interventions related to the teaching of life skills through organised competitive or elite youth sport. Camiré *et al.* (2013) examined key stakeholders' perspectives of a life skills program for male hockey players, within a sport-based high school. Findings revealed that from the program's intentional focus on life skills, players were provided opportunities to create strong relationships with their coaches, and practice using their learned life skills in sport (e.g. setting realistic long-term goals) and in their community (e.g. developing altruism through volunteering). However, there were conflicting goals between the parents, coaches, and school staff regarding how much time should be spent on personal development, and coaches struggled balancing this coaching approach with their existing duties. In a similar high school sport context, Martin *et al.* (2021) led a six-month intervention to collaboratively assist a teacher-coach in facilitating student-athletes' life skills transfer from sport to the classroom. The teacher-coach perceived that with the direct support from the researcher he gained confidence in his ability to explicitly teach life skills in both contexts (e.g. setting goals) and to reflect on his implementation of the life skills activities. The student-athletes reported learning life skills on the field and in the classroom, in addition to gaining confidence and awareness for transferring their life skills to other contexts based on their relationship with the teacher-coach.

Beyond such direct interventions, scholars have tended to qualitatively explore the perceptions and experiences of coaches in supporting child-athletes' PYD and life skills. Such studies offer insights into the types of strategies perceived as effective (e.g. implicit or explicit) and the challenges coaches may face (e.g. Marsollier *et al.*, 2020; Preston *et al.*, 2021). A common theme from this research appears to be an acknowledgement of the importance of life skills development through competitive and elite youth sport, but the limited use of explicit strategies for such developmental goals. Coaches tend to perceive that life skills development and PYD happens due to the inherent features of the sport (e.g. Portuguese field hockey's familial subculture promotes belonging; Santos *et al.*, 2018) or from the use of implicit strategies (e.g. providing opportunities for players to voice their opinions; Harrist and Witt, 2014). Even when coaches have acknowledged the use of explicit strategies in their sport contexts, they still have difficulty articulating exactly what is done to facilitate such explicit PYD (e.g. Santos *et al.*, 2018), and their athletes may perceive they developed their life skills through sport implicitly (Marsollier *et al.*, 2020).

Regardless of the coaches' intentions, a predominant challenge for coaches seems to be navigating how to balance the emphasis on young athletes' personal development within the performance-oriented and professionalised culture in elite and competitive sports (e.g. Camiré, 2015). Through observational research, elite youth sport coaches have been seen to align their actions with winning rather than promoting PYD, despite their stated motivations to facilitate PYD through sport (e.g. Preston *et al.*, 2021). The disconnect between coaches' intentions and actions for fostering PYD may also occur based on the age and cognitive maturity of their athletes. For instance, elite coaches have discussed focusing on performance-related development and PYD when coaching younger athletes (i.e. 4–14), but noted an emphasis on performance-related development with older athletes (i.e. 15–18; Santos *et al.*, 2017).

Such inconsistencies in coaches' perceived intentions versus actions and the conditionality of when PYD is relevant to coaching practice form the crux of a multi-layered problem. Coaches in competitive and elite contexts have expressed worth in learning how to facilitate PYD and teach life skills through mainstream coach education courses; however, there are limited, if any, formalised or mainstream coach education programs (Vella *et al.*, 2013; Santos *et al.*, 2017). As such, researchers have created their own PYD-focused and life skills training programs for coaches in competitive and elite sport contexts (e.g. Falcão *et al.*, 2012; MacDonald *et al.*, 2020). For example, MacDonald *et al.*'s (2020) training intervention with 30 Portuguese youth sport coaches and their athletes revealed that the coaches in the experimental group (i.e. who received the intervention) increased their frequency of their PYD-oriented coaching behaviours during the intervention compared to the control group, but then returned to levels slightly above baseline three months post-intervention. Moreover, the athletes in both the experimental and control groups reported high levels of coach-athlete relationships throughout the study, with no significant changes in their scores over time despite increases in positive coach-athlete behaviours observed throughout the intervention. Whilst researcher-led collaborative programs may heighten awareness and train coaches in how they might foster PYD and life skills in competitive and elite sport, the long-term impact of such interventions remains questionable. Moving forward, an approach may be to provide coaches with a training program that begins with a holistic perspective to development and then shifts to a sport-specific focus, to teach and train their young athletes in using life skills which are not only relevant in sport but also in other domains (see Blijlevens *et al.*, 2018).

## Implications for Children's Sport Coaching

The mosaic of literature that has been formed from attention to young athletes' psychological skills and life skills development makes for interesting debate around coaches' levels of responsibility and practice. For example, few would argue that a child's psychological skills and their personal development weren't factors for the coach to consider in their coaching of a young person. Yet the body of work in sport psychology fails to offer a convincing portrait of coherent, explicit, and strategic engagement of coaches in optimising such developmental skills and outcomes.

Competitive and elite youth sport contexts have been recognised as ideal sub-cultures for the facilitation of PYD and the teaching of life skills when the team/program is structured appropriately and coaches promote competition as an opportunity for growth and development rather than endorse a 'win at all costs' approach (e.g. Strachan *et al.*, 2011). However, this philosophy can also extend to the teaching of traditional psychological skills for performance of which a number reflect life skills in and of themselves (e.g. relaxation, decision-making). Where coaches spend time developing a well-articulated coaching philosophy that emphasises psychological and life skills teaching (e.g. Harwood, 2008; Camiré *et al.*, 2011; Santos *et al.*, 2017) in an environment characterised by shared values and supportive interactions between and among sport stakeholders (e.g. coach-athlete, coach-parent, club-coach-parent), the cultural conditions exist for optimising young athletes' experiences in both athletic and personal domains. Moreover, implementing a holistic approach to support young athletes' development may encourage stakeholders to view athletic and personal domains as integrative rather than dichotomous, helping coaches to teach psychological and life skills relevant for sport and beyond (Blijlevens *et al.*, 2018). Nevertheless, research illustrates the barriers and challenges that prevent or dilute a coach's focus on psychological and life skills development in young athletes to the same level that they might attend to technical, tactical, and physical development (Harwood, 2008).

In their study of the knowledge and perceptions of sport psychology among elite youth academy football staff, Pain and Harwood (2004) reported how some coaches and directors perceived psychology in a negative light, noted a lack of sport psychology knowledge, and struggled with time and logistical integration of psychology into the academy program. Role clarity was a further barrier in terms of differentiating the strategic input required from coaches against the input from sport psychology practitioners. Lack of coordination with practitioners and poor role clarity can lead to inefficient management of human resources and expertise. For instance, in Hardcastle *et al.*'s (2015) study within high performance youth sport, external facilitators led the life skills program for athletes without coach involvement. Whilst the athletes reported being exposed to many positive skills (e.g. managing stress), the disinvolvement from the coaches and their lack of awareness was perceived to limit sustained teaching, practicing, and reflection on life skills activities. Whether it is the development of psychological skills for performance or life skills for personal development, both represent complex and contextually specific processes consisting of purposeful, direct and indirect, and formal and informal activities (Arthur *et al.*, 2019). With coaches having more direct contact time with young athletes than other staff, it is critical that coaches are sufficiently educated, confident, and supported by the wider system.

It is perhaps this latter point that sums up where the real challenge exists in terms of mitigating less than optimal coaching attention to children and young people's psychological and life skills. Contemporary ecological approaches to talent development (see Henriksen *et al.*, 2010) view young athletes as nested in the centre of a series of social systems each influencing the other. The coach is proximal to the athlete as a key source of influence, yet a coach's priorities, behaviour, and practices are in turn influenced by the system around them. Coaches are influenced by the goals and mandates of their employers and the espoused values of the organisation. Where organisations truly value psychological skills and life skills development in youth sport (e.g. as much as investments in technology for gaining a winning edge), then such a holistic approach would presumably lead to an organisation's strategic and commensurate investment in appropriate coach education and coach key performance indicators (KPIs) in respect of engagement in more 'integrated' psychological and life skills coaching practices (see Larsen *et al.*, 2014). The question of whether psychological and life skills are on the contemporary coach's agenda is perhaps more a matter of whether this is on an organisation's agenda, reflected by a coherent approach towards holistic athlete care.

## Summary, Future Directions, and Future Research

In this chapter, the authors have positioned the coach as critical [in direct and indirect capacities] for supporting the psychological and life skills development of their athletes and examined the state of the academic literature with this role in mind. Whilst it is important not to underestimate the diverse roles that a coach plays, it is vital to consider how coaches can effectively support the growth of PS and life skills in competitive youth sport contexts. Informed by a modest body of research, there are several future directions, opportunities and research questions that remain unanswered.

## Organisational Priorities and Coach Development

A pressing area for consideration is the degree to which sport organisations, federations, and clubs invest philosophically and financially in the holistic development of children and young people, with deliberate and intentional policies and strategies aligned to psychosocial development of the 'person' and the 'performer' (Santos *et al.*, 2019a). Changes in the perceptions of coaches may only occur with changes in the values of an organisation or system employing the coach. Organisational strategies that would align to a holistic focus include critically appraising the quality and quantity of education that coaches receive in coaching psychological and life skills as part of professional accreditation curricula and continuing professional development. Such an audit would reveal the nature and degree of investment required in preparing coaches and developing their sense of confidence.

Supplementing such work would be further research into understanding the barriers coaches face towards taking an intentional approach to children and young athletes' psychosocial development with compatible and integrated attention to PS training. Methods of coach education should be carefully considered as literature suggests that brief coach training programs offered online may be limited by the absence of tangible support and feedback from expert facilitators to help embed changes in coaching behaviour and practices (e.g. Santos *et al.*, 2019b).

Scholars in youth sport psychology also need to take responsibility for how effective knowledge translation and tailoring can be achieved such that organisations take on board the science that is produced. Knowledge translation is critical to the health of the profession, and it is vital to translate findings that illustrate how coaching psychological and life skills leads to positive outcomes and experiences in young people (Holt *et al.*, 2017).

## Role Clarity, Leadership, and Collaboration with Support Staff

The overall project of psychological and life skills development in children and young athletes is not isolated to the role of the coach. Where support from sport psychology practitioners is available, it is vital to have a clear and cohesive strategy of working with the coach in terms of how PS and life skills are going to be practically and strategically nurtured in athletes. When coaches and practitioners work 'in tandem', they both gain an understanding of where the athlete is at in terms of PS and life skills development; they are able to identify areas of development through appropriate observation and assessment; and they are able to collaborate on individual development and activity plans for that athlete. Research is needed that illustrates the leadership processes and coordinated practices of coaches, psychologists, and related support staff working together such development plans and monitoring the quality of athlete outcomes through such collaborative endeavours.

## Integrative and Systemic Approaches

Extending the leadership role of the coach beyond their inner circle of support staff includes strategic collaboration with other stakeholders in a young athlete's system, such as parents and teachers. For example, it is likely that parental involvement will exert some degree of psychological influence upon a child-athlete, and that parents can be powerful reinforcement and modelling resources for the coach when supported and educated appropriately (Harwood *et al.*, 2019). Nevertheless, there is little research that has explored the integrative processes and outcomes of an athlete-centred, coach-led, and parent-supported system that is focused on specific psychological or life skill outcomes. Such triadic, relational work around valued skills and qualities may represent processes underpinning cohesive, development environments for PS and life skills (see Martindale *et al.*, 2005).

In closing this chapter, the contemporary coach is a key gatekeeper to the direction of travel a young athlete may take in terms of their psychological and life skills development through sport. Coaches can significantly influence the motivation for athletes to develop themselves, and more critically, they can guide 'what' skills athletes should work on and 'how' this skill development process best works. There is a tremendous amount of existing science and knowledge around psychological skills and life skills that may be more or less accessible to coaches, and existing internal and external barriers to the application of such knowledge into coaching practice on a day-to-day basis. Holistic sport organisational values, improved coach education, and more efficient, integrative work with practitioners, parents, and relevant stakeholders represent factors to consider in advancing the coach's agenda for psychological and life skills in children and young people.

## References

Arthur, R.A., *et al.*, 2019. Coaches coaching psychological skills—Why not? A framework and questionnaire development. *Journal of Sport and Exercise Psychology*, 41 (1), 10–23.

Bean, C., *et al.*, 2018. The implicit/explicit continuum of life skills development and transfer. *Quest*, 70 (4), 456–470.

Bell, J.J., Hardy, L., and Beattie, S., 2013. Enhancing mental toughness and performance under pressure in elite young cricketers: A 2-year longitudinal intervention. *Sport, Exercise, and Performance Psychology*, 2 (4), 281–297.

Bernier, M., *et al.*, 2014. Effects and underlying processes of a mindfulness-based intervention with young elite figure skaters: Two case studies. *The Sport Psychologist*, 28 (3), 302–315.

Bishop, D.T., Karageorghis, C.I., and Kinrade, N.P., 2009. Effects of musically-induced emotions on choice reaction time performance. *The Sport Psychologist*, 23 (1), 59–76.

Blijlevens, S., *et al.*, 2018. Psychological characteristics and skills of top-level Dutch gymnasts in the initiation, development and mastery stages of the athletic career. *Psychology of Sport and Exercise*, 38, 202–210.

Brown, D.J. and Fletcher, D., 2017. Effects of psychological and psychosocial interventions on sport performance: A meta-analysis. *Sports Medicine*, 47 (1), 77–99.

Callow, N., *et al.*, 2010. Coach education related to the delivery of imagery: Two interventions. *The Sport Psychologist*, 24 (3), 277–299.

Camiré, M., 2015. Reconciling competition and positive youth development in sport. *STAPS*, 3 (109), 25–39.

Camiré, M. and Trudel, P., 2014. Helping youth sport coaches integrate psychological skills in their coaching practice. *Qualitative Research in Sport, Exercise and Health*, 6 (4), 617–634.

Camiré, M., Trudel, P., and Bernard, D., 2013. A case study of a high school sport program designed to teach athletes life skills and values. *The Sport Psychologist*, 27 (2), 188–200.

Camiré, M., *et al.*, 2011. Strategies for helping coaches facilitate positive youth development through sport. *Journal of Sport Psychology in Action*, 2 (2), 92–99.

Coakley, J., 2016. Positive youth development through sport: Myths, beliefs, and realities. *In*: N.L. Holt, ed. *Positive youth development through sport*. 2nd ed. New York: Routledge, 21–33.

DCMS, 2017. *Duty of Care in Sport Review* [online]. Available from: https://www.gov.uk/government/publications/duty-of-care-in-sport-review [Accessed 8 April 2022].

Falcão, W., Bloom, G., and Gilbert, W., 2012. Coaches' perceptions of a coach training program designed to promote youth developmental outcomes. *Journal of Applied Sport Psychology*, 24 (4), 429–444.

Feddersen, N.B., Keis, M.A.B., and Elbe, A.M., 2021. Coaches' perceived pitfalls in delivering psychological skills training to high-level youth athletes in fencing and football. *International Journal of Sports Science & Coaching*, 16 (2), 249–261.

Fournier, J.F., *et al.*, 2005. Effects of a season long PST program on gymnastic performance and on psychological skill development. *International Journal of Sport and Exercise Psychology*, 3 (1), 59–78.

Geldhof, G.J., *et al.*, 2013. Relational developmental systems theories of positive youth development: Methodological issues and implications. *In*: P.C.M. Molenaar, R.M. Lerner, and K.M. Newell, eds. *Handbook of developmental systems theory and methodology*, New York: The Guilford Press, 66–94.

Gould, D. and Carson, S., 2008. Life skills development through sport: Current status and future directions. *International Review of Sport and Exercise Psychology*, 1 (1), 58–78.

Haddad, K. and Tremayne, P., 2009. The effects of centering on the free-throw shooting performance of young athletes. *The Sport Psychologist*, 23 (1), 118–136.

Hardcastle, S.J., *et al.*, 2015. Exploring the perceived effectiveness of a life skills development program for high-performance athletes. *Psychology of Sport and Exercise*, 16 (3), 139–149.

Hardy, L., *et al.*, 2010. Test of Performance Strategies (TOPS): Instrument refinement using confirmatory factor analysis, *Psychology of Sport and Exercise*, 11 (1), 27–35.

Harrist, C.J. and Witt, P.A., 2014. Calling the screens: Self-reported developmental outcomes in competitive basketball. *Journal of Adolescent Research*, 30 (6), 751–778.

Harwood, C., 2008. Developmental consulting in a professional football academy: The 5C's coaching efficacy program. *The Sport Psychologist*, 22 (1), 109–133.

Harwood, C., Barker, J.B., and Anderson, R., 2015. Psychosocial development in youth soccer players: Assessing the effectiveness of the 5Cs intervention program. *The Sport Psychologist*, 29 (4), 319–334.

Harwood, C.G. and Thrower, S.N., 2019. Performance enhancement and the young athlete: Mapping the landscape and navigating future directions. *Kinesiology Review*, 8 (3), 171–179.

Harwood, C.G., *et al.*, 2019. Advancing the study of parental involvement to optimise the psychosocial development and experiences of young athletes. *Psychology of Sport and Exercise*, 42, 66–73.

Hatzigeorgiadis, A., *et al.*, 2008. Investigating the functions of self-talk: The effects of motivational self-talk on self-efficacy and performance in young tennis players. *The Sport Psychologist*, 22 (4), 458–471.

Henriksen, K., Stambulova, N., and Roessler, K.K., 2010. Holistic approach to athletic talent development environments: A sailing milieu. *Psychology of Sport and Exercise*, 11 (3), 212–222.

Henriksen, K., *et al.*, 2014. Sport psychology interventions with young athletes: The perspective of the sport psychology practitioner. *Journal of Clinical Sport Psychology*, 8 (3), 245–260.

Holt, N.L., 2016. *Positive youth development through sport*. 2nd ed. New York: Routledge.

Holt, N.L., *et al.*, 2017. A grounded theory of positive youth development through sport based on results from a qualitative meta-study. *International Review of Sport and Exercise Psychology*, 10 (1), 1–49.

Larsen, C.H., *et al.*, 2014. Preparing footballers for the next step: An intervention program from an ecological perspective. *The Sport Psychologist*, 28 (1), 91–102.

Lauer, E.E., *et al.*, 2020. The creation of a mental skills training program in elite youth tennis: A coach-driven approach to developing resilient, confident competitors. *International Sport Coaching Journal*, 7 (1), 74–81.

Lerner, R.M., *et al.*, 2005. Positive youth development: A view of the issues. *The Journal of Early Adolescence*, 25 (1), 10–16.

MacDonald, D.J., *et al.*, 2020. Positive youth development related athlete experiences and coach behaviors following a targeted coach education course. *International Journal of Sports Science & Coaching*, 15 (5-6), 621–630.

MacNamara, Á., Button, A., and Collins, D., 2010. The role of psychological characteristics in facilitating the pathway to elite performance. Part 2: Examining environmental and stage related differences in skills and behaviours. *The Sport Psychologist*, 24 (1), 74–96.

Mamassis, G. and Doganis, G., 2004. The effects of a mental training program on juniors precompetitive anxiety, self-confidence, and tennis performance. *Journal of Applied Sport Psychology*, 16 (2), 118–137.

Marsollier, E., Trottier, C., and Falcão, W.R., 2020. Development and transfer of life skills in figure skating: Experiences of athletes and their coaches. *Qualitative Research in Sport, Exercise and Health*, 12 (5), 664–682.

Martin, N., Camiré, M., and Kramers, S., 2021. Facilitating life skills transfer from sport to the classroom: An intervention assisting a high school teacher-coach. *Journal of Applied Sport Psychology*. Advance online publication.

Martindale, R.J., Collins, D., and Daubney, J., 2005. Talent development: A guide for practice and research within sport. *Quest*, 57 (4), 353–375.

McCarthy, P.J., *et al.*, 2010. What do young athletes implicitly understand about psychological skills? *Journal of Clinical Sport Psychology*, 4 (2), 158–172.

Munroe-Chandler, K.J., *et al.*, 2005. Using cognitive-general imagery to improve soccer strategies. *European Journal of Sport Science*, 5 (1), 41–49.

Pain, M.A. and Harwood, C.G., 2004. Knowledge and perceptions of sport psychology within English soccer. *Journal of Sports Sciences*, 22 (9), 813–826.

Pierce, B.E. and Burton, D., 1998. Scoring the perfect 10: Investigating the impact of goalsetting styles on a goal-setting program for female gymnasts. *The Sport Psychologist*, 12 (2), 156–168.

Pierce, S., Gould, D., and Camiré, M., 2017. Definition and model of life skills transfer. *International Review of Sport and Exercise Psychology*, 10 (1), 186–211.

Post, P.G., Wrisberg, C.A., and Mullins, S., 2010. A field test of the influence of pre-game imagery on basketball free throw shooting. *Journal of Imagery Research in Sport and Physical Activity*, 5 (1), 1–15.

Preston, C., Allan, V., and Fraser-Thomas, J., 2021. Facilitating positive youth development in elite youth hockey: Exploring coaches' capabilities, opportunities, and motivations. *Journal of Applied Sport Psychology*, 33 (3), 302–320.

Rhind, D.J.A., *et al.*, 2017. Building a system to safeguard children in sport: The eight CHILDREN pillars. *Journal of Sport and Social Issues*, 41 (2), 151–171.

Santos, F., Camiré, M., and Campos, H., 2018. Youth sport coaches' role in facilitating positive youth development in Portuguese field hockey. *International Journal of Sport and Exercise Psychology*, 16 (3), 221–234.

Santos, F., Gould, D., and Strachan, L., 2019a. Research on positive youth development-focused coach education programs: Future pathways and applications. *International Sport Coaching Journal*, 6 (1), 132–138.

Santos, F., *et al.*, 2019b. Process and outcome evaluation of a positive youth development-focused online coach education course. *International Sport Coaching Journal*, 6 (1), 1–12.

Santos, F., *et al.*, 2017. Youth sport coaches' perspective on positive youth development and its worth in mainstream coach education courses. *International Sport Coaching Journal*, 4 (1), 38–46.

Sharp, L.A., *et al.*, 2013. Qualitative evaluation of the effectiveness of a mental skills training program for youth athletes. *The Sport Psychologist*, 27 (3), 219–232.

Ste-Marie, D.M., *et al.*, 2011. Self-modeling and competitive beam performance enhancement examined within a self-regulation perspective. *Journal of Applied Sport Psychology*, 23 (3), 292–307.

Strachan, L., Côté, J., and Deakin, J., 2011. A new view: Exploring positive youth development in elite sport contexts. *Qualitative Research in Sport and Exercise*, 3 (1), 9–32.

Sweeney, L., Horan, D., and MacNamara, Á., 2021. Premature professionalisation or early engagement? Examining practise in football player pathways. *Frontiers in Sports and Active Living*, 3, 1–9.

Turnnidge, J., Côté, J., and Hancock, D.J., 2014. Positive youth development from sport to life: explicit or implicit transfer? *Quest*, 66 (2), 203–217.

Vealey, R.S., 1988. Future directions in psychological skills training. *The Sport Psychologist*, 2 (4), 318–336.

Vella, S.A., Oades, L., and Crowe, T., 2013. The relationship between coach leadership, the coach-athlete relationship, team success, and the positive developmental experiences of adolescent soccer players. *Physical Education and Sport Pedagogy*, 18 (5), 549–561.

Visek, A.J., Harris, B.S., and Blom, L.C., 2009. Doing sport psychology: A youth sport consulting model for practitioners. *The Sport Psychologist*, 23 (2), 271–291.

Weiss, M.R., 2008. 'Field of dreams': Sport as a context for youth development. *Research Quarterly for Exercise and Sport*, 79 (4), 434–449.

Wylleman, P., 2018. Sport psychologists assisting young talented athletes faced with career transitions. *In*: C. Harwood, D. Gould, and C. Knight, eds. *Sport psychology for young athletes*. New York: Routledge, 141–152.

Zakrajsek, R.A., Lauer, E.E., and Bodey, K.J., 2017. Integrating mental skills and strategies into youth sport training: A tool for coaches. *International Sport Coaching Journal*, 4 (1), 76–89.

# 8

# EXPLORING CONTEXTUAL FACTORS INFLUENCING POSITIVE DEVELOPMENT THROUGH SPORT

*Leisha Strachan, Jessica Fraser-Thomas, Nickolas Kosmenko, and Craig Brown*

## Introduction

The author Urie Bronfenbrenner (1996, p. 1) has been famously quoted as saying – "There is no more critical indicator of the future of a society than the character, competence, and integrity of its youth". This chapter will venture to acknowledge the various contexts of development within sport that lead to the positive growth of children and youth. Whilst it is clear that interpersonal interactions within youths' contexts are key, the strong presence and influence of broader contextual influences have been under-researched and under-represented in the literature (Holt *et al.*, 2017). The chapter will begin by discussing Bronfenbrenner's (1979, 1999) Ecological Systems Theory (EST), followed by a description of Holt *et al.*'s (2017) model of positive youth development (PYD) through sport; the chapter will also draw upon these frameworks to explore specific contextual factors in children (and youth) sport, namely the coach-parent relationship, the role of administrators and organisations, and cultural factors related to newcomer and Indigenous communities. Actions to enhance positive development and future directions related to contextual factors in sport are also explored.

## Review of Current Research

### *Ecological Systems Theory*

Learning, growth, and development do not occur in a vacuum; everyone has experienced various settings for growth and credits these for their development as a person. Whether family, school, church, or sport, various settings provide unique opportunities to learn. One popular approach to explaining developmental processes is through EST, which assumes "that development is a function of forces emanating from multiple settings and forms the relations between these settings" (Bronfenbrenner, 1999, p. 17). The nested systems, conceptualised by Bronfenbrenner (1979), lays the groundwork for looking at different levels (or systems) of growth from proximal to distal from the developing person. The most proximal system, the

 DOI: 10.4324/9781003199359-10

microsystem, includes the individual and the relationships that are cultivated with various other individuals. The mesosystem, the next level, is focused on dyadic relationships that are developed between two or more microsystems (e.g. parent-coach); these bi-directional interactions in turn influence the child's development. Next, the exosystem discusses connections between two or more settings with at least one setting that does not include the person. For example, an exosystemic interaction could be between a sports team (i.e. involving the person) and the program administration (i.e. not directly involving the person). Finally, the most distal system is the macrosystem. This level explains the influence that systemic structures have on various developmental settings. These include, but are not limited to, sociocultural structures and barriers, policies, and culture which encompass values, beliefs, resources, and social interactions. While Bronfenbrenner continued to refine and reinterpret his work until his passing in 2005, the original EST offers a sound framework and grounding for understanding contextual influences broadly, and specifically in sport. In his paper linking sport with EST, Garcia-Bengoechea (2002, p. 8) posited that Bronfenbrenner's EST "is the conceptualisation of the environment as a hierarchy of nested structures", highlighting the importance of context on development at each system level. Further, while Bronfenbrenner's (1979, 1999) work highlights interdependence as one moves through systems, this interdependence is sometimes less obvious at the macrosystem level, given the substantive powers held at this level and the inherent difficulty in changing systems.

## Positive Development through Sport

Since the early 2000s, a growing body of research has focused on PYD through sport, with significant consideration to the nested levels of contextual influence. Holt *et al.* (2017) conducted a qualitative meta-study synthesising work completed in the field, creating a model of PYD through sport, which further emphasises the influence of context. Connecting to Bronfenbrenner's (1979, 1999) work, Holt *et al.*'s (2017) model outlines sport as a microsystem containing interactions between people. Notably, the authors acknowledge the important influence of adult leaders, parents, and peers in creating a positive developmental climate to optimally deliver programs and foster positive outcomes, with intentionality by these individuals being important to delivery. Additionally, more distal systems (e.g. macrosystem, exosystem) influence interactions, with social and cultural structures directly and indirectly impacting the individual in the sport environment. The emergence of this model, coupled with other influential frameworks and models (Fraser-Thomas *et al.*, 2005; Petitpas *et al.*, 2005; Gould and Carson, 2008; Côté *et al.*, 2020) highlight that more understanding is needed at all levels of EST to gain a more complete picture of the facilitators and barriers to youth sport participation. In the sections that follow, three specific contextual influences are explored: (a) coach-parent relationships (mesosystem), (b) administrators (exosystem), and (c) cultural considerations (macrosystem).

## A Mesosystem Influence: Coach-Parent Relationships

Parent-coach relationships fall within the mesosystem of Bronfenbrenner's (1979, 1999) EST, whereby interactions occur between specific microsystems (i.e. parents and coaches) to influence children's development. While much research has focused on the independent influence of parents and coaches upon children's development (e.g. Tamminen *et al.*, 2020; Holt *et al.*, 2021), little work has exclusively explored their shared influence and/or bidirectional interactions. Similarly, while Holt *et al.*'s (2017) model of PYD through sport highlights the importance of a PYD climate (i.e. involving parents and coaches), their specific collective influence upon athlete positive developmental outcomes has been minimally explored, despite these interactions playing an important role in shaping athletes' outcomes (Fraser-Thomas and Strachan, 2015; Holt *et al.*, 2017).

## *Narrative of Parents as Problems*

Much of the narrative around parent-coach interactions has been framed through the lens of parents as problems, with coaches often describing their frustrations of 'dealing with', 'managing', and/or resenting parents, rather than 'working with' or 'collaborating with' parents (see Knight and Harwood, 2009; Harwood, 2011; Camiré *et al.*, 2016; Preston *et al.*, 2020). For example, in their study of 70 British tennis coaches, Knight and Harwood (2009) found coaches experienced different parent-related stressors according to athletes' stage of development, with coaches of younger athletes challenged by parents' (lack of) understanding of tennis and development, and coaches of older athletes stressed by parental pressure and involvement. In a more recent study, Preston *et al.* (2020) drew upon reflective practice to understand the coach's (i.e. lead author's) interactions with parents of a Canadian elite level boys' (age 10) hockey team, finding interactions ranged on a continuum from cooperative (i.e. contributing to a collborative style of conflict resolution) to uncooperative (i.e. negatively influencing athletes' PYD). While it is often just a 'few bad apples' (i.e. parents, and/or coaches) driving this negative narrative, the impact of these interactions is often much more influential on all stakeholders' sport experiences than more frequent positive interactions (Preston *et al.*, 2020). Given the critical influence of parents and coaches in children's sport development, it is worth considering why and how this contextual element is often so toxic.

At the most fundamental level of negative parent-coach interactions, are misunderstandings of others' experiences and perspectives. This may not be surprising, given parents' primary focus is on their child's optimal development, while coaches must focus on the development and performance of the entire team (Horn, 2011). Parents are often perceived as being under, over, or extremely involved in their child's sport, rather than appropriately involved (Dorsch *et al.*, 2019, p. 435); under-involved parents may view sport as a "drop-off daycare society", while extremely involved parents can be too focused on performance, recognition, and controlling their child's participation. Parents may also have inflated beliefs regarding their sport expertise (i.e. due to spectating or past playing experience) (Holt *et al.*, 2009; Preston *et al.*, 2020), engage in group (i.e. 'gang-up') discussions criticising coaches' behaviours/performances (Preston *et al.*, 2020), or lack understanding of the time, pressures, and challenges of coaching youth sport teams (O'Connor, 2011). Yet, reciprocally, parents may perceive coaches as stressors, outlining their poor communication and lack of respect for parents, leading to frustration, confusion, and lack of trust (Knight and Harwood, 2009; Knight *et al.*, 2010; Bean *et al.*, 2016).

More distal (i.e. exosystem/macrosystem; Bronfenbrenner 1979, 1999) factors can also contribute to toxicity in parent-coach relations – namely, increasingly professionalised youth sport cultures (Smoll *et al.*, 2011), and changing social expectations around parenting. In many Western nations, children are viewed as precious and valued commodities, while simultaneously vulnerable to physical and emotional harm, contributing to a culture of potentially intrusive 'helicopter parenting' (Horn, 2011). Many parents view sport as a competitive context for their child to be successful while building self-esteem and other life skills (O'Connor, 2011). Yet youth sport organisations, leagues, and coaches are increasingly creating a culture of high performance (e.g. early specialisation, intense competition, extensive travel) with an expectation that parents are "all in" (Dorsch *et al.*, 2019; Preston *et al.*, 2020). Within this culture, parents are often seeking a 'return on investment', in the form of their child's playing time, scholarship/recruitment opportunities, and even social status within the sport (Campbell and Parcels, 2013; Bean *et al.*, 2016; Preston *et al.*, 2020). As such, while parents are often suggested to be the source of significant parent-coach relational issues, the broader culture of youth sports' increasingly singular focus on performance outcomes is likely contributing to parents' over/ extreme-involvement and resultant complex interactions.

## Understanding and Optimising Parent-Coach Interactions

Limited studies have examined the intricacy of parent-coach relationships. A notable exception is Jowett and Timson-Katchis' (2005) study of five Greek national level adolescent female swimmer-parent-coach triads, which explored the influences that parents exerted on the quality of dyadic coach-athlete interactions. They found parents' over-supportiveness or over-involvement – often perceived by athletes and coaches as interference or pressure – elicited negative affect/emotion on the coach-athlete relationship, in turn leading coaches to distance from athletes, particularly during early childhood. Preston *et al.*'s (2020) study analysing how coach-parent relationships nurtured or impeded PYD through the lens of a Canadian hockey coach extended Jowett and Timson-Katchis' (2005) research, finding parents' behaviours towards coaches also influenced athletes' performances, which tended to decrease when parents' opinions conflicted with coaches' viewpoints; this could be caused by children's stress mitigating different messages from parents and coaches and/or children feeling they had too much information to process (Knight *et al.*, 2010). These and other studies collectively contribute to several recommendations for optimising parent-coach communication and ultimately, athlete outcomes. Below we discuss (a) viewing parents as resources, (b) parent education, and (c) ongoing bi-directional communication.

Fundamental to optimising athletes' development, is for coaches to view parents as assets, rather than problems to be fixed (Dorsch *et al.*, 2019). Two-way communication is central to this approach, where parents serve as valuable sources of information, and parents and coaches work as a team. Jowett and Timson-Katchis (2005) suggested parents can give broader context to their child's training/performances by sharing information on athletes' home situation, nutrition, sleep, and/or friends. Similarly, Preston *et al.* (2020) underlined how parents provided key information for coaches to tailor their styles to individual athletes' physical and emotional health. Parents can also play key roles in interpreting children's sport experiences, acting as mediators in sport conflicts, and modelling optimal behaviours (Jowett and Timson-Katchis, 2005; Horn, 2011; Petitpas, 2011; Smoll *et al.*, 2011). Horn (2011, p.28) discussed the need for coaches to "meet parents where they are at" (i.e. in relation to the current social context of parenting), while also empowering parents with realism (i.e. realistic expectations).

Second, as parents may not always comprehend how their behaviours affect their child's experiences and outcomes in sport (Lauer *et al.*, 2010), parent education (i.e. a comprehensive pre-season parent meeting), is broadly encouraged (Jowett and Timson-Katchis, 2005; Camiré *et al.*, 2016). Smoll *et al.* (2011) recommend a 75-minute meeting with prescribed topics including the objectives of youth sport, program details, coaches' and parents' roles, responsibilities, challenges, and relationships, and extensive time for questions – suggesting this would improve parents' understanding of youth sports, while simultaneously gaining parents' co-operation and support. Further, Horn (2011) highlighted the importance of discussing varying rates of maturation, to mitigate parents' concerns about each child's "position" relative to peers. While pre-season meetings have typically been delivered by coaches, other potentially more 'neutral' delivery could be offered by researchers, former parents, sport psychologists, or even family therapists (Blom *et al.*, 2013; Dorsch *et al.*, 2019).

Finally, it is critical for coaches and parents to engage in two-way communication throughout the season. Increasingly, many coaches have 'open door' policies encouraging parents to ask questions or raise concerns, aiming to fulfill parents' inquiries about their children's activities (Smoll *et al.*, 2011). Some researchers have suggested formal interactions such as "report cards" or mid-season meetings, while others outline less formal means such as year-end team and family dinners (Jowett and Timson-Katchis, 2005; O'Connor, 2011; Smoll *et al.*, 2011). Preston *et al.* (2020) highlight the value of coaches initiating frequent honest "check-ins" with parents, with parameters set around timing and format (e.g. outside of practices/games, typically in person rather than through text/email.) Despite parent-coach relationships significantly influencing children's development within sport, this complex relationship remains understudied. Much of the research has been conducted within sport systems in Western nations, highlighting the need to better understand the nature of parent-coach relationships in other nations and within diverse cultures. Additionally, unpacking how relationships and subsequent interventions to optimise relationships may differ based on athletes' developmental stage, gender, administrators, and a child's youth sport experiences and outcomes.

## *Exosystem Influences: Administrators and Sport Organisations*

In considering more distal influences on children's development, Bronfenbrenner (1979, 1999) highlights the exosystem as involving two or more social settings that do not directly include the child; this could be reflected as interactions between sport administrators, and a child's youth sport organisation. Holt *et al.* (2017) hypothesise that PYD outcomes are more likely to occur if they are fostered intentionally (i.e. by coaches, administrators, sport organisations). Subsequently, Holt *et al.* (2018a, 2018b) spoke to Canadian provincial sport administrators, who discussed the need for more research and understanding related to long-term sport development models and creative ways to implement and assess effective developmental systems. They noted research should "focus on examining the *contextual conditions* that exist within the programs offered by particular sports and the extent to which they may contribute to, or detract from, participants' acquisition of positive developmental outcomes" (Holt *et al.*, 2018b, p. 13). However, administrators were unsure how to access or use research to assist in the development of children and youth sport programs, as research in the field of PYD grows. This barrier is disadvantageous to the macrosystemic link between sport structure and the person in the environment; if those involved in making decisions are not confident in accessing research to assist change, there is the potential for many relationships and interactions to suffer. Stronger partnerships between sport organisations and researchers is key for organisational and institutional change (Kendellen *et al.*, 2017), highlighting the need for each of these stakeholders to intentionally establish a connection.

## *Macrosystem Influences: Cultural Considerations*

Sport plays an important role as a vehicle for migration in the lives of athletes from non-Euro-originating cultures (e.g. Foo, 2015), which has necessitated calls for more attention within host cultures to how cultural transition and adjustment impact newcomers (Ryba, 2017), as well as greater effort among sport organisations to create atmospheres that promote diversity (Cooper *et al.*, 2020). Sport-based afterschool programs can contribute to the personal growth of minority youth by providing positive relationships and safe, trusting environments that allow for self-exploration (e.g. Fuller *et al.*, 2013). In Canada, researchers have noted the benefits of sport felt by Indigenous young people (Bruner *et al.*, 2016) when positive outcomes were intentional and informed. However, without proper measures in place, Euro-Canadian sport settings can be isolating for participants from diverse cultures; Blodgett *et al.*'s (2014) research with Indigenous athletes who moved from reserves to pursue sport in Euro-Canadian settings discussed feelings of culture shock and disconnect from one's home culture.

Eurocentric or "whitestream" sport (see Paraschak and Tirone, 2015, p. 104) should not be viewed as being culturally neutral, as approaches to sport vary across cultural groups (Forsyth and Paraschak, 2013). In failing to understand athletes' cultures and lived experiences, sport stakeholders (e.g. psychologists, coaches, administrators) may not be able to successfully guide athletes in handling acculturation challenges.

## *Cultural Barriers to Sport Participation*

Contrasting philosophies underlie the differences in how sport is manifested across cultures (Forsyth and Paraschak, 2013), and what is mainstream in many countries represents the colonisation of Indigenous sport, or, in other words, modifications to sport made by countries that have colonised other countries. Mainstream sport is largely guided by a Neoliberal ideology emphasising individualism, competition, hierarchies, winning, and rewards (Coakley, 2011) – particularly at higher sport levels where winning is the primary focus. Values-based approaches such as PYD (Lerner *et al.*, 2005) in Eurocentric sport contexts recognise sport as something more than the Neoliberal approach implies. Going further, values and lessons serve as the foundation upon which Indigenous sport has been built. This definition of Indigenous sport is in direct contrast to Eurocentric approaches. For example, Rice (2019) emphasised that traditional Indigenous "sports" were meant to teach skills necessary to survive, but in contemporary times, Indigenous sport has become less about developing survival skills and more about developing values important to life in and out of sport, with competition being a component, but not a primary focus (e.g. Heine and Young, 1997). Historically, there have been instances in which sport has been used to disadvantage certain groups, as was the case within residential schools in Canada, where the mainstream sport was used to instill colonial-capitalist values (Canada, 1996, as cited in Forsyth, 2007), or in Australia, where Australian rules football is seen as a site of "exclusion and marginalisation of Indigenous people" (Hallinan and Judd, 2012, pp. 984–985).

Indeed, the cultural privileging that occurs in Euro-Canadian sport can perpetuate the normalisation of racism (Yearwood, 2018), institutionalising it within the sport context. Although sport leaders can work to address overt racism that causes athletes to dropout of sport (e.g. Tirone, 1999), institutionalised racism rarely critiqued. Aquino (2015) highlighted examples of institutional racism, discussing Filipino basketball players being forced to change their style of play, dress, and overall cultural expression to fit the mainstream basketball culture. In relation to the difficulty of abolishing institutional racism, Tirone's (1999) work highlighted how some sport leaders may be unwilling to make adjustments to their sport programs to accommodate the cultural commitments of participants, such as the demands of fasting during Ramadan. In some cases, sport participants are simultaneously exposed to multiple forms of racism (manifested verbally and physically, as well as institutionally embedded) in what is known in the context of hockey as the hat-trick of racism (Sandrin, 2020).

## Implications for Children's Sport-Coaching

So as not to continue assimilative or discriminatory approaches within sport programs, leaders must ask themselves who intended practices might privilege, and who they might marginalise.

A critical lens and informed approach is the foundation of inclusive and meaningful sport contexts that support and engage, as opposed to subvert, the fluid identities of acculturating, relocated, and marginalised sport participants. Despite organisations' good intentions to create inclusive sport settings, the necessary expertise (e.g. psychological support relating to cultural transition) is often lacking (Ryba *et al.*, 2016). Multi-cultural perspectives that aid in guiding the transitions of sport participants from diverse cultural contexts are needed. One example to consider is culturally relevant pedagogies that emphasizse learning about the cultural landscapes of individual sport participants and working toward providing meaningful, culturally affirming, and supportive sport climates (Halas *et al.*, 2013).

Sport organisations, administrators and coaches must create environments that promote welcoming, inclusive attitudes that contribute to a sharing of acculturation loads (Schinke *et al.*, 2013), particularly as sport participants from outside cultures may look to teammates in their host cultures for a sense of family and belonging (Brown, 2020). Coaches can expose participants to race-related matters from an early age by clearly denouncing unacceptable conduct, and by having an independent, anonymous line for reporting incidents (Sandrin, 2020). Administrators and organisations can also work to incorporate aspects of participants' home cultures into sport settings (e.g. language learning exchanges; Schinke *et al.*, 2013). For example, Lavallée and Lévesque (2013) advocated for Morrissette *et al.*'s (1993) suggestion for an Aboriginal framework of social work within the sport setting, emphasising and recognising distinct Aboriginal world views – empowerment as a method of practice, and the development of Aboriginal consciousness, cultural knowledge and tradition. Through such approaches, coaches and administrators can take significant steps toward limiting Euro-centrism in their team settings, and help sport participants from other cultures feel more welcome and included.

## Summary, Future Directions, and Future Research

This chapter highlighted the paucity of research exploring contextual influences of child and youth development in sport, particularly at the broader meso-, exo-, and macrosystem levels of EST (Bronfenbrenner, 1979, 1999). This concern continues to resonate. Holt *et al.* (2016) discussed the 'black box' of youth sport, emphasising the need to determine the circumstances under which positive developmental outcomes can be attained. While this question has been studied extensively at the microsystem level, more attention is required at community, structural, policy and cultural levels of youth sport. Below are a few select areas necessitating further examination.

Foremost, at a macrosystem level – at the time of writing of this chapter (i.e. 2021), the COVID-19 pandemic is on-going. While a level of normalisation has settled into sport communities from local to professional levels (coupled with the 'successful' execution of a year-delayed, spectator-less, locked-down Olympic Games), there is still much to learn from the pandemic, and how it may influence sport for children and youth moving forward. One highly concerning trend has been the uneven, unequal, and unjust differences of pandemic experiences (Evans *et al.*, 2020). Assuring that already existing inequities in sport are not further exacerbated through increasingly selective, elitist, costly programming will be essential moving forward. Further, technological platforms have played an essential role in maintaining program delivery and keeping communities connected throughout the pandemic; however, questions are arising regarding the role of technology in facilitating development moving forward – and the importance of balancing unique and creative opportunities, with concerns of restricted connections or lost relationships.

Relatedly, at an exosystem level, Gould (2019) discussed how overall aims of children and youth sport organisations have not changed in recent decades, but the weight given to different objectives has shifted to be more professionalised and focused on talent, with a resultant decreased focus on sport for all, local recreation, and unstructured free play. A (presumably) unintended consequence of this shift is that children who could most benefit from sport often have least access. At organisational and structural levels, a comprehensive approach to youth sport programming is needed – with government funding, informed policies, supportive environments, educated coaches, ties to community and health, and safe spaces for unstructured free play – so that all youth have an opportunity to experience positive sport.

At a mesosystem level, the changing children and youth sport philosophies outlined above have bidirectional implications, whereby parents, coaches, and young athletes often 'buy into' program mandates. While parents are often blamed for being 'problematic', they are often existing in a context that promotes underlying philosophies of their approaches. As such, organisations must model and promote sport where healthy children's development is central to the vision and delivery, in turn guiding parents' clear understanding of positive physical, psychological, and social development through sport.

Finally, in furthering research focused on contextual influences of development in sport, the role of researchers in the translation of knowledge must be re-examined and enhanced. Research leaders (e.g. Holt *et al.*, 2016; Gould, 2019) have advocated that researchers should drive knowledge translation, moving beyond a list of implications in scientific papers and presentations, to more proactively and consistently assuring users' needs are understood; subsequently, researchers should develop "knowledge products", utilising diverse communication systems to optimally reach target audiences (e.g. coaches). Essentially, researchers need to be involved in transforming contextual influences in current sport programs to assure children and youth sport can and are really fostering positive development – in diverse sport settings – across nations and cultures.

## References

Aquino, K., 2015. More than a game: Embodied everyday anti-racism among young Filipino-Australian street ballers. *Journal of Intercultural Studies*, 36 (2), 166–183.

Bean, C.N., *et al.*, 2016. Negative parental behaviour in Canadian youth hockey: Insiders' perceptions and recommendations. *PHEnex Journal* [online], 7 (3). Available from: https://ojs.acadiau.ca/index.php/phenex/article/view/1610 [Accessed 4 April 2022].

Blodgett, A.T., *et al.*, 2014. Navigating the insider-outsider hyphen: A qualitative exploration of the acculturation challenges of Aboriginal athletes pursuing sport in Euro-Canadian contexts. *Psychology of Sport and Exercise*, 15 (4), 345–355.

Blom, L.C., Visek, A.J., and Harris, B.S., 2013. Triangulation in youth sport: Healthy partnerships among parents, coaches, and practitioners. *Journal of Sport Psychology in Action*, 4 (2), 86–96.

Bronfenbrenner, U., 1979. *The ecology of human development: Experiments by nature and design*. Cambridge: Harvard University Press.

Bronfenbrenner, U., 1996. *The state of Americans: This generation and the next*. New York: Simon and Schuster.

Bronfenbrenner, U., 1999. Environments in developmental perspective: Theoretical and operational models. *In*: S.L. Friedman and T.D. Wachs, eds. *Measuring environment across the life span*. Washington, DC: American Psychological Association, 3–28.

Brown, C., 2020. An exploration of the lived acculturation experiences of newcomer varsity athletes in Manitoba. Unpublished thesis. University of Manitoba.

Bruner, M.W., *et al.*, 2016. Positive youth development in Aboriginal physical activity and sport: A systematic review. *Adolescent Research Review*, 1 (3), 257–269.

Camiré, M., Rocchi, M., and Kendellen, K., 2016. Profiling the Canadian high school teacher-coach: A national survey. *International Sport Coaching Journal*, 3 (2), 145–155.

Campbell, K. and Parcels, J., 2013. *Selling the dream: How hockey parents and their kids are paying the price for our national obsession*. Toronto: Penguin Group.

Canada. 1996. *Report of the Royal Commission on Aboriginal peoples: Looking forward, looking back (Vol. 1)*. Ottawa: Minister of Supply and Services Canada.

Coakley, J., 2011. Ideology doesn't just happen: Sports and neoliberalism. *Revista da Associación Latinoamericana de Estudios Socioculturales del Deporto*, 1 (1), 67–84.

Cooper, J.N., *et al.*, 2020. A call for culturally responsive transformational leadership in college sport: An anti-ism approach for achieving equity and inclusion. *Frontiers in Sociology* [online], 5. Available from: https://www.frontiersin.org/articles/10.3389/fsoc.2020.00065/full [Accessed 4 April 2022].

Côté, J., *et al.*, 2020. Youth sport research: Describing the integrated dynamics elements of the personal assets framework. *International Journal of Sport Psychology*, 51, 562–578.

Dorsch, T.E., *et al.*, 2019. Parent education in youth sport: A community case study of parents, coaches, and administrators. *Journal of Applied Sport Psychology*, 31 (4), 427–450.

Evans, A.B., *et al.*, 2020. Sport in the face of the COVID-19 pandemic: Towards an agenda for research in the sociology of sport. *European Journal for Sport and Society*, 17 (2), 85–95.

Foo, C.E., 2015. Exploring sport migration through international student athlete recruitment: The sojourn of male soccer players from Trinidad and Tobago. *Journal of Physical Education and Sports Management*, 2 (2), 149–164.

Forsyth, J., 2007. The Indian Act and the (re)shaping of Canadian Aboriginal sport practices. *International Journal of Canadian Studies/Revue internationale d'études canadiennes*, 35, 95–111.

Forsyth, J. and Paraschak, V., 2013. The double helix: Aboriginal people and sport policy in Canada. *In*: L. Thibault and J. Harvey, eds. *Sport policy in Canada*. Ottawa, ON: University of Ottawa Press, 267–293.

Fraser-Thomas, J.L., Côté, J., and Deakin, J., 2005. Youth sport programs: An avenue to foster positive youth development. *Physical Edcuation and Sport Pedagogy*, 10 (1), 19–40.

Fraser-Thomas, J. and Strachan, L., 2015. Personal development and performance? Exploring positive youth development in elite sport contexts. *In*: J. Baker, J. Fraser-Thomas, and P. Safai, eds. *Health and elite sport: Is high performance sport a healthy pursuit?* New York: Routledge, 15–32.

Fuller, R.D., *et al.*, 2013. Positive youth development: Minority male participation in a sport-based afterschool program in an urban environment. *Research Quarterly for Exercise and Sport*, 84 (4), 469–482.

Garcia-Bengoechea, E., 2002. Integrating knowledge and expanding horizons in developmental sport psychology: A bioecological perspective. *Quest*, 54, 1–20.

Gould, D., 2019. The current youth sport landscape: Identifying critical research issues. *Kinesiology Review*, 8 (3), 150–161.

Gould, D. and Carson, C., 2008. Life skills development through sport: Current status and future directions. *International Review of Sport and Exercise Psychology*, 1 (1), 58–78.

Halas, J., McRae, H., and Carpenter, A., 2013. The quality and cultural relevance of physical education for Aboriginal youth: Challenges and opportunities. *In*: J. Forsyth and A. Giles, eds. *Aboriginal peoples and sport in Canada: Historical foundations and contemporary issues*. Vancouver, BC: UBCPress, 182–205.

Hallinan, C. and Judd, B., 2012. Duelling paradigms: Australian Aborigines, marn-grook and football histories. *Sport in Society*, 15 (7), 975–986.

Harwood, C., 2011. Enhancing coach-parent relationships in youth sports: Increasing harmony and minimising hassle. A commentary. *International Journal of Sports Science & Coaching*, 6 (1), 61–63.

Heine, M.K. and Young, K., 1997. Colliding identities in Arctic Canadian sports and games. *Sociological Focus*, 30 (4), 357–372.

Holt, N.L., Deal, C.J., and Smyth, C.L., 2016. Future directions for positive youth development through sport. *In*: N. Holt, ed. *Positive youth development through sport*. 2nd edition New York: Routledge, 229–240.

Holt, N.L., Jorgensen, H., and Deal, C.J., 2021. How do sport parents engage in autonomy-supportive parenting in the family home setting? A theoretically informed qualitative analysis. *Journal of Sport and Exercise Psychology*, 43 (1), 61–70.

Holt, N.L., *et al.*, 2017. A grounded theory of positive youth development through sport based on results from a qualitative meta-study. *International Review of Sport and Exercise Psychology*, 10 (1), 1–49.

Holt, N.L., *et al.*, 2018a. Factors associated with using research evidence in national sport organisations. *Journal of Sport Sciences*, 36 (10), 1111–1117.

Holt, N.L., *et al.*, 2018b. A qualitative study of research priorities among representatives of Canadian provincial sport organisations. *Psychology of Sport and Exercise*, 36, 8–16.

Holt, N.L., *et al.*, 2009. An interpretive analysis of life skills associated with sport participation. *Qualitative Research in Sport and Exercise*, 1 (2), 160–175.

Horn, T.S., 2011. Enhancing coach-parent relationships in youth sports: Increasing harmony and minimising hassle. A commentary. *International Journal of Sports Science & Coaching*, 6 (1), 27–31.

Jowett, S. and Timson-Katchis, M., 2005. Social networks in sport: Parental influence on the coach-athlete relationship. *The Sport Psychologist*, 19 (3), 267–287.

Kendellen, K., *et al.*, 2017. Integrating life skills into Golf Canada's youth programs: Insights into a successful research to practice partnership. *Journal of Sport Psychology in Action*, 8 (1), 34–46.

Knight, C.J., Boden, C.M., and Holt, N.L., 2010. Junior tennis players' preferences for parental behaviors. *Journal of Applied Sport Psychology*, 22 (4), 377–391.

Knight, C.J. and Harwood, C.G., 2009. Exploring parent-related coaching. Stressors in British tennis: A developmental investigation. *International Journal of Sports Science and Coaching*, 4 (4), 545–565.

Lauer, L., *et al.*, 2010. Parental behaviors that affect junior tennis player development. *Psychology of Sport and Exercise*, 11 (6), 487–496.

Lavallée, L. and Lévesque, L., 2013. Two-eyed seeing: Physical activity, sport, and recreation promotion in Indigenous communities. *In*: J. Forsyth and A.R. Giles, eds. *Aboriginal Peoples and sport in Canada: Historical foundations and contemporary issues*. Vancouver, BC: UBC Press, 206–228.

Lerner, R.M., *et al.*, 2005. Positive youth development, participation in community youth development programs, and community contributions of fifth-grade adolescents: Findings from the first wave of the 4-H study of positive youth development. *The Journal of Early Adolescence*, 25 (1), 17–71.

Morrissette, V., McKenzie, B., and Morrissette, L., 1993. Towards an Aboriginal model of social work practice: Cultural knowledge and traditional practices. *Canadian Social Work Review/Revue canadienne de service social*, 10 (1), 91–108.

O'Connor, D., 2011. Enhancing coach-parent relationships in youth sports: Increasing harmony and minimising hassle. A commentary. *International Journal of Sports Science & Coaching*, 6 (1), 49–52.

Paraschak, V. and Tirone, S., 2015. Ethnicity and race in Canadian sport. *In*: J. Crossman and J. Scherer, eds. *Social dimensions of Canadian sport and physical activity*. North York, ON: Pearson, 90–115.

Petitpas, A., 2011. Enhancing coach-parent relationships in youth sports: Increasing harmony and minimising hassle. A commentary. *International Journal of Sports Science & Coaching*, 6 (1), 45–46.

Petitpas, A.J., *et al.*, 2005. A framework for planning youth sport programs that foster psychosocial development. *The Sport Psychologist*, 19 (1), 63–80.

Preston, C., *et al.*, 2020. The coach-parent relationship and athlete development in elite youth hockey: Lessons learned for conflict management. *The Sport Psychologist*, 34 (2), 143–152.

Rice, B., 2019. What does it mean to Indigenise sports? *In*: N. Kosmenko, *et al.*, eds. *Indigenous youth and sport: A literature review of best practices, issues, and health outcomes*. Winnipeg, MB: University of Manitoba, 4–5.

Ryba, T.V., 2017. Cultural sport psychology: A critical review of empirical advances. *Current Opinion on Psychology*, 16, 123–127.

Ryba, T.V., Stambulova, N., and Ronkainen, N.J., 2016. The work of cultural transition: An emerging model. *Frontiers in Psychology* [online], 7. Available from: https://www.frontiersin.org/articles/10.3389/fpsyg.2016.00427/full#:~:text=Based%20on%20the%20data%20analyses,workers'%20adaptabilities%20and%20psychological%20wellbeing [Accessed 4 April 2022].

Sandrin, R., 2020. *Sour grapes: Exploring the experiences of minority hockey players in their battle against racism [online]*. Halifax, St. Francis Xavier University. Available from: https://www.sfu.ca/~palys/ACloserLookInUnusualTimes-2020-HR.pdf [Accessed 4 April 2022].

Schinke, R.J., *et al.*, 2013. Acculturation in elite sport: A thematic analysis of immigrant athletes and coaches. *Journal of Sports Sciences*, 31 (15), 1676–1686.

Smoll, F.L., Cummings, S.P., and Smith, R.E., 2011. Enhancing coach-parent relationships in youth sports: Increasing harmony and minimising hassle. *International Journal of Sports Science & Coaching*, 6 (1), 13–26.

Tamminen, K.A., *et al.*, 2020. Examining the impact of the respect in sport parent program on the psychosocial experiences of minor hockey athletes. *Journal of Sports Sciences*, 38 (17), 2035–2045.

Tirone, S., 1999. Racism, indifference, and the leisure experiences of South Asian Canadian teens. *Leisure/Loisir*, 24 (1-2), 89–114.

Yearwood, G.M.H., 2018. Heritage as hate: Racism and sporting traditions. *Leisure Studies*, 37 (6), 677–691.

# 9

# TRANSITIONS IN CHILD AND YOUTH SPORT

*Rochelle Eime*

## Review of Current Research

Globally, participation in community-based sport is very popular for children (Vella *et al.*, 2016; Eime *et al.*, 2019; Mooses and Kull, 2020). In Australia, between 64% and 85% of children and adolescents aged 5–17 years participate in organised sport, and this rate is higher than other forms of physical activity such as active transport, active play and school based physical activity (Vella *et al.*, 2016). Whilst children and youth can be active in many different settings, the majority of participation by children aged 5–14 years the majority of participation is within a sports club or setting (Eime *et al.*, 2020), and participation in sport is highest for those aged 5–14 years (Eime *et al.*, 2019).

Participation in organised sport has become a large part of children's and adolescents' lives over recent decades and has contributed to many positive outcomes (Logan and Cuff, 2019). In addition to the physical, social and mental health benefits of participation (Eime *et al.*, 2013), children who participate in sport are more likely to lead physically active lives, and have lower levels of sedentary behaviour through adolescence (Shull *et al.*, 2020). More specifically, if children participate in sport three or more times a week and are more likely to meet the physical activity guidelines for health, further demonstrating the importance of organised sport for health (Mooses and Kull, 2020).

Young sport participants often play modified sport and then transition into club competition (Farrow *et al.*, 2016; Eime *et al.*, 2018; Buszard *et al.*, 2020). Modified sports have specifically been developed for young children and they are a modified form of the adult game, where equipment and rules are modified to facilitate and promote skill development and performance (Farrow *et al.*, 2016; Buszard *et al.*, 2020). For example, changing some rules, such as the size of the playing space and game time, and equipment such as the size of the ball, can be modified to match the developmental stage of the children which can help to facilitate improved skill development and performance and promote a fun and enjoyable playing environment (Farrow *et al.*, 2016). These programs which are developmentally appropriate for young children assists in increasing participation amongst young children as well as helping to building the foundation for talent development programs and pathways (Buszard *et al.*, 2020). Further, these programs are aimed at the development of fundamental motor skills and sport-specific skills, rather than competition (Eime *et al.*, 2018).


DOI: 10.4324/9781003199359-11

The modified programs are entry-level programs for young children generally 5–9 years. From these programs children can transition into club competition. There have been several studies examining the transition rates for children and the proportion of children who transition and continue to play the sport and those that drop-out (Eime *et al.*, 2015a; Eime *et al.*, 2018). A study of 209,336 children reported that fewer than 25% of females ($n$ = 18,652; 24.5%) and fewer than 14% of males ($n$ = 18,058; 13.6%) transitioned from a modified sports program to a club sport competition within the 4-year period. Very few children continued in a modified sports program for the whole 4-year period (females: $n$ = 2,934; 3.9% and males: $n$ = 2,149; 1.6%) (Eime *et al.*, 2015a). Many modified sports participants were very young, especially males aged 4–6 years. More children withdrew from their modified sport program rather than transitioning (Eime *et al.*, 2015a). Another more recent study and utilising the same methodology tracked 13,760 female children aged 4–10 in one particular sport. The majority (59%) transitioned from the modified sport program and into club competition. However, the rate of transition varied with age, residential location and socio-economic status, and there was an interaction between region and socio-economic status, with socio-economic status having a significant influence on transition in the metropolitan region. The peak sport entry age with the highest rates of transition was 7–9 years (Eime *et al.* 2018). Not surprisingly, the highest rates of continued participation were amongst the younger commencers and especially higher in non-metropolitan compared to metropolitan participants (Eime *et al.*, 2018).

Whilst many very young children drop-out of the modified sport before transitioning into club competition the largest drop-off is consistently reported as during adolescence (Cairney and Veldhuizen, 2017; Eime *et al.*, 2019). Retention of players, or the prevention of drop-out from organised sport is an important public health issue to improve the health of individuals now and in the future (Vella *et al.*, 2016; Westerbeek and Eime, 2021).

As stated earlier, sport is very popular for children and youth with the highest participation for ages 5–14 years, however there is a significant decline from this age group with participation rates halving for the next age group 15–19 years (Eime *et al.*, 2019). Further, the drop-off in females during adolescences is much more severe decline than that of males. The participation rate for females aged 15–19 years is less than half of that of those aged 4–14 years (Eime *et al.*, 2019).

Whilst many adolescents drop-out of sport, in some instances they simply drop-out of a specific sport but still play another, or they may also transition to other non-sport physical activities. The first is known as the sampling phenomenon, whereby many individuals, mainly children, play multiple sports when they are young before specialising in one (Eime *et al.*, 2019). Sampling may involve playing a sequence of different sports, or playing multiple sports in the same year. Therefore, some of the decline in sport participation during adolescence is due to the decline in the number of sports played and not necessarily a drop-out from sport participation altogether (Eime *et al.*, 2019). Further, during adolescence when many drop-out of sport, they actually transition into other physical activities (Eime *et al.*, 2016; Shull *et al.*, 2020). For many they transition into non-competitive and also unstructured activities, which are more time and commitment flexible and don't require sport specific skills, uniform, equipment, etc, like going to the gym or a run (Eime *et al.*, 2016). Further, more recently we have seen transition of females into traditionally male-dominated sports (Eime *et al.*, 2021). A five-year longitudinal study reported that female participation increased at twice the rate for females than for males, and this was mainly due to growth in females playing male-dominated sports (Eime *et al.*, 2021).

As a result of transitions across sport and physical activity, not all individuals are actually decreasing the amount of physical activity, merely they are changing the type of activity and setting in which they are active (Eime *et al.*, 2016). For example, a recent systematic review of longitudinal changes in the domains of physical activity during childhood and adolescence reports that non-organised physical activity tended to remain stable among adolescent girls however it did decline among adolescent boys (Kemp *et al.*, 2018).

There are now many more sports and leisure activities than decades ago on offer, and this is not just for females in sport. This is a reflection of societal changes which are away from traditional sport to other activities (Australian Sports Commission, 2013). This is also reflected in changes to national sport policy in many countries and sports included in the Olympics. The definition of sport in Europe and in Australia has shifted from a focus on traditional competitive and club-based sport to one that is broader and includes a range of physical activities including informal, unstructured activities such as walking, riding, swimming and stand-up paddle boarding and "ninja" style obstacle courses (Westerbeek and Eime, 2021). The Olympics has moved with the changes of participation in society and now includes BMX freestyle, break dancing and sport climbing (Olympics, 2021).

Sport, physical activity participation and sedentary behaviour patterns change across the lifespan and there is a range of determinants influencing these behaviours. The following summarises the main determinants for sport participation and drop-out for children and youth. In doing so these determinants are categorised within the domains of the socio-ecological model (McLeroy *et al.*, 1988). These domains include the intrapersonal, interpersonal, organisational, environmental and policy. It is acknowledged that the determinants as a concept can be related to both participation and drop-out. For example enjoyment and fun are key determinants for participation, but a lack of enjoyment and fun are also key reasons why children and youth drop-out of sport (Eime and Harvey, 2018). Further, while these are discussed separately here, it is acknowledged that the determinants are connected across domains. This is because the youth sport system, the persons and contexts that can influence youth participation behaviours, attitudes, experiences and outcomes in sport are dynamic and changing (Dorsch *et al.*, 2020)

## *Intrapersonal*

Having adequate skills and competency are key factors related to participation. As discussed in a recent sport and physical activity policy paper, physical literacy is the foundation for people living an active life (Westerbeek and Eime, 2021). Physical literacy includes not just the fundamental movement skills to play sport, but also the confidence, motivation to be active, as well as the knowledge and understanding to value and take responsibility for being active (Whitehead, 2013).

The fundamental motor skills of children and youth really impact their participation in club-based sport, and motor competency can affect future participation in club-based sport (Drenowatz and Greier, 2019). And a lack of confidence in sport-specific skills is a major barrier to youth participating in sport (Fowlie *et al.*, 2020). It is supported that skills and competency are a main determinant of participation across the lifespan, but very important that children and youth develop a strong foundation to support participation across the lifespan (Eime and Harvey, 2018). If a child feels that they are no good at sport they are more likely to not play or drop-out (Somerset and Hoare, 2018).

Whilst having adequate skills and physical literacy are foundations to being active, an interconnected determinant is fun and enjoyment (Visek *et al.*, 2015; Eime and Harvey, 2018). Fun and enjoyment is the main reason children and youth give for playing organised sport, and the absence of fun and enjoyment is the number one reason for drop-out (Visek *et al.*, 2015). Eime and Harvey (2018) argue that fun should be central to all decision-making in sport as it is an integral component of participation across all ages (Eime and Harvey, 2018). They state that for participants to have fun and enjoy and therefore continue to play organised sport then the program and/or competition and environment is inclusive and conducive to having fun, and if the participants have adequate skills level to be competent and confident to play (Eime and Harvey, 2018).

In terms of barriers to participation or impacts on drop-out, sports injuries and a perceived lack, of time are recurring results (Eime *et al.*, 2015b, Somerset and Hoare, 2018; Elliott *et al.*, 2020). Lack of time for adolescents can relate to priorities to be involved with other leisure activities and other life priorities like education and study (Eime *et al.*, 2015b). In terms of the chance of sustaining a sports injury, managing the adversity and recovery from injury are important to facilitate continued participation (Elliott *et al.*, 2020). Gender is the main determinant with males consistently more likely than females to participate and have the opportunities and support to play organised sport compared to females (Somerset and Hoare, 2018; Eime *et al.*, 2019).

## Interpersonal

Family, peers and coaches play important roles in the support for youth participating in sport (Eime, 2019; Dorsch *et al.*, 2020; Howie *et al.*, 2020). Family influences include parents and siblings and the team influences include peers and coaches (Dorsch *et al.*, 2020).

The authors state that the family system is the most proximal and in many cases most salient influence with regards to participant behaviour, attitudes, experiences and outcomes (Dorsch *et al.*, 2020). Family cannot only encourage and support financially and support transport but also physical and emotional demands of playing sport (Dorsch *et al.*, 2020; Howie *et al.*, 2020). Financial support is a key influencer and families that find it difficult to meet the financial costs of playing sport, are much less likely to have children and youth participating (Eime and Harvey, 2018; Somerset and Hoare, 2018). Linked to this is lack of access which can relate to parental support and cost of travel (Somerset and Hoare, 2018). Further, it can be harder for single-parent families to support their children and youth playing sport (Somerset and Hoare, 2018).

Peers are essential, however relatively underappreciated in their contribution to participant and athlete behaviours, attitudes, experiences and outcomes in youth sport participation (Dorsch *et al.*, 2020). Peers provide a reference point for social comparison, they spend extended periods of time together and often have a relatively equal power with one another compared to parents and coaches and other adults (Dorsch *et al.*, 2020). Friendships are a key to both recruitment and retention, and parents can facilitate participation and support through transport (Howie *et al.*, 2020). Friends is the main reason why children and youth play sport, and therefore it is important to sustain the friendship network (Howie *et al.*, 2020). However, within sport, there can be peer conflict, which needs to be managed (Dorsch *et al.*, 2020).

Coaches have the potential to influence player behaviour, attitudes, experiences and outcomes in youth sport through leadership, coaching, expertise, motivation and education (Dorsch *et al.*, 2020). Coaches can impact player enjoyment, competency, persistence, teamwork and initiative (Dorsch *et al.*, 2020). However, some can experience a negative relationship with their coach (Somerset and Hoare, 2018).

For girls playing a traditionally male-dominated sport of Australian rules football, peer support, family support and involvement, and positive relationships with the football community were important facilitators for participation (Elliott *et al.*, 2020).

In addition to friends, coaches and peers, teammates influence playing behaviours and can lead to improved prosocial behaviours and self-efficacy (Howie *et al.*, 2020), and positive team behaviour can influence social identity of the team and group cohesion can lead to beneficial team outcomes (Howie *et al.*, 2020). However, peer group pressure, fear of being judged and bullying and boys dominating play can be barriers to participation (Somerset and Hoare, 2018). These factors are often more likely to be reported by females, and girls were less likely to participate in sport when boys were present because they felt they had to prove themselves to the boys to be able to play (Somerset and Hoare, 2018).

## *Organisational*

In the youth sport system, the organisations are defined as sports clubs, academies, schools and local government (Dorsch *et al.*, 2020). Within this category the authors talk about how organisations can impose numerous demands and pressure on players. These are formed through their missions, culture and standards and can lead to injuries and in some instances abuse (Dorsch *et al.*, 2020)

The increase in females playing male-dominated sports, in Australia has resulted in retention challenges due to community sport availability and quality of infrastructure and volunteer capacity (Somerset and Hoare, 2018; Casey *et al.*, 2019). This includes both human resources to deliver sport and organisational capacity to develop and implement strategies for both recruitment and retention (Casey *et al.*, 2019).

The competitive nature of sport is not attractive for many adolescent girls and some prefer more social play options (Rowe *et al.*, 2018; Somerset and Hoare, 2018), and this can be due to differences in life priorities during adolescence and not wanting to commit to the time and structures of club-based sports training and competition (Eime *et al.*, 2015b). For females playing male-dominated sports, the club culture, coaching specifically for females and development of player pathways for girls and women is important (Fowlie *et al.*, 2020).

## *Environmental*

Geographical location is a key determinant with people residing in regional and rural areas consistently reporting higher participation rates in traditional club-based sport (Eime and Harvey, 2018; Eime *et al.*, 2019), and this is often due to the lack of opportunity for other leisure activities in regional communities. Further, metropolitan growth areas are also much less likely to play organised sport and this can be related to population density and opportunities to be active in many different leisure activities (Eime *et al.*, 2021). As Dorsch *et al.* state that large cities often have increased accessibility, exposure and choice of competition. However, smaller cities and towns may provide a more integrated sport experience that fosters more engagement with parents, peers and coaches (Dorsch *et al.*, 2020).

In the youth sport system, the environment includes the design and delivery of sport as well as the norms associated with and meanings attributed to participation in sport (Dorsch *et al.*, 2020). The main contexts within the environmental system include organisations (e.g. schools, and sports clubs) communities (e.g. parents, peers and coaches) and societies. In understanding participation, we should consider how sports organisations design and deliver competitions and programs for youth based upon their values and cultures, as well as how these are shaped by parents, coaches and other club personnel (Dorsch *et al.*, 2020). The size of the community may potentially impact the value placed on social norms, and foster a sense of belonging and influence the ways that parents, coaches and organisations deliver and design sport (Dorsch *et al.*, 2020). Further, societies can influence participation in sport for youth through traditions and values and other influencing factors such as socio-economic status of communities.

## *Policy*

There is much less literature on the policies driving sport participation and how these impact participation and transitions in youth sport. Sport policy is less about mass community-level club-based participation and more about elite sporting success (Westerbeek and Eime, 2021). At the community level, sport policy is about encouraging people to engage and play sport, and maintain an active lifestyle across the lifespan, to maintain healthy individuals and communities (Westerbeek and Eime, 2021). In this paper the authors present a model that integrates physical activity and sport, into a whole of sport ecosystem model, named the Physical Activity and Sport (PASP) framework. They argue that physical literacy is the foundation to this new framework and children and youth which includes not only sport-specific skills or sport competency but also the motivation and confidence to be active (Westerbeek and Eime, 2021). Further they advocate for a reorientation of sport policy away from simply increasing participation numbers and a shift towards a more client-based focus of sports programs and competitions, and a focus on retention of players (Westerbeek and Eime, 2021). They emphasise that sport participation patterns and motivations for participation change throughout the lifespan, and these are influenced by changes in society as well as the policy context in which sport is produced, delivered and consumed (Westerbeek and Eime, 2021).

## Implications for Children's Sport Coaching

From a coaching perspective, it is important the coaches focus on the physical literacy of the participants. That is the skills and confidence to play sport. Physical literacy is the foundation to being active and playing sport. It is important to focus on skill development for all players and that training and play be in a supportive environment. This includes the social setting but also includes inclusive play and safety (Westerbeek and Eime, 2021).

Players have a wide range of sport-specific skills and coaches need to ensure that training and development is applicable to the development of each individual. Children and youth play sport to have fun and they enjoy playing with their friends. The social environment is a key driver to participation and continued participation. Ensuring the players are having fun and are engaged because a positive experience leads to retention (Howie *et al.*, 2020).

Cost is a big barrier to participation and this can include a range of things including sports membership, equipment, coaching, clothing and transport. Trying to minimise the cost for participants will make sport more inclusive to the wider community. There is evidence that society is moving towards sport but not necessarily in the competitive and heavily structured formats. Whilst club-based settings and inter-club competitions are the main setting for sport participation for children and youth, many drop-out during adolescence (Eime *et al.*, 2020). Therefore, where possible delivering organised social and recreational based play with less structure, flexibility of play and rules like strict uniforms are important especially for adolescent females, to keep them engaged in sport.

Sport can be a great vehicle for children and youth to be active, but also to reap the many social, mental and physical health benefits from participation. Further, there are many developmental aspects like learning to work as a team, striving to achieve, leadership, setting goals and learning resilience which are great lifelong skills. Coaches play an important role not just in the skill development of children and youth, but for ensuring a conducive environmental to learn, have fun, develop and play.

## Summary, Future Directions and Future Research

In summary, participation in sport is very popular for children and youth, however many drop-out during adolescence. We need to ensure that sport is accessible for all, and not just those who are very skilled and enjoy the competitive nature of competition. We need to have opportunities for children and youth to be active through sport in different ways too. Future directions and research should prioritise retention and strategies to keep children and youth playing sport. There are many determinants for participation and retention and future research and sport industry engagement could explore how social sport programs could provide an alternative for those who do not prefer the traditional competitive model of sport. Further the positive little leavers than can influence participation and retention across aspects such as sport governance, coaching, program and play structures, cost, welcoming and inclusive settings could be explored and developed into practice guides for sports organisations and for a range of different demographic groups.

## References

Australian Sports Commission., 2013. *Market segmentation for sport participation: children*. Canberra: Australian Sports Commission.

Buszard, T., *et al.*, 2020. Implementation of a modified sport programme to increase participation: Key stakeholder perspectives. *Journal of Sports Sciences*, 38 (8), 945–952.

Cairney, J. and Veldhuizen, S., 2017. Organised sport and physical activity participation and body mass index in children and youth: A longitudinal study. *Preventive Medicine Reports*, 6, 336–338.

Casey, M., *et al.*, 2019. The implications of female sport policy developments for the community-level sport sector: A perspective from Victoria, Australia. *International Journal of Sport Policy and Politics*, 11 (4), 1–22.

Dorsch, T.E., *et al.*, 2020. Toward an Integrated Understanding of the youth sport system. *Research Quarterly for Exercise and Sport*, 93 (1), 1–15.

Drenowatz, C. and Greier, K., 2019. Cross-sectional and longitudinal association of sports participation, media consumption and motor competence in youth. *Scandinavian Journal of Medicine & Science in Sports*, 29 (6), 854–861.

Eime, R. and Harvey, J., 2018. Sport participation across the lifespan: Australian trends and policy implications. *In:* Dionigi, R. and Gard, M., eds. *Sport and physical activity across the lifespan*. UK: Palgrave Macmillan, 180–197.

Eime, R., Harvey, J., and Charity, M., 2018. Girls' transition from participation in a modified sport program to club sport competition – A study of longitudinal patterns and correlates. *BMC Public Health*, 18, 1–7.

Eime, R., Harvey, J.T., and Charity, M.J., 2019. Sport drop-out during adolescence: Is it real, or an artefact of sampling behaviour? *International Journal of Sport Policy and Politics*, 11, 1–12.

Eime, R., Harvey, J., and Charity, M. 2020. Sport participation settings: Where and 'how' do Australians play sport? *BMC Public Health*, 20, 1–9.

Eime, R., *et al.*, 2013. A systematic review of the psychological and social benefits of participation in sport for children and adolescents: Informing development of a conceptual model of health through sport. *International Journal of Behavioral Nutrition & Physical Activity*, 10, 1–21.

Eime, R. *et al.*, 2015a. Participation in modified sports programs: A longitudinal study of children's transition to club sport competition. *BMC Public Health*, 15, 1–7.

Eime, R., *et al.*, 2015b. Socioecological factors potentially associated with participation in physical activity and sport: A longitudinal study of adolescent girls. *Journal of Science and Medicine in Sport*, 18, 684–690.

Eime, R., *et al.*, 2016. Changes in sport and physical activity participation for adolescent females: A longitudinal study. *BMC Public Health*, 16, 1–7.

Eime, R., *et al.*, 2021. Sport participation in Victoria, 2019. Research Summary. Victoria University and Federation University.

Elliott, S., Bevan, N., and Litchfield, C., 2020. Parents, girls' and Australian football: A constructivist grounded theory for attracting and retaining participation. *Qualitative Research in Sport, Exercise and Health*, 12 (3), 392–413.

Farrow, D., *et al.*, 2016. Using Modification to generate emergent performance (and learning?) in Sports. *Research Quarterly for Exercise and Sport*, 87 (Suppl 1), S21–S22.

Fowlie, J., Eime, R.M., and Griffiths, K., 2020. Barriers to adolescent female participation in cricket. *Annals of Leisure Research*, 24 (2), 1–19.

Howie, E.K., Daniels, B.T., and Guagliano, J.M., 2020. Promoting physical activity through youth sports programs: It's Social. *American Journal of Lifestyle Medicine*, 14 (1), 78–88.

Kemp, B.J., *et al.*, 2018. Longitudinal changes in domains of physical activity during childhood and adolescence: A systematic review. *Journal of Science and Medicine in Sport*, 22 (6), 695–701.

Logan, K. and Cuff, S., 2019. Organised sports for children, preadolescents, and adolescents. *Pediatrics*, 143 (6), 1–20.

Mcleroy, K., *et al.*, 1988. An ecological perspective on health promotion programs. *Health Education Quarterly*, 15 (4), 351–377.

Mooses, K. and Kull, M., 2020. The participation in organised sport doubles the odds of meeting physical activity recommendations in 7–12-year-old children. *European Journal of Sport Science*, 20 (4), 563–569.

Olympics., 2021. *Omympics Sports List* [Online]. Available from: https://www.google.com/search?q=sports+in+summer+olympics&rlz=1C1GCEA_enAU783AU783&oq=sports+in+summer+olympics&aqs=chrome..69i57l2j0i27113j69i65l3.2781j0j15&sourceid=chrome&ie=UTF-8 [Accessed 21st May 2021].

Rowe, K., Sherry, E., and Osborne, A., 2018. Recruiting and retaining girls in table tennis: Participant and club perspectives. *Sport Management Review*, 21 (5), 504–518.

Shull, E.R., *et al.*, 2020. Sport participation, physical activity and sedentary behavior in the transition from middle school to high school. *Journal of Science and Medicine in Sport*, 23 (4), 385–389.

Somerset, S. and Hoare, D.J., 2018. Barriers to voluntary participation in sport for children: A systematic review. *BMC Pediatrics*, 18, 1–19.

Vella, *et al.*, 2016. The contribution of organised sports to physical activity in Australia: Results and directions from the Active Healthy Kids Australia 2014 Report Card on physical activity for children and young people. *Journal of Science and Medicine in Sport*, 19 (5), 407–412.

Visek, A., *et al.*, 2015. The fun integration theory: Toward sustaining children and adolescent sport participation. *Journal of Physical Activity and Health*, 12 (3), 424–433.

Westerbeek, H. and Eime, R., 2021. The physical activity and sport participation framework—A policy model toward being physically active across the lifespan. *Frontiers in Sports and Active Living*, 3, 1–11.

Whitehead, M., 2013. Definition of physical literacy and clarification of related issues. *Journal of Sport Science and Physical Education*, 65, 21–27.

# 10

# THE ROLE OF THE COACH IN PLAYER RETENTION AND ATTRITION

*Deborah Agnew and Shane Pill*

## Introduction

The aim of this chapter is to review the role of the coach in player retention and attrition in children's and youth sport. It is internationally recognised that regular participation in physical activity and sport has benefits for individuals, communities, and countries. Solid foundations in movement abilities developed through sport are associated with continued participation in sport and physical activity throughout childhood, adolescence, and adulthood (Pill and Harvey, 2019). There are many factors that influence an individual's ability to reach their potential, and whether their interest in continued participation is maintained. Factors include the coach, the context, and the environment the athlete is in, which can change. The coach maintains a pivotal role in influencing enjoyment and contributing to player retention and attrition. Previous research indicates that there are two key age ranges where attrition occurs with both corresponding to competition changes and training intensity and the potential this brings for changes to players' relationships with coaches. Findings also suggest that the coach is the most important factor in player retention and attrition in children's and youth sport able to be directly influenced by sport clubs and associations (Agnew *et al.*, 2013, 2016). This chapter will review the current research, focussing on why children participate in sport, coaching as a social practice and the influence of coaches on player attrition and retention.

## Review of Current Research

### *Children's Involvement and Withdrawal from Youth Sport*

Parents have a key role in the sport experience of their children. Furusa *et al.* (2020) found that children want their parents to be involved in their sport experience through facilitating opportunities, by prioritising their children's sport participation, through listening to their children and providing support that goes beyond their child's sport involvement. Whilst parents are important for initiating and maintaining children's involvement in sport the reasons why children join and stay involved in sports clubs are more complex as they involve a mixture of influences that include family, previous positive experiences in sport, the commitment in terms of time, effort, enjoyment, energy, and resources that would be lost if they no longer played

 DOI: 10.4324/9781003199359-12

sport. In addition, social connectedness, and the opportunity for new friendships as well as developing existing friendships through sharing a common experience and belonging to the team also influence retention in children's and youth sport (Scanlon *et al.*, 1993; Allender *et al.*, 2006; Hamson *et al.*, 2008; Light and Curry, 2009; Agnew *et al.*, 2016). Enjoyment also has a powerful influence on continued involvement in sport (Elliott and Drummond, 2011, 2013, 2015; Iñigo *et al.*, 2015). Enjoyment from sport is derived from "positive social interactions, support and involvement from parents, coaches and peers, self-perceptions of physical activity, social recognition of physical competence, effort exerted in learning and demonstrating skills, mastery and achievement of skills and movement sensations" (Weiss, 2000, p. 2).

There are two key age ranges where children and youth are at risk of withdrawing from sport participation include around age 12 and between the ages of 16 and 18 (Agnew *et al.*, 2016). These age ranges align with significant changes in competition level within the sport but also other important transition stages such as the transition from primary to secondary school and the completion of secondary school. The Developmental Model of Sport Participation (Côté *et al.*, 2003) highlights children generally begin reducing the number of sports they participate in after the sampling years (ages 6–12), which could account for some of the attrition in some sports. Children and youth may not be withdrawing from all sports, rather starting to specialise in their chosen sport(s) through the ages of 13–15 and invest their time in one sport at 16+ (Côté *et al.*, 2003).

The 16–18 age group is identified as a critical stage to target retention strategies as it is an age group where players face transition challenges within the sport and life. For example, at this age group, players' actual and perceived efficacy with regards to competence can influence player thinking about retention. That is, if the player perceives they are not good enough or 'ready' for senior teams they may be more likely to transition out of the game. If players do not perceive themselves as having adequate skills to play, they do not then enjoy playing and drop out (Agnew *et al.*, 2013). Competitive sport requires a significant time commitment, therefore perceptions of a lack of opportunity to be involved in other pursuits (like part-time work and increasing school-work) can prompt a withdrawal from sport (Fraser-Thomas *et al.*, 2008; Hamson *et al.*, 2008; Molinero *et al.*, 2009).

## Factors Influencing Attrition in Children's and Youth Sport

The most influential factor in children and youth dropping out of sport is lack of enjoyment (Butcher *et al.*, 2002; Fraser-Thomas *et al.*, 2008; Crane and Temple, 2015). Historically, team success is often not a reason for attrition in children's and youth sport (Barnett *et al.*, 2006). The coach has been found to be a significant factor in player retention (Agnew *et al.*, 2016). Specifically, the coach–player relationship is critical in the retention of players beyond junior sport (Agnew *et al.*, 2013). The relationship and interaction between the coach and players has significant influence on the continued involvement of children and youth in sport. Poor coach–player interaction is a key contributor in the withdrawal from youth sport participation and includes perceptions of favouritism shown by coaches towards 'better' performers (Salguero *et al.*, 2003; Fraser-Thomas *et al.*, 2008; Molinero *et al.*, 2009).

If coaching is not provided appropriately the outcomes might result in poor performance and team result, however also importantly, particularly in the context of retention, the experience of the sport may result in a lowering of the child's self-esteem, elevated levels of participation anxiety, or burnout. Poor coaching can be a marginalising and potentially exclusionary experience for junior players who are slower to develop. In youth sport, players with a lower level of skill are at risk of being excluded from participation (not making the team) or 'full' participation (sitting on the bench for extended time periods or continually being played in peripheral 'away from most of the play' roles) (Agnew *et al.*, 2013). It is clear that children and youth withdrawal from sport can be strongly influenced by a perceived lack of competence in sporting ability (Butcher *et al.*, 2002; Witt and Dangi, 2018; Gould and Walker, 2019). Competition to fill places on the team, particularly when transitioning from junior to youth sport, means that competence and sporting ability is a significant component with regard to continued participation. Fewer opportunities for positions in the team can foster perceptions of a lack of ability and related feelings of not being 'good enough', which can influence the decision to leave sport and pursue other interests (Butcher *et al.*, 2002).

## *Coaching as a Social Practice*

Coaching is a social practice involving complex interactions directed at impacting player learning and performance. When looked at through the lens of a 'problematic activity' whereby coaching is not viewed as beginning application of an instruction model but a behavioural complexity existing within a culturally structured and contextually situated human dynamic, the need for coaches to have a sophisticated understanding of practice is necessary for a coach to be able to work through the ambiguities, contradictions, compromises, and complexities of coaching (Cushion, 2013). The area of 'problematic activity' we consider in this chapter is the coach role in player retention and attrition in sport. The style of coaching chosen by sport coaches is a significant way to affect players' development and sense of self as they mature and grow (Griffin *et al.*, 2018). One of the main challenges for coaches and clubs is to make sure players' experiences in sport are positive (Langan *et al.*, 2013).

## *Coaching Practice and Influence on Player Retention and Attrition*

Traditional forms of coaching focus on a direct style that stresses technical reproduction. Representing coaching as a mechanical and complex process that hinges on transferring information from coach to player to mechanically put parts together has caused concern for some time (Light, 2013). To move away from the technical coaching focus and in light of the apprehensions about the usefulness of the common directive in Australia, the Game Sense approach was developed (Australian Sports Commission: ASC, 1996; Light, 2013; Pill, 2016). The Game Sense approach continues to be the pedagogical grounding of the Sport Australia Playing for Life Philosophy of junior sport (ASC, 2013; Sport Australia, 2019) and is now associated with the Sport Australia Physical Literacy strategy through the Playing for Life Cards (Sport Australia, 2020). This approach has influenced coach development and coaching interventions at all levels of sport in Australia. Since the middle of the 1990s, the Game Sense approach has been featured in sport coaching literature.

The purpose of launching the Game Sense approach in Australian sport was to provide a coaching model that would enhance player retention by working with what motivates participation at any age, but with children in particular – playing the game. Play provides a sense of agency and ownership that encourages the motivation to continue to be active (MacDougall *et al.*, 2004). Boredom from insufficient activity has been found to be a factor in attrition, thus keeping players active through the choice of activity and teaching style is an important attrition-retention strategy (Molinero *et al.*, 2009; Monteiro *et al.*, 2017). Thus, the pedagogical style of the coach may also be a factor in attrition.

The teaching style of a coach can affect a player positively or negatively. It can reduce anxiety, increase confidence, enhance the desire to continue to play and practice, and encourage game development (Carlsson and Lundqvist, 2016). The teaching style of the coach can also have the opposite effects, inducing anger, distractions, declining motivation to continue to play and practice, and stall or introduce decrements in game development (Carlsson and Lundqvist, 2016). Coaches may often be unaware of the impact of their teaching style and overestimate the frequency of their positive behaviours (Partington and Cushion, 2011). Coaches favouring a teaching style emphasising drills and focussed on error reduction can deprive children the opportunity for the development of self-confidence. In contrast, game-based approaches such as the Game Sense approach provide opportunities for learning through coach-guided exploration, rather than critique (Light and Harvey, 2017). This fosters more positive and enjoyable experiences (Light, 2003) and increases the likelihood of player retention.

## *Athlete (Player) Centred Coaching*

What has been called game-based or game-centred coaching, an example of which is the Game Sense approach of the Playing for Life Philosophy of Australian sport, has been identified as a tenet of athlete-centred coaching (Kidman and Lombardo, 2010; Pill, 2018). Athlete-centred coaching is a comprehensive holistic model providing for sport coaches intentional links between the pedagogy (i.e. coaching), culture and climate of sport and the holistic development of players – developing good people as well as good players. Athlete-centred coaches are concerned with setting culture and climate. Culture develops over time and consists of values, norms, rituals and traditions, and communication. Climate is more immediate and short-term, influenced by the tone of athlete-to-athlete interactions, and coach-to-athlete interactions (Thompson, 2003; Kidman and Lombardo, 2010; Griffin *et al.*, 2018). Developing a coaching environment where the climate is one of coaches promoting creativity, game intelligence, personal and social responsibility is important in creating positive sporting experiences. Adults have a key role in the positive development of youth through sport. If those responsible for sport programs deliberately and intentionally create holistic and ecological learning experiences, positive development can be promoted. Holistic programs focus on the whole person in terms of physical, social, and emotional well-being and ecological factors include the various realities of the person, outside of their role as a player. Settings, where participants can train their problem-solving and decision-making skills that enable the promotion of physical and psychological safety through positive and clearly structured sessions in terms of expectations and rules are also central influencing factors. Players who are engaged in a positive sporting culture and climate show increased levels of enjoyment, motivation, and well-being, and are more likely to develop a lifelong appreciation of sport (Agnew and Pill, 2016).

Experiences as a coach create an 'everyday philosophy' that informs the understanding and practice of the coach, as experience is often the basis for reflection (Stodter and Cushion, 2014). Although coaches often acknowledge athlete-centred coaching principles such as Game Sense coaching, they experience challenges, confusion, and contradictions implementing the principles (Hewitt *et al.*, 2016a, 2016b; Stodter and Cushion, 2019a). Research by Hewitt *et al.* (2016a, 2016b) investigating the coaching practice of Australian tennis coaches found incongruence between what the coaches believed they were doing, and what was found by observation of their coaching. Coach education may lead to evident changes in coach knowledge, but that does not ensure a change in practice behaviours, and suggests there is a lack of learning that bridges the 'theory into practice' gap (Stodter and Cushion, 2019b). Coaches may believe they are being game-based and athlete-centred although observation of the coaching shows the coaching to be predominantly under the pacing, timing, and direction of the coach with the players expected to replicate the instructions and demonstrations provided by the coach.

The absence of player agency and sense of ownership, key factors in player retention, are not understood by the coach as absent from the player experience.

## Implications for Children's Sport Coaching

One of the main challenges for coaches and sports clubs is to make sure players have positive experiences (Langan *et al.*, 2013). Children want to play. 'Play' and 'sport' have significant, sometimes conflicting meanings for children. Children can perceive 'play' as being in their control and 'sport' as monitored by adults (MacDougal *et al.*, 2004). As can be seen in Figure 10.1, coaches and parents both play key roles in the sport experiences of children and youth and in their sustained participation. When the coach–athlete relationship is positive, player motivation is high, and the sport experiences are more likely to be positive. Similarly, as can be seen in the extant literature, parents have a significant influence on the participation of their children in sport and physical activity. Parents are usually the instigators of children's initial participation in sport and their ongoing support, financial assistance and perceptions of their children's competence have a strong influence over whether children and youth continue their involvement in sport.

The figure highlights that the coach is the most important factor in player retention and attrition in children's and youth sport that is able to be directly influenced by sport clubs and associations. Coaches are fundamental to the provision of sport experiences (Lyle and Cushion, 2010). The review of literature points to two messages for coaches engaging

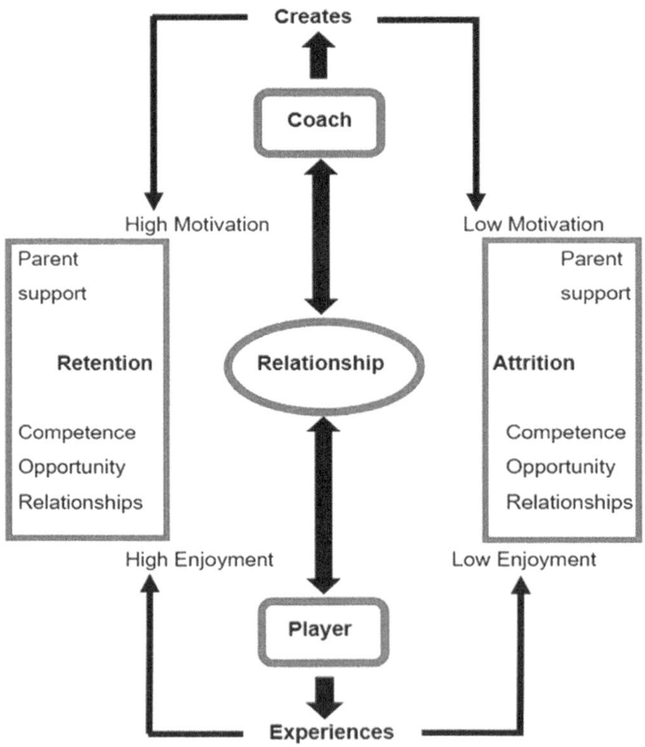


*Figure 10.1* Coach–player relationship and player retention and attrition factors: the coach creates and the player experiences

children in junior and youth sport. Firstly, children and youth should be given the chance to play with purpose through sport (Pill, 2007): that is, children and youth should have opportunities for deliberate play as a means to increase physical activity and to build movement ability through game design. Secondly, parents should be encouraged by coaches to be involved in their children's physical activity because we know that children and youth have increased enjoyment with a high level of parental support. To promote children's and youth's physical, social, emotional, and cognitive development, the benefits of sport participation should be advocated to parents. Coaches are in a key position to encourage and engage parents to play informally with their children (Pill, 2020a). Children and youth's belief in their ability becomes an influential factor in motivation around the ages of 10–12. Competence in sport may underpin overall self-esteem, in that a sense of self-worth can be defined by specific abilities such as sport competency (Atkins *et al.*, 2015). Having low movement ability has consequences for adolescence, including being more likely to be overweight due to sedentary behaviours (Pill and Harvey, 2019).

Adolescents are particularly sensitive to equal treatment and the perception of fairness. If this means they are not getting game time as an outcome of unequal or fair treatment from the coach, they are likely to pursue other interests. If an adolescent believes the coach 'doesn't like them', they are also likely to withdraw from sport (Agnew *et al.*, 2016). Into adolescence, the influence parents can have during childhood to motivate participation begins to decline, but parent support is still important. Additionally, by the time an adolescent reaches senior (high) school age, the individual generally has a good sense of what physical activities they are 'good at' and enjoy, and therefore what they want to stay involved with.

Adolescents who persist with sport participation report greater experiences of their coaches promoting a task-focused motivational environment than those who drop out (Le Bars *et al.*, 2009; Atkins *et al.*, 2015). Coaches who produce task-involving climates provide direct psychological and behavioural benefits to their players (Atkins *et al.*, 2015). Therefore, coaches engaging players aged 10–12 should be aware of the following:

- Play/playing game forms continues to be a motivator for participation. Play with purpose assists player learning and development of movement ability. Play/playing game forms is critical to player motivation; and
- Coaches have a key role in sport participation and retention in this age group (Pill, 2020a).

Coaches have an increasingly significant role in sport participation and retention as participation moves from junior to youth sport. They have a high amount of influence in two areas – progressing the game development of participants with goals to play at higher levels; and maintaining interest in engaged players through offering them game time and commitment to developing the person as well as the player. This is called athlete-centred coaching (Pill, 2018). Junior and youth sport engagement and retention revolve around two key factors:

- Creating opportunities for play through informal sport opportunities; and
- Elevating the standard of coaching.

Coach education therefore needs to be prioritised to elevate the standard of coaching. Coaching has a key influence on children's and youth retention in sport, to improve retention in youth sport the elevation of the standard of coaching at community sport levels must be a strategic priority (Pill, 2020a).

## Summary, Future Directions, and Future Research

Coaching involves a complex relationship between the coach, the player, and the context in which that dynamic occurs (Cushion, 2013). A philosophy positively positioning the coach–athlete relationship at the centre of coaching is athlete-centred coaching (Kidman and Lombardo, 2010). Athlete-centred coaching is where the coach is player-centred, concerned with the development of the player as a person as well as the person as a player (Pill, 2020b). We suggest that research is needed into the role of the coach in athlete-centred junior and youth sport and the adoption of this type of coaching on player retention/attrition. More research is also needed into coaching strategies and behaviours encouraging inclusivity and player enjoyment at the two critical stages of player retention and attrition.

## References

Agnew, D. and Pill, S., 2016. "I think it's going to save lives". Sport administrator perspectives on youth development through sport. *The Sport Journal*, 48, 1–16.

Agnew, D., Pill, S., and Drummond, M., 2016. Investigating the elements that encourage or inhibit the participation of children and youth in Australian football. *Annals of Leisure Research*, 19 (1), 27–46.

Agnew, D., *et al.*, 2013. *SANFL youth retention study*. Adelaide: Flinders University and SANFL.

Allender, S., Cowburn, G., and Foster, C., 2006. Understanding participation in sport and physical activity among children and adults: A review of qualitative studies. *Health Education Research*, 21 (6), 826–835.

Atkins, M.R., *et al.*, 2015. Peers, parents, and coaches, oh my! The relation of the motivational climate to boys' intention to continue in sport. *Psychology of Sport and Exercise*, 16(3), 170–180.

Australian Sports Commission, 1996. *Game sense: Perceptions and actions research report*. Belconnen, ACT: Australian Sports Commission.

Australian Sports Commission, 2013. *Validation of the playing for life philosophy* [online]. Available from: https://www.clearinghouseforsport.gov.au/research/smi/validation_of_playing_for_life_philosophy [Accessed 7 April 2022].

Barnett, N.P., Smoll F.L., and Smith R.E., 2006. Effects of enhancing coach-athlete relationships on youth sport attrition. *The Sport Psychologist*, 6 (2), 111–127.

Butcher, J., Lindner, K., and Johns, D., 2002. Withdrawal from competitive youth sport: A retrospective ten-year study. *Journal of Sport Behaviour*, 25 (2), 145–163.

Carlsson, A. and Lundqvist, C., 2016. The coaching behaviour scale for sport (CBS-S): A psychometric evaluation of the Swedish version, *Scandinavian Journal of Medicine and Science in Sports*, 26 (1), 116–123.

Côté, J., Baker, J., and Abernethy, B., 2003. From play to practice: A developmental framework for the acquisition of expertise in team sport. *In*: J.L. Starkes and K.A. Ericsson, eds. *Recent advances in research on sport expertise*, Champaign, IL: Human Kinetics, 89–113.

Crane, J. and Temple, V., 2015. A systematic review of dropout from organised sport among children and youth. *European Physical Education Review*. 21 (1), 114–131.

Cushion, C., 2013. Applying game-centred approaches in coaching: A critical analysis of the 'dilemmas of practice' impacting change. *Sport Coaching Review*, 2 (1), 61–76.

Elliott, S.K. and Drummond, M.J., 2011. Parental involvement in junior sport. *In*: G.D. Dodd, ed. *Moving, learning and achieving: Edited proceedings of the 27th ACHPER International Conference*. Adelaide, South Australia: ACHPER, 137–144.

Elliott, S.K. and Drummond, M.J.N., 2013. A socio-cultural exploration of parental involvement in junior Australian rules football. *Asia-Pacific Journal of Health, Sport and Physical Education*, 4 (1), 35–48.

Elliott, S. and Drummond, M., 2015. The (limited) impact of sport policy on parental behaviour in youth sport: A qualitative inquiry in junior Australian football. *International Journal of Sport Policy and Politics*, 7 (4), 519–530.

Fraser-Thomas, J., Côté, J., and Deakin, J., 2008. Understanding dropout and prolonged engagement in adolescent competitive sport. *Psychology of Sport and Exercise*, 9 (5), 645–662.

Furusa, M.G., Knight, C.J., and Hill, D.M., 2020. Parental involvement and children's enjoyment in sport. *Qualitative Research in Sport, Exercise and Health*, 13 (6), 1–19.

Griffin, L., Butler, J., and Sheppard, J., 2018. Athlete-centred coaching: Extending the possibilities of a holistic and process-oriented model to athlete development. *In*: S. Pill, ed. *Perspectives on athlete centred coaching*. London: Routledge. 9–23.

Gould, D. and Walker, L., 2019. Youth sport: Meeting unique development needs of young athletes for preventing dropout. *In*: M. Anshel. T. Petrie., and J. Steinfeldt, eds. *APA handbook of sport and exercise psychology, volume 1: Sport psychology*. American Psychological Association. 151–177.

Hamson, K., Head, L., and McDonald, L., 2008. *AFL Gold Coast juniors. Player dropout report 2007–2008*. Queensland, Australia: AFL Queensland & Griffith University.

Hewitt, M., Edwards, K., and Pill, S., 2016b. Investigating the teaching styles of a junior tennis coach using the spectrum of teaching styles. *ICHPER.SD Journal*, 44 (1), 5–32.

Hewitt, M., *et al.*, 2016a. Investigating the teaching styles of tennis coaches using the spectrum. *Sport Science Review*, 25 (5/6), 321–344.

Iñigo, M.M., Podlog, L., and Hall, M.S., 2015. Why do athletes remain committed to sport after severe injury? An examination of the sport commitment model. *The Sport Psychologist*, 29 (2), 143–155.

Kidman, L. and Lombardo, B.J., 2010. *Athlete-centred coaching: Developing decision makers*. Christchurch, NZ: Innovative Print Communications.

Langan, E., Blake, C., and Lonsdale, C., 2013. A systematic review of the effectiveness of interpersonal coach education programs on athlete outcomes. *Psychology of Sport and Exercise*, 14 (1), 37–49.

Le Bars, H., Gernigon, C., and Ninot, G., 2009. Personal and contextual determinants of elite young athletes' persistence or dropping out over time. *Scandinavian Journal of Medicine and Science in Sports*, 19 (2), 274–285.

Light, R., 2003. The joy of learning: Emotion and learning in games through TGfU. *Journal of Physical Education New Zealand*, 36 (1), 93–108.

Light, R., 2013. *Game sense: Pedagogy for performance, participation and enjoyment*. New York: Routledge.

Light, R. and Curry, C., 2009. Children's reasons for joining sport clubs and staying in them: A case study of Sydney soccer club. *ACHPER Healthy Lifestyles Journal*, 56 (1), 23–27.

Light, R. and Harvey, S., 2017. Positive pedagogy for sport coaching. *Sport, Education and Society*, 22 (2), 271–287.

Lyle, J. and Cushion, C., 2010. *Sports coaching: Professionalisation and practice*. Edinburgh, New York: Churchill Livingstone.

MacDougall, C., Schiller, W., and Darbyshire, P., 2004. We have to live in the future. *Early Child Development and Care*. 174 (4), 369–387.

Molinero, O., *et al.*, 2009. Dropout reasons in youth Spanish athletes: Relationship to gender, type of sport and level of competition. *Journal of Sport Behaviour*, 29 (3), 255–269.

Monteiro, D., *et al.*, 2017. Determinants and reasons for dropout in swimming—Systematic review. *Sports*, 5 (3), 50.

Partington, M. and Cushion, C., 2011. An investigation of the practice activities and coaching behaviors of professional top-level youth soccer coaches. *Scandinavian Journal of Medicine Science and Sports*, 23 (3), 374–382.

Pill, S., 2007. *Play with purpose*. Hindmarsh: ACHPER Publications.

Pill, S., 2016. Implementing game sense coaching approach in Australian football through action research. *Agora for Physical Education and Sport*, 18 (1), 1–19.

Pill, S., 2018. Developing thinking players: A coach's experience with game sense coaching. *In*: S. Pill, ed. *Perspectives on athlete centred coaching*. London: Routledge, 93–103.

Pill, S., 2020a. *Children, Junior and youth sport; retention messages* [online]. Available from: https://learningthroughsport.blogspot.com/2020/04/building-bridge-out-of-covid-19-for.html [Accessed 7 April 2022].

Pill, S., 2020b. Introduction. *In*: S. Pill, ed. *Athlete-centred coaching*. London: Routledge, 1–5.

Pill, S. and Harvey, S., 2019. A narrative review of children's movement competence research 1997-2017. *Physical Culture and Sport. Studies and Research*, 81, 47–74.

Salguero, A., *et al.*, 2003. Identification of dropout reasons in young competitive swimmers. *Journal of Sports Medicine and Physical Fitness*, 43 (4), 530–534.

Scanlon, T.K., *et al.*, 1993. An introduction to the sport commitment model. *Journal of Sport and Exercise Psychology*, 15 (1), 1–15.

Sport Australia, 2019. *Playing for life* [online]. Available from: https://www.sportaus.gov.au/p4l [Accessed 7 April 2022].

Sport Australia, 2020. *Playing for life – Game sense approach* [online]. Available from: https://www.sportaus.gov.au/p4l/game_sense_approach [Accessed 7 April 2022].

Stodter, A. and Cushion, C., 2014. Coaches' learning and education: A case study of culture in conflict. *Sports Coaching Review*, 3 (1), 63–79.

Stodter, A. and Cushion, C., 2019a. Layers of learning in coach developers' practice-theories, preparation and delivery. *International Journal of Sports Science and Coaching*, 6 (3), 307–316.

Stodter, A. and Cushion, C., 2019b. Evidencing the impact of coaches' learning: Changes in knowledge and practice over time. *Journal of Sports Sciences*, 37 (18), 2086–2093.

Thompson, J., 2003. *The double-goal coach*. New York: Harper Collins.

Weiss, M., 2000. Motivating kids in physical activity. *The President's Council on Physical Fitness and Sports Research Digest Series*, 3 (11), 1–8.

Witt, P.A. and Dangi, T.B., 2018. Why children/youth drop out of sports. *Journal of Park and Recreation Administration*, 36 (3), 191–199.

# SECTION II

# Protecting Child Athletes

## Introduction: Protecting Child Athletes

*Ruth Jeanes and Martin Toms*

All children have the right to play sport in a safe and supportive environment and coaches have numerous responsibilities in ensuring the safety of children in youth sport settings. As the chapters in this section illustrate, protecting child athletes can take multiple forms. When coaching children, coaches are working with individuals whose bodies are growing and developing and this has significant implications for what we might expect of children in relation to training loads. As the diverse array of chapters in this section illustrates, protecting children in sport requires coaches to have knowledge of a broad array of areas, from growth and maturation, to managing injuries through to considering social media use amongst child athletes. Considerable expectations are placed on coaches to understand multiple aspects of child protection within sport. This section captures this diversity but also illustrates the general lack of research examining key issues impacting children, such as nutritional requirements for child athletes.

The section highlights the multiple social influences that need to be considered by coaches when looking to provide a safe and supportive environment for young people. Managing parents is often one of the biggest challenges youth sport coaches face, this section considers how coaches might better support and manage the involvement of parents alongside considering other factors such as managing social media use amongst children and parents. Within this section, there is also a focus on supporting care-experienced children in youth sport contexts, considering the role of the coach when family support may be absent or at times transient. This is an important but relatively overlooked area of research particularly within a youth sport coaching context.

The section also delves into the darker side of sport, considering child protection in sport and the potential ways in which coaches can engage in abusive practices that cause significant psychological and physical harm to children. The chapters in the section emphasise the power coaches hold over children and the ways in which abuse can manifest subtly for example through practices that encourage children to scrutinize their bodies for example and lead to disordered eating.

The section discusses the ways in which coaches can develop supportive environments which act as protective settings for young people. Coaches can play an important role in supporting young people's mental health, developing children's mental health literacy as well as providing an environment where they feel safe to ask for help when struggling with their mental health. Overall the section illustrates the breadth of responsibilities placed on coaches working with children and the multiple areas they need to consider when looking to make sport safe for all children.

DOI: 10.4324/9781003199359-13

# 11

# PREPARING CHILDREN FOR SPORT: THE IMPORTANCE OF ATHLETIC DEVELOPMENT

*Rhodri S. Lloyd, Sylvia Moeskops, and Jon L. Oliver*

## Introduction

Organised sport serves as a vehicle to promote a number of physical, psychological and social benefits (Brenner, 2016). For example, young children engaged with sport are often stronger (Dotan *et al.*, 2013), more powerful (Wrigley *et al.*, 2014) and possess greater aerobic (Ballester *et al.*, 2015) and anaerobic (Ara *et al.*, 2004) fitness than their non-sporting peers. Sport also provides an opportunity to enhance self-esteem (Eime *et al.*, 2013), foster life skills (Gould and Carson, 2008) and encourage positive youth development by promoting enjoyment, challenge and motor skill mastery (Merkel, 2013). While few 'talented' young children will actually reach professional levels of sport (Brenner, 2016), it is important to remember that children participate in sport predominantly to have fun, learn new skills and foster friendships (Allender *et al.*, 2006).

Notwithstanding these benefits, it is imperative that children are suitably prepared to participate safely in the sports they choose to play. The dynamics of sports will subject children to high forces, often in reactive and unpredictable contexts, and repeatedly in sports that promote specialisation from an early age. Thus, it is imperative that all children possess adequate levels of *athleticism* to safely tolerate the demands of sports and ensure they can continue to participate long into adulthood. Athleticism is defined as the ability to frequently perform a variety of movements with precision and confidence in various environments that require competent levels of motor skills, strength, power, speed, agility, balance, coordination and endurance (Lloyd *et al.*, 2016a).

Developing athleticism in children and adolescents should not involve superimposing adult-based training programmes but rather prescribing developmentally-appropriate athletic development programmes that account for the nuances of youth populations. While the training response can be impacted by a multitude of factors (e.g. rest, recovery, nutrition, workloads, psycho-social attributes), the interaction between training, growth and maturation is a concept that has stimulated a growing interest in paediatric research over the last two decades. The purpose of this chapter is to firstly review the current research pertaining to the natural development and trainability of athleticism in youth and secondly, consider how the research can be applied synergistically within practice.

DOI: 10.4324/9781003199359-14

## Review of Current Research

### Natural Development of Athleticism

Childhood and adolescence reflect unique developmental periods when physical performance can change dramatically as a result of the biological processes that underpin growth and maturation (Faigenbaum *et al.*, 2019). This natural development can result in substantial improvements in movement competency and physical performance throughout childhood and adolescence, including improvements in agility, balance and coordination (Tomkinson *et al.*, 2018) and strength, power, speed and endurance (Viru *et al.*, 1999). However, the rate of change in function and fitness will vary over time (Viru *et al.*, 1999), the biological mechanisms that underpin change can alter throughout development (Lloyd and Oliver, 2012), and there may be periods and circumstances where natural development impairs coordination and physical performance (Quatman-Yates *et al.*, 2012). As children mature, sex-related differences in physical performance will become apparent (Faigenbaum *et al.*, 2019) and some aspects of natural development may contribute to increased risks of participants experiencing growth- and sports-related injuries (Dalton, 1992).

### The Central Nervous System and Neuroplasticity

The brain and central nervous system (CNS) grow at a rapid rate during childhood and the development of the brain is organised to help prioritise learning of movement skills early in life (Gogtay *et al.*, 2004). It is easy to observe the rapid gains in movement vocabulary of children who are provided with a stimulating physical environment, which should allow for mastery of fundamental movement skills (e.g. balance, locomotion and object control) during childhood (Lubans *et al.*, 2010). Neuroplasticity refers to the ability of the CNS to adapt in response to stimuli, with plasticity at its greatest during childhood before reducing throughout adolescence and into adulthood (Spear, 2013). As well as underpinning improvements in movement vocabulary and competence, development of the CNS likely contributes to a modest childhood spurt in strength, speed, power and endurance development observed in young boys and girls (Viru *et al.*, 1999).

The brain experiences a further spurt in maturation around late childhood and early adolescence, with a process that involves synaptic overproduction, myelination of routinely used pathways and subsequent pruning of rarely used synapses (Johnson *et al.*, 2009). Much of the support for providing children and adolescents with a sampling and diversification approach to physical activity (Côté *et al.*, 2009; Lloyd *et al.*, 2016a) can be associated with an opportunity to capitalise on CNS development and neuroplasticity. Supporting the role of sampling on the development of movement skill, young athletes following a diversification pathway have been shown to demonstrate improved jump landing mechanics compared to those who specialised in a single sport (DiStefano *et al.*, 2018; DiCesare *et al.*, 2019).

### Development of the Muscular and Cardiorespiratory Systems

The onset of sexual maturation represents a key biological event in the transition from childhood to adolescence, with puberty marking a time of substantial change in circulating hormones, rapid growth and changes in physiological function (Faigenbaum *et al.*, 2019). Increased levels of circulating androgens lead to large increases in muscle mass, heart and lung size and blood volume, driving large improvements in strength, speed, agility, power and endurance (Faigenbaum *et al.*, 2019). As boys benefit from increased testosterone during puberty they experience greater gains in muscle-mass, with sex-related differences in physical fitness becoming more pronounced during adolescence. Girls experience increased levels of estrogen during puberty and the accumulation of greater levels of body fat, which can further disadvantage girls in activities such as running, sprinting and jumping, where body mass has to be moved. Coaches should be aware that increased mass, even if resulting from increased muscle mass, may increase the risk of injury (Kemper *et al.*, 2015), particularly if increases in size are not also accompanied by concomitant increases in strength and movement control (Read *et al.*, 2017; Read *et al.*, 2018).

The onset of puberty and the period of adolescence is consequently associated with large improvements in most aspects of physical fitness, particularly in boys. However, the timing and tempo of puberty can vary considerably between individuals, and potentially by as much as five years within a given sex (Malina, 2014). This has consequences for sports selection, as sports that rely on greater size, strength, speed or power are likely to favour early maturing individuals, while sports that benefit from smaller body dimensions and lower body fat can favour late maturing individuals (Till and Baker, 2020).

## *Skeletal Development*

While skeletal maturation occurs throughout childhood and adolescence, the adolescent period is a particularly important time for skeletal development. With the onset of the growth spurt the long bones grow rapidly, and by the time a child reaches peak height velocity they will be around 92% of their adult height (Cumming *et al.*, 2017). At this stage long bones will be at near adult length, but bone mineral density will be further below adult values at this time (Boot *et al.*, 1997). This means the adolescent skeleton may be susceptible to stress fractures, particularly for youth involved in high volumes of repetitive weight-bearing exercise (Tenforde *et al.*, 2011; Difiori *et al.*, 2014). As muscle mass continues to develop this will provide increased skeletal loading and will help to stimulate increased bone mineral development, with increases in bone mass peaking at a similar time to peak increases in muscle mass (Martin *et al.*, 1997; McKay *et al.*, 1998). Engagement in exercise that involves mechanical loading, particularly rapid increases in force development as seen in plyometrics, and good nutrition should be central to promoting the development of bone health throughout adolescence (Faigenbaum *et al.*, 2019).

Muscle and tendon development will lag behind bone growth; rapid growth of the long bones will stretch muscle and tendons and provide a further stimulus for growth in those tissues. However, this can lead to muscle tightness and soreness and additional strain on still developing apophyses. Young athletes who are involved in a high-volume of repetitive training while experiencing the growth spurt may be particularly vulnerable to apophyseal injuries, such as Sever's and Osgood-Schlatter disease (Micheli and Fehlandt, 1992). The adolescent growth spurt also leads to rapid increases in limb length, which can lead to temporary disruption to coordination, a phenomenon referred to as adolescent awkwardness (Quatman-Yates *et al.*, 2012). Adolescent awkwardness may affect a large proportion of youth (~90% of boys and ~76% of girls) and it is more likely to be observed in movements that require greater levels of coordination (Hirtz and Starosta, 2002).

## *Training Responsiveness*

Existing international youth athletic development guidelines advocate the use of strength and conditioning to develop appropriate levels of athleticism in both children and adolescents (Bergeron *et al.*, 2015). Notwithstanding the natural increases in athleticism due to growth and maturation, exposure to athletic development programmes can result in both children and

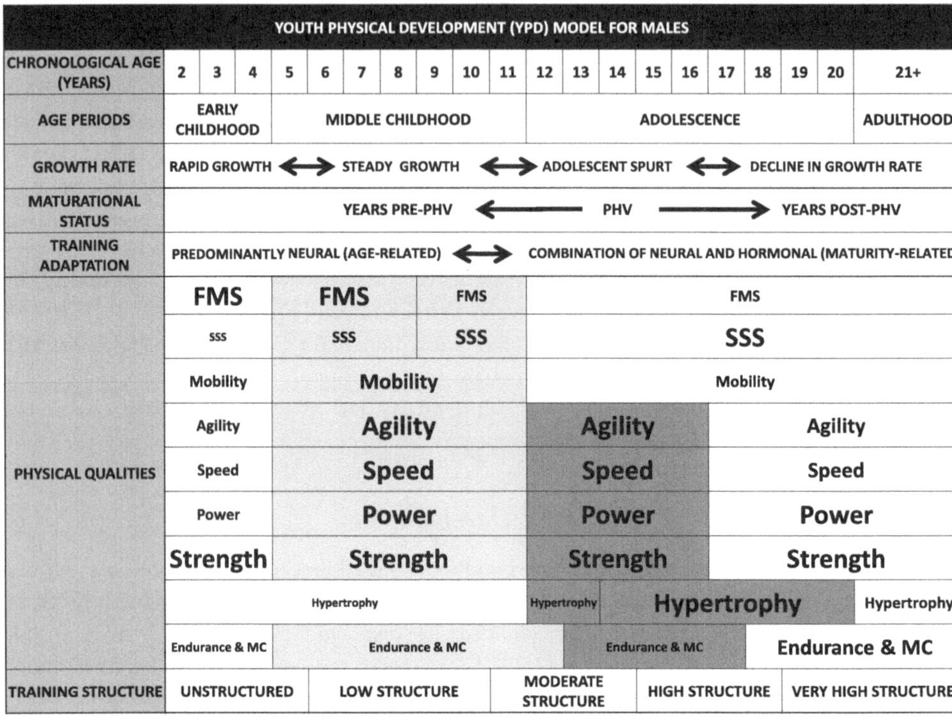


*Figure 11.1a* The Youth Physical Development (YPD) model for males

(Note: Font size refers to importance; light grey boxes refer to pre-adolescent periods of adaptation, dark grey boxes refer to adolescent periods of adaptation; PHV = peak height velocity; FMS = fundamental movement skills; SSS = sport=specific skills; MC = metabolic conditioning)

adolescents making meaningful improvements in athleticism above and beyond those of natural development. Indeed, the interest in interactions between training, growth and maturation has stimulated an increase in youth training research and led to the creation of long-term athletic development models that attempt to provide a systematic approach to exercise prescription for youth (Lloyd and Oliver, 2012; Gulbin *et al.*, 2013). The most granular detail for exercise prescription appears in the Youth Physical Development model (Figures 11.1a and 11.1b), which highlights that all youth can make meaningful improvements in athletic qualities (e.g. strength, power, speed), irrespective of maturity status (Lloyd and Oliver, 2012).

## Motor Skill Development

Muscular strength and motor skill development should be prominent features of any youth athletic development programme, starting from early childhood (Lloyd and Oliver, 2012). These two athletic qualities should be considered and developed synergistically (Cattuzzo *et al.*, 2016), given that the ability to move in a coordinated manner (motor skill competence) requires the production and absorption of force (muscle strength). Recent data, albeit from male adolescents, indicated boys with low and average relative isometric strength were nearly eight-times and four-times respectively more likely to be deemed low competency compared to boys with higher relative strength levels (Pichardo *et al.*, 2019). Research has shown that neuromuscular training,

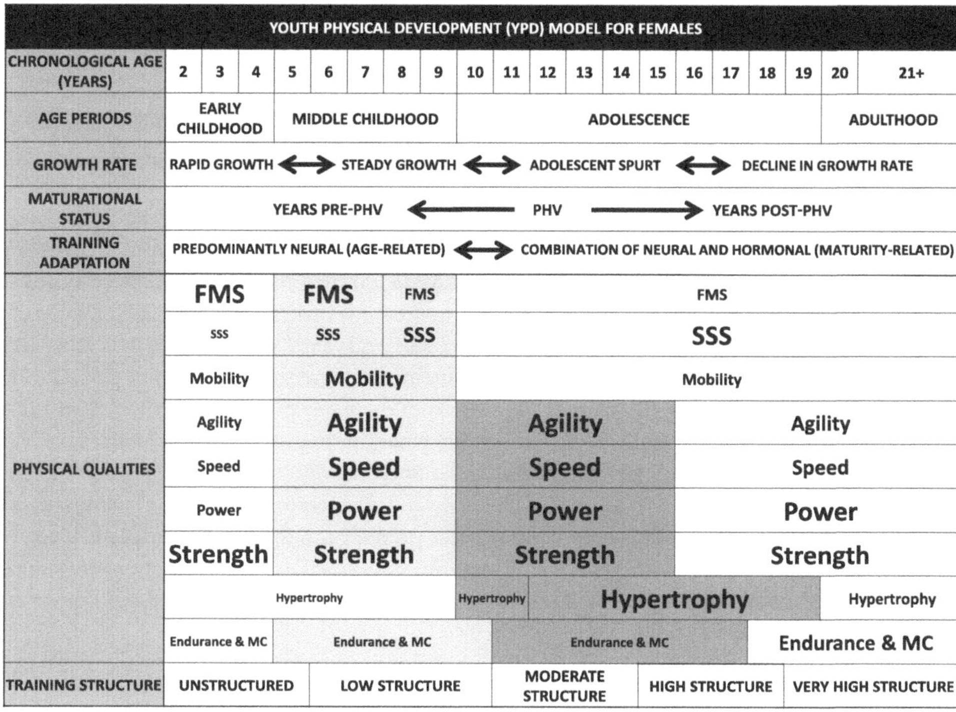


*Figure 11.1b* The Youth Physical Development (YPD) model for females

(Note: Font size refers to importance; light grey boxes refer to pre-adolescent periods of adaptation, dark grey boxes refer to adolescent periods of adaptation; PHV = peak height velocity; FMS = fundamental movement skills; SSS = sport = specific skills; MC = metabolic conditioning)

inclusive of strength and power training, plyometrics, sprinting and coordination training, can significantly improve motor skill competence and performance in children (Faigenbaum *et al.*, 2011; Duncan *et al.*, 2018; Collins *et al.*, 2019). Given the increased neuroplasticity associated with early childhood, developing a breadth and depth of motor skill competencies are deemed essential for ensuring children have the foundational "building blocks" that will enable them to withstand the rigours of organised sports and recreational physical activity (Lloyd *et al.*, 2016a).

## *Strength and Power Development*

Existing literature has shown that while adolescents are physiologically primed to make larger absolute gains in strength and power, children are also able to make significant improvements in these athletic qualities in response to resistance training (Behringer *et al.*, 2010). For example, ten-weeks of strength-dominated training increased jump performance in 4–6 year old children (Wick *et al.*, 2021), while eight-weeks of neuromuscular training has been shown to improve push-ups, curl-ups, long and single leg hop performance in primary school children (Faigenbaum *et al.*, 2011). However, in both of these studies, significant improvements were not consistently achieved for all athletic qualities tested, which is likely a function of the shorter interventions not allowing children to safely progress to the higher training intensities, which are required to maximise the training response (Lesinski *et al.*, 2016). Recent data has shown that a ten-month neuromuscular training intervention, which gradually increased in intensity (i.e. load lifted, eccentric strain), enabled prepubertal gymnasts to realise significant improvements in isometric strength, jumping kinetics, peak sprint speed and vaulting take-off velocity, with these adaptations greater than any achieved from gymnastics training or natural development alone (Moeskops *et al.*, 2022a). Therefore, it is clear that when prescribed the appropriate training dosage (i.e. duration, frequency, intensity) children can realise important improvements in strength and power.

Assuming a child has accrued a reasonable training history and is technically competent, adolescence offers a timeframe in which large improvements in athleticism can be realised as a result of the interaction between training and the natural adaptations resulting from growth and maturation (Faigenbaum *et al.*, 2019). Indeed, recent data indicated that a more advanced maturity status enabled greater increases in isometric strength and concentric jump variables (Lloyd *et al.*, 2021). However, meta-analytical data is somewhat equivocal, with some studies indicating that adolescents can make greater improvements in absolute measures of strength (Moran *et al.*, 2017b; Peitz *et al.*, 2018) and power (Slimani *et al.*, 2018) following exposure to resistance training, however, the training responses are more comparable when strength and power are made relative to body mass (Peitz *et al.*, 2018). Notwithstanding the potential differences between absolute and relative strength and power, the hormonal changes and architectural changes (Radnor *et al.*, 2020b) associated with more advanced maturity status predispose adolescents to make large gains in force production. Critically, irrespective of maturity status quality of movement must remain paramount within any youth-based training programme and training intensity should never be increased at the expense of technical competency.

## *Speed and Agility Development*

Literature indicates that children and adolescents can make meaningful training-induced gains in speed (Moran *et al.*, 2017a). Maturation induces changes in sprinting mechanics, with children increasing ground contact times and reducing stride frequency; however, these changes are more than compensated for by an increased stride length, which underpins gains in overall sprint speed (Meyers *et al.*, 2015). Producing large amounts of force during short ground contact times has also been associated with sprint performance, with changes in relative measures of vertical stiffness, leg stiffness and maximal force explaining 83% of the change in sprint speed in boys transitioning from pre- to post-peak height velocity (Meyers *et al.*, 2016). Training mode and the physiological and biomechanical adaptations underpinning training-induced improvements in speed likely differ between children and adolescents (Rumpf *et al.*, 2012; Lloyd *et al.*, 2016b). However, combining strength training and plyometrics appears to be a particularly potent training stimulus for all youth (Radnor *et al.*, 2017).

Similar to the development of linear speed, literature has shown that youth populations can make meaningful training-induced improvements in agility (Asadi *et al.*, 2017). Due to the complexities and limitations associated with attempting to test "true" reactive agility, our understanding is currently limited to change-of-direction-speed (Lloyd and Oliver, 2017). Despite the evidence base for the natural development and trainability of change-of-direction-speed being somewhat limited, existing data indicates that training-induced gains are likely a function of increased relative strength (Keiner *et al.*, 2014). Intuitively, greater levels of relative strength should enable children and adolescents to produce more force when accelerating and better tolerate forces when decelerating. Natural improvements in speed and change-of-direction-speed are related to growth-related changes in size as well as changes in neural and muscle-tendon structure and function. For example, a recent study has shown that school-aged boys experiencing, or having experienced, peak height velocity, make the largest increases in muscle thickness and sprinting performance (Radnor *et al.*, 2021). Therefore, training programmes that specifically

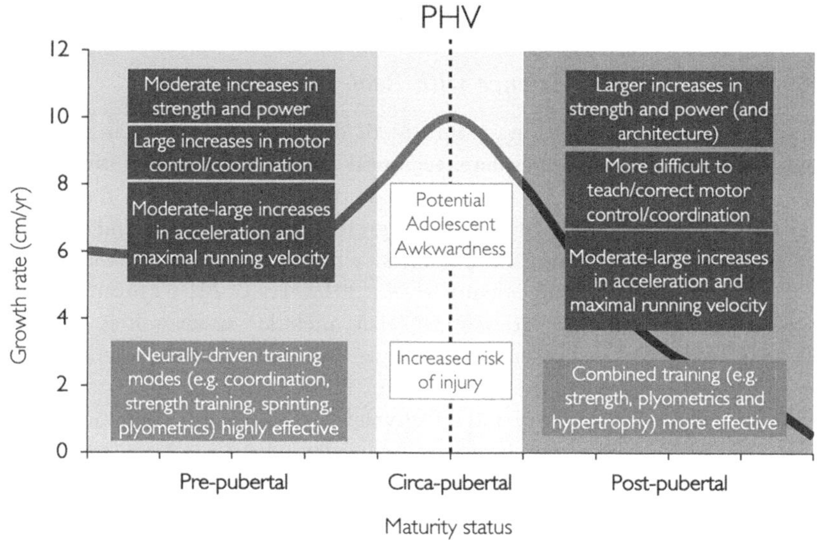


*Figure 11.2* Conceptual figure illustrating how training modalities can be synergistically aligned with naturally occurring adaptations resulting from growth and maturation

target the development of these natural adaptations, termed 'synergistic adaptation' (Lloyd *et al.*, 2016b) will hopefully result in an enhanced overall response due to the interactions between training, growth and maturation (Figure 11.2).

## *Aerobic Endurance Development*

Aerobic endurance refers to the ability to perform lower-intensity exercise over a prolonged period of time and facilitates recovery following bouts of high-intensity exercise. Maturity-related changes in body size, cardiac size and blood volume drive large changes in absolute peak oxygen uptake ($VO_{2peak}$), which is one of the primary determinants of aerobic endurance (Faigenbaum *et al.*, 2019). The other two determinants, anaerobic threshold and exercise economy, also change as a result of natural development. Children are more reliant on aerobic metabolism than adolescents and adults, with their anaerobic threshold occurring at a higher percentage of $VO_{2peak}$ than adolescents (Reybrouck *et al.*, 1985). Increases in body size, muscle strength and more efficient muscle recruitment strategies are responsible for the natural development in exercise economy (Faigenbaum *et al.*, 2019).

In light of the natural development of aerobic endurance, research has also shown that children and adolescents can realise meaningful improvements in $VO_{2peak}$ in response to appropriate training strategies (Armstrong and Barker, 2011; Harrison *et al.*, 2015). Due to their inherent physiology, data indicate that children need to exercise at >80% maximum heart rate in order to expect meaningful gains in $VO_{2peak}$ (Baquet *et al.*, 2003; Harrison *et al.*, 2015). While improvements in aerobic endurance can be obtained following interval running, small-sided games are often a fun and highly effective method of providing a high-intensity dosage of exercise (Harrison *et al.*, 2015). In addition to the endurance stimulus, it is also recommended that neuromuscular training (e.g. motor skills, strength and power) is also used to ensure youths have a robust and resilient system than can tolerate the demands of sport.

## Implications for Children's Sport Coaching

### *Merging Science with Real-World Practice*

To reap the greatest benefits from long-term athletic development programmes, longstanding buy-in and engagement from the athlete, technical coaches and parents are of paramount importance. Likewise, practitioners must have a sound understanding of the training principles (e.g. training variation and relevance, progressive overload, etc.) and paediatric physiology to design effective training programmes, which promote on-going adaptations in the desired physical qualities (Faigenbaum *et al.*, 2019; Haff, 2019). From a psychosocial perspective, designing training programmes that include opportunities to build self-confidence (e.g. tasks to create success) and increase resilience (e.g. tasks to challenge) are also important for young athletes (Till *et al.*, 2021). Therefore, both the art and science of coaching are critical to the longevity and effectiveness of any given programme. Figure 11.3 provides a "Top 10 Tips" for practitioners to consider when coaching strength and conditioning to young athletes.

Regardless of the child or adolescent's stage of development or sporting capabilities, practitioners should take a long-term, systematic and holistic approach to athletic development (Lloyd *et al.*, 2016a). With this philosophy in mind, periodising and planning training to elicit the greatest adaptive response to enhance physical performance and to reduce sport-related injury risk is recommended (Faigenbaum *et al.*, 2019).

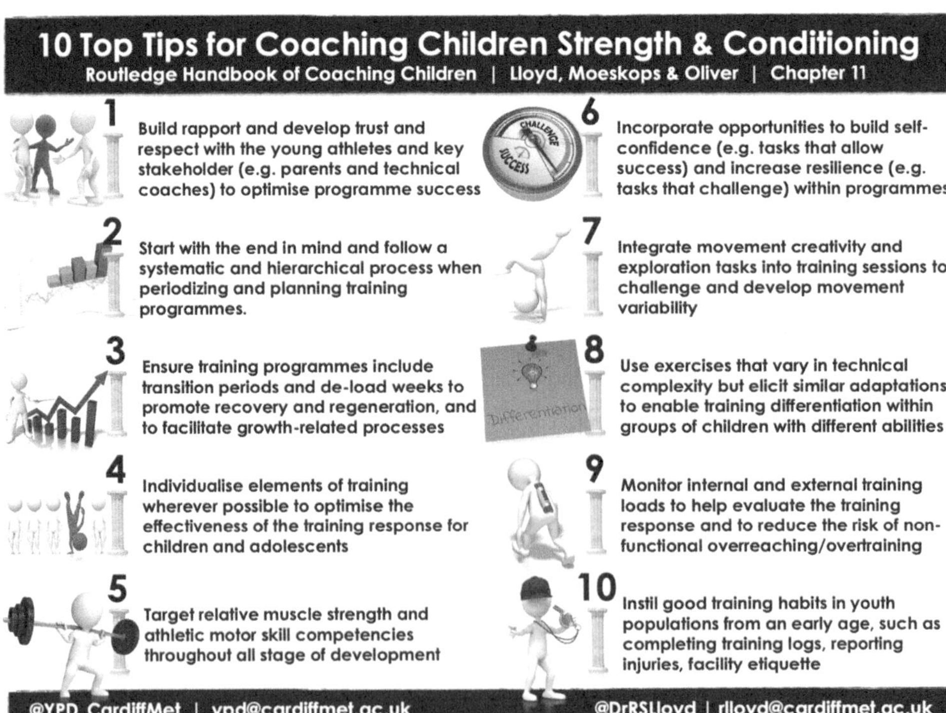


*Figure 11.3* Top 10 Tips for coaching children strength and conditioning

Following a thorough analysis of the child's sport (e.g. physical, biomechanical and injury characteristics) and their individual needs (e.g. training age, maturity status, psychological development) the planning process can commence. Practitioners are encouraged to start with the end in mind by following a hierarchical process to programming. Eight hierarchical, interlinking levels of planning (Figure 11.4) have been suggested for youth; including, the overall long-term athletic development plan, multiyear plan, annual plan, macrocycle, mesocycle, microcycle, training day and training session (Faigenbaum *et al.*, 2019). Macrocycles are often organised into periods of training, namely; preparation, competition and transition, with these training periods further sub-divided into phases, including general and specific preparation and pre-competition and competition (Haff and Haff, 2012). Placing a greater focus on specific preparation and competition is only appropriate for more advanced young athletes, when higher levels of technical competency are displayed and it is apparent that they are physically prepared to tolerate such training stimuli (Faigenbaum *et al.*, 2019). It should also be emphasised that all youth must be afforded transition periods to promote recovery and regeneration, reduce the risk of overuse type injuries (e.g. from the negative effect of accumulated fatigue, repetitive movements), and to facilitate growth-related processes (Lloyd *et al.*, 2016a).

*Figure 11.4* Hierarchical order of planning

## Realities of Implementing Long-Term Athletic Development Programmes within Youth Sport

### Individualising Training Prescription

When implementing LTAD programmes, practitioners are encouraged to consider the individual needs of each child or adolescent, such as technical competency, physical abilities, sex, growth, maturation (biological and psychosocial), goals, resource and time availability to optimise their training response (Faigenbaum *et al.*, 2019). Here, the potential possibilities for individualisation will depend upon the context and constraints of the training setting. To assist with this process, collecting data on physical performance characteristics, growth and maturation, injury risk factors, training loads, wellness and mood, as well as the young athletes' longer-term aspirations would be helpful (Read *et al.*, 2020). Irrespective of the context, creating a safe training environment must be prioritised and therefore, technical competency drives the practitioner's decision making process for progressing or regressing exercises (Lloyd *et al.*, 2014). This could be particularly important when programming for individuals who differ in levels of technical competency, training age and/or stage of maturation, but yet train alongside each other. Therefore, to aid the programming process, practitioners are encouraged to develop a 'library' of exercises (i.e. progressions and regressions) which vary in technical complexity but can elicit similar adaptations (e.g. squatting variations).

### Managing Early Specialising Athletes

Early sport specialisation (ESS) involves intense training schedules and chronic exposure to a single sport during the developmental years, which can lead to an increased risk of overuse injuries, blunting of motor skill development, psycho-social issues, overtraining syndrome and burnout (Malina, 2010; Mostafavifar *et al.*, 2013), and reduced long-term participation in sport (LaPrade *et al.*, 2016). Practitioners working with these ESS athletes have a key role in integrating developmentally appropriate, holistic and athlete-centred training programmes (Moeskops *et al.*, in press-b). When faced with this type of athlete, practitioners should prescribe training that specifically targets the development of athletic motor skill competencies that are not inherent in their specialist sports, in order to increase the breadth of athleticism and to develop well-rounded individuals (Myer *et al.*, 2016). For example, to address the 'gaps' in a young rower's training programme who is very dominant in lower-body concentric movements and upper-body pulling, a greater bias towards lower-body posterior chain (e.g. eccentric hamstring and hip-dominant exercises work) and upper-body pushing exercises could be beneficial. Encouraging movement creativity, and exploration via non-structured forms of training (e.g. obstacle courses, playground games, partner challenges) to promote greater movement variability is also recommended for early specialising athletes (Radnor *et al.*, 2020a). Designing training programmes that aim to increase movement variability could also help reduce the risk of overuse injuries in early specialising athletes, as different movement patterns will vary the point of force application and coordination demands (Lloyd *et al.*, 2016a).

Cumulatively, the existing body of paediatric literature clearly shows that both children and adolescents benefit from exposure to athletic development programmes. Possessing a sound grasp of paediatric physiology and understanding training responsiveness will hopefully enable practitioners to design and deliver programmes that take advantage of the interactions between training, growth and maturation to optimise the development of athleticism. The development of sporting talent is complex and unpredictable and it is impossible to predict the sporting journeys of children. However, it is imperative that children and adolescents are exposed to appropriate training that rewards them with the foundations to enjoy a lifetime of sport.

## Summary, Future Directions and Future Research

Despite our advances in long-term athletic development and paediatric strength and conditioning, there are three notable challenges that should direct future research studies.

1 Despite the premise of long-term athletic development, our current understanding is limited to shorter-term training studies. While training frequency is recognised as a moderating variable for training responsiveness, the effects of chronic exposure to neuromuscular training remains unclear.
2 Existing training interventions have taken an inconsistent approach to estimating maturity status, with many studies failing to report maturity in any guise. Future research needs to adopt a consistent approach to assessing maturity status to better enable comparisons between different studies.
3 There is a disproportionate number of training interventions involving adolescent cohorts in comparison to children and a greater representation of boys compared to girls. Therefore, long-term training interventions involving regular assessments of maturity status need to be conducted that track athletic development in boys and girls from early childhood through to late adolescence.

## References


Allender, S., Cowburn, G., and Foster, C., 2006. Understanding participation in sport and physical activity among children and adults: A review of qualitative studies. *Health Education Research*, 21 (6), 826–835.

Ara, I., *et al.*, 2004. Regular participation in sports is associated with enhanced physical fitness and lower fat mass in prepubertal boys. *International Journal of Obesity and Related Metabolic Disorders*, 28 (12), 1585–1593.

Armstrong, N. and Barker, A.R., 2011. Endurance training and elite young athletes. *Medicine and Sport Science*, 56, 59–83.

Asadi, A., *et al.*, 2017. Influence of maturation stage on agility performance gains after plyometric training: A systematic review and meta-analysis. *Journal of Strength and Conditioning Research*, 31 (9), 2609–2617.

Ballester, R., *et al.*, 2015. The relationship between regular sports participation and vigilance in male and female adolescents. *PLoS One*, 10 (4), e0123898.

Baquet, G., van Praagh, E., and Berthoin, S., 2003. Endurance training and aerobic fitness in young people. *Sports Medicine*, 33 (15), 1127–1143.

Behringer, M., *et al.*, 2010. Effects of resistance training in children and adolescents: A meta-analysis. *Pediatrics*, 126 (5), 1199–1210.

Bergeron, M.F., *et al.*, 2015. International Olympic Committee consensus statement on youth athletic development. *British Journal of Sports Medicine*, 49 (13), 843–851.

Boot, A.M., *et al.*, 1997. Bone mineral density in children and adolescents: Relation to puberty, calcium intake, and physical activity. *Journal of Clinical Endocrinology and Metabolism*, 82 (1), 57–62.

Brenner, J., 2016. Sports specialisation and intensive training in young athletes. *Pediatrics*, 138 (3), e20162148.

Cattuzzo, M.T., *et al.*, 2016. Motor competence and health related physical fitness in youth: A systematic review. *Journal of Science and Medicine in Sport*, 19 (2), 123–129.

Collins, H., *et al.*, 2019. The effect of resistance training interventions on fundamental movement skills in youth: A meta-analysis. *Sports Medicine Open*, 5 (17), 1–16.

Côté, J., Lidor, R., and Hackfort, D., 2009. ISSP position stand: To sample or to specialise? Seven postulates about youth sport activities that lead to continued participation and elite performance. *International Journal of Sport and Exercise Psychology*, 9, 7–17.

Cumming, S.P., *et al.*, 2017. Bio-banding in sport: Applications to competition, talent, identification, and strength and conditioning of youth athletes. *Strength and Conditioning Journal*, 39 (2), 34–47.
Dalton, S.E., 1992. Overuse injuries in adolescent athletes. *Sports Medicine*, 13 (1), 58–70.
DiCesare, C.A., *et al.*, 2019. Sport specialization and coordination differences in multisport adolescent female basketball, soccer, and volleyball athletes. *Journal of Athletic Training*, 54 (10), 1105–1114.
Difiori, J., *et al.*, 2014. Overuse injuries and burnout in youth sports: A position statement from the american medical society for sports medicine. *Clinical Journal of Sports Medicine*, 24 (1), 3–20.
DiStefano, L.J., *et al.*, 2018. Sport sampling is associated with improved landing technique in youth athletes. *Sports Health*, 10 (2), 160–168.
Dotan, R., *et al.*, 2013. Explosive sport training and torque kinetics in children. *Applied Physiology, Nutrition and Metabolism*, 38 (7), 740–745.
Duncan, M.J., Eyre, E.L.J., and Oxford, S.W., 2018. The effects of 10-week integrated neuromuscular training on fundamental movement skills and physical self-efficacy in 6-7-year-old children. *Journal of Strength and Conditioning Research*, 32 (12), 3348–3356.
Eime, R.M., *et al.*, 2013. A systematic review of the psychological and social benefits of participation in sport for children and adolescents: Informing development of a conceptual model of health through sport. *International Journal of Behavioral Nutrition and Physical Activity*, 10, 98.
Faigenbaum, A.D., Lloyd, R.S., and Oliver, J.L., 2019. *ACSM essentials of youth fitness*. Champaign, IL: Human Kinetics.
Faigenbaum, A.D., *et al.*, 2011. Effects of integrative neuromuscular training on fitness performance in children. *Pediatric Exercise Science*, 23 (4), 573–584.
Gogtay, N., *et al.*, 2004. Dynamic mapping of human cortical development during childhood through early adulthood. *Proceedings of the National Academy of Sciences of the United States of America*, 101 (21), 8174–8179.
Gould, D. and Carson, S., 2008. Life skills development through sport: Current status and future directions. *International Review of Sport and Exercise Psychology*, 1 (1), 58–78.
Gulbin, J.P., *et al.*, 2013. An integrated framework for the optimisation of sport and athlete development: A practitioner approach. *Journal of Sports Sciences*, 31 (12), 1319–1331.
Haff, G.G., 2019. Periodisation strategies for young athletes. *In*: R.S. Lloyd and J.L. Oliver, eds. *Strength and conditioning for young athletes: Science and application*. 2 edition. Oxon, England: Routledge, 281–299.
Haff, G.G. and Haff, E.E., 2012. Training integration and periodisation. *In*: J.R. Hoffman, ed. *NSCA's guide to program design*. Champaign, IL: Human Kinetics, 213–258.
Harrison, C.B., *et al.*, 2015. Development of aerobic fitness in young team sport athletes. *Sports Medicine*, 45 (7), 969–983.
Hirtz, P. and Starosta, W. 2002. Sensitive and critical periods of motor co-ordination development and its relation to motor learning. *Journal of Human Kinetics*, 7, 19–28.
Johnson, S.B., Blum, R.W., and Giedd, J.N., 2009. Adolescent maturity and the brain: The promise and pitfalls of neuroscience research in adolescent health policy. *Journal of Adolescent Health*, 45 (3), 216–221.
Keiner, M., *et al.*, 2014. Long-term strength training effects on change-of-direction sprint performance. *Journal of Strength and Conditioning Research*, 28 (1), 223–231.
Kemper, G.L., *et al.*, 2015. Anthropometric injury risk factors in elite-standard youth soccer. *International Journal of Sports Medicine*, 36 (13), 1112–1117.
LaPrade, R.F., *et al.*, 2016. AOSSM Early sport specialisation consensus statement. *Orthopaedic Journal of Sports Medicine*, 4 (4), 1–8.
Lesinski, M., Prieske, O., and Granacher, U., 2016. Effects and dose-response relationships of resistance training on physical performance in youth athletes: A systematic review and meta-analysis. *British Journal of Sports Medicine*, 50 (13), 781–795.
Lloyd, R.S. and Oliver, J.L., 2012. The youth physical development model: A new approach to long-term athletic development. *Strength and Conditioning Journal*, 34 (3), 61–72.
Lloyd, R.S. and Oliver, J.L., 2017. Speed and agility training. *In*: N. Armstrong and W. Van Mechelen, eds. *Oxford textbook of children's sport and exercise medicine*. 3rd edition. Oxford, UK: Oxford University Press, 507–518.
Lloyd, R.S., *et al.*, 2014. Position statement on youth resistance training: The 2014 International Consensus. *British Journal of Sports Medicine*, 48 (7), 498–505.
Lloyd, R.S., *et al.*, 2016a. National Strength and Conditioning Association position statement on long-term athletic development. *Journal of Strength and Conditioning Research*, 30 (6), 1491–1509.

Lloyd, R.S., *et al.*, 2016b. Changes in sprint and jump performances after traditional, plyometric, and combined resistance training in male youth pre- and post-peak height velocity. *Journal of Strength and Conditioning Research*, 30 (5), 1239–1247.

Lloyd, R.S., *et al.*, 2021. The effects of training frequency during a 6-month neuromuscular training intervention on movement competency and strength and power kinetics in male youth. *Sports Health*, 14 (1), 57–68.

Lubans, D.R., *et al.*, 2010. Fundamental movement skills in children and adolescents: Review of associated health benefits. *Sports Medicine*, 40 (12), 1019–1035.

Malina, R. (2014). Top 10 research questions related to growth and maturation of relevance to physical activity, performance, and fitness. *Research Quarterly for Exercise and Sport*, 85 (2), 157–173.

Malina, R.M., 2010. Early sport specialisation: Roots, effectiveness, risks. *Current Sports Medicine Reports*, 9 (6), 364–371.

Martin, A.D., *et al.*, 1997. Bone mineral and calcium accretion during puberty. *American Journal of Clinical Nutrition*, 66 (3), 611–615.

McKay, H.A., *et al.*, 1998. Peak bone mineral accrual and age at menarche in adolescent girls: A 6-year longitudinal study. *Journal of Pediatrics*, 133 (5), 682–687.

Merkel, D.L., 2013. Youth sport: Positive and negative impact on young athletes. *Open Access Journal of Sports Medicine*, 4, 151–160.

Meyers, R.W., *et al.*, 2015. Maximal sprint speed in boys of increasing maturity. *Pediatric Exercise Science*, 27, 85–94.

Meyers, R.W., *et al.*, 2016. The influence of maturation on sprint performance in boys over a 21-month period. *Medicine and Science in Sports and Exercise*, 48 (12), 2555–2562.

Micheli, L.J. and Fehlandt, A.F., Jr., 1992. Overuse injuries to tendons and apophyses in children and adolescents. *Clinics in Sports Medicine*, 11 (4), 713–726.

Moeskops, S., *et al.*, 2022a. Effects of a 10-month neuromuscular training program on strength, power, speed and vault performance in young female gymnasts. *Medicine and Science in Sports and Exercise*, 54 (5), 861–871.

Moeskops, S., *et al.*, 2022b. Practical strategies for integrating strength and conditioning into early specialisation sports. *Strength and Conditioning Journal*, 44 (1), 34–45.

Moran, J., *et al.*, 2017a. Variation in responses to sprint training in male youth athletes: A meta-analysis. *International Journal of Sports Medicine*, 38, 1–11.

Moran, J., *et al.*, 2017b. A meta-analysis of maturation-related variation in adolescent boy athletes' adaptations to short-term resistance training. *Journal of Sports Sciences*, 35 (11), 1041–1051.

Mostafavifar, A.M., Best, T.M., and Myer, G.D., 2013. Early sport specialisation, does it lead to long-term problems? *British Journal of Sports Medicine*, 47 (17), 1060–1061.

Myer, G.D., *et al.*, 2016. Sports specialisation, part II: Alternative solutions to early sport specialization in youth athletes. *Sports Health*, 8 (1), 65–73.

Peitz, M., Behringer, M., and Granacher, U., 2018. A systematic review on the effects of resistance and plyometric training on physical fitness in youth- What do comparative studies tell us? *PLoS One*, 13 (10), e0205525.

Pichardo, A.W., *et al.*, 2019. The influence of maturity offset, strength, and movement competency on motor skill performance in adolescent males. *Sports (Basel)*, 7 (7), 168–177.

Quatman-Yates, C.C., *et al.*, 2012. A systematic review of sensorimotor function during adolescence: A developmental stage of increased motor awkwardness? *British Journal of Sports Medicine*, 46 (9), 649–655.

Radnor, J.M., Lloyd, R.S., and Oliver, J.L., 2017. Individual response to different forms of resistance training in school-aged boys. *Journal of Strength and Conditioning Research*, 31 (3), 787–797.

Radnor, J.M., *et al.*, 2020a. Developing athletic motor skill competencies in youth. *Strength and Conditioning Journal*, 42 (6), 54–70.

Radnor, J.M., *et al.*, 2020b. The influence of maturity status on muscle architecture in school-aged boys. *Pediatric Exercise Science*, 32 (2), 89–96.

Radnor, J.M., *et al.*, 2021. Muscle architecture and maturation influence sprint and jump ability in young boys: A multistudy approach. *Journal of Strength and Conditioning Research*.

Read, P.J., Oliver, J.L., and Lloyd, R.S., 2020. Seven pillars of prevention: Effective strategies for strength and conditioning coaches to reduce injury risk and improve performance in young athletes. *Strength and Conditioning Journal*, 42 (6), 120–128.

Read, P.J., *et al.*, 2017. Hopping and landing performance in male youth soccer players: Effects of age and maturation. *International Journal of Sports Medicine*, 38 (12), 902–908.

Read, P.J., *et al.*, 2018. Altered landing mechanics are shown by male youth soccer players at different stages of maturation. *Physical Therapy in Sport*, 33, 48–53.
Reybrouck, T., *et al.*, 1985. Ventilatory anaerobic threshold in healthy children. Age and sex differences. *European Journal of Applied Physiology and Occupational Physiology*, 54 (3), 278–284.
Rumpf, M.C., *et al.*, 2012. Effect of different training methods on running sprint times in male youth. *Pediatric Exercise Science*, 24 (2), 170–186.
Slimani, M., Paravlic, A., and Granacher, U., 2018. A meta-analysis to determine strength training related dose-response relationships for lower-limb muscle power development in young atthletes. *Frontiers in Physiology*, 9, 1155.
Spear, L.P., 2013. Adolescent neurodevelopment. *Journal of Adolescent Health*, 52 (2 Suppl 2), 7–13.
Tenforde, A.S., *et al.*, 2011. Overuse injuries in high school runners: Lifetime prevalence and prevention strategies. *Physical Medicine and Rehabilitation*, 3 (2), 125–131.
Till, K. and Baker, J., 2020. Challenges and [possible] solutions to optimising talent identification and development in sport. *Frontiers in Psychology*, 11, 1–14.
Till, K., *et al.*, 2021. A coaching session framework to facilitate long-term athletic development. *Strength and Conditioning Journal*, 43 (3), 43–55.
Tomkinson, G.R., *et al.*, 2018. European normative values for physical fitness in children and adolescents aged 9-17 years: Results from 2 779 165 Eurofit performances representing 30 countries. *British Journal of Sports Medicine*, 52 (22), 1445–14563.
Viru, A., *et al.*, 1999. Critical periods in the development of performance capacity during childhood and adolescence. *European Journal of Physical Education*, 4, 75–119.
Wick, K., Kriemler, S., and Granacher, U., 2021. Effects of a strength-dominated exercise program on physical fitness and cognitive performance in preschool children. *Journal of Strength and Conditioning Research*, 35 (4), 983–990.
Wrigley, R.D., *et al.*, 2014. Long-term soccer-specific training enhances the rate of physical development of academy soccer players independent of maturation status. *International Journal of Sports Medicine*, 35 (13), 1090–1094.

# 12

# SPORT READINESS AND INJURY PREVENTION IN YOUNG ATHLETES: CURRENT RECOMMENDATIONS ON WHEN TO ENTER, COMPETE AND SPECIALISE IN SPORT

*Michelle Mullins, Emma Cronk, and Neeru Jayanthi*

## Introduction

Participation in organised sport can be a way for children to increase their physical activity and reap its many associated physical, social and cognitive benefits. Parents and coaches are integral in sport exposure/entry. A child's motor, cognitive and social development must be taken into consideration when determining when and at what level to participate in sport. Parents and coaches should seek to provide positive sport experiences with the goal of enjoyment and building a lifelong foundation for physical activity.

Once entered into sport, attention must be directed toward appropriate levels of competition and the associated training in preparation for competition. Kliethermes *et al.* (2019) demonstrated that young athletes and coaches have significant knowledge gaps regarding the risk of high-intensity training regimens. Even among athletes that are aware of these risks, notable barriers to compliance include perceived pressure from coaches and personal decision to disregard recommendations. In order to keep young athletes healthy, it is imperative that parents and coaches understand the current training guidelines and potential implications of exceeding these limits. This chapter will review the current recommendations for timing of sport entry, competition and specialisation, as well as the key injury prevention strategies to be aware of when working with young athletes.

## Review of Current Research

### *Early Childhood*

Early childhood encompasses ages three to five years old and according to the American Academy of Pediatrics, all preschool children are encouraged to participate routinely in a form

DOI: 10.4324/9781003199359-15

of physical activity appropriate for their developmental level (Committee on Sports Medicine and Fitness, 1992). A preschool child's readiness to participate in organised sport depends on a multitude of factors including the development of motor skills, interaction with coaches and teammates, and the ability to understand instructions (Committee on Sports Medicine and Fitness, 1992). Free play is also important for this age group that can support the development of these fundamental motor skills (Committee on Sports Medicine and Fitness, 1992). Children need daily opportunity for play daily (Logan *et al.*, 2019).

But what are these motor skills? How do we assess "readiness" in a young three-year-old? Preschoolers have limited attention spans and may not remember rules or understand the importance of maintaining their position. According to Purcell (2005), they learn best with egocentric activities (eg: hide and seek), and visual and auditory clues. Emphasis should be placed on developing skills, such as running, throwing, tumbling and catching. Activities should emphasize fun, playfulness, exploration and experimentation, and competition should be avoided. A typical exercise activity was demonstrated by Stodden and Brooks (2013) for this age group, which consists of approximately ten minutes of body awareness and movement creativity (squatting, bending, climbing), five minutes of object manipulation (picking up/putting down and throwing balls), five minutes of coordination (rhythm skills, hopping, jumping), five minutes of cooperation/rule following (Simon says), and 5–10 minutes of semi-structured free play. This sequence of events is coined "integrative neuromuscular training", which has been shown to be successful with young children, even with short-term exposure (Stodden and Brooks, 2013).

Balance and fundamental skills remain limited in this age range, leading to the recommendation for more basic sports/activities such as running, swimming and tumbling. A trial of informal participation in sport with family or friends can be a helpful test of a child's readiness prior to enrollment in organised sport. Coaches and parents should remain cognizant of anticipated developmental timelines of young athletes and avoid placing unrealistic expectations during their sport of play, i.e.: pressure to perform, emphasis on winning, holding longer and more intense practices, etc. Unrealistic expectations may lead to a loss of self-esteem and withdraw from sport. Despite entry into an organised sport, free play remains vital at this age, allowing children to play for fun, not only to develop the essential motor skills necessary for life's physical tasks but to strengthen these skills for future organised play.

## *Pre-adolescent*

Pre-adolescent ages range from 6 to 12 years old, and there is a notable transition from emphasizing fundamental movement skills to fundamental sport skills. This leads into the readiness aspect of this age group in terms of organised sports, which is based on the child's eagerness and enjoyment of the activity, and this typically is not seen before the age of six (Committee on Sports Medicine and Fitness, 1992). Furthermore, other factors to consider are motor skill acquisition as previously discussed, ability to combine skill sets, and the length of their attention span (Logan *et al.*, 2019). For ages six to nine years old, attention span is still relatively short, meaning instruction times should be shorter, loose rules, and not focusing solely on competition, and sport of play usually include soccer, baseball, swimming, running, gymnastics, and dance (Purcell, 2005). The 10 to 12 age group tends to start mastering more complex motor skills, i.e.: a layup in basketball, along with strengthening memory skills and having selective attention. Furthermore, skill development is observed with more emphasis on tactics and strategy, and sport of play usually include entry-level football, basketball and ice hockey (Purcell, 2005). Importantly free play is still relevant in this age group, and according to the

American Academy of Pediatrics, promoting sport-specific motor development for the sole purpose of ensuring sport ability at a later age should be discouraged (Committee on Sports Medicine and Fitness, 1992).

Whilst rules have evolved in sport to ensure player safety dependent on age, unfortunately the training loads and training patterns have not, which increases the risk for overuse injury among young athletes (LaBella and Myer, 2017). With players wanting to play for fun and slowly increasing the competition as age increases, coaches and parents blur the line between friendly competition versus high-level adult programming, leading to long-term injury risk (Stodden and Brooks, 2013). The adult programming in youth athletes stems from lack of literature in this area, with no clear definition on how youth-centric programming should be different from an adult-centric one (Stodden and Brooks, 2013). Failing to recognise the biological, psychological, and emotional factors of youth development often leads to practices and competition that are not appropriate for the player's developmental level, and neglect specific movement indications and contraindications (Stodden and Brooks, 2013). To help limit this discrepancy in programming it is essential to have qualified coaching staff to ensure proper technique and understand where the child is developmentally.

## *Early Adolescent*

As children enter adolescence, participation in competitive organised sport often becomes the focus. By the age of 12, most children have the capability to master complex motor skills and are prepared both physically and mentally for participation in competitive organised sports (Brown *et al.*, 2017). By this stage, children can begin entry-level competition in complex skill-based sports including volleyball, football, hockey and basketball. Children should be encouraged to continue sampling a variety of sports. Depending on their skill level and preference, they may become interested in specialisation in a single sport. As detailed later in this text, there is significant risk to early single-sport specialisation, particularly overuse injury and burnout in young athletes. All athletes, parents and coaches should maintain an understanding of their underlying motivation for sport competition. Too often, this motivation is skewed towards goals external to sport, such as a desire to obtain a college scholarship or become a professional athlete. Ultimately, depending on the sport, only 0.2%–0.5% of high school athletes ever make it to the professional level (Brenner *et al.*, 2007). Despite an introduction of competitive sport among this age group the focus should remain on setting the foundation for lifelong participation in physical activity and developing skills of healthy competition that can be used in all facets of future endeavors.

The early adolescent period is marked with unique challenges in terms of injury prevention. With increased competitive participation, athletes often face an increase in training demand that overlaps with a period of rapid growth and maturation. The onset of puberty is variable among individuals and can have profound effects on injury risk and sport performance. This growth spurt is associated with a temporary decrease in coordination and balance, and a loss of flexibility (Purcell, 2005). The maximal rate of growth during the adolescent growth spurt, termed the Peak Height Velocity (PHV) is a particularly vulnerable time for young athletes. Variable bone density and increased joint stiffness during this period are linked with temporary "skeletal fragility" and elevated acute fracture risk. Studies have demonstrated an increase in acute traumatic injury during PHV, with an increased susceptibility to overuse injury for one year following this period (van der Sluis *et al.*, 2014). The bone growth plate is often a weak link in the kinetic chain during periods of rapid growth. Long bones (such as the humerus of the upper arm and the tibia of the lower leg) tend to grow faster than their associated muscle tendons, leading to relative inflexibility. In addition, rapid changes in the composition of the growth plate lead to decreased strength with compressive force and traction (Jayanthi *et al.*, 2015). These changes are a setup for overuse or avulsion injuries involving the growth plate.

While the growth spurt typically classically begins at age 9–10 years for girls and 11–12 years for boys, this can be quite variable (Monasterio *et al.*, 2021). One marker to estimate where athletes fall among the course of their growth spurt is the percentage of predicated adult height (PPAH). An athlete's current height is compared as a percentage to their overall predicted adult height using the formula below.

Males [father's height (cm) + mother's height (cm) + 13 cm]/2

Females [father's height (cm) + mother's height (cm) − 13 cm]/2

PPAH values less than 85% signify the phase prior to peak growth, and represent a moderate risk time period in terms of sport-related injury. Percentages from 85% to 96% signify the period of peak height velocity and the highest risk zone for sport-related injury. Percentages greater than 96% signify the deceleration phase of adolescent growth and are considered a relatively low-risk period. In light of these risks, training schedules must consider that teammates of the same age may be at drastically different stages of growth and development. The aim should be to routinely monitor growth, identify the adolescent growth spurt and individualise training and competition workloads as needed in an effort to avoid injury. Note that the utility of this equation is limited if one or both of the parental heights is unknown. Alternative methods, such as the Khamis-Roche method are available for more accurate PPAH calculation. This formula also considers a child's age, height, mass, mid-height of biologic parents, and growth rate. Calculators are readily available online, with the details of this equation beyond the scope of this chapter.

Overuse injuries are the most frequently reported pediatric sports injury, and have been associated with certain high-risk training behaviors. Overuse injuries occur secondary to repetitive loading of the musculoskeletal system with inadequate rest/recovery periods for adaptation. Young athletes who train in an organised sport for more hours per week than their age (example 12 hours of training weekly for a 9-year-old athlete) are more likely to experience serious overuse injury (Jayanthi *et al.*, 2015). Despite the introduction of competitive play, free play remains important in this age group. An overemphasis on organised sport, with an organised sport to free play ratio> 2:1 has been associated with up to 50% increased likelihood of sport-related injury (Kliethermes *et al.*, 2019). This study also found that high training volumes in excess of 16 hours per week were associated with an increased incidence of sport-related injury requiring medical care. Additional training recommendations for this age include adherence to limits on sport-specific repetitive movements (such as pitch counts) and rest periods, including at least one day off per week, and 2–3 months off from single sport activity annually (DiFiori *et al.*, 2014).

Building and maintaining an appropriate training load has implications on training tolerance, performance and injury. The three components that must be considered to safely progress an athlete to optimal performance include the "floor", "ceiling" and time (Gabbett, 2020). The "floor" represents the athlete's current capacity, the "ceiling" represents the potential capacity to perform without injury. A challenge in most sporting environments is the time required to progress from the floor to the ceiling. If athletes' training loads are progressed too rapidly, producing spikes in the acute training load, young athletes will be at increased risk for injury and underperformance. Chronic training load is calculated by averaging the weekly training time, number of repetitions, or total distance over a four-week period. When the acute:chronic workload ratio is ≥1.5 (meaning the workload in the current week was 1.5 times greater than the four-week average training load), the risk of injury has been demonstrated to be 2–4 times greater over the subsequent seven days (Hulin *et al.*, 2014). Parents, athletes and coaches must understand the importance of gradual load progression, particularly in high-risk times such as the start of the season or return from injury/illness.

The importance of neuromuscular training, via pre-season and pre-practice workouts has also gained attention as a means for injury prevention in this age group. It is currently recommended that neuromuscular training begins in the pre-adolescent period, with a focus on building fundamental motor skills rather than enhancing sport performance (Myer *et al.*, 2011). This is of particular importance in young female athletes, who carry a 4–6 times higher risk of ACL injury than their male counterparts participating in similar activity, presumably because of anatomical, hormonal, and neuromuscular differences (Yoo *et al.*, 2010). Given the significant time-loss and rehabilitation required, in addition to a 10 times higher risk of future knee osteoarthritis than uninjured counterparts, ACL injury prevention is of particular importance. A 2018 meta-analysis of ACL prevention programs found that combination of pre-and in-season training was most advantageous and that programs which incorporate plyometric, strength, and balance exercises are effective in decreasing the ACL injury risk and improving athletic performance (Yoo *et al.*, 2010). The FIFA 11+ program is a publicly available program which incorporates these components and has demonstrated significant reductions in ACL injury risk among young athletes (Owoeye *et al.*, 2014).

## *Late Adolescent*

Athletes who have the ability to continue in competitive sport through the late adolescent phase must make the decision whether or not to make this a priority in their lives. Amplified training schedules, internal pressures to perform and outside pressures from parents and coaches can lead to burnout and withdrawal from sport. Unfortunately, by the age of 15, 75% of youth no longer participate in organised sports (Purcell, 2005). Attrition can be caused by a variety of factors including time conflicts and interest in other activities. However, early specialisation in sport has been associated not only with increased risk of injury but also with burnout and withdrawal from sport.

Sport specialisation is the idea of ceasing all other sport participation to focus on a single sport, often year-round. This has been reported in up to 30% of young athletes (Jayanthi *et al.*, 2015). The decision to specialise in a single sport should be individualised, with consideration of an athlete's talents, interests and motivations. With the exception of sports which involve peak performance prior to maturation (figure skating, gymnastics, diving), early specialisation has no clear benefit and research has demonstrated that young athletes who play a variety of sports have lower injury rates and participate in sport longer than those that specialise prior to puberty (Brenner *et al.*, 2007). In addition, diversified training during early adolescence may lead to the development of elite-level skills in the primary sport due to transfer of skills between sports. Therefore, late adolescence is generally considered the earliest that young athletes should specialise in a single sport.

Sport specialisation is associated with an increased risk of overuse injury and serious overuse injury in young athletes, regardless of age and training volume (Jayanthi *et al.*, 2015). Given the limited range of motor patterns among single sport athletes, these individuals may be more likely to develop muscle imbalances and overuse injuries through repetitive loading. Careful attention must be paid to the training load of young athletes, particularly among those that choose to specialise. The American Academy of Pediatrics currently recommends at least one day off from sport-specific training, competition or organised practice weekly, as well as 2–3 months off from single sport activity annually in order to promote physical and mental recovery (Brenner *et al.*, 2007).

Burnout, or overtraining syndrome, is a condition of physical and emotional exhaustion characterised by symptoms including chronic joint/muscle pain, fatigue, elevated heart rate, personality changes, lack of motivation for sport and decreased sport performance (Logan *et al.*, 2019). Overtraining syndrome is a maladaptive response to excessive exercise in the setting of inadequate recovery. The pathophysiology is theorised to involve a combination of hormonal changes, immune system suppression, psychological stressors and physical fatigue. Risk factors include increased training load, monotony of training, excessive competitions, sleep disturbance and life stressors. Prevention strategies include tapering training for competitions, variability/cross-training, and ensuring adequate sleep, hydration and nutrition (Kreher and Schwartz, 2012).

Overtraining syndrome is estimated to occur in 1%–9% of adolescent athletes (Logan *et al.*, 2019). Parents and coaches should be aware of the warning signs of overtraining syndrome, and should consider this condition in athletes that demonstrate declining performance despite continued or increased training. A brief period of rest from sport is recommended, typically lasting 4–12 weeks. Return to sport should be considered once all symptoms of overtraining syndrome have resolved.

## Implications for Children's Sport Coaching

A child's motor, cognitive and social development must be taken into consideration when determining when and at what level to participate in sport. Once enrolled in sport, coaches should maintain realistic expectations for performance based on anticipated motor developmental milestones. When creating training/competition plans, coaches should take into account that teammates of the same age may be at drastically different stages of growth and development. Therefore, coaches should consider age-appropriate workload recommendations and injury risk factors unique to each athlete, such as biologic maturity, training history and injury history. Table 12.1 summarises current sport readiness and injury prevention guidelines, as outlined in this chapter.

## Summary and Future Directions

Youth sports participation can be an enjoyable way to increase physical activity and improve the likelihood of sport and fitness involvement into adulthood. Children should be encouraged to sample a variety of sports, paying attention to the child's interests and developmental ability. Readiness for entry into sport is a factor of the tasks/demands of the sport relative to the child's gross motor and object control skills. Premature entry into a sport above the developmental ability of a child can lead to frustration and dropout.

Early childhood (ages 3–5 years) should emphasise play and fundamental movement skills. Middle and late childhood (ages 6–12) should focus on fundamental sport skills. With this foundation, competition should not be the focus of sport participation until early adolescence (ages 13–15). Single sport specialisation should be delayed until after puberty given the increased risk of injury, serious overuse injury and burnout.

Additional evidenced-based training recommendations across these age groups include incorporation of neuromuscular training programs pre-season and pre-practice, limiting organised

Table 12.1 Sport readiness and injury prevention guidelines

| | *Early childhood (3–5 years)* | *Pre-adolescent (6–12 years)* | *early adolescence (pre-PHV)* | *Late adolescence (post-PHV)* |
|---|---|---|---|---|
| **ATHLETE DEVELOPMENT AND SPORT SPECIALISATION** | Entry into basic organised sport once fundamental motor skills and attention span allow<br>Examples- running, swimming, tumbling | Entry into more advanced movement pattern sports<br>Examples-tennis, skiing, baseball, martial arts | Begin complex skill-based sports competition once physically and mentally appropriate<br>Examples-Volleyball, football, hockey, basketball | Delay single sport specialisation until this period |
| **NEUROMUSCULAR DEVELOPMENT** | Integrate short sessions focused on body awareness, coordination, object manipulation, and cooperation/rule following<br>Examples- climbing, hopping, throwing balls, hopping, Simon Says | Encourage broad motor development, avoiding focus on sport-specific motor skills | Integrate pre-season and pre-practice neuromuscular training programs to reduce injury risk<br>Example- FIFA 11+ | |
| **WORKLOAD AND TRAINING CONSIDERATIONS** | Focus on free play | Emphasize fun and skill development, not competition and winning | Monitor and account for peak adolescent growth and associated injury risks<br><85% PPAH: moderate risk<br>85-96% PPAH: high risk<br>>96% PPAH: low risk | |
| | Limit organised sport participation to less hours per week than the athletes age<br>Do not exceed an acute: chronic workload ratio of 1.5<br>Maintain an organised sport: free play ratio less than 2:1<br>At least one day per week and 2-3 months off per year from training/competition | | | |

sports participation to fewer hours per week than age (i.e. if 12 years old, <12 hours/week), an organised sport:free play ratio less than 2:1, maintaining an acute:chronic workload ratio less than 1.5, having at least one day off per week from training/competition, and having at least 2–3 months of rest from competition/training per year.

Given the variable training demands and injury patterns across sport, further research is needed to clarify sport-specific training load recommendations and injury prevention strategies. In addition, early detection of overtraining syndrome via quantitative markers, such as biochemical or psychomotor abnormality has been proposed, though more research is needed in this area.

## References

Brenner, J. and the Council on Sports Medicine and Fitness, 2007. Overuse Injuries, overtraining, and burnout in child and adolescent athletes. *Pediatrics*, 119 (6), 1242–1245.

Brown, K.A., Patel, D.R., and Darmawan, D., 2017. Participation in sports in relation to adolescent growth and development. *Translational Pediatrics*, 6 (3), 150–159.

Committee on Sports Medicine and Fitness, 1992. Fitness, activity, and sports participation in the preschool child. *Pediatrics*, 90 (6), 1002–1004.

DiFiori, J.P., *et al.*, 2014. Overuse injuries and burnout in youth sports: A position statement from the American Medical Society for sports medicine. *British Journal of Sports Medicine*, 48 (4), 287–288.

Gabbett, T.J., 2020. How much? How fast? How soon? Three simple concepts for progressing training loads to minimise injury risk and enhance performance. *Journal of Orthopaedics and Sports Physical Therapy*, 50 (10), 570–573.

Hulin, B.T., *et al.*, 2014. Spikes in acute workload are associated with increased injury risk in elite cricket fast bowlers. *British Journal of Sports Medicine*, 48, 708–712.

Jayanthi, N.A., *et al.*, 2015. Sports-specialised intensive training and the risk of injury in young athletes: A clinical case-control study. *American Journal of Sports Medicine*, 43 (4), 794–801.

Kliethermes, S.A., *et al.*, 2019. Benefits and challenges of serial sports training risk assessment and counselling in kids: The T.R.A.C.K. randomised intervention study. *British Journal of Sports Medicine*, 53, 243–249.

Kreher, J.B. and Schwartz, J.B., 2012. Overtraining syndrome: A practical guide. *Sports Health*, 4 (2), 128–138.

LaBella, C.R. and Myer, G.D., 2017. Youth sports injury prevention: Keep calm and play on. *British Journal of Sports Medicine*, 51 (3), 145–146.

Logan, K., *et al.*, 2019. Organised sports for children, preadolescents, and adolescents. *Pediatrics*, 143 (6), 1–20.

Monasterio, X., *et al.*, 2021. Injuries according to the percentage of adult height in an elite soccer academy. *Journal of Science and Medicine in Sport*, 24 (3), 218–223.

Myer, G.D., *et al.*, 2011. When to initiate integrative neuromuscular training to reduce sports-related injuries and enhance health in youth?. *Current Sports Medicine Reports*, 10 (3), 155–166.

Owoeye, O.B., *et al.*, 2014. Efficacy of the FIFA 11+ warm-up programme in male youth football: a cluster randomised controlled trial. *Journal of Sports Science and Medicine*, 13 (2), 321–328.

Purcell, L., 2005. Sport readiness in children and youth. *Paediatrics and Child Health*, 10 (6), 343–344.

Stodden, D. and Brooks, T., 2013. Promoting musculoskeletal fitness in youth, performance and health implications from a developmental perspective. *Strength and Conditioning Journal*, 35 (3), 54–62.

van der Sluis, A., *et al.*, 2014. Sport injuries aligned to peak height velocity in talented pubertal soccer players. *International Journal of Sports Medicine*, 35 (4), 351–355.

Yoo, J.H., *et al.*, 2010. A meta-analysis of the effect of neuromuscular training on the prevention of the anterior cruciate ligament injury in female athletes. *Knee surgery, Sports Traumatology, Arthroscopy*, 18 (6), 824–830.

# 13

# NUTRITION CONSIDERATIONS FOR CHILDREN IN SPORT

*Jennifer Hamer*

## Introduction

Children in sport frequently have higher-than-average energy expenditures (EE), therefore may require increased nutrient and energy intakes (EI) to support sporting performance as well as growth and development. Furthermore, these early years of life are foundational for the development of healthy relationships with their body image, the food they eat and the physical activity they are involved in.

The quantity and type of food and fluids consumed impact a child athlete's ability to train, compete, grow and recover. Some of the specific nutritional challenges they may encounter include the difficulty in balancing EI with EE and ensuring appropriate amounts of macro and micronutrients are consumed to provide the foundations for lifelong health. This is especially important for those on restricted diets (e.g. vegan, and vegetarian diets). Lastly, the challenge exists of supporting the development of a healthy relationship with food and body image, without the promotion of disordered eating behaviours. Having an optimal diet during childhood will help to foster an enjoyable, health-promoting and rewarding lifelong experience with athletic participation.

This chapter aims to provide coaches and those working with children guidance on how nutrition is incorporated into a child's sporting pursuits and support them to become advocates for positive nutrition messaging and sound dietary advice. Topics to be addressed in this text include nutritional issues young athletes may encounter including the challenges of balancing EI and EE. Macronutrient requirements are discussed (including carbohydrate, protein and fats), as well as addressing some micronutrients that require increased attention in developing athletes. This chapter also addresses how the coach can support a child athlete in meeting their nutritional needs. In this text, 'children' refers to those aged between 5 and 12 years.

## Review of Current Research

### *Nutritional Issues for Young Athletes*

#### *Energy Requirements*

Children require an adequate EI to support growth and development, as well as providing energy to sustain physical activity/athletic performance (Hannon *et al.*, 2020). A challenge exists in

DOI: 10.4324/9781003199359-16

attempting to define specific energy needs of children in sport due to metabolic variability between individuals and difficulties in accurately measuring EI and EE (Burke *et al.*, 2001). The recognition that children can become involved in spontaneous episodes of physical activity (e.g. social play/ games and sport) and/or inactivity (e.g. computer games, social media) provides further example to how the determination of energy needs for this population group is difficult to forecast due to their volatile nature of EE (Howe *et al.*, 2010; Mindell *et al.*, 2014).

Furthermore, organised children's sports typically target participation, foundational skill development and enjoyment as critical elements. These modified versions of traditional sports for children are likely to involve changes to the duration and equipment/facilities (e.g. field size) used, which will possibly reduce the energy demands of sport compared to when played under traditional formats. Needless to say, EE in children can vary due to a number of potential factors and the challenges of accurately measuring EI and EE make it difficult to predict energy requirements (Petrie *et al.*, 2004; Torun, 2005; Mindell *et al.*, 2014).

Despite these challenges, the recommended minimum energy requirements to support growth and development for children (across both genders) aged 4–6 are 1,800 kcal/day and 2,000 kcal/day for children aged 7–10 years. Between the ages of 11 and 14 energy requirements differ between genders, with boys requiring more than girls to compensate for their larger frames and bigger muscle mass as they approach puberty. Recommendations suggest an intake of 2,500 kcal/day for boys and 2,200 kcal/day for girls (Hoch *et al.*, 2008). EI requirements are likely to be higher for those involved in frequent sports participation, yet currently no specific recommendations for this population group have been identified (Torun, 2005; Hannon *et al.*, 2020).

For some children, excessive EI exceeding EE increases their risk of unnecessary weight gain, metabolic disease (e.g. type 2 diabetes), hyperlipidaemia and an increased risk if injury (L'allemand-Jander, 2010). Weight loss may be necessary for the overweight child to optimise their health, however prolonged energy restriction is not advised during childhood due to the negative consequences this may have on their growth and development as well as their psychological health (Petrie *et al.*, 2004; Hill *et al.*, 2020). A significant focus on weight loss predisposes a child at to a greater risk of developing poor relationships with food, increased in body image disturbances, disordered eating and/or eating disorders (Hill *et al.*, 2020). In these situations, it is important a registered dietician is monitoring the child's weight, encouraging a healthy nutritional intake, which emphasises increasing EE. The coach should avoid direct references to weight/body shape and instead emphasise training tasks/activities, which focus on skill development and performance.

In contrast, a small proportion of children may fail to meet the basic requirements of an adequate EI to match their EE and subsequently fall into an energy deficit. This is more likely to occur in the child who has specialised too early in sport, or those competitively involved in sports where the prevalence of this situation is more likely (e.g. gymnastics, endurance sports and dancing – Hutson *et al.*, 2020; Keay *et al.*, 2020; Meng *et al.*, 2020). Children who fail to meet their energy needs may enter a state of low energy availability (LEA). LEA occurs when there is inadequate energy available to support all physiological functions for sustaining optimal health (Mountjoy *et al.*, 2014). While this is considered rare in children, prolonged periods of LEA can have numerous health consequences including; risks to bone health, loss of muscle mass, increased susceptibility to fatigue, injury and illness (Meyer *et al.*, 2007). Thus, it is important for children to establish healthy eating patterns early, relative to their EE. This is especially important to monitor as they approach adolescence when EI requirements may increase as energy demands from both training and growth/ development are likely to rise substantially (Desbrow *et al.*, 2014).

As children approach adolescence, they are also likely to become increasingly aware of their body shape due to the normal changes that occur in response to puberty. Unfortunately, young children (e.g. 7-year-olds) have been identified to show signs of preoccupation over their body (Rodgers *et al.*, 2019). While no individual is immune, children involved in sports with an emphasis on leanness or aesthetics (e.g. gymnastics, ballet, athletics) appear at a greater risk of developing body image issues and disordered eating behaviours (Monthuy-Blanc *et al.*, 2012). Children approaching adolescence may engage in maladaptive dietary and training behaviours in attempt to control their body weight/shape, increasing the risk of LEA and eating disorders (Bonci *et al.*, 2008). A further chapter in this book provides greater insight into the issue of disordered eating among children in sport.

## *Macronutrients*

### *Carbohydrates Recommendations*

Children in sport require adequate amounts of carbohydrate (CHO) to fuel daily exercise and support basic health requirements (Burke *et al.*, 2001). CHO are the body's predominant fuel source used for exercise and brain function, therefore considered a cornerstone of an athlete's diet. Extensive literature supports the consumption of CHO prior, during and in acute recovery from high-intensity training and endurance-based sports for adult athletes (Burke *et al.*, 2011). Furthermore, replenishing glycogen stores (stored CHO) as soon as practical after exercise helps to initiate the refuelling and recovery process (Desbrow *et al.*, 2014).

Despite the lack of conclusive guidelines for the child athlete, it is generally accepted that children in sport have higher CHO needs than the recommended dietary reference intake of 100 g of CHO per day (Petrie *et al.*, 2004). It is likely that modifications to sports for children (e.g. reduced durations, changes to equipment and/or pitch size) may influence energy demands. Therefore, dietary CHO needs should be considered in light of training loads, intensity, duration and nutrition status, acknowledging requirements can differ somewhat from adults in several ways (Hannon *et al.*, 2020). That is, children frequently partake in numerous different sporting activities, as well as spontaneous bouts of physical activity (e.g. playground games, informal daily physical activity), which will also likely influence their energy demands and subsequent CHO requirements.

Owing to the challenges of accurately measuring EE it is currently difficult to recommend specific CHO requirements for children in sport. However, the general consensus suggests that a daily CHO intake between 6 and 10 $g{\cdot}kg^{-1}$ for young athletes will cover energy needs of most children. This may vary depending on sporting commitments (Hannon *et al.*, 2020). If CHO intake is to be guided based on reference from adult guidelines, young athletes training between 1 and 2 hours a day may require intakes between 5 and 7 g of CHO per kg of body weight and children training more than 2 hours per day may require 7–10 g/kg of body weight (Burke *et al.*, 2001). Intake should be comprised predominantly of nutrient dense CHO (e.g. whole grains, vegetables, low-fat dairy) while limiting free sugars (e.g. found in sweets, cakes, fizzy drinks, honey) to less than 10% of daily EI. Immediately before, during or after exercise simple CHO (fruits, honey, white bread, milk) may be appropriate for consumption due to their rapid absorption rates (Burke *et al.*, 2007; Meyer *et al.*, 2007). However, given the nature of organised sport for children, performance is unlikely to be limited by metabolic/substrate availability. Therefore, coaches may need to temper/adapt their messaging on CHO delivery when based off adult athlete recommendations, who may be involved in more frequent bouts of intense exercise/training for sports participation. There may be a small proportion of children who require further support in ensuring they meet CHO requirements if they are involved in frequent competitive environments, yet in these instances a sports dietician can be called upon for further guidance.

## *Protein*

A regular spread of moderate amounts of protein consumed across the day at frequent intervals is especially important in the recovery period after exercise to support lean tissue growth and repair, as well as promoting optimal growth and development (Phillips and Van Loon, 2011; Aerenhouts *et al.*, 2011). R Specific guidelines relating to protein intake for young athletes is limited; therefore population requirements are used as an initial figure to assess the possibility of inadequate consumption. Children aged 7–12 are likely to accommodate their protein requirements adhering to the following the relative recommendations.

A protein intake of 1.2–1.4 g/kg of body weight, or an intake that falls between 10% and 30% of the daily calorie intake has been suggested for the highly active child (regularly taking part in organised sport). (Meyers *et al.*, 2006). Most children living in developed countries meet or exceed their protein requirements through consuming protein at regular meal intervals (Petrie *et al.*, 2004; Heaney *et al.*, 2010). This includes the conusmption of either protein with a high biological value (e.g. presence of all essential amino acids) from animal origin (e.g. lean meat, chicken, fish, eggs and dairy). Or plant-based protein sources, such as beans, lentils, nuts and grains. However, these plant-based proteins are often deficient in one or more of the essential amino acids, and require the combining of sources to ensure the provision of all the essential amino acids is achieved (Purcell *et al.*, 2013). Children adhering to restrictive diets (e.g. vegetarian and vegan diets) may be at greater risk of not achieving adequate protein intakes. If there is concern, a registered dietician can help to ensure intake is appropriate to support optimal growth, development and sporting performance (Desbrow *et al.*, 2014). Children's protein intake should come from food sources and protein supplements are not recommended unless a registered health care practitioner or dietician has stated otherwise.

## *Fats*

Adequate fat intake is essential to provide an appropriate supply of fat-soluble vitamins and essential fatty acids promoting optimal health, as well as providing energy to support the growth and development in the child athlete (Petrie *et al.*, 2004). However, excessive intakes of fats are associated with health-related diseases. Accordingly, a child athlete's consumption should be consistent with the public health guidelines.

Fats should comprise of 25%–35% of nutritional intake and predominantly be consumed in the form of unsaturated fats, with saturated fats making up no more than 10% of total daily EI. Fat intakes >40% increase the risk of unnecessary weight gain and/or can displace other nutrients (e.g. carbohydrate and protein), resulting in a failure to meet the requirements for these nutrients. Unsaturated fats to encourage in the child's diet include oily fish (e.g. salmon, mackerel, sardines), nuts, seeds, lean meats and poultry and olive oil. Saturated fats from, fried foods, sweets, and cakes should be limited. For those children who have significantly high EE and find it challenging to meet energy requirements, increasing unsaturated fat content of their diet can help to address a suboptimal EI (Meyer *et al.*, 2007; Desbrow *et al.*, 2014).

In recent years there has been increased research to explore the role of intramuscular triacylglycerols on exercise performance and the effect of training with high fat and/or low carbohydrate availability in adult athletes (Burke, 2010). These strategies have not been studied in children and therefore should be avoided until further evidence exists to prevent unnecessary risks to a child's growth and development.

## Calcium and Vitamin D

Calcium and vitamin D are key nutrients supporting a child's growth and development. Failing to obtain adequate amounts of these nutrients during developmental years increases a child's risk of failing to meet peak bone mass and is more susceptible to developing low bone mineral density (Abrams, 2011). Calcium requirements for the child athlete are no different from non-active children, however requirements are greater than adults due to significant growth and development and bone remodelling during these early years.

The recommended daily intake of calcium appears to differ across different regions, yet the World Health Organisation advises an intake of 1300 mg for children aged 7–14 (Cormick and Belizán, 2019). Food sources highest in calcium include dairy milk, yogurt, cheese, sardines and fortified products. Concerningly, suboptimal calcium intakes in young athletes have been reported (Martínez *et al.*, 2011). It is thought that the growing interest in plant-based diets and the increasing availability and popularity of plant/seed-based milk and yogurts over dairy products may be influencing these inadequate intakes identified in children. With robust evidence that an increase in bone mineral capacity occurs when the diet is supplemented with dairy products, highest in calcium (De Lamas *et al.*, 2019), it is important children do not exclude dairy foods unless a valid reason exists (e.g. medical or ethical reasons). Ensuring calcium intake is monitored regularly is particularly important, especially for children on vegan diets, or those who omit dairy from their diet. In these instances, supplementation may be required under the guidance of a health care practitioner or registered dietician (Larsson and Johansson, 2002).

In addition to calcium, vitamin D is an important nutrient for bone health due to its involvement in the absorption and regulation of calcium. Vitamin D also contributes to the maintenance of a healthy immune system and skeletal muscle function (Hossein-Nezhad and Arashholick, 2013). Deficiencies are associated with poor bone health, inflammation and muscle pain and increase the risk of injury (Huh and Gordon, 2008). While vitamin D can be obtained from food, the majority is obtained from exposure to sunlight. Young athletes are at high risk of a deficiency if they receive little exposure to daily sunlight, they are living in northern latitudes (e.g. North America, and Northern Europe) or they have dark skin (Huotari and Herzig, 2008; Lips, 2010). Despite recommended intakes varying between regions, ranging between 5 and 20 μg for children (Spiro and Buttriss, 2014), there appears to be a consensus to encourage a daily intake of 15 μg for 4–18 years olds (Farrokhyar *et al.*, 2015). Those at risk of deficiency are advised to get their vitamin D levels checked at regular intervals throughout the year and be guided by their healthcare practitioner as to whether they need to supplement.

Due to the health detriments associated with vitamin D insufficiency, considerable scientific attention has been placed on assessing vitamin D status in adult athletes (Farrokhyar *et al.*, 2015). While there is a lack of scientific attention in this area on children in sport, recent prospective studies, suggest little correlation between serum levels of 25(OH)D and sports performance in adolescent athletes (Bezuglov *et al.*, 2019). Future research should seek to explore this relationship in children involved in sport.

## Iron

Young athletes are at an increased risk of depleted iron stores, particularly those athletes involved in endurance-based sports (Shoemaker *et al.*, 2020). Early detection and intervention for

*Table 13.1* Australian and New Zealand reference values for iron intake

| | *Age range (years)* | *EAR (mg/day)* | *RDI/RDA (mg/day)* |
|---|---|---|---|
| Children (both sexes) | 4–8 | 4 | 10 |
| Boys | 9–13 | 6 | 8 |
| | 14–18 | 8 | 11 |
| Girls | 9–13 | 6 | 8 |
| | 14–18 | 8 | 15 |

*Source:* National Health and Medical Research Council & New Zealand Ministry of Health, 2014.
*Note:* EAR – estimated energy requirements, RDI – recommended daily intake, RDA – recommended daily allowance.

young athletes with low iron stores is warranted, as the significant growth occurring during these years increases iron requirements. Early intervention (e.g. supplementation) in those identified to have low iron stores is essential to prevent iron deficiency, which can have long-term detrimental effects on health and sporting performance (Rodenberg and Gustafson, 2007).

The recommended nutrient reference values for iron in children are referenced in Table 13.1. For children aged 4–8 years an RDI of 10 mg/day is recommended and between the ages of 9 and 13 an RDI of 8 mg/day. However, it is important that individual recommendations are adjusted when individual differences are known to exist (especially in young female athletes who begin menarche earlier). Good sources of iron to encourage in the athlete diet include lean red meats, chicken, eggs, fish, and fortified products such as breakfast cereals. It is possible that vegetarian athletes may have increased requirements due to the reduced bioavailability of non-haem iron sources (Craig, 1994). While serum ferritin concentrations are consistently observed to be significantly lower in vegetarians, it is achievable to meet iron requirements that fall within the acceptable reference ranges provided a well-balanced vegetarian diet ensuring good sources of iron are frequently included (Pawlak and Bell, 2017). That said, it remains important to ensure vegan/ vegetarian children involved in sport have their iron status routinely monitored. Use of iron supplements should only be considered if medically warranted and must be guided by a qualified health care professional (e.g. medical practitioner and/or sports physician).

## Fluid Recommendations

Athletic performance can be affected by the type, amount and timing of fluid intake. Ensuring adequate fluids are taken on during physical activity helps to regulate body temperature and replace sweat losses during exercise (Rowland, 2011). Young individuals appear to have a similar capacity to adults managing thermal loads and exercise tolerance time in the heat. However, the mechanisms by which they dissipate heat loads can differ compared to adults. Children appear to demonstrate a greater reliance on peripheral blood redistribution (radiative and conductive cooling) rather than sweating (evaporative cooling) to maintain thermal equilibrium (Rowland *et al.*, 2008). Providing children are given adequate opportunities to take on fluids during before, during and after exercising, for most their intake driven by thirst should prevent dehydration (Rowland, 2011). However, some children may not respond to this drive for thirst unless reminded and subsequently may adopt poor fluid intake behaviours. Therefore, the coach and parents/ guardian must ensure to remind children in sport to consume adequate amounts of fluid before, during and after exercise, and should provide regular prompts of encouragement.

A challenge exists to be able to formulate useful and effective guidelines for fluid intake that can apply broadly to the children due to differences in age, size and varying rates of sweat fluid losses caused by climatic conditions, sporting intensity, clothing, sports skills and genetically determined 'heavy or light' sweaters. The recommended fluid intake guidelines for adults suggest an intake that prevents >2% loss of their pre-exercise body mass (Sawka *et al.*, 2007) and this can most likely be applied to children. Given that assessing a child's fluid loss by monitoring body mass before and after exercise may not be convenient and/or appropriate, the following general fluid intake guidelines should suffice for most children in sport. Children should aim to consume 400–600 mL of water 2–3 hours prior to exercise. During sporting activities, 150–300 ml of fluid every 15–20 minutes is advised for events that last ≤1 hour, with water as the preferred fluid (Sawka *et al.*, 2007). For events lasting ≥1 hour, or taking place in hot or humid environments, sports drinks containing 6% carbohydrate and 20 mEq/L to 30 mEq/L of sodium are recommended to replace energy stores, fluids and electrolyte losses. After exercise to replace sweat losses it is normally suggested to consume 1.25–1.5 × fluid lost (with 1 kg body weight loss = 1,000 mL fluid loss) (Sawka *et al.* 2007). For those children competing in elite sport more specific guidelines may be recommended under the guidance of a sports dietician.

Sports drinks are frequently marketed and consumed by young athletes, however for most children the use of sports drinks in place of water is unnecessary (O'Dea, 2003). Reasons to avoid promoting the use of sports drinks for the young athlete include the lower sweat rates of children, therefore they are likely to have a reduced loss in sodium and electrolytes when exercising compared to adults (Meyer *et al.*, 2012). Furthermore, the consumption of sports drinks can lead to excessive sugar intake, associated with undesirable health outcomes. Exceptions may occur for athletes partaking in periods of prolonged, vigorous sports participation with limited opportunity for recovery (<4 hours) between exercise sessions. Sports drinks may also be useful for the athlete who experiences gastrointestinal distress either immediately before or during prolonged exercise (<90 minutes) and may not be able to tolerate solid food. It is important to recognise that the consumption of sports drinks in these situations is different from caffeinated energy drinks, which often contain stimulants, which are inappropriate for children (O'Dea, 2003). The consumption of energy drinks (e.g. Red Bull/Monster) is not recommended for children due to a lack of evidence to ascertain their safety for this population group.

## *Supplements*

Dietary supplements and ergogenic aids to enhance sporting performance have received significant scientific attention in adults. However, there have been very few studies to explore their safety and effectiveness in younger athletes. Despite this lack of evidence to support their use in younger populations, children and adolescents (<18 years old) using supplements in an attempt to enhance sports performance is evident (Evans *et al.*, 2012). The use of supplements in athletes <12 years is largely unknown. Aspiring junior athletes may take supplements for a variety of reasons including natural curiosity, perceived pressure to achieve sporting results, and/or in pursuit of the ideal physique.

The consumption of sports supplements is inappropriate for the child athlete due to the uncertainty of the possible risks and safety concerns associated with their use (Peeling *et al.*, 2019). Dietary supplements (e.g. calcium, iron, vitamin D) are not considered performance enhancing and may be consumed by children in sport under the guidance of a health care professional (e.g. dietician, medical doctor) where appropriate. It is important children athletes are educated early to challenge their beliefs and coaches should be promoting performance enhancement through appropriate training, nutrition and rest, not supplements (Peeling *et al.*, 2019).

## Implications for Children's Sports Coaching

### *The Many Roles of a Coach*

Historically the coach's role has been embedded in performance, however the coach is increasingly becoming identified to be an important individual in not only developing sporting performance but also in developing a healthy individual. In this context the coach is seen as a role model, trainer, mentor and motivator to their athletes. This is especially important for those coaches working with children, as they have potential to play a significant role in a child's growth, development and shaping their beliefs and behaviours (Kidman and Hanrahan, 2010).

Coaches must be provided with learning opportunities to gain a basic understanding of how nutrition can affect the health and sporting performance of children in sport and translate this knowledge through advocating positive nutritional messaging within their scope of practice. When seeking educational resources, coaches should ensure they are learning from credible and reliable sources, (e.g. registered and/or accredited sports dieticians (Sports Dieticians Australia, Professionals in Nutrition for Exercise and Sport, British Dietetic Association), academic journals, formal sporting organisations educational seminars/ workshops or a licenced physician). It is important that the coach provides a healthy approach towards nutrition when supporting young athletes, ensuring they are promoting principles of variety, moderation and balance. There may be instances where the nutritional support required may go beyond a coach's professional scope (e.g. athletes presenting with possible eating disorder behaviours, those adhering to restrictive diets, athletes with allergies, or athletes who are diabetic). In these circumstances, to ensure the athlete receives the best nutrition advice, referral to an appropriate health care professional such as a registered dietician and/or family doctor would be recommended.

### *The Coach's Role in Supporting Energy Needs of the Child Athlete*

Coaches can play a key role in the prevention, identification and management of athletes at risk of not meeting their required energy needs by ensuring they are encouraging a healthy sporting environment, which discourages inappropriate language and behaviours around nutrition, physique and body image (Wells *et al.*, 2020). Additionally, it is important coaches are aware of the early signs and symptoms to look out for; including children presenting signs of overtraining, even in the presence of illness/injury, a lack of social interaction outside of sport, perfectionistic traits, poor development, low self-esteem, restrictive or obsessive eating behaviours, and reductions in sporting performance. Coaches are discouraged from conversations, which place emphasis on a child's body composition, weight, or those that encourage dieting behaviours. Instead, their role is to act as an advocate, promoting a healthy approach to nutrition and exercise, supporting the long-term health of their athletes (Ackerman *et al.*, 2020). Sporting organisations have a responsibility to be providing coaches with education and resources to ensure they have adequate knowledge of LEA and to be able to support those athletes at risk.

## Summary and Future Directions

Children in sport have unique nutritional needs. While the principles of sports nutrition are similar to adults, there are some key differences. Optimal nutrition in the age group should focus on supporting growth and development. Coaches are influential figures who can deliver basic nutrition information providing they remain within their scope of practice (e.g. basic general nutrition advice). Nutrition recommendations for the child athlete should promote a regular intake of high-quality meals and snacks that reflect energy demands, comprising of high-quality carbohydrate and protein sources over the day. Specific attention should also be placed on ensuring children are obtaining adequate amounts of calcium, vitamin D and iron. The child athlete should meet their energy requirements through food and avoid the use of supplements. A coach is not required or permitted to be providing specific nutrition advice beyond basic healthy eating guidelines unless formally trained in sports nutrition. If a coach is concerned about an athlete's nutritional intake and requires further support, seeking support from a registered sports dietician is advised.

Future research should seek to explore coach's knowledge, attitudes, and beliefs of sports nutrition for the child athlete to gain a greater appreciation of how we can better support coaches exposed to children in sport. Furthermore, with no specific guidelines exist for children in sport, yet a plethora of sport and exercise science research demonstrating the physical, physiological and metabolic differences between the child and adult involved in sport, it is important that the future research aims to provide guidelines specific to the child athlete.

## References


Abrams, S.A., 2011. Dietary guidelines for calcium and vitamin D: A new era. *Pediatrics*, 127 (3), 566–568.

Ackerman, K., *et al.*, 2020. #REDS (Relative Energy Deficiency in Sport): Time for a revolution in sports culture and systems to improve athlete health and performance. *British Journal of Sports Medicine*, 54 (7), 369–370.

Aerenhouts, D., *et al.*, 2011. Energy and macronutrient intake in adolescent sprint athletes: A follow-up study. *Journal of Sports Sciences*, 29 (1), 73–82.

Bezuglov, E., *et al.*, 2019. The dependence of running speed and muscle strength on the serum concentration of Vitamin D in young male professional football players residing in the Russian Federation. *Nutrients*, 11 (9), 1960.

Bonci, C.M., *et al.*, 2008. National athletic trainers' association position statement: Preventing, detecting, and managing disordered eating in athletes. *Journal of Athletic Training*, 43 (1), 80–108.

Burke, L.M. 2010. Fueling strategies to optimise performance: Training high or training low? *Scandinavian Journal of Medicine and Science in Sports*, 20, 48–58.

Burke, L.M., Millet, G., and Tarnopolsky, M.A., 2007. Nutrition for distance events. *Journal of Sports Sciences*, 25, 29–38.

Burke, L.M., *et al.*, 2001. Guidelines for daily carbohydrate intake. *Sports medicine*, 31 (4), 267–299.

Burke, L.M., *et al.*, 2011. Carbohydrates for training and competition. *Journal of Sports Sciences*, 29, 17–27.

Cormick, G. and Belizán, J.M., 2019. Calcium intake and health. *Nutrients*, 11 (7), 1606.

Craig, W.J., 1994. Iron status of vegetarians. *The American Journal of Clinical Nutrition*, 59 (5), 1233–1237.

De Lamas, C., *et al.*, 2019. Effects of dairy product consumption on height and bone mineral content in children: A systematic review of controlled trials. *Advances in Nutrition*, 1 (10), S88–S96.

Desbrow, B., *et al.*, 2014. Sports dietitians australia position statement: Sports nutrition for the adolescent athlete. *International Journal of Sport Nutrition and Exercise Metabolism*, 24, 570–584.

Evans, M.W., *et al.*, 2012. Dietary supplement use by children and adolescents in the United States to enhance sport performance: Results of the National Health Interview Survey. *The Journal of Primary Prevention*, 33 (1), 3–12.

Farrokhyar, F., *et al.*, 2015. Prevalence of vitamin D inadequacy in athletes: A systematic-review and meta-analysis. *Sports Medicine*, 45 (3), 365–378.

Hannon, M.P., Close, G.L., and Morton, J.P., 2020. Energy and macronutrient considerations for young athletes. *Strength & Conditioning Journal*, 42 (6), 109–119.

Heaney, S., *et al.*, 2010. Comparison of strategies for assessing nutritional adequacy in elite female athletes' dietary intake. *International Journal of Sport Nutrition and Exercise Metabolism*, 20 (3), 245–256.

Hill, K.E., Hart, L.M., and Paxton, S.J., 2020. Confident body, confident child: Outcomes for children of parents receiving a universal parenting program to promote healthful eating patterns and positive body image in their pre-schoolers—an exploratory RCT extension. *International Journal of Environmental Research and Public Health*, 17 (3), 891.

Hoch, A.Z., Goossen, K., and Kretschmer, T., 2008. Nutritional requirements of the child and teenage athlete. *Physical Medicine and Rehabilitation Clinics of North America*, 19 (2), 373–398.

Hossein-Nezhad and Arashholick, M.F., 2013. Vitamin D for health: A global perspective. *Mayo clinic proceedings*, 2013, Elsevier, 720–755.

Howe, C.A., *et al.*, 2010. Energy expenditure and enjoyment of common children's games in a simulated free-play environment. *The Journal of Pediatrics*, 157 (6), 936–942.

Huh, S.Y. and Gordon, C.M., 2008. Vitamin D deficiency in children and adolescents: Epidemiology, impact and treatment. *Reviews in Endocrine and Metabolic Disorders*, 9 (2), 161–170.

Huotari, A. and Herzig, K-H. 2008. Vitamin D and living in northern latitudes—an endemic risk area for vitamin D deficiency. *International Journal of Circumpolar Health*, 67 (2-3), 164–178.

Hutson, M.J., *et al.*, 2020. Effects of low energy availability on bone health in endurance athletes and high-impact exercise as a potential countermeasure: A narrative review. *Sports Medicine*, 51 (3), 391–403.

Keay, N., Overseas, A., and Francis, G., 2020. Awareness and indicators of low energy availability in male and female dancers. *medRxiv*.

Kidman, L. and Hanrahan, S.J., 2010. *The coaching process: A practical guide to becoming an effective sports coach.* London: Routledge.

L'allemand-Jander, D., 2010. Clinical diagnosis of metabolic and cardiovascular risks in overweight children: Early development of chronic diseases in the obese child. *International Journal of Obesity*, 34, S32–S36.

Larsson, C.L. and Johansson, G.K., 2002. Dietary intake and nutritional status of young vegans and omnivores in Sweden. *The American Journal of Clinical Nutrition*, 76 (1), 100–106.

Lips, P., 2010. Worldwide status of vitamin D nutrition. *The Journal of Steroid Biochemistry and Molecular Biology*, 121 (1-2), 297–300.

Martínez, S., *et al.*, 2011. Anthropometric characteristics and nutritional profile of young amateur swimmers. *The Journal of Strength and Conditioning Research*, 25 (4), 1126–1133.

Meng, K., *et al.*, 2020. The risk of low energy availability in Chinese elite and recreational female aesthetic sports athletes. *Journal of the International Society of Sports Nutrition*, 17, 13.

Meyer, F., O'Connor, H., and Shirreffs, S.M., 2007. Nutrition for the young athlete. *Journal of Sports Sciences*, 25, S73–S82.

Meyer, F., *et al.*, 2012. Fluid balance and dehydration in the young athlete: Assessment considerations and effects on health and performance. *American Journal of Lifestyle Medicine*, 6 (6), 489–501.

Meyers, L.D., Hellwig, J.P., and Otten, J.J., 2006. *Dietary reference intakes: The essential guide to nutrient requirements.* National Academies Press.

Mindell, J.S., Coombs, N., and Stamatakis, E., 2014. Measuring physical activity in children and adolescents for dietary surveys: Practicalities, problems and pitfalls. *Proceedings of the Nutrition Society*, 73 (2), 218–225.

Monthuy-Blanc, J., *et al.*, 2012. Physical self-concept and disturbed eating attitudes and behaviors in French athlete and non-athlete adolescent girls: Direct and indirect relations. *Body Image*, 9 (3), 373–380.

Mountjoy, M., *et al.*, 2014. The IOC consensus statement: Beyond the female athlete triad—relative energy deficiency in sport (RED-S). *British Journal of Sports Medicine*, 48, 491–497.

O'Dea, J.A., 2003. Consumption of nutritional supplements among adolescents: Usage and perceived benefits. *Health Education Research*, 18 (1), 98–107.

Pawlak, R. and Bell, K., 2017. Iron status of vegetarian children: A review of literature. *Annals of Nutrition and Metabolism*, 70 (2), 88–99.

Peeling, P., *et al.*, 2019. Sports foods and dietary supplements for optimal function and performance enhancement in track-and-field athletes. *International Journal of Sport Nutrition and Exercise Metabolism*, 29 (2), 198–209.

Petrie, H.J., Stover, E.A., and Horswill, C.A., 2004. Nutritional concerns for the child and adolescent competitor. *Nutrition*, 20 (7-8), 620–631.

Phillips, S.M. and Van Loon, L.J., 2011. Dietary protein for athletes: From requirements to optimum adaptation. *Journal of Sports Sciences*, 29, S29–S38.

Purcell, L.K., *et al.*, 2013. Sport nutrition for young athletes. *Paediatrics and Child Health*, 18 (4), 200–202.

Rodenberg, R.E. and Gustafson, S., 2007. Iron as an ergogenic aid: Ironclad evidence? *Current Sports Medicine Reports*, 6 (4), 258–264.

Rodgers, R.F., *et al.*, 2019. Low body esteem and dietary restraint among 7-year old children: The role of perfectionism, low self-esteem, and belief in the rewards of thinness and muscularity. *Eating Behaviors*, 32, 65–68.

Rowland, T., 2011. Fluid replacement requirements for child athletes. *Sports Medicine*, 41 (4), 279–288.

Rowland, T., *et al.*, 2008. Exercise tolerance and thermoregulatory responses during cycling in boys and men. *Medicine and Science in Sports and Exercise*, 40 (2), 282–287.

Sawka, M.N., *et al.*, 2007. American college of sports medicine position stand. Exercise and fluid replacement. *Medicine and Science in Sports and Exercise*, 39 (2), 377–390.

Shoemaker, M.E., *et al.*, 2020. High prevalence of poor iron status among 8-to 16-year-old youth athletes: Interactions among biomarkers of iron, dietary intakes, and biological maturity. *Journal of the American College of Nutrition*, 39 (2), 155–162.

Spiro, A. and Buttriss, J., 2014. Vitamin D: An overview of vitamin D status and intake in Europe. *Nutrition Bulletin*, 39 (4), 322–350.

Torun, B., 2005. Energy requirements of children and adolescents. *Public Health Nutrition*, 8 (7A), 968–993.

Wells, K., *et al.*, 2020. The Australian Institute of Sport (AIS) and National Eating Disorders Collaboration (NEDC) position statement on disordered eating in high performance sport. *British Journal of Sports Medicine*, 54, 1247–1258.

# 14

# SPORTS-RELATED CONCUSSIONS IN CHILDREN

*Casey Wagner, Jeff Webb, Brandon Mines, and Pooja Sharma*

## Introduction

Annually from a global perspective, it is estimated that concussions affect more than 6 per 1,000 adults and children (Hon *et al.*, 2019). In the United States of America, about 800,000 adolescents and children, ages 17 and younger, visit the emergency department yearly for traumatic brain injury (TBI). The leading concern for these visits is due to concussions. This number is likely an underestimation as many people suffering mild TBI's do not seek medical attention.

Symptoms related to concussion span across four domains – physical, cognitive, emotional, and sleep affecting the overall quality of life and potentially causing short and long-term deficits. Albeit, most athletes' concussion symptoms resolve within one month, about 20% experience long-term sequelae. Since the early 2000s, sports-related concussion, TBI, and chronic traumatic encephalopathy (CTE) have become a focal point of study and concern. The emphasis lies on the negative long-term effects of head injuries related to contact sports, especially in youth athletes whose brains are still developing and the repercussions it may have on young athletes as they mature.

Despite a multitude of available resources, a knowledge gap still exists within most athletes, parents, and coaches regarding recognising and responding to concussions as well as emphasising the importance of concussion education in student-athletes. As research advances and our understanding of sports-related concussions develops, it is crucial to disseminate the knowledge in an understandable way to improve safety and outcomes. Increased education and appreciation of concussions would be a public health benefit by promoting a stronger and safer youth sports culture.

## Review of Current Research

### *Definition of Sports-Related Concussion*

Sports-Related Concussion (SRC) is defined as a traumatic brain injury induced by biomechanical forces. This has been the definition used since the First International Symposium on Concussion in Sport in 2000 (McCrory *et al.*, 2017b). Concussion is sometimes referred to as mild Traumatic Brain Injury (mTBI), though mTBI also includes head injuries from other trauma


DOI: 10.4324/9781003199359-17

including motor vehicle accidents, so for the purpose of this book the term concussion will be used. Concussions may be caused by either a direct blow to the head, face, or neck or a blow to somewhere else on the body causing transmission of force to the head. SRC typically results in a transient impairment of neurologic function with rapid onset, though sometimes it may take minutes to hours for an athlete to show symptoms. SRC represents a functional disturbance rather than a structural problem, hence there are no abnormalities on traditional imaging including CT or MRI. SRC results in a range of clinical symptoms that may or may not include loss of consciousness. Resolution of symptoms typically follows a sequential course, however in some cases symptoms may be prolonged (Meehan and Bachur, 2009; McCrory *et al.*, 2017a).

## *Pathophysiology*

SRCs occur when an athlete receives an impact or blow causing forces to be transmitted to the brain. The forces can either be linear with a direct blow or rotational, usually with twisting of the neck. There is no defined biomechanical threshold for an impact to cause a clinical concussion. Multiple studies have been done in collision sports using devices in helmets to track forces delivered, but none have resulted in a clear clinical correlation between the amount of force it takes to cause a concussion (McCrory *et al.*, 2017a). Additionally, devices worn in helmets cannot always be translated to non-collision sports where concussions still occur and do not necessarily document the true movement of the brain. The forces that cause a concussion are generally felt to be less than those that cause skull fractures, but there are no known specific minimum levels to cause injury.

Following the impact to the head or neck, a complex neurometabolic cascade occurs involving microscopic injury to the axons/nerves in the brain along with increased metabolic demand and decreased cerebral blood flow. This imbalance in energy supply and demand results in the clinical symptoms seen in concussion. Until normal cellular function and blood flow is restored, the brain is susceptible to further injury. A second blow can cause worsening metabolic changes and significant deficits (Harmon *et al.*, 2012). For this reason, an athlete should not be exposed to a potential second injury to the brain until they are fully recovered from the first.

It is now well known that a child's brain is more susceptible to concussion than the adult brain (Halstead *et al.*, 2018). In addition, paediatric athletes take longer to recover than adults following concussion events. This is thought to be due to several factors including weaker neck musculature and the still-developing brain (Harmon *et al.*, 2012). Also, all documented cases of second impact syndrome have occurred in athletes younger than 23 years of age, with almost all severe cases occurring in teenagers. Therefore, practitioners and coaches must be even more cautious when taking care of children compared to their adult counterparts.

## *Epidemiology*

Documented SRC have increased significantly since 2000. This is thought to be due to increased recognition of what constitutes a concussion and increased education leading to better reporting. Severe brain injuries such as skull fractures and second impact syndrome have not increased over this time period. In the USA, the Centers for Disease Control (CDC) estimate that there are 1.5–3.8 million SRCs in the United States annually. The exact number of concussions is unknown and is likely much higher due to underreporting. Concussions make up an estimated 8.9% of all injuries in high school sports. In a survey of U.S. middle and high school students, 20% report that they have had at least one concussion (Kazl and Torres, 2019).

Prevalence of concussions varies with the sport played. Concussions occur in both collision sports with helmets and in non-contact sports without helmets. Boys' sports with the highest incidence per athlete exposure include American football, rugby, ice hockey, and wrestling. Girls' sports with the highest incidence include soccer, lacrosse, field hockey, and basketball. In general, boys sustain more concussions than girls, due to their higher participation in contact sports, but in sports that have the same rules such as football and basketball, girls sustain concussions at a greater rate. The reason for this is not entirely known but is thought to be due to differences in neck strength, head mass, and reporting differences as girls may be more likely to report their symptoms. Concussions occur more commonly in competition than practices. Studies across different sports have shown a 3–7 times greater risk of concussion in competition vs. practice (Kazl and Torres, 2019). The incidence per athlete exposure across different sports in the United States is shown in Table 14.1.

Children are more likely to suffer SRC than adult athletes. It has also been well-documented (Harmon *et al.*, 2012; Halstead *et al.*, 2018) that athletes with a history of concussion are more likely to sustain a second concussion. Several studies have suggested that those with underlying brain disorders may be more likely to sustain a concussion or take longer to recover from a concussion. This includes attention deficit hyperactivity disorder (ADHD), depression, learning disabilities, and chronic migraines (Halstead *et al.*, 2018). This information may be helpful to know preseason to identify those athletes who may be at increased risk for concussions.

## *Identifying the Athlete with Concussion*

The role of coaching can be intense, and it can be easy to overlook a myriad of symptoms that can show if a player is injured with a concussion. In 2014, research published in the British Journal of Sports Medicine (White *et al.*, 2013) showed that key points from concussion

*Table 14.1* Incidence of concussion by sport (Halstead *et al.*, 2018)

| *Sport* | *Concussion rates per 1,000 athlete exposures* |
|---|---|
| Boys' American Football | 0.54–0.94 |
| Girls' Soccer | 0.30–0.73 |
| Boys' Lacrosse | 0.30–0.67 |
| Boys' Ice Hockey | 0.54–0.62 |
| Boys' Wrestling | 0.17–0.58 |
| Girls' Lacrosse | 0.20–0.55 |
| Girls' Field Hockey | 0.10–0.44 |
| Girls' Basketball | 0.16–0.44 |
| Boys' Soccer | 0.17–0.44 |
| Girls' Softball | 0.10–0.36 |
| Boys' Basketball | 0.07–0.25 |
| Girls' Volleyball | 0.05–0.25 |
| Cheerleading | 0.06–0.22 |
| Boys' Baseball | 0.04–0.14 |
| Girls' Gymnastics | 0.07 |
| Boys' and Girls' Track and Field | 0.02 |
| Boys' and Girls' Swimming and Diving | 0.01–0.02 |

guidelines were unknown by coaches with regards to symptoms, recovery in youth athletes, and repeat concussions. There are common symptoms that should make a coach suspicious their young athlete may be suffering from a concussion. Meehan and Bachur (2009) showed that a headache was the most common symptom of a SRC and this was verified by American Academy of Pediatrics (AAP) in 2010 with a literature review (Halstead and Walter, 2010). The American Medical Society of Sports Medicine (AMSSM) position statement (Harmon *et al.*, 2012) showed that a headache was the most common symptom of a SRC and also showed that while loss of consciousness is not a common symptom, less than 10%, it is a clear sign that the athlete has suffered from a SRC (Harmon *et al.*, 2012). During the fifth International Conference on Concussion in Sports held in Berlin (McCrory *et al.*, 2017b), these common symptoms were again verified across all sports and nationalities. There are many signs that an athlete may have a SRC, but the symptoms can be vague. Literature review has shown that there were no differences in symptoms reported by male and female athletes, but it has been shown that females are more likely to sustain a SRC (Kerr *et al.*, 2019). This was seen across multiple sex comparable sports including football. It was discussed that potential factors explaining this difference may be the likelihood of an athlete to report a concussion, neck musculature, cerebral blood flow, and/or hormonal regulation. However, these potential factors have not yet been fully assessed. Halstead *et al.* (2018) in a children's SRC literature review illustrated five categories of concussion symptoms (Table 14.2).

A player during the game may exhibit these SRC symptoms (Table 14.2) in the following common situations: missing a play call (cognitive), looking clumsy on the field (vestibular/oculomotor), decreased performance (vestibular/oculomotor), erratic behavior with coaches and teammates (emotional), squinting at lights (somatic), covering ears if loud music is present (somatic), or forgetful of the game time, location, opponent, and/or score (cognitive). The next day the player may look drowsy (sleep).

Table 14.3 illustrates the most common reported SRC symptoms that Meehan and Bachur (2009) found in the children.

These vague symptoms do overlap with other disorders, and it can be challenging to distinguish the symptoms as a result of a prior condition versus a new SRC. Therefore, it is important to establish a baseline of symptoms prior to the season. Harmon *et al.* (2012) found that 50%–84% of children reported similar symptoms of SRC at baseline testing (Harmon *et al.*, 2012).

*Table 14.2* Concussion symptoms

| *Somatic* | *Vestibular/oculomotor* | *Cognitive* | *Emotional* | *Sleep* |
|---|---|---|---|---|
| Headache | Hearing problems | Confusion | Irritable | Drowsy |
| Nausea/ vomiting | Tinnitus | Mental fog | Increase emotions | Fatigue |
| Neck pain | Balance issues | Difficulty concentrating | Sadness | Low energy |
| Light sensitivity | Dizziness | Memory issues | Nervous | Change in sleep duration |
| Noise sensitivity | | Slow answers | Anxious | Difficulty initiating sleep |
| | | Repeats questions | | |
| | | Loss of consciousness | | |

*Table 14.3* Concussion symptoms in paediatric population

| *Paediatric sports-related concussion symptom* | *% of concussion reporting symptoms* |
|---|---|
| Headache | 93.4 |
| Dizziness/unsteadiness | 74.6 |
| Difficulty Concentrating | 56.6 |
| Confusion/disorientation | 46.0 |
| Vision changes/sensitivity to light | 37.5 |
| Nausea | 28.9 |
| Drowsiness | 26.5 |
| Amnesia/forgetfulness | 24.3 |
| Sensitivity to noise | 18.9 |
| Tinnitus | 10.7 |
| Irritability | 9.2 |
| Loss of consciousness | 4.6 |
| Hyperexcitability | 2.2 |
| Other | 7.5 |

## Sideline Tools

The initial evaluation of a suspected concussed athlete begins with an assessment of the severity of the situation. Theoretically, this assessment should be performed by coaches, athletic trainers, or parents, if medical personnel is not onsite. If it is determined that the athlete is conscious, then the athlete is to be escorted to the sideline for further evaluation. Certainly, if the athlete has any neurologic compromise or is simply not coherent/completely conscious, then it is best to defer to standard emergency evaluation of the airway, breathing, and circulation. To be on the safe side, if the athlete does exhibit any signs or symptoms that raise concern for a cervical spine injury (i.e. prolonged loss of consciousness (LOC), neck pain, neurologic changes in any extremity), it is best to have the athlete transported to the nearest emergency facility.

Once it has been determined that the athlete needs to be evaluated for a SRC, this is best done by a health care provider or athletic trainer that has experience in recognising and diagnosing SRC. In addition to this, it is quite invaluable to have a relationship with that athlete, so that one can assess if there are any subtle changes to the personality or demeanor. However, medical personnel may not always be available, hence it is important for parents and coaches to be aware of the signs and symptoms of a concussion.

Ideally, it is best to evaluate an athlete in a quiet location. There are several sideline tests available to the health care provider to diagnose a SRC. One of the most common tools is the Sport Concussion Assessment Tool (SCAT), which has been adopted globally, most notably in South Africa for rugby players (Patricios, 2014). There is a version for children ages 5–12 (Child SCAT 5), as well as one for adolescents and adults (SCAT 5). Overall, the SCAT 5 takes 10–15 minutes to complete. The information in the SCAT 5 is updated as needed, based on research that is evaluated during the Sport Concussion Group meeting that occurs at predefined intervals.

The SCAT 5 starts with observation of the athlete, to determine if they are motionless or if they have any gait abnormalities. Special attention is directed at determining if there are any unusual blank stares or a vacant look in the athlete's face. Also, inability to answer questions or general disorientation is noted. An attempt to determine the athlete's memory is accomplished using Maddocks questions (Maddocks *et al.*, 1995). A modified version of the balance error scoring system (BESS), a standard assessment of concussion (cognition evaluation), and a brief neurologic exam is also a part of the SCAT 5 and Child SCAT 5. While it is true that extensive research has gone into the development of the various sideline assessment tools, it is well known that they do not have the final say in diagnosing a SRC. It is critical that the health care provider assessing the athlete make the final decision and understand that these tools are merely that. While there is some normative data regarding baseline testing, it is better if the results of a SCAT 5 be compared to that individual athlete's baseline. While this is not always possible, an effort should be made to obtain this information prior to providing medical coverage for any sporting event.

It is important to remember that an athlete may not present with clear signs and symptoms of a SRC during the initial evaluation. Performing serial examinations after the initial testing can be important in the process of identifying a SRC. If the examiner is certain that no SRC has been diagnosed, the athlete can return to play. It can be argued that if there is any doubt on the diagnosis, it is better to keep the athlete out of sport for the rest of the day. When serial exams are done, however, one may "catch" an unsuspected SRC. Another scenario to keep in mind as it relates to sideline management of SRC, is to also make sure the athlete diagnosed with a SRC is not worsening as time passes. If there is any development of focal neurologic deficits, worsening headache, repeated vomiting, changes in consciousness, convulsions, or combative behavior, transport the athlete to the nearest medical emergency facility (McCrory *et al.*, 2017b).

When determining the return to play process for any given athlete, it is important to remember that it needs to be an individualised process. Athletes recover from SRC's at different rates so there needs to be some flexibility in how they matriculate through the various steps. It is best if an athlete follows a graduated stepwise approach, as described by the Berlin Concussion in Sport Group (Table 14.4) (McCrory *et al.*, 2017b).

*Table 14.4* Graduated return to sport approach

| *Stage* | *Aim* | *Activity* | *Goal of each step* |
|---|---|---|---|
| 1 | Symptom-limited activity | Daily activities that do not provoke symptoms | Gradual reintroduction of work/ school activities |
| 2 | Light aerobic exercise | Walking or stationary cycling at slow to medium pace. No resistance training | Increase heart rate |
| 3 | Sport-specific exercise | Running or skating drills. No head impact activities | Add movement |
| 4 | Non-contact training drills | Harder training drills, eg, passing drills. May start progressive resistance training | Exercise, coordination and increased thinking |
| 5 | Full contact practice | Following medical clearance, participate in normal training activities | Restore confidence and assess functional skills by coaching staff |
| 6 | Return to sport | Normal game play | |

*NOTE:* An initial period of 24–48 hours of both relative physical rest and cognitive rest is recommended before beginning the RTS progression.

There should be at least 24 hours (or longer) for each step of the progression. If any symptoms worsen during exercise, the athlete should go back to the previous step. Resistance training should be added only in the later stages (stage 3 or 4 at the earliest). If symptoms are persistent (e.g. more than 10–14 days in adults or more than one month in children), the athlete should be referred to a healthcare professional who is an expert in the management of concussion. (McCrory *et al.*, 2017b).

Much of what is done for a youth and adolescent athlete as it pertains to recovery from SRC has been pulled from how an adult recovers from a SRC. What is known is that youth athletes have a longer recovery from SRC's (Feiss *et al.*, 2020). It would be prudent to account for this in the return to play process. In general, no athlete should be allowed to return to play on the same day as being injured. Athletes should not be returned to sport-related activities that involve contact or collision until symptoms have resolved and they have gone through the proper return to play steps. There is an increased risk for repeat injury, severe injury, and prolonged recovery if returned to contact sport prior to resolution of SRC. Most experts agree that the concussed athlete only rests for the first 48 hours. Avoidance of electronic tablets and devices is recommended as they can exacerbate symptoms. Some modification of academic endeavors may be needed at this time. Forty-eight hours after being diagnosed with an SRC, light aerobic exercise can be allowed, provided it does not exacerbate or worsen symptoms. It is thought that it is unlikely that early light exercise will cause any harm, but it is documented that prolonged inactivity can lead to longer recovery and an increase in symptoms. As the athlete is progressing through the return to play steps, it is recommended that this process is monitored by a licensed health care professional. As it pertains to progressing through the steps, each step should take at least 24 hours. Athletes can progress to the next step if there are no symptoms. If symptoms do recur, the athlete should return to the previous stage that did not cause symptoms, then wait 24 hours. If no symptoms have returned, the athlete can resume the process again. Overall, the athlete should be able to return to full academic obligations at the same time or before they are fully returned to sport (Halstead and Walter, 2010).

## Long-Term Consequences/Post-concussion Syndrome

The AMSSM position statement (Harmon *et al.,* 2012), Berlin Consensus Statement on concussion in sports (McCRory *et al.*, 2017b), amongst other societies have all clearly stated that if a concussion is suspected the athlete should be removed from the game until there has been a medical evaluation and they are cleared to return to play (Harmon *et al.*, 2012; McCrory *et al.*, 2017b). The safety concern of our children is to protect them from long-term consequences and possible second impact syndrome, which occurs when an athlete suffers a second SRC before the first one resolves. McLendon *et al.* (2016), review of second impact syndrome in the Pediatric Neurology Journal did a literature review and found 17 cases from seven studies. SRCs were sustained during boxing, American football, skiing, and karate and all athletes were male. It was seen that all cases under 20 years of age led to permanent disability or death. The period between the two concussions ranged from one hour to four weeks and in most cases one of the concussion "hits" appeared to be minor. While the sample size is small, it does stress the importance of identifying a SRC and waiting for a full recovery no matter how minor it may appear. More studies are currently being conducted to expand on and monitor the occurrence of this rare but tragic outcome.

## Repeat Concussion Effects

Repeat concussions are a growing concern as well as their likelihood to occur. Once an athlete has sustained a concussion, they are at an elevated risk to sustain an additional concussion. Van Ierssel *et al.* (2020) conducted a systemic review looking at children, ages 5–18 years old and concluded that a child is four times more likely to sustain a repeat SRC. According to Meehan and Bachur (2009) literature review, if loss of consciousness occurs during a SRC the athlete will be six times more likely to sustain a repeat concussion with the risk most elevated during the initial 7–10 days. These elevated risks of repeated SRC's may be higher when considering that 50% of paediatric SRC's are underreported.

The increased susceptibility of sustaining a repeat SRC may be due to the aspect that adolescents take a longer time to recover as compared to adults. Van Ierssel *et al.* (2020) found that the delay in recovery may be due to residual physiological effects from the primary SRC, microstructure injury, skull structure, genetics, impaired neuromotor control, and sensorimotor deficits. Impaired neuromotor control (cervical spine postural stability) and cognitive processing may have cumulative effects after repeat SRCs. Once an athlete has suffered one SRC, their cerebral processing time slows. Guskiewicz and Valovich McLeod (2011) review of the paediatric SRC literature demonstrated that repeat SRC increases recovery time likely due to worsening the cerebral processing time. It is postulated that this occurs because the child's brain is still developing, and recurrent injury leads to disruption of the complex biological process needed for brain development and acquisition of new mental skills. It was also found that athletes (14–18 years old), who had two or more SRC's and felt otherwise healthy were found to have similar neurocognitive scores with those who sustained a recent concussion.

Long-term consequences and repeated concussion impacts are still being researched. As research has evolved and concussion sequelae are becoming well understood there is still further work that needs to be conducted. The two most discussed long-term consequences of concussions are post-concussion syndrome and chronic traumatic encephalopathy (CTE). Post-concussive syndrome (PCS) has yet to be firmly defined. Halstead *et al.* (2018) in Pediatric SRC review demonstrated that there is still no clear definition for PCS. The World Health Organization (WHO) defines it as the presence of three or greater symptoms after sustaining a head injury including: headache, dizziness, fatigue, irritability, difficulty with concentrating and performing mental tasks, impairment of memory, insomnia, and reduced tolerance to stress, emotional excitement, or alcohol. Kapadia *et al.* (2019) conducted a paediatric PCS management review and defined it as concussive symptoms lasting longer than four weeks. The prevalence of PCS has ranged from 10% to 30% of children athletes. Van Ierssel *et al.* 2021 surveyed children athletes who suffered a SRC one year later to evaluate symptom resolution. It was found that 90% of those athletes who did not suffer a repeat SRC had full recovery and 74% of those who had a repeat SCR had full recovery after one year from the initial SRC. Headache (13%–27%) was the most common residual symptom followed by fatigue (6%–12%), memory issues (5%–12%), more emotional (9%–12%), irritability (8%–12%) and difficulty initiating sleep (7%–9%). Successful management of PCS usually requires a multi-disciplinary approach to address emotional, vestibular, ocular, autonomic, sleep, and cognitive residual issues of PCS.

Chronic traumatic encephalopathy (CTE) has come to the forefront of possible long-term effects of repeated head injury or SRCs. Manley *et al.* (2017) undertook a systematic review of long-term SRC effects concluded that CTE is a post-mortem diagnosis and there is no current confirmatory test to diagnose CTE in a living athlete. CTE is believed to cause permanent emotional and neurocognitive effects, and ongoing research is trying to validate these findings. CTE prevalence in children is largely unknown. Mez *et al.* (2017) in clinicopathological evaluation of chronic traumatic encephalopathy in players of American football showed three of 14 (21%) high school and zero of two pre-high school American football players who donated their brains to research after death were found to have stage 1 (mild) CTE. It cannot be determined if these findings were a direct result of sport, outside factors, or a multifactorial effect. Solomon and Zuckerman (2014) in the Brain Injury journal found that it is likely CTE is developing from repeat concussion and/or sub-concussion impacts in mainly contact sports. Their epidemiological study, which is mostly derived from American data, has shown the most common sports are American football, boxing, hockey, wrestling, and one case of football.

However, as research has been evolving in CTE, more European data is becoming available. CTE is being seen in athletes who competed in contact and non-contact sports, which likely indicates that CTE is a very complex multifactorial disease. More research is needed globally to expand on the area of CTE as it is a complex injury involving numerous factors.

## Implications for Children's Sport

It is well known that not all concussions are reported to the proper medical staff. In fact, it is believed that 50% of concussions are not reported. This is relevant because the medical staff that are experts in recognising concussion may not be present at the time a concussion occurs. Many times, the only person available will be members of the coaching staff. It would seem reasonable that coaches be knowledgeable in recognising symptoms and signs of SRC, as well as local laws that govern the management of these injuries. One thing that has been shown is that coaches do respond with improvements in SRC recognition and management once they undergo some formalised training. It is not a given that all governments expect or require coaches to undergo educational training that would allow them to recognise the signs and symptoms of SRC.

Coaches tend to do a decent job recognising the physical and cognitive signs of concussion, however, only 16% know that youth concussions take longer to recover than adult concussions (Feiss *et al.*, 2020) One of the most striking knowledge gaps surrounds concussion management. It is important to realise that parental knowledge is key. It has been shown that while most parents recognise the cognitive symptoms of concussion, only 41% adequately know or understand the management and return to play recommendations (Feiss *et al.*, 2020). If a youth sports team does not have access to an athletic trainer (healthcare professional who manages, prevents, and assists in treatment of injured athletes),

SRC nuances may be left to coaches and parents. While the diagnosis of a SRC may occur, how to matriculate through the return to play process may be inappropriate if left to the coach and parent. Certainly, making sure an appropriate health care provider skilled in managing the return to play steps is important. An ideal situation would be to improve the knowledge base of the coaches and parents, to not put the young athlete at risk of returning to sport prior to complete resolution of the SRC.

Currently, there is a knowledge gap in the literature as it pertains to SRC and the very young youth athlete (under age 10). As a result of this, it is plausible to imagine this lack of knowledge can trickle down to the coaches of these athletes not being aware of concussion symptoms and management as it pertains to this group of athletes. This chapter's evidence and research suggest that once the sports medicine community has a better grasp on how SRC affects the very young athlete, then the sports medicine professionals in charge of taking care of this population can better educate the coaching staff about the different aspects of SRC.

## Summary, Future Directions, and Future Research

In summary, concussions are multifactorial. Underreporting by children, lack of awareness or management by coaches and parents and premature return to play all contribute to concussions. A large knowledge gap still exists about SRC between healthcare professionals and the public. Common avenues to educate children, parents, and coaches alike include community seminars, educational materials, and social media platforms. Future research should expand our understanding of SRC, so that we can educate coaches, parents, and athletes. Future studies on concussion risk in youth and return to sports should evaluate rule changes, equipment standard, concussion assessment techniques, gender-specific differences, and effectiveness of decreased contact during practice. Additionally, future studies should provide education for coaches and parents, particularly focusing on signs and symptoms, proper concussion management, and return to play protocols. For coaches, focus should target concussion management and for parents, focus should target on signs and symptoms particularly related to emotional regulation and sleep. As very young athletes (under age 10) increase participation in sports activity, it is also imperative to study this population and the risk and management of concussion.

Future research should evaluate the significance if any pertaining to biomarkers in relation to concussion injury, advanced neuroimaging, and equipment engineering including helmet technology. Brain safety is crucial in keeping our young athletes actively engaged in sports and together healthcare professionals, coaches, and parents can make this possible.

## References


Feiss, R., *et al.*, 2020. A systematic review of coach and parent knowledge of concussion. *Journal of Concussion*, 4, 1–11.

Guskiewicz, K. and Valovich McLeod, T., 2011. Pediatric sports-related concussion. *PM&R*, 3 (4), 353–364.

Halstead, M. and Walter, K., 2010. Sport-related concussion in children and adolescents. *Pediatrics*, 126 (3), 597–615.

Halstead, M., *et al.*, 2018. Sport-related concussion in children and adolescents. *Pediatrics*, 142 (6), 1–24.

Harmon, K., *et al.*, 2012. American medical society for sports medicine position statement: Concussion in sport. *British Journal of Sports Medicine*, 47 (1), 15–26.

Hon, K., Leung, A., and Torres, A., 2019. Concussion: A global perspective. *Seminars in Pediatric Neurology*, 30, 117–127.

Kapadia, M., *et al.*, 2019. Review of the management of pediatric post-concussion syndrome—A multi-disciplinary, individualised approach. *Current Reviews in Musculoskeletal Medicine*, 12 (1), 57–66.

Kazl, C. and Torres, A., 2019. Definition, classification, and epidemiology of concussion. *Seminars in Pediatric Neurology*, 30, 9–13.

Kerr, Z., *et al.*, 2019. Concussion incidence and trends in 20 high school sports. *Pediatrics*, 144 (5), 1–13.

Maddocks, D., Dicker, G., and Saling, M., 1995. The assessment of orientation following concussion in athletes. *Clinical Journal of Sport Medicine*, 5 (1), 32–35.

Manley, G., *et al.*, 2017. A systematic review of potential long-term effects of sport-related concussion. *British Journal of Sports Medicine*, 51 (12), 969–977.

McCrory, P., *et al.*, 2017a. What is the definition of sports-related concussion: A systematic review. *British Journal of Sports Medicine*, 51 (11), 877–887.

McCrory, P., *et al.*, 2017b. Consensus statement on concussion in sport—The 5th international conference on concussion in sport held in Berlin, October 2016. *British Journal of Sports Medicine*, 51 (11), 838–847.

McLendon, L., *et al.*, 2016. The controversial second impact syndrome: A review of the literature. *Pediatric Neurology*, 62, 9–17.

Meehan, W. and Bachur, R., 2009. Sport-related concussion. *Pediatrics*, 123 (1), 114–123.

Mez, J., *et al.*, 2017. Clinicopathological evaluation of chronic traumatic encephalopathy in players of American football. *JAMA*, 318 (4), 360–370.

Patricios, J., 2014. Rugby contact and collisions — Clinical challenges of a global game. *Current Sports Medicine Reports*, 13 (5), 326–333.

Solomon, G. and Zuckerman, S., 2014. Chronic traumatic encephalopathy in professional sports: Retrospective and prospective views. *Brain Injury*, 29 (2), 164–170.

Van Ierssel, J., *et al.*, 2020. What is the risk of recurrent concussion in children and adolescents aged 5–18 years? A systematic review and meta-analysis. *British Journal of Sports Medicine*, 55 (12), 663–669.

Van Ierssel, J., *et al.*, 2021. Symptom burden, school function, and physical activity one year following pediatric concussion. *The Journal of Pediatrics*, 228, 190–198.

White, P., *et al.*, 2013. Knowledge about sports-related concussion: Is the message getting through to coaches and trainers? *British Journal of Sports Medicine*, 48 (2), 119–124.

# 15

# DISORDERED EATING IN CHILD AND YOUTH SPORT: THE ROLE OF THE COACH

*Anthony Papathomas, Maria Luisa Fernanda Pereira Vargas, and Erin Prior*

## Introduction

Whether participatory, competitive, or elite, children's sporting experiences should occur in a place of physical, social, and psychological safety (Bean *et al.*, 2020). The positive youth development movement suggests sport can be a route to friendship (Howie *et al.*, 2020), personal growth (Holt *et al.*, 2020), and a variety of life skills (Ronkainen *et al.*, 2021). Beyond such psychosocial development, it is widely agreed that youth sport is principally about fun and enjoyment (Bailey *et al.*, 2013; Wellard, 2013; Jakobsson and Lundvall, 2021). Yet as sport becomes more structured and competitive, joy can give way to burdensome performance pressures. Unrealistic parental expectation (Knight *et al.*, 2017), coach criticism (Stirling and Kerr, 2014), and an overriding 'win at all costs' ethos (Pennington, 2017), are commonplace and can lead to psychological consequences and mental health issues.

Perhaps the most abundantly researched example of compromised athlete mental health is that of disordered eating. An unrelenting quest for improvement can lead some athletes to adopt an unhealthily stringent diet regime with dire consequences for physical and psychological health (Papathomas, 2018). Based on an overly simplistic belief that weight is inversely correlated to performance, the *thin to win* mantra can result in episodes of self-starvation (Papathomas and Lavallee, 2014), laxative abuse (Kong and Harris, 2015), and clinical eating disorders such as anorexia nervosa and bulimia nervosa (Plateau *et al.*, 2017). Given their central role in shaping children's sport experiences, this chapter addresses how coaches can impact disordered eating in sport. First, disordered eating is defined and key assumptions in athlete risk and prevalence discussed. Second, how sporting environments can precipitate worrisome eating behaviour in young athletes is considered, with a focus on coach culpability. Third, the role of the coach in preventing athlete disordered eating is explored. Conclusions centre on best practice recommendations for managing disordered eating cases and cultivating cultures where they are less likely to occur.

 DOI: 10.4324/9781003199359-18

## Review of Current Research

### *Athlete Disordered Eating: Definitions, Prevalence, Risk*

Disordered eating is considered a continuum of troublesome eating attitudes and behaviours, ranging from common but unhealthy dietary restraint to more severe pathology such as frequent purging of food and chronic starvation (Sundgot-Borgen and Torstveit, 2011). Although well-defined clinical illnesses such as anorexia nervosa and bulimia nervosa dominate the popular discourse, subclinical disordered eating is more prevalent and can also have a dramatic detrimental impact on health and quality of life. Movement along the continuum is common, so any pattern of problematic eating warrants concern and has the potential to worsen. This wide and inclusive approach to conceptualising food, weight, and eating problems is important as it acknowledges all issues as worthy of support, and in theory enables more of those who struggle to be attended to.

The prevalence of athlete disordered eating is notoriously difficult to quantify due to a range of methodological issues, not least a reluctance for athletes to disclose issues due to fear of stigma and even deselection (Papathomas and Lavallee, 2012). Most at risk are elite and sub-elite female athletes who participate in lean and aesthetic sports. Lean sports are those where a low body weight is especially central to performance, such as distance running and triathlon. Aesthetic sports are those where an exposed body is judged according to artistic symmetry, such as figure skating and rhythmic gymnastics. A systematic review showed that in six out of seven studies, disordered eating prevalence was higher in females participating in lean and aesthetic sports (Mancine *et al.*, 2020). This does not mean disordered eating does not occur in sports where body weight is considered less instrumental to performance. There are examples in the literature of disordered eating in power sports such as soccer (Papathomas and Lavallee, 2006), tennis (Papathomas and Lavallee, 2012), and basketball (Papathomas and Lavallee, 2014) amongst others. Youth sport coaches across all sports should be vigilant to possible cases of disordered eating. Similarly, coaches working with young male athletes should be mindful that boys experience eating disturbances too, and avoid dismissing potential concerns (Papathomas and Lavallee, 2006). This said, identifying disordered eating in boys is challenging as they will be more likely to conceal what is often portrayed as a "female disease" (Papathomas, 2014).

### *Disordered Eating Onset: A Youth Sport Concern*

Traditionally, the age of onset for disordered eating was considered late adolescence, somewhere between 16 and 20 years of age (Stice *et al.*, 2013; Potterton *et al.*, 2020). Developmental psychologists hypothesised the achievement threats associated with this time of life – school exams, sporting pursuits, peer acceptance – combine to form a perfect storm that promotes body dissatisfaction, distress, and a perceived loss of control (Levine and Smolak, 2013). There is growing evidence to suggest the illness increasingly occurs at a much younger age (Smink *et al.*, 2013), with clinical cases identified in children as young as 8 (Herpertz-Dahlmann and Dahmen, 2019). The principal risk-factors associated with disordered eating development, such as dieting, weight concern, and poor body image, can also present during early childhood. For example, pre-adolescents show high rates of body dissatisfaction – the discrepancy between an individual's perceived body and their ideal body – with half of young girls desiring a thinner body (Dion *et al.*, 2016). Unrealistic cultural ideals, slenderness for females, and overt muscularity for males, can be internalised at just 5 and 6 years of age (McLean *et al.*, 2018; Perez *et al.*, 2018). Body dissatisfaction is a major risk-factor for disordered eating as the young child seeks to move closer to their ideal (Petrie, 2020). This means that even coaches of pre-adolescent age should be prepared to encounter disordered eating attitudes and behaviours. Particularly given low energy intake in pre-adolescents carries the added complication of possible abnormal pubertal development (Weimann *et al.*, 2000).

## Coaches' Knowledge of Disordered Eating

A knowledge and awareness of core disordered eating signs and symptoms is an obvious minimum requirement for successfully identifying potentially problematic eating attitudes and behaviours. Coaches should be sensitive to behavioural or physical signs, such as extreme fatigue, excessive exercise, and secretive eating; and psychological signs, such as being self-critical about weight, low mood, and anxiety (Bonci *et al.*, 2008). Coaches who are sensitive to such eating psychopathology can play a vital role in preventing symptom deterioration (Plateau *et al.*, 2017). Despite its obvious importance, a baseline knowledge of disordered eating is distinctly lacking among coaches. Studies report that coaches identify a lack of confidence in recognising eating problems and how to manage them if they emerge (Nowicka *et al.*, 2013). There is wide acceptance within the coaching profession that more training and education on athlete disordered eating in sport is needed (Plateau *et al.*, 2014).

## How Culpable Is the Coach?

Although complex psychopathology is never the result of any one cause, elite, competitive sport cultures are implicated in the onset of disordered eating (Papathomas, 2018). Given the role of the coach in setting this culture, through the behaviours and practices they adopt and promote, the coach is regularly identified as a central figure in engendering disturbed eating among athletes (Jones *et al.*, 2005; Papathomas and Lavallee, 2010; Coker-Cranney and Reel, 2015). Ample studies offer examples of how coaches can contribute to creating an environment for disordered eating to thrive. For example, athletes have reported overt weight loss pressure from coaches, including specific instructions to engage in restrictive eating such as eliminating carbohydrates (Pereira Vargas and Winter, 2021). Coaches can also instigate overly frequent weigh-ins; a stressful event that embarrasses athletes, reinforces the thin-to-win mantra, and increases long-term body consciousness (McMahon and Dinan Thompson, 2008). When compliance is low and weight targets are not met, coaches may even enforce punishments such as deselection from the team (McMahon and Penney, 2013). At the extreme end of coach behavior, athletes have reported receiving abusive and derogatory comments about their weight and how they look (Kerr *et al.*, 2006; Muscat and Long, 2008).

Damaging coach behaviours are pertinent because young athletes often hold a coach in great esteem, seek their approval, and are likely to internalise a coach's views as their own. Even if such respect is absent, the power imbalance is such that if coaches encourage harmful behaviours, and/or hold extreme views regarding weight and the body, athletes are expected to align with these (Shanmugam *et al.*, 2013). Young athletes are unlikely to possess the maturity to think critically about dubious coach practices or the confidence to challenge authority (Stirling and Kerr, 2009). Some scholars argue that these coaches engage in *surveillance practices* – essentially weighing, monitoring, commenting – a form of disciplinary power designed to control and regulate the athlete to conform to expectation (McMahon and Penney, 2013). In time, athletes entrenched in such a culture, adopt these practices as their own and engage in *self-surveillance*; for example, body checking, weight monitoring at home, and calorie counting (McMahon and Barker-Ruchti, 2017). To this end, the athlete has been controlled to the extent they become the chief arbiter of their controller's demands. As such, athletes continuously engage in unhealthy eating and exercise practices (e.g. self-starvation, excessive exercise, purging).

## *Taking Action: Learning from Intervention Studies*

Psychoeducation interventions appear to be the chosen method in attempting to prevent disordered eating in youth sport (i.e. Elliot *et al.*, 2004, 2008; Buchholz *et al.*, 2008; Martinsen *et al.*, 2014; Martinsen *et al.*, 2015). Psychoeducation for youth athletes has focused on a range of topics including sports nutrition (Elliot *et al.*, 2004, 2008), eating attitudes and beliefs (Buchholz *et al.*, 2008), resisting pressure to diet (Buchholz *et al.*, 2008), physical activity for enjoyment (Buchholz *et al.*, 2008), enhancing self-esteem (Martinsen *et al.*, 2014), and psychological and physiological development in adolescents (Martinsen *et al.*, 2014). Psychoeducation for coaches has focused on providing knowledge and strategies regarding healthy nutrition, eating behaviour, and eating disorder symptoms, identification, management, and prevention (e.g., Martinsen *et al.*, 2015). Findings suggest such interventions result in moderate benefits such as reduced use of diet pills, reduced pressure to be thin, and improved awareness of how to manage disordered eating. Although these findings are encouraging, there are few long-term follow-ups to test benefits over time (Stice *et al.*, 2007).

In a recent review of interventions addressing eating psychopathology in athletes, Sandgren *et al.* (2020) suggest that successful eating disorder interventions are generally characterised by a long intervention duration, high frequency of intervention sessions, and often target multiple concepts within eating psychopathology, nutrition, self-efficacy, and self-esteem, using a wide range of delivery methods (e.g. lectures, workshops, hand-outs, and manuals). However, it is worth noting that the multicomponent nature of these complex interventions makes the identification of effective intervention components challenging; specifically, what element works? It is also suggested that focusing on fewer components and reducing intervention duration but increasing intervention intensity may be more efficacious and improve retention among athletes. It is worth noting that these recommendations relate to eating disorder interventions conducted with adult athletes, and therefore, considerations of intervention intensity and duration may differ for young athletes.

## Implications for Children's Sport Coaching

Within this section, the implications of the reviewed literature for the future of children's sport coaching is addressed. What follows is a series of best practice recommendations to guide coaches of children towards working in ways that might lessen disordered eating prevalence and impact.

1 *Get educated on disordered eating*

Youth sport coaches should ensure they are appropriately educated on disordered eating issues, including signs, symptoms, and risk-factors. Due to their regular contact with athletes, coaches are well-placed to identify early signs of disordered eating (Martinsen *et al.*, 2015). Coach knowledge – and their confidence in that knowledge – influences athletes' willingness to seek support for mental health issues (Swann *et al.*, 2018). More broadly, coaches should also be aware of the "reduced weight-increased performance" fallacy. Although performance improvement may occur in the early stages of weight loss, it will deteriorate, as will health, if weight loss persists (Plateau *et al.*, 2014). Performance is multi-faceted, even in lean sports, and an overemphasis on weight can detract from other important athletic attributes such as strength and power. Although knowledge of basic principles of diet and nutrition can be valuable, coaches should accept the limits of their expertise and avoid discussing such issues with athletes. This is especially true for coaches working with younger children who are still growing and may have yet to experience puberty.

2 *Cultivate a supportive coach-athlete relationship*

Although coaches may perceive that their primary role is to oversee physical training and performance improvement (Denison, 2007), supporting wider well-being and mental health is also imperative. Young athletes tend to seek support from people they trust and are comfortable with (Ferguson *et al.*, 2019), therefore cultivating an emotionally supportive coach-athlete relationship may increase the likelihood of disordered eating disclosure.

3 *Prepare to have difficult conversations*

A willingness to engage in challenging conversations is also necessary. For example, many coaches – particularly male coaches – report feeling uncomfortable and unable to discuss the menstrual cycle (Plateau *et al.*, 2014). However, menstrual dysfunction is a key physical indicator of disordered eating among female athletes. Therefore, coach knowledge and confidence in addressing this – and other – sometimes challenging subjects with athletes is of paramount importance to providing necessary support. Coaches should also consider how they orchestrate conversations with athletes to ensure that they avoid terms such as 'eating disorder' – which may exacerbate the issue – and ensure that conversations are approached in a way that encourages athletes to seek support if needed.

4 *Build a support network*

In such cases whereby athlete disordered eating symptoms are of clinical severity, coaches must ensure they do not practice outside of their remit and refer to a relevant professional for diagnosis and treatment (Joy *et al.*, 2016). Where possible, coaches should play an active role within a multidisciplinary team of professionals qualified to support athlete disordered eating (Conviser *et al.*, 2018). Coaches must also consider their own support network. Witnessing a young athlete experience serious illness is challenging and traumatic and coaches must ensure they are able to seek counsel for this.

5 *Reflect on practice*

Coaches must review and reflect upon their own practice and behaviour and consider how these can be changed to create a healthier culture less likely to promote disordered eating. There are some obvious and easy fixes. Coaches should not be commenting on the weight or aesthetics of a child athlete's body. Critical comments designed to mock and shame young athletes into stringent dieting represent a form of abuse. Regular weigh-ins, particularly public ones, should also be banned. Weight targets, and associated threats if they are not met, are unethical. Coaches entering environments where these practices are in place must accept responsibility to speak out against them. More generally, coaches should reflect on the weight-performance relationship and consider how they might be promoting an over-simplified version of it.

## Summary, Future Directions, and Future Research

Disordered eating is prevalent among athletes, particularly females in lean and aesthetic sports but not excluding males or athletes in other sports. No athlete is immune. The onset of disordered eating and associated risk-factors like body dissatisfaction and restrained eating can occur in pre-adolescence; much younger than originally thought. Coaches of young children must therefore not assume that disordered eating is merely a concern for older age-groups. Instead, all youth sport coaches should ensure a baseline knowledge of key signs and symptoms. Further, coaches must conduct an honest reflection on how their own practices might be conducive to disordered eating and change accordingly. Critically commenting on a child's weight constitutes abuse and is an unacceptable practice.

Future research must endeavour to include coaches as its focal point. Coaches may fear being blamed for athlete disordered eating, making engagement in research an unattractive prospect. Scholars should reassure coaches that disordered eating is multi-causal and that the goal is not a witch hunt but rather to learn from their experiences. Anonymity should also be assured so that coaches feel comfortable discussing all facets of their experiences, not just best practice. If more coaches can be better recruited into studies, knowledge may be advanced in terms of understanding the relationships between coaching philosophy, coach behaviour, and disordered eating risk. Studies may explore what coaching practices work to create athletic cultures that promote body satisfaction and a healthy relationship with food and weight. Reflective practice pieces on dealing with athlete disordered eating would also provide much needed insight into the practicalities of managing disordered eating.

Most research into athlete disordered eating focuses on adult athletes. Although it is possible to draw inferences from this body of work and apply it to youth sport, as is often the case in this chapter, it is imperative that the voices of young athletes are included in future research. Meeting ethical standards to research sensitive topics in children can be daunting and ultimately time-consuming, but children with experience of disordered eating in youth sport have much to teach us. At what age do children first become aware of the weight-performance relationship in sport? Are messages about the body, weight, and performance communicated explicitly (e.g. parent/coach instruction), or implicitly (e.g. watching a soccer player celebrate a goal by revealing a muscularly defined torso?). How do child athletes make sense of the barrage of nutritional information available in modern culture? What role does social media have in shaping child athletes' beliefs about their bodies? How do young athletes experience weight pressure and body dissatisfaction? Such foundational questions are yet to be answered. If we wish to fully understand the food and weight concerns of children who participate in competitive sports, researchers must speak to these children directly. Involving young athletes in our studies, through creative and compassionate methods, is the vital next step necessary to advance disordered eating in sport research. The more we know about young athletes' relationship with food and weight, the better we can tailor practical recommendations that support ethical coach behaviour and practice.

## References


Bailey, R., Cope, E.J., and Pearce, G., 2013. Why do children take part in, and remain involved in sport? A literature review and discussion of implications for sports coaches. *International Journal of Coaching Science*, 7 (1), 56–75.

Bean, C., Shaikh, M., and Forneris, T., 2020. Coaching strategies used to deliver quality youth sport programming. *International Sport Coaching Journal*, 7 (1), 39–51.

Bonci, C.M., *et al.*, 2008. National Athletic Trainers' Association position statement: Preventing, detecting, and managing disordered eating in athletes. *Journal of Athletic Training*, 43 (1), 80–108.

Buchholz, A., *et al.*, 2008. BodySense: An evaluation of a positive body image intervention on sport climate for female athletes. *Eating Disorders*, 16 (4), 308–321.

Coker-Cranney, A. and Reel, J.J., 2015. Coach pressure and disordered eating in female collegiate athletes: Is the coach-athlete relationship a mediating factor? *Journal of Clinical Sport Psychology*, 9 (3), 213–231.

Conviser, J.H., Tierney, A.S., and Nickols, R., 2018. Essentials for best practice: Treatment approaches for athletes with eating disorders. *Journal of Clinical Sport Psychology*, 12 (4), 495–507.

Denison, J., 2007. Social theory for coaches: A foucauldian reading of one athlete's poor performance. *International Journal of Sports Science & Coaching*, 2 (4), 369–383.

Dion, J., *et al.*, 2016. Correlates of body dissatisfaction in children. *The Journal of Pediatrics*, *171*, 202–207.

Elliot, D.L., *et al.*, 2004. Preventing substance use and disordered eating: Initial outcomes of the ATHENA (athletes targeting healthy exercise and nutrition alternatives) program. *Archives of Pediatrics and Adolescent Medicine*, 158 (11), 1043–1049.

Elliot, D.L., *et al.*, 2008. Long-term outcomes of the ATHENA (Athletes Targeting Healthy Exercise & Nutrition Alternatives) program for female high school athletes. *Journal of Alcohol and Drug Education*, 52 (2), 73–92.

Ferguson, H.L., *et al.*, 2019. Investigating youth sports Coaches' perceptions of their role in adolescent mental health. *Journal of Applied Sport Psychology*, 31 (2), 235–252.

Herpertz-Dahlmann, B. and Dahmen, B., 2019. Children in need—Diagnostics, epidemiology, treatment and outcome of early onset anorexia nervosa. *Nutrients*, 11 (8), 1932.

Holt, N.L., Deal, C.J., and Pankow, K., 2020. Positive youth development through sport. *In*: G. Tenenbaum and R. Eklund, eds. *Handbook of Sport Psychology*, 4th edition, 429–446.

Howie, E.K., Daniels, B.T., and Guagliano, J.M., 2020. Promoting physical activity through youth sports programs: It's social. *American Journal of Lifestyle Medicine*, 14 (1), 78–88.

Jakobsson, B.T. and Lundvall, S., 2021. Learn, have fun and be healthy! An interview study of Swedish teenagers' views of participation in club sport. *International Journal of Environmental Research and Public Health*, 18 (13), 6852.

Jones, R.L., Glintmeyer, N., and McKenzie, A., 2005. Slim bodies, eating disorders and the coach-athlete relationship: A tale of identity creation and disruption. *International Review for the Sociology of Sport*, 40 (3), 377–391.

Joy, E., Kussman, A., and Nattiv, A., 2016. 2016 update on eating disorders in athletes: A comprehensive narrative review with a focus on clinical assessment and management. *British Journal of Sports Medicine*, 50 (3), 154–162.

Kerr, G., Berman, E., and Souza, M.J.D., 2006. Disordered eating in women's gymnastics: Perspectives of athletes, coaches, parents, and judges. *Journal of Applied Sport Psychology*, 18 (1), 28–43.

Knight, C.J., Berrow, S.R., and Harwood, C.G., 2017. Parenting in sport. *Current Opinion in Psychology*, 16, 93–97.

Kong, P. and Harris, L.M., 2015. The sporting body: Body image and eating disorder symptomatology among female athletes from leanness focused and nonleanness focused sports. *The Journal of Psychology*, 149 (2), 141–160.

Levine, M.P. and Smolak, L., 2013. Toward a model of the developmental psychopathology of eating disorders: The example of early adolescence. *In*: J.H. Crowther, et al., eds. *The etiology of bulimia nervosa*. United States: Taylor & Francis, 75–96.

Mancine, R.P., *et al.*, 2020. Prevalence of disordered eating in athletes categorised by emphasis on leanness and activity type–a systematic review. *Journal of Eating Disorders*, 8 (1), 1–9.

Martinsen, M., *et al.*, 2014. Preventing eating disorders among young elite athletes: A randomised controlled trial. *Medicine & Science in Sports & Exercise*, 46 (3), 435–447.

Martinsen, M., *et al.*, 2015. Coaches' knowledge and management of eating disorders: A randomised controlled trial. *Medicine & Science in Sports & Exercise*, 47 (5), 1070–1078.

McLean, S.A., Wertheim, E.H., and Paxton, S.J., 2018. Preferences for being muscular and thin in 6-year-old boys. *Body Image*, 26, 98–102.

McMahon, J. and Barker-Ruchti, N., 2017. Assimilating to a boy's body shape for the sake of performance: Three female athletes' body experiences in a sporting culture. *Sport, Education and Society*, 22 (2), 157–174.

McMahon, J. and Dinan Thompson, M., 2008. A malleable body: Revelations from an elite Australian swimmer. *ACHPER Australia Healthy Lifestyles Journal*, 55 (1), 23–28.

McMahon, J.A. and Penney, D., 2013. (Self-) surveillance and (self-) regulation: Living by fat numbers within and beyond a sporting culture. *Qualitative Research in Sport, Exercise and Health*, 5 (2), 157–178.

Muscat, A.C. and Long, B.C., 2008. Critical comments about body shape and weight: Disordered eating of female athletes and sport participants. *Journal of Applied Sport Psychology*, 20 (1), 1–24.

Nowicka, P., *et al.*, 2013. Moving from knowledge to action: A qualitative study of elite coaches' capacity for early intervention in cases of eating disorders. *International Journal of Sports Science & Coaching*, 8 (2), 343–355.

Papathomas, A., 2014. A few good men: Male athlete eating disorders, medical supremacy and the silencing of a sporting minority. *In*: R.J. Schinke and K.R. McGannon, eds. *The psychology of sub-culture in sport and physical activity*. London: Routledge, 107–120.

Papathomas, A., 2018. Disordered eating in sport: Legitimised and stigmatised. *In*: M. Atkinson, ed. *Sport, mental illness, and sociology*. United Kingdom: Emerald Publishing Limited, 97–110.

Papathomas, A. and Lavallee, D., 2006. A life history analysis of a male athlete with an eating disorder. *Journal of Loss and Trauma*, 11 (2), 143–179.

Papathomas, A. and Lavallee, D., 2010. Athlete experiences of disordered eating in sport. *Qualitative Research in Sport and Exercise*, 2 (3), 354–370.

Papathomas, A. and Lavallee, D., 2012. Narrative constructions of anorexia and abuse: An athlete's search for meaning in trauma. *Journal of Loss and Trauma*, 17 (4), 293–318.

Papathomas, A. and Lavallee, D., 2014. Self-starvation and the performance narrative in competitive sport. *Psychology of sport and exercise*, 15 (6), 688–695.

Pennington, C.G., 2017. Moral development and sportsmanship in physical education and sport. *Journal of Physical Education, Recreation & Dance*, 88 (9), 36–42.

Pereira Vargas, M.L.F. and Winter, S., 2021. Weight on the bar vs. weight on the scale: A qualitative exploration of disordered eating in competitive female powerlifters. *Psychology of Sport and Exercise*, 52, 101822.

Perez, M., *et al.*, 2018. Body dissatisfaction and its correlates in 5-to 7-year-old girls: A social learning experiment. *Journal of Clinical Child & Adolescent Psychology*, 47 (5), 757–769.

Petrie, T.A., 2020. Eating disorders in sport: From etiology to prevention. *In:* G. Tenenbaum and R.C. Eklund, eds. *Handbook of sport psychology*. Hoboken: John Wiley & Sons, 694–710.

Plateau, C.R., *et al.*, 2014. Identifying and preventing disordered eating among athletes: Perceptions of track and field coaches. *Psychology of Sport and Exercise*, 15 (6), 721–728.

Plateau, C.R., *et al.*, 2017. Female athlete experiences of seeking and receiving treatment for an eating disorder. *Eating disorders*, 25 (3), 273–277.

Potterton, R., *et al.*, 2020. "I'm not a teenager, I'm 22. Why can't I snap out of it?": a qualitative exploration of seeking help for a first-episode eating disorder during emerging adulthood. *Journal of Eating Disorders*, 8 (1), 1–14.

Ronkainen, N.J., *et al.*, 2021. Learning in sport: From life skills to existential learning. *Sport, Education and Society*, 26 (2), 214–227.

Sandgren, S.S., Haycraft, E. and Plateau, C.R., 2020. Nature and efficacy of interventions addressing eating psychopathology in athletes: A systematic review of randomised and nonrandomised trials. *European Eating Disorders Review*, 28 (2), 105–121.

Shanmugam, V., Jowett, S. and Meyer, C., 2013. Eating psychopathology amongst athletes: The importance of relationships with parents, coaches and teammates. *International Journal of Sport and Exercise Psychology*, 11 (1), 24–38.

Smink, F.R., van Hoeken, D., and Hoek, H.W., 2013. Epidemiology, course, and outcome of eating disorders. *Current Opinion in Psychiatry*, 26 (6), 543–548.

Stice, E., Marti, C.N. and Rohde, P., 2013. Prevalence, incidence, impairment, and course of the proposed DSM-5 eating disorder diagnoses in an 8-year prospective community study of young women. *Journal of Abnormal Psychology*, 122 (2), 445–457.

Stice, E., Shaw, H., and Marti, C.N., 2007. A meta-analytic review of eating disorder prevention programs: Encouraging findings. *Annual Review of Clinical Psychology*, 3, 207–231.

Stirling, A.E. and Kerr, G.A., 2009. Abused athletes' perceptions of the coach-athlete relationship. *Sport in Society*, 12 (2), 227–239.

Stirling, A.E. and Kerr, G.A., 2014. Initiating and sustaining emotional abuse in the coach–athlete relationship: An ecological transactional model of vulnerability. *Journal of Aggression, Maltreatment & Trauma*, 23 (2), 116–135.

Sundgot-Borgen, J., and Torstveit, M. 2011. Prevalence of eating disorders in elite athletes is higher than in the general population. *Journal of Sports Medicine*, 14 (1), 25–32.
Swann, C., *et al.*, 2018. Youth sport as a context for supporting mental health: Adolescent male perspectives. *Psychology of Sport and Exercise*, 35, 55–64.
Weimann, E., *et al.*, 2000. Peripubertal pertubations in elite gymnasts caused by sport specific training regimes and inadequate nutritional intake. *International Journal of Sports Medicine*, 21 (3), 210–215.
Wellard, I., 2013. *Sport, fun and enjoyment: An embodied approach*. London: Routledge.

# 16

# PARENTAL INVOLVEMENT IN ORGANISED YOUTH SPORT

*Camilla J. Knight, Sam Elliott, Olivier Y. Rouquette, James Maurice, and Rachael A. Newport*

## Introduction

During their participation in sport, children interact with numerous people who have the potential to influence their development and experiences. However, in most cases, it is parents (or those who fulfil the parental role, including guardians, carers, and step-parents) who have the largest and most enduring impact (Knight *et al.*, 2017). Research conducted over the last 60 years has provided substantial evidence of the key role parents play in socializing children into sport (Dorsch *et al.*, 2021), as well as the influence they have on a range of psychosocial outcomes (Harwood *et al.*, 2019). Further, there is an increasing understanding of the reciprocal impact children's engagement in sport can have on parents (Knight, 2019).

How parents influence (and are influenced by) their children will vary depending upon their parenting cognitions, practices, and styles, which are in turn dictated by the culture in which parents are raised and raising their children (Bornstein, 2012). Consequently, the specific ways in which parents are involved in their children's sporting and non-sporting lives varies between individuals and across cultures. Nevertheless, in general, parents are seeking to raise children who are happy, healthy, and fulfilled (Bornstein, 2012). Unfortunately, however, this is not a simple or easy task, particularly within the emotionally charged youth sport environment (Newport *et al.*, 2021). Consequently, there is an increasing recognition that support or guidance for parents may be beneficial to maximise or enhance parents' involvement (Holt *et al.*, 2008; Dorsch *et al.*, 2018).

Coaches can play an extremely important part in facilitating parents' access to such support (Newport *et al.*, 2021). However, to do this, it is first important that coaches understand the complexity of parental involvement in youth sport settings; specifically, the consequences of parental involvement, factors influencing parental involvement, and perhaps most importantly, how parental involvement can be optimised. As such, through this chapter, we provide a critical review of the research pertaining to parental involvement in sport, with a particular focus on unpacking these various aspects.

DOI: 10.4324/9781003199359-19

## Review of Current Literature

### *How Are Parents Involved in Organised Youth Sport?*

It has been suggested that parents should demonstrate involvement that increases the chances for children to achieve their sporting potential, have positive psychosocial experiences, and develop positive developmental outcomes (Harwood and Knight, 2015). There are many ways that parents do this, not least through the provision of opportunities to participate. However, it is not simply providing opportunities that are important, but rather the selection of developmentally appropriate opportunities that complete their children's interests and desires (Holt and Knight, 2014). Having initiated children's involvement in sport, parents then facilitate involvement by, for instance, providing the funding for training, competitions, clothing, and equipment, as well as transporting children to the necessary venues (Lauer *et al.*, 2010). Parents' provision, and encouragement of, sporting opportunities not only enables children to participate in sport but also indicates the value parents place on sport participation. Subsequently, through these behaviours, parents influence children's interest in participating and continue their engagement (Fredricks and Eccles, 2004), as well as the importance of succeeding or performing well (e.g. Dunn *et al.*, 2016).

Parents also provide emotional support, which includes offering comfort and reassurance to their child when their child is experiencing stress or emotional upset (Fredricks and Eccles, 2004). For instance, emotional support is particularly valuable for children when experiencing injuries, nerves, slumps in performance, and for overcoming a loss of confidence (Knight *et al.*, 2016). The provision of such emotional support again acts as an indicator to children regarding parents' care and interest in their sport involvement, their perceptions of their sporting competence, and measures of success, among others (Furusa *et al.*, 2021).

### *Consequences of Parental Involvement in Sport*

Clearly, parents are a vital part of children's sport, fulfilling numerous tasks and roles (Dorsch *et al.*, 2021). As indicated, the ways in which parents fulfil such tasks, that is the specific behaviours they display and the comments they make, effects children's psychosocial development, as well as their ongoing engagement and performance in sport (Harwood *et al.*, 2019). Traditionally, the consequences of parents' involvement have been considered based on a dichotomous view of parental involvement as either supportive or pressuring and resulting consequences as positive or negative (Knight *et al.*, 2017).

Using this approach, it has generally been concluded that when parents' display supportive involvement, which is considered as behaviours that facilitate a child's sport participation, it will lead to positive outcomes (Knight, 2019). For instance, encouragement, providing sport opportunities, unconditional support (e.g. supporting regardless of the match/competitive outcome), emotional support (e.g. recomforting, reassuring), and tangible support has been associated with increased enjoyment and self-esteem (Furusa *et al.*, 2021), enhanced performance and importance of sport participation, and reduced anxiety (Hoyle and Leff, 1997). Moreover, supportive involvement is viewed positively by coaches (Lauer *et al.*, 2010) and can enhance the quality of the parent-coach relationship (Knight and Gould, 2016) and the coach-athlete relationship (Jowett and Timson-Katchis, 2005; Wall *et al.*, 2019).

In contrast, parental involvement that is viewed as pressuring, such as having unattainable expectations (Hoyle and Leff, 1997) or being negative and critical and overemphasising winning over other domains of development (Lauer *et al.*, 2010) are deemed to be negative. Pressuring types of involvement are generally associated with negative outcomes such as lower enjoyment, increased anxiety, amotivation, and boredom, or burnout and dropout (see Dorsch *et al.*, 2021 for review). Further, pressuring behaviours are perceived to negatively impact on coaches as it can result in parents interfering in training, criticising coaches, or questioning coaches' decisions (Gould *et al.*, 2008; Lauer *et al.*, 2010). Consequently, parental pressure can damage the parent-coach and the coach-athlete relationship (Gould *et al.*, 2008; Knight and Harwood, 2009).

Although the suggestion that supportive parental behaviours lead to positive outcomes and parental pressure to negative ones is widely accepted and appears evident, it is not that simple. For instance, the same parental behaviours can be associated with positive and/or detrimental outcomes for children (Gould *et al.*, 2008) and perceptions of pressuring and supportive types of behavior are not always clear (Dorsch *et al.*, 2016). One of the reasons for this is that rather than solely considering how parents behave, it is also necessary to consider athletes' perceptions of their parents' behaviours (Knight, 2019). For instance, in a study involving athletes and their parents, Babkes and Weiss (1999) found that athletes' perceptions of their parents' beliefs about competency and athletes' perceptions of parents' responses to successes were significantly related to their perceived competence, enjoyment, and motivation. However, parents' self-perceived attitudes and behaviours were not related to athletes' outcomes. This and other literature (e.g. Dorsch *et al.*, 2016; Dunn *et al.*, 2016) suggest that parents' reports of support and pressure are not necessarily related to athletes' perceptions of support and pressure, and that parents' attempts to be supportive may be perceived to be pressuring by children.

## Influence of Others

When looking at the consequences of parental involvement, it is also important to consider that parents are not the only people influencing children; other family members, coaches, and peers can also influence children's sporting experiences and psychosocial outcomes. Specifically, research suggests that different social agents have similar and unique influences on children (Keegan *et al.*, 2014). For instance, in a series of studies, Keegan *et al.* (2009, 2010, 2014) showed that parents', coaches', and peers' motivational climate shared similarities in terms of feedback and evaluative behaviours at early stages of sport participation (Keegan *et al.*, 2009). However, during the specialising years, parents' and coaches' influences were related to their specific roles, with a significant role of parents being support and facilitation, while coaches uniquely influenced athletes through their instructions and assessment (Keegan *et al.*, 2010). Finally, parents' influence diminished during the investment/later years, while coaches' instructions and leadership remained influential, alongside peers' emotional support and competitive behaviours (Keegan *et al.*, 2014). Recent research has also started to investigate the potential synergies and/or compensatory effects of coaches' and parents' influence on young athletes (Gaudreau *et al.*, 2016). Preliminary evidence tends to demonstrate that while coaches have the strongest positive influence on athletes' motivation (even when parent support is low), both parents and coaches could thwart athletes needs, leading to negative outcomes such as amotivation (Gaudreau *et al.*, 2016). Given such findings, it is important that parental involvement is considered within the broader social context when attempting to understand if certain behaviours and comments may be detrimental or beneficial.

## Experiences of Parents in Sport

Entering the youth sport setting is a dynamic, intricate, and complex social experience for parents and is influenced by a host of social and environmental factors (Knight *et al.*, 2017).

Although parents play a central role in socialising children into sport, parents also become socialised through their participation, making sacrifices to support children's participation, experiencing reactive emotions to their child's outcomes, and changing relationships with other parents (Newport *et al.*, 2021). Fulfilling these parental roles can be a challenging experience for parents given that many are uncertain how to behave in youth sport (Harwood and Knight, 2009), and their involvement is simply based on "trial and error" (Burgess *et al.*, 2016). As such, coaches and sporting organisations can help parents by providing them with guidance and support, however, an important step in doing this is to take time to understand parents' experiences in sport (Thrower *et al.*, 2018; Newport *et al.*, 2021).

Initial insights into this area came from Wiersma and Fifer (2008), who examined how the perceived characteristics of the sport environment (e.g. quality of officials, league quality, child's performance, processes of competition) influenced parents' behaviour and provision of support for their child. This study provided the impetus for a more empathetic understanding about parents' experiences in sport and the social and structural features that impact on parental involvement. Explicit research attention subsequently expanded upon this perspective and highlighted a range of complex stressors that can influence parental involvement including organisation-related (e.g. time and financial investments, inefficiencies of organisation), developmental (e.g., decisions about the child's future), and competitive (e.g. watching games, outcomes of games), stressors (Harwood and Knight, 2009; Burgess *et al.*, 2016; Harwood *et al.*, 2019).

Beyond stressors, research has also suggested that parents experience numerous, usually negative, emotions such as anxiety, anger, and frustration at youth sport competitions (Wiersma and Fifer, 2008; Knight and Holt, 2013). For instance, parents have reported experiencing anger and frustration when watching their child compete if the behaviours of referees, coaches, athletes, opponents, and other parents were seen as unjust, uncaring, or incompetent (Knight and Holt, 2013; Pynn *et al.*, 2019). Parents have also reported feelings of boredom and frustration arising from the long duration of competitions, along with becoming emotionally involved and affected by critical time points within competitions (such as the last minutes of a match or when scores are close; Holt *et al.*, 2008; Burgess *et al.*, 2016). Moreover, parents have high levels of empathy for their children and subsequently share the emotions their children experience and display. Consequently, parents may experience disappointment and enjoyment along with their children, which can affect how they respond to and support their children (Holt *et al.*, 2008; Knight and Holt, 2013).

However, although parents share many similar experiences, it is also important to recognise that parents are a heterogenous group and their experiences will vary based on numerous factors. For instance, parents' personal experiences and expectations (Knight *et al.*, 2016), personal circumstances (e.g. work demands, family commitments and make-up, location; Furusa *et al.*, 2021) their child's age, stage of development, and playing level (Newport *et al.*, 2021) and both sport-specific norms and societal expectations regarding parenting (Stefensen *et al.*, 2018) can all influence parents and their involvement in their child's sport. Thus, it is clear that parental involvement in youth sport is a repeated cognitive and social experience, in which individual parent characteristics and the sport context interact and change in a dynamic manner (Dorsch *et al.*, 2016) and this needs to be acknowledged in broader discussions about their involvement in youth sport.

## *Optimal Parental Involvement in Organised Youth Sport*

Given the complexity of parental involvement, it is not possible to produce a definitive list of things all parents should do or should avoid to ensure positive outcomes and avoid negative ones (Knight *et al.*, 2017). However, children's preferences provide important insights to inform parental involvement and support in sport. Several studies have employed child-centred research approaches and have indicated that children want parents to focus on effort rather than outcomes, respect sport etiquette, match their non-verbal behaviours with supportive comments, and encourage the entire team (Knight *et al.*, 2010). Moreover, children prefer parents to provide practical advice surrounding preparation for and recovery from competition (Knight *et al.*, 2010) and control their emotions during competition (Omli and Wiese-Bjornstal, 2011). In semi-professional settings, children also want parents to understand the difficulties they experience navigating changing social networks, revising sporting goals, and seeking new forms of feedback for improvement (Elliott *et al.*, 2018). Conversely, children prefer their children not to coach from the sidelines or provide technical and tactical advice unless they have sufficient knowledge (Knight *et al.*, 2010). Research also suggests that children do not want parents to draw attention to themselves by displaying embarrassing or overexcited behaviours, arguing with the coach or officials, or attempting to coach them (Knight *et al.*, 2010).

Parental verbal feedback has been theorised as a having the potential to 'make or break' relations between parents and their child by exacerbating feelings of shame, anxiety, and frustration through unsolicited and poorly timed feedback (Elliott and Drummond, 2017). Therefore, the provision of instructional comments, feedback, and encouragement can be enhanced if the nature and timing of parents' behaviours match children's preferences (Knight *et al.*, 2016; Elliott and Drummond, 2017; Furusa *et al.*, 2021), which can only occur if parents have opportunities to learn what their child prefers and how they perceive their actions and involvement in different situations (Knight and Holt, 2014).

The importance of parents' reacting to their child's individual needs and preferences aligns with the idea of responsiveness of the support (Reis *et al.*, 2004). The construct of perceived responsiveness includes three key components: Understanding, which accounts for the perception that the partner (e.g. parent) comprehend individual's (e.g. a child's) core self (e.g. needs, desires); validation, which is the perception that the partner respects or values the individual's view of the self (e.g. expresses liking and encouragements, value abilities and opinions), and; caring for, which describes the perception that the partner expresses warmth, affection, and interest to the individual (Reis *et al.*, 2004). Recent work has demonstrated that responsiveness positively influences children's experiences, specifically higher levels of self-efficacy to accomplish goals and thriving and reduced worry (Rouquette *et al.*, 2021a, 2021b). Overall, this preliminary evidence suggests that facilitating parents' responsiveness may be a key factor in enhancing their involvement and subsequently positively influencing children's self-perceptions (e.g. self-efficacy, self-esteem) and wellbeing within sporting contexts.

## Implications for Children's Sport Coaching

### *Enhancing Parental Involvement in Sport*

Given the importance of parents within youth sport, it has been suggested that coaches, clubs, and organisations should work to create more 'parent-positive' cultures (Knight, 2019), in which parents feel welcomed, respected, and valued as a positive member of their child's support team (Newport *et al.*, 2021). The provision of information and support is one such means through which this can occur. Drawing on research in this area, there are many areas about which parents may benefit from guidance or support. These include:

- Information about their child's sport, including technical information, the rationale behind a sports programme, and information about the sports organisation (Dorsch *et al.*, 2018).
- Suggestions for managing demands and developing coping strategies to make the parent experience more enjoyable (Harwood and Knight, 2009; Harwood *et al.*, 2019).
- How to develop relationships and communicate with coaches and others within their support network (Knight and Gould, 2016).
- How to create an autonomy-supportive environment and demonstrate emotional intelligence (Harwood and Knight, 2015; Pynn *et al.*, 2019).
- Identifying and acting upon children's preferences for parental support before, during, and after competitions (Knight and Holt, 2014; Elliott and Drummond, 2017; Dorsch *et al.*, 2018).
- Changes required in parental support in line with children's developmental needs and the journey ahead (Dorsch *et al.*, 2018).

The benefit of providing parents with information across these topics has been evidenced through the evaluation of a range of different parent education programmes (e.g. Thrower *et al.*, 2017, 2018; Tamminen *et al.*, 2020), which coaches may be well positioned to deliver or facilitate. Overall, it appears that parents benefit from the increased exposure to information and gain knowledge from their engagement (Thrower *et al.*, 2017). Such programmes enhance the parent experience and that of their child too, for instance following engagement with these programmes it appears that parents provide more support, have better communication with their child, report increased parenting efficacy, and there is an increase in their children's enjoyment (Thrower *et al.*, 2018). Parents find practical tasks, group discussions, and the opportunity to share experiences enjoyable, as they are able to enhance their relationship with other parents and gain social support (Thrower *et al.*, 2017). Furthermore, parents find it useful to have resources that they can take home and supplement the sessions (Thrower *et al.*, 2017).

In contrast, it is apparent that there are challenges and issues that have been experienced and identified through parent education programmes. Most notably, parent attendance has been a key issue across most programmes (Thrower *et al.*, 2017, 2018). Although, online programmes provide an alternative delivery method to overcome the issue of parent attendance, they subsequently limit opportunities for parents to interact and gain the social support that they benefit from in face-to-face sessions (Thrower *et al.*, 2018). It has, however, been recognised that if coaches support and endorse parent education and support programmes, that this may greatly enhance parents' engagement in programmes (Thrower *et al.*, 2018) as well as helping to enhance the relationships between parents and coaches.

## *Developing Effective Parent-Coach Relationships*

Beyond providing information and support to parents, a key component of "parent-positive" environments is good quality, effective parent-coach relationships (Newport *et al.*, 2021). Unfortunately, however, research has highlighted the complex nature of the coach-parent relationship (Wall *et al.*, 2019), and it is apparent that each party can negatively impact both on each other and children (Knight and Gould, 2016). Despite the complexity of the relationship, it is extremely important that steps are taken to enhance interactions because parents are gatekeepers to a plethora of information regarding their child and can provide coaches with key knowledge regarding a child's responsiveness to training, as well as information on their general wellbeing (Jowett and Timson-Katchis, 2005). Furthermore, through the development of the coach-parent relationship, parents can develop their understanding of their child's sport, a key factor underpinning optimal parental involvement within youth sport (Knight and Holt, 2014). Lastly, positive coach-parent interactions have been associated with smoother transitions within sport and successful talent development (Knight and Holt, 2014).

To work more effectively with parents, it is beneficial for coaches to proactively seek to work with parents and develop open, honest, and trusting relationships. The best parent-coach relationships do not happen by chance, rather they take time, effort, and creativity (Knight and Gould, 2016). It requires parents to be recognised as a valuable member of the team and being valued for their contribution (Harwood *et al.*, 2019). This requires coaches to allocate time and energy to parents while also providing guidance around interactions (Knight and Harwood, 2009). Although this may seem daunting, the time and effort invested to create positive relationships can save a lot of time in the long-run and minimise chances of conflict.

To do this, the first focus should be on developing communication channels. The more that coaches and parents interact, the more information that can be shared, and consequently the greater the support that each member of the athletic triangle can provide to each other (Maurice *et al.*, 2021). For example, introducing parent representative groups, where parents are provided the opportunity to have a voice and provide feedback about the programme, may lead to more effective two-way communication between coach and parent (Newport *et al.*, 2021). Additionally, ensuring there is regular communication about goals, plans, and expectations for each other and for children is important (Knight *et al.*, 2016). By taking the time to inform parents about current training and competition goals coaches have developed with their child, they are likely to receive more parental support. Similarly, communication regarding realistic expectations and anticipating any potential problems will help to keep parents on track and supporting your work with their child (Knight and Holt, 2014). Moreover, rushed conversations that take place when other things are going on can often lead to miscommunication and misunderstanding. Coaches could overcome this issue by allocating specific times for parents to contact them and indicating preferred means through which this should occur (Knight and Gould, 2016).

Beyond communication, additional strategies that may help to enhance parent-coach interactions include:

- Coaches spending time thinking about want they want from the relationship with parents and developing a parent-coach philosophy. Once this is identified, coaches should communicate it to parents and give parents a chance to ask any questions and then share their own thoughts. Having this conversation early on in the season will help coaches and parents start from the same page and hopefully reduce the chances of issues arising as the season progresses (Knight and Holt, 2014).
- Coaches should get to know the parents of the children they are coaching and help the parents get to know coaches (Harwood and Knight, 2009; cf., Burgess *et al.*, 2016). The more that coaches understand the different things happening in parents lives and the range of personal and interpersonal factors that may impact on their involvement the better positioned they are to tailor support and expectations. However, similarly, it's important that coaches help parents to understand the demands and pressures that are experienced as a coach, as well as other aspects of your life so that parents can also adapt their own expectations.
- Acknowledge that parents are trying to learn and provide them with guidance (Thrower *et al.*, 2017). For parents that are new to the sport, there is a lot to learn. Each time they encounter a new situation they are likely to have questions, concerns, or issues. If coaches can anticipate what parents might need to know and educate them about what to expect it

can help to minimise stress and concerns. This will help parent-coach relationship as it will minimise potential sources of conflict.

- Coaches should be professional and consistent in behaviours (cf. Harwood and Knight, 2009). Unfortunately, not all coaches work in a professional manner and although they may be in the minority, they can stimulate inappropriate interactions between parents and coaches. As such, ensuring that coaches are professional in all interactions with players and parents can help to reduce any negative images parents have of coaches. Moreover, the conflict between parents and coaches is often underpinned by parents perceiving that coaches were inconsistent in actions and behaviours, either between children or across different situations (Knight and Gould, 2016). This causes parents stress, particularly if they feel that it negatively impacts on their child and may cause them to become frustrated or angry (Wiersma and Fifer, 2008; Harwood and Knight, 2009).

## Summary, Future Directions, and Future Research

Without parents, children's opportunities to participate in sport and subsequently gain the associated physical, social, and psychological benefits would be limited. As such, the importance of understanding parental involvement and working to create environments and relationships that enhance parents' positive influence, while minimising detrimental consequences is vital. Coaches are particularly well positioned to help parents to optimise their involvement and consequently enhance the experiences of parents, coaches, and particularly children. Unfortunately, however, given the complexity of parental involvement, this is not an easy task and while there has been much growth in our understanding regarding this topic, there continues to be many areas needing further consideration. Specifically, further research unpacking the experiences of parents across the lifespan of a child's involvement, the various personal and environmental factors influencing involvement, and strategies to optimise parental involvement are needed. Moreover, somewhat surprisingly given the substantial influence that parents and coaches can have on each other, as well as the impact that the parent-coach relationship can have on children, this is an area that has received relatively limited research attention over the years. As such, there is a need for far more research regarding parent-coach relationships and evidence-based strategies exploring how to enhance and maximise parent and coach interactions.

## References

Babkes, M.L. and Weiss, M.R., 1999. Parental influence on children's cognitive and affective responses to competitive soccer participation. *Pediatric Exercise Science*, 11 (1), 44–62.

Bornstein, M.H., 2012. Cultural approaches to parenting. *Parenting: Science and Practice*, 12 (2/3), 212–221.

Burgess, N., Knight, C., and Mellalieu, S., 2016. Parental stress and coping in elite youth gymnastics: An interpretative phenomenological analysis. *Qualitative Research in Sport, Exercise and Health*, 8 (3), 1–20.

Dorsch, T.E., Smith, A.L., and Dotterer, A.M., 2016. Individual, relationship, and context factors associated with parent support and pressure in organised youth sport. *Psychology of Sport and Exercise*, 23 (1), 132–141.

Dorsch, T.E., *et al.*, 2018. Parent education in youth sport: A community case study of parents, coaches, and administrators. *Journal of Applied Sport Psychology*, 31 (4), 427–450.

Dorsch, T.E., *et al.*, 2021. A history of parent involvement in organised youth sport: A scoping review. *Sport, Exercise and Performance Psychology*, 10 (4), 536–557.

Dunn, C.R., *et al.*, 2016. The impact of family financial investment on perceived parent pressure and child enjoyment and commitment in organised youth sport. *Family Relations*, 65 (2), 287–299.

Elliott, S. and Drummond, M., 2017. During play, the break, and the drive home: The meaning of parental verbal behaviour in youth sport. *Leisure Studies*, 36 (5), 645–656.

Elliott, S., Drummond, M., and Knight, C., 2018. The experiences of being a talented youth athlete: Lessons for parents. *Journal of Applied Sport Psychology*, 30 (4), 437–455.

Fredricks, J.A. and Eccles, J.S., 2004. Parental influences on youth involvement in sports. *In:* M.R. Weiss ed., *Developmental sport and exercise psychology: A lifespan perspective*. Fitness Information Technology, 145–164.

Furusa, M.G., Knight, C.J., and Hill, D.M., 2021. Parental involvement and children's enjoyment in sport. *Qualitative Research in Sport, Exercise, and Health*, 13 (6), 936–954.

Gaudreau, P., *et al.*, 2016. Autonomy support from parents and coaches: Synergistic or compensatory effects on sport-related outcomes of adolescent-athletes? *Psychology of Sport and Exercise*, 25, 89–99.

Gould, D., *et al.*, 2008. The role of parents in tennis success: Focus group interviews with junior coaches. *The Sport Psychologist*, 22 (1), 18–37.

Harwood, C. and Knight, C., 2009. Stress in youth sport: A developmental investigation of tennis parents. *Psychology of Sport and Exercise*, 10 (4), 447–456.

Harwood, C.G. and Knight, C.J., 2015. Parenting in youth sport: A position paper on parenting expertise. *Psychology of Sport and Exercise*, 16 (1), 24–35.

Harwood, C.G., *et al.*, 2019. Advancing the study of parental involvement to optimise the psychosocial development and experiences of young athletes. *Psychology of Sport and Exercise*, 42 (1), 66–73.

Holt, N.L. and Knight, C.J., 2014. *Parenting in youth sport: From research to practice*. Routledge.

Holt, N.L., *et al.*, 2008. Parental involvement in competitive youth sport settings. *Psychology of Sport and Exercise*, 9 (5), 663–685.

Hoyle, R.H. and Leff, S.S., 1997. The role of parental involvement in youth sport participation and performance. *Adolescence*, 32 (125), 233–243.

Jowett, S. and Timson-Katchis, M., 2005. Social networks in sport: Parental influence on the coach athlete relationship. *The Sport Psychologist*, 19 (3), 267–287.

Keegan, R.J., *et al.*, 2009. A qualitative investigation exploring the motivational climate in early career sports participants: Coach, parent and peer influences on sport motivation. *Psychology of Sport and Exercise*, 10 (3), 361–372.

Keegan, R.J., *et al.*, 2010. The motivational atmosphere in youth sport: Coach, parent, and peer influences on motivation in specializing sport participants. *Journal of Applied Sport Psychology*, 22 (1), 87–105.

Keegan, R.J., *et al.*, 2014. A qualitative investigation of the motivational climate in elite sport. *Psychology of Sport and Exercise*, 15 (1), 97–107.

Knight, C.J., 2019. Revealing findings in youth sport parenting research. *Kinesiology Review*, 8 (3), 252–259.

Knight, C., Berrow, S., and Harwood, C., 2017. Parenting in sport. *Current Opinion in Psychology*, 16 (8), 93–97.

Knight, C., Boden, C., and Holt, N., 2010. Junior tennis players' preferences for parental behaviors. *Journal of Applied Sport Psychology*, 22 (4), 377–391.

Knight, C.J. and Gould, D., 2016. The coach-parent interaction: Support or distraction. *In*: R. Thelwell, C. Harwood, and I. Greenless, eds. *The psychology of sports coaching*. Routledge, 84–97.

Knight, C.J. and Harwood, C.G., 2009. Exploring parent-related coaching stressors in British tennis: A developmental investigation. *International Journal of Sports Science and Coaching*, 4 (4), 545–565.

Knight, C.J. and Holt, N.L., 2013. Factors that influence parents' experiences at junior tennis tournaments and suggestions for improvement. *Sport, Exercise and Performance Psychology*, 2 (3), 173–189.

Knight, C. and Holt, N., 2014. Parenting in youth tennis: Understanding and enhancing children's experiences. *Psychology of Sport and Exercise*, 15 (2), 155–164.

Knight, C., *et al.*, 2016. Parental involvement in elite junior slalom canoeing. *Journal of Applied Sport Psychology*, 28 (2), 234–256.

Lauer, L., *et al.*, 2010. Parental behaviors that affect junior tennis player development. *Psychology of Sport and Exercise*, 11 (6), 487–496.

Maurice, J., Devonport, T.J., and Knight, C.J., 2021. Toward improved triadic functioning: Exploring the interactions and adaptations of coaches, parents and athletes in professional academy soccer through the adversity of COVID-19. *Frontiers in Psychology*, 12, 1755.

Newport, R.A., Knight, C.J., and Love, T.D., 2021. The youth football journey: Parents' experiences and recommendations for support. *Qualitative Research in Sport, Exercise, and Health*, 13 (6), 1006–1026.

Omli, J. and Wiese-Bjornstal, D.M., 2011. Kids speak: Preferred parental behavior at youth sport events. *Research Quarterly for Exercise and Sport*, 82 (4), 702–711.

Pynn, S.R., Dunn, J.G.H., and Holt, N.L., 2019. A qualitative study of exemplary parenting in competitive female youth team sport. *Sport, Exercise, and Performance Psychology*, 8 (2), 163–178.

Reis, H.T., Clark, M.S., and Holmes, J.G., 2004. Perceived partner responsiveness as an organizing construct in the study of intimacy and closeness. *In:* D.J. Mashek and A.P. Aron, eds. *Handbook of Closeness and Intimacy*. Psychology Press, 211–236.

Rouquette, O.Y., *et al.*, 2021a. The positive association between perceived parental responsiveness and self-esteem, anxiety, and thriving among youth rugby players: A multigroup analysis. *Journal of Sports Sciences*, 39 (13), 1537–1547.

Rouquette, O.Y., *et al.*, 2021b. Effect of parent responsiveness on young athletes' self-perceptions and thriving: An exploratory study in a Belgian French-community. *Psychology of Sport and Exercise*, 52, 1–9.

Stefensen, K., Smette, I., and Strandbu, Å., 2018. Understanding the increase in parents' involvement in organized youth sports. *Sport, Education and Society*, 23 (2), 162–172.

Tamminen, K.A., et al., 2020. Examining the impact of the respect in sport parent program on the psychosocial experiences of minor hockey athletes. *Journal of Sports Sciences*, 38 (17), 2035–2045.

Thrower, S.N., Harwood, C.G., and Spray, C.M., 2017. Educating and supporting tennis parents: An action research study. *Qualitative Research in Sport, Exercise and Health*, 9 (5), 600–618.

Thrower, S.N., Harwood, C.G., and Spray, C.M., 2018. Educating and supporting tennis parents using web-based delivery methods: A novel online education program. *Journal of Applied Sport Psychology*, 31 (3), 303–323.

Wall, J.M., *et al.*, 2019. The coach-parent relationship in Canadian competitive figure skating: An interpretive description. *Psychology of Sport and Exercise*, 45 (2), 101577.

Wiersma, L.D. and Fifer, A.M. 2008. "The schedule has been tough but we think it's worth it": The joys, challenges, and recommendations of youth sport parents. *Journal of Leisure Research*, 40 (4), 505–530.

# 17

# MAKING THE CUT: COACHES AND THE DESELECTION OF YOUNG ATHLETES

*Kacey C. Neely and James H. Dugdale*

## Introduction

Youth sport is selective across all levels of competitive sport, whether that be school teams, club teams, high-performance squads, or talent development (TD) programmes. Typically, athletes vie for a spot on the team through a tryout process, at which time they are either selected or deselected. Butt and Molnar (2009) pointed out that given the pyramidal structure of sport, there are fewer places available the farther athletes work their way 'up' the competitive system. For the majority of children striving to make a more competitive team or move into provincial, national, or even international levels of sport, deselection is almost inevitable. For some athletes, deselection can lead to sport withdrawal or the termination of their athletic careers (Wylleman and Lavallee, 2004). For other athletes, they may continue to participate in sport after being deselected, but they must cope with a range of potentially negative psychosocial and emotional consequences. While competitive youth sport and TD programmes can undoubtedly provide positive, developmentally appropriate experiences for children, literature has highlighted how deselection from teams and TD pathways may catalyse significant challenges within this developing and potentially vulnerable population (Blakelock *et al.*, 2016; Williams and MacNamara, 2020). Since deselection (or being cut) is the elimination of an athlete from a competitive sport team based on the decisions of the coaches (Neely *et al.*, 2016), it requires coaches to make judgments and decisions about the ability of athletes and their suitability for a team or TD system. Not surprisingly, coaches consider deselection to be one of the most challenging aspects of their job. This chapter aims to provide an overview of the body of work on deselection within youth sport and highlight some practical implications for coaches. The chapter will start with a brief overview of the research examining the consequences of deselection for children and youth athletes, followed by a more detailed review of literature on coaches and deselection. A four-phase deselection process will be described as well as a focussed section on deselection within TD programmes. Implications for practice will provide practical considerations for youth sport coaches, and the chapter will conclude with future directions for research in this developing area of work.

DOI: 10.4324/9781003199359-20

## Review of Current Research

### *Consequences of Deselection on Children*

While the focus of this chapter is on coaches' roles within deselection in youth sport, it is both important and necessary to understand the consequences of deselection on children. Across studies on athletes and deselection, athletes who have been cut mostly describe deselection as a negative experience with a range of negative psychological, social, and emotional consequences. For example, deselected athletes have reported feelings of depression, anxiety, anger, and humiliation, as well as a loss of self-esteem, friendships, and connectedness to school and sport (Munroe *et al.*, 1999; Barnett, 2006, 2007; Brown and Potrac, 2009; Neely *et al.*, 2017). Deselected athletes often experience a loss of athletic identity and sense of self (Grove *et al.*, 2004; Brown and Potrac, 2009; Neely *et al.*, 2018). Furthermore, one study found that children who were deselected were also 'at risk' of developing clinical levels of psychological distress (Blakelock *et al.*, 2016).

Beyond describing the negative impact of deselection, researchers have investigated how athletes cope with being deselected and how they manage the psychosocial and emotional consequences often experienced following deselection. Neely *et al.* (2017) examined how female adolescent athletes (and their parents) coped with deselection from a provincial sport team using a communal coping perspective. Interviews were conducted with 14 child-parent dyads, 10–12 weeks after deselection. Results showed that athletes and parents shared the responsibility for coping and used both communal and individual coping strategies. Initially, parents felt responsible for protecting their daughters from the negative emotions arising from deselection and used 'a console first, talk later' approach. Parents and children then shared reasonability for coping and worked together using rationalisation and positive reframing strategus. Finally, children engaged in individual coping strategies including venting to friends, distracting, and increasing their training efforts. Such coping strategies appeared to provide ways for athletes to view deselection as an opportunity for personal growth.

Athletes' experiences following deselection are more often than not negative, but some research suggests there can be possible silver linings. For example, Williams and MacNamara (2020) reported that deselected children considered deselection experiences from the talent pathway as foundational for future success in other sports, careers, or education. Similarly, Neely *et al.* (2018) found that young women athletes who were deselected from provincial teams as adolescents experienced positive growth a few years later. The athletes in the study reported an enhanced sense of personal strength and resilience and developed stronger relationships with their parents, siblings, and other teammates as a result of the support provided as they coped with deselection. While these findings are potentially a 'positive' outcome of deselection and show that growth can occur following an adverse experience, it does not justify careless deselection practices in youth sport (Tamminen and Neely, 2016). Therefore, it is crucial for coaches and sport organisations to approach deselection in a delicate and considerate way, remembering to take into account the negative consequences of their deselection decisions (Neely *et al.*, 2018).

### *Deselection and Coaches*

Deselection most commonly occurs at the beginning of each new competitive sport season. However, competition demands and the necessity to select teams or squads (such as provincial teams) through competitive seasons may also influence the timing of when deselection can take place (Barreiros *et al.*, 2014). Currently, there is limited training and education on how coaches should carry out deselection, with almost no formal policies or procedures to follow. Throughout the athletic lifespan, deselection may occur at any point. This may range from deselection during scouting or trial/tryout periods, to athletes not being awarded professional contracts at the stage of youth-to-professional or junior-to-senior transition. Regardless of when deselection occurs, it poses significant and challenging decisions for coaches and staff, as well as negative psychological, emotional, and social consequences for deselected athletes, which was previously discussed. Accordingly, this section will explore some retrospective literature examining the experiences of coaches and deselection.

Team selection and deselection is often overlooked in the coaching literature as well as coach education training on how to make the appropriate selection and deselection decisions and handle the process (Cushion and Nelson, 2013). This is surprising, given that youth sport coaches report that deselection decisions are one of the most challenging and stressful aspects of their job (Capstick and Trudel, 2010; Neely *et al.*, 2016). Only a very small number of studies have examined deselection from coaches' perspectives at various levels of youth sport (i.e. school, competitive, and high performance). Previous studies on deselection involving coaches have focused on specific aspects of the deselection process, such as how coaches make and communicate decisions to athletes and parents (e.g. Capstick and Trudel, 2010; Bradbury and Forsyth, 2012; Seifried and Casey, 2012).

In terms of studies, Capstick and Trudel (2010) interviewed five community and club-level youth sport coaches to examine the methods they used to inform youth athletes of their non-selection. Each coach currently coached 13- to 15-year-old athletes, and had at least 5 team selection coaching experiences. Interviews were also conducted with five athletes and five unrelated parents about their experiences with deselection. In terms of communication strategies, the researchers found that coaches used a range of methods to communicate non-selection to athletes individually and to athletes and parents together. Several coaches used indirect methods to communicate deselection such as reading aloud or posting a list of players who made the team or a list of players who were deselected in a hallway or on the club's website. This was done in order to limit their contact with athletes and make the communication less burdensome for themselves. Other coaches used more direct and personable methods such as face-to-face conversations, phone calls, and written personal communication through a letter or e-mail. Coaches indicated that although these more direct methods could be quite stressful, they provided opportunities for them to give feedback to athletes, as well as allowed athletes and often parents to ask questions. While more direct strategies were valued, logistical concerns such as time and space demands were often prioritised. This is a potential concern as it moves away from an athlete-centered coaching approach, and a lack of feedback may discourage continued involvement in sport and limit athlete development.

Further, a study by Seifried and Casey (2012) interviewed 15 coaches of competitive high school boys' basketball programs in the US to identify how they deselected athletes. Similar to the coaches in Capstick and Trudel's (2010) study, these coaches used both indirect and direct communication strategies. Coaches explained that they used different approaches for selection and deselection depending on the age of athletes and level of the team. For example, coaches were more inclined to carry a larger roster at lower levels like middle school and junior high and carry one or two 'practice players' at the varsity level. Interestingly, some coaches attempted to minimise the number of athletes trying out for their team, so they had fewer players to deselect themselves by, for example, not advertising try-outs (i.e. when team selection tryouts were being held). Another strategy used by coaches was to have the athletes voluntarily cut themselves even before tryouts began. While these approaches may work in school sport settings, they are unlikely suitable at club level and higher levels of competition. Further, they do not reflect an approach that places the needs of athletes before the needs of coaches.

In the few studies that have examined coaches' experiences of deselection, a major limitation is that the literature has rarely involved the use of theory. However, some research on coaches and deselection has used theories from other domains to help understand aspects of the deselection process. For example, a study of deselection conducted with 25 provincial and national level coaches across a range of male and female sports in New Zealand adapted a model from the human resource management (HRM) literature (Bradbury and Forsyth, 2012). The study aimed to investigate athlete selection procedures implemented by the coaches with a focus on the degree to which workplace HRM hiring/selection practices were utilised or could be potentially beneficial for team selection. The workplace HRM model had the following steps: job analysis, job description, person specification, job selection, and performance appraisal. The model, which was adapted and translated to the sport context, had the following steps: athlete/position analysis, position description, athlete profile, athlete selection, and athlete debrief. Findings showed that while only six coaches had experience with two of the processes related to the HRM model, 23 of 25 coaches interviewed supported the application of some version of this HRM model. Based on the findings, Bradbury and Forsyth (2012) put forward several recommendations for coaches and sport organisations which will be discussed later in this chapter.

Research by Neely *et al.* (2016) that explored provincial youth sport coaches' experiences of deselecting female adolescent athletes was informed by the judgement and decision-making (JDM) literature, which focuses on how individuals make decisions. Programmed and non-programmed decisions, systematic decision-making, conditions of certainty and uncertainty, and intuition were relevant concepts that informed the study. These concepts contributed to a theoretical understanding of ways in which coaches carried out deselection and made some of their deselection decisions. For example, Neely *et al.* (2016) found many of the decisions that coaches made throughout the different phases of the deselection process (which will be described in detail later), fit within the rational model of decision-making (Slack and Parent, 2006). These decisions were based on conditions of certainty and involved programmed decisions (i.e. decisions that are relatively simple, repetitive, and based on clearly defined procedures; Betsch, 2008) such as when coaches had a high degree of confidence about the skill level and attitude of the athlete. However, coaches were also required to make non-programmed decisions (i.e. decisions that are relatively complex, unique, and with no pre-established procedures or guidelines; Betsch, 2008), such as decisions that involved athletes on the cusp of making the team (fringe players). In making final deselection decisions, the researchers found that intuition was an important aspect of decision-making for many coaches. This means that coaches' final decisions about fringe players can come down to 'gut' feelings and emotions (Plessner *et al.*, 2008). The Bradbury and Forsyth (2012) and Neely *et al.* (2016) studies provide a foundation for theory-informed research and highlight the value of adapting and using theories and concepts from non-sport contexts. This is necessary to advance our understanding of how coaches carry out deselection and make decisions and will contribute to developing research- and evidence-based deselection policy in sport organisation.

Overall, the few but important aforementioned studies have focused on specific aspects of deselection (e.g. communication strategies) rather than an overall deselection process. There is no doubt that youth sport coaches, and all coaches for that matter, have a difficult task when it comes to negotiating how to inform athletes of their deselection. However, there are other decisions that must be made before and during the deselection process. There is a need for continued research in the area to examine deselection as an entire process to understand more about the different components of deselection and the ways coaches negotiate 'tough' decisions at various stages of this process. Due to this lack of research, there is little empirical evidence to educate coaches on deselection procedures and guide the practice of deselection in youth sport.

## The Deselection Process

One recent empirical study that identified deselection as a process was conducted by Neely *et al.*, (2016). They examined youth sport coaches' views on deselecting athletes from competitive female adolescent sport teams. Semi-structured interviews were conducted with 22 head coaches of female provincial U14 to U18 soccer, basketball, volleyball, and ice hockey teams (similar to state or regional teams). Neely *et al.* (2016) identified and described deselection as a process that involved four phases: pre-tryout meeting, evaluation and decision-making, communication of deselection, and post-deselection reflections.

1 ***Pre-tryout Meeting.*** In this first stage, coaches held a meeting with children and their parents to explain the logistics of the tryout along with their selection criteria and expectations. While the information provided in these pre-tryout meetings was important for children, parents were actually the targeted audience, which is particularly relevant at the youth sport level where parents are still heavily involved.
2 ***Evaluation and Decision-making***. This second stage involved evaluating players and documentation. Coaches sought a fair and transparent tryout process that provided the athletes to be evaluated based on the criteria explained in their pre-tryout meeting. Part of this involved including additional coaches and evaluators to make sure that all athletes had been closely observed. Documenting the evaluation and their selection/deselection decisions was also important to coaches. This provided a paper trail which the coach felt was necessary in order to protect themselves from potential problems with parents later on. The decision-making aspect of this phase involved certainty and uncertainty. Picking the best and least-skilled players was relatively easy, as well as identifying players with poor attitudes and poor coachability. However, there was often a lot of uncertainty when it came to picking players on the fringe. The last cuts usually came down to intangible characteristics like personality or leadership qualities, and coaches relied on their intuition or 'gut feelings' to make these decisions.
3 ***Communication of Deselection.*** Arguably the most stressful aspect of the deselection process for both coaches and athletes is actually the communication of 'you didn't make it'. This is the third phase and involved informing players, providing feedback, and dealing with parents. In communicating their decisions to athletes, coaches acknowledged that athletes often appeared to display high 'stress levels'. As such, coaches felt deselection decisions should be communicated to athletes through individual face-to-face meetings that took place in a private space and where there was an exit route for athletes to avoid having to walk back through the group of athletes at the tryout. Coaches felt that specific feedback needed to be given to the athlete that identified the why behind their decision not to select them. Coaches were also concerned about dealing with a 'backlash' from parents and reported that parents' negative reactions could make the deselection process even more difficult.
4 ***Post-deselection Reflections.*** The final stage in the deselection process involved reflection. Coaches debriefed and reflected on the process with other coaches including the procedures they used, what went well, and what changes they could make in future tryouts. They also reflected on how their process contributed to athlete development and continued participation.

## *Deselection in Talent Development Pathways*

The majority of research highlighted and discussed thus far in this chapter has focused on competitive youth sport within *team* settings. In more recent years, there has been an increased research focus on talent identification (TI) and talent development (TD) of youth athletes along with an increased number of athlete TD pathway programmes (Baker *et al.*, 2018). The aim of these systems is to identify prospective talent and immerse them within TD programmes to support their development. It is widely argued that early recruitment and prolonged exposure to TD programmes is highly desirable for coaches and recruiters, as it provides a greater timeframe to develop skills and expertise necessary to succeed at the professional level (Vaeyens *et al.*, 2008; Burgess and Naughton, 2010). Therefore, recruitment of athletes into these systems is occurring at increasingly younger ages (Baker *et al.*, 2018).

The limited capacity of many TD programmes results in these pathways being largely exclusive in nature, with a high annual turnover of athletes being consistently reported between age-groups in elite sport (Güllich, 2014; Kearney and Hayes, 2018). Despite coaches attempting to identify and select young athletes most likely to succeed at the professional level, successful conversion from youth to senior ranks is low (Dugdale *et al.*, 2021b; Grossmann and Lames, 2015). This presents further challenges to both coaches; who must deliberate their deselection decision recognising implications to both the team and individual (Neely *et al.*, 2016), and the athlete; who, if deselected, faces a potential termination of their sporting career, loss of athletic identity, and reduced sense of self (Brown and Potrac, 2009). Acknowledging that the majority of athletes selected onto a talent pathway do not ultimately succeed in that sport at the highest level, it is important to understand the challenges of being on and then deselected from TD programmes from the perspective of both the athlete and coach, along with methodological considerations when making deselection decisions in sport.

Decisions regarding selection and deselection within TD programmes are largely subjective in nature but are often supported by objective data (such as fitness tests or psychometric assessments; Williams and Reilly, 2000) which is often not the case in more traditional completive and club team sport selection processes. It is well established that potential predictors of talent are multidimensional in nature. Therefore, consideration may be given to physical, sociological, and psychological attributes along with technical skill (and tactical knowledge, when appropriate) when making deselection decisions in sport (Güllich, 2014; Huijgen *et al.*, 2014; Dugdale *et al.*, 2021a). Although assessment of these attributes may provide insight on abilities related to the sport, the suitability of these assessments – when used in isolation – has been challenged (Unnithan *et al.*, 2012). Evidently, evaluation and assessment methodologies, and deselection more widely, in TD programmes, is required.

Throughout this chapter, it has been reiterated that the prevalence and inevitability of deselection within competitive youth sport. However, following deselection, the reselection of previously deselected players within TI processes has been advocated. When considering the impact of deselection and reselection on long-term TD, Güllich (2014) found that players who were successful at the professional level experienced repeated selection and deselection through youth, as opposed to early selection and continuous, long-term nurture within German TD programmes. Similarly, Dugdale *et al.* (2021a) reported that 76% of players released following the closure of a youth soccer academy were re-signed to another academy within six months. These results further evidence the non-linear nature of TD relative to professional success and demonstrates the potential route back into TD pathways for athletes following deselection.

## Implications for Children's Sport Coaching

Based on the body of evidence reviewed in this chapter, there are some implications for coaching and deselection within youth sport. Specifically, researchers have put forth recommendations and considerations for practice. A highly structured process may be useful for coaches and may help to minimise some of the stress associated with deselection. Through all phases of a deselection process, communication and transparency are key. Coaches should consider holding a pre-tryout meeting with children and parents to outline the tryout and selection process (Neely *et al.*, 2016). Clear selection criteria and procedures should be explained as well as expectations for athletes and parents such as effort and commitment (Bradbury and Forsyth, 2012; Neely *et al.*, 2016). This meeting can also be a good opportunity for coaches to pre-emptively prepare athletes (and parents) for the difficult deselection process. Based on the work by Neely *et al.* (2016), coaches are encouraged to include additional coaches when evaluating players and ensure that players are being evaluated on the criteria set out in the pre-tryout meeting and help alleviate potential subjectivity. Coaches should keep detailed notes on players' strengths and weaknesses in order to have a paper trail of evidence for the selection and deselection decisions. It is also worth coaches identifying which intangible characteristics they value as this may help them make decisions when it comes down to the last few places on the team.

While there is no consensus on 'best practices' for cutting youth athletes, most research suggests a face-to-face meeting with each child is desired (Neely *et al.*, 2016; Gleddie *et al.*, 2019). Capstick and Trudel (2010) also suggested considering including parents in this meeting. Privacy is an important aspect and coaches should try to ensure this meeting is held in a private location and has a private exit strategy. In terms of *what* to communicate, researchers recommend giving athletes a reason why they were not selected and providing feedback that is specific, actionable, and gives athletes a focus for improvement (Neely *et al.*, 2016; Gleddie *et al.*, 2019). It has also been suggested to provide written feedback to athletes so they can digest it later on when their emotions have settled.

One finding from the research is the role of parents within the deselection process. In some cases, they may make the process more challenging. Neely *et al.* (2016) suggest coaches be prepared for a possible confrontation with parents of deselected athletes by ensuring they have a paper trail of their decisions, garner support from their club or sport organisation, and implement a 24-hour rule whereby coaches wait at least 24 hours after tryouts have ended before communicating with upset parents. Finally, Bradbury and Forsyth (2012) suggested that post-selection issues are an important aspect to the overall tryout process and should be given attention. Likewise, Neely *et al.* (2016) highlighted the importance of reflection, particularly for improving how deselection is carried out in the future.

While attempts have been made to understand the deselection process in sport, it is important to recognise that many studies have adopted cross-sectional opposed to longitudinal study designs. Appreciating the non-linear nature of youth sport and TD, these studies may be limited by the design utilised; only providing a snap-shot view of a long and volatile pathway to success (Collins *et al.*, 2019). Coaches should be aware of this limitation when interpreting the research provided throughout this chapter and strive to consider the various implications discussed above when making deselection decisions. It should also be acknowledged that while this chapter presents recommendations for coaches to consider during the deselection process, further consideration should be made with the individual nature of each sports team or athlete population in mind. Cultural and philosophical differences, as well as athlete age or demographic between sports may result in the deselection process being more or less sensitive or challenging, dependent on the group/individual. The chapter thus encourages coaches to approach deselection with appropriate caution and sensitivity, considering these recommendations.

Finally, organisational structures of sport, and the impact this may have on deselection processes, must be acknowledged. While it is imperative that deselection is approached with appropriate consideration and empathy, structural constraints (such as time, finances, or facilities) may constrain coaches from adopting deselection processes outlined within this chapter. Again, the chapter recommends a thoughtful approach to deselection considering the information outlined within this chapter and the boundaries with which coaches are operating within their sport.

## Summary, Future Directions, and Future Research

As discussed throughout this chapter, deselection in sport is a challenging and consequential process for both coaches and athletes. Due to the limited capacity of team sport and TD programmes, many perceive deselection as 'necessary' but with the potential to exhibit 'unhealthy' outcomes given their design and implementation (Rongen *et al.*, 2018). Coaches must consider a variety of psychological, social, and emotional factors during the deselection process. A highly structured deselection process involving a pre-tryout meeting, evaluation and decision making, communication of deselection, and post deselection reflection may help guide deselection practices. However, given the magnitude of these decisions, consequences of deselection may be longstanding. Future research is needed that explores the long-term impact of different deselection approaches and strategies on children and young people. Given the stressful nature of deselection for coaches, research is also needed that focuses on identifying and developing coping strategies that help coaches manage their stress during this process. Further, as more research emerges on deselection, considerations for best practices need to be developed. However, who these best practices are for is critical, as what is 'easiest' for coaches may not be best for the athletes. Importantly, research examining athletes' perspectives on deselection processes is needed.

Within TD programmes, although the identification and development of talented young athletes has been a priority for scientists and practitioners working within youth sport, decision-making and processes around deselection has received substantially less attention than TI and recruitment within TD systems. Given the potential stress, and even trauma, of deselection for athletes (Neely *et al.*, 2018), future research on athlete deselection in this specific context is warranted. Specifically, research on how deselection is communicational within TD pathways will have important implications on the reselection of athletes and continued involvement in sport. In conclusion, while the practice of deselection is likely to remain in all contexts of youth sport, whether that be competitive sport, school sport, or TD programmes, coaches can work towards a deselection process that is a little less difficult for athletes.

## References

Baker, J., Schorer, J., and Wattie, N., 2018. Compromising talent: Issues in identifying and selecting talent in sport. *Quest*, 70 (1), 48–63.

Barnett, L., 2006. Flying high or crashing down: Girls' accounts of trying out for cheerleading and dance. *Journal of Adolescent Research*, 21 (5), 514–541.

Barnett, L., 2007. "Winners" and "losers": The effects of being allowed or denied entry into competitive extracurricular activities. *Journal of Leisure Research*, 39 (2), 316–344.

Barreiros, A., Côté, J., and Fonseca, A.M., 2014. From early to adult sport success: Analysing athletes' progression in national squads. *European Journal of Sport Science*, 14 (S1), S178–S182.

Blakelock, D.J., Chen, M.A., and Prescott, T., 2016. Psychological distress in elite adolescent soccer players following deselection. *Journal of Clinical Sport Psychology*, 10 (1), 59–77.

Betsch, T., 2008. The nature of intuition and its neglect in research on judgment and decision making. *In*: H. Plessner, C. Betsch, and T. Betsch, eds. *Intuition in judgment and decision making*. New York: Erlbaum, 3–22.

Bradbury, T. and Forsyth, D., 2012. You're in; you're out: Selection practices of coaches. *Sport, Business and Management: An International Journal*, 2 (1), 7–20.

Brown, G. and Potrac, P., 2009. You've not made the grade son: De-selection and identity disruption in elite level youth football. *Soccer and Society*, 10 (2), 143–159.

Burgess, D.J. and Naughton, G.A., 2010. Talent development in adolescent team sports: A review. *International Journal of Sports Physiology and Performance*, 5 (1), 103–116.

Butt, J. and Molnar, G., 2009. Involuntary career termination in sport: A case study of the process of structurally induced failure. *Sport in Society*, 12 (2), 240–257.

Capstick, A.L. and Trudel, P., 2010. Coach communication of non-selection in youth competitive sport. *International Journal of Coaching Science*, 4 (1), 3–23.

Collins, D., MacNamara, Á., and Cruickshank, A., 2019. Research and practice in talent identification and development: Some thoughts on the state of play. *Journal of Applied Sport Psychology*, 31 (3), 340–351.

Cushion, C. and Nelson, L., 2013. Coach education and learning: Developing the field. *In*: P. Potrac, W. Gilbert, and J. Denison, eds. *Routledge handbook of sports coaching*. New York: Routledge, 359–374.

Dugdale, J.H., McRobert, A.P., and Unnithan, V.B., 2021a. Selected, deselected, and reselected: A case study analysis of attributes associated with player reselection following closure of a youth soccer academy. *Frontiers in Sports and Active Living*, 3, 1–12.

Dugdale, J.H., *et al.*, 2021b. Progression from youth to professional soccer: A longitudinal study of successful and unsuccessful academy graduates. *Scandinavian Journal of Medicine and Science in Sports*, 31 (S1), 73–84.

Gleddie, D.L., *et al.*, 2019. If you must cut athletes from school sports teams, consider best practices. *Journal of Physical Education, Recreation and Dance*, 90 (2), 24–30.

Grossmann, B. and Lames, M., 2015. From talent to professional football: Youthism in German football. *International Journal of Sports Science and Coaching*, 10 (6), 1103–1113.

Grove, J., Fish, M., and Eklund, R., 2004. Changes in athletic identity following team selection: Self-protection versus self-enhancement. *Journal of Applied Sport Psychology*, 16 (1), 75–81.

Güllich, A., 2014. Selection, de-selection and progression in German football talent promotion. *European Journal of Sport Science*, 14 (6), 530–537.

Huijgen, B.C.H., *et al.*, 2014. Multidimensional performance characteristics in selected and deselected talented soccer players. *European Journal of Sport Science*, 14 (1), 2–10.

Kearney, P.E. and Hayes, P.R., 2018. Excelling at youth level in competitive track and field athletics is not a prerequisite for later success. *Journal of Sports Sciences*, 36 (21), 2502–2509.

Munroe, K.J., Albinson, J.G., and Hall, C.R., 1999. The effects of non-selection on first year female varsity athletes. *Avante*, 5, 63–81.

Neely, K.C., *et al.*, 2016. The deselection process in competitive female youth sport. *Sport Psychologist*, 30 (2), 141–153.

Neely, K.C., *et al.*, 2017. Athletes and parents coping with deselection in competitive youth sport: A communal coping perspective. *Psychology of Sport and Exercise*, 30 (1), 1–9.

Neely, K.C., *et al.*, 2018. Female athletes' experiences of positive growth following deselection in sport. *Journal of Sport and Exercise Psychology*, 40 (4), 173–185.

Plessner, H., Betsch, C., and Betsch, T., 2008. *Intuition in judgment and decision making*. New York: Erlbaum.

Rongen, F., *et al.*, 2018. Are youth sport talent identification and development systems necessary and healthy? *Sports Medicine - Open*, 4 (18), 1–4.

Seifried, C. and Casey, T., 2012. Managing the selection of highly competitive interscholastic sport teams: Recommendations from coaches on cutting players. *Journal of Sport Administration and Supervision*, 4 (1), 79–96.

Slack, T. and Parent, M.M., 2006. *Understanding sport organisations: the application of organisation theory*. Champaign, IL: Human Kinetics.

Tamminen, K.A. and Neely, K.C., 2016. Positive growth in sport. *In*: N.L. Holt, ed. *Positive youth development through sport*. 2nd ed. New York: Routledge, 193–204.

Unnithan, V., *et al.*, 2012. Talent identification in youth soccer. *Journal of Sports Sciences*, 30 (15), 1719–1726.

Vaeyens, R., *et al.*, 2008. Talent identification and development programmes in sport: Current models and future directions. *Sports Medicine*, 38 (9), 703–714.

Williams, A.M. and Reilly, T., 2000. Talent identification and development in soccer. *Journal of Sports Sciences*, 18 (9), 657–667.

Williams, G. and MacNamara, Á., 2020. "I didn't make it, but …": Deselected athletes' experiences of the talent development pathway. *Frontiers in Sports and Active Living*, 2 (March), 1–13.

Wylleman, P. and Lavallee, D., 2004. A developmental perspective on transitions faced by athletes. *In*: M.R. Weiss, ed. *Developmental sport and exercise psychology: A lifespan perspective*. Morgantown, WV: Fitness Information Technology, 503–524.

# 18

# MENTAL HEALTH AND COACHING CHILDREN IN SPORT

*Andy Smith and Kenny Greenough*

## Introduction

There is now widespread international concern about the mental health and mental illness of children and increasing interest in the role adults, including sports coaches, are expected to play in supporting mental health and the achievement of other social outcomes (Griffiths and Armour, 2014; Smith *et al.*, 2016; Smith *et al.*, 2021; Smith *et al.*, 2022). This chapter examines existing research which explores: (i) the alleged role coaches are expected to play in supporting the mental health of children; (ii) the mental health literacy of coaches and how this is related to their ability, and willingness, to provide mental health support and guidance; and (iii) mental literacy as an aspect of coach education and development programmes.

Before examining these issues, however, it is important to note that the relationship between wellbeing (e.g. quality of life, social and emotional functioning) and mental illness (e.g. depression, anxiety) is one in which the two constructs exist on distinct continua and both are necessary to understand mental health (Keyes, 2002; Westerhof and Keyes, 2010). Mental health has often been defined as "a state of well-being in which every individual realizes his or her own potential, can cope with the normal stresses of life, can work productively and fruitfully, and is able to make a contribution to her or his community" (World Health Organization [WHO], 2018). In contrast, mental illness (also referred to as mental or psychiatric disorder) is any health condition (such as depression and anxiety) which involves changes or alterations in thinking, mood, or behaviour (or any combination of these) which can result from stressful experiences but also occur in the absence of such experiences (WHO, 2014). An understanding of this two-continua model of mental health is essential if we are to adequately understand the role sports coaches are expected to play in supporting the mental health of children by optimising wellbeing and reducing the risk of developing mental illness.

## Review of Current Research

### *The Mental Health of Children and Adolescents*

Globally, between 10% and 20% of children and adolescents experience mental illness which is one of the most common burdens of disease amongst this group, though this burden varies

DOI: 10.4324/9781003199359-21

between and within countries (WHO, 2020). In Australia, for example, almost one-in-seven children and adolescents (4–17-years-old) have had a mental disorder in the last 12 months (Australian Institute of Health and Welfare, 2020), whilst in the United States one-in-six children have done so (CDC, 2021). In England, the latest data suggest that the proportion of 5–16-year-olds with a probable mental disorder increased from one-in-nine (10.8%: 11.4% boys, 10.3% girls) in 2017 to one-in-six (16.0%: 16.7% boys, 15.2% girls) in 2020 (NHS Digital, 2021; Newlove-Delgardo *et al.*, 2021). Amongst children of primary age (5–10-year-olds), 14.4% had a probable mental disorder (an increase from 9.4% in 2017) and 17.6% of secondary-aged children (11–16-year-olds) did so (an increase from 12.6% in 2017) (NHS Digital, 2021). Suicide, which is the third leading cause of death amongst 15–19-year-olds globally (WHO, 2019), is also the leading cause of death amongst the under 25s in the United Kingdom (UK) and for young females aged 10–24-years-old the suicide rate has increased significantly to its highest level in 2019 (ONS, 2020). The prevalence of self-harm which is associated with poor mental health is an additional global health concern, especially amongst adolescents, and represents a significant risk factor for subsequent suicide attempts and deaths (Rodway *et al.*, 2020; Uh *et al.*, 2021). In the UK, rates of self-harm are rising faster amongst young women than men, and in England prevalence estimates amongst adolescents range between 13.2% and 19.7% (Uh *et al.*, 2021). Engagement in non-suicidal self-harm, often as a means of coping with anxiety, depression, stress, and tension, is also increasing in all age groups for males, and especially females, and is an important indicator of the mental health of children and adolescents (McManus *et al.*, 2019). The global COVID-19 crisis and associated lockdowns have unambiguously accelerated, widened, and deepened pre-existing inequalities between and within countries in ways that have negatively impacted mental health (especially children in low-income and under-served communities) (Marmot *et al.*, 2020; Bambra *et al.*, 2021; Smith *et al.*, 2021). This has also further reinforced the positioning of sports coaches as important promoters of good mental health for children which is discussed in more detail next.

## *Mental Health, Duty of Care, and Coaching*

The public mental health challenge impacting children and adolescents is significant and the expectation that sports coaches could and should play a role in addressing this challenge has become a prominent, if contested, feature of sport policy and practice in many countries (Smith *et al.*, 2020; Vella and Liddle, 2020; Smith *et al.*, 2021; Smith *et al.*, 2022). Those who are formally identified as 'coaches' (especially in elite or professional sport) and/or are regarded as undertaking 'coaching' work (e.g. as an activator, instructor, facilitator, mentor, leader, trainer) in recreational/grassroots sports settings in particular are now increasingly required to address mental health alongside other priorities in their everyday practice (Smith *et al.*, 2022). In the UK, for example, current government policy and the strategies of non-departmental public bodies like Sport England – alongside the work of organisations including UK Coaching – have identified mental wellbeing (and, by implication, mental health, and illness, Smith *et al.*, 2016) as one of five key outcomes to which coaches are expected to contribute, particularly through the delivery of opportunities for people to become active in recreational/grassroots settings (Smith *et al.*, 2021; Smith *et al.*, 2022). Sport England's (2021) recent ten-year strategy, *Uniting the Movement*, identifies tackling social and health inequalities through movement, including sport and physical activity, as a key priority for those who deliver activity opportunities. Many recreational/grassroots sport coaches are now routinely expected to work with diverse partner organisations to tackle inequalities and address the priority social outcomes (e.g. improved mental health) of government policy through sport and physical activity opportunities (Smith *et al.*, 2021; Smith *et al.*, 2022). The coach's role frequently extends beyond traditional understandings of coaching (i.e. as someone who delivers sport-based techniques, skills, and experiences to athletes and teams). This role now also incorporates a requirement to support a wider range of participants with diverse needs, including children who may be inactive and/or experience poor mental health and mental illness because of the wider inequalities in their lives and the communities in which they live – inequalities which, as noted earlier, have been amplified and exacerbated by the impacts of COVID-19 (Marmot *et al.*, 2020; Bambra *et al.*, 2021; Smith *et al.*, 2021).

The increased emphasis on supporting mental health as an aspect of coaches' work is also part of a parallel growth in concerns about the duty of care in sport, particularly but by no means exclusively, in elite and professional sport where cultures of abuse, poor coach-athlete relationships and other welfare concerns (e.g. gender-based violence, injury) continue to be of concern globally and subject to ongoing investigation. Amongst the most recent discussions in the UK, for example, was an independent review of duty of care in sport led by Baroness Grey-Thompson which included a focus on coaches' roles in supporting the mental health of athletes, the responsibilities of organisations in supporting coaches' mental health, and coaches' experiences of their own mental health (Grey-Thompson, 2017). A Sports Ombudsman, which holds national governing bodies (NGBs) to account for the duty of care they have to groups including coaches, was proposed alongside a Duty of Care Charter informing coaches and others of how they can expect to be treated and where to go to receive appropriate support and guidance. Four specific recommendations related to mental health were also made: (i) "introduce sector standard mental health training for coaches and physical activity professionals (which can have aspects of sports specificity where required)"; (ii) "NGBs [national governing bodies] to include mental health issues in the content of coaching and other sport-related courses which filter down to clubs"; (iii) "staff, coaches and athletes to receive mental health awareness training and support, which should be included as part of induction processes as well"; and (iv) "NGBs and sports clubs should provide clear signposting to confidential support services outside of the sport (for participants, coaches and performance staff)" (Grey-Thompson, 2017, p. 22).

Various international consensus and position statements have also identified coaches, and coach education programmes in particular, as having an important role to play in supporting the diagnosis, treatment and management of mental illness, in supporting mental health referrals, and in creating mentally healthy and resilient sporting environments (Moesch *et al.*, 2018; Reardon *et al.*, 2019; Henriksen *et al.*, 2020). As part of multi-disciplinary mental health care teams, coaches have been frequently identified in these statements as playing an important role in recognising athlete mental health problems by ensuring they have high mental health literacy (Reardon *et al.*, 2019; Van Slingerland *et al.*, 2019; Henriksen *et al.*, 2020). Useful though these statements are in drawing attention to coaches' potential role in mental health support, they are disproportionately focused on elite athletes and coaches (Vella, *et al.*, 2021a) and thus do not support sub-elite participants and coaches (Smith *et al.*, 2020; Vella and Swann, 2021; Vella, *et al.*, 2021b). Since most participants and coaches engage in sport at recreational/grassroots level, there is a clear need for sports organisations and governing bodies to develop relevant evidence-based recommendations which support the mental health of all who play and work in sport at this level, including coaches of children (Smith *et al.*, 2020; Vella and Swann, 2021; Vella, *et al.*, 2021a; Vella, *et al.*, 2021b).

The findings of empirical studies, many of which have been conducted in Australia, suggest that the provision of practical evidence-based, appropriately resourced and supported, mental health guidelines would be welcome by coaches who are expected to support the mental health of others (including children). These studies have revealed how many coaches feel they have a role to play in the identification, referral, and prevention of mental health problems, in the facilitation of athlete wellbeing, and in the promotion of mental health through the development of positive coach-athlete relationships (Gulliver *et al.*, 2012; Mazzer and Rickwood, 2015a, 2015b; Ferguson *et al.*, 2019). For example, in their study of coaches' perceptions of supporting adolescent mental health, Ferguson *et al.* (2019, p. 246) noted how:

> All coaches, directly or indirectly, articulated that they can play an important role in athlete mental health with responses ranging from a role in the identification of symptoms and notification of parents as a minimum, through to discussing symptoms directly with the athlete.

Despite a general willingness by coaches to support adolescent mental health, most of them were "unsure of *what* help was necessary and unsure of *how* to provide that help" (Ferguson *et al.*, 2019, p. 247; original emphases), including in relation to the identification of signs and symptoms that adolescents were experiencing poor mental health. This was unsurprising, the authors claimed, because "coach education programs do not adequately equip coaches with the skills and knowledge to address the issue of adolescent mental health" (Ferguson *et al.*, 2019, p. 247), a view which is shared by others (e.g. Mazzer and Rickwood, 2009; Liddle *et al.*, 2017). Indeed, coaches often report being underprepared, lack sufficient confidence and skills to act, and require additional training to support the mental health of children who are more likely to confide informally in a coach (and other sources of support) than consult professional services about their mental health (Mazzer and Rickwood, 2015a, 2015b; Ferguson *et al.*, 2019; Bissett *et al.*, 2020; Duffy *et al.*, 2021). In Mazzer and Rickwood's (2009) study, coaches were most likely to refer young people to sources of mental health support in schools or work, or to family and friends, rather than specialist mental health services since they were most familiar with these sources of help. They concluded that coaches need to be given further support and confidence to refer young people to mental health professionals by increasing their awareness of relevant services and having a working knowledge of the signs and symptoms of mental health problems (Mazzer and Rickwood, 2009).

A more recent study of Gaelic games coaches in Ireland revealed that coaches' personal experience of mental illness was associated with higher levels of mental health literacy (Duffy *et al.*, 2021). Coaches' mental health literacy was also found to be indirectly associated – via coaches' role breadth and efficacy – with their engagement in mental health promotion, prevention, and early intervention (Duffy *et al.*, 2021). It was concluded that coaches can provide children and young people experiencing mental illness with an initial alternative source of support, and that improving mental health literacy will better enable coaches to "identify the early warning signs of mental illness and … support and refer young people to appropriately qualified mental health practitioners" (Duffy *et al.*, 2021, p. 55). Mental health literacy as an aspect of coach education and development programmes is explored further next.

## *Mental Health Literacy in Coach Education and Development Programmes*

Given the absence of substantial mental health content in many coach education and development programmes, especially those intended to support children who engage in recreational/grassroots sport, it has been argued that there is an urgent need to develop and implement holistic evidence-based, context-specific, mental health programmes for coaches which are accessible, practical and proportionate to the mental health needs of participants

(Bissett *et al.*, 2020; Vella and Liddle, 2020; Vella, *et al.*, 2021b). Such programmes may include activities which seek to improve mental health literacy which, as Jorm has noted (Jorm *et al.*, 1997; Jorm, 2012), refers to the knowledge, beliefs, and attitudes about mental health and mental illness, and the potential actions needed to support one's own and others' mental health through symptom recognition, management, and prevention. Indeed, brief mental health literacy training for coaches which focuses on knowledge and action (Jorm, 2012) has been advocated as a potentially effective way of increasing knowledge of the signs and symptoms of mental illness, enhancing coaches' understanding of mental illness and wellbeing as distinct components of mental health, and increasing coaches' confidence to provide mental health support (Ferguson *et al.*, 2019; Vella and Liddle, 2020). Little is currently known, however, about coaches' mental health literacy and how this is associated with the mental health of coaches and those whom they coach, including children (Gorczynski *et al.*, 2020; Smith *et al.*, 2020; Vella and Liddle, 2020; Duffy *et al.*, 2021). In a study of the mental health literacy of 103 coaches (three-quarters of whom coached children), Gorczynski *et al.* (2020) reported that women had higher mental health literacy than men, but no statistically significant differences were found between mental health literacy and age, ethnicity, sexuality, whether respondents coached children or adults, or had a UK coaching certificate. Mental health literacy was also not significantly associated with seeking help from others, distress, or wellbeing, but those who identified as heterosexual had lower scores of distress than those who identified as bisexual or gay (Gorczynski *et al.*, 2020). Overall, the findings pointed to the need to implement more gender-sensitive mental health literacy programmes for coaches which pay particular attention to the knowledge, attitudes, and actions of men and women of various sexualities and ethnicities, and how the determinants of poor mental health can be addressed in sporting contexts (Gorczynski *et al.*, 2020).

Coach education and development programmes involving mental health literacy training, such as Mental Health First Aid (MHFA) first developed in Australia (Kitchener and Jorm, 2008), have been identified as a potentially effective way of: starting conversations about mental health and suicide; reducing the stigma of mental health and illness; improving knowledge of the prevalence of mental illness; signposting to relevant professional support; and promoting an understanding of mental health as part of overall wellbeing (Mazzer and Rickwood, 2009; Pierce *et al.*, 2010; Mazzer and Rickwood, 2015a, 2015b; Ferguson *et al.*, 2019; Vella and Liddle, 2020). Reflecting the findings of a study of rural football in Australia (Pierce *et al.*, 2010), the value of MHFA in enabling community sport coaches to support the mental health of children and adolescents was recognised in a review of the *Safe, Fit, and Well* programme delivered by StreetGames in the UK (John and Mansfield, 2018). As part of a bespoke training package to enable coaches and other workers to support children living in low-income communities, MHFA was regarded as an effective way of improving coaches' knowledge, skills and confidence to deliver sports sessions which improve mental health amongst those with mental illness, and increasing engagement with mental health services (John and Mansfield, 2018). MHFA was also used as part of the national #21by21 campaign led by the Sport for Development Coalition in the UK which brought together sports organisations, business, and policy-makers, to provide 21,000 community sport coaches and volunteers with mental health awareness training by 2021, with 40,881 participants eventually being trained (Smith *et al.*, 2021). For Mazzer and Rickwood (2015a, 2015b), equipping coaches with the relevant skills and knowledge – via such courses as MHFA – to actively refer young people for appropriate mental health support and highlighting the benefits of this, could enhance their future willingness to do so. They add that

> explicitly including actions that support young people's mental health in key performance indicators, performance and development reviews, and formal job descriptions would further encourage … coaches' involvement in such behaviour.
>
> *(Mazzer and Rickwood, 2015b, p. 17)*

Despite the potential benefits of mental health literacy training and effectiveness of community sports clubs as appropriate settings for such training (Breslin *et al.*, 2017; Hurley *et al.*, 2017; Swann *et al.*, 2018; Gorczynski *et al.*, 2020; Duffy *et al.*, 2021), coach-specific mental health training has been rarely acknowledged as important, or implemented systematically, by organisations (Vella and Liddle, 2020), including those supporting children. Research in the area has also been limited and generally regarded as poor because studies often: involve low sample sizes; rarely include comparison or control groups; require more adequately powered trials and better measures of behaviour change; need more participant-level measures of coaching behaviours; involve insufficient theoretical foundations or programme theories; and require long-term follow-ups (Breslin *et al.*, 2017; Breslin *et al.*, 2019; Vella and Liddle, 2020; Vella, *et al.*, 2021b). A notable exception to this is the Ahead of the Game programme for 12–17-year-old males who participated in community-based organised sports clubs (Vella, *et al.*, 2021c). The programme involved four components (delivered as face-to-face workshops and online modules): two targeting mental health literacy, intentions to seek and provide help, and resilience for adolescents. A coach education programme supporting males' psychological needs and a parental mental health literacy programme were also included. Collectively, these resilience-focused and mental health literacy-focused components had significant benefits for depression and anxiety literacy, resilience, and wellbeing, intentions to seek help from formal sources, and confidence to seek mental health information (Vella, *et al.*, 2021c). Although no significant effects were found for addressing stigmatising attitudes, intentions to seek help from informal sources, perceived familial support, or implicit beliefs and psychological distress, the programme was successful in

> equipping young men who participate in organized sports with the knowledge, intentions, confidence, and psychosocial resources necessary to promote mental health and support better identification of and response to mental health problems.
>
> *(Vella, et al., 2021c, p. 146)*

Similar programmes, which are scalable and effective, are needed if we are to effectively improve the mental health of children and better understand the potential contribution coach education initiatives (including mental health literacy training) have on short-, medium- and long-term mental health. They are also important if parental and participant expectations of coaches' role in supporting mental health are to be addressed (Mazzer and Rickwood, 2015a, 2015b; Brown *et al.*, 2017; Hurley *et al.*, 2017; Swann *et al.*, 2018), especially in organised youth sport settings (Swann *et al.*, 2018). In a study investigating adolescent males' perspectives of mental health in organised youth sport, for example, Swann *et al.* (2018) reported how coaches alongside parents and family were key supports for mental health and other life challenges. Those adolescents who perceived their coach to be knowledgeable, trustworthy, and supportive were more likely to discuss their mental health problems with their coach (Swann *et al.*, 2018). In this regard, the authors concluded that more mental health focused coach education programmes are needed "as coaches in youth sport need to be prepared for adolescents needing/wanting to speak to them about mental health problems" (Swann *et al.*, 2018, p. 63). However, because in grassroots youth sport "coaches are often parents and/or volunteers who are unable to devote time and effort to coach education as more professional coaches" (Swann *et al.*, 2018, p. 63), brief and flexible forms of training such as that described above is needed to enhance the kinds of mental health literacy required by coaches and parents to fulfil their perceived role in supporting participant mental health. Involving coach developers, coaches and other workers in the co-creation, delivery and evaluation of mental health promotion work in this way is especially important (Breslin *et al.*, 2019).

## Implications for Children's Sport Coaching

If coaches are expected to assume an expanded role which includes the mental health promotion of children, then it is important that relevant accessible resources and support are provided to enable them to fulfil this role. As Ferguson *et al.* (2019, p. 247) have noted:

> Brief mental health literacy training tailored to youth sport coaches is a potentially effective and desirable initiative, especially if it could be woven into existing coach accreditation initiatives or provide continuing education credits for those coaches who require them to maintain their coaching accreditation.

The provision of such training might be a necessary condition for enhancing the mental health and sporting experiences of children, for supporting the mental health of coaches themselves, and for enabling the organisations for whom coaches volunteer and work to achieve their objectives (Gorczynski *et al.*, 2020; Smith *et al.*, 2020; Vella and Liddle, 2020; Duffy *et al.*, 2021; Smith *et al.*, 2021). However, the improvement of coaches' mental health literacy – through training and clearly articulated and applied mental health guidelines which can be easily understood and enacted (Vella and Liddle, 2020) – is insufficient on its own. It has been argued that there is a need for systems-wide cultural change in sporting environments which are often dominated more by performance and results concerns than by other goals, alongside change in the social relationships which impact coaches' mental health and practice (Bissett *et al.*, 2020; Vella and Liddle, 2020).

As noted earlier, there currently exists a significant public mental health challenge in relation to children, with adolescence being a period of peak presentation for mental illness. Indeed, childhood and youth are key life-stages for the development of mental illnesses (including depression and anxiety), are periods during which the risk of self-harm and suicide progressively increases, and when some disorders begin to develop burdens which persist throughout adulthood (Blakemore, 2019). Coaches are therefore highly likely to encounter these mental health challenges in their practice and, if the current policy trajectory is maintained, continue to be required to support children during periods of profound biological, psychological, and social change which have important impacts on mental health. These changes occur also in conjunction with the development of a whole range of adverse childhood experiences (e.g. abuse, neglect, parental mental illness, drug use), especially amongst those living in low-income communities (Blakemore, 2019) who are the focus of many recreational/grassroots sport-for-change programmes involving coaches (Griffiths and Armour, 2014; Smith *et al.*, 2021; Smith *et al.*, 2022). Providing children with positive and meaningful experiences of sport will thus depend partly on how these challenges can be navigated by coaches and others responsible for the delivery, organization, and management of sport for children. It will also depend – perhaps to a much greater degree – on the success of wider policy initiatives and action on the determinants of, and inequalities in, mental health which provide the very social conditions under which the use of sports-based programmes involving coaches are being encouraged and enacted in many countries (Smith *et al.*, 2021; Smith *et al.*, 2022). Indeed, the wider social determinants of mental health are an important part of the context within which coaching practice takes place and its impact on the mental health of children and coaches needs to be much better understood in future research. Some of the other areas of future research are considered next.

## Summary, Future Directions and Future Research

This chapter has reviewed existing research on the alleged role coaches are expected to play in supporting the mental health of children, the importance of coaches' mental health literacy, and mental health literacy as an aspect of coach education and development programmes. Much of the existing international research, policy, consensus statements, and guidelines have focused disproportionately on the mental health and practices of coaches in elite and professional sport (Breslin *et al.*, 2019; Vella and Liddle, 2020; Vella and Swann, 2021; Vella, *et al.*, 2021a; Vella, *et al.*, 2021b). More theoretically-informed, empirically-based, research is thus needed to better understand the needs and practice of sub-elite coaches and the impact of coach-led mental health support in recreational/grassroots sport where most coaches and participants are engaged (Smith *et al.*, 2020; Vella and Liddle, 2020; Vella and Swann, 2021; Vella, *et al.*, 2021a; Vella, *et al.*, 2021b). The development and evaluation of appropriate holistic evidence-based coach education programmes is also warranted, and these might usefully be broadened to focus on the mental health of coach developers as well as coaches themselves. Of particular importance, however, is the production of a better evidence base from which we can determine whether coaches, and the programmes they deliver, can promote positive mental health and contribute effectively to the prevention, treatment, and management of mental illness for children. There are surprisingly few studies in this area and future work might usefully incorporate the experiences and voices of children, alongside their coaches, so that we can determine whether the programmes in which they are involved achieve the mental health goals expected of them.

## References

Australian Institute of Health and Welfare, 2020. *Australia's children*. Canberra: AHIW.

Bambra, C., Lynch, J., and Smith, K., 2021. *The unequal pandemic: COVID-19 and health inequalities*. Bristol: Policy Press.

Blakemore, S., 2019. Adolescence and mental health. *The Lancet*, 393, 2030–2031.

Breslin, G., *et al.*, 2017. A systematic review of interventions to increase awareness of mental health and well-being in athletes, coaches and officials. *Systematic Reviews*, 6 (177), 1–15.

Breslin, G., *et al.*, 2019. International consensus statement on psychosocial and policy-related approaches to mental health awareness programmes in sport. *BMJ Open Sport and Exercise Medicine*, 5, 1–7.

Bissett, J., Kroshus, E., and Hebard, S., 2020. Determining the role of sport coaches in promoting athlete mental health: A narrative review and Delphi approach. *BMJ Open Sport and Exercise Medicine*, 6, 1–9.

Brown, M., *et al.*, 2017. Parents views of the role of sports coaches as mental health gatekeepers for adolescent males. *International Journal of Mental Health Promotion*, 19 (5), 239–251.

Centers for Disease Control and Prevention, 2021. *Children's mental health*. Available from: https://www.cdc.gov/childrensmentalhealth/index.html [Accessed 18 June 2021].

Duffy, J., Rooney, B., and Matthews, J., 2021. Coaches' mental health literacy and role perceptions for supporting young people's mental health. *Journal of Applied Sport Psychology*, 33 (1), 45–59.

Ferguson, H., *et al.*, 2019. Investigating youth sports coaches' perceptions of their role in adolescent mental health. *Journal of Applied Sport Psychology*, 31 (2), 235–252.

Gorczynski, P., *et al.*, 2020. Examining mental health literacy, help seeking behaviours, distress, and wellbeing in UK coaches. *European Physical Education Review*, 26 (3), 713–726.

Grey-Thompson, T., 2017. *Duty of care in sport: Independent report to government*. London: Department for Digital, Culture, Media and Sport.

Griffiths, M. and Armour, K., 2014. Volunteer sports coaches as community assets? A realist review of the research evidence. *International Journal of Sport Policy and Politics*, 6 (3), 307–326.

Gulliver, A., Griffiths, K. and Christensen, H., 2012. Barriers and facilitators to mental health help-seeking for young elite athletes: A qualitative study. *BMC Psychiatry*, 12, 157.

Henriksen, K., *et al.*, 2020. Consensus statement on improving the mental health of high performance athletes. *International Journal of Sport and Exercise Psychology*, 18 (5), 553–560.

Hurley, D., *et al.*, 2017. The role of community sports clubs in adolescent male mental health: The perspective of adolescent males' parents. *Qualitative Research in Sport, Exercise and Health*, 9 (3), 372–388.

John, A., and Mansfield, L., 2018. *Street Games: Safe, fit and well – Case study research*. London: Brunel University.

Jorm, A.F., 2012. Mental health literacy: Empowering the community to take action for better mental health. *The American Psychologist*, 67 (3), 231–243.

Jorm, A.F., *et al.*, 1997. 'Mental health literacy': A survey of the public's ability to recognise mental disorders and their beliefs about the effectiveness of treatment. *Medical Journal of Australia*, 166 (4), 182–186.

Keyes, C., 2002. The mental health continuum: From languishing to flourishing in life. *Journal of Health and Social Behavior*, 43 (2), 207–222.

Kitchener, B. and Jorm A., 2008. Mental health first aid: An international programme for early intervention. *Early Intervention in Psychiatry*, 2 (1), 55–61.

Liddle, S.K., Deane, F.P., and Vella, S. A. 2017. Addressing mental health through sport: a review of sporting organizations' websites. *Early Intervention in Psychiatry*, 11 (2), 93–103.

McManus, S., *et al.*, 2019. Prevalence of non-suicidal self-harm and service contact in England, 2000-14: Repeated cross-sectional surveys of the general population. *The Lancet Psychiatry*, 6 (7), 573–581.

Marmot, M., *et al.*, 2020. *Health equity in England: The Marmot Review 10 years on*. London: Institute of Health Equity.

Mazzer, K. and Rickwood, D., 2009. Community gatekeepers' advice to young people to seek help from mental health professionals: Youth workers and sport coaches. *International Journal of Mental Health Promotion*, 11 (2), 13–23.

Mazzer, K. and Rickwood, D., 2015a. Mental health in sport: Coaches' views of their role and efficacy in supporting young people's mental health. *International Journal of Mental Health Promotion and Education*, 53 (2), 102–114.

Mazzer, K. and Rickwood, D., 2015b. Teachers' and coaches' role perceptions for supporting young people's mental health: Multiple path analyses. *Australian Journal of Psychology*, 67, 10–19.

Moesch, K., *et al.*, 2018. FEPSAC position statement: Mental health disorders in elite athletes and models of service provision. *Psychology of Sport and Exercise*, 38, 61–71.

Newlove-Delgardo, T., *et al.*, 2021. Child mental health in England before and during the COVID-19 lockdown. *The Lancet Psychiatry*, 8 (5), 353–354.

NHS Digital, 2021. *The mental health of children and young people in England, 2020*. London: Crown Copyright.

Office for National Statistics (ONS), 2020. *Suicides in the UK: 2019 registrations*. London: ONS.

Pierce, D., *et al.*, 2010. Australian rural football club leaders as mental health advocates: An investigation of the impact of the Coach the Coach project. *International Journal of Mental Health Systems*, 4 (10), 1–8.

Reardon, C., *et al.*, 2019. Mental health in elite athletes: International Olympic Committee consensus statement. *British Journal of Sports Medicine*, 53 (11), 667–699.

Rodway, C., *et al.*, 2020. Children and young people who die by suicide: Childhood related antecedents, gender differences and service contact. *British Journal of Psychiatry Open*, 6 (3), 1–9.

Smith, A., Greenough, K., and Lovett, E., 2022. The politics and policy of community sport coaching. *In*: B. Ives, P. Potrac, L. Gale and L. Nelson. eds. *Community sport coaching: Policies and practice*. London: Routledge, 7–24.

Smith, A., Kinnafick, F., and Rogers, E., 2021. *Moving for mental health following COVID-19: The role of physical activity, sport and sport for development in promoting movement and mental health*. London: Sport for Development Coalition/Mind.

Smith, A., *et al.*, 2020. Exploring mental health and illness in the UK sports coaching workforce. *International Journal of Environmental Research and Public Health*, 17 (24), 1–14.

Smith, A., *et al.*, 2016. A political spectator sport or policy priority? A review of sport, physical activity and public mental health policy. *International Journal of Sport Policy and Politics*, 8 (4), 593–607.

Sport England, 2021. *Uniting the movement*. London: Sport England.

Swann, C., *et al.*, 2018. Youth sport as a context for supporting mental health: Adolescent male perspectives. *Psychology of Sport and Exercise*, 35, 55–64.

Uh, S., *et al.*, 2021. Two pathways to self-harm in adolescence. *Journal of the American Academy of Child & Adolescent Psychiatry*, 60 (12), 1491–1500.

Van Slingerland, K., *et al.*, 2019. Canadian Centre for Mental Health and Sport (CCMHS) position statement: Principles of mental health in competitive and high-performance sport. *Clinical Journal of Sport Medicine*, 29 (3), 173–180.

Vella, S. and Liddle, S., 2020. Coaching and athlete mental health. *In*: R. Resende and A. Rui Gomes eds. *Coaching for human development and performance in sports*. Cham: Springer, 289–304.

Vella, S. and Swann, C., 2021. Time for mental healthcare guidelines for recreational sports: A call to action. *British Journal of Sports Medicine*, 55 (4), 184–185.

Vella, S., *et al.*, 2021a. A systematic review and meta-synthesis of mental health position statements in sport: Scope, quality and future directions. *Psychology of Sport and Exercise*, 55, 1–11.

Vella, S., Swann, C., and Tamminen, K., 2021b. Reflections on the field of mental health in sport: Critical issues and ways of moving forward. *Journal of Applied Sport Psychology*, 33 (1), 123–129.

Vella, S., *et al.*, 2021c. An intervention for mental health literacy and resilience in organized sport. *Medicine and Science in Sports and Exercise*, 53 (1), 139–149.

Westerhof, G. and Keyes, C., 2010. Mental illness and mental health: The two continua model across the lifespan. *Journal of Adult Development*, 17, 100–119.

World Health Organization (WHO). 2014. *Social determinants of mental health*. Geneva: WHO.

World Health Organization (WHO), 2018. *Mental health: Strengthening our response*. Available at: https://www.who.int/news-room/fact-sheets/detail/mental-health-strengthening-our-response [Accessed 18 June 2021].

World Health Organization (WHO), 2019. *Suicide in the world: Global health estimates*. Geneva: WHO.

World Health Organization (WHO), 2020. Child and adolescent mental health. Available at: https://www.who.int/mental_health/maternal-child/child_adolescent/en/ [Accessed 18 June 2021].

# 19

# CHILD'S PLAY? SAFEGUARDING AND PROTECTING CHILDREN IN SPORT

*Melanie Lang and Laura G Purdy*

## Introduction

Children's participation in sport is generally regarded as beneficial, a component of a healthy childhood and important for a long, healthy adulthood (United Nations Children's Fund [UNICEF], 2004). In addition to its individual positive outcomes, such as fun, health benefits, opportunities to learn, interact and develop (United Nations Children's Fund UNICEF, 2004), sport can contribute to the economy, productivity in the workforce, and savings for health and social care services (Darnell, 2010; WHO, 2018). Yet these benefits are not automatic; organised sport at all levels and of all types is also a site for the abuse and exploitation of athletes (see Lang, 2021a). The sexual exploitation of athletes has resulted in high-profile criminal convictions, authoritarian coaching practices have come under scrutiny, and discrimination, overtraining, 'fat shaming', and other forms of maltreatment have garnered significant media and research attention globally (e.g. Lang and Light, 2010; McMahon and Barker-Ruchti, 2017; McPherson *et al.*, 2017; Lang *et al.*, 2018; Chavez, 2019; Seo and Griffiths, 2019; Bicknell, 2020; Tuakli-Wosornu *et al.*, 2020; Turkeri-Bozkurt and Bulgu, 2020; Wilinsky and McCabe, 2021).

Children have been identified as particularly vulnerable to such behaviours given their low social status and limited power compared with other sport stakeholders (Brackenridge, 2001; Lang, 2022). Sport is also a culture where conformity to potentially damaging norms and behaviours is often expected – unquestioning deference to the authority of the coach and others with assumed 'expertise'; adherence to idealised forms of masculinity and discourses of mental toughness and physical preparation that encourage risk-taking and playing through pain and injury; coach control and athlete compliance with intensive and potentially abusive training regimes and objectifying practices (Hughes and Coakley, 1991; Anderson, 2008; Lang, 2010a; Jacobs *et al.*, 2017). These practices are often structurally and culturally embedded in sport and have come to be the dominant model for success. Such behaviours are rationalised as 'functional' – not only leading to improved performance but *necessary* for this (Hughes and Coakley, 1991; Lang, 2021b).

Coaches play a central role in shaping children's experiences of sport. They can influence children's performance, motivation to participate, and the likelihood of continuing in sport (Purdy, 2018). They also have a moral and a legal duty to safeguard child athletes' welfare (see, Lang and Hartill, 2015) and are well placed to identify and manage athlete welfare. This is important given all forms of maltreatment can have devastating short-and long-term physical,

DOI: 10.4324/9781003199359-22

social, behavioural, educational, and psychological consequences for those affected (Norman *et al.*, 2012; Spinazzola *et al.*, 2014). Indeed, the consequences of maltreatment are dependent on the degree (frequency and severity) to which young people experience abusive behaviours rather than the type(s) of maltreatment experienced (Higgins, 2004; Spinazzola *et al.*, 2014). For sports organisations, athlete maltreatment can also lead to loss of trust, athlete dropout, legal challenges, reputational damage, and loss of sponsorship.

With this in mind, this chapter critically discusses what the International Olympic Committee (IOC) calls 'safe sport'. Later, the chapter focuses upon non-sexual forms of child maltreatment, which are the most prevalent forms in sport. The chapter uses the term 'child maltreatment', which is defined by the WHO as "the abuse and neglect that occurs to children under 18". Given space constraints, the content of this chapter focuses on the four forms of child maltreatment identified by the IOC (Mountjoy *et al.*, 2016). First, to contextualise the discussion, child maltreatment is defined, examples in sport are provided, and the extent of the problem is highlighted.

## Review of Current Research

### *Child Maltreatment in Sport: Definitions and Prevalence*

Definitions of maltreatment vary according to national legislation, however, most jurisdictions recognise four forms of child abuse: physical abuse, psychological abuse (often used interchangeably with 'emotional abuse'; this chapter uses psychological abuse in recognition this form of abuse has impacts beyond the emotions), sexual abuse, and neglect. Within global sport, the IOC (Mountjoy *et al.*, 2016, p. 1021) defines these as follows:

- "*Psychological abuse*: A pattern of deliberate, prolonged, repeated non-contact behaviours within a power differentiated relationship" – for example, yelling, shouting, belittling, threats, name-calling, humiliation and degrading comments, ignoring athletes or excluding them from training sessions and including incidents such as coaches throwing objects in the presence of athletes and punching walls and/or breaking training equipment when frustrated with an athlete (Stirling and Kerr, 2008);
- "*Physical abuse*: Non-accidental trauma or physical injury caused by punching, beating, kicking, biting, burning or otherwise [physically] harming an athlete". As well as bodily violence, in sport this could include forced or mandated inappropriate physical activity (e.g. age-inappropriate or physique-inappropriate training loads, training when injured or in pain) (Kerr, 2010; Lang, 2010b), forced alcohol consumption, or systematic doping practices;
- "*Sexual abuse*: Any conduct of a sexual nature, whether non-contact, contact or penetrative, where consent is coerced/manipulated or is not or cannot be given";
- "*Neglect*: The failure of parents or caregivers to meet a child's physical and emotional needs or failure to protect a child from exposure to danger". Neglect takes at least four forms: physical, educational, emotional, and medical (NSPCC, 2021). Physical neglect refers to not meeting a child's basic needs (e.g. clothing, food, and shelter) or inappropriate supervision of a child that threatens their safety. Educational neglect occurs when a child is not afforded the recommended education. Emotional neglect refers to situations in which a child is not nurtured or stimulated and includes behaviours that ignore, humiliate, intimidate, or isolate. Finally, medical neglect transpires when health care is not afforded to a child or if it is ignored. This extends to dental care. In sport, neglect could include exposing athletes to undue cold or heat without ensuring adequate clothing or hydration, encouraging athletes to play through

injury, failing to adhere to sport safety rules or to provide appropriate equipment, removing a child from or limiting a child's education in favour of training, or denying access to appropriate medical care for injuries (Partington, 2016).

Child maltreatment is typically perpetrated by someone well known to the child. In sport, while peer athletes commonly engage in abuse, coaches are also frequently offenders (Vertommen *et al.*, 2017; Hartill *et al.*, 2021). Given the closeness of the coach-athlete relationship, Brackenridge (2001) argues that abuse in sport is akin to familial abuse.

There is evidence of the prevalence of certain forms of child maltreatment in sport in some countries. In a retrospective self-report study of violence against children in sport, Hartill *et al.* (2021) found that 65% of the 10,302 adult respondents across six European countries reported experiencing psychological violence in sport as children, 44% physical violence, and 37% neglect. Forms of sexual violence were the least prevalent, although still substantial in number with 35% reporting experiencing non-contact sexual violence and 20% experiencing contact sexual violence in sport as children. Importantly, all the aforementioned forms of child maltreatment rarely occur on their own; rather, they tend to co-occur, with psychological abuse being a common denominator in all other forms of abuse (Mountjoy *et al.*, 2016). Ethnic minority, lesbian, gay, and bisexual athletes, disabled athletes, girls, and elite athletes appear to be most at risk of maltreatment (Parent *et al.*, 2016; Vertommen *et al.*, 2016; Ohlert *et al.*, 2018; Hartill *et al.*, 2021), although rates overall are sufficiently high that it would be erroneous to ignore athletes with other characteristics or at other performance levels.

Prevalence studies suggest maltreatment, and especially psychological abuse, is part of being an athlete; such abuse isn't the exception, it's the 'norm' (Vertommen *et al.*, 2016; McPherson *et al.*, 2017; Hartill *et al.*, 2021). Indeed, while child sexual abuse is often concealed, in sport non-sexual forms of maltreatment have become so normalised and/or are rationalised as effective training practices that they often happen in plain sight and go unchallenged by athletes, parents, and coaching staff (Stirling and Kerr, 2014; Jacobs *et al.*, 2017). Crucially, the normalisation of psychological abuse in sport, along with the high profile given to sexual abuse (see, Lang, 2021b, 2022; McVeigh and Lang, 2021) and dominant constructions of children as dependent and incompetent (Lang, 2022), can prevent athletes and bystanders in sport from recognising or reporting psychological and other non-sexual forms of maltreatment (Brackenridge, 2001; Lang, 2021b, 2022).

## Understanding Maltreatment in Practice

Given the prevalence rates of maltreatment in sport, coaches and other sports stakeholders are most likely to encounter behaviours that constitute psychological or physical abuse in their practice. However, these forms of abuse are the least likely to be reported to safeguarding authorities (Hartill and Lang, 2018) and the least likely to be recognised as problematic by coaches as such behaviours are often considered normal in sport or fall into a grey area between 'acceptable' and 'unacceptable' practice (Stirling and Kerr, 2014; Jacobs *et al.*, 2017). In line with this thinking, it is useful to draw attention to behaviours in sport that are prevalent in coaches' practices with children that constitute maltreatment.

Many of these problematic behaviours stem from coaches' perceptions of what constitutes 'good' or 'effective' training. It is widely recognised that for an individual to reach and achieve in top-level sport, significant training is needed, but the amount and intensity of this training has been, and continues to be, debated (Lang and Light, 2010; Oliver and Lloyd, 2015). Certainly, for children and young people, high-volume training and inappropriate physical conditioning can result in psychological stress and overuse injuries (Jayanthi *et al.*, 2015; Bell *et al.*, 2016). This is usually the by-product of poor coach education and a system that is (or coaches who are) focused on short-term performance outcomes as opposed to the long-term development of athletes (Lang and Light, 2010; Oliver and Lloyd, 2015). While coaches may justify their approaches to training as necessary to push athletes to better performances (Stirling, 2013), pressuring athletes to perform to unrealistically high standards has been flagged by the Sport England NSPCC Child Protection in Sport Unit (2021) as a form of psychological abuse.

There are coaches who have adopted a 'one-size-fits-all' approach to training that erroneously conflates quantity with quality, teaching the young athlete that 'more is better' and to play/train through pain and injury to demonstrate the mental toughness and desire to succeed they think is necessary to progress. In this way, there is a thin line in sport between intensive training, physically abusive practices, and neglect (Lang and Light, 2010; Oliver and Lloyd, 2015). This line is crossed when a coach introduces exercise that could cause harm (e.g. forcing an athlete to train when exhausted or injured), exercise in which there is no actual or perceived benefit, and when physical activity is used as punishment (e.g. running laps etc.) (Kerr, 2010).

Given its lengthy tradition in some sport contexts, it may surprise some to know that the use of exercise as punishment can constitute a form of physical abuse (Mountjoy *et al.*, 2016; Kerr *et al.*, 2020) and thus may be illegal. However, it is still used by some coaches who view this as 'appropriate training' or 'reasonable physical discipline' or 'just a bit of fun' as opposed to a physically abusive behaviour (Burak *et al.*, 2013; Kerr *et al.*, 2020). While some may argue that drills used as physical punishment are not abusive if the players 'buy into them', or if they are used 'good-naturedly' ('everyone knows it's in the spirit of having fun'), the process of obtaining athlete consent is problematic. Seeking consent assumes the athlete can discern between acceptable behaviour and maltreatment. Also, an athlete may feel pressure to agree but not be comfortable with that to which they have consented (Purdy, 2018).

Another problematic coaching behaviour that is often unquestioned is repeated shouting at children or young people. Studies suggest that such behaviours are used as a means of punishment for inadequate performances or training behaviour and/or to establish, maintain, and/or increase dominance and control over athletes (Kelly and Waddington, 2006; Stirling and Kerr, 2008). Indeed, coach control and maintaining discipline have been referred to as key aspects of successful coaching (Fox, 2006), prompting coaches to rely on authoritarian styles of leadership. This is not only not in athletes' best interests nor their preferred style of leadership (Fasting and Pfister, 2000); it is unlikely to result in player engagement, can cause athlete drop-out, and may facilitate and/or mask other forms of maltreatment (Mountjoy *et al.*, 2016; Jacobs *et al.*, 2017). For example, a coach might withhold praise, believing that the athlete must earn acclaim through the session and/or out of concern that too much praise could render it ineffective or meaningless (Schmidt, 1991). In contrast, praise that validates the effort and encourages hard work (Mueller and Dweck, 1998; Dweck, 2007) has been identified as essential in creating a positive learning environment (Hall *et al.*, 2016), with work dating back to the early 2000s noting that effective coaches use more praise (Potrac *et al.*, 2007).

## Parental Compliance

There are numerous problematic beliefs and behaviours that are ingrained in the culture of many sports and are often accepted or unquestioned but can have serious consequences for athletes. Often parents are witnesses to athlete maltreatment but don't recognise these actions as forms of physical, psychological, and/or sexual abuse and neglect. Furthermore, parents might be afraid to question coaches, believing that doing so would result in retaliation (e.g. the child athlete will be excluded from competition or ignored in training) so they accept the coaches' questionable behaviour in order for their child to stay involved in the sport. This may be more pronounced amongst athletes nearing or at elite level, when the high stakes of nearing the top may result in a more compliant athlete, one which is more susceptible to harm (Brackenridge, 2001).

If parents are apprehensive to confront coaches about their behaviour, questions should be raised about the type of training environment that is being promoted. For example, have child athletes whose parents have challenged coaches been left out of training/competition? Such a strategy (e.g. repeatedly being excluded or ignored by coaches) is a form of psychological abuse, can have a serious negative effect on athletes, and may have lasting consequences (Stirling and Kerr, 2008). As such, it is unsurprising that parents are reluctant to draw attention to problematic coaching practice.

Conversely, coaches should also be aware of how parents care for their child-athlete. It is vital that parents ensure that young athletes have interests outside of sport and that they and their child's coaches respect this. Long-standing scholarship has highlighted the importance of not over-investing in one (athletic) identity due to the consequences of overconforming (e.g. excessive overtraining, disordered eating) and resultant challenges if that identity is threatened or lost (e.g. depression, anxiety) (Jones *et al.*, 2005). Furthermore, if parents opt to prioritise their child's sport over their schooling, limiting the child-athlete's exposure to an education, this could not only be problematic in promoting a one-dimensional identity but may also constitute a form of neglect (e.g. educational). Coaches should also watch for signs of other forms of neglect by parents (e.g. physical, emotional, medical). These include, among others, parents who do not meet the child-athlete's basic needs; behaviours that ignore, humiliate, intimidate, or isolate; and those who refuse to seek medical treatment or ignore medical advice about their child's injuries.

## Implications for Children's Sport Coaching

Research on the abuse and maltreatment of children in sport first emerged in the 1990s (e.g. Lenskyj, 1992; Brackenridge, 1994) and was soon followed by strategies to protect children in sport (Lang, 2021b). Yet as this chapter illustrates, coaching practice has not always kept pace with these developments. Child maltreatment, and especially psychological and physical abuse and neglect, remains a common feature of sport and is often structurally and culturally embedded in sporting practices to the extent that it is rendered invisible and goes unquestioned (Hughes and Coakley, 1991; Stirling and Kerr, 2014). Coaches are well placed to challenge this and the need to do so is long overdue.

To commence this process, coaches, along with other sports stakeholders, must begin by recognising all forms of maltreatment, how the different forms of maltreatment manifest within sports settings, and the short- and long-term consequences of these. They must also actively reject the commonly held belief in a hierarchy of maltreatment, with certain forms considered 'more serious' or 'more damaging' than others, acknowledging instead that no form of maltreatment is benign; consequences for those who experience maltreatment are contingent on the frequency and severity of the experience, the nature of the relationship in which the maltreatment occurs, and the child's own life history, among other factors, rather than the form (s) of maltreatment experienced (Higgins, 2004; Spinazzola *et al.*, 2014). Doing so offers a pathway to critiquing coaching practices that are normalised but that have the potential to be harmful. Similarly, as adults working with children *in loco parentis*, coaches must be mindful of the behaviours of athletes' parents and peers and commit to challenging harmful practices. This requires coaches to problematise often taken-for-granted practices by critically reflecting on what they and others are doing, why, and in whose interests.

Adopting a child-centred approach, based on the principles of children's rights, is one-way coaches can critique their and others' practice. This approach places the welfare of the child at the heart of everything the coach and other sports stakeholders do, and promotes the holistic development, welfare, and well-being of the child above all – including over-performance and conformity to sporting norms (Kerr and Stirling, 2008; Lang, 2021b). Adopting a children's rights approach in coaching means incorporating the UN Convention on the Rights of the Child (UN General Assembly, 1989), which all but one country globally has now ratified. This includes the legal obligation to protect children from "all forms of physical or mental violence, injury or abuse, neglect or negligent treatment, maltreatment or exploitation" (UN General Assembly, 1989, Art. 19.1). But it also means recognising children as active citizens, agents in their own lives with the capacity to express an opinion "in all matters affecting the child, the views of the child being given due weight in accordance with the age and maturity of the child" (UN General Assembly, 1989, Art. 12.1). In other words, coaches and other adults in sport must ask for *and act upon* children's opinions about the entire sporting experience: why the child is involved in sport, what they would like to achieve, how they would like to be coached, how often they would like to train, etc.

Empowering children by giving them a voice that is acted upon not only enhances children's protection from maltreatment but also facilitates their personal development and learning (Lansdown, 2001; Lang, 2022). Doing so will have obvious implications for how coaches' approach and work with children in sport. It may mean coaches have to change their ambitions for child-athletes as well as their behaviours when coaching them. However, if sport is to continue to make claims to the many benefits noted at the start of this chapter, coaches and other adults in sport must commit to acting in children's best interests in everything they do.

## Summary, Future Directions and Future Research

Child maltreatment takes many forms in sport, and coaches are morally and legally obliged to safeguard child-athletes' welfare. Given their role in (child-) athletes' lives, coaches are also well placed to do so. Research since the 1990s has done much to reveal the sexual exploitation of athletes and more recent work has exposed other forms of maltreatment (David, 2005; Stirling and Kerr, 2008; Kerr, 2010; Lang, 2010b; Oliver and Lloyd, 2015; Turkeri-Bozkurt and Bulgu, 2020). However, more work is needed on how stakeholders interpret and understand maltreatment in sport and how sport can effectively mitigate it, as well as on how sport can better integrate children's rights. While many organisations have taken steps to prevent and manage maltreatment in sport, professionalised procedures are only part of the solution, especially when it comes to non-sexual forms of abuse and neglect which, as normalised behaviours, are often overlooked or embedded within sports practice (Stirling and Kerr, 2014; Lang, 2021b). As such, cultural change, including recognising and enacting children's perspectives, is needed to avoid developments becoming what McNamee (2011, p. 29) calls "institutional posturing: important but without real bite."

In this chapter suggestions as to how coaches (and parents) could address these forms of maltreatment have been provided, however more work is needed that focuses on how sport can be (re)shaped. Possible lines of future enquiry lie in examinations of effective education and training. For example, considering programmes or courses that are informed by the lived experience of athletes who have been subjected to all forms of maltreatment (and, where possible, are athlete-led) may offer a way of impressing on coaches and parents how child maltreatment is operationalised in sport, the warning signs to look out for, and the potentially devastating consequences of all forms of maltreatment for those affected. Equally, culturally relevant and culturally responsive training that is facilitated by trauma-informed 'insiders' to the sports culture has been found to help coaches and child-athletes recognise the abusive nature of many normalised behaviours in sport (in McMahon *et al.*, press). Similarly, educating coaches on ethical and athlete-centred pedagogical approaches and incorporating critical reflection can disrupt uncritical acceptance and recycling of abusive practices (Zehntner *et al.*, 2016; McMahon *et al.*, 2020). Additional possibilities lie in finding ways to include practitioners experienced with working with youth athletes to effectively mentor and co-coach coaches.

At the heart of these suggestions for safeguarding child athletes, however, is the requirement for children's rights in sport to be fully implemented (see,). Specifically, coaches should ensure their practice is in the best interests of children and based on children's desires and opinions as making sport more child-centred is key to ensuring 'safe sport' becomes a reality.

## References


Anderson, E., 2008. "I used to think women were weak": Orthodox masculinity, gender segregation, and sport. *Sociological Forum*, 23 (2), 257–280.

Bell, D.R., *et al.*, 2016. Prevalence of sport specialisation in high school athletics: A 1-year observational study. *American Journal of Sports Medicine*, 44 (6), 1469–1474.

Bicknell, G., 2020. British former gymnasts claim they were 'beaten' and 'starved' in abuse allegations. *The Mirror*, 7 July. Available from: https://www.mirror.co.uk/sport/other-sports/british-former-gymnasts-claim-were-22312953 [Accessed 15 July 2021].

Brackenridge, C.H., 1994. Fair play or fair game? Child sexual abuse in sport organisations. *International Review for the Sociology of Sport*, 29 (3), 287–299.

Brackenridge, C.H., 2001. *Spoilsports: Understanding and preventing sexual exploitation in sport*. London: Routledge.

Burak, L., *et al.*, 2013. Examining attitudes, beliefs, and intentions regarding the use of exercise as punishment in physical education and sport: An application of the theory of reasoned action. *Journal of Applied Social Psychology*, 43, 1436–1445.

Chavez, C., 2019. Inside the toxic culture of the Nike Oregon Project 'cult'. *Sports Illustrated*. Available from: https://www.si.com/track-and-field/2019/11/13/mary-cain-nike-oregon-project-toxic-culture-alberto-salazar-abuse-investigation [Accessed 22 December 2021].

Darnell, S.C., 2010. Power, politics and 'sport for development and peace': Investigating the utility of sport for international development. *Sociology of Sport Journal*, 27 (1), 54–75.

David, P., 2005. *Human rights in youth sport*. New York: Routledge.

Dweck, C.S., 2007. The perils and promises of praise. *Educational Leadership*, 65 (2), 34–39.

Fasting, K. and Pfister, G., 2000. Female and male coaches in the eyes of female elite soccer players. *European Physical Education Review*, 6 (1), 91–111.

Fox, A., 2006. The importance of coaching control. *International Journal of Sports Science and Coaching*, 1, 19–21.

Hall, E.T., *et al.*, 2016. The microstructure of coaching practice: Behaviours and activities of an elite rugby union head coach during preparation and competition. *Journal of Sports Sciences*, 34 (10), 896–905.

Hartill, M. and Lang, M., 2018. Official reports of child protection and safeguarding concerns in sport and leisure settings: An analysis of English local authority data. *Leisure Studies*, 37 (5), 479–499.

Hartill, M., *et al.*, 2021. *CASES: Child Abuse in Sport: European Statistics – Project Report*. Available from: https://figshare.edgehill.ac.uk/articles/report/CASES_General_Report_The_prevalence_and_characteristics_of_interpersonal_violence_against_children_IVAC_inside_and_outside_sport_in_six_European_countries/17086616/1

Higgins, D., 2004. Differentiating between child maltreatment experiences. *Family Matters*, 69, 50–55.

Hughes, R. and Coakley, J., 1991. Positive deviance among athletes: The implications of over conformity to the sports ethic. *Sociology of Sport Journal*, 8 (4), 307–325.

Jacobs, F., *et al.*, 2017. "You don't realise what you see!": The institutional context of emotional abuse in elite youth sport. *Sport in Society*, 20 (1), 126–143.

Jayanthi, N., *et al.*, 2015. Sports-specialised intensive training and the risk of injury in young athletes: A clinical case-control study. *American Journal of Sports Medicine*, 43 (4), 794–801.

Jones, R., *et al.*, 2005. Slim bodies, eating disorders and the coach-athlete relationship. *International Review for the Sociology of Sport*, 40 (3), 377–391.

Kelly, S. and Waddington, I., 2006. Abuse, intimidation and violence as aspects of managerial control in professional soccer in Britain and Ireland. *International Review for the Sociology of Sport*, 41 (2), 147–164.

Kerr, G., 2010. Physical and emotional abuse of elite child athletes: The case of forced physical exertion. *In*: C.H. Brackenridge and D. Rhind, eds., *Elite child athlete welfare*. London: Brunel University, 41–50.

Kerr, G.A. and Stirling, A.E., 2008. Child protection in sport: Implications of an athlete-centred philosophy. *Quest*, 60 (2), 307–323.

Kerr, G., *et al.*, 2020. Examining coaches' perspectives on the use of exercise as punishment. *International Sport Coaching Journal*, 7, 306–316.

Lang, M., 2010a. Surveillance and conformity in competitive youth swimming. *Sport, Education and Society*, 15 (1), 19–37.

Lang, M., 2010b. Intensive training in youth sport: A new abuse of power? *In:* M. Lang and K. Vanhoutte, eds., *Bullying and the abuse of power: From the playground to international relations*. Freeland: Inter-Disciplinary Press, 57–64.

Lang, M., ed., 2021a. *The Routledge handbook of athlete welfare*. London: Routledge.

Lang, M., 2021b. Developments in international policy on athlete welfare. *In:* M. Lang, ed., *The Routledge handbook of athlete welfare*. London: Routledge, 15–23.

Lang, M., 2022. Advancing children's rights in sport: Coaching, childhood agency and the participatory agenda. *Sports Coaching Review*. (Online First) DOI: 10.1080/21640629.2021.1990655.

Lang, M. and Hartill, M., 2015. *Safeguarding, child protection and abuse in sport: International perspectives in research, policy and practice*. London: Routledge.

Lang, M. and Light, R., 2010. Swimming coaches' concerns with the Long-Term Athlete Development model. *International Journal of Sports Science and Coaching*, 5 (3), 389–402.

Lang, M., *et al.*, 2018. Gender-based violence in EU sport policy: Overview and recommendations. *Journal of Gender-based Violence*, 2 (1), 109–118.

Lansdown, G., 2001. *Promoting children's participation in democratic decision-making*. Geneva: UNICEF.

Lenskyj, H., 1992. Unsafe at home base: Women's experience of sexual harassment in university sport and physical education. *Women in Sport and Physical Activity Journal*, 1 (1), 19–33.

McMahon, J. and Barker-Ruchti, N., 2017. Assimilating to a boy's body shape for the sake of performance. *Sport Education and Society*, 22 (2), 157–174.

McMahon, J., *et al.*, 2020. The fast tracking of elite athletes into coaching roles: A practice contributing to the perpetuation and recycling of abuse in sport? *European Journal for Sport and Society*, 17 (3), 265–284.

McMahon, J., *et al.*, in press. Athlete and coach-led abuse education that teaches about non-sexualised types of abuse: A critical overview of an education theory and design considerations when implemented into a programme for sport contexts. *Sport, Education and Society*.

McNamee, M., 2011. Celebrating trust: Virtues and rules in the ethical conduct of sports coaches. *In:* A.R. Hardman and C. Jones, eds., *The ethics of sports coaching*. London: Routledge, 37–56.

McPherson, L., *et al.*, 2017. Children's experience of sport in Australia. *International Review for the Sociology of Sport*, 52 (5), 551–569.

McVeigh, J. and Lang, M., 2021. The politics of safeguarding and child protection in sport: A history of the present. *In:* S. Wagg and A. Pollock, eds., *The Palgrave handbook of sport, politics and harm*. London: Palgrave Macmillan, 537–553.

Mountjoy, M., *et al.*, 2016. The IOC consensus statement: Sexual harassment and abuse (non-accidental violence) in sport. *British Journal of Sports Medicine*, 50 (17), 1019–1029.

Mueller, C.M. and Dweck, C.S., 1998. Praise for intelligence can undermine children's motivation and performance. *Journal of Personality and Social Psychology*, 75 (1), 33–52.

Norman, R., *et al.*, 2012. The long-term health consequences of child physical abuse, emotional abuse, and neglect. *PLoS Medicine*, 9 (11).

NSPCC, 2021. *Neglect*. Available from: https://www.nspcc.org.uk/what-is-child-abuse/types-of-abuse/neglect/?s=09# [Accessed 22 December 2021].

Ohlert, J., *et al.*, 2018. Sexual violence in organised sport in Germany. *German Journal of Exercise and Sport Research*, 48, 59–68.

Oliver, J. and Lloyd, R., 2015. Physical training as a potential form of abuse. *In:* M. Lang and M. Hartill, eds., *Safeguarding, child protection and abuse in sport: International perspectives in research, policy and practice*. London: Routledge, 163–171.

Parent, S., *et al.*, 2016. Sexual violence experienced in the sport context by a representative sample of Quebec adolescents. *Journal of Interpersonal Violence*, 31, 2666–2686.

Partington, N., 2016. Sports coaching and the law of negligence: Implications for coaching practice. *Sports Coaching Review*, 6 (1), 36–56.

Potrac, P., *et al.*, 2007. Understanding power and the coach's role in professional English soccer: A preliminary investigation of coach behaviour. *Soccer & Society*, 8 (1), 33–49.

Purdy, L., 2018. *Sports coaching: The basics*. London: Routledge.

Schmidt, R.A., 1991. *Motor learning and performance: From principles to practice*. Champaign, IL: Human Kinetics.

Seo, Y. and Griffiths, J., 2019. South Korea launches major investigation into abuse in sport after skating scandal. *CNN*. Available from: https://edition.cnn.com/2019/01/23/sport/south-korea-sport-abuse-investigation-intl/index.html

Spinazzola, J., *et al.*, 2014. Unseen wounds: The contribution of psychological maltreatment to child and adolescent mental health and risk outcomes. *Psychological Trauma*, 6 (S1), S18–S28.

Sport England NSPCC Child Protection in Sport Unit, 2021. *Child Abuse in a Sports Setting*. Available from: https://thecpsu.org.uk/help-advice/introduction-to-safeguarding/child-abuse-in-a-sports-setting/ [Accessed 13 July 2021].

Stirling, A., 2013. Understanding the use of emotionally abusive coaching practices. *International Journal of Sport Science and Coaching*, 8 (4), 625–639.

Stirling, A. and Kerr, G., 2008. Defining and categorising emotional abuse in sport. *European Journal of Sport Science*, 8 (4), 173–181.

Stirling, A. and Kerr, G., 2014. Initiating and sustaining emotional abuse in sport. *Journal of Aggression, Maltreatment and Trauma*, 23 (2), 116–135.

Tuakli-Wosornu, Y.A., *et al.*, 2020. Non-accidental harms ('abuse') in athletes with impairment ('para athletes'): A state-of-the-art review. *British Journal of Sports Medicine*, 54, 129–138.

Turkeri-Bozkurt, H. and Bulgu, N., 2020. Is injury part of sports? A children's rights perspective. *International Review for the Sociology of Sport*, 55 (1), 98–114.

UN General Assembly, 1989. The *Convention on the Rights of the Child*. Available from: www.unhcr.org/refworld/docid/3ae6b38f0.html

United Nations Children's Fund (UNICEF), 2004. *Sport, recreation and play*. Geneva: UNICEF.

Vertommen, T. et al., 2016. Interpersonal violence against children in sport in the Netherlands and Belgium. *Child Abuse & Neglect*, 51, 223–236.

Vertommen, T. et al. , 2017. Profiling perpetrators of interpersonal violence against children in sport based on a victim survey. *Child Abuse & Neglect*, 63, 172–182.

Wilinsky, C. and McCabe, A., 2021. A review of emotional and sexual abuse of elite child athletes by their coaches. *Sports Coaching Review*, 10 (1), 84–109.

Zehntner, C., et al., 2016. Using stories to investigate, reflect on and raise social consciousness in a sporting culture. *In:* S. Fan and J. Fielding-Wells, eds., *What's next in educational research?* San Francisco: Sense Publishers, 51–58.

# 20

# COACHING CARE-EXPERIENCED CHILDREN AND YOUNG PEOPLE IN SPORT

*Thomas Quarmby, Rachel Sandford, and Oliver Hooper*

## Introduction

Care-experienced youth are known by various terms both nationally and internationally. In England, for instance, 'children-looked after' or 'looked-after children' are the commonly used legislative terms. However, in America the term 'foster care' is more frequently used, while in Australia the term 'children in out-of-home care' is adopted (Sandford *et al.*, 2021). Regardless of terminology, each term is used to denote a group of children or young people who have been removed from their family and placed in the care of the state. This can be for various reasons – including family dysfunction, abuse, and neglect – but is often grounded in an inability of a child's immediate family to meet their basic needs (Department for Education, 2020). Throughout this chapter, the term 'care-experienced', is used to foreground the lasting impact that being in care might have on a child or young person and to better reflect the transient nature of what it means to be 'in care'. Ultimately, statistics show this group to be among the most vulnerable and disadvantaged in society, frequently exposed to a range of adverse childhood experiences that may have lasting impacts on their overall health and well-being (e.g. Simkiss, 2018). Given the notable lack of literature around coaching care-experienced youth, this chapter draws from the broader sport and physical activity literature to explore the challenges that care-experienced youth may face when engaging in youth sport contexts and the issues that coaches might need to be cognisant of when coaching children and youth who are care-experienced.

## Review of Current Research

### *Challenges of Accessing Youth Sport Contexts*

The broader literature clearly indicates that care-experienced youth face a range of obstacles that impede their participation in formal, structured sport and physical activity contexts (e.g. Sandford *et al.*, 2021; Quarmby *et al.*, 2021b). Importantly, the barriers that care-experienced youth face may differ depending on their care context (i.e. what type of care arrangement they have). For instance, in England, as of March 31, 2020, the majority of care-experienced youth were placed in foster care (72%), while 13% were in secure units, residential children's homes, or semi-independent living

 DOI: 10.4324/9781003199359-23

accommodation (e.g. hostels, lodgings or flats with staff employed to provide support and advice) (Department for Education, 2020). These different contexts can shape children's and young people's experiences in diverse ways. Being placed in foster care, for example, provides a family life for children who cannot live with their own parents, while living in secure units or children's homes normally involves living with several other children or young people who have been taken into care, supported by professional staff who work on a shift-based/rota system to provide care and supervision. The outcomes differ for children and young people placed in these different care contexts, with Strijbosch *et al.* (2015) noting that children in foster care had better outcomes (e.g. relating to health and educational achievement) than children in residential care placements, and that those living in the latter were also more likely to be involved in offending. Similarly, just as social outcomes might vary for children and youth living in different care contexts, so too may the factors that impact (positively or negatively) their engagements with developmental opportunities – including sport and physical activity.

Sport/physical activity has been identified as a pertinent vehicle for positive youth development (e.g. Holt, 2016; Morgan *et al.*, 2020) with research also emphasising the important role adults can play in supporting and facilitating children or young people's participation (Armour and Sandford, 2013). However, while all care-experienced youth have a range of official adults involved in their lives, it has been reported previously that key adults (e.g. social workers or foster carers) can lack competence in sports that young people under their care want to engage in and/or may not necessarily value such activities themselves (Safvenbom and Samdahl, 2000; Quarmby and Pickering, 2016). Moreover, those living in the more structured context of residential care may face a host of additional challenges including the organisation and timing of other activities (e.g. scheduled counselling, meetings, therapy, or medical appointments) that would normally occur during times when children may wish to engage in sport (Dowda *et al.*, 2009). Additionally, those living in residential care have reported difficulties in accessing sport due to domestic constraints and disrupted patterns of participation emanating from placement changes (Quarmby, 2014). These would appear to be key factors that hinder engagement in youth sport for care-experienced children and young people and may be unique to those living in residential care as opposed to those in foster care.

Arguably one of the most significant factors impacting on care-experienced youth's engagement in youth sport is the constraints of the care system and, especially, frequent placement moves – for example, moving between different foster carers or from foster care to residential care (Hollingworth, 2012; Murray, 2013). Indeed, care-experienced youth have reported that maintaining sport participation can be particularly problematic due to such moves, which often result in them living long distances away from friends and places (e.g. sport clubs, schools, or parks) where they usually engage in activities (Hollingworth, 2012; Quarmby, 2014). In England, in 2020, most care-experienced youth (68%) had just one placement in the year, yet 11% had three or more different placements (Department for Education, 2020). This is significant, as research has shown that the more life-course 'transitions' children or young people face, the less likely they are to participate in sport (O'Donnell *et al.*, 2020). Moreover, for care-experienced youth specifically, moving placement and, frequently, geographic location can significantly limit their capacity for sustained engagement with the same sport club/organisation. It is notable though – these challenges notwithstanding – that regular engagement in sport has been found to provide a sense of structure to care-experienced youths' lives that they may not experience elsewhere (Farineau and McWey, 2011; Hollingworth, 2012). As care-experienced youth have been identified as one of the groups most in need of regular engagement in sport/physical activity for health benefits (Armour *et al.*, 2011), facilitating their participation – by limiting placement disruption and ensuring sustained engagements with sport clubs – could be a valuable way of enhancing not only their physical but also social and psychological wellbeing (Murray, 2013).

However, despite the possibilities afforded by regular participation in sporting activities, Sandford *et al.* (2021) identified sport clubs as 'missing spaces' in the lives of many care-experienced youths in England. They reported that while 42% of respondents identified clubs as being a place they had previously engaged in sport, not all individuals found access to these spaces easy. Moreover, they noted that relatively few respondents referred to being a 'member' of – or belonging to – specific sport clubs or teams (Sandford *et al.*, 2021). Echoing some of the challenges noted earlier, both adults and young people in their study identified cost, travel, and accessibility as key issues in this respect. However, Sandford *et al.* (2021) also noted that stigma can be an additional barrier for care-experienced children and young people's engagements in youth sport contexts and can influence the extent to which these youth feel they 'fit in' (see also Quarmby and Sandford, 2021), while Green *et al.* (2021) noted that children in out-of-home care in Australia felt stigmatised in community settings. Similarly, young people have reported not wanting to be identified as care-experienced within organised activity settings, even avoiding such contexts in case their care status might be 'exposed', resulting in them being marked out as 'different' (Mannay *et al.*, 2017). For instance, a care-experienced child may be dropped off at a coaching session by a social worker or foster carer – someone other than their parents. As such, they may find themselves having to share their care-experienced status with their peers, should questions be asked about their relationship with these other adults (whether they feel comfortable doing so, or not). Taken together, these various challenges and barriers can make youth sport contexts particularly difficult for care-experienced youth to access, limiting their engagement in what might otherwise be particularly positive, developmental opportunities. Coaches can play a significant role in this regard but, as discussed below, they might not be as well-equipped to meet the needs of this youth population as they could be.

## Coaches' Knowledge of Care-Experienced Youth

It has been argued that sport clubs – as spaces of structured, purposeful activity – are well placed to provide care-experienced youth with a sense of stability and to facilitate valuable opportunities for developing positive and productive relationships with peers and trusted adults, such as coaches (Quarmby *et al.*, 2021b). However, while there is a growing evidence base to draw on in relation to care-experienced youths' engagements with sport/physical activity and physical education (O'Donnell *et al.*, 2020; Sandford *et al.*, 2021), there is currently a dearth of literature focusing on sport clubs and their potential for supporting care-experienced youths' development. Allied to this, Sandford *et al.* (2021) have argued that 'people' are a key factor in shaping sport/physical activity engagements for care-experienced youth, yet little is known about the role of sport coaches in this regard, nor about their knowledge/understanding of the complexity of care-experienced youths' daily lives. Significantly, the broader literature suggests that physical education teachers – practitioners working in a similar context to coaches – may not have adequate knowledge of the social and psychological factors that shape engagement and influence learning for care-experienced youth. Nor do they have sufficient awareness of care-experienced children and young people's prior knowledge and experiences – both in- and out-of-school – to ensure that they do not miss important opportunities to support them in accessing (and reaping the potential benefits of) sport/physical activity (Quarmby *et al.*, 2019; Sandford *et al.*, 2021). On this, Green *et al.* (2021) identified that community sport clubs in Australia lack understanding and resources to support children living in residential care. Indeed, research suggests that while there is much goodwill, there may be some practitioners (physical educators and sport coaches delivering in school) who are simply not aware of who might be 'in care' in their lessons, nor necessarily appreciate the difficulties that these young people may face (Quarmby *et al.*, 2019).

Similarly, O'Donnell *et al.* (2020) have noted that there is often a lack of shared knowledge in schools concerning the behaviours of care-experienced youth and, at times, a lack of understanding regarding the challenges they may encounter within broader life contexts. Teachers have also pointed to a lack of specific training and continuing professional development (CPD) in this area. Hence, given the dearth of literature from the perspectives of sport coaches, and the fact that coaching and physical education share similar pedagogical ground, these findings may usefully translate to coaching contexts too. Therefore, there may be a need for coaches to engage in specific CPD that focuses on the lived experiences and everyday realities of care-experienced youth, so they are better placed to support their engagement in sport-related contexts.

## *Challenging Childhoods and the Implications for Sport Coaching*

The literature outlined above would suggest that it is important for coaches to be aware of care-experienced youth and their complex lives if they are to develop positive pedagogical contexts. This is particularly important given the physical nature of sport – and the centrality of the body within sport practices – which may present challenges for care-experienced youth, especially those who have experienced abuse and/or neglect. In Australia, for example, emotional abuse was reported to be the most common type of abuse or neglect that led to children being placed in out-of-home care in 2020 – accounting for 54% of cases (Australian Institute of Health and Wellbeing, 2021). Similarly, within England, 65% of care-experienced children and young people enter the care system because they have been subject to abuse or neglect (Department for Education, 2020), while figures show that experiencing abuse or neglect is a common reason for children entering the care system in the US (Administration on Children, Youth, and Families, Children's Bureau, 2020). Such findings are significant as abuse and neglect have been identified as two forms of 'adverse childhood experience' (ACE) that can lead to trauma. Ultimately, ACE is a term used to describe a range of stressful events that children and young people, up to the age of 18 years, can be exposed to whilst growing up (Felitti *et al.*, 1998). Importantly, it is an individual's response to ACEs that determines whether they are considered traumatic or not (Substance Abuse and Mental Health Services Administration [SAMHSA], 2014). Trauma, defined in various ways, occurs when an individual is exposed to an experience that engulfs both the internal and external coping resources available to them, creating a sense of extreme threat that has lasting negative effects on their functioning and wellbeing (Substance Abuse and Mental Health Services Administration, 2014).

The work of Simkiss (2018, p. 26) suggests that children who enter care because of abuse and/or neglect are likely to have experienced the 'toxic trio' of domestic violence, substance misuse, and mental illness, which inevitably leads them to experience multiple ACEs. Care-experienced youth are more likely to disproportionately experience ACEs in comparison to their non-cared for peers, with Denton *et al.* (2016) noting that they may be exposed to a range of prolonged traumatic events in their early development and that such exposure to multiple ACEs is associated with poorer outcomes in adulthood (see also Simkiss, 2018). Importantly, if a child experiences trauma, the effects can be both short- and long-term and can impact on neurological, physiological, and psychological development (Dye, 2018). With regard to the implications for coaching children in sport, Nolin and Ethier (2007) suggest that children who have experienced neglect and/or abuse can have difficulties with problem-solving and planning and tend to have poorer attention, thus they are more easily distracted and more impulsive than their peers who have not had such experiences.

It is worth noting that while ACEs may be more widespread in care-experienced youth, any child could have encountered adversity. In fact, ACEs, and as a result, trauma, are increasingly prevalent, with childhood trauma having been recognised as a global health epidemic (Department of Health and Department for Education, 2017). For instance, a 2014 survey of 3,885 individuals aged 18–69 years in England revealed that 47% of respondents had experienced at least one type of adversity prior to the age of 18, while 9% had experienced multiple (four or more) ACEs (Bellis *et al.*, 2014). Likewise, in Australia in 2015, approximately 5 million adults were found to have experienced childhood trauma (Kezelman *et al.*, 2015), with 25% of Australian children impacted by child abuse alone (Segal, 2015). Finally, the National Child Traumatic Stress Network reported in 2017 that two-thirds of American children had experienced at least one traumatic event. Hence, while much of this chapter relates explicitly to care-experienced youth, ACEs (and trauma more broadly) have important implications for youth sport practitioners at large.

The depth of vulnerability felt by children exposed to trauma – which can be significantly heightened within youth sport contexts – is unlikely to be recognised by sport coaches who, as noted earlier, may have limited understanding of the complexities of care-experienced youths' lives. Indeed, childhood trauma can have significant implications for children and young people's engagements (or otherwise) with youth sport contexts. Hence, there are a range of potential 'flashpoints' that coaches should be aware of that may stem from difficulties processing information, being able to distinguish between threatening and non-threatening situations, forming trusting relationships, and being able to regulate their emotions (Cole *et al.*, 2005). Within youth sport contexts, the symptoms of trauma may therefore manifest in small fouls that escalate into physical conflict, refusal to be part of a team, or a reluctance to form connections with teammates. Some children may also struggle to adhere to the rules and demonstrate an inability to handle pressure situations during competition (Bergholz *et al.*, 2016). The interactions that frequently take place in coaching contexts may also further exacerbate the anxieties of care-experienced youth – particularly those involving physical contact and 'touch'. While touch is often necessary in youth sport contexts, it can be far from straightforward. Within physical education, for example, Caldeborg *et al.* (2019) have noted that while physical contact between a teacher and a pupil can be important – for example, to support a movement or to offer reassurance – it is highly context-relevant and there may be instances where it is unwelcomed. A coach's lack of awareness of a child's 'cared-for' status and the trauma they may have experienced can therefore unknowingly (and unwittingly) cause further distress for the child.

## Implications for Children's Sport Coaching

Although the literature suggests that many care-experienced youths are not accessing sport clubs, for those who do, there is a need to ensure that they have positive and constructive experiences. In particular, it is imperative that those working with children and young people – including coaches – help to generate inclusive coaching contexts for care-experienced youth, so that their pedagogical practices do not serve to further alienate this already marginalised group of children and young people. In that sense, sport coaches might wish to consider drawing from a growing body of work relating to trauma-aware pedagogies in physical education (e.g. Ellison *et al.*, 2019; Quarmby *et al.*, 2021a). Such pedagogies could help coaches to cater for the behavioural and learning needs of trauma-affected children and create an environment that promotes inclusion, healing, and personal growth (Avery *et al.*, 2020).

Before considering what trauma-aware pedagogies might look like in youth sport contexts at the micro level, Substance Abuse and Mental Health Services Administration (2014) suggest four guiding assumptions – known as the four 'R's' – that operate at a macro level that sport clubs/ organisations should be aware of. The first R – *realisation* – indicates that people (in this instance coaches) need to have a basic understanding of trauma and the impact it can have on individuals. This would necessitate viewing children and young people's actions in the context of their experiences and realising that any negative behaviours may be the result of an individual's coping strategies to survive an overwhelming situation. The second R – *recognise* – reflects the needs for coaches to notice the signs of trauma, while the third – *respond* – suggests that the system (i.e. the club/organisation, the coaches, the programme) responds in a way that embraces an understanding of trauma (i.e. coaches are trained in evidence-based trauma practices and the club provides a physically and psychologically safe environment). The final R – *resist re-traumatisation* – assumes that any practices at a micro level do not interfere with an individual's healing or recovery.

Building on this 4R framework, Quarmby *et al.* (2021a) proposed five interrelated principles – at the micro level – for enacting trauma-aware pedagogies in the context of physical education. These are: (1) ensuring safety and wellbeing, (2) establishing routines and structures, (3) developing and sustaining positive relationships that foster a sense of belonging, (4) facilitating and responding to youth voice, and (5) promoting strengths and self-belief. These principles – drawn from research with care-experienced youth in England and Australia and underpinned by the four R's – point to the need for creating safe environments, shaped by consistency, positive connections, and opportunities for interaction and engagement. While there is no particular order to the principles, it is suggested that considering safety and wellbeing first may serve to lay the foundations on which some of the other principles may be built (Quarmby *et al.*, 2021a). Although initially proposed for the context of physical education, it is argued that these principles reflect core aspects of pedagogical practice and may therefore also hold relevance for broader youth sport contexts.

It is important to note that, in many ways, trauma-aware pedagogies share common ground with existing pedagogical strategies linked to effective and inclusive ('good') coaching, such as problem-solving and reflective practice. Moreover, given the nature of the principles, trauma-aware pedagogies are, in essence, relational since they draw on mutual respect between coach and child. However, as Quarmby *et al.* (2021a) note, trauma-aware pedagogies are not simply a means of 'reinventing the wheel' but encourage an important focus on the broader landscapes that comprise young people's lives and shape their attitudes towards/engagements with sport and physical activity contexts. The development of trauma-aware pedagogies necessitates an understanding of the impact of trauma on the whole child, their learning, development, relationships, and life-course trajectory (Quarmby *et al.*, 2021a). Importantly, relational approaches have already been advocated for within the sport coaching literature with Cronin and Lowes (2019) noting that coaches have a responsibility to care for the participants with whom they work. Such relational approaches are reflected in recent guidance from UK Coaching – the representative body for (sport) coaches within the UK – around coaches' 'duty to care'. Indeed, UK Coaching are increasingly advocating for such 'person-centred' approaches to coaching whereby relationships that are 'positive, motivational, caring and rewarding' can be facilitated (UK Coaching, 2021, para. 3). There is then, it would seem, a good foundation on which to build with regard to shaping more engaging and inclusive coaching practices for care-experienced youth.

Finally, while these considerations might be helpful for care-experienced children and young people once they are 'in' sport clubs/youth sport contexts, it is also worth briefly considering how initial access to these settings might be improved. Notwithstanding the acknowledged challenges that children face in relation to transport and adult support within their care context (Sandford *et al.*, 2021) – which reflect structural barriers somewhat beyond the control of sports clubs – there are perhaps some ways in which individual clubs might endeavour to facilitate greater participation for care experienced children or youth. For example, sport clubs might consider reducing fees/subscriptions for care-experienced children or young people, or having greater flexibility with regard to financial obligations. On this, Green *et al.* (2021) noted that care-experienced children could not always pay their fees on time and were subsequently turned away, without clubs recognising the complexity of the broader care system and the extended negotiations required to provide funds to support children's participation. Moreover, clubs could potentially seek to provide kit or equipment to care-experienced youth, especially in those sports where participation is contingent on such resources. Research within the school sport context has suggested that such provision can be conducive to enhanced participation for care-experience children and youth (Sandford *et al.*, 2021). Finally, recognising the transient nature of care experiences – with frequent placement moves and required processes – clubs may need to be accommodating of the sporadic nature of care-experienced children and youths' participation. Ultimately, such suggestions all point to the need for a greater understanding within the coaching community of the complex social landscapes that these young people are required to navigate daily (Sandford *et al.*, 2021; Quarmby *et al.*, 2021b).

## Summary, Future Directions and Future Research

The discussion above has shown that despite positive benefits to be gleaned from participation in youth sport, many care-experienced children and young people struggle to access sport club and coaching contexts. Moreover, many sport coaches lack sufficient knowledge and understanding of care-experienced youth's lives that could help them shape more engaging and inclusive practices. Research has shown that there is a clear need for a more joined-up approach to support care-experienced children and young people's access to and (sustained) engagement with sport clubs and broader youth sport contexts (Sandford *et al.*, 2021). Certainly, stronger communication between agencies and organisations (e.g. local authorities, schools, and care contexts) would help in this respect. In relation to sport and physical activity, sport clubs and coaches can also play a central role. To enhance practice in this respect it is important for sports clubs to consider what they could do to better facilitate the involvement of care-experienced children and young people and what support they may need to achieve this. Equally, what role representative bodies (such as UK Coaching) as well as individual National Governing Bodies may play in supporting care-experienced youth's engagement in youth sport contexts requires consideration. Indeed, it may be that there is a need for specific CPD opportunities for coaches that could be facilitated by these organisations. Such CPD might learn from the work carried out in the broader field of physical education that addresses the role of trauma in shaping engagement and identifies trauma aware pedagogies that can serve to shape more inclusive practices. Finally, there is perhaps a need for more youth voice research to feed into this process and generate understanding of care-experienced children and young people's experiences of coaching and thoughts about how it might be developed.

## References

Administration on Children, Youth, and Families, Children's Bureau. 2020. *The AFCARS Report, Preliminary FY2019 Estimates as of June 23, 2020 –No. 27* [online]. Washington, DC: HHS. Available from: https://www.acf.hhs.gov/cb/report/afcars-report-27 [Accessed 19 March 2022].

Armour, K. and Sandford, R., 2013. Positive youth development through an outdoor physical activity programme: evidence from a four-year evaluation. *Educational Review*, 65 (1), 85–108.

Armour, K., Sandford, R., and Duncombe, R., 2011. Right to be active: looked-after children in physical education and sport. *In*: K. Armour, ed. *Sport pedagogy: an introduction for teaching and coaching*. London: Prentice Hall, 214–225.

Australian Institute of Health and Wellbeing, 2021. *Child protection Australia: 2019-2020*. Canberra: Australian Institute of Health and Wellbeing.

Avery, J., *et al.*, 2020. Systematic review of school-wide trauma-informed approaches. *Journal of Child and Adolescent Trauma*, 14 (3), 81–397.

Bellis, M., *et al.*, 2014. National household survey of adverse childhood experiences and their relationship with resilience to health-harming behaviours in England. *BMC Medicine*, 12 (72), 1–10.

Bergholz, L., Stafford, E., and D'Andrea, W., 2016. Creating trauma-informed sports programming for traumatised youth: core principles for an adjunctive therapy approach. *Journal of Infant, Child and Adolescent Psychotherapy*, 15 (3), 244–253.

Caldeborg, A., Maivorsdotter, N., and Öhman, M., 2019. Touching the didactic contract—a student perspective on intergenerational touch in PE. *Sport, Education and Society*, 24 (3), 256–268.

Cole, S., *et al.*, 2005. *Helping traumatised children learn: supportive school environments for children traumatised by family violence*. Boston: Massachusetts Advocates for Children.

Cronin, C. and Lowes, J., 2019. Care in community sports coaching. *In*: L. Gale and B. Ives, B, eds. *Sports coaching in the community: developing knowledge and insight*. Manchester: Manchester Metropolitan University, 79–95.

Denton, R., *et al.*, 2016. The assessment of developmental trauma in children and adolescents: a systematic review. *Child Clinical Psychology and Psychiatry*, 2, 1–28.

Department for Education, 2020. *Children looked after in England including adoptions (reporting year 2020)* [online]. London: Department for Education. Available from: https://explore-education-statistics.service.gov.uk/find-statistics/children-looked-after-in-england-including-adoptions/2020 [Accessed 19 March 2022].

Department of Health and Department for Education, 2017. *Transforming children and young people's mental health provision: a green paper* [online]. London: Department of Health & Department for Education. Available from: https://www.gov.uk/government/consultations/transforming-children-and-young-peoples-mental-health-provision-a-green-paper [Accessed 19 March 2022].

Dowda, M., *et al.*, 2009. Physical activity and sedentary pursuits of children living in residential children's homes. *Journal of Physical Activity and Health*, 6, 195–202.

Dye, H., 2018. The impact and long-term effects of childhood trauma. *Journal of Human Behaviour in the Social Environment*, 28 (3), 381–392.

Ellison, D., Walton-Fisette, J., and Eckert, K., 2019. Utilising the teaching personal and social responsibility (TPSR) model as a trauma-informed practice (TIP) tool in physical education. *Journal of Physical Education, Recreation & Dance*, 90 (9), 32–37.

Farineau, H.M. and McWey, L.M., 2011. The relationship between extracurricular activities and delinquency of adolescents in foster care. *Children and Youth Services Review*, 33, 963–968.

Felitti, V., *et al.*, 1998. Relationship of childhood abuse and household dysfunction to many of the leading causes of death in adults: the adverse childhood experiences (ACE) study. *American Journal of Preventative Medicine*, 14 (4), 245–258.

Green, R., *et al.*, 2021. "We're trying so hard for outcomes but at the same time we're not doing enough": barriers to physical activity for Australian young people in residential out-of-home care. *Child Care in Practice*.

Hollingworth, K., 2012. Participation in social, leisure and informal learning activities among care leavers in England: positive outcomes for educational participation. *Child and Family Social Work*, 17, 438–447.

Holt, N., 2016. *Positive youth development through sport*. 2nd ed. London: Routledge.

Kezelman, C., *et al.*, 2015. *The Cost of unresolved childhood trauma and abuse in adults in Australia*. Sydney: Adults Surviving Child Abuse & Pegasus Economics.

Mannay, D., *et al.*, 2017. The consequences of being labelled 'looked-after': exploring the educational experiences of looked-after children and young people in Wales. *British Educational Research Journal*, 43 (4), 683–699.

Morgan, H., *et al.*, 2020. Participation in sport as a mechanism to transform the lives of young people within the criminal justice system: an academic exploration of a theory of change. *Sport, Education and Society*, 25 (8), 917–930.

Murray, C., 2013. Sport in care: using freedom of information requests to elicit data about looked after children's involvement in physical activity. *British Journal of Social Work*, 43 (7) 1347–1363.

Nolin, P. and Ethier, L., 2007. Using neuropsychological profiles to classify neglected children with or without physical abuse. *Child Abuse and Neglect*, 31, 631–643.

O'Donnell, C., Sandford, R., and Parker, A., 2020. Physical education, school sport and looked-after-children: health, wellbeing and educational engagement, *Sport, Education and Society*, 25 (6), 605–617.

Quarmby, T., 2014. Sport and physical activity in the lives of looked-after children. *Sport, Education and Society*, 19 (7), 944–958.

Quarmby, T. and Pickering, K., 2016. Physical activity and children in care: A scoping review of barriers, facilitators, and policy for disadvantaged youth. *Journal of Physical Activity and Health*, 13 (7), 780–787.

Quarmby, T. and Sandford, R., 2021. The sport and physical activity practices of care-experienced youth: standing out and fitting in. *In*: D. Trussell and R. Jeanes. eds. *Families, sport, leisure and social justice*. London: Routledge, 139–150.

Quarmby, T., Sandford, R., and Elliot, E., 2019. 'I actually used to like PE, but not now': understanding care-experienced young people's (dis)engagement with physical education. *Sport, Education and Society*, 24 (7), 714–726.

Quarmby, T., *et al.*, 2021a. Developing evidence-informed principles for trauma-aware pedagogies in physical education. *Physical Education and Sport Pedagogy*, 1–15.

Quarmby, T., *et al.*, 2021b. Narratives and marginalised voices: storying the sport and physical activity experiences of care-experienced young people. *Qualitative Research in Sport, Exercise and Health*, 13 (3), 426–437.

Safvenbom, R. and Samdahl, D.M., 2000. Leisure for youth in residential care: an important context for intervention. *International Journal of Social Welfare*, 9 (2), 120–127.

Sandford, R., *et al.*, 2021. Navigating complex social landscapes: examining care experienced young people's engagements with sport and physical activity. *Sport, Education and Society*, 26 (1), 15–28.

Segal, L., 2015. Economic issues in the community response to child maltreatment. *In*: B. Mathews, and D. Bross, eds. *Mandatory reporting laws and the identification of severe child abuse and neglect*. New York: Springer, 193–216.

Simkiss, D., 2018. The needs of looked after children from an adverse childhood experience perspective. *Paediatrics and Child Health*, 29 (1), 25–33.

Strijbosch, E., *et al.*, 2015. The outcome of institutional youth care compared to non-institutional youth care for children of primary school age and early adolescence: a multi-level meta-analysis. *Children and Youth Services Review*, 58, 208–218.

Substance Abuse and Mental Health Services Administration, 2014. *SAMHSA's concept of trauma and guidance for a trauma-informed approach* [online]. Rockville, MD: Substance Abuse and Mental Health Services Administration. Available from: https://ncsacw.acf.hhs.gov/userfiles/files/SAMHSA_Trauma.pdf

UK Coaching. 2021. *Duty to care toolkit and digital badge* [online]. Available from: https://www.ukcoaching.org/duty-to-care [Accessed 19 March 2022].

# SECTION III

# Talent Identification and Development

## Introduction: Talent Identification and Development

*Martin Toms and Ruth Jeanes*

The focus upon ability, competition and performance in children's sport is a contentious one that also differs within cultures and contexts across the world. This approach has led to questionable activities and also coaches, parents, and influential others pushing some children towards high-performance contexts. Allied to many professional sports clubs (noticeably soccer) 'talent identifying' children at a young age and putting them into elite sports systems, this area has become a significant one for study since before the turn of the millenium. The fact that the research is still ongoing and the impact that this can have on policy and practice can be considerable for those who engage in it – not least the children who are sucked into such a system. Whilst all children should have the chance to play and engage with sport, the problematic notion of 'talent' has become part of the lexicon of children's sport – and one that will not change any time soon.

This section explores and highlights some of the key topics around Talent Identification and Development in children's sport, and aims to integrate the most recent research into exploring the challenges and practices around talent identification. The focus on particular topics is a result of the current research emphasis, and whilst this will no doubt change over time, the section explores a number of perspectives. Each of these is important and highlight current practice and theoretical considerations that are part of children's sport experiences.

The section explores the realities and considerations around not just the physical and psycho-social development of children, but also the realities of coaching elite children within elite systems. They emphasise that the focus upon the individual athlete is key – but can also be lost within structures and systems that are focused upon success. Both physical and psycho-social development is obviously also not linear, so engaging children in such systems comes with multiple risks.

The section also delves into some of the broader areas of talent identification where not only are discussions around the relative value of multi-sport sampling versus specialising in single sports are reviewed, but also how such behaviours can impact dropout and performance when children develop at such different rates compared to their peers. Such a focus upon measuring children's performance and refining skill levels leads to considerations around skill performance and development and whether such practice is beneficial in the long term.

DOI: 10.4324/9781003199359-24

The section considers the nature of talent development strategies, exploring the contextual area of age group banding strategies as a way of attempting to 'even up' the playing field in terms of children's development and age, not to mention the questioning of the entire nature of talent identification and development in the first place and its value in the 21st century. Questions will no doubt continue to challenge everyone involved in children's sport for a very long time indeed.

# 21

# COACHING ELITE JUNIOR ATHLETES

*Frode Moen, Stig Arve Sæther, and John Anders Bjørkøy*

## Introduction

Young athletes who are ambitious and talented in their sports need optimal nurturing and years of commitment to intensive quality training to become future elite athletes. Thus, even though genetics play a role in the development process of successful athletes, athletic success is mainly explained by an epigenetic nature. The epigenetic nature claims that genes alone cannot explain the development of athletic success and that specific experiences from training on specific skills are needed to fully develop the potential of an athlete (Moen *et al.*, 2018). Athletes' motivation and stamina to commit to high loads and quality in training over years, and being exposed to stimulating environments, are therefore two important keys for young athletes on their path to achieve future successes in their sport. An effective nurturing of athletes' genetic heritage depends on the quality of the training process, the cultural environment that athletes are exposed to, and their abilities to relax and recover from the training loads and their daily demands including with school, families, friends, and other activities that they are exposed to. Therefore, successes in the early years in sports do not necessarily predict later elite athletic success since this is mainly depended on the quality work young elite athletes do daily over years (Rees *et al.*, 2016).

Most governing bodies and sporting federations across the world highlight the importance of securing these athletes' opportunities to develop in their sport and research within sport science postulates that coaches are the key to help and support athletes' learning and development. Coaches are especially essential among children and young athletes (age < 16 years old) since such young athletes are more socially, psychologically, and physically vulnerable, while also trying to prepare them for future athletic successes. Thus, it is key to build a solid foundation at this age, socially, physically, and psychologically. Athletic environments that focus exclusively on performance and results at this age, and not the development of fundamental capacities and skills that are needed to grow their talent in the long run, could be contrary to the athletes' need for social, physical, and psychological stimulus. If these needs of young athletes are not met they might be introduced to the standards and expectations of adult elite athletes coaching and training, including styles of leadership and the underestimating of the importance of joy and fun.

Coaches working with young talented athletes also have to deal with the unpredictable nature of athletic talent, which makes talent identification challenging work. Thus, dilemmas related to differentiation, skill levels, athletic environments, early specialisation, and working

DOI: 10.4324/9781003199359-25

with parents are common among coaches in this age group. To succeed with developing talented child athletes, coaches need to: (1) Stimulate the athletes' motivation to complete quality training over years; (2) Establish social environments that stimulate young athletes socially, physically, and psychologically; (3) Develop coaches who have the necessary skills and competence at this age group; and (4) Be aware of the challenges that coaches meet in their work with young elite athletes. These subjects will be considered in turn within this chapter.

## Review of Current Research

A great majority of junior athletes attending high schools specialising in sport in Norway are found to have ambitions to become future elite athletes at an international level in their sport (Raanes *et al.*, 2019; Moen *et al.*, 2021). Thus, athletic success often starts with young athletes who have an ambition to achieve great performances within their sport (Locke and Latham, 2002). However, in all sport, high and lasting motivation is key in the work to achieve challenging goals and to grow any athletic talent (Deci and Ryan, 2002; Moen and Firing, 2016). Ambition and motivation are therefore important aspects of talent development. Ericsson's (1993) theory of "deliberate practice" claims that it takes thousands of hours over years with quality practice to become an expert in both sport and in any other field (Ericsson and Harwell, 2019). Deliberate practice is here defined as a highly structured activity that is explicitly aimed at improving performance (Ericsson *et al.*, 1993). Thus, young elite athletes' need to work continuously to grow their talents over many years to achieve elite senior levels. The work required need to complete the development of their capacities and skills might often be challenging both physically and mentally. Therefore, their ability to maintain their effort and interest within their sport, despite potential experiences of failures and adversities, and continue their strenuous work towards challenging goals is essential among young ambitious athletes (Buzzetto-Hollywood and Mitchell, 2019). To achieve such efforts over time, young elite athletes need to be highly motivated. The tendency athletes have to pursue such long-term challenging goals with perseverance and passion is defined as grit (Duckworth *et al.*, 2011). Grit is viewed as a personality trait that enables people to have stamina and work hard day in and day out, not for weeks and months, but for years (Duckworth and Eskreis-Winkler, 2013, Larkin *et al.*, 2015). Thus, some athletes have a more inherent extraordinary motivation, and others need more help to nurture their motivation and stamina. Gritty athletes also have the tendency to make sacrifices when this is needed and remain in love with what they do, while other athletes need more help from their coaches to do the same (Lee and Duckworth, 2018). However, young elite athletes also need to recover from their training sessions and therefore need to detach their focus to gain suitable recovery. Sleep is found to influence young elite athletes' ability to train, improve their performances, prevent injuries and gain optimal recovery. In line with the principle of physiological and psychological recovery strategies, sleep is crucial for optimal functioning of all major systems of the body and is the most important recovery tool for the body (Mah *et al.*, 2011; Zee *et al.*, 2014). Thus, young elite athletes also need optimal scheduling, quality, and quantity of sleep to progress towards athletic excellence (Hrozanova *et al.*, 2019). Therefore, one important task for coaches who are coaching young ambitious athletes is to influence their athletes' motivation and stamina in the long term, to gain both optimal training quality and recovery. However, athletes' abilities to keep their motivation and maintain their efforts over time towards their goals are highly associated with their beliefs in their capabilities to master the tasks they need to fulfil to achieve their goals (Bandura, 1997). Thus, the most important task for a coach in youth elite sport is to develop resilient self-beliefs among their athletes since their self-beliefs are predicting their motivation to continue to pursue their goals in the long run.

## *Mastery Experiences and Self-Beliefs*

The self-belief that is highly associated with athlete development and performance is defined as self-efficacy beliefs (Feltz *et al.*, 2008; Wurtele, 2011). Thus, self-efficacy is found to be one of the most predictive variables of performance and athletic successes in any sport (Guay *et al.*, 2003). Self-efficacy is here defined as athletes' beliefs in their abilities to perform the tasks that are necessary for successful and anticipated outcomes in specific domains (Bandura, 1997). Since self-efficacy is both task- and situation-specific, it is important that young elite athletes are exposed to both task- and situational demands that are relevant in their sports, and ultimately experience mastery and success when they execute their sport-specific tasks. Thus, authentic experiences of mastery and successful performances are claimed to be the most essential and dependable source of self-efficacy. Importantly, since self-efficacy is both task- and situation-specific it is important that young elite athletes learn to handle both training tasks in different situations and competitions. Thus, the ability to perform at your best under pressure in competitions is key in all elite sports. However, young elite athletes often complete their daily training sessions in psychosocial environments together with other athletes. When young athletes observe the performance of their peers, they might use this information to form their own expectancies about their own capabilities to perform similar tasks. This source of self-efficacy is defined as vicarious experiences and is based on the athlete's perception of similarity with the model athlete, the number and variety of models, the perceived power of the models, and the perceived similarity between the problem faced by the observing athlete and the model (Feltz *et al.*, 2008). Thus, coaches must be aware of this effect and develop psychosocial environments for young elite athletes that both challenge their skills and capacities and also facilitate athletes' experiences of mastery compared to the other peer athletes in the environment.

A further source of self-efficacy is when the coach tries to persuade the athlete to be confident that he or she is capable of achieving a task (Wurtele, 2011). This source is defined as verbal persuasion. Verbal persuasion can be done by any person, but the effect is higher when the person is significant and trustworthy for the athlete, such as the coach or other staff members of the team. Physical arousal can also affect self-efficacy. If athletes associate comfortable physiological arousal with successful performances, it can lead to raised confidence in the athlete's ability to master the situation when they experience such physical arousals. On the other hand, if unpleasant physical arousal is associated with unsuccessful performances, athletes are more likely to doubt their skills and capacities in the situation if they experience unpleasant physical arousals. Self-efficacy beliefs therefore result from a confluence based on information from the athletes' past experiences and information from the current situation from some of the sources discussed above.

Self-efficacy is also strongly associated with a variety of other outcomes than performance: engagement, persistence, greater cognitive flexibility for example, through effective use of goal setting, resistance to negative feedback, and self-regulation, strategy use and reduced anxiety (Pajares and Schunk, 2001). Research also shows that self-efficacy influences athletes' choice of goals and goals-directed activities, expenditure of effort, and persistence in the face of challenges and obstacles (Locke and Latham, 1990). One important task for coaches is therefore to help their athletes to complete their sport-specific tasks with high quality, give them constructive feedback, establish a stimulating environment and thus give them the opportunity to experience masteries on their path towards elite sport level. Thus, young elite athletes' abilities to remain motivated will be influenced by their experience of mastery on sport-specific tasks, and if unable to do this, their motivation will be influenced negatively.

## *Stimulating Talent Development Environment*

Most young elite athletes will experience some sort of adversities on their paths towards elite senior sport (Raanes *et al.*, 2019). In fact, research claims that many elite senior athletes have experienced different "traumas" during their early years as young athletes, indicating that adversities and "traumas" are possible to overcome (Sarkar *et al.*, 2015; Hardy *et al.*, 2017). Thus, the ability to handle adversities, failures, and potential 'traumas' is key in the work to develop young elite athletes. Psychological resilience is defined as an athlete's ability to overcome adversity and adapt during times of stress (Raanes *et al.*, 2019). The importance of developing resilient athletes is therefore key to talent development and coaches are claimed to have a key responsibility to influence their athletes' resilience (Fletcher and Sarkar, 2012). The most effective way to influence young elite athletes' resilience is to provide both challenging and supportive sport environments. Young elite athletes need to be exposed to levels that are both within and beyond their current skills and capacities to learn and develop to higher levels as described in the paragraph above. However, they also need to feel physically and psychologically accepted, understood and safe in their psychosocial environment.

## *Psychosocial Environment*

Both social competence and social resources affect the psychological resilience in young elite athletes (Fletcher and Sarkar, 2012). Social competence is the ability of young elite athletes to participate socially and create new friendships. Optimal nurturing of young elite athletes involves teaching social skills including how to communicate openly with their coaches, staff members, and peer-athletes, about their thoughts, feelings, and ideas. Athletes' experience of supporting significant others in their environments and their experiences of receiving social support, defines the resilience dimension social resources.

Team-building is designed to enhance group cohesiveness and is found to improve athletes' social skills and their bonding within the team (Dohme *et al.*, 2020). A typical approach in team building is to stimulate athletes to achieve an enhanced understanding of both themselves and their peer-athletes by reciprocally sharing their thoughts, feelings, and ideas about relevant topics (Dunn and Holt, 2004). Thus, effective team-building has also the potential to stimulate athletes' perception of themselves as well, as their self-disclosures are designed to be met with understanding and acceptance from their team-members. Team-building therefore has the potential to build resilient young elite athletes and should be used systematically and continually by coaches for youth elite athletes.

Key themes that are found to be apparent in effective development of sporting talent are long-term aims and methods, emphasis on appropriate development rather than early selection, wide-ranging coherent messages and support, individualised and ongoing development, and finally, integrated, holistic, and systematic development as the five most important features (Martindale *et al.*, 2005). The same overview however also highlighted the importance of quality and appropriateness of the coaching environment, and that it is recognised that athletes have different needs at different stages in their development process, and that they then often require different coaching environments as they develop (Martindale *et al.*, 2005). Based on the review Martindale *et al.* (2010) developed the Talent Development Environment Questionnaire (TDEQ), which measures key holistic and generic processes involved in the effective development of talented athletes. The questionnaire contained five dimensions: long-term development, holistic quality preparation, support network, communication, and alignment of expectations, all found to be important in the talent development environment (Martindale *et al.*, 2013; Gangsø *et al.*, 2021).

Simultaneously, Henriksen *et al.* (2010) developed a qualitative Holistic Ecological Approach (HEA) to talent development environments through Athletic Talent Development Environments (ATDE) and included features on Environment Success Factors (ESF). The results showed that successful ATDEs' shared a number of features that may explain the environment's success in developing talented athletes: (1) training in groups with supportive relationships, (2) environments have proximal role models, (3) receiving the support of their athletic goals by the wider environment, (4) receiving support for the development of psychosocial skills, (5) being exposed to training that allows for diversification, (6) the focus is on long-term development, (7) strong and coherent organisational culture, and (8) integrations of efforts in their work to develop (Henriksen *et al.* 2010, Larsen *et al.*, 2020). These studies on the talent development environment have highlighted the importance of a holistic approach to talent development including both their sporting and non-sporting psychosocial environment, and the athlete's perception of self as a resilient factor, their social resources, and development of their social competence. Talent development is continually becoming more challenging while it requires more aspects and larger coaching teams to help the athletes in their efforts to become senior elite athletes (Rees *et al.*, 2016).

## Implications for Children's Sport Coaching

Young elite athletes will normally be exposed to both heavy physical and psychological loads from several sources (Vitali *et al.*, 2015; Gustafsson *et al.*, 2017). Particularly, childhood and adolescence is suggested to be a stressful period in life for young athletes, with school, their sports, and peer groups as potential impactful stressors (Compas *et al.*, 2001). Research shows that these loads might potentially, if not balanced properly, affect performance negatively and eventually lead athletes into non-functional states such as lasting exhaustion and ultimately athlete burnout (Van Cutsem *et al.*, 2017). Disturbingly, researchers claim that the occurrences of non-functional states among young athletes are rising (Moen *et al.*, 2016). Ultimately, young athletes who take their sports seriously will normally experience non-functional states and negative performance development as highly stressful (Moen et al., 2019a; Raanes *et al.*, 2019). Thus, being a coach for young elite athletes is an important and challenging responsibility, and the coach's role in youth elite sports can be described as a very complex endeavor. It is therefore important to simplify and clarify the main responsibilities of coaches to make their coaching beneficial for their athletes. If coaches do not balance their workload and responsibilities properly, they might also end up exhausted (Olsen *et al.*, 2020).

The main responsibility of coaches in youth elite sport is to take care of their athletes' well-being and to grow their talent. Research claims that athletes' well-being is a key task for coaches (Olympiou *et al.*, 2008), and a recent study documents that young athletes' perceived performance development in their sports uniquely explains their satisfaction with their coaches (Moen *et al.*, 2021). Thus, the expectation among young elite athletes of the coach-athlete relationship is to receive help from their coaches and research suggests that the coach-athlete relationship plays a key role in the process of developing young elite athletes (Jones *et al.*, 2004). There is a long history of research that documents the importance of coaches on their athletes' and significant associations are found between effective coach-athlete relationships and improvements in performance, personal treatment, well-being, team cohesion and motivation (Olympiou *et al.*, 2008; Blom *et al.*, 2010).

A Coach-Athlete Working Alliance Inventory (CAWAI) describes the main responsibilities of coaches through the three terms "bond", "goals", and "tasks" (Moen et al., 2019b). Bond is the mutual trust and genuine interest the athletes experience from their coaches when they work together. Research suggests that effective coach-athlete relationships are experienced as intersubjective fellowships, where coaches and athletes gain a mutual understanding of their different perspectives, and base their relationships on trust and respect (Moen and Federici, 2017). Thus, coaches' empathic understanding of their athletes forms the fundamental foundation of effective coach-athlete relationships, and bond is the dimension that defines this coach responsibility. Goal defines the degree of mutual agreement and understanding between the coach and the athlete about the desired outcomes from their work together. There is a long history of research that document the importance of goalsetting and how clear and challenging goals affect their performance development (Locke and Latham, 2002). The task dimension defines the degree of mutual agreement between the coach and the athlete regarding the tasks and strategies that are supposed to help the athletes to achieve their goals. Goalsetting theory claims that the athlete's capability to develop, possess and effectively execute efficient and effective strategies to achieve goals is essential for goals to affect their performances. Coaches' abilities to design and define tasks that help their athletes to experience mastery is therefore defined as a main responsibility in the CAWAI. It is however essential to remember that puberty starts in this age group, and that puberty often has great impact on the development of physical attributes. Therefore, especially in this age group, training and preparation towards goals should reach beyond physical attributes. Improvements in performance is greatly influenced by athletes' psychological states and processes, such as their mental well-being and coping strategies (Moen *et al.*, 2016). Such psychological variables are perhaps less obvious than athletes' physical attributes or excellent training outcomes, but they are certainly not any less important contributors to an athlete's performance development in the long run.

A coach's sport-specific understanding and ability to develop strategies that help their athletes to achieve their goals in their specific sport are therefore essential and influence the effectiveness of the coach-athlete relationship. Both the goal and the task dimension relate to the athletes' learning and development in the coach-athlete relationship and refer directly to performance outcomes. Thus, an effective coach-athlete relationship is therefore supposed to positively influence a young elite athlete's self-efficacy, motivation, and satisfaction, and an optimal coach-athlete relationship refers to a situation where feelings, thoughts, and behaviors are inter-related between coaches and their athletes. If the coach-athlete relationship leads to improvements in the athletes' sport, athletes are most likely to experience positive reactions and reduce their concerns, since the strategies they are using are experienced as effective (Moen *et al.*, 2016). If it does not lead to improvements in athletes' sport, athletes are more likely to experience negative affect and increased concerns, since they are not able to use their strategies to cope with situational demands (Ursin and Eriksen, 2004). Thus, the coach has the responsibility to develop both physical, technical, mental, and social attributes of young elite athletes.

## Coaches' Challenges in the Junior to Senior Transition

Coaches of young elite athletes must deal with a range of dilemmas in their work to influence their athletes' personal and performance development. A well-known challenge in professional sport is however the fact that most environments for young elite athletes encourage and highlight a self-referential focus related to their sport-specific development, while results are more focused at the senior elite level (Till and Baker, 2020). Even though the optimal age of athletes varies across different sports (Allen and Hopkins, 2015), most coaches need to expose their young athletes to high training loads, critique, feedback, and high expectations. Since young athletes differ in personality, age of puberty and their developed levels of sport-specific skills and capacities, this balance is a challenge for coaches. While most training groups are characterised by high expectations of both performance level and motivation, there might still be large within group differences in skill and performance levels. A challenge for coaches in youth elite sport is therefore to remember that there will be natural differences in skills, capacities, and performance levels within the team environment, while some young elite athletes are closer to actually making the transition into elite sports and others are further behind because of differences in personality, age of puberty and their developed levels of sport-specific skills and capacities (Drew *et al.*, 2019).

Most coaching team and talent development environments for young elite athletes have their coaching and training philosophy that describes 'their way of doing things' in their environments. The philosophy defines what they believe in related to skills and capacity development, learning and development, attitudes and values, visions and goals, team building, and competition plans. A philosophy does not necessarily fit for all athletes in the environment. An overvalued belief in the philosophy can therefore be a barrier for young elite athletes if it doesn't work for exactly them. The coach's way of communicating, giving feedback, making team selections, and recruiting athletes implicitly send signals to the athletes about their position in the environment, and could also therefore be a barrier for young elite athletes' development.

Furthermore, since most junior elite athletes fail in becoming senior elite athletes, coaches of youth athletes have a responsibility of developing not only the athlete but also the person, in a safe, supportive and positive environment (Holt *et al.*, 2020). Many coaches still experience dilemmas because their main task is to contribute to the athlete's skill development. While on the one hand the road to an elite career could be described as hard, it is also arguably a privilege – both for the coaches and athletes given the opportunity to invest time and effort to test their limits on how much the athletes could develop and progress. Still, many young athletes are aware of their skills compared to their peer athletes and must find other or longer "roads" to a potential professional career. Many junior athletes (especially during the end of their time as a junior elite) experience the dilemma between keeping on trying to become an elite athlete or to stop their efforts and pursue other tasks such as studying, starting work or continuing their quest for success through a Dual Career (DC) (Stambulova *et al.*, 2015) system. Other athletes may, however, try other paths to senior elite sports, where some try their luck in other sports, which the literature has named as Talent Transfer (TT) (MacNamara *et al.*, 2010), which means a transfer to a new sport – which is often based on common features or demands between the two sports. Even though there are examples of successful talent transfer or a "talent recycling", the literature highlights that some sports are more suitable as donor sports such as gymnastics, swimming, and figure skating, while other sports, such as biathlon, rowing, canoeing, bobsleigh, and skeleton seem to tend more as recipient sports (Vaeyens *et al.*, 2009). A recent review paper on TT concluded that much remains unknown about TT, hence future research is needed to increase our understanding and its contribution as an extra pathway to the top (van Harten *et al.,* 2021).

## Summary, Future Directions, and Future Research

Coaches of young elite athletes in sport have an essential responsibility to help their athletes to develop sport-specific skills and capacities, and to gain needed levels of recovery. Also, their abilities to establish stimulating psychosocial environments are key to help the young person achieve optimal personal and sport-specific development. Talent development is also about developing resilient persons who believe in themselves on a personal level. The relationship between the coach and the athlete is key to achieving successful talent development, and through working alliances built on clear goals, strategies and emphatic bonds between their coaches and their athletes. Future directions in research should focus on building in-depth knowledge about how coaches influence talent development in the long run, and how the psychosocial environment influences talent development. Future research should also investigate optimal paths for boys and girls regarding talent development and how potential sex differences must be considered. Finally, since quality training is a key in talent development, the process of gaining optimal quality in training and needed recovery after training, should also be investigated in depth.

## References


Allen, S.V. and Hopkins, W.G., 2015. Age of peak competitive performance of elite athletes: A systematic review. *Sports Medicine*, 45, 1431–1441.

Bandura, A., 1997. *Self-efficacy: The exercise of control*. New York: Freeman.

Blom, L.C., Watson II, J.C., and Spadaro, N., 2010. The impact of a coaching intervention on the coach-athlete dyad and athlete sport experience. *Athletic Insight: The Online Journal of Sport Psychology*, 12 (3), 187–203.

Buzzetto-Hollywood, N. and Mitchell, B.C., 2019. Grit and persistence: Findings from a longitudinal study of student performance. *Issues in Informing Science and Information Technology*, 16, 377–391.

Compas, B.E., *et al.*, 2001. Coping with stress during childhood and adolescence: Problems, progress and potential in theory and research. *Psychological Bulletin*, 127, 87–127.

Deci, E.L. and Ryan, R.M., 2002. *Handbook of self-determination research*. Rochester, NY: University of Rochester Press.

Dohme, L.C., Lefebvre, J.S., and Bloom, G.A., 2020. Team building in youth sport. *In*: M.W. Bruner, M.A. Eys, and L.J. Martin, eds. *The power of groups in youth sport*. London: Academic Press, 165–182.

Drew, K., *et al.*, 2019. A meta-study of qualitative research on the junior-to-senior transition in sport. *Psychology of Sport and Exercise*, 45, 101556.

Duckworth, A.L. and Eskreis-Winkler, L., 2013. True grit. *The Observer*, 26(4), 1–3.

Duckworth, A.L., *et al.*, 2011. Deliberate practice spells success: Why grittier competitors triumph at the national spelling bee. *Social Psychological and Personality Science*, 2(2), 174–181.

Dunn, J.G.H. and Holt, N.L., 2004. A qualitative investigation of a personal-disclosure mutual-sharing team building activity. *The Sport Psychologist*, 18 (4), 363–380.

Ericsson, K.A. and Harwell, K.W., 2019. Deliberate practice and proposed limits on the effects of practice on the acquisition of expert performance: Why the original definition matters and recommendations for future research. *Frontiers in Psychology*, 10, 1–19.

Ericsson, K.A., Krampe, R.T., and Tesch-Römer, C., 1993. The role of deliberate practice in the acquisition of expert performance. *Psychological Review*, 100 (3), 363–406.

Feltz, D.L., Short, S.E., and Sullivan, P.J., 2008. *Self-efficacy in sport*. Champaign, IL: Human Kinetics.

Fletcher, D. and Sarkar, M.A., 2012. A grounded theory of psychological resilience in olympic champions. *Psychology of Sport and Exercise*, 13 (5), 669–678.

Gangsø, K., *et al.*, 2021. Talent development environments in football—comparing top-five and bottom-five ranked football academies in Norway. *International Journal of Environmental Research and Public Health*, 18 (3), 1–7.

Guay, F., Marsh, H.W., and Boivin, M., 2003. Academic self-concept and academic achievement: Developmental perspectives on their causal ordering. *Journal of Educational Psychology*, 95 (1), 124–136.

Gustafsson, H., Sagar, S.S., and Stenling, A., 2017. Fear of failure, psychological stress, and burnout among adolescent athletes competing in high level sport. *Scandinavian Journal of Medicine and Science in Sports*, 27, 2091–2102.

Hardy, L., *et al.*, 2017. Great British medalists: Psychosocial biographies of super-elite and elite athletes from Olympic sports. *In*: V. Walsh, M. Wilson and B. Parkin, eds. *Progress in brain research*. London: Elsevier, 1–119.

Henriksen, K., Stambulova, N., and Roessler, K.K., 2010. Holistic approach to athletic talent development environments: A successful sailing milieu. *Psychology of Sport and Exercise*, 11 (3), 212–222.

Holt, N.L., Deal, C.J., and Pankow, K., 2020. Positive youth development through sport. *In*: G. Tenenbaum and R.C. Eklund, eds. *Handbook of sport psychology*. Hoboken: John Wiley & Sons, 429–446.

Hrozanova, M., Moen, F., and Pallesen, S., 2019. Unique predictors of sleep quality in junior athletes: The protective function of mental resilience, and the detrimental impact of sex, worry and perceived stress, *Frontiers in Psychology*, 31 (10), 1256.

Jones, R.L., Armour, K.M., and Potrac, P., 2004. *Sports coaching cultures: From practice to theory*. London: Routledge.

Larkin, P., O'Connor, D., and Williams, A.M., 2015. Does grit influence sport-specific engagement and perceptual-cognitive expertise in elite youth soccer? *Journal Of Applied Sport Psychology*, 28 (2), 129–138.

Larsen, C.H., *et al.*, 2020. A world class academy in professional football: The case of Ajax Amsterdam. *Scandinavian Journal of Sport and Exercise Psychology*, 2, 33–43.

Lee, T.H. and Duckworth, A.L. 2018. Organisational grit. *Harvard Business Review*, 96 (5), 98–105.

Locke, E.A. and Latham, G.P., 1990. *A theory of goal setting and task performance*. Englewood Cliffs, NJ: Prentice Hall.

Locke, E.A. and Latham, G.P., 2002. Building a practical useful theory of goal setting and task motivation: A 35-year odyssey. *American Psychologist*, 57 (9), 705–717.

MacNamara, Á., Button, A., and Collins, D., 2010. The role of psychological characteristics in facilitating the pathway to elite performance part 2: Examining environmental and stage-related differences in skills and behaviors. *The Sport Psychologist*, 24 (1), 74–96.

Mah, C.D., *et al.*, 2011. The effects of sleep extension on the athletic performance of collegiate basketball players. *Sleep*, 34 (7), 943–950.

Martindale, R.J.J., Collins, D., and Daubney, J., 2005. Talent development: A guide for practice and research within sport. *Quest*, 57 (4), 353–375.

Martindale, R.J.J., *et al.*, 2010. Development of the talent development environment questionnaire for sport. *Journal of Sports Sciences*, 28 (11), 1209–1221.

Martindale, R.J.J., *et al.*, 2013. Examining the ecological validity of the talent development environment questionnaire. *Journal of Sports Sciences*, 31 (1), 41–47.

Moen, F. and Federici, R., 2017. Can athlete-centered coaching stimulate need satisfaction and prevent athlete burnout? *International Journal of Sport Management*, 18, 1–18.

Moen, F. and Firing, K., 2016. No pain no gain: Feelings and performance in sport. *Journal of Athletic Enhancement*, 5 (3), 1–7.

Moen, F., Hrozanova, M., and Stenseng, F., 2019a. Validating the working alliance inventory as a tool for measuring the effectiveness of coach-athlete relationships in sport, *Cogent Psychology*, 6 (1).

Moen, F., Hrozanova, M., and Stiles, T., 2018. The effects of perceptual-cognitive training on executive brain functions among elite athletes. *Cogent Psychology*, 5 (1).

Moen, F., Myhre, K., and Stiles, T.C., 2016. An exploration about how passion, perceived performance, stress and worries uniquely influence athlete burnout. *Journal of Physical Education and Sports Management*, 3 (1), 88–107.

Moen, F., Olsen, M., and Bjørkøy, J.A., 2021. Investigating possible effects from a one-year coach-education program. *Sports*, 9 (1), 3.

Moen, F., *et al.*, 2019b. Burnout and subjective perfomance among junior athletes- associations with affective and cognitive components. *Sports*, 7 (7), 1–11.

Olsen, M.G., *et al.*, 2020. Coping among elite level sports coaches: A systematic review. *International Sport Coaching Journal*, 8 (1), 34–47.

Olympiou, A., Jowett, S., and Duda, J.L., 2008. The psychological interface between the coach-created motivational climate and the coach-athlete relationship in team sports. *The Sport Psychologist*, 22 (4), 423- 438.

Pajares, F., and Schunk, D.H., 2001. Self-beliefs and school success: Self-efficacy, selfconcept, and school achievement. *In*: R. Riding and S. Rayner, eds. *Self-perception*. London: Ablex Publishing, 239–266.

Raanes, E.F.W., Hrozanova, M., and Moen, F., 2019. Identifying unique contributions of the coach-athlete working alliance, psychological resilience and perceived stress on athlete burnout among Norwegian junior athletes. *Sports*, 7 (9), 212.

Rees, T., *et al.*, 2016. The great British medalists project: A review of current knowledge on the development of the world's best sporting talent. *Sports Medicine*, 46 (8), 1041–1058.

Sarkar, M., Fletcher, D., and Brown, D.J. 2015. What doesn't kill me … : Adversity-related experiences are vital in the development of superior Olympic performance. *Scandinavian Journal of Medicine and Science in Sports*, 18 (4), 475–479.

Stambulova, N.B., *et al.*, 2015. Searching for an optimal balance: Dual career experiences of Swedish adolescent athletes. *Psychology of Sport and Exercise*, 21, 4–14.
Till, K. and Baker J., 2020. Challenges and [possible] solutions to optimising talent identification and development in sport. *Frontiers in Psychology*, 11, 1–14.
Ursin, H., and Eriksen, H.R., 2004. The cognitive activation theory of stress. *Psychoneuroendocrinology*, 29 (5), 567–592.
Vaeyens, R., *et al.*, 2009. Talent identification and promotion programmes of Olympic athletes. *Journal of Sports Sciences*, 27 (13), 1367–1380.
Van Cutsem, J., *et al.*, 2017. The effects of mental fatigue on physical performance: A systematic review. *Sports Medicine*, 47 (8), 1569–1588.
van Harten, K., *et al.*, 2021. Talent transfer: A systematic review. *Current Issues in Sport Science* (CISS), 6 (2021), 006.
Vitali, F., *et al.*, 2015. Motivational climate, resilience, and burnout in youth sport. *Sport Sciences for Health*, 11, 103–108.
Wurtele, S.K., 2011. Self-efficacy and athletic performance: A review. *Journal of Social and Clinical Psychology*, 4 (3), 290–301.
Zee, P.C., *et al.*, 2014. Strategic opportunities in sleep and circadian research: Report of the joint task force of the sleep research society and American academy of sleep medicine. *Sleep*, 37 (2), 219–227.

# 22

# WHAT MAKES CHAMPIONS? CHILDHOOD MULTI-SPORT PRACTICE FACILITATES LONG-TERM PERFORMANCE DEVELOPMENT

*Arne Güllich, Michael Barth, Brooke N. Macnamara, and David Z. Hambrick*

## Introduction

What is the optimal path for young people to achieve elite performance in sports – one that involves intensive specialised practice or one that includes diversified, multi-sport practice? This question is the subject of a longstanding controversy in sports science (Hill and Hansen, 1987; Côté *et al.*, 2007; DiSanti and Erickson, 2019; Kliethermes *et al.*, 2021). Although there is consensus that extensive practice in a sport, accumulated over multiple years, is required to develop exceptional performance in that sport, the question of how types and amounts of *childhood* sport activities relate to later performance is the subject of an ongoing debate. The patterns of *early specialisation* and *early diversification* are implied in the most popular (i.e. most-cited) frameworks of talent development in sports science literature: the *deliberate practice* view (Ericsson *et al.*, 1993; with special reference to sports, e.g. Ericsson, 2003) and the *Developmental Model of Sport Participation* (DMSP, Côté *et al.*, 2007).

In their classic article, Ericsson *et al.* (1993) suggested that individual differences in performance are monotonically related to individual differences in the amount of *deliberate practice* accumulated through one's career: task-specific practice under the instruction and monitoring of a coach that is undertaken to improve one's performance, involves frequent repetition of a task, is highly effortful, and is not inherently enjoyable. Ericsson *et al.* (1993) asserted that deliberate practice is the most effective type of activity to improve one's performance. Consequently, they advocated for a focus on and maximisation of deliberate practice with an early start: "[T]he higher the level of attained performance, the earlier the age of first exposure as well as the age of starting deliberate practice" (Ericsson *et al.*, 1993, p. 389). Relatedly, the authors highlighted the importance of early, rapid performance progress (for similar views from a giftedness perspective, see Heller *et al.*, 2005; Gagné, 2015).

In the *early diversification* path of their DMSP, Côté *et al.* (2007) countered that although deliberate practice is necessary to achieve elite performance, athletes should not specialise in a

DOI: 10.4324/9781003199359-26

single sport and should not emphasise deliberate practice until late adolescence. This relatively late specialisation should be preceded by extensive childhood/adolescent peer-led *deliberate play* in various sports: neighbourhood 'pick-up' games in informal settings that are regulated by the participants, not by a coach, and are undertaken for the inherent enjoyment of the game itself rather than to improve performance (e.g. pick-up soccer, basketball, table tennis, hockey in playgrounds, parks, and streets).

This chapter will review the available evidence concerning associations between participation patterns and subsequent performance. It focuses especially on the effects of different childhood/adolescent participation patterns and distinguishes the effects of these patterns on short-term performance at the junior level from their effects on long-term performance at the senior level.

## Review of Current Research

In the scientific literature, early specialisation and early diversification have typically been regarded as two contrasting, *dichotomous* participation patterns (e.g. Côté *et al.*, 2007; DiSanti and Erickson, 2019; Carder *et al.*, 2020; Giusti *et al.*, 2020; Mosher *et al.*, 2020; Kliethermes *et al.*, 2021). However, this is an imprecise characterisation of youth's participation patterns. An athlete's participation pattern is generally characterised by several continuous, metric-scaled variables including: starting age in one's main sport and amounts of coach-led practice and peer-led play in both one's main sport and other sports (Güllich *et al.*, 2021). These metric-scaled participation variables provide a more accurate and detailed description of athletes' participation patterns. At the same time, they enable us to determine in which aspects, and how closely, an athlete's participation pattern corresponds to facets of a specialisation/diversification construct.

A dichotomous 'specialisation vs. diversification' construct is thus neither necessary nor conducive to research. The research seeks to describe, explain, and predict relationships between participation variables and outcomes (here: performance): that is, the extent to which higher (lower) amounts of defined types of sport activity predict higher (lower) eventual performance. Both participation variables and performance can be quantified, whereas such research is not possible when comparing only two dichotomised participation constructs, 'specialisation vs. diversification.'

### *Systematic Literature Review*

In research on sports, the primary methods used to measure athletes' developmental 'milestones' and sport activities from childhood through adolescence and adulthood are retrospective sport-biographic interviews and questionnaires. The empirical evidence from studies using the participation variables discussed above is mixed (Macnamara *et al.*, 2016; Güllich *et al.*, 2020a, 2020b). Table 22.1 shows results from systematic reviews of studies comparing amounts of coach-led practice and peer-led play, both in athletes' respective main sport and in other sports, between higher and lower-performing samples. The table shows the results separately for comparisons between higher and lower-performing juniors, then higher and lower-performing seniors, and then between the highest performance levels, senior world-class and national-class athletes.

Results concerning relationships between participation variables and performance are inconsistent. Each of the participation variables was found to be positively correlated with performance in some studies, but was found to be uncorrelated or negatively correlated with

*Table 22.1* Systematic review of findings from studies that investigated associations of junior and senior performance with amounts of coach-led practice and peer-led play, both in one's main sport and in other sports. (Figures represent numbers of studies that revealed positive, no, or negative effects of each activity type on performance. Juniors: athletes competing in youth competitions; seniors: adult athletes competing in open-age competitions, typically in their 20s or 30s; overall: across all performance levels). Data adapted from the systematic reviews of Güllich *et al.* (2020a, 2020b)[a]

| | | | *Effect on performance* | | |
|---|---|---|---|---|---|
| | | | *Negative* | *None* | *Positive* |
| Juniors: Overall | | | | | |
| Amount of | Main-sport | Coach-led practice | 2 | 5 | 12 |
| | | Peer-led play | 0 | 4 | 3 |
| | Other-sports | Coach-led practice | 7 | 2 | 0 |
| | | Peer-led play | 5 | 3 | 0 |
| | | Practice/play[b] | 8 | 4 | 3 |
| Seniors: Overall | | | | | |
| Amount of | Main-sport | Coach-led practice | 15 | 8 | 22 |
| | | Peer-led play | 5 | 6 | 9 |
| | Other-sports | Coach-led practice | 0 | 1 | 21 |
| | | Peer-led play | 3 | 9 | 7 |
| | | Practice/play[b] | 0 | 10 | 26 |
| Seniors: World-class[c] vs. national-class athletes | | | | | |
| Amount of | Main-sport | Coach-led practice | 12 | 5 | 3 |
| | | Peer-led play | 1 | 4 | 1 |
| | Other-sports | Coach-led practice | 0 | 0 | 19 |
| | | Peer-led play | 3 | 8 | 5 |
| | | Practice/play[b] | 0 | 1 | 19 |

*Notes*

a Comparisons of extreme contrast performance groups were excluded (e.g. Olympic medallists vs. local-level competitors).

b Some studies did not distinguish coach-led practice and peer-led play in other sports, but pooled them.

c Top ten in the world.

performance in other studies. However, when studies are considered by athletes' age category (juniors, seniors) and performance levels compared (senior world class vs. national class), some consistency becomes apparent (Table 22.1). In numerous studies, higher early junior performance was associated with greater amounts of main-sport coach-led practice and less coach-led other-sports practice. By contrast, numerous studies comparing the highest adult performance levels, senior world class vs. national class, suggested that the achievement of world-class performance was associated with greater amounts of (earlier, childhood/adolescent) coach-led practice in sports other than one's main sport, but was uncorrelated or negatively correlated with one's amount of main-sport coach-led practice. Results regarding peer-led play, both in one's main sport and in other sports, were generally inconclusive.

An evaluation of the quality of the entire body of evidence using GRADE (Grading of Recommendation Assessment, Development, and Evaluation; Schünemann *et al.*, 2013) revealed moderate to high quality for all predictors except main-sport and other-sports peer-led play. Their quality of evidence was low due to negligibly small and inconsistent effects, yielding no dose-response relationship (Barth *et al.*, 2022).

## *Meta-Analysis*

The samples from previous studies were heterogeneous in terms of athletes' age category (juniors, seniors), types of sports, and performance levels compared. To establish more robust and generalizable findings, the available empirical evidence was synthesised in a *meta-analysis* (Barth *et al.*, 2022). Two sets of questions were investigated:

1 Did higher and lower-performing athletes differ in early performance progress, starting age, and amounts of coach-led practice or peer-led play, in either their respective main sport or in other sports? In particular, did they differ in *early* sport activities up to age 15 years?
2 Do effects of predictor variables differ across athletes' age category (junior vs. senior) or types of sports?

The literature search and selection procedure (through February 28, 2021) identified 71 relevant study reports presenting 131 studies, comprising 685 effect sizes from 9,241 athletes, 812 of whom achieved top-ten placings, 474 won medals, and 219 were gold medallists at Olympic Games, senior world and continental championships. Participants were from North America, Central/South America, Europe, Africa, Asia, and Oceania; 67% were male and 33% female. The athletes were from a wide range of sports: 24% from cgs sports (performance is measured in centimetres, grams, or seconds, e.g. athletics, swimming, weightlifting), 67% from game sports (e.g. basketball, soccer, tennis), 2% from combat sports (e.g. fencing, judo, wrestling), 6% from artistic-composition sports (e.g. artistic gymnastics, figure skating, platform diving), and 2% from other types of sports (meeting none or multiple criteria of the aforementioned sports types, e.g. modern pentathlon, mogul slope skiing, ski jumping).

Of the total sample, 1,003 competed at a world-class level (i.e. they achieved medals or top-ten placings at Olympic Games, senior or junior world or continental championships); 4,818 achieved a national competition level (top-ten placings at national championships and/or playing in the highest national league); 2,541 competed at a regional level (e.g. national second, third, etc. tier league, minor-league baseball, NCAA conferences, state- or provincial-level leagues or championships); and 879 competed at a local or up to county level. Across study reports, 48% to 100% of athletes participated in various sports in childhood and/or adolescence; of these athletes, 69% to 88% also *competed* in those sports.

Analyses were done separately for short-term junior (i.e. youth) performance and long-term senior performance (adults competing in the highest, open-age category, typically in their 20s or 30s). This distinction is important because evidence reveals there is relatively little overlap between the populations of successful junior athletes and of successful senior athletes: Most junior elites do not become senior elites, and most senior elites were not junior elites (Güllich and Cobley, 2017). The sample included 62% junior and 38% senior athletes.

Predictor effects are first reported across all performance levels, separately among juniors and among seniors. The question of whether participation variables – especially childhood/adolescent participation patterns – predict differences between the highest performance levels is critical from both a theoretical perspective and a practical perspective. We therefore then report comparisons between the most outstanding performers and those just below – senior world class vs. national class. In contrast, comparisons of athletes on the extreme ends of the performance distributions (e.g. Olympic medallists vs. local-level competitors) were excluded because they are less relevant both theoretically and practically.

The meta-analysis considered effects of six predictor variables on performance:

- The age at which athletes reached defined performance-related 'milestones' (*age to reach milestones*; first nomination for a selection team or squad, first participation in national championships and in international championships)
- The age at which athletes started playing their main sport (*starting age*; start of practice and/or competitions)
- Athletes' accumulated amount of coach-led practice in their respective main sport (*main-sport practice*)
- Athletes' accumulated amount of peer-led play in their respective main sport (*main-sport play*)
- Athletes' accumulated amount of coach-led practice in sports other than their respective main sport (*other-sports practice*)
- Athletes' accumulated amount of peer-led play in sports other than their respective main sport (*other-sports play*)

Amounts of the different sport activities included accumulated numbers of sessions, accumulated hours, years of engagement in an activity and, for other sports, the number of sports.

Figure 22.1 shows the central results, separately for junior athletes across all performance levels, senior athletes across all performance levels, and comparisons of senior world-class vs. national-class athletes. The figure displays the effects of age-related predictors (age to reach milestones, starting age; panel A, left), effects of amounts of the different sport activities accumulated through one's entire athletic career (panel B, centre), and effects of only *early* sport activities up to 15 years old (panel C, right).

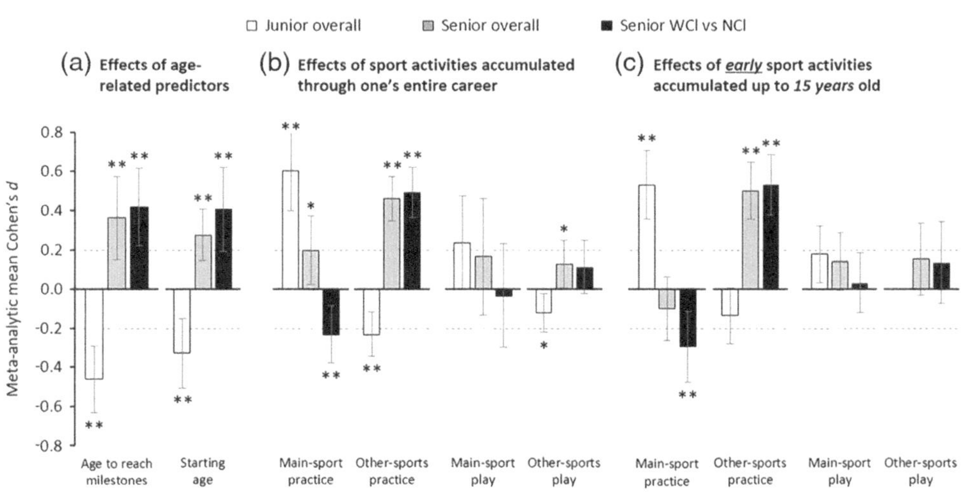


*Figure 22.1* Effects of participation variables on performance. White bars: effects on differences in junior performance overall, i.e. across all junior performance levels; grey bars: effects on differences in senior performance overall, i.e. across all senior performance levels; black bars: effects on differences between senior world-class versus national-class athletes (WCl vs NCl). (a) Effects of age-related predictors; (b) Effects of sport activities accumulated through one's entire career. (c) Effects of only *early* sport activities up to 15 years old. Juniors' early other-sports play: not enough effect sizes ($k < 5$). Error bars: 95% CI, * $p < .05$, ** $p < .01$. Original figure; results based on data from Barth *et al.* (2022)

Note the sign of effects for age-related and activity-related predictors: A *positive* effect indicates that higher performance was associated with *higher* (later) *ages* and with *greater activity amounts*.

Differences in participation patterns predicted differences in performance. Moreover, childhood/adolescent participation patterns predicted both junior and senior performance. Childhood/adolescent participation patterns even predicted the difference between senior world-class and national-class athletes. However, predictors of short-term junior performance and of long-term senior performance were opposite.

Overall, higher *junior* performance was associated with *earlier* milestone achievement, *earlier* starting age (Figure 22.1, panel A), *more* main-sport practice, and *less* other-sports practice (panel B). Higher junior performance was also associated with more *early* main-sport practice, but was unrelated to the amount of *early* other-sports practice (panel C). In contrast, higher *senior* performance was associated with *later* milestone achievement, *later* starting age (Figure 22.1, panel A), and *more* other-sports practice. Furthermore, amount of main-sport practice was less predictive of senior performance than it was of junior performance (panel B). Higher senior performance was *unrelated* to *early* main-sport practice, but was associated with more *early* other-sports practice (panel C).

Senior world-class athletes differed from their national-class counterparts in that they achieved performance-related milestones at a *later* age and started playing their main sport *later* (Figure 22.1, panel A); they also accumulated *less* main-sport practice, but *more* other-sports practice (panel B). Furthermore, world-class performance was associated with *less early* main-sport practice and *more early* other-sports practice (panel C).

Peer-led play, whether main-sport or other-sports and whether through one's entire career or only *early* peer-led play (Figure 22.1, panels B, C), generally had *negligible* effects on junior and senior performance overall as well as senior world-class vs. national-class performance (Cohen's $d < |0.20|$ and/or $p > .05$).

The major findings are consistent with recent studies that controlled for differences in the 'micro-structure' of athletes' main-sport practice (e.g. types of exercises and game formats, ways of executing them) and for potential confounds of athletes' age, sex, sport, discipline, and baseline performance through matched-pairs design, including multi-year quasi-experiments, and multivariate linear and non-linear analyses (Barth *et al.*, 2022).

Additional details concerning these findings have been revealed by four discoveries from several previous studies (Johnson *et al.*, 2006; Moesch *et al.*, 2011; Hardy *et al.*, 2013; Barth and Güllich, 2020; Barth *et al.*, 2022).

1 The performance development of senior world-class and national-class athletes was similar through their junior years, and only diverged in early adulthood. The world-class athletes achieved this greater performance improvement in adulthood with equivalent or less main-sport practice – i.e. they had greater main-sport *efficiency of practice* in adulthood: greater performance improvement per practice amount. That is, world-class athletes' childhood/adolescent multi-sport practice did not have a direct effect on main-sport performance, but a *delayed moderator effect* on their later main-sport *efficiency of practice*.
2 Associations were non-linear: The effect of childhood/adolescent other-sports practice on practice efficiency in adulthood displayed a *saturation pattern*. Furthermore, the relationship between childhood/adolescent main-sport practice and the efficiency of main-sport practice in adulthood was represented by an inversed-s-shaped, *sigmoid pattern*.

3 Childhood/adolescent multi-sport practice was associated with greater (later) improvement of sport-specific *perceptual-motor skills*, but not *physical* abilities such as power or endurance, over time. This finding suggests that childhood/adolescent multi-sport practice was associated with better subsequent skill learning, but not better physical development.
4 Associations between multi-sport practice and (later) sport-specific performance were not moderated by the relatedness of an athlete's main sport with the other sports they engaged in.

## Types of Sports

Different types of athletes' main sports were grouped based on the analytical categories of tasks in competition (Güllich and Emrich, 2014): cgs sports, game sports, combat sports, artistic compositions sports, and others. Predictor effects on performance were generally similar and did not significantly differ between types of sports. In particular, the opposite effects of participation variables on rapid junior performance and on long-term senior performance were robust across all types of sports.

## Theoretical Implication

The smaller amounts of main-sport practice and slower early progress of senior world-class compared to national-class athletes do not call into question the importance of multi-year main-sport coach-led practice and of juvenile performance progress. All the senior world-class and national-class athletes had accumulated substantial amounts of main-sport practice, and all had remarkable performance progression in their early years. However, the eventual national-class athletes had even more main-sport practice and even faster early progress. The data indicate that athletes who had a particularly accelerated development during their early years, mostly associated with reinforced specialised main-sport practice, were frequent among eventual senior national-class athletes (and also among the most successful junior athletes), but were infrequent among the eventual senior world-class performers.

How can the complex pattern of findings be explained? In particular: Why is senior world-class performance associated with less main-sport practice than national-class performance? Why do childhood/adolescent participation patterns have contrasting short- and long-term effects? And why does childhood/adolescent other-sports practice facilitate later main-sport performance?

The aforementioned concepts – deliberate practice, deliberate play, as well as giftedness (Ericsson *et al.*, 1993; Heller *et al.*, 2005; Côté *et al.*, 2007; Gagné, 2015) – are partly consistent with the predictors of early junior performance. However, they cannot provide adequate approaches to explain the highest adult performance levels, primarily because their central premises are at odds with the empirical evidence.

In their deliberate practice approach, Ericsson *et al.* (1993) only focused on task-specific practice and did not investigate the relevance of non-specific practice or play. They proposed a monotonic relationship of performance with amount of deliberate practice. However, the evidence indicates that performance differences between athletes were parabolically, not monotonically, related to main-sport practice amounts: Across athletes, increasing main-sport practice amount was associated with increasing performance from the local up to the national level, but beyond national class, *less* main-sport practice was associated with higher performance. Ericsson *et al.* also recommended an early start and subsequent maximisation of task-specific deliberate practice – a recommendation that is not only inconsistent with the empirical evidence, but contrary to it.

The proposal of extensive childhood/adolescent deliberate play in various sports (Côté *et al.*, 2007) is at odds with the evidence that childhood/adolescent peer-led play, main-sport or other-sports, generally had negligible effects both on junior and senior performance. These authors suggested that extensive childhood/adolescent participation in deliberate play promotes long-term intrinsic motivation and prolonged engagement. However, to date, empirical evidence to support this notion is lacking, and the results of several studies run counter to the hypothesis (Hendry *et al.*, 2014; Hendry and Hodges, 2019; Thomas and Güllich, 2019). Côté *et al.*'s (2007) second argument was that perceptual-motor skills and physical conditioning can be directly transferred across related sports (sports that share common movement, perceptual, conceptual, or physical conditioning elements). Indeed, such transfer exists (Schmidt and Wrisberg, 2000; Abernethy *et al.*, 2005; Causer and Ford, 2014). However, this direct transfer cannot explain why practice in other sports is more beneficial than using the time for extended main-sport practice, why other-sports coach-led practice, but not peer-led play, correlated with later main-sport performance, or why this benefit is independent of the relatedness of the sports an athlete has engaged in.

Finally, traditional views of giftedness, or what is commonly referred to as 'innate talent,' have conceptualised a fast rate of initial performance progress as an indicator of giftedness, and thus a predictor of eventual performance (e.g. Heller *et al.*, 2005; Gagné, 2015). The notion is inconsistent with the evidence that the world's best athletes initially progressed more slowly than did less accomplished senior performers.

In sum, these established theoretical views fail to explain the full pattern of evidence, most notably, the development of the highest performance level. One of the reasons for some of the misdirection in existing theoretical concepts of talent development is presumably that former theorists commonly based their hypotheses on observations of very young athletes and/or extreme group comparisons (e.g. Ericsson *et al.*, 1993; Baker *et al.*, 2003; Duffy *et al.*, 2004; Côté *et al.*, 2007; Ward *et al.*, 2007; Elferink-Gemser *et al.*, 2011; Hutchinson *et al.*, 2013; Ford *et al.*, 2016). The present evidence implies that predictors of the highest senior performance level cannot be concluded by extrapolating findings from junior athletes, moderate performance levels, or extreme contrast comparisons. In fairness, many studies comparing senior world-class and national-class athletes have only recently become available. Theorists may thus have been incapable of understanding predictors among the highest performance levels.

Alternatively, approaches from neoclassical economics provide a fruitful heuristic, especially the concepts of *efficiency* and *sustainability*. The approach rests on three premises:

1. The goal of athletes, coaches, and stakeholders is international senior success, which has greater value than only junior success (prestige, financial income). However, international senior success is an extremely scarce good, which many compete for but only a few achieve; an athlete's career is thus characterised by great *uncertainty* of success.
2. Resources for practice are restricted (available time, the length of one's athletic career, the athlete's body, load tolerance, health, coaching and facilities).
3. Sport activities yield short and long-term positive and negative outcomes, i.e. benefits and costs.

Figure 22.2 shows a simplified, schematic illustration. Expanding a child's specialised practice – e.g. from two to four weekly sessions – may boost current perceptual-motor skill learning, physiological adaptations, short-term performance, and expand one's enjoyable time in sports (*benefits*). But it reduces the child's scope for future long-term perceptual-motor learning and physiological adaptations and increases their opportunity costs (i.e. the lost benefit of foregone

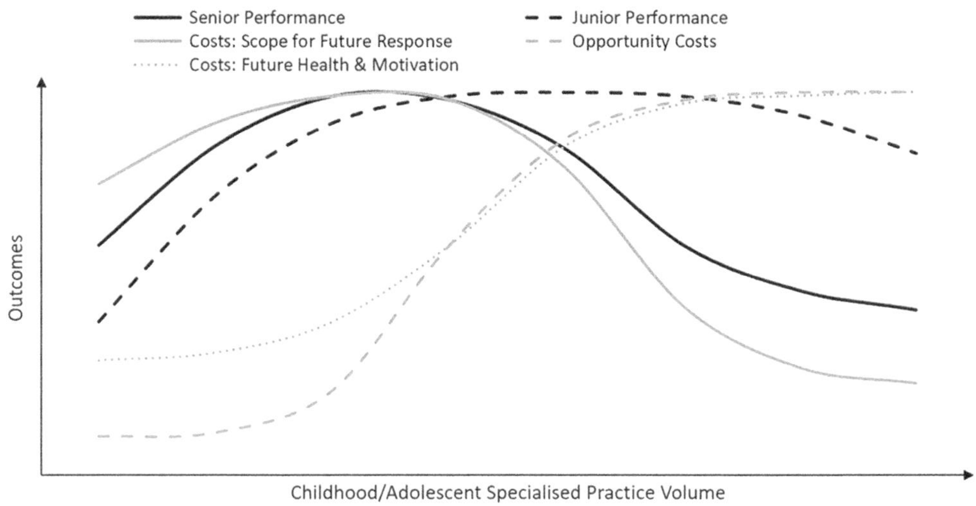


*Figure 22.2* Schematic illustration of hypothesised relationships between childhood/adolescent amount of specialised practice and senior performance, junior performance, scope for future response to practice, opportunity costs, and future risks of overuse injuries and motivational decline

other activities). Furthermore, expanded main-sport practice may increase risks of future motivational decline, burnout, and dropout (Giusti *et al.*, 2020; Waldron *et al.*, 2020), may shift one's load-recovery balance towards the 'load' pole, and may increase one's risks of later overuse injuries (Bell *et al.*, 2018; Carder *et al.*, 2020) (*costs*).

Benefits and costs can be estimated as value × probability of occurrence. The relationships between the amount of childhood main-sport practice and the different outcomes are presumably nonlinear. Yet, at some point, the ratio of benefits and costs turns negative (Figure 22.2).

The economic interpretation is further underpinned by two inter-related hypotheses discussed in the literature (Güllich, 2017; Barth *et al.*, 2022):

1 Practice and competition experiences in various sports increase the likelihood that an athlete finds the sport that best matches their talent and preferences (economic 'search and match theory,' McCall, 1970; Neal, 1999). Individual preferences may include one's rate of skill learning and performance progression, enjoyment, coach-athlete relationship, and peer interaction in a sport. Athletes' choice of a focus sport emerges from their experiences in different sports – i.e. 'talent identification' for a sport occurs *a posteriori*, not a priori (cf. Pion, 2015; Hohmann *et al.*, 2018). According to this hypothesis, the (few) senior world-class athletes who specialised early in a single sport either fell into a suitable sports match largely by luck or were talented in multiple sports, one of which was their specialisation sport.
2 Varied learning experiences (tasks, situations, methodologies) facilitate the athlete's ability to adapt to different learning tasks, situations, methodologies, and available information for learning (Bransford and Schwartz, 1999; Araújo *et al.*, 2010; Güllich, 2017). The athlete becomes a more adaptive learner and can better exploit learning opportunities. In addition, these experiences help the athlete understand which learning methodologies are individually more or less athlete-functional learning solutions. This may also facilitate their competencies for self-regulation in learning (see Jordet, 2015 for a review). At the same time, experience of varied learning methodologies increases the odds of *encountering*

particularly athlete-functional learning solutions (i.e. an intra-individual selection effect). In this way, young athletes may expand their *learning capital* for future sport-specific perceptual-motor learning.

Because resources are limited and one endeavours to increase benefits while limiting costs, *efficiency of practice* is paramount – i.e. the benefits per practice amount. At the same time, short and long-term outcomes differ – i.e. a classical problem of *sustainability*. According to this economic perspective, senior world-class athletes' childhood/adolescent investment pattern was relatively resource-preserving (time, the athlete's body, load-recovery balance, health), cost-reducing (opportunity costs, one's future potential), and risk-buffering (motivation, burnout, health, while distributing one's 'risk capital' to various sports), which led to gradual initial progress, but *sustainable* long-term *efficiency* of practice and performance development. Conversely, the best juniors engaged in intensive childhood/adolescent specialised main-sport practice and had an accelerated short-term performance development, but they likely reduced their scope for subsequent response to long-term future training (learning, adaptations) and had expanded opportunity costs, increased risks of (later) motivational decline, burnout, and overuse injuries, and, when focusing on only a single sport, a greater risk that this sport may not be their optimal sports match. This background helps explain why the populations of successful juniors and of successful seniors are not identical, but are widely distinct populations – i.e. why most junior elites do not become senior elites and why most successful seniors did not achieve an equivalent competition level in former junior years.

## Implications for Children's Sport Coaching

Managers of youth sport programmes make a choice, which may be more or less intentional and well-informed: To reinforce rapid junior success at the expense of long-term senior success or to facilitate long-term development of senior performance at the expense of early junior performance. To facilitate long-term senior performance (and also youth athletes' physical and psychological wellbeing), practitioners should avoid excess specialised single-sport practice during childhood and adolescence and encourage youths to participate in practice and competitions in various sports. Furthermore, coaches in a given sport may proactively search for promising athletes from other sports (cf. 'talent transfer,' Vaeyens *et al.*, 2009).

Talent promotion programmes (TPPs) such as youth sport academies, selection teams, and federations' youth squads often start to select young athletes around pubertal age ranges. They typically select those young athletes who show the most advanced performance at this age – mostly athletes who have already done great amounts of sport-specific training but little or no other-sports practice before the age of selection. Once selected, the TPPs aim to further expand the young athletes' sport-specific practice (Güllich and Cobley, 2017). The strategy will likely increase the probability of the early selected athletes to achieve success at junior championships but compromises long-term perspectives for senior success. In addition, the selection strategy may encourage all young athletes (together with their parents and coaches) who seek to be selected for youth sport academies, selection teams, squads, and sport scholarships to focus on intensified single-sport training. Senior world-class performers who were involved in TPPs were selected at a later age than national-class athletes (and also than successful juniors; Güllich *et al.*, 2022). That is, early selection for TPPs correlated negatively with senior world-class performance.

Detrimental effects of early TPPs may be mitigated by postponing selection to later age ranges. Furthermore, the sport biography of the young athletes at the time of selection should be considered – a multi-sport background with moderate main-sport practice is a predictor of long-term future potential. In addition, youth coaches should not be evaluated by their athletes' current performance, but by fulfilment of their actual *task* as a youth coach: Inspiring great numbers of youth athletes to engage in competitive sports and expanding their *potential* for *sustainable* long-term development.

## Summary, Future Directions and Future Research

Current theoretical views of talent development cannot adequately explain the full range of empirical evidence concerning performance development in sports, most notably, the acquisition of the highest performance level. Individual differences in childhood/adolescent participation patterns predict individual differences in later junior and senior performance. However, predictors of short-term junior performance and of long-term senior world-class performance are opposite. Compared to national-class counterparts, *senior* world-class athletes engaged in greater amounts of childhood/adolescent multi-sport coach-led practice and, relatedly, started playing their main sport later, accumulated less main-sport practice, and initially progressed more slowly. Conversely, compared to lower-performing counterparts, higher-performing *juniors* started playing their main sport at a younger age, accumulated greater amounts of main-sport practice, but less other-sports practice, and had faster initial performance progress. Childhood/adolescent peer-led play, main-sport or other-sports, had negligible effects on both junior and senior performance.

Predictors of the highest senior performance level cannot be extrapolated from findings concerning lower performance levels or junior samples. The goal for future research is to further investigate the best senior performers' earlier childhood/adolescent participation patterns. In particular, researchers should seek to understand the causal processes that underpin the contrasting short-term and long-term effects of early participation patterns and to explain how early other-sports practice benefits later efficiency of main-sport practice. The economic concepts of *efficiency* and *sustainability* provide a fruitful heuristic, and lead to three questions:

1 Which short-term and long-term benefits and costs do different childhood/adolescent participation patterns yield, to what magnitude, and at what probability?
2 What (material and immaterial) value does each of these benefits and costs have?
3 What is the eventual ratio of the summed value of all benefits relative to the summed value of all costs emerging through adolescence and adulthood?

Investigating these questions will advance a theory of the development of athletic excellence that considers the concepts of *efficiency* and *sustainability*, explains why effects of childhood participation patterns differ at short versus long terms, and how childhood non-specific practice facilitates later specific performance. This research will shed new light on our initial question: What makes champions?

## References

Abernethy, B., Baker, J., and Côté, J., 2005. Transfer of pattern recall skills may contribute to the development of sport expertise. *Applied Cognitive Psychology*, 19(6), 705–718.

Araújo, D., *et al.*, 2010. The role of ecological constraints on expertise development. *Talent Development and Excellence*, 2(2), 165–179.

Baker, J., Côté, J., and Abernethy, B., 2003. Sport-specific practice and the development of expert decision-making in team ball sports. *Journal of Applied Sport Psychology*, 15(1), 12–25.

Barth, M. and Güllich, A., 2020. Non-linear association of efficiency of practice of adult elite athletes with their youth multi-sport practice. *Journal of Sports Sciences*, 39(8), 915–925.

Barth, M., *et al.*, 2022. Predictors of junior versus senior elite performance are opposite: A systematic review and meta-analysis of participation patterns. *Sports Medicine*, 51, advance online publication, doi: 10.1007/s40279-021-01625-4

Bell, D.R., *et al.*, 2018. Sport specialization and risk of overuse injuries: A systematic review with meta-analysis. *Pediatrics*, 142(3), *September 2018*: e20180657.

Bransford, J.D. and Schwartz, D.L., 1999. Rethinking transfer: A simple proposal with multiple implications. *Review of Research in Education*, 24(1), 64–100.

Carder, S.L., *et al.*, 2020. The concept of sport sampling versus sport specialization: Preventing youth athlete injury: A systematic review and meta-analysis. *American Journal of Sports Medicine*, 48(11), 2850–2857.

Causer, J. and Ford, P.R., 2014. "Decisions, decisions, decisions": Transfer and specificity of decision-making between sports. *Cognitive Processing*, 15, 385–389.

Côté, J., Baker, J., and Abernethy, B., 2007. Practice and play in the development of sport expertise. In R. Eklund and G. Tenenbaum, eds. *Handbook of sport psychology*. Hoboken, NJ: Wiley, 184–202.

DiSanti, J.S. and Erickson, K., 2019. Youth sport specialization: A multidisciplinary scoping systematic review. *Journal of Sports Sciences*, 37(18), 2094–2105.

Duffy, L.J., Baluch, B., and Ericsson, K.A., 2004. Dart performance as a function of facets of practice amongst professional and amateur men and women players. *International Journal of Sport Psychology*, 35, 232–245.

Elferink-Gemser, M.T., *et al.*, 2011. What discriminates elite and sub-elite youth field hockey players. *Annals of Research in Sport and Physical Activity*, 1, 50–68.

Ericsson, K.A., 2003. Development of elite performance and deliberate practice: An update from the perspective of the expert performance approach. In J.L. Starkes, ed. *Expert performance in sports: Advances in research on sport expertise*. Champaign: Human Kinetics, 49–83.

Ericsson, K.A., Krampe, R.T., and Tesch-Römer, C., 1993. The role of deliberate practice in the acquisition of expert performance. *Psychological Review*, 100(3), 363–406.

Ford, P.R., *et al.*, 2016. Deliberate practice in sport. In J. Baker and D. Farrow, eds. *Routledge handbook of sport expertise*. New York: Routledge, 347–362.

Gagné, F., 2015. From genes to talent: The DMGT/CMTD perspective. *Revista de Educación*, 368(April-June), 12–37.

Giusti, N.E., *et al.*, 2020. Comparing burnout in sport-specializing versus sport-sampling adolescent athletes: A systematic review and meta-analysis. *Orthopaedic Journal of Sports Medicine*, 8(3), 2325967120907579.

Güllich, A., 2017. International medallists' and non-medallists' developmental sport activities—A matched-pairs analysis. *Journal of Sports Sciences*, 35(23), 2281–2288.

Güllich, A., and Cobley, S., 2017. On the efficacy of talent identification and talent development programmes. In J. Baker *et al.*, eds. *The routledge handbook of talent identification and development in sport*. New York: Routledge, 80–98.

Güllich, A. and Emrich, E., 2014. Considering long-term sustainability in the development of world class success. *European Journal of Sport Science*, 14(sup1), S383–S397.

Güllich, A., Macnamara, B.N., and Hambrick, D.Z., 2022. What makes a champion? Early multidisciplinary practice, not early specialization, predicts world-class performance. *Perspectives on Psychological Science*, 17(1), 6–29.

Güllich, A., *et al.*, 2020a. On the empirical substantiation of the definition of "deliberate practice" (Ericsson et al., 1993) and "deliberate play (Côté et al., 2007) in youth athletes. *Journal of Expertise*, 3(1), 1–19. Online publication at: www.journalofexpertise.org/articles/volume3_issue1/JoE_3_1_Gullich.pdf

Güllich, A., *et al.*, 2020b. Coach-assessed skill learning progress of youth soccer players correlates with earlier childhood practice in other sports. *International Journal of Sports Science & Coaching*, 15(3), 285–296.

Güllich, A., *et al.*, 2021. Further muddying the water? A comment on Bell et al.'s 2021 definition of "youth sport specialization". *Journal of Athletic Training*, 56(11), 1252–1254.

Hardy, L., *et al.*, 2013. *A comparison of the biographies of GB serial medal and non-medalling Olympic athletes*. London: UK Sport.

Heller, K.A., Perleth, C., and Lim, T.K., 2005. The Munich model of giftedness designed to identify and promote gifted students. In R.J. Sternberg and J.E. Davidson, eds. *Conceptions of giftedness, 2nd ed.* Cambridge: Cambridge University Press, 147–170.

Hendry, D.T., Crocker, P.R.E., and Hodges, N.J., 2014. Practice and play as determinants of self-determined motivation in youth soccer players. *Journal of Sports Sciences*, 32(11), 1091–1099.

Hendry, D.T., and Hodges, N.J., 2019. Pathways to expert performance in soccer. *Journal of Expertise*, 2(1), 1–13.

Hill, G.M., and Hansen, G.F., 1987. Sport specialization in high school: A complex issue. *The Physical Educator*, 44(4), 422–426.

Hohmann, A., Siener, M., and He, R., 2018. Prognostic validity of talent orientation in soccer. *German Journal of Exercise and Sport Research*, 48, 478–488.

Hutchinson, C.U., Sachs-Ericsson, N.J., and Ericsson, K.A., 2013. Generalizable aspects of the development of expertise in ballet across countries and cultures: A perspective from the expert-performance approach. *High Ability Studies*, 24(1), 21–47.

Johnson, M.B., Tenenbaum, G., and Edmonds, W.A., 2006. Adaptations to physically and emotionally demanding conditions: The role of deliberate practice. *High Ability Studies*, 17(1), 117–136.

Jordet, G., 2015. Psychological characteristics of expert performers. In J. Baker and D. Farrow, eds. *Routledge handbook of sport expertise*. New York: Routledge, 106–120.

Kliethermes, S.A., *et al.*, 2021. Defining a research agenda for youth sport specialisation in the USA: The AMSSM Youth Early Sport Specialization Summit. *British Journal of Sports Medicine*, 55(3), 135–143.

Macnamara, B.N., Moreau, D., and Hambrick, D.Z., 2016. The relationship between deliberate practice and performance in sports: A meta-analysis. *Perspectives on Psychological Science*, 11(3), 333–350.

McCall, J.J., 1970. Economics of information and job search. *The Quarterly Journal of Economics*, 84(1), 113–126.

Moesch, K., *et al.*, 2011. Late specialization: The key to success in centimeters, grams, or seconds (cgs) sports. *Scandinavian Journal of Medicine & Science in Sports*, 21(6), e282–e290.

Mosher, A., Fraser-Thomas, J., and Baker, J., 2020. What defines early specialization: A systematic review of literature. *Frontiers in Sports and Active Living*, 2, 596229.

Neal, D., 1999. The complexity of job mobility among young men. *Journal of Labor Economics*, 17(2), 237–261.

Pion, J., 2015. The Flemish Sports Compass: From sports orientation to elite performance prediction. Thesis (PhD). University of Gent.

Schmidt, R.A. and Wrisberg, C.A., 2000. *Motor learning and performance: A problem-based learning approach*. Champaign, Il: Human Kinetics.

Schünemann, H., Brozek, J., Guyatt, G., and Oxman, A., 2013. *GRADE Handbook*. https://gdt.gradepro.org/app/handbook/handbook.html. Accessed 2 April 2021.

Thomas, A. and Güllich, A., 2019. Childhood practice and play as determinants of adolescent intrinsic and extrinsic motivation among elite youth athletes. *European Journal of Sport Science*, 19(8), 1120–1129.

Vaeyens, R., *et al.*, 2009. Talent identification and promotion programmes of Olympic athletes. *Journal of Sports Sciences*, 27(13), 1367–1380.

Waldron, S., *et al.*, 2020. Exploring early sport specialization: Associations with psychosocial outcomes. *Journal of Clinical Sport Psychology*, 14(2), 182–202.

Ward, P., *et al.*, 2007. The road to excellence: Deliberate practice and the development of expertise. *High Ability Studies*, 18(2), 119–153.

# 23

# THE IMPACT OF GROWTH AND MATURATION UPON CHILDREN'S PARTICIPATION IN SPORT AND PHYSICAL ACTIVITY

*Sean Cumming*

## Introduction

Physical activity contributes positively towards the physical and psychosocial development of children and adolescents. Benefits of activity in youth include stronger bones, improved metabolic health, healthy body composition, physical fitness, and enhanced cognitive and emotional health (Sherar and Cumming, 2022). Those interested in the study and promotion of physical activity in youth should adopt a bio-cultural perspective recognising the combined effects of biological, psychosocial, cultural, and environmental factors (Malina *et al.*, 2016). Physical activity is, at its most basic level, a biological process that occurs within a biological organism, yet it is also a behaviour that exists within a sociocultural context in which various meanings and values are ascribed to it. Two biological processes fundamental to understanding children and adolescents' participation in sport and physical activity are growth and maturation.

## Review of Current Research

Growth refers to changes in body size, physique, and composition and can be considered in terms of the whole body or specific parts (Malina *et al.*, 2016). Growth results from a combination of processes, including increases in cell size (hyperplasia) and number (hypertrophy), and increases in intra-cellular substances (accretion) (Malina *et al.*, 2004). With age, children become taller and heavier, reflecting increases in skeletal length, mass, lean and fat mass, and the size of various connective tissues and organs. Growth occurs on a distal-to-proximal gradient (extremities then torso) with different body parts growing at separate times and at different rates.

Growth in childhood is modest and linear (steady) making it an ideal stage to develop and teach fundamental and more complex motor skills. There is also limited variation in growth between boys and girls during childhood (Malina *et al.*, 2004). In children, growth in height occurs predominantly in the extremities (i.e. legs and arms) approximating a rate of 5 to 6 cm per year, with a slight deceleration from early-to-late childhood (Baxter-Jones, 2019). Some children may experience a mid-childhood growth spurt between 6 and 8 years; however, such increases are small in magnitude and difficult to detect. Growth in mass during childhood is also


DOI: 10.4324/9781003199359-27

linear, with boys and girls gaining approximately 2-to-3 kg per year, with a slight acceleration in growth rate from early-to-late childhood.

Childhood gains in physical fitness (i.e. speed, strength, power, and aerobic capacity) are also relatively linear during childhood with limited variance between the sexes. Gains in fitness result from improvements in motor and neural coordination/capacity and increases body size and lean-mass (Lloyd and Oliver, 2012). Boys possess a slight athletic advantage over girls in most tests of physical fitness (i.e. speed, strength, power, aerobic capacity) from early-to-late childhood (Malina, 2007; Golle *et al.*, 2015; Latorre Román *et al.*, 2017); although girls tend to perform marginally better on tests of mobility and agility. Sex-associated differences in fitness and motor skills in childhood may, to some degree, reflect differences in activity/sport choice between boys and girls. Sex differences in physical fitness are, however. marginal during childhood and there are no substantive reasons to separate boys and girls in physical education or sporting activities during this stage of development.

It is with the onset of puberty that we first observe sex-associated differences in size, physique, appearance, and fitness (Malina *et al.*, 2004). The age at which children enter puberty is, however, highly variable with some individuals experiencing the event well in advance or delay of their same-age peers (Baxter-Jones *et al.*, 2005). Puberty generally occurs one year earlier in girls than boys. The first signs of puberty include the development of breasts in girls and pubic hair for both boys and girls. These changes are quickly followed by the adolescent growth spurt, which occurs first in height and then, 3 to 6 months later, in mass.

The pubertal growth spurt in height is one of the most salient features of adolescence and occurs about one-to-two years earlier in girls than boys. As girls tend to experience the growth spurt earlier than boys, there is a period around 11 to 12 years when many girls are significantly taller than their same-age male peers. Pubertal gains in height occur predominantly in the torso, reaching peak rates of approximately 9 to 11 cms. per year. The point of most rapid growth in adolescence is referred to as Peak Height Velocity (PHV). The mean age of PHV in girls and boys is 12.1 and 13.8 years, respectively. Boys and girls who experience PHV one year earlier than the mean (i.e. <11.1 or <12.8 years) are considered early maturing; whereas those that achieve PHV more than one year following the mean values (>13.1 or >14.8) are considered late maturing (Baxter-Jones *et al.*,2005). After PHV, growth decelerates steadily, terminating in adulthood (i.e. the mature state). Sex differences in the growth of body proportions can also be observed during adolescence, contributing towards sexual dimorphism. Boys experience greater proportional growth in shoulder width than girls, resulting in a higher shoulder-to-hip ratio. Girls, in comparison, experience a widening in the lower half of the pelvis, creating a birth canal and greater Q-angle (i.e. angle between the quadricep muscles and patellar tendon (Fieseler, 1996). These patterns of growth are generally observed across children from different races and cultures but can be influenced by behaviours and/or environmental factors.

Pubertal gains in mass occur about 3-to-6 months after PHV, with peak weight velocity (PWV) approximating 8 to 10 kg. per annum in boys and girls. Whereas pubertal gains in girls are largely due to increases in fat-mass, the equivalent gains in boys occur largely because of increases in lean-mass (Malina *et al.*, 2004). From the point of PWV, gains in mass decelerate before stabilising in early adulthood. Weight can, however, continue to fluctuate in adulthood due to a range of behavioural factors (i.e. diet, exercise). Greater pubertal gains in lean mass provide adolescent boys with a distinct advantage in test of strength, speed, and power. This advantage emerges with puberty and increases with age. Although girls also experience pubertal gains in strength, speed, and power, these improvements are more modest and linear in nature (Handelsman *et al.*, 2019). It is at this stage of development that the majority of sports organisations encourage boys and girls to compete separately, for the purpose of competitive equity, opportunity, and safety.

## Maturation

Maturation is the process of progression towards the adult (i.e. mature) state (Malina *et al.*, 2015). Maturation occurs and can be assessed in multiple biological systems (skeletal, hormonal, sexual, dental, and somatic), and can be described in terms of status, tempo and/or timing (Malina *et al.*, 2004). Status refers to the stage of maturity attained at a specific time point (e.g. pre-pubertal, pubertal, post-pubertal); whereas tempo describes the rate at which maturation progresses. Timing describes the age at which specific maturity milestones (PHV, menarche) occur and varies considerably among children of the same age. Variation in the timing of maturity results from genotypic and environmental factors and has been shown to impact physical, athletic, and psychosocial development in youth (Malina *et al.*, 2015).

## Maturation and Physical Activity

The age-related decline in children's physical activity is one of the most well-documented phenomena in paediatric exercise science (Rowland, 1998; Eisenmann and Wickel, 2009). It is observed in boys and girls and across cultures and nationalities, suggesting a biological and/or developmental basis to physical activity (Eisenmann and Wickel, 2009).

Active play is arguably the most common and salient form of physical activity from early-to-mid childhood (Byers, 1998). As a behaviour, active play has been described as biologically driven, time-sensitive, and purposeful, and as playing an important role in physical, psychological, and social development (Byers and Walker, 1995; Byers, 1998). Left to their own devices, young children naturally create and/or gravitate towards movement and/or play-related activities involving running, chasing, jumping, throwing, or catching (Eisenmann and Wickel, 2009). As children enter puberty they do, however, engage less in active play; favouring activities that are more socially oriented and sedentary in nature (Blakemore *et al.*, 2010). A study of physical activity behaviours in British youth revealed that even those children who maintain the recommended levels of physical activity demonstrated a reduction in active play as they enter adolescence (Payne *et al.*, 2013). What differentiates these individuals from their less-active peers, however, is that they substitute play for socially constructed forms of activity, such as sport and exercise.

The concept of active play as a biological determined and time-limited behaviour has implications for those involved in the promotion of the physical activity. Firstly, interventions designed to promote activity in children should be judged successful if they are able to maintain activity levels in youth, let alone increase them. Encouraging children to engage in more socially constructed forms of physical activity, such as sport and exercise, may help offset reductions in activty resulting from the natural decline in active play. Secondly, early years education programmes should be structured and designed to take optimal advantage of the time-sensitive and purposeful nature of active play, delaying entry into formal education and prioritising learning through creative and active play in natural environments (e.g. forests, coastlines). The benefits of such approaches can be seen in many Scandinavian countries where late entry into primary education is common and there is a greater emphasis on learning through active play, often in natural surroundings. In such systems, children are encouraged to engage in active play at an age when it is developmentally most appropriate for them and of optimal value for learning. Not surprisingly, children from Scandinavian countries generally perform generally rank the highest on indices of physical and psychological health and well-being, and educational attainment (UNICEF, 2020).

## Maturity Timing and Physical Activity

Puberty is considered an inflection point for health-related behaviours and adverse outcomes in youth (i.e. smoking, drug use, alcohol use, delinquency, depression, anxiety) (Cumming *et al.*, 2012). Youth who experience earlier onset of puberty are at particular risk for such outcomes, including reductions in physical activity and increases in sedentary behaviour. The adverse effect of early puberty upon physical activity is, however, largely limited to girls (Sherar *et al.*, 2010; Moore *et al.*, 2020), reflecting sex-related differences in how puberty is perceived, and socio-cultural expectations and values related to both maturation, gender roles, and physical activity.

As noted, girls who enter puberty early experience greater gains in height, and absolute lean- and fat-mass (Malina *et al.*, 2004). Whereas greater gains in size and lean-mass may afford an athletic advantage in activities requiring size or strength; greater gains in absolute and relative fat mass are considered less conducive to successful engagement in activities that involve endurance, movement of the body through space, and/or aesthetic qualities (Baxter-Jones *et al.*, 2002). Consequently, early maturing girls are more likely to withdraw from sports participation at this stage of their development (Malina *et al.*, 2015). Perceptions of pubertal change and the evaluations and reactions of others (i.e. peers, teachers, coaches) may, however, be as, if not more, important than the change itself. Girls who mature early tend to perceive themselves as less athletic, less attractive, and possess lower physical self-worth which, in turn, predicts lower levels of physical activity (Cumming *et al.*, 2011, 2020; Smart *et al.*, 2012). Early maturing girls who hold positive perceptions of the self and perceived higher levels of peer support are, however, as active as their late maturing peers (Pindus *et al.*, 2014); suggesting that such risks may be mitigated if girls are encouraged to perceive puberty as a natural and attractive consequence of becoming an adult, not as a barrier to physical activity and better supported by peers and significant others (i.e. parents, coaches, teachers). Early maturing North American and European males appear to be no more or less active than their late maturing peers (Sherar *et al.*, 2010; Moore *et al.*, 2020). They do, however, hold more positive perceptions of physical self-concept and are more likely to be represented in most sports (Baxter-Jones, 2019). It is possible that late maturing boys, though underrepresented in sport, remain equally active through engagement in less formal and/or more recreational activities such as active play, skateboarding and/or cycling.

## Growth and Maturation and Sport

Outside of physical education, sport is the most common and visible form of structured physical activity in childhood and adolescence. In many countries, organised competitive sport is available to children from as early as 5 years of age. The primary purpose of most youth sports programmes is fun, participation, and the development of physical, psychological, and social competence. The professionalisation of youth sports has, however, resulted in an increased number of more formal and structured youth sports programmes/academies where the primary objective is of athletic excellence. Talented children are being scouted and recruited to these programmes from as early as 6 years. Individual differences in growth and maturation have been shown to have a number of important implications for sport, including (1) participation and the processes of talent identification and development (2) the design, implementation, and evaluation of training and conditioning programmes, and (3) the grouping of children in competition (Cumming *et al.*, 2017).

## *Sport Participation, Talent Identification, and Development*

Athletic competence is an important predictor of sport participation in youth. Children who are, or perceive themselves as being, more athletic tend to gravitate towards those sports in which they are best suited to succeed (Weiss, 2019). Those children who are the most physically and athletically gifted receive more reinforcement and encouragement for their participation and are more likely to be recruited and/or selected onto such programmes where they receive greater access to and investment in professional coaching, training resources, and sports science/medical support. Conversely, children who are less physically gifted or successful in sports are more likely to avoid and/or withdraw from sports, especially in programmes where there is a greater emphasis upon competitive outcomes than general participation (Babic *et al.*, 2014; Henrique *et al.*, 2016).

Individual differences in the timing of maturation have consistently been shown to influence athletic performance and participation (Baxter-Jones, 1995). From puberty, early maturing boys are taller, heavier, and generally outperform their later developing peers on tests of upper and lower body strength, speed, power, agility, and endurance (Malina *et al.*, 2004). The physical and functional advantages of advanced maturation in boys are substantial and maintained through adolescence, yet attenuated and in some cases, reversed in early adulthood (Lefevre *et al.*, 2000). Girls who mature early are also taller and heavier than their peers and may possess an athletic advantage in sports that demand greater size and/or absolute strength and power. Advanced maturity in girls is, however, less conducive to performance in sports that require relative strength and power, muscular and/or aerobic endurance, or the movement of the body through space (Baxter-Jones *et al.*, 2002).

Differences in the size and athleticism of early and late maturing youth have been shown to contribute towards the emergence of maturity-associated selection biases in youth sports. Maturity selection biases emerge with the onset of puberty and vary relative to the nature and demands of the sport (Baxter-Jones, 2019). Boys who mature in advance of their peers are more likely to be selected and/or represented in sports that require greater size, strength, speed, and power (e.g. tennis, soccer, rugby). This bias increases in magnitude with age and is most evident in select and elite level programmes (i.e. professional academies, national junior squads). For the most part, late maturing boys are generally absent from competitive sports programmes from 14 years of age, except in some sports that may place a less emphasis upon size and/or prioritise endurance or technical aesthetic qualities (gymnastics, diving) (Malina *et al.*, 2015). The representation of early and late maturing girls across sport also varies relative to the demands of the sport (Malina *et al.*, 2015). Whereas early maturing girls are more likely to be represented in sports that require size and/or absolute strength (tennis, swimming) (Myburgh *et al.*, 2016), they are much less likely to be represented in those sports that emphasize endurance and/or aesthetics. Some sports, such as soccer appear to show maturity selection biases that vary relative to the stage of development (Malina *et al.*, 2021). Whereas early maturing girls are more likely to be represented in soccer during late childhood and early adolescence; late maturing girls are more likely to be represented from mid-to-late adolescence, and in adulthood (Malina *et al.*, 2021). Individual differences in the timing of maturation can enhance or confound evaluations of physical fitness and/or athletic performance in youth, ultimately impacting the selection and retention of young athletes (Baxter-Jones *et al.*, 2005; Hill *et al.*, 2020b). Early maturing boys, for example, are judged as having greater athletic ability and/or future potential due to the inherent physical and athletic advantages conferred through advanced maturation. Maturity-associated gains in size and fitness also make it challenging for practitioners to evaluate the extent to gains in physical fitness have occurred as a result of specific training or conditioning programmes or the natural processes of growth and maturity (Cumming *et al.*, 2017).

Maturity-associated differences in athleticism can also be observed in metrics of game performance. Early maturing boys cover greater distances at a higher speed, achieve higher peak speeds, engage in more individual and repeated high-intensity actions, and accelerations and decelerations, than their late maturing peers (Buchheit and Mendez-Villanueva, 2014; Parr *et al.*, 2021). This effect was, however, attenuated when the repeated performances of boys across games were controlled for, indicating that the observed association was largely due to the early maturing boys repeatedly outperformed their peers in these metrics across games. Using performance analysis data from across an academy season, Johnson *et al.*, found early maturing males to receive more match minutes than their late maturing peers. Controlling for differences in match minutes played, early maturing boys were also found to engage in more offensive and defensive actions (Johnson, 2021).

## Practical Implications

The assessment and monitoring of growth and maturation is recommended for the optimal development and safeguarding of young athletes. In 2015, the English Premier League implemented an academy-wide growth and maturity screening programme. Maturity data was integrated with fitness testing and injury data to generate league wide age and maturity standards for all tests of physical fitness (Cumming, 2018), allowing staff to effectively identify individual player's strengths and weaknesses. Similarly, Lawn Tennis Association has generated age and maturity for fitness attributes, such as 5-meter speed, enabling staff to evaluate the fitness of players more accurately on their performance pathways (Myburgh *et al.*, 2020). An early maturing girl, for example, might approximate the 75th centile for upper body strength for her age, yet only the 25th for her maturity status (Myburgh *et al.*, 2020). Developmentally fitness standards also enable practitioners to differentiate between fitness gains resulting from training and those associated with normal growth and maturation. If an athlete progresses from the 35th centile to the 75th centile in strength for their maturational status, for example, we can assume that the gains observed occurred above and beyond those associated with growth and maturation.

Individual differences in maturational status should also be considered making an evaluative decision regarding athletic ability and/or potential. Maturity timing and status have been shown to influence coaches' and scouts' evaluations of actual performances in competition. Considering five seasons of data from competitive academy football games, Hill and colleagues found coaches to award higher match grades to the most mature players in the under-14 and under-15 age groups (Hill *et al.*, 2020b). Coach evaluations of game performance were also found to decline temporarily as players entered the growth spurt, before returning to previous standards post-growth spurt (Hill *et al.*, 2020a). This finding highlights the need to consider both maturity timing (i.e. early, on-time, late) and status (pre-, circa-, post-PHV) when evaluating young athletes. Coaches should be especially careful when evaluating players' mid-growth spurt. Professional football players in the UK, such as Gareth Bale, a product of the and Southampton Academy was almost released following a decline in performance that accompanied his growth spurt. Fortunately, academy staff recognised that he was currently during his growth spurt and were able to adjust his training programme, allowing him to transition through this phase of his development more effectively (Maw, 2013).

## Maturation and Training

Strength and conditioning practitioners have long recognised the importance of accommodating individual differences in growth and maturity for the prescription, design, implementation, and evaluation of training programmes. The Youth Physical Developmental Model holds that training effects and athlete safety are optimised when training is aligned with, and takes advantage of, the physiological changes that accompany the maturation process; a concept known as 'synergistic adaptation' (Lloyd and Oliver, 2012). In childhood, gains in strength, speed, and power are best achieved through activities that enhance neuro-muscular activation and co-ordination. From mid-to-late, puberty, optimal gains in strength, power, speed, and anaerobic capacity are best achieved through a combination of neural and structural (i.e. hypertrophy) adaptation. Allowing for technical competence and psychological readiness, trainers should group athletes by maturational status in strength and conditioning programmes (Lloyd and Oliver, 2012). Potential groupings include athletes who are pre-growth spurt (80%–85% PPAH), early-t0-mid growth spurt (85%–90% PPAH), mid-to-late growth spurt (90%–95%), and post growth spurt (95%–100% PPAH) (Cumming *et al.*, 2017).

Maturity matching for training can also reduce injury risk in young athletes (McKay *et al.*, 2019). Growth-related injuries are of particular concern in sports where children specialise early and engage in high training loads at a young age. The adolescent growth spurt is a developmental stage where athletes are more susceptible to growth-related and overuse injuries (Johnson, 2015). The prevalence of growth-related injuries in young athletes follows a distal-to-proximal gradient, with those injuries associated with specific anatomical sites following a sequence that is consistent with skeletal growth (McKay *et al.*, 2019). Peak rates of Sever's disease (heel) occur at the onset of the growth spurt, whereas Osgood-Schlatter's disease (knee) and Spondylosis (lower back) peak at mid and deceleration stages of the growth spurt, respectively (Monasterio *et al.*, 2020).

Injury risk and burden can be reduced by adapting training load and content during the growth spurt. Jan Willem Teunnisen, a movement scientist at Ajax football club, used maturity matching training principles to allow academy players to transition more safely through the adolescent growth spurt (Wormhoudt *et al.*, 2017). Players entering the growth spurt were assigned to a 'conditioning program' that involved a reduction in training and competition load and activities involving accelerations and decelerations. In place of these activities, players engaged in tasks that focussed upon coordination, balance, core strength, and mobility, and the re-training of fundamental and sport-specific skills. Implementing an equivalent training programme for players experiencing the adolescent growth spurt, sports scientists at AFC Bournemouth in the UK observed significant reductions in both injury incidence and burden (Johnson, 2021). Further research is, however, required to substantiate these findings. It is equally important that research be conducted to better identify the specific changes in training load and content that optimal for mitigating injury risk at different stages of the adolescent growth spurt. The effectiveness of such programmes may also be increased through the education and inclusion of medical staff and coaches, highlighting the need for an integrated approach towards athlete development. Knowledge pertaining to injury symptomology, fatigue, and/or adolescent awkwardness may help practitioners better detect those athletes at greater risk for injury during this stage of their development (Johnson, 2015).

## *Maturation and Competition*

In most countries, young athletes are grouped by age for competition. Age groups are often limited to a single year (e.g. U11s, U12s, U13s), but may span two-to-three years in recreational programme (e.g. 11–13 years, 13–15 years) or in less densely populated communities. Age groups are ideal for matching children based on attributes closely aligned with age (e.g. experience, cognitive, social, and motor development), yet have their limitations. Maturity-associated differences in size and athleticism within age groups are substantial and can adversely impact competitive equity.

As noted, children of the same chronological age can vary by as much as five-to-six years in skeletal age (Johnson, 2015). Thus, it is entirely possible for an U14's age group to include some individuals who are close to fully mature competing alongside others who have yet to enter puberty. Such David versus Goliath scenarios are not uncommon in sports and are of little value to both the early and late developers. Whereas early maturing athletes are insufficiently challenged, the challenges for the late developers may be insurmountable, irrespective of their technical and/or tactical ability (Zuber *et al.*, 2016). The pressure to produce results can also encourage early developers to rely upon their physical advantages, at the expense of their technical, tactical, or psychological development. While this strategy may bring immediate rewards, its long-term value and effectiveness is limited.

To account for individual differences in maturation, scholars and practitioners have suggested grouping athletes by maturity rather than age. The most recent iteration of this concept is known as bio-banding (Cumming *et al.*, 2017) and involves grouping athletes by attributes relative to combinations of age, size, and/or maturity. Examples of bio-banding already exist in sports where variance in size and maturity has implications for safety and competitive equity (Malina *et al.*, 2019). For example, in boxing and judo children are grouped by age and weight criteria (Delorme, 2014). Similarly, some collision sports have implemented aged and weight-based rules for grouping players in the competition and/or permitting players to play specific roles (e.g. ball carrier in American Football) (Cassidy, 2018). More recently, the English Premier League organised soccer games where players were grouped by maturity (Cumming *et al.* 2018), with the aim of limiting the maturity-associated difference in size and athleticism and presenting players with new challenges and learning opportunities. Competing against older yet physically matched players, early developers must work harder, think, make decisions, release the ball more quickly, and place greater emphasis upon the use of their technical, tactical, and psychological skills. In contrast, late developers had more opportunities to use, develop, and demonstrate their technical and tactical attributes and assume positions of leadership. Research on bio-banding in football has consistently supported the differential benefits of maturity-matched competition for early and late maturing players (Thomas *et al.*, 2017; Abbott *et al.*, 2019; Bradley *et al.*, 2019; Towlson *et al.*, 2020). Analysis of game performance in bio-banded competitions also suggests a greater emphasis upon technical and tactical rather than the physical style of play and greater equity in physical, technical tactical, and psychological challenges across players of varying maturity status.

Although the practice of bio-banding has been endorsed by the English Premier League and, more recently, FIFA, it is not without its critics. Advocates of the ill-christened 'talent needs trauma' idiom (Savage et al,. 2017) describe bio-banding as a misplaced solution for the relative age effect (Collins and MacNamara, 2017); arguing that it removes the challenge necessary for late maturing athletes to succeed at the highest level. These criticisms are, however, naive on several counts. First, bio-banding is not designed as solution for the relative age effect. Rather it is designed to address individual differences in biological maturation. Maturation and relative age are separate constructs that exist and operate independent of one another and require separate solutions. Second, as bio-banding is an adjunct to, and not replacement for, age group competition, late maturing players continue to be challenged in age group games. As late maturing players are, however, largely absent from academy football from 14 years (Hill *et al.*, 2020a) it is difficult to envisage how these individuals would experience such challenges at all.

## Implications for Children's Sport Coaching

As noted previously, the regular assessment and monitoring of growth and maturation in young athletes is recommended as best practice. All youth sports programmes should, where possible, implement systems for assessing the growth and maturity status of their athletes. In doing so, coaches be more aware of and capable of accommodating individual differences in growth and maturation. It is equally important that those working with young athletes (i.e. coaches, scouts, sports science, and medical practitioners) are educated upon the processes of growth and maturation in youth and understand their implications for athletic performance and development.

When working with young athletes, coaches need to be aware of and account for individual differences in maturation, adjusting their perceptions and expectations in relation to athletic ability and future potential. In many instances, early maturing will naturally outperform their late maturing peers based upon their inherent physical and athletic advantages. Coaches need to look beyond these temporary advantages and encourage early developing youth to focus upon those abilities and skills that are necessary to perform and succeed at the highest-level adults. Similarly, coaches need to be more nuanced and patient in their evaluation of late maturing youth. As noted, it may not be until early adulthood that maturity-associated differences in size and athleticism are attenuated and the true potential of these players is realised.

It is also important that coaches are aware of the adolescent growth spurt and the challenges that it presents in terms of athletic performance and athlete health. Through the regular screening of growth and maturation in young athletes, coaches can better identify when athletes enter this phase of their development, Coaches can then adjust their expectations in relation to athletic performance and modify training load and content accordingly. Reductions in training load and changes in training content may entail less engagement in certain training activities and competitive games/contests, however, it does increase the likelihood that athletes stay healthy during this stage of their development and have the time and opportunity to adjust to accommodate for growth-related changes in size, physique, and function. As athletes exit the adolescent growth spurt, training and competition loads can return to normal, affording athletes with a safer and healthier pathway to success at the adult level.

## Summary, Future Directions, and Future Research

It is well established that individual differences in growth and maturation can positively and/or adversely impact towards children's experiences in sport and physical activity. Although it may not be possible to change the age or rate at which children mature, adults can increase their awareness of growth and maturation and alter their expectations, perceptions, and behaviours accordingly. To ensure that all children have optimal opportunities to be active and engage successfully in sport, whether it be at an elite or recreational level, it is important that adults recognise and accommodate for individual differences in growth and maturation. It is equally important that we educate children about the processes of maturation. Children should be encouraged to view the changes that accompany puberty as a normal and natural consequence of becoming an adult and as opportunities for and not barriers towards activity. Future research should adopt a bicultural approach to better understand the impact of growth and maturation upon children's experiences in sport and physical activity. Particular attention should be paid to the role of the scouts and coaches in relation to the emergence of maturity-associated selected biases in sport and the impact of puberty upon injury risk during the growth sport. It is equally important that research move beyond the study of maturity-associated differences in physical fitness, to examine the potential impact of maturation upon the quality of play and decision-making in sport. Finally, research should continue to work with practitioners to develop and evaluate strategies to best optimise the development and learning opportunities for early and late developers.

## References


Abbott, W., *et al.*, 2019. Effects of bio-banding upon physical and technical performance during soccer competition: A preliminary analysis. *Sports*, 7 (8), 193–205.

Babic, M.J., *et al.*, 2014. Physical activity and physical self-concept in youth: Systematic review and meta-analysis. *Sports Medicine*, 44 (11), 1589–1601.

Baxter-Jones, A.D., 1995. Growth and development of young athletes. *Sports Medicine*, 20 (2), 59–64.

Baxter-Jones, A.D., 2019. Physical growth and development in young athletes: Factors of influence and consequence. *Kinesiology Review*, 8(3), 211–219.

Baxter-Jones, A.D., Eisenmann, J.C., and Sherar, L.B., 2005. Controlling for maturation in pediatric exercise science. *Pediatric Exercise Science*, 17 (1), 18–30.

Baxter-Jones, A.D., Thompson, A.M., and Malina, R.M., 2002. Growth and maturation in elite young female athletes. *Sports Medicine and Arthroscopy Review*, 10 (1), 42–49.

Blakemore, S., Burnett, S., and Dahl, R.E., 2010. The role of puberty in the developing adolescent brain. *Human Brain Mapping*, 31 (6), 926–933.

Bradley, B., *et al.*, 2019. Bio-banding in academy football: Player's perceptions of a maturity matched tournament. *Annals of Human Biology*, 46 (5), 400–408.

Buchheit, M. and Mendez-Villanueva, A., 2014. Effects of age, maturity and body dimensions on match running performance in highly trained under-15 soccer players. *Journal of Sports Sciences*, 32 (13), 1271–1278.

Byers, J.A., 1998. The biology of human play. *Child Development*, 69 (3), 599–600.

Byers, J.A. and Walker, C., 1995. Refining the motor training hypothesis for the evolution of play. *The American Naturalist*, 146 (1), 25–40.

Cassidy, T., 2018. 'I didn't have to tackle humungus people': An ecological investigation into a dispensation policy in New Zealand junior rugby. *International Journal of Sports Science & Coaching*, 13 (6), 947–957.

Collins, D. and MacNamara, A., 2017. *Talent development: A practitioner guide*. London: Routledge.

Cumming, S.P., 2018. A game plan for growth: How football is leading the way in the consideration of biological maturation in young male athletes. *Annals of Human Biology*, 45 (5), 373–375.

Cumming, S.P., *et al.*, 2011. The mediating role of physical self-concept on relations between biological maturity status and physical activity in adolescent females. *Journal of Adolescence*, 34 (3), 465–473.

Cumming, S.P., *et al.*, 2012. A biocultural model of maturity-associated variance in adolescent physical activity. *International Review of Sport and Exercise Psychology*, 5 (1), 23–43.

Cumming, S.P., *et al.*, 2017. Bio-banding in sport: Applications to competition, talent identification, and strength and conditioning of youth athletes. *Strength & Conditioning Journal*, 39 (2), 34–47.

Cumming, S.P., *et al.*, 2018. Premier League academy soccer players' experiences of competing in a tournament bio-banded for biological maturation. *Journal of Sports Sciences*, 36 (7), 757–765.

Cumming, S.P., *et al.*, 2020. Maturational timing, physical self-perceptions and physical activity in UK adolescent females: Investigation of a mediated effects model. *Annals of Human Biology*, 47 (4), 384–390.

Delorme, N., 2014. Do weight categories prevent athletes from relative age effect? *Journal of Sports Sciences*, 32 (1), 16–21.

Eisenmann, J.C. and Wickel, E.E., 2009. The biological basis of physical activity in children: Revisited. *Pediatric Exercise Science*, 21 (3), 257–272.

Fieseler, C.M., 1996. Special considerations for the female runner. *Journal of Back and Musculoskeletal Rehabilitation*, 6 (1), 37–47.

Golle, K., *et al.*, 2015. Physical fitness percentiles of German children aged 9–12 years: Findings from a longitudinal study. *PloS One*, 10 (11).

Handelsman, D., Hirschberg, A., and Bermon, S. 2018. Circulating testosterone as the hormonal basis of sex differences in athletic performance. *Endocrine Reviews*, 39 (5), 803–829.

Handelsman, D.J., *et al.*, 2019. Effects of bio-banding upon physical and technical performance during soccer competition: A preliminary analysis. *Sports*, 7 (8), 193–205.

Henrique, R.S., *et al.*, 2016. Association between sports participation, motor competence and weight status: A longitudinal study. *Journal of Science and Medicine in Sport*, 19 (10), 825–829.

Hill, M., *et al.*, 2020a. Relative age and maturation selection biases in academy football. *Journal of Science in Sport and Exercise*, 38 (11), 1359–1367.

Hill, M., *et al.*, 2020b. Are relative age and biological ages associated with coaches' evaluations of match performance in male academy soccer players? *International Journal of Sports Science and Coaching*, 16 (2), 227–235.

Johnson, A., 2015. Monitoring the immature athlete. *Aspetar Sports Medicine Journal*, 4 (4), 114–118.
Johnson, D., 2021. *Growth, maturation and bio-banding in youth football*. Stockholm: Svensk Fotboll Webanariet, 19 April, 2021.
Latorre Román, P., *et al.*, 2017. Physical fitness in preschool children: Association with sex, age and weight status. *Child: Care, Health and Development*, 43 (2), 267–273.
Lefevre, J., *et al.*, 2000. Daily physical activity and physical fitness from adolescence to adulthood: A longitudinal study. *American Journal of Human Biology: The Official Journal of the Human Biology Association*, 12 (4), 487–497.
Lloyd, R.S. and Oliver, J.L., 2012. The youth physical development model: A new approach to long-term athletic development. *Strength & Conditioning Journal*, 34 (3), 61–72.
Malina, R., 2007. Physical fitness of children and adolescents in the United States: Status and secular change. *Pediatric Fitness*, 50, 67–90.
Malina, R.M., Bouchard, C., and Bar-Or, O., 2004. *Growth, maturation, and physical activity*. Illinois: Human Kinetics.
Malina, R.M., Cumming, S.P., and e Silva, M.J.C., 2016. Physical activity and movement proficiency: The need for a biocultural approach. *Pediatric Exercise Science*, 28 (2), 233–239.
Malina, R.M., *et al.*, 2015. Biological maturation of youth athletes: Assessment and implications. *British Journal of Sports Medicine*, 49 (13), 852–859.
Malina, R.M., *et al.*, 2019. Bio-banding in youth sports: Background, concept, and application. *Sports Medicine*, 49 (11), 1671–1685.
Malina, R.M., *et al.*, 2021. Growth and maturity status of female soccer players: A narrative review. *International Journal of Environmental Research and Public Health*, 18 (4), 1448–1464.
Maw, J., 2013. *The day Gareth Bale almost got booted out of Southampton* [online]. Four Four Two. Available from: https://www.fourfourtwo.com/features/day-gareth-bale-almost-got-booted-out-southampton [Accessed 1 April 2022].
McKay, C.D., Cumming, S.P., and Blake, T., 2019. Youth sport: Friend or Foe? *Best Practice & Research Clinical Rheumatology*, 33 (1), 141–157.
Monasterio, X., *et al.*, 2020. Injuries according to the percentage of adult height in an elite soccer academy. *Journal of Science and Medicine in Sport*, 24 (3), 218–223.
Moore, S.A., *et al.*, 2020. Exploring the relationship between adolescent biological maturation, physical activity, and sedentary behaviour: A systematic review and narrative synthesis. *Annals of Human Biology*, 47 (4), 365–383.
Myburgh, G.K., *et al.*, 2016. Growth and maturity status of elite British junior tennis players. *Journal of Sports Sciences*, 34 (20), 1957–1964.
Myburgh, G.K., *et al.*, 2020. Developmental fitness curves: Assessing sprint acceleration relative to age and maturity status in elite junior tennis players. *Annals of Human Biology*, 47 (4), 336–345.
Parr, J., Winwood, K., Hodson-Tole, E., Deconinck, F. J., Hill, J. P., and Cumming, S. P., 2021. Maturity-Associated Differences in Match Running Performance in Elite Male Youth Soccer Players. *International journal of sports physiology and performance*, 1 (aop), 1–9.
Payne, S., Townsend, N., and Foster, C., 2013. The physical activity profile of active children in England. *International Journal of Behavioral Nutrition and Physical Activity*, 10 (1), 1–8.
Pindus, D.M., *et al.*, 2014. Maturity-associated variation in physical activity and health-related quality of life in british adolescent girls: Moderating effects of peer acceptance. *International Journal of Behavioral Medicine*, 21 (5), 757–766.
Rowland, T.W., 1998. The biological basis of physical activity. *Medicine and Science in Sports and Exercise*, 30 (3), 392–399.
Savage, J., Collins, D., and Cruickshank, A., 2017. Exploring traumas in the development of talent: What are they, what do they do, and what do they require? *Journal of Applied Sport Psychology*, 29 (1), 101–117.
Sherar, L. and Cumming, S., 2022. Physical activity and growth. *In*: N. Cameron and L. Schell, eds. *Human growth and development*. London: Elsevier, 469–490.
Sherar, L.B., *et al.*, 2010. Adolescent biological maturity and physical activity: Biology meets behaviour. *Pediatric Exercise Science*, 22 (3), 332–349.
Smart, J.E.H., *et al.*, 2012. Maturity associated variance in physical activity and health-related quality of life in adolescent females: A mediated effects model. *Journal of Physical Activity and Health*, 9 (1), 86–95.
Thomas, C.H., *et al.*, 2017. A pilot study of the demands of chronological age group and bio-banded match play in elite youth soccer. *Graduate Journal of Sport Exercise and Physical Education Research*, 5 (1), 211.

Towlson, C., *et al.*, 2020. The effect of bio-banding on physical and psychological indicators of talent identification in academy soccer players. *Science and Medicine in Football*, 5 (4), 280–292.

UNICEF, 2020. *Worlds of influence understanding what shapes child well-being in rich countries* [online]. Florence: UNICEF Office of Research–Innocenti. Available from: https://www.unicef-irc.org/child-well-being-report-card-16 [Accessed 1 April 2022].

Weiss, M.R., 2019. Youth sport motivation and participation: Paradigms, perspectives, and practicalities. *Kinesiology Review*, 8 (3), 162–170.

Wormhoudt, R., *et al.*, 2017. *The athletic skills model: Optimising talent development through movement education*. London: Routledge.

Zuber, C., Zibung, M., and Conzelmann, A., 2016. Holistic patterns as an instrument for predicting the performance of promising young soccer players–a 3-years longitudinal study. *Frontiers in Psychology*, 27 (7), 1088–1098.

# 24

# DIGGING FOR DIAMONDS? THE ABSTRACT AND QUESTIONABLE NATURE OF TALENT IDENTIFICATION IN CHILDREN'S SPORT

*Kathryn Johnston, Nick Wattie, and Joseph Baker*

## Introduction

The term 'talent' means different things to different people under different contexts (Gagné, 2004; Baker and Wattie, 2018; Jones *et al.*, 2020). You may hear the term being used when referring to exceptional human performance across multiple spheres (e.g. music, visual art, education, sport). Typically, it's used when we are in awe of someone's abilities that seemingly extend beyond what the average person can accomplish. This is especially true when we think of the superstar athletes such as Roger Federer, Serena Williams, Lionel Messi, and Tiger Woods. What is it that makes them talented? Are they genetically superior, or did they find smarter ways to train? Can we measure that 'talent'? These are some of the questions puzzling athletes, coaches, parents, and sport scientists alike and remain at the forefront of conversations because of talent's elusive nature.

## Review of Current Research

Recent work has sought to uncover what talent is and what qualities, attributes, and characteristics comprise talent (McCardle *et al.*, 2019; Jones *et al.*, 2020; Pino-Ortega *et al.*, 2021). The majority of the work to date has focused on the physical components of talent such as the anthropometric and physiological measures of superior athletes (e.g. Johnston *et al.*, 2018; Millet *et al.*, 2021), but there is growing interest in the psychological and perceptual cognitive attributes as well. In an effort to highlight the research findings, multiple systematic reviews have been conducted spanning multiple sports (Johnston *et al.*, 2018; Roberts *et al.*, 2019; Baker *et al.*, 2020; Pino-Ortega *et al.*, 2021).

This elusive nature of talent is a likely contributor to the reason why sports are not very good at assessing and selecting athletes. Even at the highest level of sport, the predictive capabilities are poor (Koz *et al.*, 2012; Farah and Baker, 2020). For example, in the USA, Koz *et al.* (2012) examined the relationship of career performance and draft round for the NHL, NBA, NFL,

 DOI: 10.4324/9781003199359-28

and MLB. Even when selection decisions were made later in an athlete's career (early adulthood instead of youth, childhood, or adolescence), the level of predictive accuracy was relatively low. If this is the level of predictive accuracy at the most elite levels when athletes are more mature (when attributes are more stable than during puberty), it is not difficult to imagine the magnitude of these errors at earlier levels of sport participation!

Before the chapter can answer important (and necessary) questions such as the ones listed earlier, it is important to examine *what* makes talent so elusive. The following sections will review current research on the reasons why we are still far away from accurate talent selection.

## *Definition Challenges*

To date, there is no universally accepted definition of talent. Some definitions take a more nature-centric perspective, some nurture-centric, and others embrace the more widely accepted understanding that the combination of both is necessary for advancing to the next level of competition. But regardless of what talent actually is, the term is almost always defined vaguely and in an abstract way. As many researchers emphasise, until there is an agreed-upon definition, the ability to identify, measure and track talent will be limited. Furthermore, some definitions of talent and its properties fall short of being useful for practitioners. In particular, many definitions do not provide a clear sense of what to look for, when, or how. Work by Baker *et al.* (2019) has tried to remedy this, by providing a clear definition of the *properties* of talent, but whether it is taken up by researchers and practitioners remains to be seen.

To explore coaches' definitions of talent, Jones *et al.* (2020) interviewed collegiate-level coaches across various sports at a Canadian academic institution and asked them 'what does talent mean to you in the context of sport?' Through thematic analyses, superior physical attributes such as anthropometric measures and physiological abilities were commonly found in coaches' descriptions. Moreover, coaches believed these abilities stemmed from an athlete's genetics and were often regarded as 'unteachable' or 'untrainable' qualities. In addition to the physical attributes, coaches highlighted important psychological attributes such as work ethic, game sense, coachability, resilience, perseverance, and positivity, speaking to the belief that talent is multi-dimensional. What was perhaps the most surprising finding was that collegiate-level coaches recognised talent is likely coach-dependent. One coach stated outright,

> I think every coach has their own criteria, their own things that they look for and it can vary greatly from coach to coach. I think what one coach looks for, another coach could be totally turned off by, so it really just depends on your own- your own beliefs as a coach and your own evaluation criteria.
>
> *(Jones et al., 2020, p. 91)*

This finding aligns with previous work in the field and speaks to the arduous, and potentially fruitless, task of arriving at a unified and operational definition of talent.

In a similar vein, Johnston and Baker (2022) interviewed ten expert distance running coaches across Canada and asked them to describe the 'best' athletes they had coached. During their explanations coaches typically used the term talent in their descriptions which led to interesting conversations when unpacking their conceptualisations of the term. This group of coaches commonly believed talent had physical and psychological qualities, but also that it existed in multiple forms (either trained or untrained) and can be obvious or non-obvious in the way it presents itself. To add another layer of complexity to the discussion, the coaches used terms like 'gift' and 'potential' when explaining athlete talent. When asked to compare and contrast with their notions of all three terms, they found it difficult to untangle the web of these intertwined and abstract terms. These findings emphasise the complexity of talent and echo the sentiments of Jones *et al.* that talent may mean different things to different coaches and likely in different countries.

## Diversity of Influential Factors

Perhaps one of the driving factors affecting the variability in definitions is the variability in the way talent presents itself, particularly in sport. Significant attention has been directed at identifying the factors related to performance and attainment in sport – such as genetics, training, resources, friend groups, parent/ family support, psychology, birth date, coaches, geographic location, and personality (e.g. Côté *et al.*, 2006; Wattie *et al.*, 2015; Hardy *et al.*, 2017; Jacob *et al.*, 2018). Some may have a more significant impact than others, either due to differences between individuals or in the key performance indicators of their sport relative to other sports, but the exact degree of importance is still unknown. One way to consider the relative impact of these factors on the development of sport expertise was suggested by Baker and Horton (2004) who categorised the factors into two groups, primary (direct influences on expertise) and secondary factors (indirect or moderating influences). Primary factors include genetic influences, training/practice, and psychological factors that have a clear path in how they affect performance and expertise. Secondary factors, on the other hand, include indirect influences such as access to resources, the involvement of the family, and the culture of the society, which work as 'buffers' to the primary factors (e.g. greater access to resources and/or cultural support facilitates training quantity and quality). Stemming from this work, researchers have shown the many different combinations and magnitude of factors that affect eventual attainment, speaking to the complexly intertwined relationship between the athlete and his/her/their environment (Baker *et al.,* 2019). Some even believe this infinite number of combinations makes predicting talent a near impossible feat (Den Hartigh *et al.*, 2018; Cox *et al.*, 2019).

## Measurement Challenges

At many levels of competitive sport, a battery of tests is used to assess athletes' capabilities, with physical and technical skills dominating the types of tests used (Unnithan *et al.*, 2012; Fernandez-Fernandez *et al.*, 2014; Johnston *et al.*, 2014). Obviously, elite sport performance extends beyond physical and technical skills. In addition, 'intangible' variables such as perseverance, resilience, and self-regulation are gaining attraction in talent identification models and are receiving more research attention (Tedesqui and Young, 2018; McCardle *et al.*, 2019). Despite their perceived importance, only pockets of isolated studies have examined psychological variables believed to play an important role in elite performance (see Martinent *et al.*, 2018; Dohme *et al.*, 2019 for reviews). For this reason, it becomes a challenge for practitioners looking to integrate valid and reliable testing measures to their assessment protocols, especially for a category of variables so diverse and far-ranging.

Even with the studies completed to date, common criticisms exist for both subjective and objective measures. In particular, the tests used to assess athlete abilities do not always reflect the performance demands of the sport, reflecting a low degree of 'representativeness' (Lidor *et al.*, 2005). For example, questionnaires are a popular method, but may contain biases which affect how accurately or reliably scores represent the variable being considered. Furthermore, given zeitgeists about the importance of resilience, grit, mindset, and the like, questionnaires also create the risk of

Hawthorn Effects (i.e. participants modify their responses as a result of being observed). Moreover, few have tracked these variables longitudinally, undoubtedly because it can be difficult to follow enough athletes who stay in competitive sport to track changes over time (Morris, 2000; Johnston *et al.*, 2018).

Another criticism relates to the degree of applicability of these measurement tools to different, often quite distinct, groups of athletes. Much of the work in talent identification in sport has been conducted on male samples, in the sport of soccer, and in adolescents or adults, who live in Europe (Baker *et al.*, 2020). Without greater diversity and representativeness in the samples reflected in high-quality research studies (e.g. females, across different sports, spanning various ages and stages (especially youth and children), and across cultures), the ability to assess, select, and develop athletes effectively will continue to be significantly limited.

## Time Constraints

In addition to being complex, talent is dynamic. Simply put, not everyone who is 'talented' early in life remains 'talented' later in life, and vice versa. We tend to think of athletic success as a relatively linear process, meaning an athlete who appears talented at an early age continues to be talented throughout his/her/their athletic endeavours. However, the evidence here is largely equivocal. In one study by Hollings and Hume (2010), nearly half of all World Champions, Olympic Champions, and Beijing Olympic medalists did not compete at the World Junior Championships. While there is plenty of evidence to support the opposite (that junior success is important for senior success), the variability in the findings highlights the non-linear path that many athletes may take to reach the top. This is likely due to the fact that the rate and stage of maturity complicates the ability to assess and predict future sport performance (Burgess and Naughton, 2010; Cobley and Till, 2015). This is especially true during puberty, when not only are athletes' bodies changing, but their attitudes and motivation to train and work hard are changing as well (Pearson *et al.*, 2006; Vaeyens *et al.*, 2008). This maturational change happens at different ages for example, for girls typically between 10 and 12, and boys typically between 12 and 14 (Philippaerts *et al.*, 2006), and it is accompanied by a time of unpredictability and variability. During these periods of fluctuations, it can be challenging for coaches to assess an athlete's 'potential'.

In addition to these growth and maturational influences on the time course of athlete development, research also suggests talent is best considered as an 'emergenic' concept, involving not simply linear and additive relationships, but immensely complex, multiplicative relationships between countless genetic and environment variables (Baker *et al.*, 2019). Consider the influence of height, a relatively straightforward variable which has clear implications for many sports (e.g. basketball, volleyball, gymnastics). This simple outcome results from a complex pattern of interactions between hundreds of genetic and environmental variables (e.g. proper nutrition). Increase the level of complexity in the variable being considered and you increase the complexity of the genetic-environment interactions, and decrease the likelihood of capturing these relationships in simple models of athlete development. For instance, sport- and training-related variables such as creativity, leadership, personality traits, and interest in specific types of recreational activities are best considered as emergenic.

## Decision-Making Errors

Entire fields of research are dedicated to understanding how people make decisions under uncertain circumstances, much of which has relevance for selection decisions in sport settings. A prevailing finding is humans are prone to making poor judgements and inaccurate decisions.

Two major areas for this error are wrongful inclinations (biases) and within- and between-person variability (noise).

To date, there are hundreds of different, known cognitive biases that affect our thinking. Some of these biases are useful as they can act as time-saving strategies, while others can be hurtful and nudge us towards making illogical and inaccurate judgments. One example of a prevalent bias in sport is the relative age bias (Wattie *et al.*, 2015; Leyhr *et al.*, 2021). Depending on the sport and age of the athletes you are coaching, there is a possibility there could be large variability between the relatively youngest and the relatively oldest athlete on the team. For example, a cut off day of December 31 would mean a child born on January 1 would be nearly one year older than a child born December 30. This difference in age can result in relative age effects where there is an increased likelihood of coaches selecting the relatively older child because he/she/they appears more talented because they are more mature, and more likely to be larger, stronger, and more capable in peer-to-peer comparisons (i.e. because they were 'relatively older'). This effect is likely more pronounced in childhood when maturational changes are happening at a rapid rate. Interestingly, what appears to be an initial advantage may hold negative consequences later in development. A 2007 study found that there were more players drafted into the National Hockey League (competitive hockey league in Canada and the United States) who had birthdays in the first four months of the year compared to athletes with birthdates in the last four months of the year (Baker and Logan, 2007). But surprisingly, the relatively younger players (born later in the year) were more likely to be chosen in earlier rounds of the draft, suggesting they were more sought after. Others have also observed a reversal of relative age advantages in favour of relatively younger athletes with respect to career length (Gibbs *et al.*, 2012; Grossmann and Lames, 2013; Steingröver *et al.*, 2016; Fumarco *et al.*, 2017) games played (Deaner *et al.*, 2013; Ramos-Filho and Ferreira, 2021), points (Deaner *et al.*, 2013), and notable career achievements (Gibbs *et al.*, 2012). Similarly, in soccer and ice hockey, relatively younger players were better paid than the relatively older players (Ashworth and Heyndels, 2007; Fumarco *et al.*, 2017).

In addition to these more system-level biases, many other individual biases exist during decision-making processes. While many of these biases have not been studied within the context of athlete selection specifically (although they have been speculated to; see Johnston and Baker, 2020), the extent of many of these biases shown to affect decision-making in other disciples such as medicine, economics, and education would indicate they could be (and likely are) present in sport. For instance, the 'affinity bias' (sometimes known as the 'self-mirroring bias') represents an unconscious gravitation to people who are most similar to us (Persaud, 2019). It is not a far stretch of the imagination that a coach (either rationally or irrationally) would select an athlete with similar values, traits, and interests. For example, a coach who had an aggressive playing style as an athlete may be more drawn towards a similar aggressive style in an athlete. Sometimes this approach can be strategic and advantageous, but sometimes it can come at a cost of de-selecting an athlete for his/her/their differences rather than athletic 'potential'. Another prominent bias affecting an individuals' judgement and decision-making is the 'confirmation bias', the tendency to search for information corroborating pre-existing beliefs (Nickerson, 1998). In this case, a coach may look for confirmatory cues to attach to and reject information that does not align with the coach's narrative, and subsequently may miss out on critically analysing more of the athlete's strengths and weaknesses. Both biases (affinity and confirmation) share similar properties, and while they can be helpful from a time- and energy-saving perspective, they can also lead to systematic and costly errors. Other common mental quirks that influence the way we store and recall memories include discarding specifics to form generalities (overgeneralisation), storing memories differently based on how they were experienced, noticing things primed in memory or repeated often, drawn to details that confirm our own existing beliefs (halo effect) (for a list of other biases in relation to sport, see Johnston and Baker, 2020). The challenge is to better understand which cognitive biases and shortcuts are adaptive, innocuous, and maladaptive, and in which specific contexts they are found (e.g. levels of sport).

Equally harmful is the degree of 'noise' present when making decisions (Kahneman *et al.*, 2021). Even experts with years of education and experience and who are trained to be objective in their decision-making strategies (such as judges and insurance underwriters) do not arrive uniformly at an answer as often as we might think. In one example, 48 underwriters were tasked with assigning premiums to various cases containing pertinent information. Overwhelmingly, the underwriters did not agree on a premium amount for these cases. In fact, the average difference between two randomly selected underwriters was 55% (Kahneman *et al.*, 2021). While this example is not situated in athlete selection, we have seen similar variability in studies examining expert coaches when selecting for talent. For example, Andersson *et al.* (2005) investigated the forecasting performance and confidence of experts and non-expert coaches in predicting the soccer World Cup outcomes. They discovered expert coaches' predictions were outperformed by a simple prediction calculation using world ranking. Similarly, Schorer *et al.* (2017) compared the predictive accuracy of handball coaches at different competitive levels, along with handball players and lay people. When asked to watch a video of handball athletes and determine who the most talented performers were, the study revealed little difference between the levels of coaches (regional and national), laypersons, and players.

Going forward, decision-making for athlete selection may not get easier. The drive to consider talent as a multidimensional and dynamic construct necessitates that more data is collected to inform selections. As a result, the 'data deluge' (Cukier, 2010) that has occurred in sport over recent decades will likely grow. Increasingly, selectors are able to supplement their observations with advanced analytics and machine learning algorithms. As these technologies become more accessible, the degree to which selectors abdicate decision-making to these technical tools, and the resultant influence on the accuracy of athlete selections, will need to be scrutinised. Indeed, it may even be useful to consider whether ardent devotion and faith in analytics and AI may itself be a manifestation of certain cognitive biases. More to the point, the power of these tools is not without limitation. For example, a recent mass scientific collaboration allowed 160 research teams to build their respective machine learning approaches to predict life outcomes from the same dataset (Salganik *et al.*, 2020). Even though the dataset contained thousands of variables, research teams were not able to make accurate predictive models. Even the most accurate models using complex machine learning methods did little better than simple linear and logistic regressions with four predictor variables selected by an expert. With respect to talent, which is dynamic, emergenic, and multidimensional, the role of supplementing human cognition with technological 'cognition' offers both risk and reward.

## Implications for Children's Sport Coaching

As sport at all levels becomes more 'professionalised' (aka mirroring elite sport programming), the values and philosophies of many youth and childhood programs may not align with the principles of talent identification or talent selection. Although athlete selection is a necessary process in many sports where developmental resources are limited, given the aforementioned reasons why talent is so elusive, it begs the question, should we be selecting for talent at all? It is important to note the distinction between making selections and making selections based on talent. Making selection decisions is a component of competitive sport, however, selections may be more accurate if 'talent' is not at the centre of the decision.

This in turn may have more positive implications for athletes as well, as being told an athlete has talent or not, can have some lasting ramifications. For example, the messages and language we use to describe athletes (e.g. 'a natural', 'gifted' vs. 'hard worker', 'hustle player', 'coachable') may impact how they view themselves, their abilities, and ultimately their behaviour. Research in education, physical activity, and sport suggests that believing abilities to be innate and unchangeable, can result in amotivation (Biddle *et al.*, 2003), higher anxiety and helpless patterns of behaviour in the face of adversity/failure (Ommundsen, 2001a), decreased effort and persistence (Spray *et al.*, 2006), and self-handicapping strategies (Ommundsen, 2001b). In contrast, believing abilities to be modifiable and predominantly the result of effort and practice has been associated with higher levels of enjoyment, adaptive responses to failure, and better skill acquisition (Jourden *et al.*, 1991; Wulf and Lewthwaite, 2009), the skills we want to engender in young athletes. We want children who respond to challenges and adversity in adaptive ways. Indeed, meta-cognitive self-regulation skills have been shown to be a consistent predictor of current and future performance (see McCardle *et al.*, 2019 for a review).

Evidence suggests our language can mould athletes' beliefs about the nature of their abilities (see Dweck, 2003; Spray *et al.*, 2006; Wulf and Lewthwaite, 2009). Labelling an athlete as 'talented' could risk instilling a mindset prone to helpless patterns of motivation and behaviour. In contrast, while coaches and parents should encourage kids to pursue their dreams, expectations need to be realistic. Not all children can become elite level athletes, for a variety of reasons. As such, telling them their inability to reach 'the top' is the result of lack of effort and perseverance is both inaccurate and cruel (see Wattie and Baker, 2017).

Moreover, due to the lack of scientific grounding and poor predictive capabilities for most talent identification models, some programs have moved away from early identification and towards inclusive talent development and guidance programs (Vaeyens *et al.*, 2008). The allure of allowing everyone to participate in sport on the team of their choosing seems enticing, however, making de-selections is a fairly important and inevitable component of competitive sport. If executed with the athlete's feelings first, and with the inclusion of options for future participation and ways to improve, it can be a powerful tool to help drive intrinsic motivation and the desire to invest in deliberate and meaningful practice. It is important to explain that a de-selection (as mentioned in another chapter in this text) does not mean elimination from that sport for life, there are more ways to enter back into the competitive sport system. A paradigm shift is needed to re-frame selection and de-selection, as 'streaming' into optimal athlete development environments.

In contrast to talent identification (the process of assessing athlete potential), talent development is thought to be the provision of the most appropriate environments to support athletes and to accelerate their learning and performance (Abbott and Collins, 2004). Sport can be an important vehicle for personal development in a young person's life. The goal in many of these talent development programs is to enhance the physical, social, and psychological wellness in children and help them reach their potential. Social interactions and development of physical literacy skills are thought to result in strong developmental outcomes (Côté *et al.*, 2008).

To help combat the poor selection accuracy, some suggestions are provided. More accurate decisions are believed to be made when the decision maker considers multiple perspectives and takes the time to assess the situations for sound evidence and logic. In contrast, fast, reactive, and impulsive decisions do not typically help us make 'better' decisions. Evidence also highlights that having an awareness of one's thought processes and biases may help to minimize the use of unnecessary biases and lead to more informed decisions. Work from the cognitive behavioural therapy (Stallard, 2018) domain encourages the use of the 3Cs to combat some of the irrational and illogical ways of thinking and decision-making:

- Catch it – before a decision has been made, take some extra time to acknowledge what information you are using to craft a judgment.
- Check it – check in with yourself to see if you are forming a judgment without sound evidence and potentially influenced by a bias. Consider also the opportunity to consult with a more neutral third party to help gather a different perspective.
- Change it – consider your other options and whether those options have more substantiating evidence to help you craft a decision. Upon closer examination, is a change in your thinking necessary?

## Summary, Future Direction, and Future Research

Overly simplistic notions of what talent is and how it changes across development, as well as the lack of appropriate and reliable measurement tools, could mean there is a real possibility that high rates of accuracy are just not feasible. Evidence to date indicates that while talent may be reasonable from a theoretical standpoint, it may not be valid from a practical sense (Baker and Wattie, 2018). Practitioners should be cautious when making decisions about who to select based on the notion of talent, especially given the measurement concerns and complexities associated with this concept. Instead, those working with children should focus on elements where the evidence is clearer. These include providing appropriate feedback, maximising opportunities for engagement and learning, and ensuring a balance between challenge and enjoyment. A focus on these elements will not only improve the experiences of more children but also improve the development of those lucky enough to be 'talented' … whatever that might mean.

## References


Abbott, A. and Collins, D., 2004. Eliminating the dichotomy between theory and practice in talent identification and development: Considering the role of psychology. *Journal of Sports Sciences*, 22 (5), 395–408.

Andersson, P., Edman, J., and Ekman, M., 2005. Predicting the World Cup 2002 in soccer: Performance and confidence of experts and non-experts. *International Journal of Forecasting*, 21 (3), 565–576.

Ashworth, J. and Heyndels, B., 2007. Selection bias and peer effects in team sports: The effect of age grouping on earnings of German soccer players. *Journal of Sports Economics*, 8 (4), 355–377.

Baker, J. and Horton, S., 2004. A review of primary and secondary influences on sport expertise. *High Ability Studies*, 15 (2), 211–228.

Baker, J. and Logan, A.J., 2007. Developmental contexts and sporting success: Birthdate and birthplace effects in national hockey league draftees 2000-2005. *British Journal of Sports Medicine*, 48 (8), 516.

Baker, J. and Wattie, N., 2018. Innate talent in sport: Separating myth from reality. *Current Issues in Sport Science*. 3 (2018), 1–9.

Baker, J., Wattie, N., and Schorer, J., 2019. A proposed conceptualisation of talent in sport: The first step in a long and winding road. *Psychology of Sport and Exercise*, 43, 27–33.

Baker, J., *et al.*, 2020. Talent research in sport 1990–2018: A scoping review. *Frontiers in Psychology*, 11, 607710.

Biddle, S.J.H., *et al.*, 2003. Motivation for physical activity in young people: Entity and incremental beliefs about athletic ability. *Journal of Sports Sciences*, 21 (12), 973–989.

Burgess, D.J. and Naughton, G.A., 2010. Talent development in adolescent team sports: A review. *International Journal of Sports Physiology and Performance*, 5 (1), 103–116.

Cobley, S. and Till, K., 2015. Talent identification, development, and the young rugby player. *In*: C. Twist and P. Worsfold, Eds. *The science of rugby*. New York: Routledge, 237–252.

Côté, J., Strachan, L., and Fraser Thomas, J., 2008. Participation, personal development and performance through youth sport. *In*: N. Holt, ed. *Positive youth development through sport*. New York: Routledge, 34–45.

Côté, J., *et al.*, 2006. When "where" is more important than "when": Birthplace and birthdate effects on the achievement of sporting expertise. *Journal of Sports Sciences*, 24 (10), 1065–1073.

Cox, R.F., *et al.*, 2019. Complex dynamical systems in human development. *Hindawi: Complexity*, 5010413.

Cukier, K., 2010. Data, data everywhere. *Economist*, 394 (8671), 3–5.

Deaner, R.O., Lowen, A., and Cobley. S., 2013. Born at the wrong time: Selection bias in the NHL draft, *PLoS ONE*, 8 (2), e57753.

Den Hartigh, R.J., Hill, Y., and Van Geert, P.L., 2018. The development of talent in sports: A dynamic network approach. *Hindawi: Complexity*, 9280154.

Dohme, L.C., *et al.*, 2019. Psychological skills and characteristics facilitative of youth athletes' development: A systematic review. *The Sport Psychologist*, *33*(4), 261–275.

Dweck, C.S., 2003. Ability conceptions, motivation and development. In *BJEP Monograph Series II, Number 2-Development and Motivation*, *13* (27), 13–27.

Farah, L. and Baker, J., 2020. Accuracy from the slot: Evaluating draft selections in the national hockey league. *Scandinavian Journal of Medicine and Science in Sports*, 1 (3), 564–572.

Fernandez-Fernandez, J., Ulbricht, A., and Ferrauti, A., 2014. Fitness testing of tennis players: How valuable is it? *British Journal of Sports Medicine*, 48, (Suppl 1), 22–31.

Fumarco, L., *et al.*, 2017. The relative age effect reversal among the national hockey league elite. *PLoS ONE*, 12 (8), e0182827.

Gagné, F., 2004. Transforming gifts into talents: The DMGT as a developmental theory. *High Ability Studies*, 15 (2), 119–147.

Gibbs, B.G., Jarvis, J.A., and Dufur, M.J., 2012. The rise of the underdog? The relative age effect reversal among Canadian-born NHL hockey players: A reply to Nolan and Howell. *International Review for the Sociology of Sport*, 47 (5), 644–649.

Grossmann, B. and Lames, M., 2013. Relative age effect (RAE) in football talents: The role of youth academies in transition to professional status in Germany. *International Journal of Performance Analysis in Sport*, 13 (1), 120–134.

Hardy, L., *et al.*, 2017. Great British medalists: Psychosocial biographies of super-elite and elite athletes from Olympic sports. *Progress in Brain Research*, 232, 1–119.

Hollings, S.C. and Hume, P.A., 2010. Is success at the World Junior Athletics Championships a prerequisite for success at World Senior Championships or Olympic Games?–Prospective and retrospective analyses. *New Studies in Athletics*, 25 (2), 65–77.

Jacob, Y., *et al.*, 2018. The potential role of genetic markers in talent identification and athlete assessment in elite sport. *Sports*, 6 (3), 88.

Johnston, K. and Baker, J., 2020. Waste reduction strategies: Factors affecting talent wastage and the efficacy of talent selection in sport. *Frontiers in Psychology*, 10 (2925), 1–11.

Johnston, K. and Baker, J., 2022. The complex and (sometimes) conflicting beliefs about talent: A case study of elite distance running coaches. *Journal of Expertise*, 5 (1), 38–57.

Johnston, R.D., Gabbett, T.J., and Jenkins, D.G., 2014. Applied sport science of rugby league. *Sports Medicine*, 44 (8), 1087–1100.

Johnston, K., *et al.*, 2018. Talent identification in sport: A systematic review. *Sports Medicine*, 48 (1), 97–109.

Jones, J., Johnston, K., and Baker, J., 2020. "I can't teach you to be taller": How Canadian, collegiate-level coaches construct talent in sport. *Case Studies in Sport and Exercise Psychology*, 4 (1), 84–94.

Jourden, F.J., Bandura, A., and Banfield, J.T., 1991. The impact of concepts of ability on self-regulatory factors and motor skill acquisition. *Journal of Sport and Exercise Psychology*, 8 (1), 213–226.

Kahneman, D., Sibony, O., and Sunstein, C.R., 2021. *Noise: A flaw in human judgment*. London: Little, Brown.

Koz, D., Fraser-Thomas, J., and Baker, J., 2012. Accuracy of professional sports drafts in predicting career potential. *Scandinavian Journal of Medicine and Science in Sports*, 22 (4), 64–69.

Leyhr, D., *et al.*, 2021. Relative age-related biases in objective and subjective assessments of performance in talented youth soccer players. *Frontiers in Sports and Active Living*, 3, 664231.

Lidor, R., *et al.*, 2005. Measurement of talent in team handball: The questionable use of motor and physical tests. *Journal of Strength and Conditioning Research*, 19 (2), 318–325.

Martinent, G., *et al.*, 2018. The prognostic relevance of psychological factors with regard to participation and success in table-tennis. *Journal of Sports Sciences*, 36 (23), 2724–2731.

McCardle, L., *et al.*, 2019. Self-regulated learning and expertise development in sport: Current status, challenges, and future opportunities. *International Review of Sport and Exercise Psychology*, 12 (1), 112–138.

Millet, G.P., Brocherie, F., and Burtscher, J., 2021. Olympic sports science—Bibliometric analysis of all summer and winter olympic sports research. *Frontiers in Sports and Active Living*, 3, 772140.

Morris, T., 2000. Psychological characteristics and talent identification in soccer. *Journal of Sports Sciences*, 18 (9), 715–726.

Nickerson, R.S., 1998. Confirmation bias: A ubiquitous phenomenon in many guises. *Review of General Psychology*, 2 (2), 175–220.

Ommundsen, Y., 2001a. Pupils' affective responses in physical education classes: The association of implicit theories of the nature of ability and achievement goals. *European Physical Education Review*, 7 (3), 219–242.

Ommundsen, Y., 2001b. Self-handicapping strategies in physical education classes: The influence of implicit theories of the nature of ability and achievement goal orientations. *Psychology of Sport and Exercise*, 2 (3), 139–156.

Pearson, D.T., *et al.*, 2006. Predictability of physiological testing and the role of maturation in talent identification for adolescent team sports. *Journal of Science and Medicine in Sport*, 9 (4), 277–287.

Persaud, S., 2019. Addressing unconscious bias: A nurse leader's role. *Nursing Administration Quarterly*, 43 (2), 130–137.

Philippaerts, R.M., *et al.*, 2006. The relationship between peak height velocity and physical performance in youth soccer players. *Journal of Sports Sciences*, 24 (3), 221–230.

Pino-Ortega, J., *et al.*, 2021. Training design, performance analysis and talent identification—A systematic review about the most relevant variables through the principal component analysis in soccer, basketball and rugby. *International Journal of Environmental Research and Public Health*, 18 (5), 1–19.

Ramos-Filho, L. and Ferreira, M.P., 2021. The reverse relative age effect in professional soccer: An analysis of the brazilian national league of 2015. *European Sport Management Quarterly*, 21 (1), 78–93.

Roberts, A.H., *et al.*, 2019. Coach knowledge in talent identification: A systematic review and meta-synthesis. *Journal of Science and Medicine in Sport*, 22 (10), 1163–1172.

Salganik, *et al.*, 2020. Measuring the predictability of life outcomes with a scientific mass collaboration. *PNAS*, 117 (15), 8398–8403.

Schorer, J., *et al.*, 2017. Long-term prognostic validity of talent selections: Comparing national and regional coaches, laypersons and novices. *Frontiers of Psychology*, 8 (1146),1–8.

Spray, C.M., *et al.*, 2006. An experimental test of self-theories of ability in youth sport. *Psychology of Sport and Exercise*, 7 (3), 255–267.

Stallard, P., 2018. Cognitive behavioural therapy. In Pattison, et al., Eds. *The handbook of counselling children and young people*. London: Sage, 49–63.

Steingröver, C., *et al.*, 2016. Does relative age affect career length in North American professional sports? *Sports Medicine-Open*, 2 (1), 1–7.

Tedesqui, R.A. and Young, B.W., 2018. Comparing the contribution of conscientiousness, self-control, and grit to key criteria of sport expertise development. *Psychology of Sport and Exercise*, 34, 110–118.

Unnithan, V., *et al.*, 2012. Talent identification in youth soccer. *Journal of Sports Sciences*, 30 (15), 1719–1726.

Vaeyens, R., *et al.*, 2008. Talent identification and development programmes in sport. *Sports Medicine*, 38 (9), 703–714.

Wattie, N. and Baker, J., 2017. Why conceptualizations of talent matter. In J. Baker, *et al.*, Eds. *The routledge handbook of talent identification and development in sport*. London: Routledge, 69–79.

Wattie, N., Schorer, J., and Baker, J., 2015. The relative age effect in sport: A developmental systems model. *Sports Medicine*, 45 (1), 83–94.

Wulf, G. and Lewthwaite, R., 2009. Conceptions of ability affect motor learning. *Journal of Motor Behavior*, 41 (5), 461–467.

# 25

# THE CHILD AND ADOLESCENT SPORT DROPOUT PROBLEM: COULD MODIFYING THE COACHING MICRO-SYSTEM CLIMATE HELP?

*Stephen Cobley and Kylie Moulds*

## Introduction

### *The Big Picture of Child and Adolescent Health Problems and Benefits from Sport Participation*

*Lack of activity destroys the good condition of every human being, while movement and methodical physical exercise save it and preserve it.* (Plato)

Globally, within developed(ing) countries, childhood and adolescent physical inactivity and obesity represent societal health concerns due to their immediate and longer-term impact on health (Ng *et al.*, 2014). Research has identified how sustained sedentary behaviour is associated with several negative developmental outcomes, including psychological well-being (e.g. self-esteem – Tremblay *et al.*, 2011; Suchert *et al.*, 2015); clinical psychological conditions (e.g. depression – Hoare *et al.*, 2016; Liu *et al.*, 2016), physical health (e.g. less favourable cardiometabolic risk profiles – Chastin *et al.*, 2015) and social health development (e.g. Iannotti et al., 2013). Meanwhile, childhood obesity in the short-term has been negatively associated with fundamental movement skill development (Tompsett *et al.*, 2017; Han *et al.*, 2018) and increased risks of psychological co-morbidities, including depression as well as emotional (e.g. anxiety; Sanders *et al.*, 2015) and behavioural disorders (e.g. ADHD; Cortese et al., 2015). In the longer-term, childhood obesity has been associated with negative health trajectories into adulthood, including greater risks of multiple physiological conditions such as type II diabetes (Morrison *et al.* 2010), cardiovascular disease (Tirosh *et al.*, 2011; Ajala, 2017), and multiple forms of cancer (Ahlgren *et al.*, 2004; Biro and Wien, 2010).

Given broader societal health concerns, the importance of physical activity opportunities within the child and adolescent years (i.e. 5–18 years – WHO, 2020) across multiple locations (e.g. backyard – national park spaces) and societal organisations (e.g. local school & community provision) would seem of paramount importance. And, by logical extension, the multiple


DOI: 10.4324/9781003199359-29

modalities of localised sport provision should have a prominent role to play. In fact, studies suggest children who use sport as a platform to be physically active, and who sustain engagement throughout adolescence, are associated with multiple physical, psychological, and social health benefits (e.g. Eime *et al.*, 2013). Sustained regular sport participation has been associated with increased aerobic fitness (Janssen and LeBlanc, 2010), lower body fat (Ortega *et al.*, 2008), favourable cardiovascular and metabolic disease risk profiles (Biddle *et al.*, 2004), enhanced bone health (Smith *et al.*, 2014) and reduced likelihoods of reporting psychological symptoms related to conditions like depression and anxiety (Bailey, 2006). Thus, sport participation could help counteract negative health trends and provide an avenue for positive health trajectories. However, sabotaging the argument is evidence suggesting how a substantial proportion of children either temporarily or permanently dropout from sport before adolescence (Armentrout and Kamphoff, 2011), reducing the likelihood of accruing physical, psychological and social benefits. On these grounds, this chapter emphasises how Child and Adolescent Sport Dropout (CASD) should be viewed as (generally) problematic, unhealthy, and be addressed where possible.

## Review of Current Research

### *Definitions and Measurements of Child and Adolescent Sport Dropout (CASD)*

Sustained sporting participation has previously been referred to as maintained involvement within one (or more) sporting activity for over one year or more (Weiss *et al.*, 2001). Yet, by contrast, dropout has been more challenging to define due to behavioural nuances (Alfermann, 2014). Most commonly, 'dropout' has referred to those who have discontinued involvement in a sport context across a given time-period of tracking, and who have not re-registered to participate over one or more successive seasons or annual periods (Butcher *et al.*, 2002; Balish *et al.*, 2014; Crane and Temple, 2015; Fraser-Thomas and Côté, 2016). Still, inter-changeable terms have been utilised, including sport 'attrition', 'discontinuation', 'disengagement', and 'dropoff', with their commonality referring to forms of temporary to permanent behaviour cessation. Alternative terms (e.g. dropoff) have been applied, particularly when not implying permanent withdrawal, acknowledging the possibility of returning to participate at a later age-group or stage (Lindner *et al.*, 1991).

While CASD is negatively framed for the purpose of this chapter, it is also noteworthy to recognise circumstances when CASD may be normatively or positively framed. Several authors (e.g. Pion *et al.*, 2015; Battaglia and Kerr, 2020) have characterised CASD as a normative decision-making process about (less-)preferred activity engagement. They regard 'trying-out' or 'sampling' (Côté, 1999) of different sporting activities in childhood as a process inevitably involving short-term 'dropoff'. Such behaviours may precede later (more permanent) decisions on whether to pursue a sporting activity (or not); thus, both 'dropoff' and 'dropout' terms may be relevant. By comparison, intentional withdrawal should be considered positive and protective when physical and/or psychosocial sporting environments are harmful, abusive or toxic (Lindner *et al.*, 1991; Bean *et al.*, 2014). Withdrawal here may speak more about the unhealthiness of a sporting system, including its policies, values, social structures (Cobley, 2016) and/or the potential actions, social skills, and activities deployed by those who operate within them (e.g. coaches, program managers etc.; Rongen *et al.*, 2020). These circumstances serve to act as caveats to CASD framing. If the latter types of culture or social milieu exist within child/adolescent segments of sporting organisations, then arguably an additional set of 'societal problems' could be considered.

Bar noted exceptions, CASD assessment can be considered an easily measured rudimentary behavioural indicator of dissatisfaction from sport engagement. Still, dropout is not consistently tracked or critically examined as part of normative practice within sporting organisations. In research studies, dropout has most commonly been assessed using frequency counts of participants who have (not) re-registered in the same sport for successive seasons (Balish *et al.*, 2014; Crane and Temple, 2015). However, more recently, studies have begun to track participants across multiple years using (re-)registration data and numerous analytical techniques. These include hazard ratios (e.g. Pion *et al.*, 2015), hazard rates (e.g. Moulds *et al.*, 2020), relative risk ratios (Manz *et al.*, 2016), and retention rates relative to baseline norms (e.g. Sabo and Veliz 2016). Such indices have the benefit of estimating dropout rates while accounting for exposure time-periods (Blagoev *et al.*, 2012); help account for sample size in respective comparison groups (e.g. Hazard Ratios – Bradburn *et al.*, 2003), and provide estimates relative to normative trends (e.g. prior years of dropout rate). Collectively, these progressions help improve estimation accuracy as to the prevalence and rapidity of CASD. That said, dropout rates may still fail to unpack the influential factors and explanatory narratives for why dropout may be occurring in a given context.

CASD may occur due to either specific or multiple psychological, social, physical, or environmental factors. CASD may also occur due to interactions between such factors (i.e. simple-complex processes) and could be relatively stable or dynamic (i.e. [not] changing over time). These factors, processes and dynamics may apply at a group or cohort level but not at an idiosyncratic level (and vice versa). Thus, being able to unpack and understand what may influence CASD at an individual-cohort level requires the application of a comprehensive, multi-factorial, meta-theoretical framework. Bronfenbrenner's Bio-Ecological Human Development Theory (1979, 2005) is considered as one such framework.

## CASD According to Bronfenbrenner's Bio-Ecological Development Theory and Process-Person-Context-Time (PPCT) Model

According to Bronfenbrenner's (1979) original Ecological Human Development Theory (1979), positive (e.g. psychological, social and physical health) or negative development (e.g. CASD; psychological problems) occur via means of frequent social and behavioural (dis-)functional exchanges and interactions over time between the biological, psychological, and socially functioning individual (including their pre-existing characteristics) with other individuals within proximal micro-systems (e.g. family members at home; Bronfenbrenner and Morris, 1998). The theory proposes how functional exchanges and interactions beyond the home (i.e. nested within meso-systems), with coaches in childhood/adolescent sport settings – alongside locations, spaces, resources, symbols, objects, and meaning in such settings – can lead to bi-directional development (Bronfenbrenner, 2005). Further, broader cultural values, regulations, and policies in distal macro-systems (e.g. sport governing policies) are also proposed to (potentially) impact the nature of developmental activities and inter-relationships within more localised tiers of the ecological system (Bronfenbrenner, 2005; Bronfenbrenner and Morris, 2006). Thus, for example, state/national sport systems, structures and their ascribed purpose or meaning at specific participation or athlete development stages can all come to influence the nature of individual-coach as well as individual-peer interactions and the nature of their relationships.

To help explain how interactions across levels of the social-ecological system could influence individual functioning and development, Bronfenbrenner and Morris (2006) proposed the *Process-Person-Context-Time* (PPCT) model. Here, *Process* refers to factors associated with the direct and reciprocal nature of interactions (i.e. verbal, non-verbal) over time, between the individual and others across layers of the ecological system (Bronfenbrenner and Morris, 1998).

*Person* considers the pre-existing bio-psycho-social feature characteristics of individuals (i.e. age, sex, motivations, attitudes) that may interact and influence others within a micro-system. *Context* refers to the constant or dynamic factor features within an individual's ecology. Notably, where the individual devotes significant proportions of time in particular locations or spaces and with others. Parental encouragement (i.e. social support in the micro-system), financial support from the sport context (e.g. club – meso-system), as well as local sporting facility provision (i.e. exo-system and macro-system characteristics; Bronfenbrenner and Morris, 1998) are examples of context-related factors. Lastly, *Time* refers both to the existence and (in-)stability of activities and (in-)stability of interactions over time. For example, *Micro-time* refers to interactions and events occurring within relatively short time-courses of a specific activity (e.g. training or competition). *Meso-time* relates to the frequency of events and/or exchanges transpiring with a degree of consistency over longer time-periods, such as weeks or months (e.g. consistency of social support); while *macro-time* considers the influence of stable or changeable interactions and/or activities over extended time-periods within the ecosystem (e.g. years of sporting involvement). Based on information obtained across the PPCT model, explanations (known as *processes*) for how distinguishing factors and their interactions across and within tiers of an individual's ecological system can be identified to account for (dis-)functional development. On this basis, the PPCT model provides a multi-factorial reference frame for helping identify a greater range of *factors* and *processes* involved in CASD within particular sporting contexts.

## A Case Study Application of the PPCT Model: Australian State Swimming

As a case study example, in Australia, swimming is a popular sport for children and adolescents (Sport Australia, 2019). Akin to other sports, Swimming Australia has a structural pathway connecting initial participation to respective competition levels for junior-senior members. Swimming New South Wales (SNSW) is a state affiliate that implement participation and competition structures. These structures expand with age into several competitive tiers (i.e. club, district, region, state and national). In their large-scale examination of CASD in SNSW swimming, Moulds *et al.* (2020) examined the CASD trends of N = 17,161 swimmers (10–15 years old) over a five-year tracking period using survival analysis techniques. Moulds *et al.* (2020) identified that the median number of years of sustained participation before dropout (i.e. no re-registration after two years) was four years. However, 48% and 50% of females and males respectively dropped out from swimming within two years at 10 and 11 years old. Based on available data and when aligned with the PPCT model, several influential factors were identified. The *Person* characteristic of age was influential, with a 184.9% higher hazard rate of dropout apparent for 10- vs. 15-year-olds, irrespective of sex (see Figure 25.1a). In *Context* terms, residential proximity to major cities was influential, with swimmers registered with urban (NSW city-based) clubs reporting a 24.8% higher dropout risk than rural club-based swimmers. Further, in a subsample of competitive female ($n$ = 1,011) and male ($n$ = 811) swimmers (12–15 years), the influence of competition level was identified, with an 86% increased dropout risk for swimmers participating at lower competition levels (i.e. club/district v national; see Figure 25.1b). These trends were relatively stable over time (i.e. annual macro-cycles) irrespective of age and other factors and were not affected by the time point of assessment. These findings also aligned large cohort studies in international multi-sport contexts, where age and competition level were also identified as influential to CASD (i.e. Rottensteiner *et al.*, 2015; Vella *et al.*, 2020).

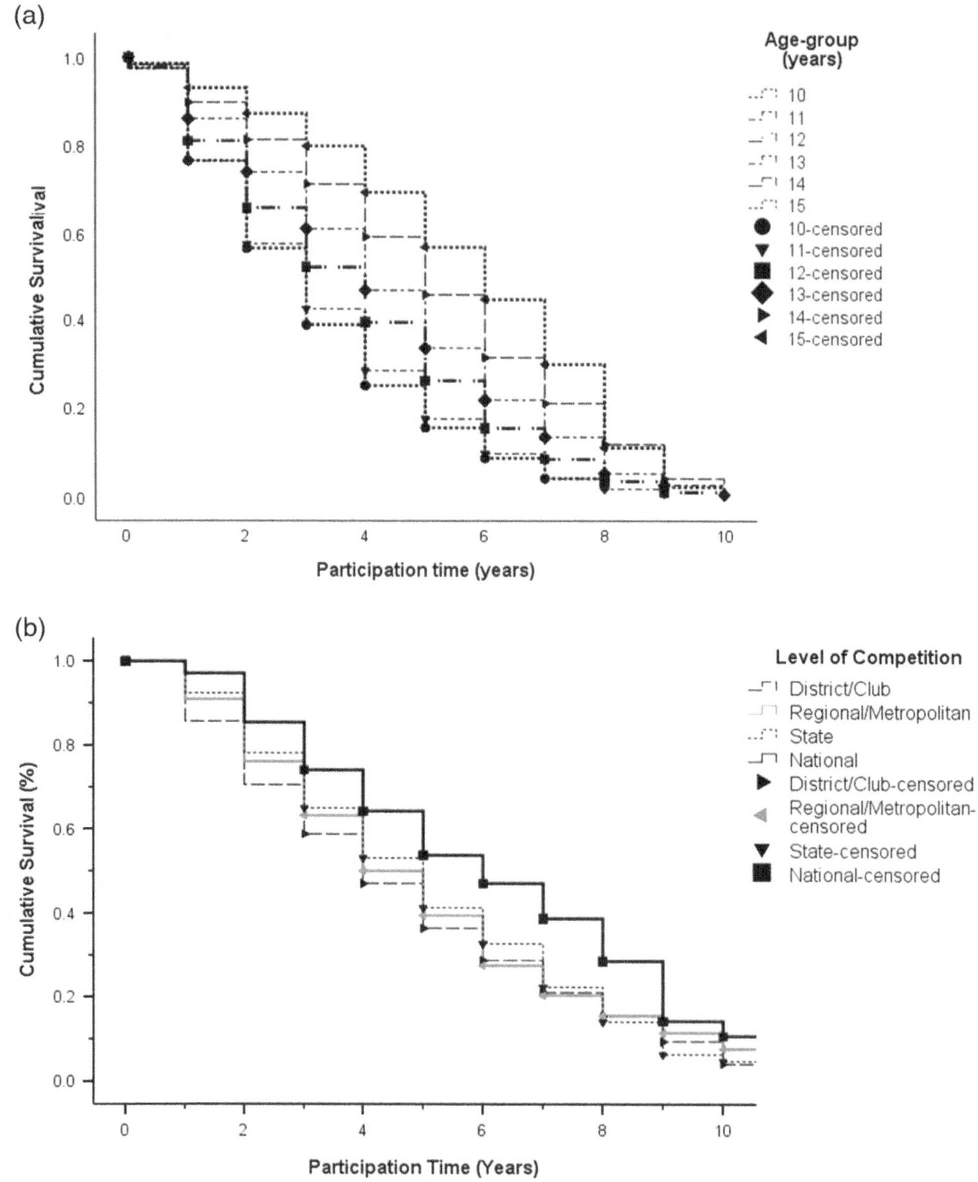


*Figure 25.1* a & b Kaplan-Meier survival curves illustrating dropout (or conversely sustained participated over years) according to the influence of age-group (25.1a) and competition level (25.1b)

Theoretically, findings from Australian and Canadian swimming international studies suggest the possibility of similar or different explanatory processes. For instance, in swimming, given the strength of association between age and competition level with dropout, Fraser-Thomas *et al.* (2008) and Moulds *et al.* (2020) proffered how early age changes in emphasis from 'learn to swim' programs to 'competitive swimming', and their differential valuing or treatment of swimmers based on early-age performance, may be significant to

CASD. Many early age participants may enter club swimming with different, or alternative, motives for swimming which may not match/align with coaching, club, or broader sport system motives and priorities (Light *et al.*, 2013). Such an account may align with Canadian ice-hockey, where youth who progressed into a more advanced playing level received additional coaching, competition opportunities and were more valued. By contrast, negative experiences for those not selected may have accentuated their motive to dropout (Lemez *et al.*, 2014).

To further illustrate the bio-ecological framework's benefits, Moulds *et al.* (2022) recently utilised the PPCT model in their systematic review of all CASD literature. Based on 69 identified studies who collectively attempted to assess the influence of approximately 90 independent factors on CASD, they categorised all examined factors according to the PPCT model (i.e. *Process* – $n$ = 23; *Person* – $n$ = 27; *Context* – $n$ = 30; *Time* – $n$ = 10). While not all factors were associated with CASD across contexts examined worldwide, Moulds *et al.* (2022) were able to identify the most consistently (i.e. ≥4 studies) identified influential factors within each PPCT category (see Table 25.1 for a summary). These included: (Process – *coach-athlete relationships, competition structure)*, (Person – *competence perception, enjoyment)* and (Context – *coach social support).* On this basis themes or constructs are considered which may connect across identified factors whilst recognising the possibility of multiple implications and strategies to address CASD.

*Table 25.1* An overview of common (identified in ≥4 studies) influential factors in YSD. Grouped according to Bronfenbrenner and Morris's (2006) PPCT model

| *Process* | *Person* | *Context* | *Time* |
|---|---|---|---|
| Coach-athlete relationships[>] | Age | Parental support | Time use characteristics[*] (e.g. time demand v alternative activities) |
| Competition structure[+] | Sex | Peer support | Sport game/practice scheduling conflict |
| Relative age | Injury/illness | Coach support[<] | Frequency of practice sessions/competitions overtime |
| Type of sport (e.g. Individual v Team) | Perceived enjoyment | Resource demands (e.g. parental socio-demographics/work commitments; transport availability/costs) | Duration of sport competition events |
| Perceived pressure to perform | Perception of competence<br>Types of motivation | Geographic location (e.g. urban/rural) | |

*Notes*: Literature indicates individual factors are associated dropout (i.e. not inter-related factors across the PPCT levels).> = Coach-athlete relationship variables include communication, coaching styles, technical instruction (knowledge and teaching new skills) and feedback (Lyle, 2005). + = Competition structure refers to sub-types of a competition structure assessed for an association with dropout, (e.g. competition level, junior ranking, performance levels, team selection); < = Coach social-support refers to a supporting relationship illustrated through the creation of a positive, fair and caring emotional environment (e.g. mentorship); * = Time use characteristics refer to a perceived lack of time (i.e. weekly time in hours spent on sports, school, work, social activities).

## Implications for Child and Adolescent Sport Coaching

### *Why Coaching Climates Matter in Child and Adolescent Sport*

Bio-ecological theory and accompanying PPCT model also provides a framework to identify possible CASD solutions and potential intervention points across multiple levels of a sport ecological system. These may range from soliciting national sport governing structural or policy change at the macro-system level to parent/coach education at the micro-system level. However, given the more consistent factors influential to CASD and the intention to achieve more immediate impact at a localised level, targeting coaching behaviours and the psychosocial characteristics of childhood/adolescent sporting micro-systems maybe most appropriate. Considered as architects at the epicentre of childhood/adolescent sport, coaches both design and implement learning as well as training activities (Lyle, 2005), and facilitate inter-individual social interactions (i.e. coach-participant, peer-peer; Temple and Crane, 2016). Scaffolding engagement, coaches provide ongoing technical, tactical, and instructional feedback to support learning and development. Junior coaches frequently interact (i.e. x hours within a week) with participants, providing consistent, stable, social support and encouragement across activity sessions (micro-time periods) and training/competition periods (i.e. meso- and macro-cycles; Fraser-Thomas *et al.*, 2008; Rottensteiner *et al.*, 2013). Further, from their created challenges and experience, coaches aid the learning of 'life-skill lessons' learned' which may have valuable spillover effects into other life areas (e.g. education, employment; Bean *et al.*, 2020; Martin *et al.*, 2021). But what kind of coaching climate is associated with helping maintain sport participation and achieving positive developmental outcomes?

### *Coaching Climates Favourable to Sustained Child and Adolescent Sport Participation*

An emerging body of research emphasises the importance of coach-created motivational climates to sustained child and adolescent sport participation (Appleton *et al.*, 2016). Put another way, what coaches do and how they do it shapes an individual's interpretation (i.e. perceptions, meaning) and subsequent behaviour (e.g. individual learning; social experience). Integrating constructs from Achievement Goal (Nicholls, 1984) and Self-Determination (Deci and Ryan, 1985; Deci and Ryan, 2000) theory, Duda (2013) presents a dualistic conceptualisation of motivational climate, known as a coach-created *Empowering* or *Disempowering* climate.

An empowering motivational climate is characterised as having a combination of task-involving, autonomy-supportive and socially supportive characteristics. More specifically task-involving refers to coaches implementing encouraging and reinforcing values related to personal task effort; a work ethic toward personal skill improvement and self-betterment; as well as individual contribution toward collective (social or team) tasks. The coach may implement skill learning drill/activities orientated toward these values or may encourage such values during activities where individuals are focused on skill mastery, problem-solving or effective teamwork. Autonomy-supportive coaching is evident when the coach takes the participants' perspective into account, encourages choice and decision-making during problem-solving or learning, as well as acknowledges and recognises participant emotions or feelings (Mageau and Vallerand, 2003). Socially-supportive coaching refers to a genuine interest in athlete welfare. The coach demonstrates care and concern for athlete's well-being and provides social encouragement and support during learning/training activities. A socially supportive coach respects his or her athletes and does not demand respect in return (Reinboth and Duda, 2004).

By comparison, disempowering climates are commonly characterised by features of ego-involving (e.g. result focussed) and controlling (e.g. authoritarian) instruction, social interaction patterns, and behaviours (Duda, 2013; Duda and Appleton, 2016). Ego-involving coaching often refers to differential treatment based on (perceived) capability or present competence differences. In this climate, the coach may create a competitive rivalry between participants, focus on out-performing others (Newton *et al.*, 2000), and create inequity in participation and social engagement opportunities. Finally, the controlling dimension refers to how a coach will dictate participant behaviours, social interaction, and performance within training and competition settings. Controlling behaviour includes pressurising, coercing, intimidation and threatening behaviours during interactions. Such coaches may more likely use extrinsic rewards/reinforcements to manipulate participant behaviour (Bartholomew *et al.*, 2010). For further definitions and examples of empowering and disempowering climates, see Table 25.2.

*Table 25.2* Summary examples of empowering and disempowering coaching behaviours according to training and contexts (Duda, 2013; Smith *et al.*, 2015; Cobley, 2016)

| *Empowering coaching climates to prevent CASD* | *Recommended coaching behaviours in a training environment* | *Recommended coaching behaviours in environment a competition environment* |
|---|---|---|
| **Autonomy supportive** | Encourages athlete choice and decision-making within the training setting.<br>Encourages athletes to participate in regular training for intrinsic reasons (e.g. enjoyment, curiosity, self-learning) | Encourages athlete choice to participate in competition.<br>Encourages participation for intrinsic reasons (e.g. enjoyment, curiosity, self-challenge). |
| | Facilitates and provides the rationale for appropriate age and context-related training drills/activities/tasks. | Before, during (where possible) and after competition, the coach answers athletes' questions openly and honestly. |
| | Communicates in a way during training to allow for athlete self-exploration, problem-solving, self-choice and volition. | Communicates in a way before and after competition to allow the athlete to self-explore, problem-solve, providing choice and volition. |
| | Encourages and acknowledges athletes' feelings and perspectives within training situations, providing opportunities for athlete input/feedback. | Encourages and acknowledges athletes' feelings and perspectives towards competition, providing opportunities for athlete input/feedback. |
| **Task involving** | Creates training drills/activities/tasks with variety and novelty but geared toward individual development.<br>Provides individual task-focused feedback and individual encouragement. | Encourages athletes to practice new skills (technical, tactical, physical, psychological) in a competitive game situation with the overall goal of achieving personal skill mastery. |
| | Explains the importance of different athlete roles on a team and creates situations to facilitate cooperative learning with an emphasis on learning and developing new skills. | Emphasises self-based skill improvement (technical, tactical, physical, psychological) in a game situation above winning or losing. |

(*Continued*)

*Table 25.2* (Continued)

| *Empowering coaching climates to prevent CASD* | *Recommended coaching behaviours in a training environment* | *Recommended coaching behaviours in environment a competition environment* |
|---|---|---|
| **Socially supportive** | Recognises/emphasises athlete personal effort and creates a feeling of success if athletes invested effort and persistence during training. | Recognises/emphasises athlete effort and contribution to the broader goals/objectives. Creates a feeling of success if athletes tried hard and persistence during game situations. |
| | Facilitates an inclusive environment (i.e. all athletes are included in drills, tasks, activities), emphasising connection, inclusion, fun, enjoyment, fosters a sense of belonging during training. | Encourages all athletes to contribute their effort, personal skills, whilst working toward individual or team goals during a game situation. |
| | Listens openly and without judgement regarding athletes' personal feelings | Provides all athletes with an equally important role to play on the team. |
| | Adopts a warm and inviting communication style | Encourages peer social support and encouragement during a game situation. |
| | Appreciates each athlete as a person. The coach can be relied upon for support as a teacher, mentor, leader regardless of the training outcome | Provides a shared social and emotional experience – facilitating connection, inclusion, fun, enjoyment. Fosters a sense of belonging within the competitive setting. |
| | | Coach can be relied upon for support as a teacher, mentor, leader regardless of the performance outcome. |
| *Disempowering coaching climates potentially associated with CASD* | *Coaching behaviours to avoid in a training environment* | *Coaching behaviours to avoid in a competition environment* |
| **Controlling** | Relies on controlling language and intimidation to get athletes to complete training drills/ activities/tasks | Threatens to punish athletes after poor performances, displays social judgement, labelling and competency fixation. |
| | Devalues the athlete's perspective, provides little opportunity for athlete input/feedback | Less supportive of athletes if they perform poorly |
| | Uses extrinsic rewards when completing training sessions | Uses rewards for winning |
| | Shouts at athletes during training to make them do things | Shouts at athletes before, during and after a match to make them do things |
| | Training drills/activities/tasks are often tedious and unvaried, punishes athletes for mistakes during a training session | |

(*Continued*)

*Table 25.2* (Continued)

| *Disempowering coaching climates potentially associated with CASD* | *Coaching behaviours to avoid in a training environment* | *Coaching behaviours to avoid in a competition environment* |
|---|---|---|
| **Ego- involving** | Excludes/substitutes athletes from training drills/activities/tasks when they make mistakes | Excludes/substitutes athletes when they make mistakes |
| | Coach may have favourite athletes and provides additional opportunities in training to athletes with perceived ability | Coach may have favourite athletes and provides additional competitive opportunities to athletes with perceived ability |
| | Emphasises superior/inferior performance over skill development in a training situation | Emphasises superior/inferior performance over skill development |
| | Devalues peer support and teamwork | Devalues peer support/teamwork and encourages success via inter/intrateam rivalry |

To date, coaching motivational climates have been assessed using two psychometric instruments, namely The Empowering and Disempowering Motivational Climate Questionnaire (EDMCQ-C – Appleton *et al.*, 2016) and The Multidimensional Motivational Climate Observation System (MMCOS – Smith *et al.*, 2014). Drawing on Duda's (2013) conceptualisation, the EDMCQ-C uses 34 items on a 5-point Likert scale to capture the extent to which athletes perceive their coach to be: Autonomy Supportive, Task-Involving, Socially Supportive, Controlling and Ego-Involving. Meanwhile, the MMCOS is an observational rating system where coaching behaviours are coded according to empowering and disempowering dimensions. Both instruments have been utilised to help assess the effect of coaching climate change. For instance, based on the Promoting Adolescent Physical Activity (PAPA) project conducted across five European countries (N = 7,661) in junior soccer, findings identified that when empowering coaching climate dimensions were successfully implemented, child and adolescent enjoyment was facilitated and participation was sustained (e.g. Quested *et al.*, 2015). Thus, coaches who can create and establish higher perceived empowerment and lower-rated disempowerment have the potential to generate positive cognitive and emotional outcomes and achieve sustained sport participation (Appleton and Duda, 2016).

## Summary, Future Directions and Future Research

From a research and sport organisational standpoint, future studies which address the definitional, theoretical causes (factors/processes involved), measurement and analytical limitations of sport dropout would be most beneficial. For instance, within a multi-level, multi-factorial framework (e.g. PPCT model), longitudinal assessment of dropout patterns within sport contexts are recommended. Correspondingly, advanced analytical approaches including survival analysis (e.g. Pion *et al.*, 2015), structural equational modelling (e.g. Sarrazin *et al.*, 2016), and multiple logistic regression could either help better estimate dropout odds or rates, or help identify the influence of independent (or interacting) factors. Such future directions would subsequently help identify CASD-targeted intervention or prevention strategies.

For sport contexts with heightened rates of CASD, perhaps the most immediate recommendation and future direction is to establish system-wide stakeholder knowledge and awareness of the problem and consider intervention options across and within the sport. Causal factor identification via application of the PPCT model would help identify courses for action. As forms of coaching behaviour (i.e. *coach-athlete relationship, coach social-support)* were identified as most frequently influential to CASD in a recent systematic review, the assessment of motivational climates or coaching culture across the CAS aspects of a sport system may prove valuable. At present, many sport system operators (e.g. managers and administrators) may not fully understand how coaching climates may associate with CASD, and how micro-climate change at a local level could be significantly beneficial to participation. Implementing coach education or professional development programs targeted at improving coach motivational climates could be a viable, organisation-wide, cost-effective strategy. The positive immediate outcomes may be a greater likelihood of sustained sport participation, while in the longer-term an increased likelihood to accrue multiple health benefits from child and adolescent sport.

## References

Ahlgren, M., *et al.*, 2004. Growth patterns and the risk of breast cancer in women. *New England Journal of Medicine*, 351 (16), 1619–1626.

Ajala, O., *et al.*, 2017. Childhood predictors of cardiovascular disease in adulthood: A systematic review and meta-analysis. *Obesity Reviews*, 18 (9), 1061–1070.

Alfermann, D., 2014. Drop-out. *In:* R.C. Eklund and G. Tenenbaum, eds. *Encyclopedia of sport and exercise psychology*. Thousand Oaks: Sage, 216–217.

Appleton, P.R., *et al.*, 2016. Initial validation of the coach-created empowering and disempowering motivational climate questionnaire (EDMCQ-C). *Psychology of Sport and Exercise*, 22, 53–65.

Appleton, P.R. and Duda, J.L., 2016. Examining the interactive effects of coach-created empowering and disempowering climate dimensions on athletes' health and functioning. *Psychology of Sport and Exercise*, 26, 61–70.

Armentrout, S.M. and Kamphoff, C.S., 2011. Organisational barriers and factors that contribute to youth hockey attrition. *Journal of Sport Behavior*, 34 (2), 121–136.

Bailey, R., 2006. Physical education and sport in schools: a review of benefits and outcomes. *Journal of School Health*, 76 (8), 397–401.

Balish, S.M., *et al.*, 2014. Correlates of youth sport attrition: A review and future directions. *Psychology of Sport and Exercise*, 15 (4), 429–439.

Bartholomew, K.J., Ntoumanis, N., and Thorgersen-Ntoumani, C., 2010. The controlling interpersonal style in a coaching context: Development and initial validation of a psychometric scale. *Journal of Sport and Exercise Psychology*, 32 (2), 193–216.

Battaglia, A. and Kerr, G., 2020. Exploring sport stakeholders' interpretations of the term dropout from youth sport. *Journal of Applied Sport Psychology*, 34 (1), 1–22.

Bean, C., Kramers, S., and Harlow, M., 2020. Exploring life skills transfer processes in youth hockey and volleyball. *International Journal of Sport and Exercise Psychology*, 20 (1), 1–20.

Bean, C.N., *et al.*, 2014. Understanding how organised youth sport may be harming individual athletes within the family unit: A literature review. *International Journal of Environmental Research and Public Health*, 11 (10), 10226–10268.

Biddle, S.J.H., Gorely, T., and Stensel, D.J., 2004. Health-enhancing physical activity and sedentary behaviour in children and adolescents. *Journal of Sports Sciences*, 22 (8), 679–701.

Biro, F.M. and Wien, M., 2010. Childhood obesity and adult morbidities. *American Journal of Clinical Nutrition*, 91 (5), 1499–1505.

Blagoev, K.B., Wilkerson, J., and Fojo, T., 2012. Hazard ratios in cancer clinical trials-a primer. *Nature Reviews Clinical Oncology*, 9 (3), 178–183.

Bradburn, M.J., *et al.*, 2003. Survival analysis part II: Multivariate data analysis–An introduction to concepts and methods. *British Journal of Cancer*, 89 (3), 431–436.

Bronfenbrenner, U., 1979. *The ecology of human development: Experiments by nature and design*. United Kingdom: Harvard University Press.

Bronfenbrenner, U., 2005. Bioecological theory of human development. *In:* U. Bronfenbrenner, ed. *Making human beings human: Bioecological perspectives on human development*. India: SAGE Publications, 15–33.

Bronfenbrenner, U. and Morris, P., 1998. The ecology of human developmental processes. *In:* W. Damon and R.M. Lerner, eds. 5th ed. *Handbook of child psychology: Theoretical models of human development*. New York: Wiley, 993–1028.

Bronfenbrenner, U. and Morris, P., 2006. The ecology of human developmental processes. *In*: W. Damon and R.M. Lerner, eds. 6th ed. *Handbook of child psychology: Theoretical models of human development*. New York: Wiley, 793–828.

Butcher, J., Lindner, K.J., and Johns, D.P., 2002. Withdrawal from competitive youth sport: A retrospective ten-year study. *Journal of Sport Behavior*, 25 (2), 145–163.

Chastin, S.F., *et al.*, 2015. Combined effects of time spent in physical activity, sedentary behaviors and sleep on obesity and cardio-metabolic health markers: A novel compositional data analysis approach. *PloS One*, 10 (10), 1–37.

Cobley, S., 2016. Talent identification and development in youth sport. *In*: K. Green and A. Smith, eds. *Routledge handbook of youth sport*. Abingdon: Routledge, 506–521.

Cortese, S., *et al.*, 2015. Cognitive training for attention-deficit/hyperactivity disorder: Meta-analysis of clinical and neuropsychological outcomes from randomized controlled trials. *Journal of American Academy of Child and Adolescent Psychiatry*, 54 (3), 164–174.

Côté, J., 1999. The influence of the family in the development of talent in sport. *Sport Psychologist*, 13 (4), 395–417.

Crane, J. and Temple, V., 2015. A systematic review of dropout from organised sport among children and youth. *European Physical Education Review*, 21 (1), 114–131.

Deci, E.L. and Ryan, R.M., 1985. Conceptualisations of intrinsic motivation and self-determination. *In:* E.L. Deci and R.M. Ryan, eds. *Intrinsic motivation and self-determination in human behavior*. Boston: Springer, 11–40.

Deci, E.L. and Ryan, R.M., 2000. The "what" and "why" of goal pursuits: Human needs and the self-determination of behavior. *Psychological Inquiry*, 11 (4), 227–268.

Duda, J.L., 2013. The conceptual and empirical foundations of Empowering Coaching™: Setting the stage for the PAPA project. *International Journal of Sport and Exercise Psychology*, 11 (4), 311–318.

Duda, J.L. and Appleton, P.R., 2016. Empowering and disempowering coaching climates: Conceptualisation, measurement considerations, and intervention implications. *In:* M. Raab, *et al.*, eds. *Sport and exercise psychology research: From theory to practise*. London: Academic Press, 373–388.

Eime, R.M., *et al.*, 2013. A systematic review of the psychological and social benefits of participation in sport for adults: Informing development of a conceptual model of health through sport. *International Journal of Behavioral Nutrition and Physical Activity*, 10 (1), 1–14.

Fraser-Thomas, J. and Côté, J., 2016. Understanding adolescents' positive and negative developmental experiences in sport. *The Sport Psychologist*, 23 (1), 3–23.

Fraser-Thomas, J., Cote, J., and Deakin, J., 2008. Examining adolescent sport dropout and prolonged engagement from a developmental perspective. *Journal of Applied Sport Psychology*, 20 (3), 318–333.

Han, A., *et al.*, 2018. Effectiveness of exercise intervention on improving fundamental movement skills and motor coordination in overweight/obese children and adolescents: A systematic review. *Journal of Science and Medicine in Sport*, 21 (1), 89–102.

Hoare, E., *et al.*, 2016. The associations between sedentary behaviour and mental health among adolescents: A systematic review. *International Journal of Behavioral Nutrition and Physical Activity*, 13 (1).

Iannotti, L., *et al.*, 2013. Review of the safety and efficacy of vitamin A supplementation in the treatment of children with severe acute malnutrition. *Nutrition Journal*, 12, 125.

Janssen, I. and LeBlanc, A.G., 2010. Systematic review of the health benefits of physical activity and fitness in school-aged children and youth. *International Journal of Behavioral Nutrition and Physical Activity*, 7 (40).

Lemez, S., *et al.*, 2014. Examining the relationship between relative age, competition level, and dropout rates in male youth ice-hockey players. *Scandinavian Journal of Medicine & Science in Sports*, 24 (6), 935–942.

Light, R., *et al.*, 2013. Why children join and stay in sports clubs: case studies in Australian, French and German swimming clubs. *Sport, Education and Society*, 18 (4), 550–566.

Lindner, K.J., Johns, D.P., and Butcher, J., 1991. Factors in withdrawal from youth sport: A proposed model. *Journal of Sport Behavior*, 14 (1), 3–18.

Liu, M., Wu, L., and Yao, S., 2016. Dose–response association of screen time-based sedentary behaviour in children and adolescents and depression: A meta-analysis of observational studies. *British Journal of Sports Medicine*, 50 (20), 1252–1258.

Lyle, J., 2005. *Sports coaching concepts: A framework for coaches' behaviour*. London: Routledge.

Manz, K., *et al.*, 2016. Determinants of organised sports participation patterns during the transition from childhood to adolescence in Germany: Results of a nationwide cohort study. *BMC Public Health*, 16 (1), 939–952.

Mageau, G.A. and Vallerand, R.J., 2003. The coach athlete relationship: A motivational model. *Journal of Sports Sciences*, 21 (11), 883–904.

Martin, N., Camiré, M., and Kramers, S., 2021. Facilitating life skills transfer from sport to the classroom: An intervention assisting a high school teacher-coach. *Journal of Applied Sport Psychology*, 1–25.

Morrison, J.A., *et al.*, 2010. Childhood predictors of adult type 2 diabetes at 9- and 26-year follow-ups. *Archives of Pediatrics and Adolescent Medicine*, 164 (1), 53–60.

Moulds, K., *et al.*, 2020. Sink or swim? A survival analysis of sport dropout in australian youth swimmers. *Scandinavian Journal of Medicine and Science in Sports*, 30 (11) 2222–2233.

Moulds, K., *et al.*, 2022. Youth sport dropout according to the process-person-context-time model: A systematic review. *International Review of Sport and Exercise Psychology*, 1–42.

Newton, M., Duda, J.L., and Yin, Z., 2000. Examination of the psychometric properties of the perceived motivational climate in sport questionnaire-2 in a sample of female athletes. *Journal of Sports Sciences*, 18 (4), 275–290.

Nicholls, J.G., 1984. Achievement motivation: Conceptions of ability, subjective experience, task choice, and performance. *Psychological Review*, 91 (3), 328.

Ng, M., *et al.*, 2014. Global, regional, and national prevalence of overweight and obesity in children and adults during 1980-2013: A systematic analysis for the global burden of disease study 2013. *The Lancet*, 384 (9945), 766–781.

Ortega, F.B., *et al.*, 2008. Physical fitness in childhood and adolescence: A powerful marker of health. *International Journal of Obesity*, 32 (1), 1–11.

Pion, J., *et al.*, 2015. Talent in female gymnastics: A survival analysis based upon performance characteristics. *International Journal of Sports Medicine*, 36 (11), 935–940.

Quested, E.J., *et al.*, 2015. The impact of the empowering coaching training programme on the motivational climate and player responses. In *14th FEPSAC congress*, Bern, Switzerland.

Reinboth, M. and Duda, J.L., 2004. The motivational climate, perceived ability, and athletes' psychological and physical well-being. *The Sport Psychologist*, 18 (3), 237–251.

Rongen, F., *et al.*, 2020. Psychosocial outcomes associated with soccer academy involvement: Longitudinal comparisons against aged matched school pupils. *Journal of Sports Sciences*, 38 (11–12), 1387–1398.

Rottensteiner, C., *et al.*, 2013. Personal reasons for withdrawal from team sports and the influence of significant others among youth athletes. *International Journal of Sports Science and Coaching*, 8 (1), 19–32.

Rottensteiner, C., *et al.*, 2015. Sustained participation in youth sports related to coach-athlete relationship and coach-created motivational climate. *International Sport Coaching Journal*, 2 (1), 29–38.

Sabo, D. and Veliz, P., 2016. Inequalities in athletic participation during adolescence: A nationwide study of attrition rates in organised sports in the United States. *Health Behavior and Policy Review*, 3 (2), 88–98.

Sanders, R.H., *et al.*, 2015. Childhood obesity and its physical and psychological co-morbidities: A systematic review of Australian children and adolescents. *European Journal of Pediatrics*, 174 (6), 715–746.

Sarrazin, F., *et al.*, 2016. Global sensitivity analysis of environmental models: Convergence and validation. *Environmental Modelling & Software*, 79, 135–152.

Suchert, V., *et al.*, 2015. Sedentary behavior, depressed affect, and indicators of mental well-being in adolescence: Does the screen only matter for girls? *Journal of Adolescence*, 42 (1), 50–58.

Smith, J.J., *et al.*, 2014. The health benefits of muscular fitness for children and adolescents: A systematic review and meta-analysis. *Sports Medicine*, 44 (9), 1209–1223.

Smith, N., *et al.*, 2015. Development and validation of the multidimensional motivational climate observation system. *Journal of Sport and Exercise Psychology*, 37 (1), 4–22.

Sport Australia, 2019. *Australia's top 20 sports and physical activities revealed* [online]. Canberra: ACT. Available from: https://www.sportaus.gov.au/media_centre/news/australias_top_20_sports_and_physical_activities_revealed [Accessed 1 October 2021].

Temple, V.A. and Crane, J.R., 2016. A systematic review of drop-out from organised soccer among children and adolescents. *Soccer and Society*, 17 (6), 856–881.

Tirosh, A., *et al.*, 2011. Adolescent BMI trajectory and risk of diabetes versus coronary disease. *Survey of Anesthesiology*, 55 (6), 296–297.

Tompsett, C., *et al.*, 2017. Pedagogical approaches to and effects of fundamental movement skill interventions on health outcomes: A systematic review. *Sports Medicine*, 47 (9), 1795–1819.

Tremblay, M.S., *et al.*, 2011. Systematic review of sedentary behaviour and health indicators in school-aged children and youth. *International Journal of Behavioral Nutrition and Physical Activity*, 8, 98.

Vella, S.A., Schweickle, M.J., and Sutcliffe, J.T., 2020. Prevalence of drop-out from organised extra-curricular sports and associations with body fat percentage during childhood and adolescence. *BMJ Open Sport and Exercise Medicine*, 6 (1).

Weiss, M.R., Kimmel, L.A., and Smith, A.L., 2001. Determinants of sport commitment among junior tennis athletes: Enjoyment as a mediating variable. *Pediatric Exercise Science*, 13 (2), 131–144.

World Health Organization, 2020. *Who Guidelines on Physical Activity-WEB ANNEX Evidence Profiles* [online]. Switzerland: World Health Organisation. Available from: https://www.who.int/publications/i/item/9789240015111 [Accessed 27 February 2021].

# 26

# PSYCHO-SOCIAL MATURATION AND THE IMPLICATIONS FOR COACHING CHILDREN

*Fieke Rongen, Ian Cowburn, Sergio Lara-Bercial, Tom Mitchell, and David Piggott*

## Introduction

Understanding who we are coaching is fundamental to coaching practice. In order to understand 'the who' of children's coaching and bring about the benefits that sport has to offer, coaches must be knowledgeable about and consider their athletes in terms of their physiological, physical, cognitive, emotional, and social development (e.g. Abraham *et al.*, 2014; Kipp, 2018). There is a wealth of research literature about physiological and physical development (for a recent example, see Eisenmann *et al.*, 2020), but despite calls for more developmentally orientated sport research since 1983 (Weiss and Bredemeier, 1983) there is scant literature that has explored what children of different ages are typically capable of (or 'are like') psycho-socially in the context of sport (Pankhurst, 2016; Weiss, 2019). Therefore, this chapter will draw on mainstream developmental theories (e.g. Piaget, 1952; Erikson, 1959; Kohlberg, 1963, 1981; Harter, 1999, 2012) to describe *typical* psychological and social milestones and developmental processes and their implications for coaching practice. Where available, this will be supported by research from the sport domain.

The chapter offers representations of 'typical' development, though coaches should be aware there will be considerable variability around this. Development is individual and non-linear, and sport is but one developmental environment in which children are engaged (e.g. school). Consequently, the chapter aims are to allow coaches (1) to articulate 'typical' (expected) participant behaviours and plan developmentally appropriate activities and (2) to reflect on where their participants are in relation to 'typical' expectations and recognise where it may be appropriate to facilitate the development of desirable psycho-social attributes.

## Review of Current Research

This chapter will outline an amalgamated view of what participants may be expected to 'be like' in terms of psycho-social development in the following age-based stages: early childhood (3–6 years old), mid-to-late childhood (6–11 years old), early-to-mid adolescence (11–16 years old).


DOI: 10.4324/9781003199359-30

## *Early Childhood (3–6 Years Old)*

Cognitively, children in this age group are in the pre-operational stage (Piaget, 1952) and possess a relatively short attention span with limited selective attention (Crain, 2016). In this stage, children can represent (and perform) physical actions mentally. They can picture an action/object and manipulate this in their mind which allows for deferred imitation (i.e. seeing a demonstration of a skill and only later trying it themselves). Children of this age like using their newfound skill of imagination and pretend play and activities that allow them to be creative, including theming sessions/activities on familiar topics such as superheroes, popular cartoons or animals will engage them. Children this young typically still rely on perceptual reasoning instead of logic, as they see things in very concrete terms (not abstract representations), it is helpful to show them things rather than rely on descriptions of activities. They can do simple tasks, with few steps/elements, explained in simple language or by copying what they see without really understanding why or how they are doing them, and can be taught a few simple rules (Pankhurst, 2016). This could be a simple game of 'catch' where the ball can only bounce once or a target activity where all they have to do is throw a ball or beanbag towards a target. If more than two instructions need to be remembered they need visible/memorable cues to stay on task (Kushner *et al.*, 2015). As information processing speed and reaction time are relatively slow, planned events are more likely to be successful than unplanned ones (i.e. catch a ball if they know where it will land) and coaches should try to capitalise on this by making activities more predictable.

In terms of a sense of self, children of this age typically have a very positive image of their own abilities and often over-estimate these (Harter, 2012). Equally, their self-attributions lack nuance and they are either 'good' or 'bad' at something (Harter, 2012). Global self-esteem is lacking as children cannot yet combine perceptions of their adequacy across domains such as school and sport (Harter, 2012). They have an undifferentiated view of effort and ability (Nicholls, 1989), meaning that putting in effort and simple task completion will lead children to judge they are good at something. Therefore, it is important to offer many opportunities to explore and repeatedly practice skills (e.g. movements, trying to hit different targets of various sizes and distances with different pieces of equipment), as well as detaching success and failure from winning and losing (e.g. not losing or being knocked out of the game, having unlimited opportunities to go again or defining success differently such as trying another way or persisting, etc).

In terms of how they relate to others, children of this age are egocentric; they regard their needs and desires as their primary focus which may result in easily becoming frustrated when those needs are not met (Feldman, 2004; e.g. when playing football, a child may judge their success based on how many times they kicked the ball, even if their team lost). Although they are beginning to share, they often prefer to still be the centre of attention (Pankhurst, 2016) and are only minimally able to take someone else's perspective (Crain, 2016). Consequently, particularly at younger ages, children prefer individual (by themselves) or parallel play (alongside each other but each working towards their own objectives such as a simple target-based activity) (Kipp, 2018). Toward the end of this age-group cooperative play becomes more feasible but needs to be scaffolded and very simple (e.g. a relay race). Furthermore, what is wrong or right is largely related to what 'authority' figures will permit and/or punish (Gibbs, 2010; Crain, 2016). Although moral decision-making largely relies on what avoids punishment (Crain, 2016), egocentrism also means that children will prefer to break or bend the rules in order to win (Feldman, 2004). To allow fair play, activities need clear rules that decide what is 'right' and 'wrong' and should be balanced without disproportionate advantages for one side. At the same time, some rule breaking should be expected, and coaches should not place too much emphasis on 'playing by the rules' or at least not punishing too harshly when this does not happen.

## *Mid-to-Late Childhood (6–11 Years Old)*

Cognitively, at this stage, children are described as 'concrete operational' (Piaget, 1952). They begin to 'reason' and they start to apply logical operations, including:

- Seriation – ordering along a qualifiable dimension,
- Conservation – something stays the same in quantity even if its appearance changes,
- Classification – categorising/putting together based on a criteria,
- Transitivity – relationship between concepts,
- Decentring – considering more than one aspect of a problem at a time,
- Reversibility – going back and forward between steps.

In a sporting context, if four defenders were positioned across the pitch and they were to spread out, children would now be able to reason there must therefore be more space between the defenders. Equally, the size of a target may now be understood to stay the same no matter the distance away from it. Instructions/tasks can now consist of multiple steps and the concrete operational child can recall them in any order and repeatedly move back and forth between steps. As a result, activities can begin to look like simplified (i.e. low number of players) versions of games/sports with very early notions of time and space, although initially should not focus strongly on strategies or managing new (and unpredictable) situations (Vealey and Chase, 2016).

Children also have an expanded vocabulary and improved memory and attention span but (particularly the younger children in this age-group) will still benefit from instructions delivered in explicit basic and memorable language, alongside visual cues, close to when skills need to be executed and repeated from previous training sessions as well as from immediate feedback (Kushner *et al.*, 2015). Later in this stage children are more able to reflect on what they are doing and what they want to achieve. Equally their ability to plan more consciously, coordinate actions, evaluate progress and modify plans and strategies based on this emerges (Eccles, 1999). They are increasingly capable of understanding verbal feedback, can engage in basic reflection on various aspects of their development (e.g. running vs. passing) and can start to self-adjust form and technique and plan for improvement (e.g. changing the angle of approach to kick a ball in the air) (Visek *et al.*, 2013; Kipp, 2018). However, as hypothetical (future) thinking is limited (Piaget, 1952) and long-term consequences are not yet considered (Visek *et al.*, 2013) for now these skills are largely used to plan and reflect on proximal, concrete situations (i.e. today's practice session; Kipp, 2018).

The main developmental challenge for children this age is establishing a sense of competence (Erikson, 1959), as children start developing a sense of pride in their achievement and a sense of being able to complete projects and reach goals. At the start of this stage children are typically still very optimistic about their abilities, but as their expectations for success tend to decline, by age 10 their self-evaluations become increasingly more accurate but also more negative (Eccles, 1999; Harter, 1999, 2012). For this reason, it is important for coaches to pitch activities at the right level to guarantee sufficient levels of success. Although children start to incorporate more aspects into their self-descriptions, these tend to still focus on general competencies (e.g. nice, smart, sporty) (Harter, 2012).

Mid to late childhood is also characterised by a move away from spending most of their time at home with family into the wider social context of formal education and perhaps more organised afterschool and sporting activities with similar-aged peers. This more homogenous environment (i.e. similar-aged peers, particularly in sport where children are often grouped by age) wherein success and failure are relatively public, may introduce more overt comparison to peers in terms of ability domains (Eccles, 1999; Kipp, 2018). Further, children shift to a partially differentiated view of ability (i.e. ability can explain performance, but effort is still believed to result in improved ability; Nicholls, 1989). Sources of competence information now increasingly include comparison to peers and performance outcomes alongside effort put in, as well as feedback from significant others including peers, teachers (and coaches!) as well as parents and siblings (Harter, 2012). Consequently, to promote the development of a healthy sense of competence, both activities and pedagogy should minimise comparison to others through actively promoting a task-involved focus where success is experienced through skill mastery and achievement of personal-bests (Kipp and Bolter, 2020). This is particularly important as motivation will come mostly from present, task-specific enjoyment rather than perceived future benefits (Kipp, 2018). Although children still need many opportunities to explore and experience success, some experiences of 'safe failure' (with limited, particularly public, consequences) may be introduced via fun-oriented competitions such as a timed target-based task.

At this age children develop the ability to take perspective (Piaget, 1952) and establish a theory of mind (i.e. beliefs guide actions and other people's beliefs may be different from mine) (Piaget, 1952). Awareness of their own complex emotions grows, and although they may still struggle to always understand those emotions (Vernon, 2004) children develop the ability to be empathetic (Crocker *et al.*, 2004). Although they may initially experience stronger connections with parents and other adults (like coaches) than with their peers (Horn and Butt, 2014), as children progress through this stage social acceptance and peer group social status become increasingly important (Kipp, 2018). They become more and more aware of what matters to others and want to contribute to friends' happiness. Equally, a 'we-feeling' beyond cooperation starts to emerge as children can and want to work towards a shared interest (Eccles, 1999). In sports, coaches should promote cooperation and positive interaction (Zakrajsek *et al.*, 2017), for example through working as a team toward a shared, relatively simple objective (e.g. playing doubles in racket sports, or designing a team routine to achieve a score in gymnastics). Moral decision-making shifts somewhat from avoiding punishment to receiving reward for good behaviour, acknowledging that avoidance of punishment does not mean something is 'right'. In line with this, children will need a coach to provide clear rules and regulations and ensure these are consistently modelled and applied with an emphasis on rewarding appropriate behaviours even in the face of unfairness. As with the previous stage, what is right/wrong is about that particular moment or incident rather than a wider appreciation of societal right/wrong or set of values (Gibbs, 2010; Crain, 2016), although children will not only focus on their own experiences and are increasingly able to consider peers and how they might feel about being treated unfairly.

## *Early-to Mid-Adolescence (11–16 Years Old)*

Cognitively, adolescents are described as moving into the formal operational stage (Piaget, 1952), where thinking changes in three fundamental ways (Sanders, 2013). Young people can now explore the full range of possibilities inherent in a situation, consider multiple dimensions of a problem at once, and as such start to plan, reflect and problem solve in greater complexity. Further, this increased rational thinking can be applied to abstract (i.e. non-directly observed or experienced) situations (Strandjord and Rome, 2016). The ability to reason not only inductively (from observed/experienced events to what will typically happen) but also deductively (from general to specific – 'if-then') emerges, and young people are not only able to consider what is, but also increasingly able to think through what could be ('the hypothetical'). Finally, meta-cognition, the ability to think about thinking, develops too (Sanders, 2013). These higher-order cognitive abilities help adolescents in several ways. For example, symbols, signs and code words can be used for communication (Kushner *et al.*, 2015), and instructions can be shorter. Equally, they can now cope with more complicated, elaborate and unpredictable activities that involve adapting 'on the move', multitasking, strategy, tactics and problem-solving (Strandjord and Rome, 2016; Brown *et al.*, 2017; Kipp, 2018). Where coaches may start by introducing simpler game types to younger children (e.g. target and net/wall games), here they can introduce more complex activities such as striking/fielding and territorial/invasion games (Almond, 1986), and increasingly in their full-sized variants (i.e. progressively moving closer to adult-sized pitches and team sizes).

At the same time, adolescence is a period of significant ongoing brain development and maturation, including a steady increase in the sophistication of information-processing (Strandjord and Rome, 2016). Over time, these developments will result in improved prefrontal cortex executive function (Nigg, 2017), which underpins a range of self-regulatory mechanisms, such as emotional regulation and attentional and behavioural regulation (Dennison *et al.*, 2013). As such, adolescents are still (slowly) developing their ability to problem-solve around their own (athletic) development (e.g. goal set or make plans to achieve these goals over long term). Equally, despite cognitive readiness to understand risks and think through long-term consequences, impulsive, emotion-driven, and irrational behaviour remains prominent well into mid-adolescence (Blakemore, 2018). For example, we may expect athletes to take what coaches may consider 'rash decisions' or 'unnecessary' risk both as part of (e.g. choose an extra risky manoeuvre, play on while injured) and away from (e.g. stay out with friends despite a big game the next day) sport. Nonetheless, as the brain is still 'plastic' during this period, it is a good time to practice the development of these regulatory skills, through the anticipation of and preparation for regulatory challenges (e.g. anything that creates a gap between the desired state and current state, such as wanting to be in the team vs. not being picked for the team) and by scaffolding increasingly self-directed reflection and direction of learning.

The central task in adolescence is developing a sense of self as an autonomous individual (Erikson, 1959). Adolescence is characterised by an increased need for independence, particularly from parents (Eccles, 1999), and acceptance, particularly from peers (Sanders, 2013). As such, peers, their social standing within the peer group, and a sense of fitting in become increasingly salient for adolescents, and they crave opportunities for establishing close friendships (Brown *et al.*, 2017). Adolescents' ability to think abstractly also leads to more intense self-awareness and an increased detection of contradictions about self, potentially leading to a sense of confusion, conflict and distress (Harter and Monsour, 1992). Throughout this period, and through experimenting with different roles and personas (e.g. different clothes, hairstyles, friends), adolescents slowly figure out a coherent sense of who they are (i.e. a personal identity; Harter, 2012), of where (and with whom) they fit in, for example in a sports team, as well as what their future goals and aspirations are (Sanders, 2013). Coaches must exercise caution and not pre-judge or ridicule young athletes as they go through this period of exploration.

Linked to cognitive maturation, self-evaluations across multiple domains are now integrated into global self-esteem which tends to decline into mid-adolescence (Harter, 2006). Domain-specific self-evaluations become increasingly differentiated and complex (not just sporty, but good at athletics and swimming but perhaps less so at racket sports) (Harter, 2006, 2012) and accurate (Smith *et al.*, 2012), with young people showing much greater awareness of their own strengths and weaknesses (Harter, 2012; Brown *et al.*, 2017). This more accurate perception of their own abilities is also partly informed by the ability to integrate multiple sources of competence information. Alongside all previously used sources, early adolescents compare and weigh up feedback from significant others to other sources of information including peer comparison, performance outcomes, and skill improvement (Harter, 1999; Horn, 2004). At this age, young people shift to a differentiated view of effort and ability; needing to put in more effort may be interpreted as having lower ability (Nicholls, 1989). As a result, given the importance of the peer group and peer group norms, there is a renewed need to support a task-specific climate and mitigate the inevitable ego-orientated persuasions of particularly the early adolescent stage. Moving into mid-adolescence the sources of information are further expanded to also include comparisons to one's own internal standards and previous performances (Harter, 1999; Horn, 2004; Weiss and Amorose, 2005), which would allow for more stability in competency judgements, along with a potential shift back towards task-involvement. However, this may also lead to frustration if the young athlete perceives they are not reaching their expected standards and coaches must be ready to offer technical and emotional support during these times (Zakrajsek *et al.*, 2017).

In the initial part of this stage, complex emotions develop, and emotional outbursts may be common (Vealey and Chase, 2016). However, as they progress through this stage, adolescents become more aware of and able to identify, understand and express their own feelings (Vernon, 2004). As adolescents are more capable of taking perspective (including third person – understand what a third person may feel as the result of a second person's action) and become more aware of and able to identify the feelings of others (Sanders, 2013), their ability to show empathy expands further (Crocker *et al.*, 2004). They are increasingly focused on gaining a deeper understanding of self and others (Eccles, 1999) and why people behave the way they do. Yet, as a result of this increased cognitive sophistication, adolescent egocentrism can occur with young people thinking about what others think about them, leading to increased self-consciousness and easy embarrassment (Harter, 2012; Strandjord and Rome, 2016). Consequently, instead of persecuting outbursts, coaches should assist athletes in understanding and managing their emotions in a sport setting (Zakrajsek *et al.*, 2017). Further, although more complex cooperation becomes feasible and something adolescents enjoy/crave, peer interactions may need careful management, such as when there may be a clear winner or a player of a significantly lower standard in the group, as peer rejection can have a large impact on self-esteem.

At this stage, moral development beings to move from something that concerns the individual toward understanding that moral actions could and perhaps should align with broader societal norms and expectations. Adolescents may gradually move to thinking people should live up to expectations of family and community and behave in 'good' ways – predicated on good motives and interpersonal feelings such as love, trust, empathy, concern, etc. for others. This can be most easily seen when there is a direct relation (e.g. friend, family) where feelings can be known and empathised with (Kohlberg, 1963; Crain, 2016). Here the motto 'treat others as you would like to be treated' becomes relevant. When relating it to sport, adolescents will start to have an understanding that behaving in line with rules and norms of clubs or sport – such as club 'values' (e.g. respect opposition, referees, be kind) or ethos of the sport (e.g. play fair) becomes more important, especially if affiliation to that club/sport is high. Initially, the peer group may predominantly help decide what kind of behaviour is good/acceptable (Hart and Carlo, 2005), but as young people progress through this stage, moral thinking may develop further into personal ideals around why behaving in good ways is important (Kohlberg, 1981); or into understanding that moral behaviour is important for sustaining social order (Crain, 2016). For example, a greater understanding of behaving in ways that uphold the standard within their sport may also begin to emerge (e.g. "I shouldn't dive/cheat because that means anyone/everyone should dive/cheat").

## Implications for Children's Sport Coaching

Coaches require knowledge and understanding of psycho-social development in order to plan appropriate activities and judge when/why psycho-social skills may be introduced. For example, if a coach aims to promote pro-social behaviours, they may realistically expect this to look like a willingness to take turns in early childhood, compared to a selflessness in setting up opportunities for a teammate to score a goal in mid to late adolescence. In order to translate descriptive knowledge of 'typical' development into coaching practice, Table 26.1 offers coaching practice considerations that align to the developmental summaries discussed in the chapter. The table can be used to plan both short-term and long-term developmental curricula and pedagogy.

Development does not happen in a vacuum but is driven by the interaction between individuals and their environment. Coaches need to be cognisant of participants' lives (e.g. changes in social environment) and how these may interact with typical developmental challenges (e.g. transition to secondary school), as well as the coaching context (e.g. participation/performance) and participants' reasons for engagement. Consequently, coaches should consider individual, contextual, and environmental factors alongside those presented in Table 26.1. Overall, the implications are offered as reflective tools for coaches and are not prescriptive. Indeed, the purpose of the chapter is to increase coach flexibility in developing activities in response to where their participants 'actually are' in terms of development, rather than where they 'ought' to be.

## Summary, Future Directions and Future Research

This chapter offers an insight into the various aspects of 'typical' psycho-social maturation of children for coaches. Over time their abilities to remember, retrieve, and process information as well as to reason and problem solve develop. These changes in cognitive development go hand in hand with being able to recognise their own abilities and attributes, shaping an increasingly complex sense of self. Furthermore, children grow to recognise, and understand their own and others' emotions and perspectives, allowing for increasing cooperation but also introducing challenges in terms of social interaction. Over time children face the challenge of establishing independence, identity, and a sense of direction for the future.

While there is a wealth of research informing coaches about the psycho-social aspects they could and should be developing, there is limited sport-specific literature that has explored what coaches may expect their participants to 'be capable of' from a psycho-social perspective. Equally, acknowledging that development is idiosyncratic, there are few studies that explore the 'bandwidth' in terms of typical development. Therefore, future research should take a developmental approach and explore (and describe) between-and within-age variations in psychological and social maturity. Following Weiss (2019), researchers should select specific participants based on theoretically informed psycho-social developmental criteria, compare different age groups in terms of psycho-social maturity as well as follow participants longitudinally to track their development. In addition, future research should take a 'whole person' approach and explore the interaction between typical developmental challenges and contextual and environmental factors (e.g. participation vs. performance). For example, selective contexts with high levels of scrutiny may be hypothesised to be particularly challenging for the already self-conscious adolescent.

*Table 26.1* Coaching practice considerations

| | *Cognitive* | | | | *Social-emotional* | | | | | |
|---|---|---|---|---|---|---|---|---|---|---|
| | *Material complexity* | *Cognitive complexity* | *Responsibility and ownership* | *Feedback format* | *Cooperation & relationships* | *Sense of fairness* | *Probability of failure* | *Consequences of failure* | *Feedback tone* | *Motivational climate* |
| Simple Description | Number of moving pieces | Amount of information processing required | Level of ownership given and self-organisation | Frequency and amount of feedback | Level and type of cooperation | Participant perception of how just the activity is | Likelihood of participant success / failure | Implications of failing a task | Level of positivity and demand | Personal improvement or external comparison |
| More Developed | • More complex, less predictable tasks.<br>• Increased questioning<br>• Reduced instruction | • Strategy and tactics.<br>• Problem based pedagogies | • Ownership, leadership and decision making. | • Increased complexity of feedback<br>• Encourage self-evaluation | • Complex cooperation in terms of tasks and empathy<br>• Acknowledge need to avoid embarrassment and to 'fit in' | • Unjust decisions as learning moments<br>• Support behaviours consistent with values | • Challenging tasks where probability of success lower than failure<br>• Artificial and real pressure to learn how to perform under pressure.<br>• Help participants respond to poor decisions<br>• Beware peer rejection due to failure | | • Challenge alongside positivity<br>• Increased demands from feedback | • Support a task-climate to challenge ego-orientations<br>• Balanced task- and ego-climates may be appropriate for performance contexts |
| Less Developed | • Simple tasks with few steps/elements<br>• Simple language used<br>• Visible cues required (e.g. demonstration) | • Pretend play, imagination.<br>• Reduced speed tasks | • Limited, basic choices<br>• Encourage self-referenced improvement | • Immediately, simple, effort-based feedback.<br>• Simple cues and reminders | • Individual or parallel play<br>• Scaffolded cooperation | • Clear rules of 'right and wrong' from coach model<br>• Activities without dispropor-tionate advantages for one side | • Limited failure and consequences of failure<br>• Opportunities to explore and achieve success<br>• Effort and task completion emphasised as success | | • Positive feedback tone<br>• Low demand from feedback | • Focus on self, improvement, and effort mastery-involving climate |

## References


Abraham, A., *et al.*, 2014. Planning your coaching: A focus on youth participant development. *In:* C. Nash, ed. *Practical sports coaching*. London: Routledge, 16–53.

Almond, L., 1986. A games classification. *In:* R. Thorpe, D. Bunker, and L. Almond, eds. *Rethinking games teaching*. Loughborough: Loughborough University, 71–72.

Blakemore, S.J., 2018. Avoiding social risk in adolescence. *Current Directions in Psychological Science*, 27 (2), 116–122.

Brown, K.A., Patel, D.R., and Darmawan, D., 2017. Participation in sports in relation to adolescent growth and development. *Translational Pediatrics*, 6 (3), 150–159.

Crain, W.C., 2016. *Theories of development: Concepts and applications*. New York: Routledge.

Crocker, P.R.E., *et al.*, 2004. Emotional experience in youth sport. *In*: M.R. Weiss, ed. *Developmental sport and exercise psychology: A lifespan perspective*. Morgantown, WV: Fitness Information Technology, 197–221.

Dennison, M., *et al.*, 2013. Mapping subcortical brain maturation during adolescence: Evidence of hemisphere-and sex-specific longitudinal changes. *Developmental Science*, 16 (5), 772–791.

Eccles, J.S., 1999. The development of children ages 6 to 14. *The Future of Children*, 9 (2), 30–44.

Eisenmann, J.C., Till. K., and Baker, J., 2020. Growth, maturation and youth sports: Issues and practical solutions, *Annals of Human Biology*, 47 (4), 324–327.

Erikson, E.H., 1959. *Psychological issues*. New York: International University Press.

Feldman, D.H., 2004. Piaget's stages: The unfinished symphony of cognitive development. *New Ideas in Psychology*, 22 (3), 175–231.

Gibbs, J.C., 2010. *Moral development and reality: Beyond the theories of kohlberg and hoffman*. 2nd ed. Boston, MA: Pearson Higher Education.

Hart, D. and Carlo, G., 2005. Moral development in adolescence. *Journal of Research on Adolescence*, 15 (3), 223–233.

Harter, S., 1999. *The construction of the self: A developmental perspective*. New York: Guilford Press.

Harter, S., 2006. Developmental and individual difference perspectives on self-esteem. *In*: D.K. Mroczek and T.D. Little, eds. *Handbook of personality development*. Hillsdale, NJ: Lawrence Erlbaum Associates, 311–334.

Harter, S., 2012. *The construction of the self: Developmental and sociocultural foundations*. 2nd ed. New York: The Guilford Press.

Harter, S. and Monsour, A., 1992. Developmental analysis of conflict caused by opposing attributes in the adolescent self-portrait. *Developmental Psychology*, 28, 251–260.

Horn, T.S., 2004. Developmental perspectives on self perceptions in children and adolescents. *In*: M.R. Weiss, ed. *Developmental sport and exercise psychology: A lifespan perspective*. Morgantown, WV: Fitness Information Technology, 101–143.

Horn, T.S. and Butt, J., 2014. Developmental perspectives on sport and physical activity participation. *In*: A. Papaloannou and D. Hackfort, eds. *Routledge companion to sport and exercise psychology: Global perspectives and fundamental concepts*. London: Taylor & Francis, 3–21.

Kipp, L., 2018. Developmental considerations for working with young athletes. *In*: K.J. Knight, C.G. Harwood, and D. Gould, eds. *Sport psychology for young athletes*. London: Routledge, 32–42.

Kipp, L.E. and Bolter, N.D., 2020. Motivational climate, psychological needs, and personal and social responsibility in youth soccer: Comparisons by age group and competitive level. *Psychology of Sport and Exercise*, 51, 1–10.

Kohlberg, L., 1963. The development of children's orientations toward a moral order: I. sequence in the development of moral thought. *Human Development*, 6 (1/2), 11–33.

Kohlberg, L., 1981. *Essays in moral development: The philosophy of moral development: Moral stages and the idea of justice*. Cambridge: Harper and Row.

Kushner, A.M. *et al.*, 2015. Training the developing brain part II: Cognitive considerations for youth instruction and feedback. *Current Sports Medicine Reports*, 14 (3), 235–243.

Nicholls, J.G., 1989. *The competitive ethos and democratic education*. Cambridge, MA: Harvard University Press.

Nigg, J.T., 2017. Annual research review: On the relations among self-regulation, self-control, executive functioning, effortful control, cognitive control, impulsivity, risk-taking, and inhibition for developmental psychopathology. *Journal of Child Psychology and Psychiatry*, 58 (4), 361–383.

Pankhurst, A. (2016). 10u Tennis: The essentials of developing players for the future. *In*: Colvin, A.C. and Gladstone, J.N., eds. *The young tennis player: Injury prevention and treatment*. Cham: Springer, 1–17.

Piaget, J., 1952. *The origins of intelligence in children*. New York: International University Press.
Sanders, R.A., 2013. Adolescent psychosocial, social, and cognitive development. *Pediatrics in Review*, 34 (8), 354–358.
Smith, A.L., Dorsch, T.E., and Monsma, E.V., 2012. Developmentally informed measurement in sport and exercise psychology research. *In*: G. Tenenbaum, R.C. Eklund, and A. Kamata, eds. *Measurement in sport and exercise psychology*. New York: Human Kinetics, 131–141.
Strandjord, S.E. and Rome, E.S., 2016. Growth and development in the young athlete. *In*: A.C. Colvin and J.N. Gladstone, eds. *The young tennis player: Injury prevention and treatment*. Cham: Springer, 19–36.
Vealey, R.S. and Chase, M.A., 2016. *Best practice for youth sport*. Leeds: Human Kinetics.
Vernon, A., 2004. Working with children, adolescents, and their parents: Practical application of developmental theory. *In*: A. Vernon, ed. *Counselling children and adolescents*. Denver, CO: Love Publishing Company, 1–34.
Visek, A.J., Harris, B., and Blom, L.C., 2013. Mental training with youth sport teams: Developmental considerations & best practice recommendations. *Journal of Sport Psychology in Action*, 4 (1), 45–55.
Weiss, M.R., 2019. Youth sport motivation and participation: Paradigms, perspectives, and practicalities. *Kinesiology Review*, 8 (3), 162–170.
Weiss, M.R. and Amorose, A.J., 2005. Children's self-perceptions in the physical domain: Between-and within-age variability in level, accuracy, and sources of perceived competence. *Journal of Sport and Exercise Psychology*, 27 (2), 226–244.
Weiss, M.R. and Bredemeier, B.J., 1983. Developmental sport psychology: A theoretical perspective for studying children in sport. *Journal of Sport Psychology*, 5 (2), 216–230.
Zakrajsek, R.A., Lauer, E.E. and Bodey, K.J., 2017. Integrating mental skills and strategies into youth sport training: A tool for coaches. *International Sport Coaching Journal*, 4 (1), 76–89.

# 27

# INTEGRATING SPECIFICITY AND GENERALITY OF PRACTICE TO ENRICH CHILDREN'S LEARNING IN SPORT

*Martyn Rothwell, James Rudd, and Keith Davids*

## Introduction

Participation and high-performance sport systems have seen a shift towards early identification and selection of children into specialised training pathways in a single sport. This radical change has led to children's sport becoming increasingly professionalised in formalised athlete development programmes when they are still in primary education (i.e. 4 to 11 years). The value of such sport systems continues to stimulate debate amongst academics and practitioners, who have highlighted the challenges of early specialisation to the mental, physical, and social development of children and youth (Baker *et al.*, 2021). Indeed, an editorial in the British Journal of Sports Medicine, identified early specialisation in elite sports development programmes as a major threat to the health and wellbeing of future generations (Roetert *et al.*, 2018).

The fundamental problem of how to motivate, encourage and develop skills and talent in children without causing them mental, physical, and social harm, is framed in the longstanding *specificity versus generality* of practice dualism in motor learning (Ribeiro *et al.*, 2021). Specificity of practice involves learners engaging in highly repetitious drills in dedicated performance contexts to develop 'optimal' movement techniques for performance in a targeted sport. Too much specificity of practice may exacerbate intensity of specialised training in children. The result could be problems related to physical, psychological, and emotional loading and intensity (Forsman *et al.*, 2016). Generality of practice involves providing learners with variable play and practice experiences (structured and unstructured learning experiences in different sports (Coutinho *et al.*, 2016)) to develop a foundation of functional movement skills which can interact with later specialised training to enhance talent (Ribeiro *et al.*, 2021).

This chapter discusses the *complementary nature* of specificity and generality of play and practice experiences to enrich children's learning. These ideas highlight the importance of infusing variability and specificity of task constraints at appropriate times during children's learning. Principles of contemporary pedagogical models of learning, Non-linear Pedagogy (NLP) and the Athletic Skills Model (ASM), are discussed to highlight how they can be implemented by coaches and sports teachers integrating both types of practice experiences. In this approach, the developmental needs of each child can be satisfied whether seeking to specialise


DOI: 10.4324/9781003199359-31

in sport on an elite pathway or to maintain long-term physical literacy for health and wellbeing benefits.

## Review of Current Research

Motor learning has been one of the most relevant sub-disciplines to influence learning designs in sport coaching practice (Chow *et al.*, 2022). Traditionally, however, the motor learning domain was consumed in a heated debate about the putative nature of internalised, representational mechanisms for controlling movements (for reviews see Singer, 1975; Schmidt, 1982). As motor control and learning process theories developed, the *specificity versus generality* debate emerged between the 1960s and 1980s, side-tracking understanding of both characteristics for motor learning principles for coaches and teachers. In the 1960s, this debate was centralised on key issues, such as whether an internalised movement representation was specific (a motor programme for each movement) or more general (a schema to control a class of movements such as locomotion, throwing, kicking, or catching) (Williams *et al.*, 1999).

These theoretical and empirical insights were adopted by applied scientists, motor learning specialists and sport pedagogy researchers focusing on examining the benefits and effects of *either* specificity or generality of learning experiences. However, the possibility that both types of experiences were of relevance for children's skill learning and development has rarely been considered, exemplifying a 'dualism' often observed in other areas of science. Indeed, the tendency to *juxtaposition* specificity and generality of play and practice experiences was also apparent in physical education, being highlighted in some of the most influential research papers published in the early years of the sub-discipline's development (Table 27.1). The word 'versus' in the title captures the thinking at that time.

In contrast to research programmes in physical education, sport science practitioners such as Anatoly Bondarchuk (1994, 2007) advocated a more nuanced understanding of general and specific experiences for learning and practice in sport. Bondarchuk's insights have important implications for understanding how to coach children, enhance their movement development, and prevent physical and mental problems common in early specialisation programmes. Bondarchuk (1994, 2007) proposed that more general training should be concerned with developing general athletic skills, whereas specific training is dedicated to performance enhancement and preparation in one sport. He advocated a unification of general and specialised preparation for sport performance, proposing a " … . principle of unity of general and specialised preparation" (Bondarchuk, 2007, p.5). He noted that, experienced separately, each type of training has some benefits for athletes, but integrated together they provide a significant platform for athlete development. His ideas highlight how infusing variability and specificity of

*Table 27.1* Scientific dualism in the titles of research papers focusing on investigating the benefits of either specific or general learning, practice, and training experiences, rather than seeking to understand their complementarity

| |
|---|
| Henry, F.M. 1958. Specificity vs. Generality in Learning Motor Skills. *Proceedings of College of Physical Education Association*, 61, 126–128. |
| Bachman, C. 1961. Specificity vs. Generality in Learning and Performing Two Large Muscle Motor Tasks. *Research Quarterly*, 32, 3–11. |
| Smith, L. 1973. Specificity versus Generality of relationships between individual differences in motor abilities. *Educational Perspectives*, 12, 19–28. |

practice at appropriate timepoints, can support successful athletic performance and preparation by emphasising the all-round development through improving children's skill adaptation (Button *et al.*, 2020).

## *An Ecological Dynamics Rationale for Specificity and Generality of Practice*

An extensive body of research informed by an ecological dynamics framework, over the past few decades, has evidenced the value of specificity and generality of learning experiences. Research investigating specificity of learning (conceptualised as *representative learning design*) has been conducted in a diverse range of sports contexts including cricket batting (Pinder *et al.*, 2011), springboard diving (Barris *et al.*, 2013), futsal (Travassos *et al.*, 2012) and ice climbing (Seifert *et al.*, 2014). Barris *et al.* (2013), for example, studied Olympic level springboard divers when they practised diving into a pool and in a dry-land facility which simulated the diving action (coaches used the latter because it enabled more repetitions of the preparatory phase prior to take off). Observations indicated different coordination tendencies under the two distinct task constraints, leading to performance differences at key stages of the dive (second approach step, hurdle step, hurdle jump height and board angles during the hurdle and at landing). These differences emerged during the preparation phase of dive take-offs completed in the dry land and aquatic training environments. For example, the elite divers showed significantly less board angle depression at landing (from the hurdle jump) during take-offs completed under the task constraints of the dry-land area than when diving into the pool.

These findings support the importance of representative learning design principles when using specificity of practice to advance skill levels and expertise in high performance sport organisations. In more specific practice experiences (i.e. learning to hit a backhand shot in tennis), a challenge is to ensure that learning designs represent contextual task (e.g. temporal, spatial, presence of opposition and competition) constraints which children can use as information to regulate their actions. By way of example in competitive sport, Browne *et al.* (2019) sampled 29,153 kicks from across different competition levels in Australian Rules Football to determine key task constraints on kicking skill performance. Analysis revealed that low kicking success was associated with physical pressure (37%), whereas high efficiency emerged when kicking to an open target (70%). Data of this nature can ensure specificity of practice experiences are more effective for replicating competition environments and enhancing skilled behaviour. While getting access to this level of data to enrich children's learning experiences may be unrealistic for many children's coaches, implementing the concept of representative co-design can alleviate this challenge by drawing on children's knowledge of the environment, inviting them to consider how to change rules to produce practice conditions that feel more demanding and challenging when needed as in competition (for a detailed overview see Woods *et al.*, 2021).

Research has also demonstrated the precise value of generality of practice and play (captured in variable and unstructured play and activities) (see Phillips *et al.*, 2010, 2014; Cairney *et al.*, 2018; Machado *et al.*, 2019; Lascu *et al.*, 2020). Indeed, the results of the study by Cairney *et al.* (2018) refute the idea of juxtaposing organised sports participation (structured specific practice) *versus* free play (unstructured and generalised play and practice experiences). Their evidence showed observations of a relationship between tendencies to participate in structured physical activity, closely allied with tendencies to engage in unstructured practice and play (termed 'free play' by the authors). This point was previously exemplified by Phillips *et al.* (2014), who interviewed 11 past or present Australian international elite fast bowlers who had taken more than 2,400 international test wickets in over 630 international test matches. This group was truly elite with all of them having taken at least 75 international test wickets and appearing in at least 20 international test matches. In terms of their early childhood experiences, unstructured practice activities were found to be important, with 73% of the expert bowlers saying that they did not specialise in fast bowling until the late teens. Several experts were not even involved in structured cricket until late in their teenage years. This factor questions the value of over-emphasising specificity of practice in early specialisation programmes. Their data also confirmed that a particular advantage of late specialisation for future fast bowlers in cricket was that it limits their exposure to injury associated with high bowling workloads during maturation.

### *Facilitating Skill Integration and Enrichment in Practice*

A unified approach to general and specific training and practice challenges coaches of children and youth to understand how to integrate these dualistic positions to enhance developmental experiences (e.g. Bondarchuk, 2007). An ecological dynamics rationale explains how general preparation for performance advocated by Bondarchuk (1994, 2007), is relevant for the enrichment of athletic performance in every individual from early childhood onwards (Rudd *et al.*, 2021). Enrichment in practice supports the transfer of functional abilities and capacities, allowing a learner to use perception, action, and cognition during performance, as expertise in one sport increases (Chow *et al.*, 2020). As discussed later in this chapter, ecological-dynamics informed pedagogical frameworks (The Athletic Skills Model, Constraints-Based Coaching and Non-Linear Pedagogy) can support coaches and teachers to integrate a range of general and specific activities during practice to enhance the movement repertoire and athleticism of young athletes during development (Chow *et al.*, 2020; Rudd *et al.*, 2020; Woods *et al.*, 2020).

Learning through the process of enrichment aims to develop children's capacities (e.g. psychological, emotional, cognitive, perceptual, and physical) to interact meaningfully with environmental demands. This idea relates to an *individual environment fit* across diverse movement contexts (O'Sullivan *et al.*, 2020), where evolving capacities can support engagement in everyday movement tasks, skill adaptation in sport, and continued physical health across the lifespan. In developing this fit, children learn to perceive action opportunities (i.e. affordances) (Gibson, 1979, Cordovil *et al.*, 2015) to regulate their performance in different contexts. Through this process, functional movement solutions emerge when children develop the capacities to satisfy a range of specific and varying task and environmental constraints to achieve intended task goals (Sigmundsson *et al.*, 2021). Over time, it is crucial that children develop the capacities to perceive and distinguish between the multitude of affordances available in the environment that invite or repel actions (Adolph and Hoch, 2019). Play and practice experiences in childhood need to help learners to navigate a rich landscape of action possibilities across sport and physical activity settings (Cordovil *et al.*, 2015).

### *Pedagogical Frameworks to Integrate Generality and Specificity Practice Designs*

While theoretical and conceptual arguments for generality and specificity of practice are well advanced (e.g. Rudd *et al.*, 2020; Chow *et al.*, 2022), pedagogical guidance is needed to navigate the nuances associated with integrating these juxtaposed positions in learning designs. Non-linear Pedagogy and the ASM are contemporary models of pedagogical practice, informed by ecological dynamics, and provide a start point for practitioners interested in integrating generality and specificity of practice in sports training. The ASM supports enrichment of functional movement skills through learning, movement, perception, physiological, and competence transfer in generalised practice and learning experiences (for a detailed overview see Wormhoudt et al., 2018). The ASM advocates that children take part in multisports (i.e. playing and sampling many sports for fun) and donor sports (i.e. playing in sports that can enhance relevant skills for a chosen target sport), to encourage holistic movement competencies pre-, during, and post-engagement with specialised pathways. Engagement in these varied activities is based on specific phases of development and in the ASM biological age, and not chronological age, influences what stage a child should be experiencing at a specific time point. Passing through these stages of development aims to enrich children's capacities so they can cope with specialised training programmes when excelling in a target sport.

Aligned with the ASM, NLP provides specific theoretical design principles to facilitate learning at the microstructure of practice (for a detailed overview see Correia *et al.*, 2019; Chow *et al.*, 2022). To exemplify how NLP can support sport practitioners to integrate generality and specificity of practice designs, the principle of exploratory learning in representative learning design is highlighted. In general practice experiences, coaches can facilitate exploratory learning to support children in developing a functional range of individualised movement solutions to different problems posed in environmental settings (i.e. exploring multiple ways to beat a defender in a 1 v 1 situation). Hacques *et al.* (2020) have suggested that supporting exploratory behaviours through carefully designed practice, and the facilitation of a child's search for specifying information sources, contributes to highly skilled coupling of perception and action. This coupling process helps to develop a functional fit between a child's action capabilities and the relevant properties of the environment.

When a coach is upskilled to deliver contemporary pedagogies, they are faced with the challenge of knowing when generality or specificity of practice is relevant and important at different times to enrich children's development experiences. Individualising the learning process is central to the ASM and NLP, with the ASM philosophy stating *first the child, then the athlete, then the specialist.* A nuanced balance between specificity and generality of practice is, therefore, a question of timing, based on the development status of a child at a specific timepoint, and not dependent on an age-based model of performance. To manage the challenges of identifying and supporting multiple individual differences at the same time, Button *et al.* (2020) have suggested several strategies to support coaches in this process. Aligned to concepts within the ASM and NLP, these principles relate to a learner-centred approach where a 'one size fits all' philosophy is rejected in favour of individual challenge (e.g. equipment changes or varied task challenges), facilitating exploration and adaptation to constraints. Through this approach, coaches can become more attuned to individual differences in development status, with a greater focus on performer (e.g. needs, prior experience or motivation), task (e.g. design features like information and intentions), and environmental (e.g. social support or economic status) constraints specific to each child. Next, we provide practical examples to support coaches and teachers to implement the concepts discussed thus far.

## Implications for Children's Sport Coaching

### *Learning to Move: Practical Examples for Sport Practitioners*

A high proportion of children do not have sufficient opportunities to play outdoors, unlike previous generations who had the freedom to play games in the street, roam around their neighbourhoods and explore local fields and woodlands (Bates *et al.*, 2020). Considering this change in play opportunities, it is hardly surprising that many children possess a foundational movement skills repertoire that is more limited than that of their parents, and grandparents at the same age (Bardid *et al.*, 2015). One of the key reasons for the ASM's success is that children are provided with rich opportunities to interact and explore a multitude of varied movement environments. In the ASM, learning environments are devised as *skills gardens* where learners are encouraged to innovate and adapt actions through interacting with task designs which challenge them to explore and learn. The coaches working with children using the ASM model are continually traversing across a spectrum of generality to specificity in their learning and development settings.

To support coaches and teachers to adopt and make sense of their own practice and delivery we provide an example nonlinear pedagogy lesson plan created as part of the SAMPLE-PE project (see Figure 1.0 in Rudd *et al.*, 2020) (Figure 27.1). The first thing to notice is that the session plan does not follow a traditional linear format that lists a set of tasks that should be completed in a set amount of time i.e. 10 minutes warm up, 30 minutes conditioned/small-sided game, and lastly 20 minutes of game play. Instead, a cyclical session plan is presented in which a coach would have developed three of these activity plans. Each activity plan works towards the same session objective. The three activities are not progressions from one to another, but rather they create different learning environments that will lead to the emergence of similar skills but under a variety of constraints. This adaptive approach means that there is no pressure for a coach to progress beyond one activity plan if learning is progressing in the current task. Instead, they can move on when the activity naturally runs its course, or the coach or learners have run out of ideas on how to perturb movement behaviours. For each activity plan five pedagogical principles informed by an ecological dynamics framework are utilised. These

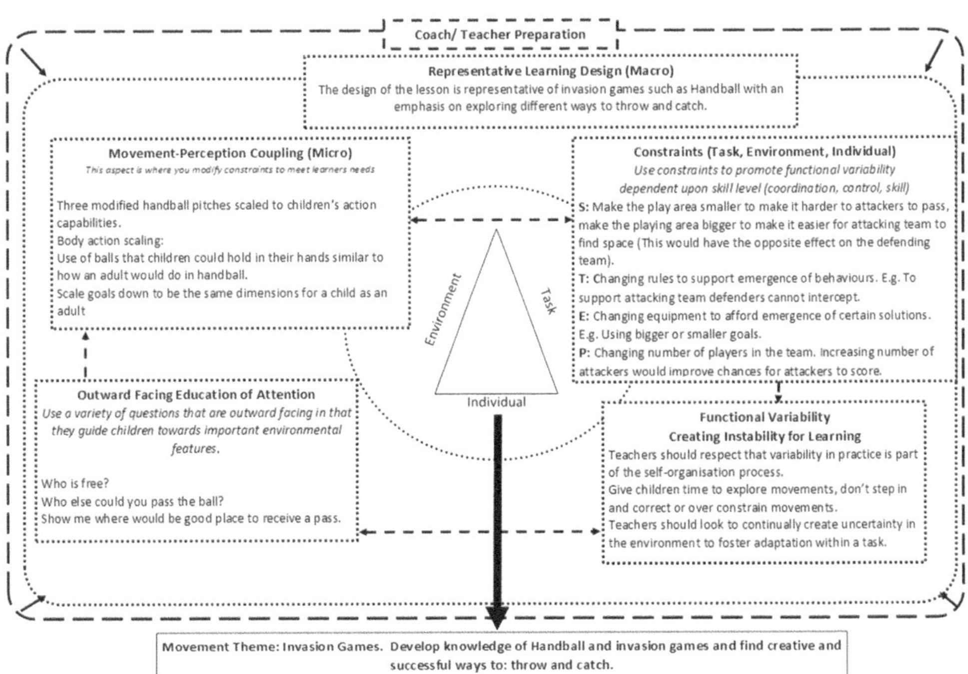


*Figure 27.1* Example activity/learning environment plan this one is for a games lesson for young children (Rudd *et al.*, 2020)

are representative learning design, movement perception coupling, outward-facing attention, constraints manipulation, and functional variability.

To help coaches and teachers understand the planning process, examples of how the key pedagogical principles can be used to plan sessions are presented.

1 *Representative learning design* emphasises the importance of skill transfer between practice environment and performance environment. Informational constraints sampled from competition (i.e. opponents, ground surfaces, time of day) are carefully designed into practice tasks to support learning transfer.

Example: In the NLP activity plan the coach is creating a handball game to improve young children's catching and throwing skills. The coach will introduce some general constraints, such as you cannot run with the ball and must throw the ball to pass and to score. This approach creates a representative environment for sports like handball, but also for a variety of functional throwing and catching opportunities to emerge.

2 *Movement-perception coupling* must be maintained when performing skills. This means that skills are practised in their entirety, rather than broken down into component parts or in a decontextualised fashion.

Example: In the NLP activity plan the coach builds and develops a more learner-centred activity plan, thereby starting to manipulate the environment to meet the children's action capabilities and body scaling constraints, for example scaling the dimensions of the playing space, ball, and goal targets.

3 *An outward-facing education of attention* allows for self-organisation of movement patterns to meet the goal of the task and develops knowledge of the environment.

Example: In the NLP activity plan a coach pre-plans a variety of questions that are outward-facing to guide children towards important environmental features that will help them attune to more functional movements within their environment. A coach may show a child where to look, but does not tell them what to see, using verbal information to guide interactive search activities in play, such as: "Which of your teammates is free, where can you throw the ball in the goal to beat the keeper … don't tell me show me".

4 *The manipulation of constraints* – careful manipulation of task constraints will lead to self-organisation and the emergence of new functional movement patterns.

Example: Coaches can take a simple S.T.E.P (space, task, equipment, people) approach to create nonlinear changes to movement behaviour. Increasing or decreasing the space will lead to greater, or less pressure, on the attack or defence. Manipulating the task (i.e. implementing a rule that a child cannot hold the ball for longer than three seconds) is likely to increase scanning behaviours prior to catching the ball. Changing the equipment size of goals will lead to varying degrees of success in scoring. Manipulating the number of people playing, creating uneven teams, changing teammates and opponents will create different dynamics and lead to nonlinear changes in performance behaviours.

5 *Infusing perturbations within the learning process.* This means that we see variability as exploration of movement possibilities, and not as error in the system as would be the case with traditional theories of motor learning and pedagogies.

Example: This is fundamental to skill adaptation and is important for a coach to understand as this is how we observe learning in action. Children's movements skills may transition from one stable state to another. Once movement skills are in a stable state, little to no learning will take place. The coach, therefore, needs to perturb the current movement pattern to create innovation in the child-environment system. A skilled coach uses a combination of education of attention and constraint manipulation to achieve this outcome for learning to occur and progress.

## Summary, Future Directions and Future Research

This chapter has discussed the importance of generality and specificity of practice experiences that are traditionally viewed as a dualism. Contemporary motor learning theory, in the form of ecological dynamics recommends a nuanced balance between these practice contexts can provide more integrated motor learning experiences to enrich children's skills repertoire. Based on this conceptualisation, contemporary pedagogical models, such as NLP and ASM, can support coaches to implement individualised learning approaches, where a balance of generality and specificity of practice can support the development of each child at specific timepoints. Identifying and supporting individual differences is essential to support children's enriched functionality throughout their development. This approach can go some way to avoiding the defects of an early specialisation approach and build a platform for children to thrive in specialised performance environments later in their development.

While there are applied examples of contemporary pedagogical models in practice (e.g. Roberts *et al.*, 2019), future research studies should aim to document sport coaches' and practitioners' lived experiences of transitioning between generality and specificity of practice in learning programmes. Studies of this nature can provide important insights into the complex relationship between the practices that coaches design and the psychological, physical, and emotional dimensions that influence children's capacity to adapt to new challenges in practice and competition.

## References

Adolph, K.E. and Hoch, J.E., 2019. Motor development: Embodied, embedded, enculturated, and enabling. *Annual Review of Psychology*, 70, 141–164.

Baker, J., Mosher, A., and Fraser-Thomas, J., 2021. Is it too early to condemn early sport specialisation? *British Journal of Sports Medicine*, 55 (3), 179–180.

Bardid, F., *et al.*, 2015. Cross-cultural comparison of motor competence in children from Australia and Belgium. *Frontiers in Psychology*, 6 (964), 1–8.

Barris, S., Davids, K., and Farrow, D., 2013. Representative learning design in springboard diving: Is dry-land training representative of a pool dive? *European Journal of Sport Science*, 31, 305–313.

Bates, L.C., *et al.*, 2020. COVID-19 impact on behaviors across the 24-hour day in children and adolescents: Physical activity, sedentary behavior, and sleep. *Children*, 7 (9), 1–9.

Bondarchuk, A., 1994. General and special training. *Fitness and Sports Review International*, 29, 163–165.

Bondarchuk, A., 2007. *Transfer of training in sport*. Michigan: Ultimate Athlete Concepts.

Browne, P.R., *et al.*, 2019. Prevalence of interactions and influence of performance constraints on kick outcomes across Australian football tiers: Implications for representative practice designs. *Human Movement Science*, 66, 621–630.

Button, C., *et al.*, 2020. *Dynamics of skill acquisition: An ecological dynamics approach*. Champaign: Human Kinetics Publishers.

Cairney, J., *et al.*, 2018. A longitudinal study of the effect of organised physical activity on free active play. *Medicine & Science in Sports & Exercise*, 50 (9), 1772–1779.
Chow, J.-Y., *et al.*, 2020. Ecological dynamics and transfer from practice to performance in sport. *In*: A.M. Williams and N. Hodges, eds. 3rd ed. *Skill acquisition in sport: research, theory and practice*. Oxon: Routledge, 330–344.
Chow, J.-Y., *et al.*, 2022. *Nonlinear pedagogy in skill acquisition*. Oxon: Routledge.
Cordovil, R., *et al.*, 2015. An ecological stance on risk and safe behaviours in children: The role of affordances and emergent behaviours. *New Ideas in Psychology*, 36, 50–59.
Correia, V., *et al.*, 2019. Principles of nonlinear pedagogy in sport practice. *Physical Education and Sport Pedagogy*, 24 (2), 117–132.
Coutinho, P., *et al.*, 2016. How structured and unstructured sport activities aid the development of expertise in volleyball players. *Psychology of Sport & Exercise*, 25, 51–59.
Forsman, H., *et al.*, 2016. The role of sport-specific play and practice during childhood in the development of adolescent Finnish team sport athletes. *International Journal of Sport Science and Coaching*, 11 (1), 69–77.
Gibson, J., 1979. *The ecological approach to visual perception*. Hillsdale, NJ: Lawrence Erlbaum Associates.
Hacques, G., *et al.*, 2020. Exploring to learn and learning to explore. *Psychological Research*, 85 (4), 1367–1379.
Lascu, A., *et al.*, 2020. Practical application of ecological dynamics for talent development in cricket. *International Journal of Sports Science & Coaching*, 15 (2), 227–238.
Machado, J.C., *et al.*, 2019. Enhancing learning in the context of Street football: A case for nonlinear pedagogy. *Physical Education and Sport Pedagogy*, 24 (2), 176–189.
O'Sullivan, M., *et al.*, 2020. Conceptualising physical literacy within an ecological dynamics framework. *Quest*, 72 (4), 448–462.
Phillips, E., *et al.*, 2010. Developmental trajectories of fast bowling experts in Australian cricket. *Talent Development and Excellence*, 2 (2), 137–148.
Phillips, E., *et al.*, 2014. Acquisition of expertise in cricket fast bowling: Perceptions of expert players and coaches. *Journal of Science and Medicine in Sport*, 17 (1), 85–90.
Pinder, R., *et al.*, 2011. Representative learning design and functionality of research and practice in sport. *Journal of Sport and Exercise Psychology*, 33 (1), 146–155.
Ribeiro, J., *et al.*, 2021. Talent development in sport requires athlete enrichment: Contemporary insights from a nonlinear pedagogy and the athletic skills model. *Sports Medicine*, 51 (6), 1115–1122.
Roberts, W.M., Newcombe, D.J., and Davids, K., 2019. Application of a constraints-led approach to pedagogy in schools: Embarking on a journey to nurture physical literacy in primary physical education. *Physical Education and Sport Pedagogy*, 24 (2), 162–175.
Roetert, E.P., Ellenbecker, T.S., and Kriellaars, D., 2018. Physical literacy: Why should we embrace this construct? *British Journal of Sports Medicine*, 52 (20), 1291–1292.
Rudd, J.R., *et al.*, 2020. Physical literacy – A journey of individual enrichment: An ecological dynamics rationale for enhancing performance and physical activity in all. *Frontiers in Psychology*, 11, 1904.
Rudd, R.J., *et al.*, 2021. An ecological dynamics conceptualisation of physical 'education': Where we have been and where we could go next. *Physical Education and Sport Pedagogy*, 26 (3), 293–306.
Schmidt, R.A., 1982. *Motor control and learning: A behavioural analysis*. Champaign, IL: Human Kinetics.
Seifert, L., *et al.*, 2014. Neurobiological degeneracy and affordance perception support functional intra-individual variability of inter-limb coordination during ice climbing. *PloS One*, 9 (2), 1–12.
Sigmundsson, H., *et al.*, 2021. Exploration of the specificity of motor skills hypothesis in 7–8-year-old primary school children: Exploring the relationship between 12 different motor skills from two different motor competence test batteries. *Frontiers in Psychology*, 12, 1–8.
Singer, R.N., 1975. *Motor learning and human performance: An application to physical education skills*. New York: Macmillan.
Travassos, B., *et al.*, 2012. Practice task design in team sports: Representativeness enhanced by increasing opportunities for action. *Journal of Sports Sciences*, 30 (13), 1447–1454.
Woods, C., *et al.*, 2020. Wayfinding: How ecological perspectives of navigating dynamic environments can enrich our understanding of the learner and the learning process in sport. *Sports Medicine*, 6 (1), 1–11.
Woods, C.T., *et al.*, 2021. Representative co-design: Utilising a source of experiential knowledge for athlete development and performance preparation. *Psychology of Sport and Exercise*, 52, 1–9.
Williams, A.M., Davids, K., and Williams, J.G., 1999. *Visual perception and action in sport*. London: Routledge.
Wormhoudt, R., *et al.*, 2018. *The athletic skills model: Optimising talent development through movement education*. Oxon: Routledge.

# 28

# SAMPLING AND SPECIALISING IN CHILDREN'S SPORT: IMPLICATIONS FOR RESEARCH AND COACHING PRACTICE

*Colin D. McLaren, Mark W. Bruner, Alex Murata, Luc J. Martin, and Jean Côté*

## Introduction

Stadiums full of adoring fans chanting your name, wearing your uniform, and more fortune and fame than you ever thought possible – indeed, becoming a professional athlete certainly has appeal. Getting to the highest levels of competition, however, and acquiring the requisite skill set for continued success is a challenge that has confounded researchers, practitioners, parents, and athletes alike. One dominant position pertaining to achievement is that athletes should be engaging earlier in intensified practice in one activity during childhood. By doing so, it is thought this deliberate and specific practice will provide a performance advantage to children by increasing their chances of reaching an elite level of performance as an adult. This orientation generally represents the foundation of the early specialisation movement that has influenced the sport landscape for children.

A consequence of early specialisation is the professionalisation of sport for children – an issue identified as the single biggest problem facing young athletes today (Gould, 2019). Under this type of sport model, the goal is to implement year-round training in a single sport and have athletes motivated by extrinsic rewards and the long-term pursuit of elite performance. Elite training programs exist with the objective of helping young athletes gain an advantage over their competitors and increase their chances of being selected to competitive teams where scouts (i.e. talent identifiers) are more likely to recognise them. In essence, the belief is that the type of athletic abilities needed to reach the highest levels of competition should be acquired during childhood and cannot be fostered in an enjoyable and personal development oriented atmosphere. This approach to children's sport is based on an adult competitive model that is influenced by a limited number of athletic scholarships and spots on professional or other elite teams (Erdal, 2018). It is worth noting that this prevailing viewpoint of early specialisation originates from research conducted mainly in Western cultures (Storm *et al.*, 2012; Murata *et al.*, 2021).

Despite the potential to identify 'success stories' based on athletes who have followed a traditional early specialisation route, it is equally likely to find those that have achieved while following divergent approaches. Prominent examples of this can be seen in the many successful

DOI: 10.4324/9781003199359-32

athletes whose previous participation in sport mirrored engagement and experiences more closely aligned with Côté *et al.* proposed developmental pathway known as 'early sampling' (Côté, 1999; Côté *et al.*, 2009; Côté and Vierimaa, 2014). Here, athletes are introduced to a variety of sporting activities and sporting environments at a range of intensities as children (e.g. non-adult led, adult led, recreational, competitive) before gradually intensifying their level of engagement and focusing more on the activities that they like most during late adolescence. Compared to early specialisation, research suggests that this more incremental and explorative-based approach to sport participation may be more likely to foster long-term interest in sport while simultaneously protecting young athletes against injury and burnout (Fraser-Thomas *et al.*, 2008b; Fraser-Thomas and Côté, 2009). Additionally, given that more than 99% of children who participate in sport do not progress to a full-time athletic career (Côté and Erickson, 2015), the availability of a pathway that can help to build, potentially, life-long interest *in* and engagement *with* sport and exercise for 'as many as possible for as long as possible' (Erikstad *et al.*, 2021) may be a more beneficial approach to adopt. In this regard, child sport programs should not be built solely around the variables that affect skill development and performance (e.g. amount of practice) and must, instead, be designed to foster more general and inclusive outcomes (e.g. enjoyment, interest, personal development). Such an approach is critical and recognises the impact of child sport programs on the quality of the experience and short-term consequences of the young people involved. A focus on skill acquisition and expert development is not itself a problem, however such programs need not be mutually exclusive from programs that emphasise positive youth development (e.g. Harwood and Johnston, 2016).

## Review of Current Research

As detailed in the chapter introduction, young athletes can navigate sport through a number of different pathways, based on various factors such as personal interest and social influences from important others (e.g. parents). On one hand, there is extensive evidence indicating that physical, mental, and social outcomes increase as a result of sport participation during childhood and adolescence (Eime *et al.*, 2013; Bruner *et al.*, 2021). On the other hand, it is important to note that mere participation in sport does not automatically guarantee positive development or outcomes (i.e. personal and social skills; Côté *et al.*, 2020). With the rise in adult-led youth sport programming, experiences layered with high levels of commitment, intensity, and cost are far less desirable for young athletes, and often drive them to pursue other extracurricular activities that may not be physical-activity based (Crane and Temple, 2015; Erdal, 2018). When sport participation becomes more about intensified training at increasingly younger ages, and less about challenging activities in fun environments, young athletes may turn away from sport prematurely (Fraser-Thomas *et al.*, 2008a). In light of these findings, many researchers, sport practitioners, and pediatric specialists have promoted early sampling during development as opposed to early specialising (Bergeron *et al.*, 2015; Côté and Hancock, 2016; DiFiori *et al.*, 2018)

A vast amount of research and popular discussion was triggered by Ericsson *et al.* (1993) related to the role of practice in the development of expertise. Ericsson *et al.* suggested that engagement in a specific type of practice labelled as *deliberate practice* was the most important variable for the development of expertise. Deliberate practice was defined as a training activity that (a) is undertaken with the specific purpose of increasing performance (e.g. not for enjoyment or external rewards), (b) requires cognitive and/or physical effort, and (c) promotes skill development. Ericsson et al. also reported, through their work with musicians, a linear relationship between time spent in deliberate practice and measures of performance. Building upon Ericsson's work, early studies investigating the deliberate practice framework in sport supported the contention that the number of hours invested in deliberate practice was directly linked to the development of skills and level of achievement in different sports (e.g. Starkes *et al.*, 1996; Helsen *et al.*, 1998; Deakin and Cobley, 2003). This body of research led some sport organisations to adopt this idea and design programs that focus heavily on early involvement in deliberate practice – often at the cost of participant interest, motivation, and well-being.

The Developmental Model of Sport Participation (DMSP – Côté, 1999; Côté and Vierimaa, 2014) has been recognised as one of the most influential sport involvement models (Bruner *et al.*, 2010). The DMSP emphasises the importance of early sampling and consists of progressive stages of development towards both sport expertise as well as continued engagement in recreational sport that includes: (a) the sampling years, (b) the specialising years or recreational years, and (c) the investment years.

Two concepts predicting sport involvement throughout an athlete's lifespan consistently emerged from the empirical data that support the DMSP and an early sampling approach, these being the practice of (a) sampling between sports and (b) sampling within sports. More specifically, the concept of sampling *between* sports describes the pattern of an athlete's involvement in different types of sport experiences during childhood (i.e. participating in different sports) while the concept of sampling *within* sport refers to a pattern of varied engagement experienced by an athlete within the context of a singular sporting activity (i.e. deliberate play, playing multiple positions within a single sport, participating in more game-like versions of a single sport, organised practice). In terms of the greater deliberate play element that occurs through sampling sport, less structured or child-led activities are thought to aid in fostering interest more easily due to involvement in activities that are enjoyable and promote intrinsic regulation. Within the DMSP, the concepts of sampling between and sampling within sport act as the backbone of recommended engagement with sport during a child's sampling years (Erickson *et al.*, 2018; Murata *et al.*, 2021).

In addition to the important distinction involving between and within sport sampling, the DMSP carries seven postulates. Generally speaking, these postulates detail the evidence that early sampling (a) does not hinder later elite sport performance where peak performance is reached after maturation, (b) has positive implications for longer-term sport participation, (c) allows for participation in a wider range of social contexts, and (d) establishes a range of motor and cognitive skills that children can eventually bring to a principal sport of interest. As a guideline, the DMSP advocates for the entry into adolescence (around age 13) as an optimal timeframe for athletes to determine if they would like to specialise in one sport, and posits that it is not until later adolescence (around age 16) that athletes possess the appropriate physical, cognitive, social, emotional, and motor skills needed to invest their efforts into highly specialising training in a single sport.

The most important aspect of sampling between and within sport during the sampling years is the idea that these pathways reduce the intensity of involvement in one sport and the need to have selective teams that favour only a chosen number of athletes during childhood. Further, child sport programs built around these concepts, as well as deliberate play, have a protective effect against burnout, dropout, and injuries (Law *et al.*, 2007; Wall and Côté, 2007; Fraser-Thomas *et al.*, 2008a, 2008b). These key elements of the sampling years remind adults to focus on the needs of all children involved in sport instead of a select number of children that have been unreliably chosen. Through the practice of sampling various sports and engaging in different activities within the same sport, the sampling years are considered essential building blocks for self-regulated investment in elite sport during adolescence and adulthood (Côté *et al.*, 2009). In relation to empirical evidence, participating in a variety of sports can increase the likelihood of improving motor skills and enjoying prolonged and rewarding sport experiences (e.g. Côté and Vierimaa, 2014; Gould, 2019). Specialising in sport, on the other hand, is more closely tied to overuse injuries, anxiety due to high-performance expectations, and a higher tendency to encounter burnout (Myer *et al.*, 2015, 2016; DiSanti and Erickson, 2019, 2020 for reviews). The following paragraphs outline the evidence based on recent systematic reviews in sport that speak to the postulates of the DMSP, but also offer insight regarding the type of research conducted to attain these broad conclusions.

Recently, Güllich *et al.* (2021b) conducted a meta-analysis involving 51 international studies with over 6,000 athletes, including nearly 800 of the world's top sport performers, to understand if intensive specialised practice or multidisciplinary practice backgrounds better predicted performance. The main variables of interest for this review were sport starting age, age of reaching performance milestones, and amounts of coach-led practice and child-led play in the athlete's main sport and in other sports. Three main conclusions were drawn from this review of nearly 500 effect sizes. The first finding was that adult world-class athletes engaged in more multisport practice as a child and adolescent, started their main sport later in life, accumulated less main-sport practice, and initially progressed more slowly than did national-class athletes. Second, higher performing athletes started playing their main sport earlier, engaged in more main-sport practice but less other-sport practice, and had faster initial progress than did lower performing athletes. Finally, child-led play appeared to have negligible effects on both child and adult performance. In sum, the major takeaway from this meta-analysis supported the sampling trajectories of obtaining elite sport performance insofar that practice that is diverse in nature was associated with more gradual initial discipline-specific progress (i.e. athletes may not have performed as high during childhood), but importantly sustainability of long-term development of excellence as an adult.

Looking to test the hypothesis that young athletes who engage in early specialisation are also more likely to experience burnout, Giusti *et al.* (2020) reviewed the evidence that compared early specialisers against samplers on a specific measure of psychological burnout. Comparable to accepted definitions, qualifying as a sport specialiser meant that athletes had to participate in only one sport more than eight months of the year, to the exclusion of other sports. Data were compiled from a total of 1,429 athletes aged 12 to 17 across eight unique studies. Overall, meta-analysis revealed that early specialisers were more likely to report higher scores for reduced sense of accomplishment, exhaustion, and sport devaluation, which supports consensus statements from different governing bodies advising against early specialisation (e.g. AOSSM – LaPrade *et al.*, 2016).

In another review, Murata *et al.* (2021) sought to better understand the nature of the sport sampling literature using a scoping review methodology. In hopes of adding new knowledge to the early sampling and specialisation discussion, the main impetus behind conducting this review was to seek out and highlight scholarship that specifically looked at the effects of sampling multiple sports as opposed to the effects of playing a single sport. More specifically, the research team hoped to explore what kinds of findings had been previously published linking the practice of sampling between sports to the developmental metrics of athlete performance, continued sport participation, and personal development outside of sport (i.e. the 3Ps: Côté *et al.*, 2020). Upon completion of the project's search procedure, the research team located and then assessed a total of 53 articles, which sought to explore the effects of playing multiple sports on at least a single outcome within the 3Ps.

Following article assessment and coding, Murata *et al.* found that evidence linking the practice of sampling between sports and the attainment of sporting skill – either through the assessment of skills learned between groups of samplers and specialisers or through the exploration of successful athletes' past histories – was plentiful. Additionally, it also appeared evident that those athletes who played a variety of sports in lieu of specialising seemed much less likely to sustain a variety of injury types (i.e. soft tissue, overuse) and, therefore, were more likely to enjoy sustained sport participation across multiple stages of their lives (i.e. in childhood, adolescence, and adulthood). Perhaps somewhat surprisingly, researchers did not find evidence that linked sampling between sports to a reduction in levels of burnout or burnout acquisition across captured studies. Similarly, few articles sought to explore how the practice of sampling between sports might affect athlete's lives positively or negatively outside of the sporting context.

In addition to exploring the effects that sampling multiple sports might have on athlete development, the research team also sought to provide additional clarity regarding the sampling topic as a whole. For example, it was found that particularly in articles that discussed sampling but did not report empirical data (i.e. editorials, non-systematic reviews, position papers) it was often assumed that sampling a variety of sports might be both protective against athlete burnout as well as facilitative of positive outcomes outside of sport (i.e. personal development: increased social networks, life satisfaction) despite little evidence supporting these claims. Finally, a lack of uniformity regarding the various terms used to describe authors' choices in the description of opposing pathways to early specialisation were quite common and lacked a uniformity in definition (e.g. diversification, multi-sport participation, non-specialisation).

As detailed throughout this chapter, retrospective studies of expert athletes have supported the benefits of an early sampling approach leading towards elite performance in one sport during adulthood. More precisely, an early sampling trajectory has been supported by a large body of qualitative (e.g. Bloom, 1985; Carlson, 1988; Côté, 1999) and quantitative studies (e.g. Baker, 2003; Baker *et al.*, 2003; Soberlak and Côté, 2003; Baker *et al.*, 2005; Leite *et al.*, 2009; Barreiros and Fonseca, 2012; Güllich and Emrich, 2012, 2014; Bridge and Toms, 2013; Barreiros *et al.*, 2014; Güllich, 2014, 2018; Fahimi *et al.*, 2016). Despite this body of evidence, there is no consistent definition of sampling. In fact, many conceptualisations of sampling exist in the literature and most of the writing has restricted the term sampling to diversification between sports without providing a consistent definition. On the contrary, as the athlete development research evolves, multiple definitions of early specialisation have been presented (e.g. Laprade *et al.*, 2016; Bell *et al.*, 2021) in the literature, some of which have been criticised for lacking scientific rigor (Güllich *et al.*, 2021a). A single definition of sport sampling is essential to move the field forward and suggest an alternative pathway to early specialisation. To provide a starting point for a definition, we bring together past research in the area with the results of the Murata *et al.* (2021) review to forward the following parameters for a definition of early sport sampling. This foundation will help to ensure the construct is defined and measured accurately and appropriately.

## *Towards a Definition of Sport Sampling*

Sport sampling is a period of discovery during childhood. Sport sampling consists of exploring different sports (*sampling between sports*) and/or different ways of engaging in one sport (*sampling within sports*) so that interest and investment in one or multiple sports during adolescence and adulthood is maintained. It is also important to acknowledge that sport experiences can take place in organised, adult-led settings (e.g. deliberate practice) or unorganised, child-led settings (e.g. deliberate play). Differentiating between sampling that takes place between and within sports, and in play and practice settings is important if we are to understand the diverse sampling experiences that contribute to positive emotions and the ability to make an informed decision about future engagement. A more comprehensive definition of sport sampling is needed and, therefore, this chapter presents the following three postulates (i.e. sport engagement, time, and decision-making) as critical elements required within any such formalised definition.

Young sport participants may be considered samplers if their engagement in sport encompasses each of the following elements during their childhood sport involvement (approximately between the ages of 6 and 12):

1 Sport engagement:

   a Sampling between sports: A child would be considered a sport sampler if they are engaged in more than one (i) organised sport and/or (ii) unorganised sport.
   b Sampling within sports: A child would be considered a sport sampler if they are engaged in (i) multiple positions within one organised/unorganised sport or (ii) various versions of the same organised/unorganised sport (e.g. soccer and futsal).

2 Time:

   a A child should sample between or within sport on a regular basis (i.e. at least one hour a week).
   b A child should sample between or within sport for a minimum of three months within a 12-month period.
   c A child should sample between or within sport for at least two years to establish a pattern of behavior.

3 Decision-making:

   a The choice to sample between and within sports is made collaboratively between adults (parents) and the child, and is motivated by curiosity, participating in different activities, and exploring different social settings. After a period of sampling, children can make an autonomous and informed decision about their engagement in one or multiple sports at a recreational or more competitive level.

Importantly, these postulates (and the sub-points within) should not be thought of as prescriptive. Instead, it is best to consider each as a pillar within the broader structure of behaviours encompassing the practice of sport sampling. For instance, individual differences and the type of experiences will dictate how long the sampling period needs to last to lead to long-term engagement and autonomous decision. The ultimate consequence of sampling is to develop children's ability to make an informed decision about their future involvement in sport.

## Implications for Children's Sport Coaching

Coaching effectiveness should be representative of not only a coach's professional knowledge but also their interpersonal and intrapersonal knowledge (Côté and Gilbert, 2009). Gleaned from this definition is the notion that whereas coaches certainly require requisite knowledge about sport-specific skills, activities, and strategies, they must also emphasise positive interactions with athletes and engage in self-reflection to understand how their behaviors impact those around them. In the child sport setting, perhaps one of the most important implications from the research listed above is that coaches must diligently work against the professionalisation of childhood sport and actively downplay the need for immediate performance (i.e. winning) while promoting a person-centered developmental mindset.

For coaches in the child sport setting, it is important to be considerate of the offseason and work with athletes to ensure a healthy dose of diversification for their sport participation. As made clear in the DMSP, it is recommended that young athletes are afforded the opportunity to progress through stages of sport participation: (a) the sampling years (roughly between the ages of 6 and 12), characterised by a high level of diversity both between and within sports; (b) the specialising years (between roughly 13 and 16), wherein athletes begin to focus solely on the activities they enjoy most; or recreational years (as an extension of the sampling years; ages 13 and up) and (c) the investment years (approximately from the age of 17 and onwards), in which athletes may safely specialise in a single activity at an elevated level of intensity (generally in the pursuit of elite performance). Evidence accumulated over the past two decades suggests this more varied and gradual approach to sport participation may help to protect young athletes from the risks of early specialisation while also cultivating a climate better suited to hone athletic performance, sustain long-term sport participation, and provide more opportunities for personal development (i.e. the 3Ps).

As coaches, we may push our athletes to enroll in specialised offseason training programs so that they can return the following season further ahead, and give your team the best chance to succeed. Further, parents may solicit a coach regarding the options available for their child to improve for a future season. In either case, it is important to set aside a personal agenda, and make sure that athletes and parents both understand the wide range of sport options available. These options for diversification should be compared against the DMSP levels of sport participation, and should include opportunities for sampling between and within sport.

## Summary, Future Directions, and Future Research

Throughout this chapter, two distinct pathways are detailed through which young athletes may pursue expertise and long-term engagement in sport. On the one hand, we have early specialisation, in which athletes participate year round in a single sport at the expense of other sport experiences (even those within the same sport type). Alternatively, early sport sampling is promoted as a more viable pathway to achieve personal and social skill development through sport. With the knowledge that more than 99% of children who participate in sport do not progress to a full-time sport career (Côté and Erickson, 2015), it is critical for coaches to advocate for 'as many as possible for as long as possible.'

In terms of limitations of existing research, the majority of what we know about sampling between sports and athlete development has been discovered through work completed with male team sport athletes. As such, more research on this topic must be completed with female athletes and with athletes participating in individual sports to gain a more complete picture of the mechanisms behind sampling multiple sports and its potential benefits. Related to more female athletes, this is a critical future direction because adolescence is a recognised time period for increased sport dropout (Pfeiffer *et al.* 2006), and the nuances of sampling and specialising in sport could further contribute to this issue. It will also be important to expand cultural consideration, as this research tends to focus on athletes in WEIRD (Western, Educated, Industrialised, Rich, and Democratic) countries, and these participants may be far less indicative of the global population as researchers assume. Finally, research also relies heavily on retrospective accounts of athletes who 'made it' to tell their lived experiences. Although these stories are interesting and informative, it does not represent the majority of athletes who did not make it to professional sport levels. Therefore, more longitudinal research to track athletes that achieved different levels of performance and outcomes will help to understand how participation along different DMSP pathways relates to psychosocial outcomes over time.

## References

Baker, J., 2003. Early specialisation in youth sport: A requirement for adult expertise? *High Ability Studies*, 14 (1), 85–94.

Baker, J., Cote, J., and Abernethy, B., 2003. Sport-specific practice and the development of expert decision-making in team ball sports. *Journal of Applied Sport Psychology*, 15 (1), 12–25.

Baker, J., Côté, J., and Deakin, J., 2005. Expertise in ultra-endurance triathletes early sport involvement, training structure, and the theory of deliberate practice. *Journal of Applied Sport Psychology*, 17 (1), 64–78.

Barreiros, A., Côté, J., and Fonseca, A.M., 2014. From early to adult sport success: Analysing athletes' progression in national squads. *European Journal of Sport Science*, 14 (sup1), S178–S182.

Barreiros, A.N. and Fonseca, A.M., 2012. A retrospective analysis of Portuguese elite athletes' involvement in international competitions. *International Journal of Sports Science and Coaching*, 7 (3), 593–600.

Bell, D.R., *et al.*, 2021. Consensus definition of sport specialisation in youth athletes using a Delphi approach. *Journal of Athletic Training*, 56 (11), 1239–1251.

Bergeron, M.F., *et al.*, 2015. International olympic committee consensus statement on youth athletic development. *British Journal of Sports Medicine*, 49 (13), 843–851.

Bloom, B., 1985. *Developing talent in young people.* New York: Ballantine Books.

Bridge, M.W. and Toms, M.R., 2013. The specialising or sampling debate: A retrospective analysis of adolescent sports participation in the UK. *Journal of Sports Sciences*, 31 (1), 87–96.

Bruner, M.W., *et al.*, 2010. An appraisal of athlete development models through citation network analysis. *Psychology of Sport and Exercise*, 11 (2), 133–139.

Bruner, M.W., *et al.*, 2021. The effect of sport-based interventions on positive youth development: A systematic review and meta-analysis. *International Review of Sport and Exercise Psychology*. 1–28. 10.1080/1750984X.2021.1875496

Carlson, R., 1988. The socialisation of elite tennis players in Sweden: An analysis of the players' backgrounds and development. *Sociology of Sport Journal*, 5 (3), 241–256.

Côté, J., 1999. The influence of the family in the development of talent in sport. *The Sport Psychologist*, 13 (4), 395–417.

Côté, J. and Erickson, K., 2015. Diversification and deliberate play during the sampling years. *In*: J. Baker and D. Farrow, eds. *Routledge handbook of sport expertise.* London: Routledge, 305–316.

Côté, J. and Gilbert, W., 2009. An integrative definition of coaching effectiveness and expertise. *International Journal of Sports Science and Coaching*, 4 (3), 307–323.

Côté, J. and Hancock, D.J., 2016. Evidence-based policies for youth sport programmes. *International Journal of Sport Policy and Politics*, 8 (1), 51–65.

Côté, J., Lidor, R., and Hackfort, D., 2009. ISSP position stand: To sample or to specialise? Seven postulates about youth sport activities that lead to continued participation and elite performance. *International Journal of Sport and Exercise Psychology*, 7 (1), 7–17.

Côté, J. and Vierimaa, M., 2014. The developmental model of sport participation: 15 years after its first conceptualisation. *Science and Sports*, 29, S63–S69.

Côté, J., *et al.*, 2020. Youth sport research: Describing the integrated dynamics elements of the personal assets framework. *International Journal of Sport Psychology*, 51 (4), 562–578.

Crane, J. and Temple, V., 2015. A systematic review of dropout from organised sport among children and youth. *European Physical Education Review*, 21 (1), 114–131.

Deakin, J.M. and Cobley, S., 2003. A search for deliberate practice: An examination of the practice environments in figure skating and volleyball. *In*: J. Starkes and K.A. Ericsson, eds. *Expert performance in sports: Advances in research on sport expertise.* Champaign, IL: Human Kinetics, 115–135.

DiFiori, J.P., *et al.*, 2018. The NBA and youth basketball: Recommendations for promoting a healthy and positive experience. *Sports Medicine*, 48 (9), 2053–2065.

DiSanti, J.S. and Erickson, K., 2019. Youth sport specialisation: A multidisciplinary scoping systematic review. *Journal of Sports Sciences*, 37 (18), 2094–2105.

DiSanti, J.S. and Erickson, K., 2020. Challenging our understanding of youth sport specialisation: An examination and critique of the literature through the lens of bronfenbrenner's person-process-context-time model. *International Review of Sport and Exercise Psychology*, 14 (1), 28–50.

Eime, R.M., *et al.*, 2013. A systematic review of the psychological and social benefits of participation in sport for children and adolescents: Informing development of a conceptual model of health through sport. *International Journal of Behavioral Nutrition and Physical Activity*, 10 (1), 1–21.

Erdal, K., 2018. *The adulteration of children's sports: Waning health and well-being in the age of organised play.* New York: Rowman & Littlefield.

Ericsson, K.A., Krampe, R.T., and Tesch-Römer, C., 1993. The role of deliberate practice in the acquisition of expert performance. *Psychological Review*, 100 (3), 363–406.

Erickson, K., *et al.*, 2018. Play during childhood and the development of expertise in sport. *In*: Z. Hambrick, G. Campitelli, and B. Macnamara, eds. *The Science of Expertise: Behavioral, neural, and genetic approaches to complex skill.* London: Routledge, 398–416.

Erikstad, M.K., *et al.*, 2021. "As many as possible for as Long as possible"—A case study of a soccer team that fosters multiple outcomes. *The Sport Psychologist*, 1, 1–11.

Fahimi, M., *et al.*, 2016. The effect specialisation and diversification involvement on learning of sports skills according to deliberate practice and deliberate play. *International Journal of Medical Research and Health Sciences*, 5 (12), 110–116.

Fraser-Thomas, J. and Côté, J., 2009. Understanding adolescents' positive and negative developmental experiences in sport. *The Sport Psychologist*, 23 (1), 3–23.

Fraser-Thomas, J., Coté, J., and Deakin, J., 2008a. Examining adolescent sport dropout and prolonged engagement from a developmental perspective. *Journal of Applied Sport Psychology*, 20 (3), 318–333.

Fraser-Thomas, J., Côté, J., and Deakin, J., 2008b. Understanding dropout and prolonged engagement in adolescent competitive sport. *Psychology of Sport and Exercise*, 9 (5), 645–662.

Giusti, N.E., *et al.*, 2020. Comparing burnout in sport-specialising versus sport-sampling adolescent athletes: A systematic review and meta-analysis. *Orthopaedic Journal of Sports Medicine*, 8 (3), 2325967120907579.

Gould, D., 2019. The current youth sport landscape: Identifying critical research issues. *Kinesiology Review*, 8 (3), 150–161.

Güllich, A., 2014. Many roads lead to Rome–Developmental paths to Olympic gold in men's field hockey. *European Journal of Sport Science*, 14 (8), 763–771.

Güllich, A., 2018. Sport-specific and non-specific practice of strong and weak responders in junior and senior elite athletics–A matched-pairs analysis. *Journal of Sports Sciences*, 36 (19), 2256–2264.

Güllich, A. and Emrich, E., 2012. Individualistic and collectivistic approach in athlete support programmes in the German high-performance sport system. *European Journal for Sport and Society*, 9 (4), 243–268.

Güllich, A. and Emrich, E., 2014. Considering long-term sustainability in the development of world class success. *European Journal of Sport Science*, 14 (sup1), S383–S397.

Güllich, A., Macnamara, B.N., and Hambrick, D.Z., 2021b. What makes a champion? Early multidisciplinary practice, not early specialisation, predicts world-class performance. *Perspectives on Psychological Science*, 17 (1), 6–29.

Güllich, A., *et al.*, 2021a. Further muddying the waters? A comment on Bell *et al*'s 2021 definition of youth sport specialisation. *Journal of Athletic Training*, 56 (11), 1252–1254.

Harwood, C. and Johnston, J., 2016. Positive youth development and talent development: Is there a best of both worlds? *In*: N. Holt, ed. *Positive youth development through sport*, London: Routledge, 113–125.

Helsen, W.F., Starkes, J.L., and Hodges, N.J., 1998. Team sports and the theory of deliberate practice. *Journal of Sport and Exercise Psychology*, 20 (1), 12–34.

LaPrade, R.F., *et al.*, 2016. AOSSM early sport specialisation consensus statement. *Orthopaedic Journal of Sports Medicine*, 4 (4), 2325967116644241.

Law, M.P., Côté, J., and Ericsson, K.A., 2007. Characteristics of expert development in rhythmic gymnastics: A retrospective study. *International Journal of Sport and Exercise Psychology*, 5 (1), 82–103.

Leite, N., Baker, J., and Sampaio, J., 2009. Paths to expertise in Portuguese national team athletes. *Journal of Sports Science and Medicine*, 8 (4), 560–566.

Murata, A., *et al.*, 2021. Sampling between sports and athlete development: A scoping review. *International Journal of Sport and Exercise Psychology*, 1–25. 10.1080/1612197X.2021.1995021

Myer, G.D., *et al.*, 2015. Sport specialisation, part I: Does early sports specialisation increase negative outcomes and reduce the opportunity for success in young athletes?. *Sports Health*, 7 (5), 437–442.

Myer, G.D., *et al.*, 2016. Sports specialisation, part II: Alternative solutions to early sport specialisation in youth athletes. *Sports Health*, 8 (1), 65–73.

Pfeiffer, K.A., *et al.*, 2006. Sport participation and physical activity in adolescent females across a four-year period. *Journal of Adolescent Health*, 39 (4), 523–529.

Soberlak, P. and Côté, J., 2003. The developmental activities of elite ice hockey players. *Journal of Applied Sport Psychology*, 15 (1), 41–49.

Starkes, J.L., *et al.*, 1996. Deliberate practice in sports: What is it anyway. *In*: K.A. Ericsson, ed. *The road to excellence: The acquisition of expert performance in the arts and sciences, sports, and games*. Mahwah, NJ: Lawrence Erlbaum Associates. 81–106.

Storm, L.K., Kristoffer, H., and Krogh, C.M.K., 2012. Specialisation pathways among elite danish athletes: A look at the developmental model of sport participation from a cultural perspective. *International Journal of Sport Psychology*, 43 (3), 199–222.

Wall, M. and Côté, J., 2007. Developmental activities that lead to dropout and investment in sport. *Physical Education and Sport Pedagogy*, 12 (1), 77–87.

# 29

# GROUP BANDING STRATEGIES IN CHILDREN'S ORGANISED SPORT: LOOKING BEYOND FIXED CHRONOLOGICAL AGE

*Adam L. Kelly and Jennifer Turnnidge*

## Introduction

The primary purpose of grouping children by chronological age is to facilitate developmentally appropriate levels of challenge and equitable competition (Baxter-Jones, 1995). However, the reality of lived youth sport experiences may not always meet these intended outcomes (e.g. Kelly *et al.*, 2021b). For instance, it has become well documented that (bi)annual age grouping can create a relative age bias towards those born earlier in the selection year (Barnsley *et al.*, 1985). Broadly, relative age effects (RAEs) refer to the overrepresentation of those born near the start of the cut-off date and the underrepresentation of those born near the end of the cut-off date throughout male and female youth sport participation and performance pathways (Kelly and Williams, 2020). This is often contingent on a number of contextual factors (e.g. age, gender, playing level, sport type; Wattie *et al.*, 2015; Smith *et al.*, 2018), which can result in relatively older children possessing superior physiological characteristics (Cobley *et al.*, 2009), advanced psychosocial skills (Hancock *et al.*, 2013), and an older training age (Doncaster *et al.*, 2020) when compared to their relatively younger peers.

As a result of RAEs occurring due to children competing in fixed (bi)annual age groups, there is a growing body of literature that has explored alternative group banding concepts to offer more appropriate settings in youth sport (Webdale *et al.*, 2019). As such, this chapter aims to encapsulate the existing research that proposes alternative group banding strategies, including (a) 'flexible chronological approach' (i.e. *playing-up* and *playing-down*), (b) 'birthday-banding', and (c) 'average team age'. Moreover, based on these discussions of the current research, this chapter will offer possible implications for children's sport coaching, as well as directions for future research and practice.

## Review of Current Research

### *Flexible Chronological Approach*

Despite a large amount of research that has focussed on talent identification, athlete development, and youth sport participation, there is a lack of literature on children who participate outside of their chronological age groups. For example, when youth athletes demonstrate that they are more

DOI: 10.4324/9781003199359-33

skilled than their same-aged peers, they may be allowed to compete at higher age levels. This concept is commonly known as *playing-up* (Goldman *et al.*, 2021a). In comparison, *playing-down* occurs when players participate at lower age levels. Playing-down may create more suitable developmental settings by promoting greater selection opportunities and increased participation amongst low-achieving children (Goldman *et al.*, 2021b). The term 'flexible chronological approach' depicts the organisational structures that allow young athletes to play-up or play-down a (bi)annual age group (Kelly *et al.*, 2020b). Although these approaches are regularly used throughout youth sport organisations, they have received little attention within the literature.

Given the paucity of research in youth sport, it may be useful to understand how similar issues to playing-up have been examined in education. For example, in the same way that coaches may play-up athletes who show advanced sport-specific skills, teachers may move high-achieving students into advanced streams of study to provide them with developmentally appropriate learning experiences. Current literature has associated student grouping in education with numerous benefits and drawbacks for youth. One such method of student grouping that can be compared to playing-up is *acceleration* (i.e. students enter into school early or skip a grade; Steenbergen-Hu *et al.*, 2016). Previous studies have shown acceleration can have positive effects on childrens' academic achievement and psychosocial development. For instance, meta-analyses conducted by Steenbergen-Hu and Moon (2011) showed that accelerated students recorded higher academic achievement than their non-accelerated peers. From a psychosocial perspective, researchers have suggested that children's mental age (i.e. how old an average person with their intellect would be) may be a greater determinant of their emotional maturity compared to their chronological age (Janos and Robinson, 1985). Overall, the body of literature on acceleration implies that accelerated learning has the potential to facilitate children's holistic development.

In order to better understand the concept of playing-up in children's sport, two empirical studies have been conducted. First, Kelly *et al.* (2021b) investigated *what* factors differentiated English academy soccer players who played-up from those who did not. Broadly, their study highlighted the multidimensional nature of the athlete development process that was implicated through playing-up and dependent on age phase. More specifically, results in the Foundation Development Phase (FDP; U9 to U11) demonstrated significant factors that were technical and tactical in nature, whereas the Youth Development Phase (YDP; U12 to U16) revealed significant factors that offered a more holistic representation. These findings suggest it is important for practitioners to use a multidimensional approach when considering children's suitability to play-up. Second, Goldman *et al.* (2021a) explored youth soccer players perceptions of playing-up to understand *how* and *why* it may have affected their sport-specific skills and psychosocial outcomes. They found how athletes perceived playing-up to involve a combination of *challenge* and *progress*. However, the authors noted that athletes' perceptions of playing-up varied greatly from player to player. As such, playing-up should not be considered as a heterogeneous experience and it would be inappropriate to examine using a *one-size-fits-all* approach. Moving forward, further playing-up research is warranted across a diverse range of sporting contexts to advance our sport-specific knowledge (Table 29.1).

In comparison to playing-up, playing-down is yet to be empirically studied. Although this approach is perhaps used less commonly, there are still important implications for practitioners to consider. Drawing from an education context, playing-down in children's organised sport may be compared to *grade retention* (i.e. being held back a grade in school). Interestingly, previous research shows that grade retention may have limited positive effects on student outcomes. For instance, Jimerson *et al.* (2002) conducted a systematic review on the relationship between grade retention and dropout amongst high school students. Across 17 studies, students who were held back were up to 11 times more likely to drop out than those who were not. More recently, researchers showed that grade retention had neither positive nor

*Table 29.1* Evidence-based recommendations for practitioners working with children who play-up (adapted from Goldman *et al.*, 2021b)

| *Recommendations* | *Desired outcomes* | *Example behaviors* |
|---|---|---|
| Get to know children and include them in team activities | Social integration with older peers; Improved team cohesion; Positive perceptions of belongingness | Introduce oneself; Participate in bonding activities; Invite children to be partners or to join a group |
| Offer constructive feedback that tailors to the child's needs | Positive coach-athlete and athlete-athlete relationships; Improved intrinsic motivation to play-up | Compliment children on their abilities; Teach children to improve technique |
| Provide opportunities for children to demonstrate skills | Mutual trust and respect between children and older peers; Reduced pressure for children to prove themselves | Ask children to lead practice activities; Offer equal playing time; Create activities whereby older and younger children must work together to succeed |

negative effects on students' attendance and discipline, although it was associated with a decrease in students' motivation (Martorell and Mariano, 2018; Kretschmann *et al.*, 2019). Overall, the current literature outlines the potential benefits and drawbacks of moving relatively younger individuals into lower age groups, such as in the case of playing-down. From a children's organised sport perspective, playing-down may offer a useful strategy to moderate RAEs (e.g. for relatively younger athletes). In contrast, however, it could lead to negative outcomes (e.g. dropout, de-motivation, low self-esteem) if used in the wrong context. Since the implications of playing-down have yet to be empirically evaluated in children's organised sport, further study is needed to better understand its potential to influence athletes' experiences and developmental outcomes.

Together, playing-up and playing-down offer useful strategies to moderate equity in youth soccer and may provide children with a more appropriate learning environment. Within a youth soccer setting, Kelly *et al.* (2020b) termed the adoption of playing-up and playing-down as a flexible chronological approach, as opposed to a traditional *fixed* chronological approach. Specifically, during their investigation into RAEs at a professional soccer academy, the authors suggested that playing-up may facilitate greater development for relatively older players by creating a *birth quarter four effect* (i.e. players who are relatively older within their age group become relatively younger by playing-up against older peers). Likewise, playing-down may offer a more suitable developmental setting for relatively younger children, as well as possibly offering a more challenging environment for earlier-born players in a younger age group. Moreover, rather than competing in a *fixed* chronological age group (i.e. being relatively older or relatively younger throughout development), playing-up and playing-down facilitate more diverse experiences throughout players' developmental pathways (i.e. opportunities to be both relatively older *and* relatively younger; Kelly *et al.*, 2020b). Whilst these examples focus on how RAEs could be moderated, other performance-related outcomes could also be mediated through holistic approach, such as maturation status, sport-specific skills, and psychosocial behaviours. Therefore, further research is required across a range of sporting contexts to explore how a flexible chronological approach can be used to foster rich sport experiences for children that facilitate performance, participation, and personal development outcomes in the long term.

## *Birthday-Banding*

'Birthday-banding' refers to a grouping strategy whereby children move up to their next birthdate group on their birthday in organised youth sport (Kelly *et al.*, 2020a). The aim of this grouping policy is to remove particular selection time-points, fixed chronological age groups, and moderate RAEs. As a practical example, within an annual age group, an U14 child would move up to the U15 age group on their birthday and remain in that age group until their following birthday (Figure 29.1). As such, recruitment remains continual to ensure there is an equal opportunity for all athletes to be selected during the entire selection year. It also denotes that in any 12-month (or 24-month) period, a child will be both the oldest and youngest in their (bi)annual age group. Despite being quietly implemented by England Squash approximately eight years ago, the introduction and preliminary exploration of this strategy has only recently been studied (Kelly *et al.*, 2020a; Jeffreys *et al.*, 2021).

In an attempt to test its ability to moderate RAEs, a preliminary study by Kelly *et al.* (2020a) explored the birth quartiles (BQs; i.e. 12 months of the (bi)annual selection year divided into four quartiles) of the athletes in the five-step England Squash Talent Pathway. Contrary to a large body of existing relative age literature in sport (Cobley *et al.*, 2009; Smith *et al.*, 2018), and more specifically racket sports (Loffing *et al.*, 2010; Romann *et al.*, 2018; Faber *et al.*, 2020), their results showed there were no differences in all of the cohorts' BQ distributions (BQ1 = 21% vs. BQ4 = 25.6%) when compared to national norms. Further, there were no differences in the BQ distributions based on gender when compared to national norms. Overall, these findings served as a useful opening to the potential of birthday-banding to moderate RAEs.

In addition to its potential to moderate RAEs, birthday-banding offers children the opportunity to consistently shift between being the relatively oldest *and* the relatively youngest based on their individual age throughout development. As a result, this strategy may better reflect the dynamic nature of the athlete development process (e.g. the 'rocky road' effect; Collins and MacNamara, 2012; Collins *et al.*, 2016). More specifically, rather than competing in

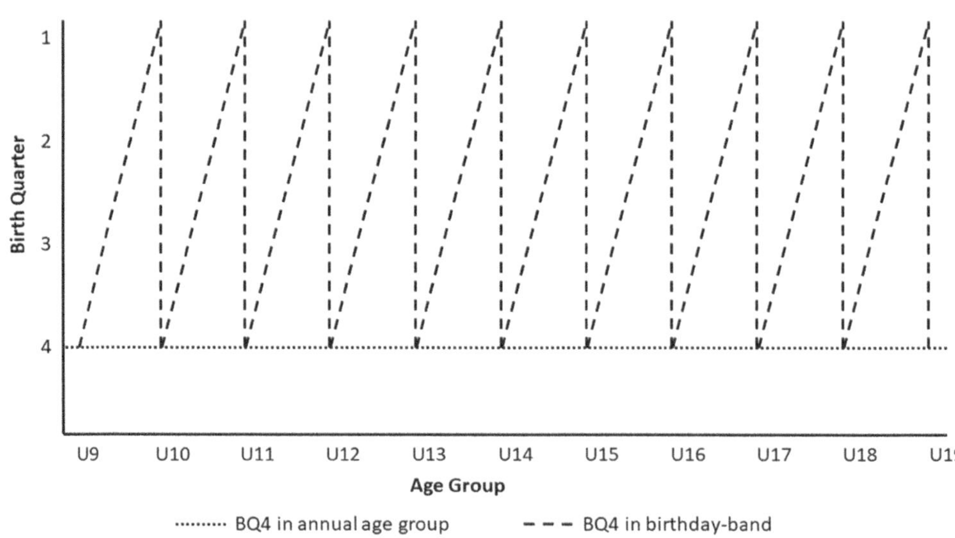


*Figure 29.1* A comparison between the U9 to U19 developmental trajectories of annual age grouping and birthday-banding (adapted from Jeffreys *et al.*, 2021)

*fixed* (bi)annual age groups (i.e. being relatively older or relatively younger throughout development), more diverse experiences may be offered by the birthday-banding strategy (i.e. being both relatively older and relatively younger throughout development). This could also lead to various other possible benefits, such as providing opportunities for *mixed-aged activities* and broader *social comparisons*. With regard to mixed-aged activities, evidence exists to suggest that there are positive outcomes from younger and older athletes playing together. For instance, both Côté *et al.* (2007) and Jarvis (2007) identified that children who are relatively older can gain leadership opportunities by helping to develop relatively younger children. On the other hand, relatively younger children may be able to develop their skills by competing against older teammates, which has resulted in possible reversal effects of relative age in English rugby union and cricket (McCarthy *et al.*, 2016), higher average earnings in German soccer (Ashworth and Heyndels, 2007), and a longer career duration in Canadian ice hockey (Gibbs *et al.*, 2012). These diverse experiences may well extend beyond athletes' relative age within their peer group. For example, children may also have increased opportunities to interact with different coaches, as well as engage in a wider range of activities.

In relation to social comparison theory, it has been suggested that children utilise peers and teammates as a frame of reference to compare themselves, and subsequently build self-perceptions such as competence and identity (Wood and Wilson, 2003). Applied to the birthday-banding strategy, opportunities to be relatively older may provide a setting for children to compare themselves positively with others, as well as enabling a greater number of children to experience being amongst the higher performers within their group. Alternatively, however, when children move to the older age groups and become the youngest in that age group, they may be required to re-evaluate their self-perceptions in relation to their new peer group (Goldman *et al.*, 2021a). By heightening opportunities for children to compare themselves against others, the birthday-banding approach may establish a more dynamic, realistic, and resilient sense of self throughout development. However, given the limited body of literature on this topic, further research is encouraged to substantiate these suggestions.

Gender (i.e. male vs. female), sport type (i.e. team vs. individual), and competition level (e.g. recreational participation vs. talent development) may all play a vital role in constructing RAEs. For example, stronger RAEs have generally been identified in males when compared to females (e.g. Kelly *et al.*, 2021a). Furthermore, team sports are often associated with higher RAE estimates when compared to individual sports (Smith *et al.*, 2018). Additionally, previous studies have documented higher RAEs with increased competition levels across various sports, which is also dependent on the sport popularity (Cobley *et al.*, 2009). Since empirical research on birthday-banding is very much in its infancy, further empirical research across a wide range of sporting contexts is encouraged to better understand the viability of the birthday-banding approach based on these relative age origins (i.e. gender, sport type, and competition level). Moreover, there is more to understand about how this approach is viewed and experienced by children, coaches, and practitioners. As such, future investigations with a variety of key stakeholders may extend beyond our existing knowledge of this grouping approach.

## Average Team Age

It has been proposed that using the average age of a team can create more equitable opportunities for relatively younger children in youth sport when compared to (bi)annual age grouping (Helsen *et al.*, 2000). Based on the 'average team age' (ATA) grouping strategy, the bandings apply to the team and not the individual, which is comprised of two components:

a The average (mean) age of the starting team in a match shall be no more than "Y" years.
b No child in the squad shall be more than "Z" years older than the youngest child in the squad (see Lawrence *et al.*, 2019).

In addition to adjusting the average age of a team to a predetermined maximum, the ATA grouping strategy also addresses the maximum age difference between the oldest and youngest children in a given team (Figure 29.2). More specifically, the ATA grouping strategy allows a child to be selected based on a predetermined maximum age difference (e.g. two years), while the team meets the average age maximum. This enables a child of a certain age to compete in one of three ATA bands. As such, it may increase the opportunity to participate and develop at an appropriate age level, which may change over time depending on an individual's development trajectory. Moreover, a child can either be younger in an older ATA team, average in the middle ATA team, or older in the younger ATA team. Indeed, this flexibility for coaches does not exist in traditional (bi)annual age group structures.

Although the ATA grouping strategy is yet to be empirically tested, it is important to consider the potential benefits that this policy may have on RAEs, as well as the wider impact on participation and performance outcomes. Given the complexity of RAEs, there is a need for a so-called *hybrid approach* that offers more than one solution to diminish RAEs (Webdale *et al.*, 2019). For instance, it has been shown that single-age-focused grouping strategies to mitigate RAEs (e.g. postponing the age at which youth athletes can get drafted to the senior level) only partially addressed RAEs in the Australian Rules football talent pathway (Haycraft *et al.*, 2018). The ATA grouping strategy may qualify as a hybrid approach because it requires coaches to consider the relative age of all the athletes when computing the average age of a team. Thus, it is suggested that coaches may become explicitly aware of the birthdate distribution of the available athletes, which has been shown to reduce relative age biases during talent identification procedures (Mann and van Ginneken, 2017).

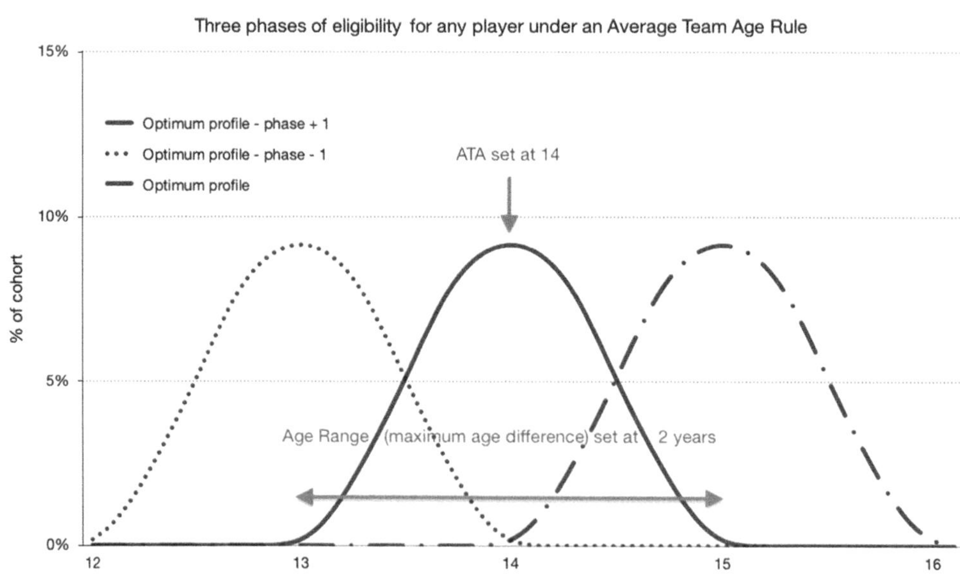


*Figure 29.2* Optimum age profiles for the ATA grouping strategy (adapted from Verbeek *et al.*, 2021)

In addition to potentially moderating RAEs in youth sport, the ATA grouping strategy may have broader benefits. In terms of creating fair and equitable competition, comparisons can be drawn from team selection in wheelchair rugby. That is, teams are not allowed to exceed a total of '8.0 points' at any time during a game, which is determined per athlete based on a classification system. The purpose of classification is to ensure fair and equitable competition at all levels and allow children to compete at the highest level, regardless of individual differences in physical function. In the context of the ATA grouping strategy, a maximum combined average age to which a team should adhere to is created, to provide more fair and equitable competition, as well as allowing children to compete at varying levels regardless of their relative age. Moreover, the ATA grouping strategy may also enable coaches to better group children according to their current development age rather than being restricted to fixed (bi)annual age groups. This not only allows younger athletes to *play-up*, but also the opportunity for older players to *play-down*. In turn, the ATA approach could facilitate more diverse developmental experiences by allowing a child to be both relatively older and relatively younger in different ATA teams. As such, the ATA approach may be a well-suited grouping strategy that is more representative of the non-linear pathway in youth sport development and thus provides more appropriate learning opportunities (Phillips *et al.*, 2010). Indeed, this may create a wide range of developmental experiences for children, such as mixed-age activities (Côté *et al.*, 2014), broader social comparison (Wood and Wilson, 2003), leadership opportunities (Jarvis, 2007), and underdog benefits (Gibbs *et al.*, 2012).

There have been some preliminary examples of in-house soccer competitions organised using the ATA grouping strategy. For instance, in England, Stoke City Football Club Academy trialled the ATA approach by mixing their male U9 to U12 age groups. According to their staff, the grouping policy showed positive developmental opportunities for athletes in terms of social cohesion and additional challenges. Moreover, they stated how older athletes took on leadership roles when playing with younger academy teammates (Cope, 2018). The Royal Netherlands Football Association has also studied small-sided games using the ATA grouping strategy with U9 to U13 recreational males and females. Their preliminary results highlighted that the ATA grouping strategy enabled coaches to group children according to a maximum average age and subsequently decreased the bias in birthdate distributions that is often present in (bi)annual age grouping (de Hoog 2020).

Although the ATA grouping strategy appears promising, it is important to consider that it is very much in its infancy and has only been explored in the context of soccer. A logical next step should be to study this approach using experimental tournaments. This may include the collection of quantitative data during matches (e.g. physical, technical) or qualitative approaches following tournaments (e.g. semi-structured interviews, surveys) to gain key stakeholders perceptions (e.g. players, practitioners). Moreover, possible concerns with applying the ATA approach include the uncertainty about how practitioners will deal with grouping older and younger children together, while the practical feasibility of implementing it should also be considered (Verbeek *et al.*, 2021). Thus, empirical research is encouraged across a range of sporting contexts to explore its practical effectiveness, from both children's development outlook and administrative perspective. This will enable researchers and practitioners to better understand the ecological validity of the ATA grouping strategy, as well as its potential mechanisms in creating more appropriate settings in children's organised youth sport.

## Implications for Children's Sport Coaching

It is important to consider that there are group bandings strategies that are available beyond those discussed in this chapter. Except chronological age, 'age and anthropometric bandings' appear to be the most studied throughout the grouping literature (Webdale *et al.*, 2019). Examples of age and anthropometric bandings in organised youth sport include grouping children into categories based on height, weight, and/or maturity status in relation to chronological age (Malina *et al.*, 2019). In combat sports (e.g. boxing, judo), for instance, *weight-based bandings* are often used to group athletes, since having a considerable disparity in weight can have implications on both performance and injury risk (Albuquerque *et al.*, 2016). Weight-based bandings have also been used in team sports (e.g. rugby, American football) for some time (Malina *et al.*, 2019). For example, they are implemented in New Zealand youth rugby from the ages of U8 to U13, with set weight restrictions for each age group. Thus, if an athlete does not fall within the weight band for their age group, they will have to *play-up* or *play-down* accordingly (Thomas *et al.*, 2021). Moreover, weight-based bandings have been implemented as an organisational policy in youth American football. In contrast to many other team sports (Cobley *et al.*, 2009), previous research has identified no RAEs in American football (MacDonald *et al.*, 2009; Jones *et al.*, 2019), which may lend credibility to this approach. Taken together, weight-based bandings may provide a useful approach in an attempt to moderate both maturity-related biases *and* RAEs in youth sport (Helsen *et al.*, 2021).

In an attempt to remove RAEs in timed sports, 'corrective adjustments' has been designed and evaluated as a method in children's athletics (Romann and Cobley, 2015) and swimming (Cobley *et al.*, 2019). This is whereby regression equations are applied through birthdate distributions and raw performance times, with the disseminations of performance levels subsequently re-examined for a greater chronological age equality. Moreover, *proficiency level-based competition* in youth sport, such as the 'belt' or 'colour' used in some combat sports, indicates that it may be a useful approach to moderate age-related performance advantages (Chiodo *et al.*, 2011). In taekwondo for instance, since children begin to compete at aged 10 years, organised youth competitions are based on a progression to meet the physiological characteristics of the child to preserve them from an excessive physiological strain, as well as facilitate the development of their technical and tactical skills (Casolino *et al.*, 2012). For this reason, Casolino *et al.* (2012) suggest how the Italian Taekwondo Federation establishes the proficiency level of children, by taking into account their training experience (i.e. from 1 to 3 years) and technical capabilities (i.e. belt or colour).

Based on the extant evidence base, it is plausible to suggest how different grouping approaches may be required depending on the sport-specific context. As an example, a flexible chronological approach, the average team age method, and age and anthropometric bandings may be more suitable for team sports (e.g. basketball, rugby, soccer), whereas birthday-banding, corrective adjustments, and proficiency level-based competition may be more useful for racket (e.g. badminton, squash, tennis), timed (e.g. cycling, sprinting, swimming), and combat (e.g. boxing, judo, taekwondo) sports, respectively. Moreover, practitioners are encouraged to realise that there is no 'copy and paste' template, and that they should seek to comprehend the grouping requirements based on a sport-specific perspective alongside considering contextual complexities of cultures, communities, and individual circumstances (Sullivan *et al.*, 2021).

It is important to consider the potential implications of group banding strategies in children's organised sport when looking beyond fixed chronological age grouping. Indeed, implementing alternative grouping approaches to organisational structures in youth sport has a range of potential positive outcomes, including:

- Moderates RAEs and offers a broader repertoire of strategies for coaches to use and children to engage in.
- Creates diverse technical, tactical, physical, and psychosocial developmental outcomes for children.

- Generates greater opportunities for mixed-age play, social comparison, and leadership skills.
- Presents the opportunity for children to experience a more dynamic, non-linear pathway rather than competing as a fixed birth quartile.
- Provides more accurate indicators of potential during talent identification procedures.
- Produces more equitable opportunities for participation, performance, and personal development in the long-term time scale.

## Summary, Future Directions and Future Research

Despite RAEs and maturity-related biases in youth sport being well documented within the academic literature, there has been little attempt to design, implement, and evaluate possible solutions in practice. This chapter has presented a small, growing body of literature that has attempted to shine light on potential strategies to mitigate these biases through alternative group banding strategies. As a result of these concepts only recently being proposed, they require further research to test their effectiveness. More specifically, researchers are encouraged to (a) actively design, implement, and evaluate group banding strategies across various children's settings, (b) adopt novel qualitative approaches (e.g. content analysis, composite narratives) to better understand the lived experiences and developmental trajectories of children throughout a variety of group banding strategies, and (c) ensure gender equity when designing research methodologies to facilitate the most appropriate developmental settings for both boys and girls.

## References

Albuquerque, M.R., *et al.*, 2016. Do weight categories prevent athletes from the relative age effect? A meta-analysis of combat sports. *Sport Sciences for Health*, 12 (2), 133–139.

Ashworth, J., and Heyndels, B., 2007. Selection bias and peer effects in team sports: The effect of age grouping on earnings of german soccer players. *Journal of Sports Economics*, 8 (4), 355–377.

Barnsley R.H., Thompson, A.H., and Barnsley, P.E., 1985. Hockey success and birthdate: The relative age effect. *Canadian Association of Health, Physical Education and Recreation Journal*, 51 (1), 23–28.

Baxter-Jones, A., 1995. Growth and development of young athletes: Should competition be age related? *Sports Medicine*, 20 (2), 59–64.

Casolino, E., *et al.*, 2012. Technical and tactical analysis of youth taekwondo performance. *Journal of Strength and Conditioning Research*, 26 (6), 1489–1495.

Chiodo, S., *et al.*, 2011. Stress-related hormonal and psychological changes to official youth taekwondo competitions. *Scandinavian Journal of Medicine and Science in Sports*, 21 (1), 111–119.

Cobley, S., *et al.*, 2019. Removing relative age effects from youth swimming: The development and testing of corrective adjustments procedure. *Journal of Science and Medicine in Sport*, 22 (6), 735–740.

Cobley, S., *et al.*, 2009. Annual age-grouping and athlete development. *Sports Medicine*, 39 (3), 235–256.

Collins, D. and MacNamara, Á., 2012. The rocky road to the top: Why talent needs trauma. *Sports Medicine*, 42 (11), 907–914.

Collins, D.J., MacNamara, Á., and McCarthy, N., 2016. Putting the bumps in the rocky road: Optimising the pathway to excellence. *Frontiers in Psychology*, 7 (1482), 1–6.

Cope, N. (2018). *Academy trial birth bias concept* [online]. Retrieved from: https://www.stokecityfc.com/news/academy-trial-birth-bias-concept [Accessed 25 March 2022].

Côté, J., Baker, J., and Abernethy, B., 2007. Practice and play in the development of sport expertise. *In*: G. Tenenbaum and R.C. Eklund, eds. *Handbook of sport psychology* (3rd Ed.). Hoboken, NY: Wiley, 184–202.

Côté, J., Turnnidge, J., and Evans, M.B., 2014. The dynamic process of development through sport. *Kinesiologia Slovenica*, 20 (3), 14–26.

de Hoog, M. (2020). *Waarom deze voetbalclub experimenteert met een gemiddelde leeftijd voor jeugdteams* [online]. Retrieved from: https://decorrespondent.nl/10913/waarom-deze-voetbalclub-experimenteert-met-een-gemiddelde-leeftijd-voor-jeugdteams/963707004645-0dbc4ba4 [Accessed 25 March 2022].

Doncaster, G., *et al.*, 2020. Appreciating factors beyond the physical in talent identification and development: Insights from the FC Barcelona sporting model. *Frontiers in Sports and Active Living*, 2 (91), 1–9.

Faber, I.R., *et al.*, 2020. Are performance trajectories associated with relative age in French top 100 youth table tennis players? – A longitudinal approach. *PLOS ONE*, 15 (4), e0231926.

Goldman, D.E., *et al.*, 2021a. Athlete perceptions of playing-up in youth soccer. *Journal of Applied Sport Psychology* [ePub ahead of print].

Goldman, D.E., *et al.*, 2021b. "Playing-up" in youth soccer. *In*: A.L. Kelly, J. Côté, M. Jeffreys, and J. Turnnidge, eds. *Birth advantages and relative age effects in sport: Exploring organisational structures and creating appropriate settings*. London: Routledge, 77–94.

Gibbs, B.G., Jarvis, J.A., and Dufur, M.J., 2012. The rise of the underdog? The relative age effect reversal among Canadian-born NHL hockey players: A reply to nolan and howell. *International Review for the Sociology of Sport*, 47 (5), 644–649.

Hancock, D.J., Adler, A.L., and Côté, J., 2013. A proposed theoretical model to explain relative age effects in sport. *European Journal of Sport Science*, 13 (6), 630–637.

Haycraft, J.A.Z., *et al.*, 2018. The influence of age-policy changes on the relative age effect across the Australian Rules football talent pathway. *Journal of Science and Medicine in Sport*, 21 (10), 1106–1111.

Helsen, W.F., Starkes, J.L., and Van Winckel, J., 2000. Effect of a change in selection year on success in male soccer players. *American Journal of Human Biology*, 12 (6), 729–735.

Helsen, W.F., *et al.*, 2021. Levelling the playing field: A new proposed method to address relative age- and maturity-related bias in soccer. *Frontiers in Sports and Active Living*, 3, 1–17.

Janos, P.M. and Robinson, N.M., 1985. Psychosocial development in intellectually gifted children. *In*: F.D. Horowitz and M. O'Brien, eds. *The gifted and talented: Developmental perspectives*. Washington DC: American Psychological Association, 149–195.

Jarvis, P., 2007. Dangerous activities within and invisible playground: A study of emergent male football play and teachers' perspectives of outdoor free play in the early years of primary school. *International Journal of Early Years Education*, 15 (3), 245–259.

Jeffreys, M., Turnnidge, J., and Kelly, A.L., 2021. Birthday-banding in the England squash talent pathway. *In*: A.L. Kelly, J. Côté, M. Jeffreys, and J. Turnnidge, eds. *Birth advantages and relative age effects in sport: Exploring organisational structures and creating appropriate settings*. London: Routledge, 95–106.

Jimerson, S.R., Anderson, G.E., and Whipple, A.D., 2002. Winning the battle and losing the war: Examining the relation between grade retention and dropping out of high school. *Psychology in the Schools*, 39 (4), 441–457.

Jones, C., *et al.*, 2019. Association between relative age effect and organisational practices of American youth football. *Journal of Sports Sciences*, 37 (10), 1146–1153.

Kelly, A.L. and Williams, C.A., 2020. Physical characteristics and the talent identification and development processes in male youth soccer: A narrative review. *Strength and Conditioning Journal*, 42 (6), 15–34.

Kelly, A.L., *et al.*, 2020a. "Birthday-banding" as a strategy to moderate the relative age effect: A case study into the England squash talent pathway. *Frontiers in Sports and Active Living*, 2, 1–9.

Kelly, A.L., *et al.*, 2020b. A longitudinal investigation into the relative age effect in an English professional football club: Exploring the 'underdog hypothesis'. *Science and Medicine in Football*, 4 (2), 111–118.

Kelly, A.L., *et al.*, 2021a. The relative age effect in male and female English age-grade rugby union: Exploring the gender-specific mechanisms that underpin participation. *Science and Medicine in Football* [ePub ahead of print].

Kelly, A.L., *et al.*, 2021b. Talent identification and the relative age effect in male professional and international rugby union: From entry to expertise. *Frontiers in Sports and Active Living*, 3, 1–9.

Kretschmann, J., *et al.*, 2019. Effects of grade retention on students' motivation: A longitudinal study over 3 years of secondary school. *Journal of Educational Psychology*, 111 (8), 1432–1446.

Lawrence, S., Jonker, L., and Verbeek, J., 2019. The age advantage in youth football. *In*: D. Karlis, I. Ntzoufras, and S. Drikos, eds. *Proceedings of the mathsport international congress*. Athens: Propobos Publications, 228–233.

Loffing, F., Schorer, J., and Cobley, S.P., 2010. Relative age effects are a developmental problem in tennis: But not necessarily when you're left-handed!, *High Ability Studies*, 21 (1), 19–25.

MacDonald, D.J., *et al.*, 2009. Place but not date of birth influences the development and emergence of athletic talent in American football. *Journal of Applied Sport Psychology*, 21 (1), 80–90.

Malina, R.M., *et al.*, 2019. Bio-Banding in youth sports: Background, concept, and application. *Sports Medicine*, 49 (11), 1671–1685.

Mann, D.L. and van Ginneken, P.J.M.A., 2017. Age-ordered shirt numbering reduces the selection bias associated with the relative age effect. *Journal of Sports Sciences*, 35 (8), 784–790.

Martorell, P. and Mariano, L.T., 2018. The causal effects of grade retention on behavioural outcomes. *Journal of Research on Educational Effectiveness*, 11 (2), 192–216.

McCarthy, N., Collins, D., and Court, D., 2016. Start hard, finish better: Further evidence for the reversal of the RAE advantage. *Journal of Sports Sciences*, 34 (15), 1461–1465.

Phillips, E., *et al.*, 2010. Expert performance in sport and the dynamics of talent development. *Sports Medicine*, 40 (4), 271–283.

Romann, M. and Cobley, S., 2015. Relative age effects in athletic sprinting and corrective adjustments as a solution for their removal. *PLOS ONE*, 10 (4), e0122988.

Romann, M., *et al.*, 2018. Relative age effects in Swiss talent development – A nationwide analysis of all sports. *Journal of Sports Sciences*, 36 (17), 2025–2031.

Smith, K.L., *et al.*, 2018. Relative age effects across and within female sport contexts: A systematic review and meta-analysis. *Sports Medicine*, 48 (6), 1451–1478.

Steenbergen-Hu, S., Makel, M.C., and Olszewski-Kubilius, P., 2016. What one hundred years of research says about the effects of ability grouping and acceleration on K–12 students' academic achievement: findings of two second-order meta-analyses. *Review of Educational Research*, 86 (4), 849–899.

Steenbergen-Hu, S. and Moon, S.M., 2011. The effects of acceleration on high-ability learners: A meta-analysis. *Gifted Child Quarterly*, 55 (1), 39–53.

Sullivan, M.O., *et al.*, 2021. The learning in development research framework for sports organisations. *Sport, Education and Society* [ePub ahead of print].

Thomas, C., Oliver, J., and Kelly, A.L., 2021. Bio-banding in youth soccer: Considerations for researchers and practitioners. *In*: A.L. Kelly, J. Côté, M. Jeffreys, and J. Turnnidge, eds. *Birth advantages and relative age effects in sport: exploring organisational structures and creating appropriate settings*. London: Routledge, 125–126.

Verbeek, J., *et al.*, 2021. The average team age method and its potential to reduce relative age effects. *In*: A.L. Kelly, J. Côté, M. Jeffreys, and J. Turnnidge, eds. *Birth advantages and relative age effects in sport: exploring organisational structures and creating appropriate settings*. London: Routledge, 107–124.

Wattie, N., Schorer, J., and Baker, J. 2015. The relative age effect in sport: A developmental systems model. *Sports Medicine*, 45 (1), 83–94.

Webdale, K., *et al.*, 2019. Solving sport's "relative age" problem: A systematic review of proposed solutions. *International Review of Sport and Exercise Psychology*, 13 (1), 187–204.

Wood, J.V. and Wilson, A.E., 2003. How important are social comparisons for self-evaluation? *In*: M.R. Leary and J.P. Tangney, eds. *Handbook of self and identity*. New York: Guilford Press, 344–366.

# SECTION IV

# Diversity and Inclusion

## Introduction: Diversity and Inclusion in Children's Coaching

*Ruth Jeanes and Martin Toms*

The capacity to work inclusively and engage all children in sporting activity is fundamental to quality coaching. In exploring the reasons why children drop out of formal sport the most frequent reasons young people give is that participation was not fun anymore, it was too competitive and they did not feel a sense of belonging within the sport environment. Coaches who are able to support the participation and progress of a spectrum of children are essential for positive youth sport experiences. Decades of research have illustrated that sport at all levels can be a hostile place for its participants. Whilst participating in sport provides children with many benefits, it can potentially expose them to discrimination and prejudice from an early age. The coach plays a vital role in creating a culture that refuses to tolerate discrimination, which can also help foster positive attitudes towards diversity amongst the children they coach. The chapters in the following section speak to the important role that the coach holds in both fostering inclusive environments for all young people but also in challenging and addressing discrimination.

The chapters in this section also have significant implications for coach education. The importance of coaches having the skills to respond sensitively and inclusively to diversity and difference in sport is emphasised by all contributors, yet working inclusively is rarely a core component of coach education curriculum. Education focusing on inclusive practice is often an optional addition, a short course that can be taken alongside main coaching qualification. The chapters emphasise the need for inclusive practice to be a core component of all foundational coach education curriculums. It is hoped the chapters in the following section can go someway toward filling the educational gap that exists when considering how coaches can work.

Within the following section, the chapters explore various aspects of diversity and implications for coaching children. They do so utlising a single lens to explore for example children with disabilities or Indigenous children. What is missing in this analysis, due to a lack of available literature, is an exploration of what intersectional approaches to inclusive coaching look like and how they can be enacted. Research considering inclusion in coaching using an intersectional lens remain limited, yet coaches work with children with intersectional identities, LGBTQ+ young people of colour for example. Whilst studies within physical education have begun to grapple with how teachers can respond to intersectionality this level of analysis remains absent within the coaching literature. This is an important and productive avenue for future research.

DOI: 10.4324/9781003199359-34

# 30

# CHILDREN'S RIGHTS AND SPORTS COACHING

*Peter Donnelly and Gretchen Kerr*

## Introduction

This chapter outlines how children's rights became an issue in adult organised/coached sports for children. Consideration is given to the autonomy and structural inertia of organised sports in resisting attempts to introduce reforms intended to establish organised sports for children as key sites for child development – sites where responsible adults understood their 'duty of care' for children. Attention is also paid to a growing understanding of children's rights, showing promise that such reforms are achievable.

Human rights are most evident when they are neglected or ignored. Adult coaches in children's sports have a key role here. Not all coaches violate children's rights, but there are far too many reports about those with win-at-all-costs attitudes who neglect or ignore the rights of children. It is important to acknowledge that coaches are not the only adults in sport organisations with child athletes. Coaches have the closest contact with children in the sporting context, spend the most time with them, teaching, evaluating and making decisions about them, and organising everything from practices to travel. They often find themselves under pressure from parents who are seeking additional playing time and other favours for their children, and from sport organisation administrators demanding success, often defined in the most limited terms of winning a tournament or championship. In the zero-sum game of competitive sports there is only ever one winner under this definition.

The chapter outlines the context in terms of the emergence of children's rights, and the emergence of organised/coached sports for children. This is followed by an examination of children's rights and sports coaching by tracking the growing recognition of problems in adult organised sport for children, and the way that the language of children's rights has come to be applied to addressing those problems. The chapter concludes by considering the implications of these changes, and suggesting some next steps in reform.

## Review of Current Research

### *Context – The Emergence of Children's Rights*

In the *age of rights* (Bobbio, 1982), beginning with the French and American Revolutions, the realisation of children's rights was a long and slow process. Agencies such as the NSPCC in the

DOI: 10.4324/9781003199359-35

UK, Children's Aid Societies in Canada and the Gerry Society in the USA began to appear in the 1880s and 1890s, followed shortly by the first pieces of legislation to protect children from abuse and neglect. While the rights of children are implicit in these agencies and laws, they were not framed specifically in those terms. The same reformist urges, beginning in the same time period, saw the first protests against child labour. Economic implications made ending child labour more difficult to realise until emerging trade unions recognised that child labour helped to maintain low wages; unions were the main drivers for legislation against child labour.

During the 20th century it was increasingly acknowledged that children were not just small adults, that childhood was a period of time during which there was a special need for attention and protection, and that adults had a 'duty of care' with regard to children. Following the horrors of World War II, United Nations (UN) adoption of the Universal Declaration of Human Rights (UDHR) in 1948 reified the age of rights and helped to unleash widespread rights seeking movements in terms of decolonisation and anti-discrimination. The UDHR was followed by a series of International Conventions outlining rights that pertained to specific population segments, with the Convention on the Rights of the Child (CRC) being ratified in 1989.

While there are mechanisms in place to monitor and attempt to enforce our rights as human beings, and while more humans than ever are conscious of their rights and aware when they are being violated, "human rights are still easier to endorse than to enforce" (Hunt, 2007, p. 211). The UDHR proclaims that "childhood is entitled to special care and assistance" (Article 25), and the CRC states that "In all actions concerning children … the best interests of the child shall be the primary consideration" (Article 3). In the case of child athletes and children in sport, scholars have pointed to 14 or more of the CRC rights to which children are entitled that are occasionally or routinely violated in sporting contexts.

## *The Emergence of Organised/Coached Sports for Children*

Adult-organised sport systems for children vary significantly by country; and while there is evidence from many countries of adults/coaches violating children's rights in sport, this chapter focuses more specifically on Canada and the United States, and countries such as the UK, Australia and Japan where there are similar systems. In a disturbing coincidence, organised sports for children, and the violation of children's rights in those settings, emerged in the period following ratification of the UDHR. Adult supervision of children's sports existed in schools and in urban recreation before the UDHR, but the major growth of sport organisations and coaching for children resulted from two related trends: (1) the rationalisation of high-performance sports, and (2) the 'baby boom' and the growth of the suburbs.

*First*, with regard to high-performance sports, during the Cold War international sport became a *War Without Weapons* (Chataway and Goodhart, 1968). Cantelon (1981) argued that the "quest for international [and political] superiority … transformed [international sport] into a rationalized work world" (pp. 261–262). One consequence involved developing a system to train athletes (workers) at much younger ages so that they might reach their peak level of athletic achievement at an earlier age, and sustain it longer – a system of early talent identification and intensive and specialised training for those identified. By the 1970s scholars began to critique the system, and Ommo Grupe (1985, p. 10) outlined the following concerns: Children in elite sport programmes:

- are not permitted to be children
- are denied important social contacts and experiences
- are victims of disrupted family life

- are exposed to excessive psychological and physiological stress
- may experience impaired intellectual development
- may become so involved with the sport that they become detached from the larger society
- face a type of abandonment on completion of their athletic careers

Variations of this system of early specialisation and intensive training are still widely evident, although beginning to face increasing criticism from athletes, activists and academics.

*Second*, with regard to community-based sports, the trends are less global than is the case with high-performance sport, but – at least in much of the Anglosphere – changes in society, in family and child relations, and in sport since the middle of the 20th century led to a massive growth in organised, adult-directed sports for children. Coakley and Donnelly (2009) outline these interconnected changes, beginning with the return of troops from World War II, the resulting housing and economic booms and the growth of the suburbs. Subsequent changes in family structure and the expectations of parents; in beliefs about health and child development; and in the mediatisation and commercialisation of sport all contributed to the growth in organised sport for children.

## *Children's Rights and Sports Coaching*

A growing awareness of problems in adult organised sports

As early as the late 1960s researchers were beginning to identify the 'professionalisation' of youth sports (Webb, 1969). The interpretation given to this consistent finding was that adults – usually male coaches, and to some extent parents – along with mediated sports coverage, were normalising a focus on outcome ('victory') as opposed to the process of participation implicit in 'equity' and 'skill'.

Since the 1970s, Canadian Bill L'Heureux has often been cited to summarise concerns about adult organised sports for children: "The only problem with kids' sports is adults". Proposals to ban adults proved unrealistic for mainstream sports, but lasting effects of the idea may be seen in the growth of alternative sports, 'new games' (Fluegelman, 1976) and 'cooperative games' (Orlick, 1977).

Perhaps the earliest concern in adult organised youth sports was the *right to participate*, although it was never expressed in human rights terms. In addition to class, race and gender, exclusions were based on ability. Leagues and clubs were happy to sign up children and receive their annual fees, coaches involved all children in the practices, but most attention was paid to the more able players who were given the most time playing/competing – an ongoing concern in youth sports. (While a number of the following examples are Canadian similar examples exist in other countries.) One solution that emerged in the 1970s was the introduction of 'house leagues' for team sports – players received equal amounts of playing time and teams were balanced in terms of skill. Coaches, usually parent volunteers, were encouraged to emphasise skill development and de-emphasise the outcome of games. House leagues are still popular for younger children, but the better players are often recruited to more competitive travel teams. House leagues rarely continue with participants beyond their early teens.

Of equal concern was the lack of qualified leadership – children coached by adults with little knowledge of child development, and little sense of what was appropriate for different age levels. Coaches often adapted practice sessions, game strategies and motivational techniques from those in adult and professional levels of the sport. The introduction of coach education programmes in the 1970s, which became mandatory in some Canadian jurisdictions, was an attempt to ensure that novice level coaches had at least a minimal understanding of what was involved in coaching children. The *right to qualified leadership* has become an aspect of many charters of children's rights in sport, but the introduction of coach education has not had a major effect in improving leadership. Unlike almost every other sector of volunteerism, there is little, if any, monitoring, supervision and evaluation of volunteer coaches, especially at the lower levels of sport (Donnelly and Harvey, 2011; see also Stewart, 2021). Without volunteer coaches, children would not be able to play in organised sports; many organisations struggle to find volunteers for all of their teams; and organisations are hesitant to introduce standards or supervision that may lead to the loss of those volunteers.

Third, children's *right to safety and security* when participating in sports is a concern that began to emerge during the 1990s. In a culture that normalises injury some coaches are responsible for, for example, children experiencing over-use injuries from excessive training and competitions; encouraging children (especially the more skilled participants) to play when injured and to return early from an injury; and encouraging violent (and injurious) play in contact sports – especially problematic when there are significant size differences between same age players. Several innovations have been introduced to reduce violence and injury – and to reduce the increasing withdrawal of children from contact sports. In Canada these include non-contact leagues, and 'fair play' or *franc jeu* leagues where teams with fewer fouls are rewarded. However, these alternatives often have the same fate as 'house leagues' since they are considered a less important level of competition.

Some coaches are also involved in the use of psychological and physical abuse, and neglectful and bullying behaviour intended to motivate or punish children. The latter behaviours have become so normalised as part of the 'culture' of sport that some child and adult athletes refuse to see them as abusive (see, for example, Donnelly, 1993; Willson *et al.*, 2021). Finally, what has been recognised as an act more concerned with power than with sex, is the involvement of some coaches in the sexual abuse of child athletes. Although Willson, *et al.* (2021) found that this is the least frequent form of abuse reported by athletes, it is the one that has garnered the most attention with major scandals involving coaches in, for example, boys' football in the UK and girls' gymnastics in the US (coaches were enablers/bystanders in the Nassar case).

The revelations about current and historical cases of sexual abuse have drawn attention to the more prevalent forms of maltreatment. The Universal Code of Conduct to Prevent and Address Maltreatment in Sport (UCCMS, 2019), which is now in effect for Canadian National Sport Organizations (NSOs), is perhaps the most comprehensive Code, including all of the forms of abuse cited above and specifically identifying, for example, racial, homophobic and online abuse as aspects of psychological abuse. The independent mechanism for enforcing the UCCMS and imposing sanctions is currently being developed.

The autonomy of sport organisations means that each organisation determines what constitutes unethical and illegal behaviour. Everything from cronyism to turning a blind eye to offences by someone who coaches winning athletes and teams has helped to create an unregulated culture of control. There is a preference for an authoritarian style of coaching and, where there is maltreatment of children, it may be ignored or excused as part of the culture of that sport; a culture that can routinely violate the rights of children. For example, in an earlier draft of the UCCMS (2019), some coaches and NSOs attempted to maintain this 'traditional' sport culture by including a statement indicating that Neglect/Physical Misconduct/Psychological Misconduct "does not include coaching methods that are professionally-accepted to Canadian standards ...."

A growing awareness of the violation of children's rights in sport

Human rights are relational; they "derive from a foundational community relationship that human beings stand in with one another *qua* human beings" (Susienka, 2017, p. ii). It is crucial to acknowledge this in order to examine children's rights and sport coaching. In relational terms, coaches may be *in loco parentis*, they have a duty of care for the children they coach, they are teachers, task leaders, and they may be mentors. In human rights terms, they are to protect the autonomy and dignity of the children in their care, and the CRC provides a specific outline of the rights to which children are entitled. Coaches are in a position to ensure, or to violate children's rights.

The idea of the *right to participate in sport* and the *right to qualified leadership* first appeared in the 1964 UNESCO *Declaration on Sport* (Maheu, 1972), which also recognised the problems of early specialisation and intensive training by children. The *Declaration* developed into a global rights document, the *International Charter on Physical Education and Sport* (1978) (now the *International Charter of Physical Education, Physical Activity and Sport,* 2015).

The 1978 *Charter* helped to establish the idea of rights in relation to sport and physical education, and in the US, Martens and Seefeldt (1979) produced the *Bill of Rights for Young Athletes* (1979). Other rights-based documents followed (e.g. Galasso, 1988), and Kidd and Eberts (1982) produced the first legal/academic document on athletes' rights. However, since 1989 the CRC has (slowly) changed everything with regard to children's rights in sport. Donnelly (1993) and David (1993) were among the first to acknowledge the importance of the CRC for children's sport, and then the research proliferated (e.g. David, 1999; DeMartelaer, *et al.*, 2000; Weber, 2009; Turkeri-Bozkurt and Bulgu, 2020).

Of course, each of these rights, and others (e.g. to be consulted, to be free of child labour, exploitation, sexual abuse and so on) are occasionally, or even routinely violated in high-performance sport. Whenever children are in an unregulated environment, under the supervision of adults whose livelihood depends on the performance of those children, there is reason to be concerned for the rights of those children (Donnelly, 1997). The research literature on children's rights in sport proliferated, but the most significant impact of the CRC on children's rights and sports coaching was its incorporation into sport policy in Norway and Sweden.

Researchers in Norway (e.g. Farstad, 2007; Skirstad, *et al.*, 2012; Ellingsen and Danielsen, 2017) and Sweden (e.g. Carlsson and Fransson, 2005; Fransson, 2009; Eliasson, 2015; Eliasson *et al.*, 2017) have a well-established interest in sport and children's rights and the way that coaching practices may violate those rights. Children's rights were first included in sport policy in Norway, in a preliminary way in 1987, shortly before the ratification of the CRC, and more formally by the Norwegian Olympic and Paralympic Committee and the Confederation of Sport (NIF, 2007), and updated in 2015. The policy outlines the specific rights to which children are entitled in sport and was approved by the General Assembly of the NIF. The preamble states:

> Children are engaged in sports because they enjoy it. Together with their friends they have experiences and learn lessons that will last them a lifetime. This is the foundation that all coaches, managers and parents must safeguard and develop further.
>
> *(NIF, 2007, p. 2)*

Following the achievements of Norwegian athletes at the 2018 Winter Olympics (from a country of 5.3 million people, athletes won 39 medals – more than any other country had achieved at the Winter Olympics), Tom Farrey (2019), in an unflattering comparison with youth sports in the US, praised the Norwegian system:

> Imagine a society in which 93% of children grow up playing organized sports. Where costs are low, the economic barriers to entry few, travel teams aren't formed until the teenage years – and where adults don't start sorting the weak from the strong until children have grown into their bodies and interests.

With respect to coaching, the policy is explicit, among other things, about developmentally appropriate activity, no inappropriate pressure, children being heard and children having a choice.

Sweden followed a different trajectory – the Swedish Sports Confederation recommended, in 2009, that children's sports were to comply with the CRC by being grounded in children's rights.

Eliasson's (2015, Eliasson *et al.*, 2017) research tracked some of the measures and difficulties involved in introducing a children's rights perspective. On January 1, 2020, the CRC became law in Sweden, to be applied to every sector involving children including sports (O'Sullivan, 2019). Early reports suggest that there are some difficulties in implementation, despite the fact that CRC compliance in sports was supposed to have started in 2009, and various documents have been developed to assist sport organisations (e.g. Sportidealisten, 2020).

The coaching practices that have led to the negative experiences of children in adult organised sports outlined in this chapter have become so well entrenched in many high-income countries that changing the culture of children's sport is extraordinarily difficult. Norway and Sweden have taken courageous steps in the direction of children's rights and towards building a culture of sport in which the best interests of the child is of primary importance.

## Implications for Children's Sport Coaching

While there are a number of alternatives to promote a more inclusive culture of participation in children's sports (e.g. 'house leagues', the US-based *American Development Model* in ice hockey (admkids.com), and initiatives being developed by Project Play in the US (www.aspenprojectplay.org)) the dominant structure of sport for children developed some 60 years ago is still largely in place. Early specialisation and intensive training are still the norm for children whose athletic abilities are evident early (and, in many societies, limited to children from families with the means to fund their participation); competition is more focused on outcome rather than process or 'fun'; authoritarian styles of coaching predominate, among coaches with little or no training relevant to coaching children; and children's voices are frequently silenced or ignored. This structure has persisted and been reproduced despite some 50 years of ongoing criticism and attempts to introduce alternatives to the dominant model. In fact, as the political and economic significance of 'prolympic' sport (Donnelly, 1996) has increased, the prestige of having a child win an athletic scholarship, be recruited by a professional team, or achieve membership in a national team has often assured parents' involvement in support of the existing sport structure.

Although coaches are in an ideal position to affirm and assure children's rights, this chapter points to ample research and anecdotal and experiential evidence of coaches in children's sports who have violated those rights. Violations range from denying children the right to choose or to be consulted, to physical abuse and neglect (e.g. exercise as punishment (Kerr *et al.*, 2016, 2020a), or failure to care appropriately for a child's illness or injury), to psychological abuse and bullying (see extensive research by Gretchen Kerr and Ashley Stirling), to sexual abuse. However, there are some indications that what has been referred to as a 'culture of abuse' in children's (and adults') sport may be in retreat. There is evidence that the autonomy of sport is being challenged, governance of sport is being enhanced as a consequence of widespread pressure, and there is a growing recognition of athletes' rights.

The greatest focus has been on sexual abuse in children's sport and, following major scandals in the Boy Scouts and the Catholic Church, sport organisations have increasingly become aware of the costs and damage to reputation that result from a sexual abuse scandal. Although important policy and legal steps are being taken in countries such as Australia, Canada, the UK and the US, it seems likely that the safe reporting measures being introduced to prevent sexual abuse in sport are also likely to encourage athletes and former athletes to reveal cases of historical abuse. These will have to be addressed as part of the culture change in sport. And while coaches are often at the centre of such scandals, research is increasingly showing that sexual and other abuses could not occur without enablers and bystanders (Tuakli-Wosornu *et al.*, 2022). As a recent book on abuse in Christian youth camps explains, "We learned from Savile that abusers can only abuse in a culture that enables it" (Graystone, 2021, p. 7).

Physical and psychological abuse, and the high rate of injuries (e.g. Clarsen *et al.*, 2021) are so normalised in children's (and adult) sports that many athletes and sport organisations were surprised as they have increasingly come to be defined as abusive. The sexual abuse scandals have led to a wider examination of abuse, but the normalisation of controlling and abusive coaching practices – practices that usually fall below the criminal threshold – is proving to be the most difficult step to overcome to achieve rights-based sports for children. However, attempts to regulate non-sexual abuses have been enabled by a growing body of research shows, for example, that the long-term effects of psychological abuse can be at least as damaging as those from sexual abuse (e.g. Kerr *et al.* 2020b).

The moral suasion of children's rights is combined with a growing body of scientific evidence to help bring about change. A significant part of the growing demands for human rights in sport concerns coaching practices and child athletes. Major reports on the abuse of child athletes in Japan (Human Rights Watch, 2020), and on abusive practices in gymnastics in Australia (Australian Human Rights Commission, 2021) are an indication that leading human rights organisations are beginning to address children's rights in sport; and the Centre for Sport and Human Rights is currently engaged in a project connecting children's rights in sport to child labour. The system of early specialisation and intensive training, which is at the basis of so much abuse of child athletes, is also now being questioned in new research with regard to its efficacy in terms of identifying talent and achieving international success in sports (e.g. Baker *et al.*, 2020; Güllich *et al.*, 2021). It seems that the calls to consider the best interests of children and to 'let children be children' in sport are finally being heard.

## Summary, Future Directions and Future Research

Researchers, activists and athletes have been aware, for at least 50 years, of the troubles (rights violations) that too often result from adults coaching children in competitive sports. These troubles have been reproduced from generation to generation, and have become more problematic as sport has become more economically and politically important, and as parents have increasingly attempted to provide a competitive advantage (in sport, education and future careers) for their children.

While children's rights were often implicit in the early critiques, they have become much more explicit since the ratification of the CRC. However, the autonomy of sport organisations has provided a sense of immunity from human rights obligations, recently asserted by World Athletics identifying itself as "a private body exercising private (contractual) powers … [and] not subject to human rights instruments such as the [UDHR]" (IAAF, 2019). The United Nations High Commissioner for Human Rights recently pointed out that sport organisations do have human rights obligations, but reported that there is no existing mechanism to assure compliance by the International Olympic Committee and the International Federations (UNHCHR, 2020).

The autonomy of sports is being challenged on many fronts at this time. With regard to children's rights and coaching, it is crucial that researchers continue to provide activists and sport organisations with reliable evidence in support of children's rights and appropriate coaching practices. Research should also monitor policy developments such as the effectiveness of sports policy grounded in children's rights in Norway and Sweden, and the implementation of the UCCMS in Canada. These changes have real implications for the behaviour and practices of coaches, and the way that children are treated in sport. In particular, these changes are emphasising the need for a rights-based and developmentally-appropriate sport that is congruent with the physical and psychosocial development of children at various ages, and the best interests of the child (Kerr, 2021).

## References

Australian Human Rights Commission, 2021. *Change the routine: report on the independent review into gymnastics in Australia* [online]. Available from: https://humanrights.gov.au/sites/default/files/document/publication/ahrc_gymnastics_review_2021_final_.pdf [Accessed 25 March 2022].

Baker, J., Wattie, N., and Schorer, J., 2020. Issues in athlete identification and selection: Are we compromising talent? *SIRC Blog*, February 24: Available from: https://sirc.ca/blog/issues-in-athlete-identification-and-selection-are-we-compromising-talent/. [Accessed 25 March 2022].

Bobbio, N., 1982. *The age of rights*. Cambridge: Polity.

Cantelon, H., 1981. High performance sport and the child athlete: Learning to labour. *In*: A. Ingham and E. Broom, eds. *Career patterns and career contingencies in sport*. Vancouver: University of British Columbia, 257–286.

Carlsson, B. and Fransson, N., 2005. Youth sports, official policy, and children's rights in society. Idrottsforum [online]. Available from: https://www.idrottsforum.org/articles/carlsson/carlsson_fransson/carlsson_fransson051130.pdf [Accessed 30 November 2021].

Chataway, C. and Goodhart, P., 1968. *War without weapons*. London: W.H. Allen.

Clarsen, B., *et al.*, 2021. Methods, challenges and benefits of a health monitoring programme for norwegian olympic and paralympic athletes: The road from London 2012 to Tokyo 2020. *British Journal of Sports Medicine*, 55 (23), 1342- 1349.

Coakley, J. and Donnelly, P., 2009. *Sports in society: Issues and controversies* (2nd Canadian edition). Toronto: McGraw-Hill Ryerson.

David, P., 1993. Children and sport: Accomplishment or exploitation? *International Children's Rights Monitor*, 10 (4), 8–12.

David, P., 1999. Children's rights and sports – Young athletes and competitive sports: Exploit and exploitation. *The International Journal of Children's Rights*, 7, 53–81.

De Martelaer, K., *et al.*, 2000. The UN Convention as a basis for elaborating the rights of children in sport. *Journal of Leisurability*, 27 (2), 3–10.

Donnelly, P., 1993. Problems associated with youth involvement in high performance sport. *In*: B. Cahill and A. Pearl, eds. *Intensive participation in children's sports*. Champaign, IL: Human Kinetics, 95–126.

Donnelly, P., 1996. Prolympism: Sport monoculture as crisis and opportunity. *Quest*, 48 (1), 25–42.

Donnelly, P., 1997. Child labour, sport labour: Applying child labour laws to sport. *International Review for the Sociology of Sport*, 32 (4), 389–406.

Donnelly, P. and Harvey, J., 2011. Volunteering and sport. *In*: B. Houlihan and M. Green, eds. *Handbook of sport development*. London: Sage,55–71.

Eliasson, I., 2015. The gap between formalised children's rights and children's real lives in sport. *International Review for the Sociology of Sport*, 52 (4), 470–496.

Eliasson, I., Karp, S., and Wickman, K., 2017. Developing sports with a children's rights perspective? Intentions, methods, and priorities of development projects in local Swedish sports clubs. *European Journal for Sport and Society*, 14 (3), 244–264.

Ellingsen, J. and Danielsen, A., 2017. Norwegian children's rights in sport and coaches' understanding of talent. *International Journal of Children's Rights*, 25, 412–437.

Farrey, T. (2019). *Does Norway have the answer to excess in youth sports?* [online]. *New York Times*, 28 April. Available from: https://www.nytimes.com/2019/04/28/sports/norway-youth-sports-model.html. [Accessed 25 March 2022].

Farstad, S., 2007. Protecting children's rights in sport: The use of minimum age. *Human Rights Law Commentary*, 3, 1–20.

Fluegelman, A., 1976. *The new games book. Play hard, play fair, nobody hurt*. New York: Doubleday.

Fransson, K., 2009. *Children's sport, a question of rights: Children, childhood and the Swedish sports movement* [online]. *Idrottsforum*, Available from: www.idrottsforum.org/articles/fransson/fransson090429.html [Accessed 25 March 2022].

Galasso, P., 1988. Children in organised sport: Rights and access to justice. *In*: P. Galasso, ed. *Philosophy of sport and physical activity: Issues and concepts*. Toronto: Canadian Scholars' Press, 324–342.

Graystone, A., 2021. *Bleeding for Jesus: John Smyth and the cult of the iweme camps*. London: Darton, Longman and Todd.

Grupe, O., 1985. Top level sport for children from an educational viewpoint. *International Journal for Physical Education*, 22 (1), 9–16.

Güllich, A., Macnamara, B., and Hambrick, D., 2021. What makes a champion? Early multidisciplinary practice, not early specialisation, predicts world-class performance. *Perspectives on Psychological Science*, 17 (1), 6–29.

Human Rights Watch, 2020. "*I was hit so many times I can't count:" abuse of child athletes in Japan* [online]. New York: Human Rights Watch, Available from: https://www.hrw.org/report/2020/07/20/i-was-hit-so-many-times-i-cant-count/abuse-child-athletes-japan. [Accessed 25 March 2022].

Hunt, L., 2007. *Inventing human rights: a history*. New York: W.W. Norton.

IAAF, 2019. *IAAF publishes briefing notes and Q&A on Female Eligibility Regulations*[online]. May 7: Available from: https://www.worldathletics.org/news/press-release/questions-answers-iaaf-female-eligibility-reg. [Accessed 25 March 2022].

Kerr, G., 2021. *Next steps in the safe sport journey: from prevention of harm to optimising experiences* [online]. Available from: https://sirc.ca/blog/next-steps-in-the-safe-sport-journey. [Accessed 25 March 2022].

Kerr, G., Willson, E., and Stirling, A., 2020b. "It was the worst time in my life": The effects of emotionally abusive coaching on female Canadian national team athletes. *Women in Sport and Physical Activity Journal*, 28 (1), 81–89.

Kerr, G., *et al.*, 2016. Exploring the use of exercise as punishment in sport. *International Journal of Coaching Science*, 10 (2), 34–52.

Kerr, G., *et al.*, 2020a. Examining coaches' perspectives on the use of exercise as punishment. *International Sport Coaching Journal*, 7 (3), 306–316.

Kidd, B. and Eberts, M., 1982. *Athletes' rights in Canada*. Toronto: Ministry of Tourism and Recreation.

Maheu, R., 1972. Declaration on sport prepared by ICSPE in cooperation with UNESCO after consulting the governments and private organizations concerned. [Reproduction in English of the 1964 document.] *International Review for the Sociology of Sport*, 7 (1), 151–168.

Martens, R. and Seefeldt, V., 1979. *Guidelines for children's sports*. Reston, VA: American Alliance for Health, Physical Education, Recreation and Dance.

NIF, 2007. *Children's Rights in Sport: Provisions on Children's Sport* [online]. Available from: https://www.aspeninstitute.org/wp-content/uploads/2019/04/Childrens-Right-to-Sport-in-Norway.pdf. [Accessed 25 March 2022].

Orlick, T., 1977. Cooperative games. *Journal of Physical Education and Recreation*, 48 (7), 33–35.

O'Sullivan, M., 2019. *The quiet revolution and its evolution (United Nations Convention on the Rights of the Child to become law in Swedish sport on January 1st 2020*) [online]. *Footblogball*, 12 November. Available from: https://footblogball.wordpress.com/2019/11/12/the-quiet-revolution-and-its-evolution-united-nations-convention-on-the-rights-of-the-child-to-become-law-in-swedish-sport-on-january-1st2020/. [Accessed 25 March 2022].

Skirstad, B., Waddington, I., and Säfvenbom, R., 2012. Issues and problems in the organisation of children's sport: a case study of Norway. *European Physical Education Review*, 18 (3), 309–321.

Sportidealisten, 2020. *How to implement the convention on the right of the child in sport* [online]. Available from: https://sportidealisten.se/how-to-implement-the-convention-on-the-rights-of-the-child-in-sports/). [Accessed 25 March 2022].

Stewart, C., 2021. The say they can coach, but can they teach? *Academia Letters*, July, 1–7.

Susienka, C., 2017. *Human responsibilities: a relational account of human rights*. Doctoral thesis, Columbia University [online]. https://academiccommons.columbia.edu/doi/10.7916/D84J0SP8. [Accessed 25 March 2022].

Tuakli-Wosornu, *et al.*, 2022. Athlete abuse hurts everyone: Vicarious and secondary traumatic stress in sport. *British Journal of Sports Medicine*, 56 (3), 119–120.

Turkeri-Bozkurt, H. and Bulgu, N., 2020. Is injury part of sports?: A children's rights perspective. *International Review for the Sociology of Sport*, 55 (1), 98–114.

UCCMS, 2019. Universal code of conduct to prevent and address maltreatment in sport [online]. Available from: https://www.tribc.org/wp-content/uploads/2020/01/UCCMS-v5.1-FINAL-Eng.pdf. [Accessed 4 March 2022].

UNHCHR – United Nations High Commissioner for Human Rights, 2020. Report: Intersection of race and gender discrimination in sport. June 15: A/HRC/44/26.

Webb, H., 1969. Professionalisation of attitudes toward play among adolescents. *In*: G. Kenyon, ed. *Aspects of contemporary sport sociology*. Chicago: Athletic Institute, 161–178.

Weber, R., 2009. Protection of children in competitive sport: Some critical questions for London 2012. *International Review for the Sociology of Sport*, 44 (1), 55–69.

Willson, E.G., *et al.*, 2021. Prevalence of maltreatment among Canadian national team athletes. *Journal of Interpersonal Violence*, 1–23.

# 31

# COACHING DISABLED CHILDREN: A BRIEF LOOK AROUND AND FORWARD

*Robert C. Townsend*

## Introduction

From a critical perspective, the study of disability and disablement demands that we shift our focus to the various ways that children and young people with impairments are unnecessarily excluded from participation in social life. Disability can be experienced through interaction with a multitude of individual, structural, social and attitudinal barriers (Oliver, 1990). These barriers overlap, compound and create structured disadvantages that limit their opportunities for participation in social life.

In policy at least, the rights of children to participate fully in social life are well established. The UN Convention on the Rights of the Child (UNCRC) provides primary oversight for children as rights bearers; indeed, article 23 outlines that state parties must create conditions which ensure dignity, promote self-reliance and facilitate active participation in the community while promoting equal access to education, health care, preparation for employment and, of particular interest here, leisure, active recreation and play. However, it cannot be assumed that initiatives to improve children's rights in general will benefit the most marginalised children. In foregrounding the rights of *disabled* children, the UN Convention on the Rights of Persons with Disabilities (CRPD) states that disabled children should participate in recreation, leisure and sport *on an equal basis* with other children (United Nations, 2006). The CRPD further states that disabled children should access "*appropriate instruction and training*" to ensure full participation in sport (United Nations, 2006, 30.5b).

With inclusion and inclusive practice firmly embedded in international social policy and legislation, it is worth critically assessing 'where we are at' in relation to disabled children, youth sport and coaching. This is especially important considering the heightened interest in, and recognition of, disability sport in contemporary society. This interest is matched by scholarship across youth disability sport, including for example its organisation and genesis (e.g. DePauw and Gavron, 2005; Fitzgerald, 2009), representation and media framing (e.g. Hardin *et al.*, 2001), the participation experiences of disabled children (e.g. Fitzgerald, 2005; Carter *et al.*, 2014), as well as the implications for youth identity development (e.g. Anderson, 2009). Further research has explored youth disability sport itself, in particular its psychosocial aspects (e.g. Martin, 2006) and associated talent identification and development practices (e.g. Houlihan and Chapman, 2017). Curiously, in youth sport *coaching* research, disabled children are absent and unaccounted for. This chapter is a brief and modest attempt at addressing this silence.

DOI: 10.4324/9781003199359-36

## Review of Current Research

### *Coaching in Youth Sport*

Over the last thirty years youth sport coaching has garnered significant and sustained research interest. Coaches are generally positioned as central figures in the delivery of youth sport; as supporters of the personal and social development of children and young people (Holt *et al.,* 2017; Lara-Bercial and Mckenna, 2018), facilitators of the development of lifelong physical activity, and developers of skill and performance (Stafford, 2011). Many of these same messages hold true for disabled children and their involvement in sport. In broad terms, disability sport is often assumed a 'non-disabling' site and is commonly associated with disability 'empowerment' and identity work, that is, resisting and challenging negative disability-specific associations (Ashton-Schaeffer et al., 2001). These same discourses circulate in youth disability sport, where sport provides crucial opportunities for the physical and psychosocial development of disabled children and youth (King *et al.,* 2003; Martin, 2006;). Specifically, research with disabled children has suggested improved feelings of physical competence, development of friendships, and increased sense of belonging and connection (Martin, 2006). Together, existing research paints a somewhat 'rosy' picture, where the provision of youth disability sport is positive, and "ultimately leading to greater inclusion in society" (Spencer-Cavaliere *et al.,* 2017, p. 121).

Despite this, existing research also shows that for disabled children sport can represent a site of exclusion, isolation, anxiety, bullying, stigma and ableist micro-aggressions (e.g. Fitzgerald *et al.,* 2003; Fitzgerald, 2005, 2009; Spencer-Cavaliere *et al.,* 2017). Commonly, exclusion from youth sport (including physical education) is a consequence of both covert and overt forms of discrimination, that is, 'ableism' and its attendant, 'disablism'. Ableism is a system of beliefs, practices and discourses that, implicitly and explicitly, shape social, economic and built environments in ways that privilege able-bodiedness. Ableism has at its centre the notion of the 'normative individual', resulting in divisive practices that separate normative individuals from those that deviate from this norm, namely, people with impairments (cf. Campbell, 2009). Thus, ableism is observable in youth sport, where the provision of sporting opportunities is often targeted at the 'most able' children, while separate structures and practices are made available for disabled children.

While ableism privileges normalcy and able-bodiedness (Campbell, 2009), the term 'disablism' has been used to describe socio-political processes that marginalize and oppress disabled people (Oliver, 1990; Thomas, 1999). Together, ableism and disablism permeate the structure of youth sport, restricting opportunities to participate and solidifying conceptions of ability and performance through which disabled children are judged (Fitzgerald, 2005; cf. Goodley, 2014). Indeed, the ways in which ableism and disablism are embedded within youth sport are well-documented. Leisure facilities can be inaccessible, there are often fewer structured opportunities for disabled children to participate, train and compete, and participation is marked by negative attitudes of others (e.g. peers), resulting in bullying, non-participation, and the internalisation of stigma resulting in feelings of exclusion and isolation. Furthermore, there is a lack of knowledge from those delivering sport about how to effectively include disabled children (Jones, 2003; Hodge & Runswick-Cole, 2013), a situation observable in the broader disability coaching literature (Townsend *et al.*, 2017; Townsend, *et al.*, 2022).

Hence it might be reasonably argued that despite the 'enlightened' rhetoric of inclusion framing youth sport discourse (Dagkas & Armour, 2011), the reality is one of marginalisation for disabled children. A critical factor in enacting and facilitating change in these contexts is the engagement, recruitment, education, and development of coaches (Stafford, 2011). Indeed,

Hammond *et al.* (2014) argued that there is a strong link between coaches' knowledge and their attitudes towards inclusion. As such, inclusion is predicated on a high-quality coaching workforce equipped with the skills and knowledge to effectively include disabled children (Townsend *et al.,* 2021). However, as Hammond *et al.* (2019) have argued there is a distinction between inclusive rhetoric within organisational coaching policy and actual coaching practices. In particular, evidence suggests that coaches are more willing to include disabled people when major changes to existing competition and practice structures are not required. Where impairment presents a direct and unavoidable consideration for coaches, research repeatedly confirms that youth sport practitioners feel unprepared and uncertain about their abilities to effectively support these children (Morley *et al.,* 2005; Fitzgerald & Jobling, 2009; Townsend *et al.,* 2017). Another factor to consider is that most children's coaches are volunteers who, by definition, have neither the time nor the support to develop their knowledge and skills, which can impact on the quality of opportunities afforded to athletes (Townsend & Peacham, 2021). With these constraints in mind, it is worth examining existing research to understand how coaches are situated within youth disability sport.

## Inclusive Coaching

As Black (2011) argues, for disabled children it is the "everyday access to opportunities in physical activity and sport in school and community that restricts choice and defines difference" (p. 198). Disability sport is a complex term in that it captures a variety of activities, modes of delivery and contexts for coaches to negotiate. Following Spencer-Cavaliere *et al.* (2017) in looking closely at coaching, it is necessary to understand the visibility and viability of sport pathways for disabled children. There are range of options theoretically available for disabled children to access coaching, and while an attempt has been made to differentiate coaches' roles, behaviours and practices according to domains (e.g. Lyle, 2002), these are complicated by the presence of disability. Goodwin and Peers (2011) outlined three broad settings in which 'inclusive' coaching might be observed. The first is commonly referred to as disability sport, that is, sports that are typically comprised of only disabled children and youth. This might include participants with similar impairments or may be 'pan-disability'. Disability sports are considered a direct response to exclusionary 'mainstream' sports structures, necessitating the establishment of segregated contexts designed to meet individual needs.

An example of a segregated sports context for people with intellectual impairments is Special Olympics, in which over 5 million athletes with learning disabilities and 1 million coaches and volunteers participate across 170 countries (Townsend and Peacham, 2021). Segregated contexts have been promoted as a means of developing a sense of belonging, competence and athletic identity (Shapiro & Martin, 2010; Spencer-Cavaliere *et al.,* 2017). While some disability sports are gaining popularity, there is ongoing criticism that promoting segregated sport is based on a false assumption that it is a "desirable and equitable" context for people who experience disability (Fay & Wolff, 2009). Other sports provision might involve adapted versions of the 'normal' game, such as blind football or visually impaired cricket. By contrast, 'mainstream' settings tend to be those created for non-disabled children but may be able to either fully accommodate disabled children with little to no modifications, or involve disabled children superficially by coaching them separately – usually with the help of an assistant coach or support worker – from one another within the same session (Spencer-Cavaliere *et al.,* 2017). Finally, disability sports provision can be conceptualised as 'reverse integration', where disabled children and able-bodied children participate and compete in sports where impairment is a 'levelling factor'. Examples of these might include boccia, goalball, sitting volleyball and wheelchair sports (e.g. rugby, basketball) (Goodwin and Peers, 2012). Despite this, segregated settings are most commonly associated with disability sport provision and in which coaches are routinely positioned as influential figures. Yet research on coaching in these contexts is almost non-existent.

One exception is the work of Spencer-Cavaliere and colleagues (2017). Drawing on interview data with a range of practitioners responsible for delivering in segregated sports programmes, the authors highlighted a unique tension between inclusion and exclusion framing the coaches' practice. Commonly, coaches described the importance of the social environment for disabled young people to develop connections with their peers and build relationships, while questioning the role of segregated programs in reproducing disabled children's exclusion from wider society. Importantly, while the coaches' expectations of the athletes were similar to those in 'mainstream' programs, and the coaching role closely related to supporting their psychological and social development, the diversity and range of needs present in segregated programs created difficulties for coaches' practice adaptations and as such impacted on their ability to positively impact the athletes' skill development. This meant that the coaching environment was framed by a particular orientation towards 'ability', and the ways that ability can act as a source of differentiation, separation, and comparison for coaches. As such, the authors demonstrate that while the empowering language of disability sport rejects the language of individual deficit, ableism (overt or covert) remains entrenched in sport. As such, the extent to which segregated programmes mask the continuation of coaching practices that marginalise disabled people is an important line of future inquiry - a discourse reflective of 'enlightened' ableism (cf. Lyons, 2013). As Spencer-Cavaliere *et al.* (2017) argued, addressing the various ways that ableism is embedded and enacted through youth sport coaching practices requires a critical focus on coach education to enhance the reflexive capacities of coaches (Hay, 2012) and question ableist assumptions.

## *Models of Inclusion*

In youth sport the achievement of inclusion is a fundamental component of the experience of coaches and policy makers, and there is an enduring concern of how to actually *practice* inclusivity in youth sport. Coach education and professional development is positioned as crucial in bridging the gap between policy, knowledge and practice. Yet, the extent to which coaches are adequately trained, educated, or supported to practice inclusion is questionable. Most notably, disability is often viewed as an 'add on' to coach education or overlooked entirely in sport-specific coach education pathways (Townsend *et al.*, 2021). This has led to a proliferation of frameworks and models that, as Black (2011) wryly observed, can be captured under the banner of 'the accursed acronym'. This refers to the trend of providing coaches with resources – typically drawn from physical education – that encourage activity differentiation and are easily assimilated into coaching practice. A primary example of this is the Activity Inclusion Model (AIM). Dubbed a 'structural and functional model', the Activity Inclusion Model is derivative of the Inclusion Spectrum, first developed in 1996 by Ken Black drawing on Winnick's (1987) 'Integration Continuum for Sport Participation'. Later refined by Black and Stevenson (2011), this model provides coaches with a range of participation options based on the central principle of the 'least restrictive environment'. In the most recent iteration of this model developed specifically to address disability, coaches are encouraged to explore a range of delivery options on a continuum of participation ranging from *open, modified, parallel and specific* tasks. To help with the tricky business of modifying tasks for a diverse group of learners, coaches can draw on tools such as the United Kingdom's 'STEP' model, or the Australian Sports Commission's 'TREE' acronym (see Black, 2011). Both 'models' emphasise changing one or more conditions of practice, whether that be the rules and regulations of the sport, modifying the space in which activity occurs, group size, or the use of various types of equipment. Positioned as 'thinking tools' for fostering thoughtful and reflective coaches, these models undoubtedly occupy a central place in disability coaching discourse and are based on the recognition of barriers to sports participation. The extent to which they are a primary point of reference for coaches in practice, however, requires further investigation.

## Implications for Children's Sport Coaching

As the number and range of sports opportunities for disabled people have grown, so too has heightened awareness of the need for high quality, inclusive provision, resulting in a clear focus on coaches and coaching in this context. However, expanding the range and scope of sports for disabled children brings challenges for coaches to respond to the diverse range of participants that wish to participate, and this is compounded by the inclusive discourses, policies and strategies circulating in coaching. Given their prominence and widespread circulation as a foundational discourse in inclusive coaching it is worth looking closely at such models. Such is the inclusion imperative in popular sports discourse that it, arguably, loses meaning and few dare argue against it (Bailey, 2005). This is not to dismiss calls for inclusive practice or diminish its significance in youth sport. Instead, this can be considered as part of an ongoing interchange of ideas regarding the conceptualisation of inclusion implicit in such coaching pedagogy, and to carefully examine what is meant when practitioners are referred to 'models for' inclusive coaching practice.

Concepts of inclusivity vary considerably across historical, theoretical, and practical contexts. In youth sport coaching a critical examination of the theoretical roots of the models outlined above reveals a variety of preconceived ideas about child development and ability, that is, a particular view of the 'normative' individual and their ability to participate in sport. This reflects an integration paradigm, rather than inclusion, and is concerned with building up the capacity of the person to fit into existing structures. Grounded historically in educational discourse, integration perspectives precede inclusion as the first step towards involvement in 'mainstream' education from special education, where disabled children are positioned as 'outsiders' and understood through a deficit model of disability. Integration therefore might be understood as 'pre' social model, whereby disabled children are 'included' in practice activities yet are still excluded by a set of existing practice structures that privilege able-bodied athletes, and in so doing, reproduces ableism. In youth sport, this perspective translates to improving existing initiatives to integrate children with special needs into sport and is accentuated through changes to coaching practice. As such, by reducing issues of inclusion to a battery of strategies and frameworks for adapting practice structures, coach educators and policy makers risk perpetuating integration when meaning to focus on inclusion. Coaching practice is thus framed with a level of instrumentalism and disabled children as a 'problem' to 'deal with' (Townsend *et al.*, 2017). This deficit position in relation to disabled children undermines the most fundamental objectives of inclusion, that is, to fulfil the basic rights of all in an equitable manner. It is worth questioning the extent that coach education programmes, and the view of inclusion these models reproduce, prepares coaches to move beyond mainstreaming or integrating disabled children into 'normal' sports programs, in order to trouble the notion of 'normal' that organizes standardized programs in the first place.

## Summary, Future Directions and Future Research

A key part of advancing research in youth disability sport is the role of the researcher in constructing knowledge about coaching. Despite a considerable body of knowledge developing in youth sport coaching, disabled children are invisible in existing coaching research. In physical education there is a notable emphasis on engaging with disabled children to inform practice (e.g. Fitzgerald *et al.*, 2003; Goodwin, 2009). This trend is not observable in the youth coaching literature. For researchers interested in disability sport and coaching, there is a continued need to expose the effects of ableism and disablism on disabled children, however crucially the research gaze should be turned *from* disabled people and the disabling effects of ableism, towards ableism itself and how it sustains ableist structures, practices and discourses. Methodologically, participatory and emancipatory research traditions and their associated methods provide researchers with the tools to focus the analytical gaze on issues that disabled children identify as important and worthwhile, while valuing their contribution to coaching knowledge and centralising their perspectives. For example, co-production is one such method that is spreading quickly across public health, disability and physical activity. Co-production methods enable researchers to engage with potentially multiple knowledge user communities to provide necessary perspectives on, for example, enhancing the provision of youth disability sport, or informing coach education. In this instance, research that engages with disabled children, coaches, parents and policy-makers directly challenges the value of conventional research practices, from 'pre-proposal' through to the translation of research (see, for example, Carroll *et al.*, 2018).

Looking ahead there are both immediate and enduring challenges for researchers and practitioners interested in enhancing the quality of sport for disabled children and promoting inclusion. The immediate and perhaps most pressing challenge is the requisite need to respond to both the experiences of disabled children in youth sport coaching contexts, as well as practitioners working at the sharp end of disability sport. In providing coaches with theoretically informed, practically relevant guidance (see Stevenson, 2009), researchers can start to address the fundamental issue of securing access for disabled children *and* ensuring quality of participation once access has been secured (Kiuppis, 2018). The second is the need for coach education reform to centralise the knowledge and skills required to enact inclusion across the coaching pathway (cf. Townsend *et al.*, 2021). As such, the limited discussions around coaching disabled children have largely been instrumental, centralising 'best practice' discourses and encouraging the use of coaching frameworks designed to encourage disabled children to participate alongside their age-peers in mainstream or integrated sports sessions. While questions of 'best practice' necessarily occupy a central place in discussions of coaching, it is important to remember disability itself is not a cause for prescriptions, and that best practice is not fixed and absolute. Third, there is a clear need to engage with the communities that we are writing about and researching to inform practice.

This chapter provides a brief examination of the existing literature with a view to establishing some productive lines of inquiry in coaching and disability youth sport. Coaches have a critical influence on how children engage and participate in sport. For disabled children, significant responsibility is placed on coaches when it comes to inclusion, yet little is known about their experiences and challenges in doing so or how best to support them. To ensure that disabled children are not denied their basic right to sport there is a need to consider the education and support required for coaches, alongside the active inclusion of disabled children's experiences and views informing coach education provision.

## References

Anderson, D. 2009. Adolescent girls' involvement in disability sport: implications for identity development. *Journal of Sport and Social Issues*, 33, 427–449.

Ashton-Shaeffer, C, Gibson, HJ, Autry, CE, *et al.* 2001. Meaning of sport to adults with physical disabilities: A disability sport camp experience. *Sociology of Sport Journal*, 18 (1), 95–114.

Bailey, R. 2005. Evaluating the relationship between physical education, sport and social inclusion. *Educational Review*, 57 (1), 71–90.

Black, K., 2011. Coaching disabled children in sport. *In:* I. Stafford, ed. *Coaching Children in Sport.* London: Routledge, 197–212.

Black, K. and Stevenson, P. 2011. The inclusion spectrum. http://www.sportdevelopment.info/index.php/browse-all-documents/748-the-inclusion-spectrum

Campbell, F.K. 2009. *Contours of ableism: The production of disability and abledness.* London, UK: Palgrave Macmillan.

Carroll, P., *et al.*, 2018. Enabling participation for disabled children: Study protocol. *BMC Public Health*, 18 (712), 1–11.

Carter, B., *et al.*, 2014. 'Just kids playing sport (in a chair)': Experiences of children, families and stakeholders attending a wheelchair sports club. *Disability & Society*, 29 (6), 938–952.

Dagkas, S., and Armourk, K. (eds.). 2011. *Inclusion and exclusion through youth sport.* New York: Routledge.

DePauw, K. and Gavron, S. 2005. *Disability and sport*, 2nd ed. Champaign, IL: Human Kinetics.

Fay, T. and Wolff, E., 2009. Disability in sport in the twenty first century: Creating a new sport opportunity spectrum. *Boston University International Law Journal*, 27, 231–248.

Fitzgerald, H. and Jobling, A. 2009. 'Future directions in disability and youth sport: Development, aspirations, and research.' *In:* H. Fitzgerald, ed. *Disability and youth sport.* New York: Routledge, 160–170.

Fitzgerald, H., Jobling, A., and Kirk, D., 2003. Valuing the voices of young disabled people: Exploring experience of physical education and sport. *European Journal of Physical Education*, 8 (2), 175–200.

Fitzgerald, H. 2005. Still feeling like a spare piece of luggage? Embodied experiences of (dis)ability in physical education and school sport. *Physical Education and Sport Pedagogy*, 10, 41–59.

Fitzgerald, H., 2009. *Disability and youth sport.* London: Routledge.

Goodley, D. 2014. *Dis/ability studies: Theorising disablism and ableism.* London, UK: Routledge.

Goodwin, D., 2009. The voices of students with disabilities: Are they informing inclusive physical education practice?. *In:* H. Fitzgerald, ed. *Disability and youth sport.* London: Routledge, 53–75.

Goodwin, D. and Peers, D. 2011. Disability, sport and inclusion. *In:* S. Dagkas and K. Armour, eds. *Inclusion and exclusion through youth sport.* London: Routledge, 186–202.

Hammond, A., *et al.*, 2019. "'I feel we are inclusive enough': Examining swimming coaches" understandings of inclusion and disability. *Sociology of Sport Journal*, 36 (4), 311–321.

Hammond, A., Young, J.A., and Konjarski, L. 2014. Attitudes of Australian Swimming Coaches towards Inclusion of Swimmers with an Intellectual Disability: An Exploratory Analysis. *International Journal of Sports Science and Coaching*, 9 (6), 1425–1436.

Hardin, B., *et al.*, 2001. Missing in action? Images of disability in sports illustrated for kids. *Disability Studies Quarterly*, 21 (2). Retrieved from: http://dsq-sds.org

Hay, P.J., 2012. Ability as an exclusionary concept in youth sport. *In:* S. Dagkas and K. Armour. eds. *Inclusion and exclusion through youth sport.* London, UK: Routledge, 87–99.

Hodge, N. and Runswick-Cole, K., 2013. 'They never pass me the ball': Exposing ableism through the leisure experiences of disabled children, young people and their families. *Children's Geographies*, 11 (3), 311–325.

Holt, N.L., *et al.*, 2017. A grounded theory of positive youth development throught youth sport participation report 36 sport based on results from a qualitative meta-study. *International Review of Sport and Exercise Psychology*, 10 (1), 1–49.

Houlihan, B. and Chapman, P., 2017. Talent identification and development in elite youth disability sport. *Sport in Society*, 20 (1), 107–125.

Jones, D.B., 2003. "Denied from a lot of places": Barriers to participation in community recreation programs encountered by children with disabilities in maine: Perspectives of parents. *Leisure/Loisir*, 28(1/2), 49–69.

King, G., *et al.*, 2003. A conceptual model of the factors affecting the recreation and leisure participation of children with disabilities. *Physical & Occupational Therapy In Pediatrics*, 23(1), 63–90.

Kiuppis, F. 2018. Inclusion in sport: Disability and participation. *Sport in Society*, 21 (1), 4–21.

Lara-Bercial, S. and McKenna, J., 2018. No coach, no gain: The central role of the coach in the personal development of youth performance athletes. *Revista de psicología del deporte*, 27 (3), 50–59.

Lyle, J. 2002. *Sports coaching concepts: A framework for coaches' behaviour.* London: Routledge.

Lyons, L. 2013. Transformed understanding or enlightened ableism? The gap between policy and practice for children with disabilities in Aotearoa New Zealand. *International Journal of Early Childhood*, 45 (2), 237–249.

Martin, J.J., 2006. Psychosocial aspects of youth disability sport. *Adapted Physical Activity Quarterly*, 23 (1), 65–77.

Morley, D., Bailey, R., Tan, J., and Cooke, B. 2005. Inclusive physical education: Teachers' views of teaching children with special educational needs and disabilities in physical education. *European Physical Education Review*, 11 (1), 84–107.

Oliver, M. 1990. *The politics of disablement*. London: Macmillan Press.

Shapiro, D.R. and Martin, J.J. 2010. Athletic identity, affect and peer relations in youth athletes with physical disabilities. *Disability and Health Journal*, 3, 79–85.

Spencer-Cavaliere, N., Thai, J., and Kingsley, B., 2017. A Part of and Apart from Sport: Practitioners' experiences coaching in segregated youth sport. *Social Inclusion*, 5 (2), 120–129.

Stafford, I. (ed.). 2011. *Coaching children in sport*. London: Routledge.

Stevenson, P., 2009. The pedagogy of inclusive youth sport: working towards real solutions. *In:* H. Fitzgerald, ed. *Disability and youth sport*. London: Routledge, 199– 130.

Thomas, C. 1999. *Female forms: Experiencing and understanding disability*. Buckingham, UK: Open University Press.

Townsend, R. and Peacham, G. 2021. Reflections on coaching policy and practice in community disability sport. *In:* B. Ives, L. Gale, P. Potrac, and L. Nelson, eds. *Community sports coaching: Policies and practice*. Routledge.

Townsend, R.C., Cushion, C.J., and Smith, B. 2017. A social-relational analysis of an impairment-specific mode of coach education. *Qualitative Research in Sport, Exercise and Health*, 10 (3), 346–361.

Townsend, R.C., Huntley, T., Cushion, C.J., and Culver, D. 2022. Infusing disability into coach education and development: a critical review and agenda for change. *Physical Education and Sport Pedagogy*, 27 (3), 247–260.

United Nations. 2006. *Convention on the rights of persons with disabilities*. Geneva: United Nations.

Winnick, J.P., 1987. An integration continuum for sports participation. *Adapted Physical Activity Quarterly*, 4 (3), 157–161.

# 32

# "I TREAT EVERY PLAYER EQUALLY": COACHING CULTURALLY DIVERSE CHILDREN IN SPORT

*Brent McDonald*

## Introduction

"I treat every player equally" is a consistent statement from coaches when reflecting on their individual coaching philosophy and practices. The quote is indicative of a general trend in coaching towards inclusivity and a subsequent belief that this is being achieved. In many coaching contexts "equally" can be replaced by "the same", and therefore poses the question: How do ideas about "same" interact with contexts that are "diverse" when it comes to coaching? This chapter examines coaching culturally diverse children (CDC) in the context of community sport.

CDC are not a monolithic category, rather this is a multidimensional descriptor that acknowledges their individual and collective complexity shaped variously through the intersection of ethnicity, gender, experiences, ability, and class (to name just a few). Importantly though, CDC *are* positioned as a category outside of, or different to, some form of dominant (in both a statistical sense and in relation to power) majority. In coaching this dominant majority can be characterised as white, more male than female, and as having lifelong connections to the sport context. Further these coaches tend to have coached younger people who also fit under the dominant majority umbrella and hence share some common cultural identity with their athletes. This is not to say that there aren't situations in sport where these majority/minority positions are turned on their head, where cultural diversity is the majority, or where coaches come from outside the dominant majority. However, this chapter focuses on the often-dichotomous relationship between CDC and the mainstream (majority culture) context.

The following chapter begins by briefly contextualising coaching in mainstream community sport before moving to an examination of the popular rhetoric of inclusive coaching practices. This rhetoric involves taken-for-granted and common-sense understandings of the value of sport (character building), and neo-liberal ideology expressed through the core beliefs of meritocracy and colour-blindness. Further to this rhetoric, the practices of ethno-racialisation, and issue of whiteness, are discussed. Following this the concept of microaggressions is introduced, as a reflection of popular rhetoric, and as conscious and unconscious practices of coaching that, in fact, achieves the opposite of "treating every player equally". Finally, the

DOI: 10.4324/9781003199359-37

chapter discusses the possibilities of transforming microaggressions into micro-affirmations (Gearity and Henderson Metzger, 2017) through the development of reflexive and relational coaching practices.

## Review of Current Literature

### *Contextualising Sport Coaching*

Coaching occurs at a variety of levels and in settings that can be quite different. For example, for young people it might be any of the following: a local "come and try" program; an intervention program for "at risk" young people; a community club, participation-based, non-competitive experience; a community club competitive, seasonal format; a school-based representative sport; a talent identification or high-performance format (including State and National representation); a semi-professional context. Some children's engagements with sport may be through a singular setting, however it is entirely possible that they may also experience each of these settings on their sporting journey. The context of coaching that is considered in this chapter is the mainstream community sport model, as it is through this model that most CDC will have their first engagement with sport and coaches.

The mainstream sport model can generally be characterised as competitive, club-based, fee-based, organised into leagues, and featuring weekday training/s followed by weekend matches based on a home and away format. The clubs are predominantly formed on the community model, namely the members (players, coaches, volunteers, etc) come from the local community. Most sports are 'governed' by sport organisations who are responsible for fixturing, providing officials, accrediting coaches, maintaining behavioural standards of clubs, and developing entry-level, modified versions of the sport aimed at attracting new players as children. Most clubs incorporate teams from juniors through to seniors. The participatory focus of each sport tends to shift towards performance from about the age of 12 as league tables, finals series, and premierships become more important. In adult competition, players (especially men) may be paid to play, and home grounds and clubrooms are adorned with various memorabilia and serviced by a canteen and, in many cases, a bar as well. This description of the mainstream sport model is not necessarily exhaustive, nor is it necessary to possess all these features to fit under the 'mainstream' umbrella.

Coaches within this model are mostly volunteers, though some are paid, and operate with relatively large amounts of autonomy. How coaches use this autonomy is dependent on their individual philosophy about sport. For example, a coach whose focus is on participation and skill development may operate quite differently to a coach who is driven to win premierships, or a coach who is looking to further their own coaching opportunities. Further coaching practice is also shaped by the type of club the coach operates in, for example the importance the club has for the performance of its teams or the cultural history of the club. In coaching contexts, it may often be difficult to directly identify forms, both overt and covert, of racial aggressions and exclusion because they simultaneously exist with 'happy discourses of diversity, racial transcendence, and cosmopolitanism' (Manning, 2021, p.196).

The sport/coach/club nexus is where CDC engage with and experience both sport and majority culture. In relation to coaching CDC a coach has multiple responsibilities when considering the idea of creating inclusive practices. The first is in relation to their own practices as a coach. How does the coach who has good intentions, for example treating everyone equally, ensure that this occurs? The second is in relation to managing the various interactions that CDC have in sport that maybe be considered negative, hostile, alienating and 'othering'.

These interactions could be between teammates, or opponents, or even parents, spectators, and other coaches (Farquharson *et al.*, 2019). How does a coach provide a safe and positive environment for CDC? Whilst this range of responsibility may in one sense be onerous and disproportionate for any coach to have to contend with, it is nevertheless an important realisation for a coach to have. The reality is that sport is never just the activity itself. It doesn't occur in a vacuum, rather it is embedded always in multiple overlapping political, situational, historical, and physical contexts. Coaching CDC requires a reflexive, culturally responsive coaching praxis in which it is necessary to recognise the coaches' own positionality in these contexts and the subsequent taken-for-granted epistemological and common-sense logics that shape coach actions, both verbal and physical.

## *The Rhetoric of Inclusive Coaching Practices*

Considering the rhetoric of inclusive practices for CDC, "treating everyone equally" usually occurs in conjunction with "our club accepts anyone" or "everyone is welcome". Of course, there is usually an unspoken caveat to these statements, namely "if they want to". It is here that the responsibility for being included falls on the young person, and therefore suggests that CDC may be required to change something about themselves to fit in. Hallinan *et al.* (2007, p.295) comment that coaching, both in relation to management of players and selection of teams, is 'inherently assimilationist'. Anyone can play: "If they want it enough"; "If they show determination and commitment"; "If they turn up to training"; "If they follow the team rules"; "If they pay their membership fees and register". What we have in this list of "ifs" are some common taken-for-granted assumptions used by coaches and which, in each case, requires the labour of inclusion to be carried out by the person seeking to be included. If we were to deconstruct all the taken-for-granted aspects of involvement in sport, we would go some way to understanding the variety of practices and processes that contribute to the exclusion of CDC and their families in sport. Research into the barriers to participation in sport for CDC is extensive (see for example: Cortis, 2009; Smith *et al.*, 2019; Fox and Paradies, 2020), and yet coaches often ignore or are ignorant about these issues.

Recognising the taken-for-granted assumptions regarding access to sport needs to be followed by a critique of the common-sense understanding of the value of coaching. A common driver in coaching philosophy are approaches that reflect the logic of sport as being "character building" for young people. Many coaches in community-level sport hold a strong belief that sport contributes to positive development in young people, that it keeps them out of trouble, that it teaches positive traits, and that it makes players better people in their societies. For many coaches this is why they coach; they feel they can contribute positively to the lives of CDC, and in many cases they do. However, the idea of character building is far from a neutral concept, rather it reflects certain values and norms that are culturally grounded. Recognition of this is essential in developing reflexive coaching practices that ensures that coaching CDC doesn't become a form of neo-colonialisation (McDonald *et al.*, 2019). Sport was historically used as an effective tool of the coloniser and the mantra of building character could be seen conversely as 'civilising the savage' as the values espoused through sport on the colonised were very much those of self, and social, control. In a contemporary sense therefore, coaches must beware of the evolutionary trajectory of character building, namely positive development. Coakley (2011) provides an extensive critique of sport as positive development for young people, and this is especially the case with CDC. This is because coaches often assume that CDC are coming from a deficit ('at risk') position and therefore positive development is demonstrated through forms of self-control and self-discipline that don't necessarily benefit CDC (Coakley, 2011;

McDonald *et al.*, 2019). This is not to say that sport can't contribute to the positive development of CDC, rather that it doesn't happen by default.

The idea of coaches providing guidance and opportunities for the positive development of CDC is supported further by the fact that much of sport effectively reflects neoliberal ideology present in many societies in the Global North. Coaches actively invoke aspects of neoliberalism in their speech and approaches to team selection, especially when framed in the language of treating everyone equally. Neoliberal ideology is apparent in its ahistoricism, its tendency to locate all responsibility for success/failure in demonstrating character and being a player at the level of individual agency, and its reliance on the myth of the "level playing field" (a favourite sporting metaphor) to insist on the absence of bias in the coach/athlete relationship.

The approach of treating every player equally is flawed because it assumes a system of equality is present in the first place. Neoliberalism ignores the various historical, social, and cultural inequalities faced both by individual CDC, and the collective groupings that they belong to (or are assigned to) (Hylton, 2018). The "level playing field" is essential to support the concept of meritocracy, namely people end up where they deserve to, based on their natural ability combined with work ethic. The meritocracy relies on two fallacies, namely that sport is value neutral, and that coaching decisions are made via objective practices. When coaching CDC this is probably most prominent through the belief in colour-blindness. Colour-blindness, or the belief in not seeing 'race', is seen as a positive. However, Hylton (2018) identifies that colour-blindness has the effect of reinforcing the myth of meritocracy and producing aversive racism, whereby coaches are absolved of responsibility for identifying and addressing forms of systemic and institutional racism present in sport settings and their own practices. Colour-blindness focuses on incremental and superficial changes that have occurred slowly over time, for example the reduction in the use of overt racial slurs in coaching, and in doing so obscures other forms of racism that continue to thrive. Reflexive coaching practices would pay attention to these other forms of racism when engaging with CDC.

Whilst the raison d'etre for many coaches is found in the positive development of their players (character traits), many are also highly motivated to win and to that end possess a strong desire to find and/or develop talent. Recruiting talented players can be an end in itself, or it can be utilised as part of aspiring coaches' trajectory of moving through the ranks and building their coaching CV. Either way, eschewing colour-blindness, coaches' decisions on who to recruit and who possesses talent when it comes to CDC invariably draw on the practice of ethno-racialisation.

Ethno-racialisation refers to the practice of consciously and unconsciously stereotyping individuals based on either cultural identity or more commonly some phenotypic difference, for example skin colour. The practice of ethno-racialisation is the process whereby people make sense of those around them by relying on reducing individuals to a collective identity that involves assumptions about physical, social, and psychological behaviour. These assumptions are based on a confusing mix of myth, erroneous science, and regular representations of ethno-racialised people in mass media. Whilst this process can be multi-directional, it is predominantly involved when the majority culture operationalises it to understand minority culture. A clear example of ethno-racialisation is when racial profiling is employed in policing, the result of which means higher representation of these groups in the criminal justice system and incarceration (McDonald *et al.*, 2019). This then leads to stereotypes that certain cultural groups are more prone to criminality than majority culture. This form of ethno-racialisation, namely racial profiling, would be seen by many people as highly problematic and as a form of racism.

However, the practices of ethno-racialisation in sport and coaching are harder to identify and problematise, as the outcomes are seen as positive. Ethno-racialisation in coaching has the tendency to produce two distinct explanations for the performances of CDC in sport. The first is a surplus model, that relies on problematic and fundamentally flawed ideas tied to biological 'race' and 'natural' sporting talent (McDonald and Spaaij, 2020). The surplus model is almost always linked to a fallacious relationship between skin colour and particular physiological characteristics that are advantageous in certain sports. In other words, this is a focus on the Black athlete and the search for talent. For example, in the Australian context, 'Black' often conflates young people from Indigenous, Pasifika, and African backgrounds into a sought after, naturally gifted commodity (McDonald, 2013). This conflation can occur differently across national contexts, but does so in juxtaposition to the unmarked (White) majority culture (Hylton, 2018). Research across a range of sports has demonstrated the ways in which stereotypes about natural ability results in positional segregation which is the statistical overrepresentation of ethno-racialised people in particular positions on the field/court that are deemed suited to their 'natural' abilities (see for example Spaaij *et al.*, 2015). These positions are most often in peripheral, non-decision making, roles on the team, with central and leadership roles being occupied by the cultural majority, White, athletes. In the context of CDC, if the diversity comes in the form of a Black athlete, then coaches believe having such diversity as advantageous. Equally not having this diversity is often regarded as being at a disadvantage (McDonald, 2016). This therefore poses the question about how coaches interact with, or seek out, potential athletes who are culturally diverse but fall outside of the Black athlete category.

The flip side of ethno-racialised thinking is the deficit model that applies cultural stereotypes to explain CDC's absence from sport. For example, in the Australian context this is seen in the underrepresentation of CDC from Asian backgrounds in multiple sport settings. This absence may be explained away as either being not physically suited or not culturally interested, in sport. Again, the logic of neoliberalism, when applied to both explanations, places the absence in the hands of the agency of CDC. Further this absence is often problematised, especially in relation to culturally diverse girls from Muslim backgrounds (Cortis, 2009; Ekholm *et al.*, 2019).

If ethno-racialisation influences coaches' understanding about who is/isn't suited to sport, then it has the potential to also shape coach interactions with CDC, especially in relation to the coaches' expectations about CDC's performance and behaviour in the sport setting. It is these expectations, and the ways in which they are communicated, both to the CDC and the rest of the team, that have a significant influence on the experiences of CDC. As ethno-racialisation occurs mostly at a subconscious level, the way this plays out in the coach/athlete relationship is at a micro-level, including through body language, patterns of speech, and attempted humour. When seen as a one-off occurrence such micro-interactions may appear harmless, however when they are repeated, they have the potential to be harmful and dangerous. Identifying and understanding micro-aggressions is therefore of vital importance to coaches of CDC who genuinely want to be inclusive and supportive.

## Micro-Aggressions and Coaching

The rhetoric of inclusive coaching practices reflects a larger macro-system of policies and ideologies that are present in many countries in the Global North. Such macro-systems include neoliberalism and ethno-racialisation, but also involve debates between issues such as immigration and multiculturalism; systemic racism and anti-racist movements; Islamophobia, religious freedoms, and identity politics. Macro-systems create the context where micro-aggressions can flourish (Lin *et al.*, 2016). For example, when certain migrant groups are demonised in various media, held responsible for crime waves, or described as "not fitting in", then these are ripe conditions for micro-aggressions to thrive. Micro-aggressions are commonplace and regular, intentional or unintentional, forms of communicating consistent insensitivities to CDC in ways that are detrimental to their overall well-being (Lin *et al.*, 2016). Micro-aggressions that occur in the context of coaching CDC can produce alienation, marginalisation, anxiety, low self-esteem, dropout, or conformity and 'quiet disengagement' (Johnston-Goodstar and Roholt, 2017, p.39). A further consideration is that microaggressions experienced by CDC in sporting contexts are regularly like those experienced in other social and institutional contexts. Such microaggressions have also been noted in a variety of settings including education, public transport, and across a range of media. Hence it is the accumulative nature of microaggressions that is particularly damaging for CDC (Burdsey, 2011), and it is here that coaches, through attention and recognition of microaggressions in their interactions with CDC, have the potential to make sport, not only a safe space, but also one that allows for young people to learn to resist microaggressions.

Microaggressions fall into three categories, micro-assaults, micro-insults, and micro-invalidations. Micro-assaults are the most overt form of microaggression and the easiest to identify. These can be categorised as explicit and intentional attacks (e.g. racist, sexist, xenophobic language) whose goal is to harm CDC. As they are conscious acts, micro-assaults are less likely to occur in the coach/athlete relationship and more in the interactions between CDC and teammates, opponents, spectators, and opposition coaches. Managing and stopping these micro-assaults often falls on the victim of the assault, namely CDC, making a formal complaint and advocating for themselves. As Farquharson *et al.* (2019) have observed, this is an inadequate process and does little to support CDC nor change racist behaviours they experience. Coaches need to actively support CDC and not only when they report a micro-assault. They need to be sensitive to the interactions that occur and be proactive in addressing such micro-assaults, rather than waiting for the CDC to lodge a complaint.

The micro-aggressions that are most likely to occur in the coach/CDC relationship are micro-insults and micro-invalidations. There are a range of coaching settings that these might take place in including in the context of language used in both coaching and casual interactions (including humour), tactical considerations, team selection, match reports, engagement and conversations with players' families (especially parents), and use of communication platforms to connect with team members.

Micro-insults are mostly covert because the coach is unaware that their language is insensitive to the recipient's identity. These might take the form of throwaway lines, negative stereotyping, or stigmatisation. Coaches making comments about CDC and them not being punctual, being lazy or not putting in effort, or failing to follow tactics or staying in position, do so in a way that draws on assumptions about cultural deficiency or pathology (Johnston-Goodstar and Roholt, 2017). In the same way labelling CDC as 'naturals' strips them of some of the cognitive elements of performance and makes assumptions that their abilities come without the need to work hard (as opposed to the majority culture athlete). Micro-insults are particularly common when coaches are trying to discipline their athletes, as both racial and gendered language, becomes normalised as part of coaching vernacular (Gearity and Henderson Metzger, 2017). Another form of micro-insult is misrepresenting CDC, for example lumping players into collective categories or conflating one cultural identity with other identities (for example assuming that all players who have migrated from Africa are Muslim).

Finally, micro-invalidations are covert and unintended or unwitting. These would be seen as unconscious communication that 'exclude, negate, or nullify' the ideas, emotions, or 'experiential reality' of CDC (Sue *et al.*, 2007 in Gearity and Henderson Metzger, 2017, p.161). Micro-invalidations can also occur when a coach acts in what they believe as the CDC's best interests. An example might be pushing CDC towards a high-performance team or putting them in a high-pressure position on the field because of ethno-racialised assumptions about ability and/or motivations for playing, when in fact the young person has little interest in the competitive aspects of the sport and is involved because of social relationships and a wanting to be involved in a low stress, fun, recreational environment. Micro-invalidations can also take the form of invalidating the voices of CDC. This can be ignoring their suggestions (for example playing a certain position), not asking for their input at training (but regularly asking majority culture players), or not taking them seriously when they have a problem (for example if they experience racial taunts when on the field). Micro-invalidations could involve constantly getting a culturally diverse player's name wrong (because no effort is made to learn how to pronounce it) or giving them a nickname that may confuse or stereotype, always using famous players from the majority culture for a role model and never mentioning similarly famous CD players, ignoring major religious events important to CDC whilst celebrating other religious events (for example ignoring Ramadan but recognising Christmas), making no effort to have any engagement with CD players' parents and yet demonstrating strong connections to other players' families.

The above are simply a few examples of the potential list of micro-aggressions that could occur between coaches and CDC. As many of these are often subconscious, they can be difficult to identify, and if challenged, coaches often respond that they have been misunderstood, that they were only joking, or that those challenging are overreacting. However, if the goal is to become an inclusive coach who believes in equality, then developing a capacity to recognise one's own micro-aggressions is central to achieving this goal. Language and mannerisms of coaches become automatic as similar words, phrases, sentences, and body language are repeated during the coaching performance. Reflexive and relational coaching starts therefore with a linguistic turn, changing micro-aggressions into micro-affirmations.

## Implications for Children's Sports Coaching

### *Micro-Affirmations and Relational Coaching*

Authors such as Gearity and Henderson Metzger (2017, p.160) argue for a move towards a 'layered cultural praxis of sport coaching with a social justice end' and suggest that a step towards achieving this by changing micro-aggressions into micro-affirmations. Micro-affirmations are not only linguistic, but include listening, gestures, and caring actions, and they have the effect of building strength and facilitating further opportunities for CDC. Just as micro-aggressions are regular and repeated, for micro-affirmations to be successful they need to be consistent and specific and do the work of reducing the 'dominating effects of' existing power relations (Gearity and Henderson Metzger, 2017, p.164). The following are a few examples of how this might work:

> Micro-aggression: A CD player is fasting as part of Ramadan, shows low energy at training and the coach continually calls her lazy whilst praising other players for their effort.
>
> Micro-affirmation: The coach talks to the player about Ramadan and asks if she is happy to explain its significance to the rest of the team. Based on conversations with the player the coach changes some of her workload at training and praises her for her effort.
>
> Micro-aggression: Yelling at CD players for failing to follow team rules and match tactics.

Micro-affirmation: Think about alternative ways of communicating tactics and develop strategies to ensure these are understood. Consider how language is used, including speed of delivery and slang. Think of ways for the team to generate their own rules and tactics.

Micro-aggression: Ethno-racialisation, CDC are always selected in peripheral positions suited to their "natural" abilities.

Micro-affirmation: Rotate positions, ask players which positions they would like to play and give them a chance to play there.

Micro-aggression: The coach mispronounces a CD player's name. Other players find the mispronunciation funny and start copying the coach when interacting with the player.

Micro-affirmation: On first meeting ask the CD player how to pronounce their name and check with them that you are saying it correctly.

Micro-aggression: The opposition team has several CDC. Before the match, as a form of motivation, the coach makes disparaging comments about them being physically inferior.

Micro-affirmation: Before the match the coach focuses on her own team's strengths and game plan. She refers to the opposition with respect.

Micro-aggression: The coach notices that a CD player's parents seem reluctant to make conversation and assumes it is because they are not interested in their child's sport or don't speak English very well. The coach leaves them alone.

Micro-affirmation: The coach makes a concerted effort to include the CD player's parents. The coach approaches them and makes conversation, learns their names, and actively works to include them with other parents and in club activities.

To create genuine micro-affirmations, however, one needs to be careful not to rely on assumptions (lest one ends up unintentionally creating new micro-aggressions) to formulate positive communication. Relational approaches are the most significant starting point to develop a coaching practice that is culturally responsive. Acting on behalf of CDC is problematic as it can unintentionally rely on stereotyping and 'othering'. A relational approach would seek to coach *with* CDC, building relationships, listening, and working to understand their individuality and cultural identity. Treating all players equally is all well and good as long as the coach knows all players equally.

## Summary, Future Directions and Future Research

Coaching any young person can be a challenging, confusing, and immensely rewarding activity. Each young person comes to sport with their own motivations, physical and sporting history, knowledge, and social characteristics. Coaches can be responsible for micro-aggressions towards any athlete under their charge, but this is much more likely the case when the athlete comes from a culturally diverse background different to the coach. The principles of inclusive coaching discussed in this chapter apply to all coaching practices but are especially connected to CDC. Reflexive and relational coaching requires a willingness to apply a critical lens to one's own practice and to deconstruct the various taken-for-granted aspects of both access to sport, and the values and beliefs behind why one coaches.

Considering that most sports now expect coaches to undertake some form of training or accreditation it would be entirely possible to include an emphasis on a reflexive and relational coaching framework that focused on understanding micro-aggressions and micro-affirmations.

Whilst learning how to prepare athletes to avoid injury or where to put the witches' hats to effectively run a drill is important for coaches, most training and accreditation does little to instruct on pedagogical aspects of working with young people and especially not CDC. Such changes would also demonstrate that sport organisations are committed to diversity and inclusion in more ways than just rhetoric.

Research with CDC in the context of mainstream sport is also relatively limited. Often the focus has been on intervention or CDC only programs and there is a need for more ethnographic-based work that engages with both coaches and CDC (Flensner *et al.*, 2021). Another research approach that offers new insights and directions for coaches are participatory action research and activist research frameworks (Luguetti *et al.*, 2021). In these approaches the research goal is not only to understand a problem, but to affect some form of change through the research process. This type of research is applicable to reflexive and relational coaching practices as it approaches CDC from a strengths-based perspective and utilises the concept of co-creation to engage CDC. The concept of co-creation suggests that through social interaction all participants are responsible for and able to contribute to the development of something new (Luguetti *et al.*, 2021). In a coaching context this would mean a shift from coaching 'to' or 'for' CDC to an intention of coaching 'with'.

The performative nature of coaching means that micro-aggressions can become part of a coaches' repertoire without them being fully aware. Assumptions and stereotypes about CDC are shaped by various ideologies, and decontextualised experiences with CDC. In other words, coaches make sense of the behaviour of CDC (based on perhaps four or five hours engagement a week) by using causal logic between that behaviour and what they think they know about a particular cultural group. This has the effect of removing from CDC their individual sense of agency. Considering that CDC may experience similar micro-aggressions in other parts of society, reflexive and relational coaching has the potential to make the sport environment one that is more inclusive and safer for CDC. In this way creating micro-affirmations to counter micro-aggressions presents coaches with a clear path on how to be a better, more inclusive coach, and in doing so achieve their stated intention of "treating every player equally".

## References

Burdsey, D., 2011. That joke isn't funny anymore: Racial microaggressions, colour-blind ideology and the mitigation of racism in English men's first-class cricket. *Sociology of Sport Journal*, 28 (3), 261–283.

Coakley, J., 2011. Youth sports: What counts as "positive development?". *Journal of Sport and Social Issues*, 35 (3), 306–324.

Cortis, N., 2009. Social inclusion and sport: Culturally diverse women's perspectives. *Australian Journal of Social Sciences*, 44 (1), 91–106.

Ekholm, D., Dahlstedt, M., and Ronnback, J., 2019. Problematising the absent girl: Sport as a means of emancipation. *Sport in Society*, 22 (6), 1043–1061.

Farquharson, K., *et al.*, 2019. Managing racism on the field in australian junior sport. *In*: P. Essed *et al.*, eds. *Relating worlds of racism: Dehumanisation, belonging, and the normativity of European Whiteness*. Switzerland: Palgrave Macmillan, 165–189.

Flensner, K., Korp, P., and Lindgren, E., 2021. Integration into and through sports? Sport-activities for migrant children and youths. *European Journal for Sport and Society*, 18 (1), 64–81.

Fox, B. and Paradies, Y., 2020. Youth sport and community segregation: A study of kids' participation in Australian rules football and soccer clubs in an Australian community. *Race Ethnicity and Education*, 23 (5), 732–746.

Gearity, B.T. and Henderson Metzger, L., 2017. Intersectionality, microaggressions, and microaffirmations: Toward a cultural praxis of sport coaching. *Sociology of Sport Journal*, 34 (1), 160–175.

Hallinan, C., Hughson, J., and Burke, M., 2007. Supporting the 'world game' in Australia: A case study of fandom at national and club level. *Soccer & Society*, 8 (2/3), 283–297.

Hylton, K., 2018. *Contesting 'race' and sport: Shaming the colour line*. London: Routledge.
Johnston-Goodstar, K. and Roholt, R.V., 2017. "Our kids aren't dropping out: They're being pushed out": Native American students and racial microaggressions in schools. *Journal of Ethnic and Cultural Diversity in Social Work*, 26 (1-2), 30–47.
Lin, A.R., *et al.*, 2016. "They will post a law about playing soccer" and other ethnic/racial microaggressions in organised activities experienced by Mexican-origin families. *Journal of Adolescent Research*, 31 (5), 557–581.
Luguetti, C., Singehebhuye, L., and Spaaij, R., 2021. 'Stop mocking, start respecting': An activist approach meets African Australian refugee-background young women in grassroots football. *Qualitative Research in Sport, Exercise and Health*, 14 (1), 119–136.
Manning, A., 2021. Racial and ethnic diversity and racist ruptures in US youth soccer. *In*: M. Lang, ed. *Routledge handbook of athlete welfare*. London: Routledge, 196–205.
McDonald, B., 2013. The reproduction of biological 'race' through physical education textbooks and curriculum. *European Physical Education Review*, 19 (2), 183–198.
McDonald, B., 2016. Coaching whiteness: Stories of 'Pacifica exotica' in Australian high school rugby. *Sport, Education and Society*, 21 (3), 465–482.
McDonald, B., Rodriguez, L., and George, J.R., 2019. 'If it weren't for rugby I'd be in prison now': Pacific Islanders, rugby and the production of natural spaces. *Journal of Ethnic and Migration Studies*, 45 (11), 1919–1935.
McDonald, B. and Spaaij, R., 2020. Finding the 'natural': Talent identification and racialisation in sports coaching and selection practices in Australia. *In*: S. Bradbury, J. Lusted, and J. van Sterkenburg, eds. *'Race', ethnicity and racism in sports coaching*. London: Routledge, 97–111.
Smith, R., Spaaij, R., and McDonald, B., 2019. Migrant integration and cultural capital in the context of sport and physical activity: A systematic review. *Journal of International Migration & Integration*, 20, 851–868.
Spaaij, R., Farquharson, K., and Marjorinbanks, T., 2015. Sport and social inequalities. *Sociology Compass*, 9 (5), 400–411.

# 33

# ADDRESSING THE NEEDS OF INDIGENOUS CHILDREN?: COACH EDUCATION PROGRAMS IN CANADA, AOTEAROA NEW ZEALAND, AND AUSTRALIA

*Andrew Bennie, Jeremy Hapeta, Dan Henhawk, and Audrey R. Giles*

## Introduction

Canada, Australia, and Aotearoa New Zealand (NZ) all share histories of devastating acts of colonialism against Indigenous Peoples. In the present moment, the continued education of Indigenous children through coaching is overflowing with tensions from the legacies of colonialism that continue to permeate the spaces of sport and physical education. This chapter examines coach education programs in Canada, Australia, and Aotearoa New Zealand (NZ). These three countries enable comparisons between countries of the white diaspora (Ashcroft *et al.*, 2013, p. 18); indeed, they share similar histories in which the church and state have conspired to create sporting spaces, including coaching programs that reinforce Euro-centric beliefs and values.

This chapter outlines a need for cultural safety in coaching if sport is to be a safe space for Indigenous children in Canada, Australia, and Aotearoa NZ. This chapter begins with an overview of cultural safety before providing a summary of coach education programs in each of the three countries. It then draws on examples to illustrate the ways in which cultural safety can be infused into coach education programs.

## Review of Current Literature

### *Cultural Safety*

Fundamental to the coaching of Indigenous children is a recognition of sport as a contentious space that has created many struggles around issues of race and identity. Contemporary coach education programs must interrupt neo-colonial interventions that maintain racist notions of Indigeneity and create safe spaces for Indigenous children to engage in sport while strengthening understandings of Indigenous culture and identity. This requires coaches to be educated in cultural safety (Ramsden, 1993).

DOI: 10.4324/9781003199359-38

Cultural safety is an approach that nursing educators in Aotearoa NZ developed to address colonial practices in healthcare and health disparities between Māori and Pākehā (white) peoples (Ramsden, 1993). Those who engage in this approach emphasise the necessity of addressing the ways in which social, political, historical, and economic structures influence relations of power between Indigenous and non-Indigenous peoples (Smye and Browne, 2002) – for example, a Māori patient and a non-Indigenous practitioner. The focus on the interaction between *two* cultures makes cultural safety distinct from concepts such as cultural sensitivity and cultural relevancy, which often rely on the idea that the practitioner is in the position of deciding whether or not she/he/they are providing culturally sensitive or relevant services (Brascoupé and Waters, 2009). Crucially, in cultural safety, it is only the recipient of the service or care who can determine if an encounter has been one that is culturally safe.

The likes of Giles and Darroch (2014) have argued that cultural safety needs to be extended to physical activity and sport settings. They suggested that practitioners in such settings need to reframe the question of "Why are the actions or plans of this Indigenous client/participant not in line with my cultural worldview, which informs my program?" to "Why do my actions or plans not fit into the cultural worldview of this Indigenous client/participant and how will we together negotiate this difference?" (p. 318). The principles of cultural safety in a coaching context require coaches to understand their own cultural beliefs and attitudes towards Indigenous children; have an awareness of the impact of history on Indigenous children's engagement in sport; and to make every effort to be conscious and deliberate in creating the safest sporting spaces possible for Indigenous children. Below, the chapter offers a review of the current coach training programs in Canada, Australia, and Aotearoa NZ, and situates them within each country's colonial history.

## *Canada*

In Canada, coach education takes place through the National Coaching Certification Program (NCCP). This program was created by the Coaching Association of Canada in 1971 (Coaching Association of Canada, 2021) with the goal of providing training and certification to coaches involved in grassroots development and high-performance sport. In 1994, the National Aboriginal Coaching and Leadership Program (NACLP) was developed and initially followed the framework set forth by the NCCP. The NACLP offered NCCP theory courses that were focussed on coaching pedagogies and technical skills. However, the framework for the NALCP eventually changed as the NCCP moved to a "Competency Based Evaluation Training" model focusing on five core competencies: problem-solving, valuing, critical thinking, leading, and interacting (Aboriginal Sport Circle [ASC], 2017). In 1998, the ASC, which is the national voice for Indigenous sport and recreation in Canada, assumed responsibility of the NACLP and began the process of "developing culturally relevant reference material for the NCCP" (ASC 2017, p. i). This led to the development of the Aboriginal Coaching Modules (ACM), which launched in 2003 and were subsequently updated in 2015.

According to the ASC (2021), the ACM was a response to an identified need to provide a coach training curriculum that reflected Indigenous cultures and values. The program was originally envisioned to cater to coaches of First Nation, Métis, and Inuit heritage, but the program eventually expanded to include non-Indigenous coaches working in Indigenous contexts. The ACM outlines the following as purposes for the guiding reference material: Improve the understanding of the application of Aboriginal culture in sport and coaching; provide a culturally relevant learning experience for Aboriginal coaches and athletes; increase the capacity of non-native coaches to coach Aboriginal athletes; improve the quality of the sport experience for Aboriginal athletes; increase the number of Aboriginal certified coaches; make the wisdom of Aboriginal culture available to mainstream sport. These purposes are addressed through three modules: (i) A Holistic Approach to Coaching, (ii) Dealing with Racism in Sport, and (iii) Individual and Community Health and Wellness.

Of note is the use of the Medicine Wheel as a basis for conceptualising a holistic approach to coaching in the ACM:

> The medicine wheel represents a view of life that is whole and shows the inter-dependence of all facets of life. The medicine wheel also represents the ongoing and cyclical nature of change and transformation that is fundamental to all living creatures … One of the fundamental principles in using the medicine wheel is that harmony and balance in all four directions is the goal of learning and change.
>
> (ASC, 2017, p. 2)

The ACM has noted that while the medicine wheel is not universal to all Indigenous cultures in what is now known as Canada, it does provide a basis upon which to conceptualise a holistic approach to coaching and an Indigenous understanding of interconnectedness.

The ACM in Canada operates in a sporting space filled with tensions that reflect the profound impacts of historical settler-colonialism. The Canadian government's creation of the Indian Act of 1876 and the Department of Indian Affairs in 1880 formalised the state's interference in Indigenous peoples' lives. Educational spaces were created by missionaries from virtually every Christian denomination, leading to the formalised Indian residential school system. These schools were created for the purpose of eradicating Indigenous cultures and assimilation of Indigenous children (Truth and Reconciliation Commission of Canada, 2015), and they implemented strategies ranging from the banning of cultural and ceremonial practices through law to creating a physical education curriculum that utilised Euro-centric sports and games to inculcate Indigenous children with settler-colonial values (Forsyth, 2007). Indeed, within these institutions and in broader sporting spaces, Indigenous physical cultural practices were deemed as deficient in the face of Euro-centric values and moral judgements (Paraschak, 1998), often being mis-interpreted or dismissed entirely. In their place, Euro-centric sport and games were (and continue to be) utilised in attempts to transform Indigenous children into citizens who embody the goals of the nation state.

Researchers have not yet specifically addressed coaching Indigenous children in the Canadian context; however, investigations of older, high-performance Indigenous athletes' experiences in Canadian sport prove instructive and provide a basis upon which to analyse the ACM and coach education in general. For example, Schinke *et al.*'s (2007) research into Indigenous athletes' experiences of being coached in Canadian mainstream sport revealed that they would like to see coaching education include culture-specific curriculum and training, as well as a focus on how coaches could more effectively mobilise Indigenous resources to support athletes throughout the process of their sporting careers. The authors noted the prevalence of racist stereotypes and a lack of knowledge of culturally relevant strategies of engagement of the athletes, a situation that continues in Canada today.

## Australia

Sport Australia is the national sporting body responsible for governing coach education in partnership with more than 70 National Sporting Organisations (NSOs) across Australia (Sport Australia, n.d.). Under the National Coaching Accreditation Scheme (NCAS), NSOs design their own coach education pathways, including the number and type of accreditation levels. These levels sit alongside general coaching principles coursework developed by the NCAS, setting the minimum competency standards coach accreditation in Australia (Sport Australia, n.d.). The general principles course (Australian Sports Commission, 2006) is for coaches with little to no previous experience in coaching and coaches who are working with children. Coaches learn about the coach's role, group management, planning and reviewing training, inclusive coaching, and risk management, including the ethical responsibilities of a coach. While they are assessed via practical coaching demonstrations, session planning, and a written component, at no point are they introduced to coaching athletes from a diverse range of backgrounds.

While Australia's sports industry attempts to connect with Indigenous communities through sport development and sport for development programs, these programs tend to focus on promoting the physical, mental, and social health of youth. Although not strictly confined to an athlete's skill development, sport becomes the mechanism for connecting young people to broader outcomes like physical activity, general health, and nutritional awareness (Forneris *et al.*, 2016; Schulenkorf and Siefken, 2018). More specifically, pathway programs like these are used in attempts to nurture life skills (behavioural, cognitive, and interpersonal competencies like effective communication, responsibility, problem-solving, decision making and goal setting) to "help" support a young person's ability to adapt and succeed in both sport and non-sport settings (Camiré *et al.*, 2013; Hodge *et al.*, 2017). However, Sheppard *et al.* (2021) noted that such sport development programs for Indigenous youth in Australia have been critiqued for becoming means for "domestic development" (p. 1) rather than achieving their intended outcomes. Therefore, based on recent critiques of existing sport development programs, caution needs to be taken when coaching Indigenous children.

The current national sources of information for coaching Indigenous children – the *Beginning coaching principles manual* (Australian Sports Commission, 2006) and Sport Australia's dedicated webpage for coaching Indigenous athletes (Sport Australia, n.d.) – briefly acknowledge the great diversity of First Nations peoples within Australia and introduce various cultural concepts relating to the importance of family, communication, respect, and community protocols. However, they fail to provide necessary and detailed information about the strengths and resilience of Indigenous peoples, their role in sporting contexts over time, and the broader impacts and legacies of colonisation in Australia – and how they may influence sport participation. Indeed, Indigenous peoples in Australia have shown incredible resilience in the face of colonialism. Settler attempts to "civilize" Indigenous Australians were (and in some cases remain) remain very similar to those used in Canada: the establishment of missions, the use of boarding schools for Indigenous children, land theft, and the denial of the use of Indigenous languages and cultural practices (Armitage, 1995; Tatz, 1995) – and, importantly, the use of sport (Sheppard *et al.*, 2021).

As there are no dedicated courses offered by Sport Australia and NSOs to upskill coaches with the know-how to coach Indigenous children, the currently available information does not adequately cater for the multitude of experiences of Indigenous athletes in Australian urban, rural, and remote contexts. These issues raise concerns about structural blindness within sporting organisations and inevitable invisibility of Indigenous peoples within coach education settings (e.g. texts, coaching positions, and course delivery). The question then remains, how do we coach Indigenous children effectively if there exists negligible information within sporting bodies that drive coach education in Australia?

## Aotearoa New Zealand (NZ)

Similar to Canadian and Australian contexts, Watson *et al.* (2016) argued that Aotearoa NZ's settler history has led to the demise of the inclusion of traditional Maori knowledge in the sport sector. According to Hokowhitu (2003), disinterest in traditional Māori games occurred because the social usages with which they were connected decreased. The stories that accompanied these activities had practically disappeared due to colonial efforts to have them replaced by Pākehā (European) games and sports. Indeed, Māori games as sports were seen as heathen or barbaric and thus inappropriate for inclusion in institutions such as schools. The mātauranga (knowledge) embedded within them, which allowed for the regeneration of whakapapa (genealogy) and tikanga (customs), was thus dismissed. Hokowhitu also argued that the implementation of settler sports was a form of social control that "further oppressed Maori by perpetuating their physical stereotype" (p. 192) and, by way of social Darwinism, constrained them to physical ("non-intellectual") arenas, such as sport and physical education, where they apparently "naturally" excelled. Meanwhile, at the same time, Hokowhitu also acknowledged that Māori have achieved more in sport than many other areas of Aotearoa NZ society, as "sport was the only mainstream activity where Māori could achieve success and compete with Pākehā on an "even playing field' ... and could gain mana (respect/esteem)" (p. 209).

Currently, Ihi Aotearoa / Sport New Zealand (Sport NZ) is the kaitiaki (guardian) of the Play, Active Recreation and Sport (PARS) system in Aotearoa NZ. It includes High Performance Sport NZ (HPSNZ), which leads the sport system in supporting high-performance athletes and coaches to deliver performances that inspire the nation, helping to build national identity and promote Aotearoa NZ internationally. As a government agency, Sport NZ (and HPSNZ) promotes and supports quality experiences in PARS, including elite sport, to improve levels of physical activity and, through this, ensure the greatest impact on wellbeing for all residents of Aotearoa NZ. Together, Sport NZ and HPSNZ provide end-to-end leadership of the sport system. This national sport agency is also responsible for governing coach education in partnership with the NSOs across Aotearoa NZ (Sport New Zealand, 2021).

A decade ago, in 2012, Sport NZ refreshed its National Coaching Strategy (NCS), which was influenced then by the International Council of Coaching Excellence (ICCE) thinking. Subsequently, in 2014, Sport NZ launched its Coach Developer training programme, signalling a move away from predominantly content-driven "professional" (technical/tactical) approaches towards more interpersonal (effective communication, leadership) and intrapersonal (reflection, self-regulation), competency-based approaches (Walters *et al.*, 2020). At approximately the same time as this paradigm shift, Hippolite and Bruce's (2013) research highlighted the need for the sport sector in Aotearoa NZ to move towards being more "culturally competent" and less "culturally blind" (Cross *et al.*, 1989) when it came to the Māori population. In an attempt to be more culturally competent and responsive to the Crown's Māori partners, two key resources were developed in partnership with Sport NZ: Te Whetū Rehua (McKegg *et al.*, 2013) a developmental evaluation framework, and more recently the "Balance is Better" (2021) website. These initiatives signified clear intent from the sport sector in Aotearoa NZ to better connect with Māori peoples in a way that embraces rather than admonishes cultural practices when working with young people. While Sport NZ's Balance is Better website is "the home of youth sport" in Aotearoa NZ, only one of the 69 resources under the "for coaches" tab is authored by a Māori coach practitioner. Indeed, there is still more work that Sport NZ could do to become culturally safe providers of sport for children in Aotearoa NZ.

This section outlined the approach to coaching more broadly and coaching Indigenous children more specifically in each of Canada, Australia, and Aotearoa NZ. Below, articulates more specific strategies that can be embedded when coaching Indigenous children, drawing on examples from each context.

## Implications for Children's Sport Coaching

### *Coaching Indigenous Children*

When compared to Aotearoa NZ, there is a generally less of an emphasis on culturally safe frameworks to guide coach education and evaluate how responsive sporting organisations are to meeting Indigenous children's needs in the Canadian and Australian contexts. As such, we have chosen to structure this section based on Burden and Lambie's (2011) broad principles for developing sociocultural competencies for coaches to develop to generate positive coach-athlete relationships that could underpin coach education and be localised to best suit coaching Indigenous children in various sport contexts. Coaches can develop these competencies as part of a "growth model continuum" (see Figure 33.1), where they move from little to no knowledge (or potentially having destructive beliefs) to sociocultural competence at varying rates, which can then play a key role in the provision of culturally safe sporting spaces. Burden and Lambie (2011) proposed three main principles that involve developing

1 Self-Awareness of Personal Beliefs/Biases
2 Knowledge of Athletes' Worldviews
3 Coaching Skills and Strategies

### *Sociocultural Coaching Competency (SCC) 1: Self-Awareness of Personal Beliefs/ Biases*

First, coaches must develop a level of self-awareness about their personal beliefs, their own sociocultural background, potential biases that might influence the coaching environments, and how they perceive those who are different from them (Burden and Lambie, 2011). Robillard (2019) explained this well in his Canadian text *Kihcite Metawewina (Playing with a Great Heart),* stating that "to know what is true, we must recognise our pre-conceived assumptions, then apply information, evaluation, and re-examination" (p. 13). In Aotearoa NZ, Sport NZ recently advocated for a move away from traditional content-driven delivery approaches towards context-driven delivery that considers coaches/coach developers holistically as human beings, "grounded in the ability to know and regulate oneself" (Walters *et al.*, 2020, p. 156). When coaches are self-reflexive and open to respecting and understanding athletes' identities, they can begin to demonstrate socio-cultural competencies that might assist when coaching children with belief systems that may be different to their own.

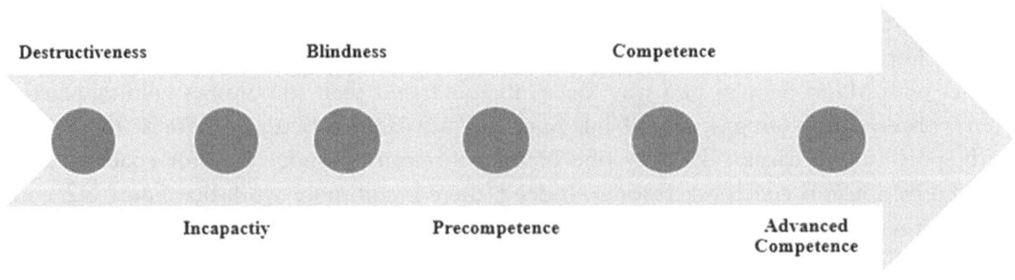


*Figure 33.1* Sociocultural competence for sport coaches continuum (Burden and Lambie, 2011, pp. 26–28).

With respect to coaching Indigenous children, for instance, it is critical to avoid making assumptions based on misinformed constructions of their identity (e.g. that an athlete is not Indigenous because they have fair skin; Shay, 2018). Similarly, negative cultural stereotypes about Indigenous people being lazy, drug-users, and naturally suited to physical rather than intellectual pursuits have devastating consequences for young people, particularly in sport settings (Apoifis *et al.*, 2018; Bennie *et al.*, 2019). Shay (2018) recommended that best practice involves getting to know Indigenous young people and their families as people with individual strengths and goals to minimise deficit discourses that have been normalised in curricular, media, politics, and social interactions by non-Indigenous peoples.

Sport NZ's recent shift towards "cultural competency" for sports coaches of Indigenous children identified its intent to move away from merely focussing on the professional domain to the promotion of the interpersonal and intrapersonal "effective coaching domains" (Côté and Gilbert, 2009). A way of doing this has been to integrate and employ the kaupapa Māori principle of ako, "whereby teaching and learning is acknowledged as a two-way process as teachers and learners learn from each other" (Walters *et al.*, 2020, p. 162). These ideas tie in well with the need for coaches to develop culturally responsive pedagogy (CRP), which include "those pedagogies that actively value, and mobilise as resources, the cultural repertoires and intelligences that students bring to the learning relationship" (Morrison *et al.*, 2019, p. v). While CRP has received limited attention in the coaching context (Hapeta *et al.*, 2021), education researchers have shared positive outcomes specifically amongst members of student populations who experience marginalisation (Morrison *et al.*, 2019).

To enact CRP, coaches must support all athletes to experience success, develop cultural understanding and critical consciousness, and create learning atmospheres where athletes and coaches feel respected by, and connected to, one another (e.g. including and valuing young peoples' knowledges). Further, privileging Indigenous knowledges and voices may provoke emancipatory and anti-deficit views about Indigenous identity (Rigney, 1997, cited in Morrison *et al.*, 2019, p. 23). Each of these skills can be practiced on a day-to-day basis by coaches working with Indigenous youth before, during and after training sessions.

## *SCC 2: Knowledge of Athletes' Worldviews*

In terms of this, Burden and Lambie (2011) stated that if coaches come to realise their worldviews are different to their athletes, or that their knowledge is lacking with respect to diverse perspectives and practices, it is crucial that they acquire information about athletes' background, upbringing, personal values, and cultural norms. This ties in with becoming knowledgeable about broader social, economic, and economic disparities that might influence access to sport resources such as facilities, talent pathways, and resources for general participation (Bennie *et al.*, 2017; Bennie *et al.*, 2021). Furthermore, coaches must be conscious of how their communication styles might positively or negatively affect their athletes based on their cultural practices, gender, capability, and sexual orientation (Burden and Lambie, 2011).

To become more knowledgeable about Indigenous athletes, individual coaches could take the time to read publicly available information like *The Little Red Yellow Black Book: An introduction to Indigenous Australia* (Pascoe, 2018) to gain important background information cultural insights about Indigenous young people before coaching them. Although not specifically tied to coaching, this book has been used within secondary teacher education in Australia and forms an appropriate starting point for those willing to make their own time to learn. In Canada, coaches of Indigenous children can develop cultural knowledge through the Aboriginal Coaching Modules and information shared on the ASC's Website (https://www.

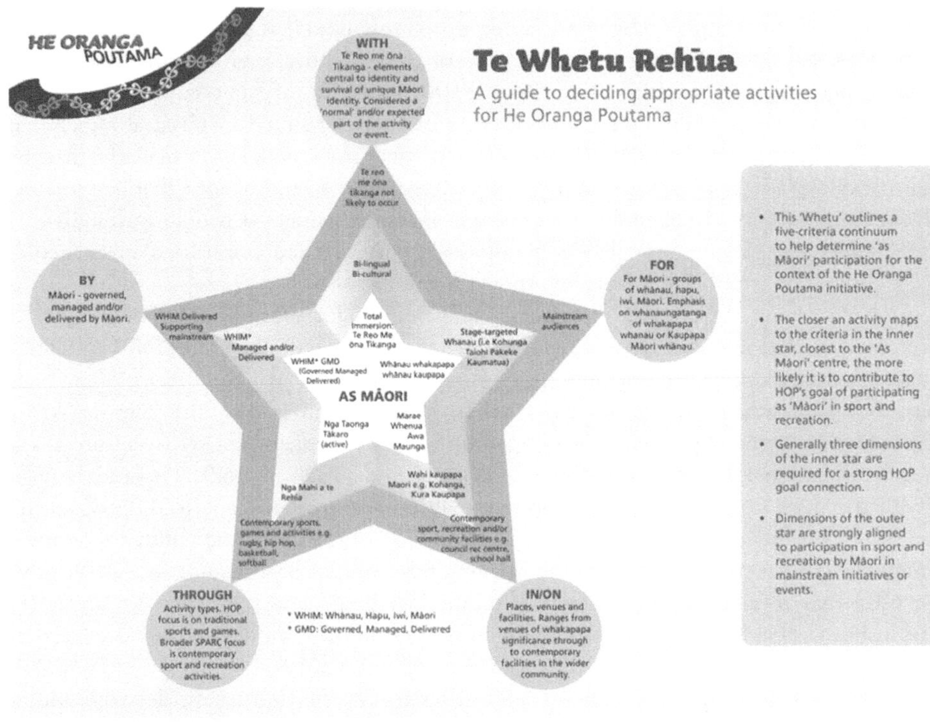


*Figure 33.2* Te Whetu Rēhua concepts and principles (see McKegg *et al.*, 2013, p. 17).

aboriginalsportcircle.ca/). However, it is in Aotearoa NZ where perhaps the broadest culturally-informed sport resources have been developed. The Te Whetu Rēhua guide to using culturally appropriate activities has been utilised to be more inclusive of Māori culture and practices when coaching Indigenous children (see McKegg, *et al.* 2013, p. 16–17, Figure 33.2). As an analytical tool, this framework can guide organisational decisions when catering for, and responding to, the needs of Māori through, in, and on Māori spaces and places.

If coach education courses better infuse Indigenous perspectives into their mainstream course curriculum – like McKegg *et al.* (2013) suggest through Te Whetu Rēhua – sport may have more positive impacts on the non-Indigenous peoples' knowledge about Indigenous histories and experiences, and therefore enable a better understanding of Indigenous young people and their needs within sport.

## *SCC 3: Coaching Skills and Strategies*

The third competency focuses more specifically on the nature of the coaching process before, during, and after training. Burden and Lambie (2011) claimed that coaches need to make efforts to develop culturally sensitive coaching behaviours that exhibit strategies focused on inclusion, sensitivity to issues of social injustice, and able to accommodate athletes' diverse needs. Within SCC 3, professional development is encouraged in similar ways to SCC 2 with the view that taking part in learning experiences underpinned by sociocultural principles will help coaches in their understanding of athletes' worldviews and become more actively involved with athletes beyond their athletic identities. Relatedly, sport organisations might prioritise cultural training led by Indigenous organisations to deepen coach developers' understanding of Indigenous worldviews and experiences before delivering coach education workshops.

This chapter would further Burden and Lambie's (2011) call for cultural sensitivity by emphasising the necessity of Indigenous children experiencing cultural *safety* in sport setting. Ideas for creating culturally safe sessions can be generated by partnering with local Indigenous communities, athletes, and their families to identify the practices that they deem important or necessary as, crucially, it is only Indigenous peoples themselves who can determine if a sport environment is culturally safe. More specific to activities within the training context, coaches can access specialised resources that incorporate Traditional Indigenous Games (Edwards and Meston, 2008) that are appropriate to the local context. Indeed, there is every reason to include Indigenous games as a sincere part of training to connect culture to sport on a regular basis. Such an approach can create opportunities for Indigenous children to keep traditional knowledges alive while also presenting a chance for non-Indigenous peoples to engage in a strengths-based learning experience and build greater awareness of Indigenous culture.

## Summary, Future Directions and Future Research

Though continued progress can be seen in recognising the importance of Indigenous cultures in Canada, Australia, and Aotearoa NZ, much more work needs to be done, including in the coaching context. Sport coaches have a responsibility to ensure that they provide athletes with safe environments. The notion of safety in sporting contexts needs to be extended to be seen as including cultural safety (Giles and Darroch, 2014). It is crucial that coaches receive high-quality training so they can provide the best possible environments in which Indigenous children can play, grow, and thrive. While this chapter has provided a few approaches and strategies that might be used in enhancing the likelihood of the provision of a culturally safe sport context, it is important that coaches build relationships and work with local Indigenous communities to ensure that their practices are informed by local knowledge and practices and take into account the ways in which knowledge and practices may vary from community to community.

Future research should focus on developing and evaluating strategies for promoting culturally safe coaching practices with Indigenous children. It will be crucial for Indigenous researchers, children, parents, coaches, and community members to be involved in this work. Culturally safe coaching environments must be made central to the provision of sport opportunities for Indigenous children to ensure that those in sport coaching address the legacy of colonialism that continues to result in inequities for Indigenous children in Canada, Australia, and Aotearoa NZ.

## References


Aboriginal Sport Circle, 2017. *Aboriginal coaching modules: Reference material*. Toronto: Aboriginal Sport Circle Inc. in partnership with the Coaching Association of Canada and Sport Canada.

Aboriginal Sport Circle, 2021. *Aboriginal coaching modules* [online]. Available from: https://www.aboriginalsportcircle.ca/aboriginal-coaching-modules [Accessed 13 May, 2021].

Apoifis, N., Marlin, D., and Bennie, A., 2018. Noble athlete, savage coach: how racialised representations of aboriginal athletes impede professional sport coaching opportunities for aboriginal australians. *International Review for the Sociology of Sport*, 53 (7), 854–868.

Armitage, A., 1995. *Comparing the policy of aboriginal assimilation: Australia, Canada and New Zealand*. Vancouver: UBC Press.

Ashcroft, B., Griffiths, G., and Tiffin, H., 2013. *Post-colonial studies: the key concepts*. London: Routledge.

Australian Sports Commission, 2006. *Beginning coaching* [online]. Available from: https://bmxaustralia.com.au/wp-content/uploads/2018/10/Sport-Australia-Beginning-Coaching-4th-edition.pdf [Accessed 21 September, 2020].

Bennie, A., *et al.*, 2017. A guide to conducting systematic reviews of coaching science research. *International Sport Coaching Journal*, 4 (1), 191–205.

Bennie, A., *et al.*, 2019. Cultural connections and cultural ceilings: exploring the experiences of Aboriginal Australian sport coaches. *Qualitative Research in Sport, Exercise and Health*, 11 (3), 299–315.

Bennie, A., *et al.*, 2021. 'We were made to feel comfortable and … safe': co-creating, delivering, and evaluating coach education and health promotion workshops with aboriginal australian peoples. *Annals of Leisure Research*, 24 (1), 168–188.

Brascoupé, S. and Waters, C., 2009. Cultural safety: Exploring the applicability of the concept of cultural safety to aboriginal health and community wellness. *Journal of Aboriginal Health*, 5 (2), 6–41.

Burden, J.W., Jr. and Lambie, G.W., 2011. Sociocultural competencies for sport coaches: a proposal for coaches and coach education. *Journal of Coaching Education*, 4 (3), 3–28.

Camiré, M., Trudel, P., and Bernard, D., 2013. A case study of a high school sport program designed to teach athletes life skills and values. *The Sport Psychologist*, 27 (2), 188- 200.

Coaching Association of Canada, 2021. Coaching association of canada celebrates milestones *at this year's partners congress* [online]. Available from: https://coach.ca/coaching-association-canada-celebrates-milestones [Accessed 15 July, 2021].

Côté, J. and Gilbert, W., 2009. An integrative definition of coaching effectiveness and expertise. *International Journal of Sports Science and Coaching*, 4 (3), 307- 323.

Cross, T., *et al.*, 1989. *Towards a culturally competent system of care: A monograph on effective services for minority children who are severely emotionally disturbed.* Washington DC: Georgetown University Child Development Center.

Edwards, K. and Meston, T., 2008. *Yulunga: Traditional Indigenous games*. Canberra: Australian Sports Commission.

Forneris, T., Bean, C., and Halsall, T., 2016. Positive youth development programing with marginalised populations. *In:* N. Holt, ed. *Positive youth development through sport*. London: Taylor and Francis, 168–179.

Forsyth, J., 2007. The Indian Act and the (re)shaping of canadian aboriginal sport practices. *International Journal of Canadian Studies*, 35 (1), 95–111.

Giles, A.R. and Darroch, F.E., 2014. The need for culturally safe physical activity promotion and programs. *Canadian Journal of Public Health*, 105 (4), e317–e319.

Hapeta, J., Evans, J.R. and Smith, G.H. 2021. Ako and Indigenous athletes: Kaupapa Māori principles and game sense pedagogy. *In:* R. Light and C. Curry, eds. *Game sense for coaching and teaching: international perspectives*. London: Routledge, 84–95.

Hippolite, H.R., and Bruce, T., 2013. Towards cultural competence: How incorporating Māori values could benefit New Zealand sport. *In:* C. Hallinan and B. Judd, eds. *Native games: Indigenous peoples and sports in the post-colonial world.* United Kingdom: Emerald Group Publishing Limited, 85–106.

Hodge, C.J., *et al.*, 2017. A family thing: Positive youth development outcomes of a sports-based life skills program. *Journal of Park and Recreation Administration*, 35 (1), 34–50.

Hokowhitu, B., 2003. 'Physical beings': Stereotypes, sport and the 'physical education' of New Zealand Māori. *Culture, Sport, Society*, 6 (2–3), 192–218.

McKegg, K., Wehipeihana, N., and Pipi, K., 2013. He Oranga Poutama. What have we learned. A report on the developmental evaluation of He Oranga Poutama [online]. Wellington, Sport New Zealand. Available from: https://www.srknowledge.org.nz/wp-content/uploads/2012/12/HOP-What-We-Have-Learned-LR.pdf [Accessed 21 August, 2021].

Morrison, A., *et al.*, 2019. *Toward an Australian culturally responsive pedagogy: A narrative review of the literature* [online]. Available from: https://apo.org.au/sites/default/files/resource-files/2019-08/apo-nid262951.pdf [Accessed 30 June, 2021].

Paraschak, V., 1998. "Reasonable amusements": Connecting the strands of physical culture in native lives. *Sport History Review*, 29 (1), 121–131.

Pascoe, B., 2018. *The little red yellow black book: An introduction to Indigenous Australia*. Canberra: Aboriginal Studies Press.

Ramsden, I., 1993. Cultural safety in nursing education in Aotearoa (New Zealand). *Nursing Praxis in New Zealand*, 8 (3), 4–10.

Robillard, B., 2019. *Kihcite Metawewina: Playing with a great heart.* Manitoba: Manitoba Aboriginal Sports and Recreation Council.

Schinke, R.J., *et al.*, 2007. Canadian Aboriginal elite athletes: The experiences of being coached in mainstream cultures. *International Journal of Sport and Exercise Psychology*, 5 (2), 123–141.

Schulenkorf. N. and Siefken, K., 2018. South Pacific: Fostering healthy lifestyles. *In:* H. Collison, *et al.*, eds. *Routledge handbook of sport for development and peace*. London: Routledge, 520–530.

Shay, M., 2018. More than cultural celebrations. *In:* T. Ferfolja, C. Jones-Diaz, and J. Ullman, eds. *Understanding sociological theory for educational practices*. Cambridge: Cambridge University Press, 102–120.

Sheppard, L.K., Rynne, S.B., and Willis, J.M., 2021. Sport as a cultural offset in Aboriginal Australia? *Annals of Leisure Research*, 24 (1), 29–50.

Smye, V. and Browne, A., 2002. "Cultural safety" and the analysis of health policy affecting Aboriginal people. *Nursing Research*, 9 (3), 42–56.

Sport Australia, n.d. *Coaching Indigenous athletes* [online]. Available from: https://www.sportaus.gov.au/coaches_and_officials/coaches/coaching_specific_groups#coaching_indigenous_athletes [Accessed 21 September, 2020].

Sport New Zealand, 2021. *Balance is better. The role of coaches in developing participants* [online]. Available from: https://balanceisbetter.org.nz/coaches/ [Accessed 6 February, 2021].

Tatz, C., 1995. *Obstacle race: Aborigines in sport*. Randwick: UNSW Press.

Truth and Reconciliation Commission of Canada, 2015. *Honouring the truth, reconciling for the future: Summary of the final report of the truth and reconciliation commission of Canada* [online]. Available from: https://ehprnh2mwo3.exactdn.com/wp-content/uploads/2021/01/Executive_Summary_English_Web.pdf [Accessed 21 April, 2021].

Walters, S., Rogers, A., and Oldham, A., 2020. A competency-based approach to coach learning: The sport New Zealand coach developer program. *In:* B. Callary and B. Gearity, eds. *Coach education and development in sport: Instructional strategies*. London: Routledge, 154–165.

Watson, G., Palmer, F., and Ryan, G., 2016. Aotearoa/New Zealand. *In:* J. Nauright and D.K. Wiggins, eds. *Routledge handbook of sport, race and ethnicity*. London, Routledge, 131–145.

# 34

# COACHING CHILDREN AND YOUTH WITH REFUGEE BACKGROUNDS

*Carla Luguetti, Christopher Hudson, and Ramón Spaaij*

## Introduction

Over the last decades, systemic human rights abuses, conflict, war, and violence have increased humanitarian migration. The gravity of the global crisis is represented in the most recent figures from the United Nation High Commissioner for Refugees (UNHCR, 2020), which reports that there are almost 82 million forcibly displaced people worldwide. In addition, it is estimated that 42% of this population are children and youth below 18 years of age. The term 'refugee' can be confusing as it is informally applied in varying contexts and may refer to people at various stages of migration and settlement. Alternative, more precise and inclusive terminologies are becoming more common in the literature, for example, the use of 'refugee background' or 'with refugee backgrounds' (Spaaij *et al.*, 2019). The chapter uses the term 'children and youth with refugee backgrounds' in order to attend to the complexities of migration and settlement. Holistically, the term signifies a movement away from using terminology that labels an individual's identity and instead takes into consideration the wider social structures that shape young people's lives.

If designed well, sport-based programmes may benefit children and youth with refugee backgrounds as a supportive environment that facilitates increased well-being, inclusion, and feelings of belonging (Spaaij, 2015; Fader *et al.*, 2020). To achieve the benefits, sport-based programmes must validate the cultural knowledge that young people possess and translate this knowledge into more culturally responsive programmes (Luguetti *et al.*, 2022). This chapter aims to critically examine international research in sport, coaching, and children and youth with refugee backgrounds. The chapter critically examines the current state of academic knowledge on the relationship between sport and settlement of children and youth with refugee backgrounds, by focusing on the identification of key themes in the research as well as current knowledge gaps. This is followed by a discussion of implications for children's sport coaching. The conclusion outlines directions and critical challenges for future research on sport and children and youth with refugee backgrounds.

## Review of Current Research

The review of literature is divided into four subsections. The first section draws a connection between participation in sport and settlement for children and youth with refugee backgrounds.

 DOI: 10.4324/9781003199359-39

Section two brings attention to a deficit view of children and youth with refugee backgrounds that surfaces in sport coaching research, which gives rise to interventions that are paternalistic and controlling in nature. Section three discusses current literature in relation to the different pedagogies that have been implemented when coaching children and youth with refugee backgrounds. Lastly, section four advocates for pedagogies to be co-designed *alongside* children and youth by using community-based participatory action research (CBPAR).

## *Children and Youth with Refugee Backgrounds and Settlement through Participation in Sport*

Participation in sport can provide health benefits across different population groups. Given that children and youth with refugee backgrounds often face significant social challenges as a result of forced migration (Ha and Lyras, 2013), participation in sport also has the ability to break down the barriers that impede settlement in a new community (Block and Gibbs, 2017). In this context, there are opportunities to move beyond more traditional aspects of coaching, notably through supporting children and youth with refugee backgrounds with settlement in and through sport. Settlement should not be seen as a one-way process. Rather, it affects *all* members of society – those who seek to be included, and those who have the power to include. Thus, the support role of the coach encompasses an important social equity lens. It is through this lens that coaches can build the conditions necessary to encourage all players, staff and spectators to advocate for cultural plurality alongside social integration rather than cultural assimilation in which newcomers are expected to adapt unilaterally to the dominant values and norms of the 'host society' (Bartsch and Rulofs, 2020). When such an environment exists, sport participation can play a significant role in carving out a successful settlement path for children and youth with refugee backgrounds.

Post-migration life can be challenging for children and youth with refugee backgrounds as they contend with cultural and linguistic isolation and attending school in unfamiliar physical and social landscapes (Harwood *et al.*, 2021). Additionally, migration during adolescence adds more depth to the issue as the challenge of identity formation during this pivotal phase of life is compounded by displacement. The provision of a sporting environment in which a sense of belonging is evident, is paramount to ensuring a successful settlement process for children and youth with refugee backgrounds. Fader *et al.* (2020) conducted a quantitative investigation of the relationship between a sense of belonging, resilience, and the settlement process for children and youth with refugee backgrounds through a refugee soccer club. The researchers show that participation in sport allows children and youth with refugee backgrounds the opportunity to engage with others who face similar challenges, receive support and guidance from adults and coaches, and also a space in which to build a strong sense of belonging where they feel that they could connect with others. In the study, having a strong sense of belonging led to children and youth with refugee backgrounds reporting higher levels of resilience and higher levels of perceived settlement.

A significant inference from the Fader *et al.* (2020) is that a sense of belonging is, in essence, a psychological construct that is not reliant on material support. This is a pertinent factor to consider when *intentionally* designing a sports programme aimed at assisting settlement. 'Intentional', because as Anderson *et al.* (2019) suggest, the social benefits of participation in sport for children and youth with refugee backgrounds are not always inherent through participation alone. The authors explain that such benefits are highly dependent upon the coach being intentional and conscious of including additional supportive elements to their sport programmes. Supportive conditions whereby children and youth with refugee backgrounds feel listened to, valued, included, and treated fairly by the community, can all be incorporated in a sport programme to promote a positive settlement environment. Given the benefits associated with settlement of children and youth with refugee backgrounds discussed, there is a strong case for coaches being mindful of affording opportunities for children and youth with refugee backgrounds to develop a sense of belonging in and through sport.

## *Challenging Cultural Deficit Perspectives of Young People with Refugee Backgrounds in Sport*

A concerning theme that emerges in the literature, is the cultural deficit perspectives of children and youth with refugee backgrounds in sport (Bartsch and Rulofs, 2020). Researchers have drawn connections between such perspectives and the prevailing connotations of refugee background people's culture and values, which, to a large extent, are seen as incompatible with those of the dominant group (Anderson *et al.*, 2019; Bartsch *et al.*, 2021). These cultural deficit perspectives have major ramifications for coaching children and youth with refugee backgrounds. As discussed below, it is critical that coaches extend their understanding of how best to coach and support diverse groups of children and youth in times of increasing cultural plurality, as well as deploy a strengths-based approach to their coaching practices.

The study by Bartsch and Rulofs (2020) interviewed coaches to ascertain how they manage coaching heterogeneous groups of students. The authors reveal that the coaches' assumptions about children and youth with refugee backgrounds tend to be gendered – girls and young women with refugee backgrounds are seen through the lenses of victimisation and vulnerability, whereas boys and young men with refugee backgrounds are seen through the lens of suspicion and threat. Coaches tend to describe girls and young women with refugee backgrounds as fragile, weak, shy, and passive and as victims, therefore requiring an extended level of paternalistic protectionism against feelings of vulnerability when engaging in sport. Bartsch and Rulofs explain that such preconceptions are often built upon assumptions rather than on actual knowledge of the young person's backgrounds and experiences. Therefore, when a coach attaches a cultural deficit perspective to a girl or young woman with a refugee background, and resultantly deploys paternalistic pedagogical techniques, this constrains the agency, individualism, and freedom of girls and young women with refugee backgrounds in sport. Bartsch and Rulofs warn that having girls and young women with refugee backgrounds identify with these clichés and assumptions may negatively impact their trajectories in life far beyond the sporting fields insofar as they may be discouraged, or withheld, from developing self-confidence and a desire to engage in leadership positions within and beyond sport.

In terms of boys and young men with refugee backgrounds, Bartsch and Rulofs (2020) found that the coaches' perceptions were overarchingly composed by notions of impulsivity and threat. These perceptions, which are rooted in historically and colonially influenced societal belief systems, are typically based on unconsciously internalised images that ignore the fact that male bodies are vulnerable in the face of suffering, trauma, violence, and war. In doing so, the boys and young men are stereotyped by a colonial discourse that paints non-Western men as dominant and aggressive. This, in turn, influences the way that they are coached in sport, through a method of disciplining and controlling their bodies. Bartsch and Rulofs explain that the boys and young men with refugee backgrounds were often made to engage in intensive, strenuous, one-dimensional forms of movement such as fitness and strength training. Such pedagogical techniques only serve to reinforce the existing hierarchical structures within sport, and as such, a more critical lens needs to be applied to the preconceptions of coaches that precede and govern such approaches.

A major ramification of these cultural deficit perspectives is the process of 'Othering', which has contributed to the ongoing issue of racism and cultural tensions that exist within sport today. Othering occurs when children and youth with refugee backgrounds are described through the use of hierarchical language which maintains an existing social power structure that keeps them marginalised in society (Bartsch and Rulofs, 2020; Luguetti *et al.*, 2022). Such language typically includes the use of pronouns such as 'they', 'them', and 'their', when talking about children and youth with refugee backgrounds. Although studies have shown that coaches are enthusiastic about supporting children and youth with refugee backgrounds (Dagkas *et al.*, 2011; Jeanes *et al.*, 2015; Bartsch *et al.*, 2021), there still exists a stark dichotomy between settlement intentions, and the suppression and controlling of non-white culture that leads to Othering and racism in sport (Bartsch and Rulofs, 2020; Jeanes *et al.*, 2015).

Othering can occur in more subtle acts than the use of separatory language. Coaches who romanticise an almost evangelical approach to their coaching and believe that they are "saving" children and youth with refugee backgrounds through sport, engender a contradictory discourse of individualism and decontextualisation, which, as Fine (1994) explains, brands a person as an Other amidst the incongruity born from distorted preconceptions. It is therefore important that a coach does not seek to *solve* the social struggles of children and youth with refugee backgrounds through sport (Freire, 1987, 1996). Rather, they must choose to engage in social struggles *with* and *alongside* them through sport. Fine (1994) believes that doing this erodes the fixedness of racial categories by creating a space in which it is possible to challenge the structural forces that support the proliferation of Othering. To shift from pedagogical practices that seek to protect and control, as well as language that divides and suppresses, coaches must learn to observe and critically analyse our preconceptions and be willing to challenge and change them. Only then can the existing hierarchical structures that constrain children with refugee backgrounds within sport be transformed.

## Pedagogies Implemented in Sport Programmes with Children and Youth from Refugee Backgrounds

Pedagogies implemented in sport programmes with children and youth with refugee backgrounds that have been examined in research include positive youth development (PYD) (Pink *et al.*, 2020), teaching personal and social responsibility (TPSR) (Whitley and Gould, 2010; Whitley *et al.*, 2016), and the integrated second language (L2) acquisition approach (Krüger, 2018). Both TPSR and PYD are well-recognised models that focus on the development of life skills.

An evaluation of the promotion of PYD model among children and youth from refugee and migrant backgrounds (Pink *et al.*, 2020) found that it supports children and youth to develop positive behaviours and competencies that help them deal with daily adversities and contribute to the world. This pedagogy aims to teach personal skills such as emotional control, respect, teamwork, and focus through participation in sport, which can be transferred to other environments such as school, home, or community. In a study with children and youth with refugee backgrounds, Pink *et al.* (2020) interviewed ten participants (six youth participants and four stakeholders) concerning their experiences with a PYD programme in Australia. Personal outcomes related to PYD included increased confidence, improved networking skills, and enhanced employment opportunities. Social outcomes included improved communication, development of intercultural understanding and acceptance, improved teamwork and leadership, and a greater sense of belonging to a wider and more inclusive community. In addition, they found that PYD was useful in exploring the coherence between the participants' experiences and desires, the features of the PYD climate and programme, and PYD outcomes.

Studies by Whitley and Gould (2010) and Whitley *et al.* (2016) investigated the impact of TPSR in working with children and youth with refugee backgrounds. TPSR connects personal and social responsibility with specific values, and these values are represented by five progressive levels: (I) self-control and respecting the rights and feelings of others; (II) participating and giving good effort; (III) being self-directed; (IV) helping others and demonstrating leadership; and (V) transferring the previous levels to outside the gym. In a first study, Whitley and Gould (2010) investigated psychosocial development in children and youth with refugee backgrounds through the TPSR model in the US. According to the authors, the most valuable outcome of the programme was the cultivation of a caring environment where the coaches consistently showed care for each participant as a person and not just as an athlete. In a second study, Whitley *et al.* (2016) interviewed 16 boys and young men with refugee backgrounds who participated in the TPSR model. The findings demonstrated the participants' positive experiences in the programme, including general enjoyment, experiencing and learning new sports, and a sense of belonging. Participants also reported the TPSR concepts of respect, teamwork, and leadership, along with the transference of these concepts into their everyday lives.

Finally, Krüger (2018) examined an L2 acquisition approach with children and youth in Germany. The L2 intervention consisted of six lessons that used language-enriched physical activities. The approach combined strategies from sport pedagogy with principles of usage-based approaches to second language acquisition. The study used an intervention group and a control group, both of which were tested pre- and post-intervention. Krüger found that the L2 intervention improved domain-specific vocabulary and listening comprehension within the context of sport games.

PYD, TPSR, and L2 pedagogies for the most part do not foreground the voices of children and youth with refugee backgrounds or community participation. Rather, they represent models and approaches to sport programming that are primarily researcher-led with some modification in practice by practitioners. In researcher-designed approaches, outcomes are mainly defined in terms of pro-social behaviour (e.g. controlling the levels of responsibility, teaching emotional control and other personality skills). As such, these pedagogies might be seen to reflect assimilationist sport-based interventions instead of participant-driven and culturally responsive pedagogies (Spaaij *et al.*, 2019; Luguetti *et al.*, 2022).

## *Moving from Assimilationist to Co-designed Ways of Working alongside Children and Youth with Refugee Backgrounds in Sport*

As an alternative to assimilationist pedagogies, scholars have engaged with children and youth with refugee backgrounds through CBPAR in sport (Rosso and McGrath, 2016; Robinson *et al.*, 2019; Luguetti *et al.*, 2021; Middleton *et al.*, 2021). CBPAR is a relational research approach in which researchers and participants become co-investigators seeking to co-construct new knowledge that benefits the participants' community. This research is often situated within a critical pedagogy and feminist studies paradigm. The aim is to generate changes within communities by prioritising local knowledge in the development of practical solutions to problems identified by the community itself. The value of CBPAR in the sport context has been evidenced by previous projects published in the last five years, as discussed below.

In a study on the use of CBPAR, Luguetti *et al.* (2021) implemented it to co-create a sport programme with young African Australian women in grassroots football. Programme co-creation lasted four months and the authors utilised multiple data sources to evaluate the co-construction process. The first eight weeks were designed to identify what facilitated and hindered the young women's engagement in sport. The authors identified the lack of female representation in the sport programme as their main concern. Given what Luguetti *et al.* learned from the young African Australian women, they co-created and implemented a coaches' workshop where the young women shared the data collected and brainstormed ideas for future change. The young women reported that they learned that "together we have power" (p. 14) as well as the importance of "speaking up to those in charge" (p. 14). The approach in this study highlighted the need for action beyond simply understanding the barriers to sport participation evidenced in most studies, and particularly in female football.

This has further been explored by Middleton *et al.* (2021) explored CBPAR as a way to change the meaning of sport during children and youth from refugee backgrounds acculturative journeys in Canada. The authors utilised get-to-know-you arts-based conversational interviews held at the onset of a CBPAR. Centralising children and youth with refugee backgrounds and their parents in the research process facilitated different ways of thinking about how sport can help youth feel safe and able to share their stories, which can result in the development of a shared acculturation process. Through developing a central narrative, the authors provided insight to future researchers and practitioners as to how they may provide opportunities for children and youth with refugee backgrounds to voice their opinions about sport as a part of a positive settlement environment. This was achieved by creating a space for children and youth with refugee backgrounds to openly listen to and reflect upon shared stories with one another. In addition, Robinson *et al.* (2019) implemented CBPAR with young Syrian refugees in a rural Canadian area. Drawing upon multiple data sources to inform their research cycles, they co-created and implemented a 'Syrian Youth Sports Club.' The results of the study indicated that the refugee-background young people experienced improvements in physical literacy as well as a sense of belonging.

Finally, Rosso and McGrath (2016) delivered a CBPAR in partnership with a university in Australia. In line with CBPAR, the programme aimed to build capacity with refugee background community leaders to address the issues faced by their communities by working side by side with academics. The authors acknowledged that despite the care taken in rendering the CBPAR process as democratic as possible, they observed power relations and potential coercion with recruitment (especially children). The authors concluded that most of the participants expressed general satisfaction with the programme.

## Implications for Children's Sport Coaching

As discussed, coaches need to challenge the status quo and recognise the strengths and capabilities of children and youth with refugee backgrounds. This requires coaches to establish a culturally safe environment in which young people with refugee backgrounds can thrive. Aligning with Luguetti *et al.* (2022), coaches should:

- Connect young people to different resources in and outside of sports contexts to develop their success in sport and in life;
- Be willing to nurture and support cultural competence by sharing power with the participants and their community, and;
- Develop spaces for young people with refugee backgrounds to build awareness of, and subsequently critique, the social inequities that hinder their social integration in and through sport.

When coaches adopt these approaches, community-driven sport programs will offer meaningful opportunities for them to practice and cultural responsiveness. In that sense, CBPAR offers an innovative pedagogy to work with children and youth with refugee backgrounds by moving towards a more critical and transformative paradigm (Freire, 1987, 1996). Coaches can potentially learn a lot from the CBPAR experiences described in this chapter. First, coaches need to build relationships with children and youth to co-design sport programmes and invite the whole community to be part of this process. This is important because so many of the barriers that children and youth with refugee backgrounds face on a day-to-day basis are not topics that they will easily discuss with strangers. To gain the understanding necessary to co-design a sport programme, coaches must firstly promote a safe space where children and youth feel comfortable to talk. Second, coaches should champion democratic decision-making and engage children and youth in inquiry (e.g. asking questions) to identify the barriers and enablers they experience in sport. As part of this process, it is important that coaches help children and youth with their ability to name and label their sporting experiences. Finally, coaches and children and youth with refugee backgrounds should work together to develop strategies that speak to overcoming any identified barriers to participation in sport. This collective action is the first stage in the longer-term process of micro-level change. The steps outlined here address a need for co-creating sport programmes with children and youth through culturally responsive pedagogies.

There are several challenges that coaches might face in enacting culturally responsive pedagogical approaches. These approaches require coaches to understand and negotiate existing preconceptions and relationships. First, coaches may be uncomfortable with the necessary change in power relations that results from the adoption of a more democratic pedagogical process. Such change challenges conventional conceptions of young people as subordinate to the expert coach. Coaches must be prepared to engage in what can be a very personal struggle with their assumptions about, and their relationships to, the people they are working with; ultimately challenging the 'us' and 'them' dichotomy that occurs through the process of Othering children and youth with refugee backgrounds.

As discussed earlier, existing alongside cultural deficit perspectives towards children and youth with refugee backgrounds in sport, is the lack of specific knowledge and awareness of working with children and youth with refugee backgrounds (Baldwin, 2015; Anttila *et al.*, 2018; Bartsch and Rulofs, 2020), which is of grave concern. Coaching education courses need to include more culturally responsive training as a core component of the progression from beginner coach levels to advanced coach levels. As Bartsch and Rulofs (2020) explain, topics such as Othering, cultural stereotypes, and positionality, have so far been largely neglected in the training and education of sport coaches. It is our hope that by incorporating such topics into coaching education courses, coaches can develop a higher awareness around sport being a means of promoting positive settlement for children and youth with refugee backgrounds.

This chapter thus posits that coaches should see sport as a way for children and youth with refugee backgrounds to build social capital, a sense of belonging, and leadership skills as part of their settlement journey. Through this, children and youth with refugee backgrounds can gain a stronger voice in sport, and coaches can enact more culturally responsive pedagogical approaches that assist settlement and nullify the process of Othering children and youth with refugee backgrounds in sport.

## Summary, Future Directions and Future Research

This chapter has critically examined the body of research on sport, coaching and children and youth with refugee backgrounds. It has explored the benefits of sport participation for children and youth with refugee backgrounds, the importance of challenging deficit views and perspectives, the pedagogies implemented in sport programmes, and the need to move from assimilationist pedagogies to co-designed ways of working with children and youth. Based on this synthesis, the chapter advocates for the use of culturally responsive pedagogies when coaching children and youth with refugee backgrounds in order to develop culturally safe sporting environments. It also suggests that collaborative and democratic practices be extended to these pedagogical approaches.

Future studies should keep moving towards a more critical and transformative paradigm. Researchers should continue to prioritise local knowledge and invite children and youth with refugee backgrounds and the (local) community as co-participants in research projects, to engage with the social struggles of children and youth with refugee backgrounds in order to develop practical solutions to the structural and cultural issues they identify in sport participation. Further, the chapter suggests that future research should bring attention to the perspectives that children and youth with refugee backgrounds have on how their relationships with coaches assist or hinder their settlement through sport (Dagkas *et al.*, 2011). By doing so, it is our hope that researchers can ensure that the voices of children and youth with refugee backgrounds are amplified within the literature, and, resultantly, a more holistic and inclusive lens be applied to the issue of how to challenge and change the cultural deficit perspectives towards children and youth with refugee backgrounds in sport moving forward.

## References


Anderson, A., *et al.*, 2019. Managerial perceptions of factors affecting the design and delivery of sport for health programs for refugee populations. *Sport Management Review*, 22 (1), 80–95.

Anttila, E., Siljamäki, M., and Rowe, N., 2018. Teachers as frontline agents of integration: Finnish physical education students' reflections on intercultural encounters. *Physical Education and Sport Pedagogy*, 23 (6), 609–622.

Baldwin, C.F., 2015. First-year physical education teachers' experiences with teaching African refugee students. *SAGE Open*, 5 (1), 1–10.

Bartsch, F. and Rulofs, B., 2020. Intersections of forced migration and gender in physical education. *Frontiers in Sociology*, 5, 1–14.

Bartsch, F., Wagner, I., and Rulofs, B., 2021. Students from refugee backgrounds in physical education: A survey of teachers' perceptions. *European Physical Education Review*, 27 (4), 854–870.

Block, K. and Gibbs, L., 2017. Promoting social inclusion through sport for refugee-background youth in Australia: Analysing different participation models. *Social Inclusion*, 5 (2), 91–100.

Dagkas, S., Benn, T., and Jawad, H., 2011. Multiple voices: Improving participation of Muslim girls in physical education and school sport. *Sport, Education and Society*, 16 (2), 223–239.

Fader, N., Legg, E., and Ross, A., 2020. Finding a sense of community in youth soccer: A composite vignette of the refugee experience. *Journal of Park and Recreation Administration*, 38 (2), 97–115.

Fine, M., 1994. Working the hyphens: Reinventing self and other in qualitative research. *In*: N.K. Denzin and Y.S. Lincoln, eds. *Handbook of qualitative research*. Thousand Oaks, CA: Sage Publications, 70–82.

Freire, P. 1987. *Pedagogia do Oprimido [pedagogy of the oppressed]*. 17th ed. Rio de Janeiro: Paz e Terra.

Freire, P. 1996. *Pedagogia da autonomia: Saberes necessários à prática educativa [pedagogy of autonomy: Necessary knowledge for educational practice]*. São Paulo: Paz e Terra.

Ha, J. and Lyras, A., 2013. Sport for refugee youth in a new society: The role of acculturation in sport for development and peace programming. *South African Journal for Research in Sport, Physical Education and Recreation*, 35 (2), 121–140.

Harwood, G., *et al.*, 2021. A Bourdieusian analysis exploring the meaning of sport for young women from refugee backgrounds in an Australian state high school. *Sport, Education and Society*, 26 (2), 175–187.

Jeanes, R., O' Connor, J., and Alfrey, L., 2015. Sport and the resettlement of young people from refugee backgrounds in Australia. *Journal of Sport and Social Issues*, 39 (6), 480–500.

Krüger, M., 2018. Second language acquisition effects of a primary physical education intervention: A pilot study with young refugees. *PloS One*, 13 (9), 1–13.

Luguetti, C., Singehebhuye, L., and Spaaij, R., 2021. 'Stop mocking, start respecting': An activist approach meets African Australian refugee-background young women in grassroots football. *Qualitative Research in Sport, Exercise and Health*, 14 (1), 119–136.

Luguetti, C., Singehebhuye, L., and Spaaij, R., 2022. Towards a culturally relevant sport pedagogy: Lessons learned from African Australian refugee-background coaches in grassroots football. *Sport, Education and Society*, 27 (4), 449–461.

Middleton, T.R.F., *et al.*, 2021. The changing meaning of sport during forced immigrant youths' acculturative journeys. *Psychology of Sport and Exercise*, 54 (3). 1–9.

Pink, M.A., Mahoney, J.W., and Saunders, J.E., 2020. Promoting positive development among youth from refugee and migrant backgrounds: The case of Kicking Goals Together. *Psychology of Sport and Exercise*, 51 (2020), 1–12.

Robinson, D.B., *et al.*, 2019. The Syrian Canadian sports club: A community-based participatory action research project with/for Syrian youth refugees. *Social Sciences*, 8 (6), 1–15.

Rosso, E. and McGrath, R., 2016. Promoting physical activity among children and youth in disadvantaged South Australian CALD communities through alternative community sport opportunities. *Health Promotion Journal of Australia*, 27 (2), 105–110.

Spaaij, R., 2015. Refugee youth, belonging and community sport. *Leisure Studies*, 34 (3), 303–318.

Spaaij, R., *et al.*, 2019. Sport, refugees, and forced migration: A critical review of the literature. *Frontiers in Sports and Active Living*, 1, 1–18.

UNHCR, 2020. *Global trends: Forced displacement in 2020.* Geneva: United Nations High Commissioner for Refugees.

Whitley, M.A., Coble, C., and Jewell, G.S., 2016. Evaluation of a sport-based youth development programme for refugees. *Leisure/Loisir*, 40 (2), 175–199.

Whitley, M.A. and Gould, D., 2010. Psychosocial development in refugee children and youth through the personal-social responsibility model. *Journal of Sport Psychology in Action*, 1 (3), 118–138.

# 35

# TOWARDS A CRITICAL INCLUSION OF LESBIAN, GAY, OR BISEXUAL YOUTH IN COACHING CONTEXTS

*Dawn E. Trussell, Kyle A. Rich, and Jake Quinton*

## Introduction

Although there have been subtle shifts in how diverse sexual identities are perceived in sport, homophobia and prejudice persist. The collective evidence points to the need to understand and address the sometimes hostile sport contexts for young athletes of lesbian, gay, bisexual, transgender, or queer (LGBTQ) identities (e.g. Petty and Trussell, 2018; Kulick *et al.*, 2019). This chapter will review current literature on lesbian, gay, or bisexual identities in sport and discuss implications for coaches and organisations who provide youth sport programs. Understanding the experiences, opportunities, and barriers of these key sport stakeholders is an important, yet understudied area of research (Shaw and Cunningham, 2021). As there is a movement to understand the complexities and nuances of diverse gender and sexual identities, we focus our discussion on sexual identities. However the variation in LGBTQ/LGBT+ acronyms used throughout this chapter reflect differences in the sample characteristics of studies cited and the importance of understanding how diverse identities intersect.

A key perspective that underpins this chapter is examining lesbian, gay, or bisexual athletes through a lens of *critical inclusion* (see Kokozos and Gonzalez, 2020) that critiques normative conceptualisations of inclusion and recognises the erasure of other forms of social identities (e.g. race, gender, social class, [dis]ability). Using examples from current research, the first section will examine implications of sexual identities for how lesbian, gay, or bisexual youth experience sport. In the second section, emphasis is placed on research pertaining to coaches. Finally, the third section focuses on organisational cultures that reproduce and/or resist exclusionary behaviours and heteronormativity in youth sport. Through a politics of hope (Lincoln and Denzin, 2000), five strategies are recommended that embody doing critical inclusion in youth sport. In enacting these strategies coaches and other leaders (e.g. decision-makers, managers, and directors in and of sports organisations) that facilitate inclusion may not only create a welcoming space for lesbian, gay, or bisexual athletes but may also enhance sport performance within their team(s) and/or organisation.

DOI: 10.4324/9781003199359-40

## Review of Current Research

### *Lesbian, Gay, or Bisexual Youth Experiences*

Participating in sport has many positive effects on the physical and mental health of youth (Rodriguez-Bravo *et al.*, 2020). For example, sports can offer increased opportunities for socialisation, development of life skills such as teamwork and leadership, and decreased experiences of poor mental health (Rodriguez-Bravo *et al.*, 2020). Unfortunately, many lesbian, gay, or bisexual youth miss the benefits of sport due to a variety of barriers to entry, resulting in decreased sports participation among lesbian, gay, or bisexual youth compared to heterosexual youth (Greenspan *et al.*, 2017). For lesbian, gay, or bisexual youth who remain in sport, their experiences may be negatively impacted and/or they may intentionally seek out sport activities in which they feel less stigmatised (Petty and Trussell, 2018).

Factors keeping lesbian, gay, or bisexual youth from actively engaging in sports can be both real, such as overt homophobic remarks and actions, or perceived, such as expecting poor treatment due to other experiences in their lives (Kulick *et al.*, 2019). Sport scholars have revealed how sexual stigma is experienced by youth and how it negatively impacts sport experiences during the high school years (Melton and Cunningham, 2012; Petty and Trussell, 2018). Young athletes experience multiple forms of sexual stigma (i.e. enacted, felt, and internalised) from multiple stakeholders in the sporting context (i.e. coaches, teammates, teachers, and parents) and these relationships influence their sport engagement (see Petty and Trussell, 2018). As Petty and Trussell (2018) illustrated, while sexual stigma does not necessarily lead to overt homophobic behaviours and violence towards lesbian, gay, or bisexual athletes, sexual stigma is omnipresent in the athletes' stories – and coaches play an important role in shaping their experiences.

One of the most prevalent reasons lesbian, gay, or bisexual youth do not participate in sports as often as their heterosexual counterparts is because they feel unsafe in sport contexts. While feeling unsafe is something experienced by two thirds of lesbian, gay, or bisexual youth (Greenspan *et al.*, 2017, 2019), the nature of the experience differs between boys who identify as gay, girls who identify as lesbians, and anyone who identifies as bisexual. Experiences with overt homophobia tend to be the most prevalent in male locker rooms with young people using harmful language, like denoting the word gay with something that is bad, whether it is intentional or not (Greenspan *et al.*, 2019). Smits *et al.* (2021) suggest that homonegative and heteronormative microaggressive speech acts may have a devastating impact on gay young male athletes' experiences. Smits *et al.* (2021) illustrate how despite increased acceptance of diverse sexual identities, heteronormative privilege is maintained through appropriating words such as 'gay' and 'queer' and linking them to weakness, mistakes, and errors, while normalising homonegative discourses through humour and antigay physical aggression.

While boys who identify as gay may experience more outward displays of homophobic behaviour from their peers, lesbian and bisexual youth also experience homo-and bi-phobia in sport contexts, whether that be through experiencing it firsthand or witnessing others' experiences (Greenspan *et al.*, 2017; Hartmann-Tews *et al.*, 2020). Consequently, how an organisation or team presents themselves plays a significant role in whether lesbian, gay, or bisexual youth choose to engage with programming (Flett, 2021). For that reason, it is imperative that leaders (including coaches) make it clear that lesbian, gay, or bisexual athletes will be welcomed in sport contexts and are prepared to support these young people by managing others in the environment. Denison *et al.* (2021) make it clear that young athletes who 'come out' to teammates are significantly more likely to be a target of homophobic behaviour and emphasise the importance of sports administrators to develop programs and enforce policies that create safe sports environments.

Perceived barriers to entry for lesbian, gay, or bisexual youth in sport contexts can be difficult to combat (Kulick *et al.*, 2019). However, considering a variety of lived experiences and using these understandings to create safe sporting contexts is of utmost importance for lesbian, gay, or bisexual youth. Although LGB athletes may experience multiple forms of sexual stigma in sport, research also highlights how beneficial it can be during their identity development. For example, Petty and Trussell (2018) illustrated how sport has the potential to bring joy, distraction, and mindfulness that frees lesbian, gay, or bisexual youth from worry and fear in other domains of their lives. For some athletes, team sports may also provide important social connections and forms of support as they negotiate their developing lesbian, gay, or bisexual identities (Petty and Trussell, 2018).

In sum, many lesbian, gay, or bisexual youth have negative associations with sports and are therefore missing out on the physical and emotional benefits that come with youth sport (Greenspan *et al.*, 2019; Rodriguez-Bravo *et al.*, 2020). Coaches and other leaders should be active in their support of lesbian, gay, or bisexual youth and not assume that simply opening a program will make all potential participants feel safe and welcome. Indeed, the behaviours, actions, and words of authority figures such as coaches are constantly being monitored and evaluated by lesbian, gay, or bisexual youth (Wolowic *et al.*, 2018), which makes it even more apparent that coaches should be informed on matters concerning lesbian, gay, or bisexual youth.

## Coaching

Coaches play a vital role in shaping athletes' engagement in and experiences of sport. Therefore, supportive coaches are an integral part of lesbian, gay, or bisexual youth's ability to feel safe and to thrive in sporting contexts (Halbrook *et al.*, 2019). Unfortunately, not all coaches feel equipped or prepared to support lesbian, gay, or bisexual youth and organisational practices to guide coaches are not always readily available. Research with coaches at both the high school and collegiate level highlights that coaches often feel unprepared or that they have low efficacy for working with lesbian, gay, or bisexual athletes (Vargas-Tonsing and Oswalt, 2009; Halbrook and Watson, 2018). While there is a growing body of literature examining coaching frameworks to welcome youth and enhance the development of life skills, little research focuses explicitly on the role of the coach in supporting lesbian, gay, or bisexual youth. This section reviews some of the recent literature focused on the intersection of coaching and lesbian, gay, or bisexual youth, supplemented with examples from the broader literature situated in schools and other education contexts.

Sporting constructs are often structured explicitly by expressions and hierarchies of sexuality and gender (Messner, 2002). As coaches and other leaders are often (current or former) athletes themselves, they are likely to embody the (hetero)normative expectations of these social hierarchies. Therefore, coaches may unintentionally express homonegative attitudes or insinuations within their sport and coaching practice (Krane, 2016). The (in)actions and comportment of coaches have important implications for the social environment of the team and sport experience.

As alluded to above, lesbian, gay, or bisexual young people often have a variety of unique lived experiences that have implications for their engagement with sport, which make them relevant concerns for coaches. Halbrook *et al.* (2019) identify several important considerations for coaches of lesbian, gay, or bisexual athletes: team norms and social environments (including how sexuality is treated and discussed); fundamental beliefs of parents, coaches, and other athletes (e.g. related to religion, culture, or upbringing), and the impact of these beliefs on attitudes and perceptions of lesbian, gay, or bisexual people; the ways and timing of sexual orientation disclosure (i.e. athletes' experiences of coming out), and; the diversity of lesbian, gay, or bisexual athletes and their experiences in relation to sport participation. Each of these issues present unique considerations for coaches, particularly if they do not have prior life or coaching experiences to inform how these issues may influence athletes' experiences in sport.

Coach characteristics are also an important and growing area of study. Halbrook and Watson (2018) examined coach efficacy for working with lesbian, gay, or bisexual athletes and found that coaches who were younger, those who reported no religious affiliation, and those with previous experience working with lesbian, gay, or bisexual athletes reported higher efficacy. Interestingly, their findings did not identify a significant relationship between efficacy and having participated in diversity training – which suggests that these trainings are unlikely to either challenge pre-existing attitudes and beliefs or to adequately prepare coaches to work with lesbian, gay, or bisexual athletes. Importantly, research highlights that participation in coach training is not sufficient to ensure buy in and effective implementation of policies, as coaches learn and make decisions based on knowledge from a variety of sources both within and outside of a sport organisation (Bolter *et al.*, 2017). Rather, Tseng and Sum (2021) suggest coach attitudes and understandings appear to change following experiences working with athletes of diverse sexual orientations.

In one study, Scheadler *et al.* (2021) examined attitudes about coaches and found that students had negative attitudes towards anti-LGBT+ coaches, however, students also perceived sexual orientation of gay coaches as a weakness. These recent studies build on previous work (e.g. Krane and Barber, 2005) that calls attention to the complex and sometimes nefarious ways that homophobia operates within sport contexts and organisations. As such, coaches need to be aware of the role that they play in shaping the social context of sport, but also cognisant of the complex ways that experiences or perspectives outside of the team or organisation have implications for lesbian, gay, or bisexual youth.

There is a growing interest in both academic and practitioner spheres in understanding how coaches can work to develop life skills through sport (e.g. see Hermens *et al.*, 2017; Holt *et al.*, 2017; Kramers *et al.*, in press). While this work provides valuable insights regarding how youth can be better served through sport, it is also important to consider how critical, radical, and transformative ways of thinking about sport and coaching may be an effective way of serving lesbian, gay, or bisexual youth. For example, Christensen *et al.* (2021) examined the use of a school-wide coaching model designed to create safe and inclusive spaces for LGBTQ youth. Similarly, Greenspan *et al.* (2019) discussed a professional development model for physical education teachers designed to develop comprehensive understandings of LGBTQ youth experiences in sport settings to better prepare teachers to engage in affirming and inclusive practices. These models go beyond dyadic understandings of coach/teacher-athlete/student and circumscribed environments like the team or classroom and challenge us to think critically about how sport and coaching practices are a situated element of young peoples' lives that do not exist only in the silo of sport. Therefore, effectively serving lesbian, gay, or bisexual youth in sport may require radical changes to thinking about the way we coach, and the ways that coaches are embedded in schools, organisations, and communities.

## *Sport Organisations*

Despite commitment to, and support for, diversity in sport organisations, leaders' lack of expertise in diversity principles, may reflect individual prejudicial attitudes and beliefs (Cunningham and Pickett 2018, Shaw 2019). Current evidence suggests that while supportive attitudes towards LGBT+ identities may have developed, they may not have converted into actual changes in behaviours (Storr *et al.*, 2021). Those in positions of leadership (i.e. decision makers, coaches, managers, and directors in and of sports organisations) may even intentionally engage in "rhetoric that endorses the value of institutional diversity while also engaging in resistance to the actual implementation of diversity" (Spaaij *et al.*, 2019, p. 365). These differences, helps to explain why sport organisations, on the whole, have not become significantly diverse.

Moreover, Kokozos and Gonzalez (2020) question the effectiveness of LGBTQ inclusion projects that are shaped by normative views of gender and sexuality and may be complicit in the reproduction of heteronormativity. For example, the authors posit that inclusion projects such as *safe spaces* "run the risk of failing to be disruptive to the social hierarchy and the system of power that put them there remain intact" (p. 155). As the authors explain, these programs and

LGBTQ terminology represent a micro-political change, yet, also give the illusion of safety in addressing homophobia without addressing structural practices.

Problematically, organisations use the language of diversity without changing ideologies, values or practices. For example, speech acts such as "we are inclusive", "there are equal opportunities here", and "everyone is welcome" does not recognise systematic inequalities and difference is understood as an individual attribute (for a more detailed discussion on speech acts, see Spaaij *et al.*, 2019; Storr *et al.*, 2021). Other discursive practices, Spaaij *et al.* (2019) contend, reinforce and maintain dominant power relations such as: in-group essentialism (e.g. using homogenising language to justify the status quo – we've always done it this way), denial/silencing (e.g. use of sexist/homophobic jokes), self-victimisation (e.g. pointing out lack of capacity and resources), and bodily inscription (e.g. degrading women who challenge traditional ideas about femininity and heterosexuality).

It is clear, too, that policies, programs, and spaces that are designed to enhance inclusivity are often underscored by values that reproduce white privilege (Knee, 2018; Kokozus and Gonzalez, 2020; Flett, 2021). Synthesizing the literature, Knee (2018) points out, LGBTQ spaces are "dominated by neoliberal, white, upper-class, normative values to the detriment of those who are gender nonconforming, of lower socioeconomic status, and racial minorities" (p. 499). As such, the taken-for-granted assumptions of staff as well as organisations that do LGBT work may serve to reproduce hierarchies that (unintentionally) reproduce exclusionary practices of those that do not conform to idealised versions of white queerness.

As alluded to earlier, existing research serves to emphasise the importance of education to better understand the needs and complex challenges facing LGBTQ youth through an intersectional lens (e.g. Trussell *et al.*, 2018; Flett, 2021). It is clear that education and awareness initiatives are required for social change to disrupt a heterosexist organisational culture. Within school-based research, Barber and Krane (2007) argued that the pervasive silence about gender identity and sexual orientation is the greatest barrier for LGBTQ student athletes. Fear and anxiety may also heighten the pervasive silence as well as the questioning of roles and responsibilities in the implementation of programs and policies (e.g. When is it even appropriate to discuss issues of gender and sexuality with children and young people? Am I responsible? Is it even my role?). However, when youth sport administrators and coaches create intentional discussion concerning issues related to lesbian, gay, or bisexual youth (as well as other diverse social identities) a more open, inclusive, and fluid dialogue can emerge. As Satore and Cunningham (2010) write: "[t]he vital roles that interpersonal contact, power, and status play in mitigating the stigmatisation process and its effects cannot be overstated" (p. 497). Through leadership that facilitates inclusion (e.g. language, behaviours), a more welcoming environment may be created that, in turn, has the potential to facilitate not only social benefits that build community and evoke principles of social justice (Trussell, 2020a), but also enhance young athletes' meaningful participation in sport.

Families are a key resource for educational support as well as leadership for sport organisations. Studies examining family diversity (i.e. lesbian, gay, or bisexual parents) and sport participation point to the important role that families have in challenging and changing existing exclusionary structures within sport to access opportunities that are more inclusive and appropriate for their children (Trussell *et al.*, 2018; Trussell, 2020a, 2020b). Families can be crucial activists, campaigners, and educators within youth sport. Drawing on personal experiences (as a lesbian, gay, or bisexual parent or as a parent of an lesbian, gay, or bisexual child), parents can play an important role in helping lesbian, gay, or bisexual youth navigate the sporting context, calling out homophobic behavior and heteronormative policies and practices, raising questions about the provision of programs, offering a diverse perspective on boards inclusive of intersectional identities, and reshaping how coaches and other leaders work within community sport organisation contexts (Trussell *et al.*, 2018; Trussell, 2020a). At the same time, parents do not always want to be a 'flag waver' responsible for minimizing sexual stigma. Experiences of fatigue speak to the importance of allyship by those in leadership roles as allies too can help negotiate and challenge the cultural narrative of heteronormativity and work towards more equitable and inclusive practices.

## Implications for Children's Sport Coaching

Through a politics of hope (Lincoln and Denzin, 2000), this chapter calls for more just and equitable coaching and organisational practices that not only support LGBTQ young athletes, but actively seek to disrupt the heteronormative structures that shape experiences in sport. Further, coaches and other leaders in sport should consider the way that other identities (e.g. related to class, gender, race, etc.) intersect with and complicate experiences of sexual stigma in sport. This section moves beyond describing oppression to also focus on advocacy and challenging the status quo to address power differences (Parry and Johnson, 2015; Wetherly *et al.*, 2017). It is in this spirit that five strategies are recommended that embody doing critical inclusion in youth sport.

1. *Recognise that participation alone does not equate to inclusion* – Regardless of how many LGBTQ athletes are participating and whether or not diverse identities have been disclosed, develop an environment in which everyone is respected, equal, and experiences a sense of belonging (Spaaij *et al.*, 2014).
2. *Engage in education and self-reflection* – Those in coaching and other leadership roles should examine and understand sexual prejudices and work to find ways to counter these negative beliefs in themselves and others (Barber and Krane, 2007; Norman, 2013; Flett, 2021). Coaches could be positioned and celebrated as allies. Further, training must consider issues beyond those that may be evident in the coach-athlete relationship. Educational workshops that focus on inclusive organisational cultures may result in a more welcoming environment and enhanced social connections among all youth sport stakeholders, and in turn, has the potential to enhance athlete/team participation and performance.
3. *Develop partnerships* – Collaborative relationships with local and national LGBTQ advocacy groups can help youth sport organisations develop educational sessions through finding the resources and training they need. In particular, these organisations may help develop resources that might be free and easy to download (Young *et al.*, 2017) for all stakeholders within a youth sport organisation. In many instances, these organisations are already doing this work (e.g. Around the Rainbow, 2010; Mauer, 2013; Wells, 2015; Asakura, 2016; Rummell, 2016; YouthREX 2017, 2019; Queersmart, 2018; Gaunt, 2020; The Trevor Project, 2020). In cases where organisations or individuals work on initiatives specific to teams and/or organisations, they should be remunerated or supported in equally meaningful ways.
4. *Recruit individuals who identify as LGBTQ* – The intentional recruitment of LGBTQ young people as well as LGBTQ parents in volunteer positions (e.g. coach, director) is one way to build diversity within sport contexts. These individuals can provide diverse perspectives by raising questions about heteronormative policies and practices and providing lived-experiences and knowledge to move towards equitable and inclusive organisational cultures (Kokozus and Gonzalez, 2020; Trussell, 2020a). These individuals however, should not be tokenised or expected to contribute inequitably to work being done in organisations.
5. *Evaluate organisational policies and practices* – Evaluation may consider if the organisation and coaches are using inclusive language and representations of diverse identities in policy and practice (e.g. representational statements on diversity on websites, inclusive language on registration forms, LGBTQ friendly images and promotional materials, special events). Websites, and the language used, are often an important marker for families to evaluate if a

sport organisation will be a welcoming space or not (Trussell *et al.*, 2018; Trussell, 2020a). Further, organisations should establish clear guidelines and conduct for how instances of abuse are treated. Athletes and families need to know how they can report when they are uncomfortable and that they will be supported. Coaches need to communicate these expectations and enforce these policies no matter the consequences on or off the field. Clear and severe consequences need to be articulated and enforced.

Through these and other strategic as well as everyday actions and behaviours, possibilities for transformational and meaningful experiences for LGBTQ young athletes exist.

## Summary, Future Directions and Future Research

The health of all youth "is influenced by where they live, learn, work, and play, and the relationships they form within communities that promote health and well-being" (Gower *et al.*, 2019, p. 327). For lesbian, gay, or bisexual young athletes, sport participation is also influenced by the ways in which coaches and sport organisations acknowledge their intersectional lived realities and provide supports that embody strategies of critical inclusion. This chapter has reviewed some of the ways that lesbian, gay, or bisexual youth experience sport and how their experiences outside of sport may also frame their (dis)engagement with sport. It has also discussed current literature related to coaching and lesbian, gay, or bisexual athletes. Finally, the chapter has considered how organisations and families play a role in shaping sport participation.

Lesbian, gay, or bisexual youth have a variety of unique lived experiences that are intertwined with their home, school, community, and broader leisure activities. Effectively supporting lesbian, gay, or bisexual youth may require empathy and support in these various spheres. Transformative thinking about sexuality and its implications for coaching require coaches and organisations to recognise the potential role of a coach as a supporter, ally, and mechanism of change for athletes, teams, schools, families, and communities. While these insights provide an important starting point in thinking through the implications of sexual stigma in sport, there is still much work to be done.

Importantly, much of the current literature on coaching and lesbian, gay, or bisexual youth is taking place in Western countries like Canada, the USA, and Australia. Future research should seek to unpack the complex ways that sexuality is embedded in diverse cultural understandings and ways of seeing the world as well as how different social and political contexts shape experiences of lesbian, gay, or bisexual youth. As communities are increasingly diverse and interconnected, coaches need access to knowledge and resources to help them navigate complex interrelationships between sport, leisure, sexuality, and culture.

Clearly, it will be important in future research and professional practice to consider the diverse experiences of lesbian, gay, or bisexual athletes in sport. Coaches and other sport leaders can play an impactful role in creating safe, welcoming, and supporting sport contexts as well as acting as allies and agents of change in the many spheres of young peoples' lives. To do so, all of the stakeholders involved in sport need to think critically about inclusion and the complex ways that sport participation is shaped. Future research may play a key role in these developments by problematising diverse experiences, challenging normative sport practices, and advocating for a more just and equitable sport system that serves all youth.

## References

Around the Rainbow, 2010. *Toolkit for educators and service providers: Working with LGBTTQ parents and their children*. Ottawa: Family Services Ottawa.

Asakura, K., 2016. Paving pathways through the pain: A grounded theory of resilience among lesbian, gay, bisexual, trans and queer youth. *Journal of Research on Adolescence*, 27 (3), 521–536.

Barber, H. and Krane, V., 2007. Creating a positive climate for lesbian, gay, bisexual, and transgender youths. *The Journal of Physical Education, Recreation and Dance*, 78 (7), 6–52.

Bolter, N., Petranek, L.J., and Dorsch, T.E., 2017. Coach, parent, and administrator perspectives on required coaching education in organised youth sport. *International Journal of Sports Science & Coaching*, 13 (3), 362–372.

Christensen, J.E., Larson, K.E., and Dykes, F.O., 2021. Using a school-wide coaching framework to create safe and inclusive spaces for students who identify as LGBTQ. *Preventing School Failure: Alternative Education for Children and Youth*, 65 (4), 371–378.

Cunningham, G.B. and Pickett, A.C., 2018. Trans prejudice in sport: Differences from LGB prejudice, the influence of gender, and changes over time. *Sex Roles*, 78, 220–227.

Denison, E., *et al.*, 2021. The relationship between 'coming out' as lesbian, gay, or bisexual and experiences of homophobic behaviour in youth team sports. *Sexuality Research and Social Policy*, 18, 765–773.

Flett, J., 2021. Youth-serving organisations' inclusivity of LGBTQ newcomers in Canada-a content analysis. *Journal of Gay & Lesbian Social Services*, 33 (3), 356–375.

Gaunt, K., 2020. Approaching intersectional conversations. *The Trevor Project*. Available from: https://www.thetrevorproject.org/wp-content/uploads/2020/07/intersectional-conversations.pdf Accessed 12.2.2022.

Gower, A.L., *et al.*, 2019. The LGBTQ supportive environments inventory: Methods for quantifying supportive environments for LGBTQ youths. *Journal of Gay & Lesbian Social Services*, 31 (3), 314–331.

Greenspan, S.B., Griffith, C., and Murtagh, E.F., 2017. LGBTQ youths' school athletic experiences: A 40-year content analysis in nine flagship journals. *Journal of LGBTQ Issues in Counseling*, 11 (3), 190–200.

Greenspan, S.B., Whitcomb, S., and Griffith, C., 2019. Promoting affirming school athletics for LGBTQ youth through professional development. *Journal of Educational and Psychological Consultation*, 29 (1), 68–88.

Greenspan, S.B., *et al.*, 2019. LGBTQ+ and ally youths' school athletics perspectives: A mixed-method analysis. *Journal of LGBT Youth*, 16 (4), 403–434.

Halbrook, M. and Watson, J.C., 2018. High school coaches' perceptions of their efficacy to work with lesbian, gay, and bisexual athletes. *International Journal of Sports Science & Coaching*, 13 (6), 841–848.

Halbrook, M.K., Watson, J.C., and Voelker, D.K., 2019. High school coaches' experiences with openly lesbian, gay, and bisexual athletes. *Journal of Homosexuality*, 66 (6), 838–856.

Hartmann-Tews, I., Menzel, T., and Braumüller, B., 2020. Homo- and transnegativity in sport in Europe: Experiences of LGBT+ individuals in various sport settings. *International Review for the Sociology of Sport*, 56 (7), 997–1016.

Hermens, N., *et al.*, 2017. A systematic review of life skill development through sports programs serving socially vulnerable youth. *Research Quarterly for Exercise and Sport*, 88 (4), 408–424.

Holt, N.L., *et al.*, 2017. A grounded theory of positive youth development through sport based on results from a qualitative meta-study. *International Review of Sport and Exercise Psychology*, 10 (1), 1–49.

Knee, E., 2018. Gay, but not inclusive: Boundary maintenance in an LGBTQ space. *Leisure Sciences*, 41 (6), 499–515.

Kokozos, M. and Gonzalez, M., 2020. Critical inclusion: Disrupting LGBTQ normative frameworks in school contexts. *Equity & Excellence in Education*, 53 (1–2), 151–164.

Kramers, S., *et al.*, In press. Development of a life skills self-assessment tool for coaches. *Journal of Sport Psychology in Action*, 1–11.

Krane, V., 2016. Inclusion to exclusion: Sport for LGBT athletes. In: R.J. Schinke, K.R. McGannon, and B. Smith, eds. *Routledge international handbook of sport psychology*. Milton Park, NY: Routledge, 238–255.

Krane, V. and Barber, H., 2005. Identity tensions in lesbian intercollegiate coaches. *Research Quarterly for Exercise and Sport*, 76 (1), 67–81.

Kulick, A., *et al.*, 2019. Three strikes and you're out: Culture, facilities, and participation among LGBTQ youth in sports. *Sport, Education, and Society*, 24 (9), 939–953.

Lincoln, Y. and Denzin, N., 2000. The seventh moment: Out of the past. *In:* N. Denzin and Y. Lincoln eds. *Handbook of qualitative research*. Thousand Oaks, CA: Sage, 1047–1065.

Mauer, L., 2013. *LGBTQ inclusion in youth program environments* [online]. ACT for Youth Center of Excellence. Available from: https://youthrex.com/wp-content/uploads/2019/05/pm_lgbtq_0613.pdf Accessed 12.2.2022.

Messner, M.A., 2002. *Taking the field: Women, men, and sports*. Minneapolis: University of Minnesota Press.

Melton, E., and Cunningham, G., 2012. When identities collide. *Journal for the Study of Sports and Athletes in Education*, 6 (1), 45–66.

Norman, L., 2013. The concepts underpinning everyday gendered homophobia based upon the experiences of lesbian coaches. *Sport in Society*, 16 (10), 1326–1345.
Parry, D.C. and Johnson, C.W., 2015. Theoretical perspectives for social justice inquiry. *In:* C.W. Johnson and D.C. Parry eds. *Fostering social justice through qualitative inquiry*. Walnut Creek, CA: Left Coast, 23–41.
Petty, L. and Trussell, D.E., 2018. Experiences of identity development and sexual stigma for lesbian, gay, and bisexual young people in sport: 'Just survive until you can be who you are'. *Qualitative Research in Sport, Exercise and Health*, 10 (2), 176–189.
Queersmart, 2018. *Queer terminology from A to Q*. Qmunity: Queersmart.
Rodriguez-Bravo, A.E., De-Juanas, Á.E., and Garca-a-Castilla, F.J., 2020. Effect of physical-sports leisure activities on young people's psychological wellbeing. *Frontiers in Psychology*, 11, 543951- 543951.
Rummell, C.L., 2016. *Mentoring lesbian, gay, bisexual, transgender, questioning, intersex, and gender non-conforming youth* [online]. National Mentoring Resource Center. Available from: https://youthrex.com/wp-content/uploads/2019/12/Mentoring-LGBTQI-GNC-Youth.pdf Accessed 6.1.2022.
Satore, M. and Cunningham, G., 2010. The lesbian label as a component of women's stigmatisation in sport organisations: An exploration of two health and kinesiology departments. *Journal of Sport Management*, 24, 481–501.
Scheadler, T.R., *et al.*, 2021. Student-athlete attitudes toward gay, ally, and anti-LGBT+ prospective coaches. *Journal of Issues in Intercollegiate Athletics*, 14, 135–151.
Shaw, S., 2019. The chaos of inclusion? Examining anti-homophobia policy development in New Zealand sport. *Sport Management Review*, 22, 247–262.
Shaw, S. and Cunningham, G.B., 2021. The rainbow connection: A scoping review and introduction of a scholarly exchange on LGBTQ+ experiences in sport management. *Sport Management Review*, 24 (3), 365–388.
Smits, F., Knoppers, A., and Elling-Machartzki, A., 2021. 'Everything is said with a smile': Homonegative speech acts in sport. *International Review for the Sociology of Sport*, 56 (3), 343–360.
Spaaij, R., Knoppers, A., and Jeanes, R., 2019. "We want more diversity but … ": Resisting diversity in recreational sports clubs. *Sport Management Review*, 23 (3), 363–373.
Spaaij, R., Magee, J., and Jeanes, R., 2014. *Sport and social exclusion in global society*. New York: Routledge.
Storr, R., *et al.*, 2021. Are we there yet? (illusions of) inclusion in sport for LGBT+ communities in Australia. *International Review for the Sociology of Sport*, 57 (1), 92–111.
The Trevor Project, 2020. *How to support bisexual youth: Ways to care for bisexual, pansexual, fluid, and queer youth who are attracted to more than one gender*. West Hollywood: The Trevor Project.
Trussell, D.E., 2020a. Building inclusive communities in youth sport for lesbian-parented families. *Journal of Sport Management*, 34 (4), 367–377.
Trussell, D.E., 2020b. Lesbian-parented families: Negotiating the cultural narrative of heteronormativity through leisure and sport experiences. *In:* K. Levasseur, S. Paterson, and L. Turnbull eds. *Thriving mothers/depriving mothers: Mothering and welfare*. Toronto, Canada: Demeter Press, 243–258.
Trussell, D.E., Kovac, L., and Apgar, J., 2018. LGBTQ parents' experiences of community youth sport: Change your forms, change your (hetero) norms. *Sport Management Review*, 21 (1), 51–62.
Tseng, Y.H. and Sum, R.K.W., 2021. The attitudes of collegiate coaches toward gay and lesbian athletes in Taiwan, Hong Kong, and China. *International Review for the Sociology of Sport*, 56 (3), 416–435.
Vargas-Tonsing, T.M. and Oswalt, S.B., 2009. Coaches' efficacy beliefs towards working with lesbian, gay, and bisexual athletes. *International Journal of Coaching Science*, 3, 29–42.
Wells, K., 2015. *GSAs and QSAs in alberta schools: A guide for teachers* [online]. The Alberta Teacher's Association. Available from: https://youthrex.com/wpcontent/uploads/2019/05/gsasandqsasinalbertaschools2015.pdf Accessed 12.11.2021.
Wetherly, P., Watson, B., and Long, J., 2017. Principles of social justice for sport and leisure. *In:* J. Long, T. Fletcher, and B. Watson eds. *Sport, Leisure, and Justice*. New York: Routledge, 15–27.
Wolowic, J.M., *et al.*, 2018. Come along with me: Linking LGBTQ youth to supportive resources. *International Journal of Child, Youth, and Family Studies*, 9 (3), 1–20.
Young, S.R., *et al.* 2017. LGBTQ organising beyond "low-hanging fruit": A qualitative examination of safe schools coalitions in the United States South. *Journal of Community Practice*, 25 (3–4), 524–541.
YouthREX, 2017. *Bringing our whole selves: Inclusive programs with and for racialized LBGBTTQQ2SIA youth*. Toronto: YouthREX.
YouthREX, 2019. *Delivering group programming for LGBTQ+ youth*. Toronto: YouthREX.

# 36

# EXPLORING THE IMPLICATIONS OF ABILITY IN CHILDREN'S SPORT

*Tania Cassidy*

## Introduction

Young people's involvement in sport is shaped by their own perceptions of ability as well as the perceptions of others. Yet, in the context of youth sport there has been limited debate around the concept of ability. This is not the case in other fields or disciplines. For example, in education and psychology the concept of ability has been debated for over a century. The debates have focused on the impact that grouping children by ability has on learning in the cognitive and affective domains (Liem *et al.*, 2015; Francis *et al.*, 2020). In this chapter, the term ability grouping is used to describe "the common educational practice of separating students based on actual or purported ability in the same grade into different instructional groups with differing levels of aptitude or achievement" (Lleras, 2013, p. 1). One aim of ability grouping is to create more homogenous groupings but this fails to recognise that there will still be within-group variability in a homogenous group, even more so if learning is viewed as occurring in the cognitive, psychomotor and affective domains.

In education, Chmielewski's (2014) reviewing of ability grouping in school contexts suggests that explicit, and implicit, types of ability grouping are still occurring in schools around the globe and both types "have the same purpose of differentiating curricula by students' achievement levels, and both types often have the consequence of segregating students by socioeconomic status (SES) and ethnicity, which can exacerbate achievement disparities between these groups" (p. 294). The purpose of the chapter is two-fold: (i) to provide coaches working with children an insight into the history and debates that have informed our understanding of ability, ability grouping, mixed ability grouping and coaching, and; (ii) to provide opportunities for coaches to reflect upon current coaching practices, and consider the implications of ignoring these debates, specifically what it could mean for children and their involvement in youth sport.

## Review of Literature

Due to the limited literature examining ability grouping in children's sport, this chapter firstly examines literature from the disciplines of psychology and education to explore the concepts of ability, ability grouping as well as mixed ability grouping and mixed ability teaching. The chapter will subsequently connect knowledge from these broader areas to discuss key concepts in the context of sport coaching.

 DOI: 10.4324/9781003199359-41

## *Ability Grouping*

Upon reviewing the history of Western public education Marklund (1984) noted that initially

> no great attention appears to have been paid to the question of how pupils should be divided into groups. The school was a unit. Pupils of differing ages were mixed together. Nor was any distinction made between the more able and the less able.
>
> *(p. 101)*

Yet, in the late 19th to early 20th century classes began to be grouped according to ability. When Reulecke (1977) analysed why this practice arose in Germany he contended that the system of 'ability grouping' was an outcome of the population growth and urbanisation that was occurring at that time. In the early 1880s, the French education system underwent dramatic changes as a consequence of a law being passed to make it mandatory for primary aged children to attend school (Brickman, 2014). As other Western countries in Central and Northern Europe, as well as in the UK and USA, also faced issues around urbanisation, increasingly diverse populations and compulsory schooling for children, they increasingly followed Germany's response and adopted the system of 'ability grouping' in schools. The justification of such a practice then was, as is often the case now, that "less gifted pupils should be allowed to develop according to their abilities" (Marklund, 1984, p. 102). However, even in these early stages of ability grouping, questions were being asked as to the fairness of the system and the contribution the practice was making "to a social division in the nation at large which many regarded as unjust" (Marklund, 1984, p. 102).

In the early 20th century Alfred Binet, with the assistance of Theodore Simon, created the Binet-Simon scale to classify a "hierarchy of intellectual qualities" (Michell, 2012, p. 1). It was subsequently used to determine the educational abilities of a child and the ability group into which a child was placed. Despite this widespread use, Binet and Simon identified the limitations of the scale being used in a way that reduced "intelligence to a single number" rather than recognising the "remarkable diversity of intelligence" (Siegler 1992, p. 179). This limitation was mostly disregarded by psychologists who "reified the notion that intelligence is a unitary inherited trait that could be assessed in one general score – an intelligence quotient (IQ)" (Turiel, 2020, p. 105). Binet and Simon were also concerned about the lack of recognition given to the "multitude of factors other than intellectual ability that could influence performance on the test … [eg] family and school background, health, and past effort in school … [as well as recognising] intellectual development progressed within individuals at variable rates" (Siegler, 1992, p. 182).

Fast forward over a century and politicians, researchers and educators continue to debate the merits of the Binet-Simon intelligence scale and its subsequent iterations, and the practice of grouping by ability. Yet it appears, at least at the rhetorical level, the 'tide is turning' away from grouping young people by cognitive ability. For, example in March 2021, New Zealand's Minister of Education, The Hon Chris Hipkins in an document entitled '*End Streaming in Aotearoa*' said:

> All of the international research is very clear, streaming does more harm than good, it isn't justified, it's wrong, it's discriminatory, it's unfair and … I acknowledge in the NZ context where streaming exists, and it shouldn't exist, that it's Māori and Pasifika who are disadvantaged by that. NZ based research has been very, very clear, streaming leads to lower expectations for Māori and Pasifika students and that's not okay [sic].
>
> *(Tokona Te Raki, 2021, p. 7)*

Despite such public statements rallying against the practice of grouping students by cognitive ability the practice is entrenched in many education systems. For example, the 2012 Programme for International Student Assessment (PISA) identified that "95% of New Zealand [15-year-old] students attended schools where streaming [grouping by ability] occurred in at least some of their school's maths classes, compared to 76% on average for OECD nations" (One News, 2021)

The above illustrates a bias that occurs in the discussions around ability, notably the primarily focus is on cognitive ability at the expense of ability in the affective or psychomotor domains of learning. Moreover, it highlights the complexities, environmental factors, and tensions surrounding the conceptualisation and practices associated with 'ability grouping'. These complexities and biases have implications for those working with children in the sports context because there are few resources to draw on to develop a comprehensive understanding of ability and therefore to make an informed contribution to the debates.

## *Adopting a Reflexive Lens on Ability*

In the 19th century, not only was there a preoccupation with quantifying intelligence, there was also the eugenics movement that attempted to, amongst other things, link intelligence with the superiority of the white race. According to Turiel (2020) some American psychologists were "influential in connecting eugenics with IQ" (p. 105). For example, Lewis Terman developed the Stanford-Binet scale, which he claimed could measure "innately determined intelligence – which, in turn, reflected racial differences, social class differences, and the usual eugenic moral features" (p. 105). These were not 'fringe' ideas, instead they were used to form the basis of many policies in numerous countries e.g. Australia, USA, UK and Germany. After the exposure of eugenic inspired atrocities undertaken by the Nazis in the Second World War the eugenic movement lost some of its momentum (Turiel, 2020). While eugenics may have lost some of its legitimate momentum, the ideas are still implicit in many practices that occur in, and outside of, sport.

Making a race-based assessment of physical ability is a longstanding eugenic practice. Hokowhitu (2003) mapped the way in which Māori have historically, and continue to be, regarded as achievers in the physical realm, yet limited in the academic. He gave the example of 19th-century Māori being constructed as "physical, unintelligent and savage" by missionaries and European settlers (p. 193). Such a view was still evident in the 20th (and arguably the 21st) centuries and can be seen through comments about Māori men having a "warrior instinct 'in the blood'" or sporting "ability among blacks due to 'natural rhythm'" (Tait, 1999, p. 207). These comments, and the like, still prevail in the 21st century, which has implications for those working with young people in the sporting context.

Wright and Burrows (2006) draw on the work of Hokowhitu (2003) to identify some of the practices that are implicitly informed by the eugenic-inspired view that Māori and Pacific Islanders have 'physical capital', which has been 'inherited' by virtue of race. Specifically: Māori and Polynesian boys are overrepresented in school sport 'academies'; professional rugby is actively promoted as a lifestyle choice for Māori and Pacific Islanders, and; young people of Māori and Pacific descent (with sporting prowess) are deliberately targeted for recruitment into elite state and private schools. Hokowhitu (2003, p. 193) argued that normalising the above depictions and practices "are undoubtedly tied to a bio-racist history contrived by colonizer privilege" and are "implicitly linked" to the Cartesian mind/body dualism, which assumes the "natural physical ability is paralleled by an inherent lack of mental resolve" (p. 212).

These eugenic-inspired race-based assessments of ability do not only occur in Aotearoa/ New Zealand. In the USA, Shane Battier, of the National Basketball League fame, described his experience of growing up as the son of a black father and a white mother in the suburbs of an American city. He said "[e]verything I have done since then [8th grade] is because of what I went through with this". He said the "[s]uburban kids ... treated him like a visitor from the planet where they kept black people", while the "[i]nner city kids ... treated him like a suburban kid with a white game" (Lewis 2009). Battier's experiences illustrate the way in which judgements of ability are socially constructed and encouraged Lewis (2009) to ask the question

> [i]s it a coincidence that many of the things a player does in [so-called] 'white basketball' to prove his character – take a charge, scramble for a loose ball – are all more pleasantly done on a polished wooden floor than they are on inner-city asphalt?

While Battier's example illustrates links between psychomotor ability and race in the USA, links are still being made between cognitive ability and race. Recently, the National Football League in the USA has been under scrutiny for how it settles concussion lawsuits, specifically their use of a "race-based formula that assumes black players have a lower level of cognitive function" (Malik, 2021). This practice is known as 'race-norming'. Despite the initial introduction of race norming being linked to affirmative action programmes, any assessment of people's ability due to their racial grouping is rooted in a bio-racist history (Malik, 2021).

In contrast to the eugenic position, Evans (2004) views ability as dynamic and a 'socio-cultural construct and process' (p. 99). Moreover, he contends "[w]e cannot 'read' or interpret 'ability' ... without reference to a person's gender, age, ethnicity, 'disability' and the values prevailing within and across particular fields" (p. 101). Evans's (2004) work encourages us to question the basis on which coaches, administrators and selectors make judgments on athletes' abilities. Wright and Burrows (2006) have also challenged the eugenic perspective of ability by pointing out that making judgments as to who has the ability "contributes to differentiating effects for young people in relation to gender, race and social class" (Wright and Burrows, 2006, p. 287). They explained that ability is classed because of the 'unequal opportunities' people have to develop ability due to available physical and human resources as well as "the ways particular cultural and social capital are associated with particular abilities and capacities". (p. 283).

Recently, two sporting examples illustrate the unequal opportunities young people have to develop their sporting abilities. First are the experiences of Nia Dennis, whose gymnastic floor routine "celebrating 'Black excellence' went viral" (Silva, 2021). Her routine included performing to "a mashup of music by Black artists" and incorporated "viral dances like the woah and the snap, as well as stepping". While Nia is successfully competing now she reflects that growing up loving gymnastics was tough "without role models that mirrored her style or identity". It was also difficult because her coaches told her "you don't look good or you're not in shape because you don't fit into those typical styles of gymnastics:", which she said was such a 'cookie-cutter' way of viewing who could be a gymnast. She went on to say

> Black gymnasts are kind of rare in the sport of gymnastics. And Black culture is not really recognized or known in the sport of gymnastics, so it was really important to me to bring that into the light of gymnastics — to raise awareness of Black culture.
>
> *(Silva, 2021)*

The second example is FINA's (the international governing body for swimming) ban of the 'Soul Cap' from competitions, including the Tokyo Olympic Games. The Soul Cap makes "swimming caps to fit over and protect dreadlocks, afros, weaves, hair extensions, braids, and thick and curly hair", which helps people with these hair types and styles to become more involved in swimming (Evans, 2021). The reason FINA gave for banning the Soul Cap was because it does not conform to "the natural form of the head". One swimming coach said he is 'disappointed' by FINA's wording saying "[i]t just shows misunderstanding and ignorance". He went on to say that "There's [already] so many barriers for black swimmers and [FINA have] kind of put another barrier up – defeating the whole purpose of the work that I'm doing" with young people (Evans, 2021).

## *Mixed Ability Grouping and Mixed Ability Teaching*

Mixed ability grouping:

As with ability grouping, the discussions and debates occurring around the concept of mixed ability grouping and practices of mixed ability teaching have also been influenced by prevailing social and political contexts, albeit as Cheung and Rudowicz (2003) pointed out, primarily through an Eurocentric lens. In the West, prominent and influential 20th century psychologists such as Dewey, Piaget and Vygotsky argued for recognition to be given to the role social interactions play in a learner's cognitive development and challenged the then dominant thinking that young people are empty vessels waiting to be filled by their knowledgeable teacher. Their ideas, and those of their associates, have subsequently informed constructivist inspired teaching practices. Furthermore, Dewey (1916), amongst others, was interested in education and social reform and their ideas gained more attention at the end of World War II where, in countries like the USA, increased efforts were made to achieve greater economic and social equality. In education, one of the strategies adopted to achieve this aim was to challenge the practice of grouping young people by their perceived cognitive abilities. The challenge was supported by research that was showing the practice of grouping young people by their perceived ability was less effective in developing cognitive function, specifically for those grouped in the lower and middle groups (Pallas *et al.*, 1994).

More recently, and outside of the education context, the business sector has been calling for educators to move towards mixed ability groupings because employers are wanting employees who are able to work in diverse teams (Schullery and Shullery, 2006). In psychology, Dweck's (2006) work on 'mindsets' has led her to ask questions about talents and abilities, which has subsequently influenced discussion around mixed ability grouping and mixed ability teaching. In summarising her research findings Dweck (2015) noted that "students who believed their intelligence could be developed (a growth mindset) outperformed those who believed their intelligence was fixed (a fixed mindset)." (p. 1). This is consistent with what has been observed in the context of mathematics where it has been observed that "ability grouping often leads to a fixed mindset … ie they are either a maths person, or they are not" (Pine, 2018).

Contributing to the debates around mixed ability grouping are the associate discussions on the merits of homogenous and heterogenous groups. Schullery and Shullery (2006) provided insight into the merits and complexities of both positions, which is worth quoting at length.

> Heterogeneous groups tend to avoid groupthink, consider more options, match roles with individuals who are predisposed to their tasks, and lead to better task outcomes … .On the other hand, homogeneous groups tend to be happier and have

> less conflict. Intimidation and control by a domineering member is less likely, and out of necessity these group members may feel compelled to develop valuable skills in unfamiliar tasks or roles. Although heterogeneous groups might be preferable in the workplace, where the group's task productivity is the top priority, homogeneous groups might be more appropriate in the classroom, where the students' development is the top priority.
>
> *(pp. 544–545)*

It is not often valuable, or even ethical, to position practices in dichotomous ways e.g. mind/body or black/white. This could be the same when debating the merits around ability or mixed ability grouping especially when a person could be judged as having a high ability in one subject and a low ability in another subject (Marklund, 1984). Also much of the debate around the merits of mixed ability grouping has focused on the impact the practice has on ability in the cognitive and, to a lesser extent, the affective domains of learning. There is little discussion on what it means for ability in the psychomotor domain, which is of concern for those working with young people in a sporting context.

Mixed ability teaching:

There is some slippage in the discussion around mixed ability grouping and mixed ability teaching, with assumptions often being made that putting people into mixed ability groups will result in the occurrence of mixed ability teaching. The error of this assumption is illustrated in the wide-spread, and time honoured, practice of two sport captains alternating their picks as to who they want on their team, with those perceived the most able (at least in the psychomotor domain) being chosen first. Some might argue that such a practice provides an opportunity for mixed ability grouping, but ample anecdotal evidence suggests that this practice, and often what happens after the teams are picked, are not good examples of mixed ability *teaching*, and do little to enhance learning in the psychomotor, cognitive or affective domains.

In 1982 Sands and Kerry published an edited collection which highlighted the 'lively' debates that surround mixed ability teaching. That this book was republished in 2020 suggests the debates have not subsided. Also, in the 1980s questions were asked as to whether mixed ability grouping had "led to new [teaching] methods" (Marklund, 1984, p. 110). The response then to such a question was;

> changes in this respect appear to have been considerably slower. Thus one conclusion to be drawn is that an organizational change does not automatically produce the desired change in methods. All it can do is render the latter more accessible, and more probable.
>
> *(p. 110)*

Arguably, the above response is similar to what would be given now, some 40 years later. Yet, there is not a uniform pattern when it comes to the quality adoption, or not, of mixed ability teaching. In a recent analysis Tereshchenko *et al.* (2019) stated that mixed ability teaching is prevalent in subjects like the arts, humanities and music, but uncommon in subjects like mathematics, and less common in science and English. No mention was made of the status of mixed ability teaching in physical education or sport.

Despite, or because of, the findings reflected in analyses like the one conducted by Tereshchenko *et al.* (2019), mathematic teachers in Aotearoa/New Zealand have been using blogs to share how they are teaching mixed ability groups. They are clear that mixed ability teaching is 'more than just mixing students up and continuing to teach the same way' (Pine, 2018). Some of the suggestions made by these mathematic teachers are also relevant to those working with young people in the sports context. For example;

> [s]tudents need to be taught how to work collaboratively … be supported so that they can explain their thinking, ask questions, and justify their solutions. Teachers have to be comfortable with the locus of control moving to the students and be able to facilitate discussions through effective questioning. Promoting productive struggle is an important part of learning and the ability to design tasks which develop a conceptual understanding as well as being accessible to all students … . Developing positive mindsets and providing a safe environment focused on learning rather than performing is paramount, and this all takes time.
>
> *(Pine, 2018)*

Some educators are rethinking the approaches they are using to form groupings. One approach has been to use flexible groupings, which has been described as a method where students work together sometimes in heterogeneous, and at other times, homogeneous groups. The key point of difference between flexible groupings and the use of stable mixed ability or ability groupings is that the flexible groups are formed "only for the length of time necessary for them [the learner] to develop an identified skill or to complete a learning activity" (Rubie-Davies, 2017). Proponents of flexible grouping argue that the arrangement benefits the learners and the teacher. The benefits to the students include: (1) not being 'pigeon holed' as able, or not, and the potential for value to be placed on all learning domains; (2) 'feeling valued' because everyone is considered to be able to add value to the learning community, which in turn can support the development of a culturally responsive teaching (Gay, 2000) and culturally relevant education (Aronson and Laughter, 2016) being prepared for the workforce where working in diverse teams is increasingly becoming commonplace (Morin, n.d.). It has also been claimed that teachers benefit from adopting a flexible group arrangement because it builds a 'team-oriented culture' where students learn from each other as well as the teacher. Because the groups are only designed to stay together for the length of time needed for the learning activity it requires teachers to gather data so they can confidently design subsequent groupings and sessions and reflect on their practices (Morin n.d.)

## Implications for Coaching Children in Sport

By extrapolating the observation in mathematics that "ability grouping often leads to a fixed mindset … i.e. they are either a maths person, or they are not" (Pine, 2018) to a sporting context, the practice of grouping young people based on their psychomotor ability into a low ability group could result in them developing a fixed mindset that they are not a 'sporty person'. One intrapersonal reason why young people drop out of sport is "low perceptions of physical competence" (Witt and Dangi, 2018, p. 194). If we genuinely want to find ways to reduce drop out of youth sport and/or re-engage young people in sport then we need to reflexively explore the concept of ability and practice in a way that challenges the development of a fixed mindset.

By default, many community sport coaches work with mixed ability groups because they work in a context that if a young person is in the right age group, or weight category, then they have the right to play. But if mixed ability *groupings* are often not purposefully established, a result is that the coaches do not undertake mixed ability *teaching*. Arguably, a lack of knowledge, and/or desire to, engage with mixed ability teaching is evident by those who continue to promote early specialisation and select young people primarily on perceived psychomotor ability. The implications of this practice is that the young people chosen to be in the high ability group develop a growth mindset, which may be assisted by setting challenging activities. However, those young people not selected may often be given low-level tasks, which as the literature has suggested, supports the development of a fixed mindset (Rubie-Davies, 2017). Given what we know about the socially constructed nature of ability, and its assessment, and the implications of being consigned to low ability groups, early specialisation practices do little to redress the 'unequal opportunities' many young people face when attempting to develop their sporting potential.

In a sporting context, team work (i.e. affective domain), decision-making (i.e. cognitive domain) and physical skill (i.e. psychomotor domain) are all considered key components of a successful sporting performance. If coaches adopted a flexible approach to grouping by ability it may be possible to genuinely acknowledge the importance of learning across all domains and thereby not disadvantaging the late developers who could be very able decision-makers or those young people who may not be the best in psychomotor domain but they are very capable leaders.

## Summary, Future Directions and Future Research

The chapter highlighted the way in which much of the existing literature on ability has focused on cognitive ability, with limited attention being given to understanding ability in the psychomotor domain. Nonetheless, findings from the existing literature do provide insight into the challenges that exist for those working with young people in the sporting context. Moreover, the chapter exposed the way in which ability is socially constructed and used contemporary sporting examples to illustrate the consequences this has on young people's opportunities to participate in sport. There is limited academic literature around ability in the sporting context and there are gaps in how we understand, and assess, ability across the cognitive, affective and psychomotor learning domains. Future research agendas could focus on the above as well as explore ways in which judgements of ability "contributes to differentiating effects for young people in relation to gender, race and social class" (Wright and Burrows 2006, p. 287) and expose the ways in which young people have 'unequal opportunities' to develop their abilities.

## References

Aronson, B. and Laughter, J., 2016. The theory and practice of culturally relevant education: A synthesis of research across content areas. *Review of Educational Research*, 86 (1), 163–206.

Brickman, M., 2014. *Expanding the education universe: A fifty-state strategy for course choice*. Washington: Thomas B. Fordham Institute.

Chmielewski, A., 2014. An international comparison of achievement inequality in within- and between-school tracking systems. *American Journal of Education*, 120 (3), 293–324.

Cheung, C-K. and Rudowicz, E., 2003. Academic outcomes of ability grouping among junior high school students in Hong Kong. *The Journal of Educational Research*, 96 (4), 241–254.

Dewey, J., 1916. *Democracy and education: An introduction to the philosophy of education*. New York: Macmillan.

Dweck, C., 2006. *Mindset: The new psychology of success*. New York: Ballantine Books.

Dweck, C., 2015. *Carol Dweck revisits growth mindset, Education week* [online], 35 (5), 20–24. Available from: https://www.edweek.org/leadership/opinion-carol-dweck-revisits-the-growth-mindset/2015/09 [Accessed 10 July 2021].

Evans, J., 2004. Making a difference? Education and 'ability' in physical education. *European Journal of Physical Education*, 10 (1), 95–108.

Evans, A., 2021. Soul Cap: Afro swim cap Olympic rejection 'heartbreaking' for black swimmers [online]. Available from https://www.bbc.com/news/newsbeat-57688380 [Accessed 10 July 2021].

Francis, B., *et al.*, 2020. The impact of tracking by attainment on pupil self-confidence over time: Demonstrating the accumulative impact of self-fulfilling prophecy. *British Journal of Sociology of Education*, 41 (5), 626–642.

Gay, G., 2000. *Culturally responsive teaching: Theory, research, and practice*. New York: Teachers College Press.

Hokowhitu, B., 2003. 'Physical beings': Stereotypes, sport and 'physical education' of New Zealand Māori'. *Culture, Sport and Society*, 6 (2/3), 192–218.

Lewis, M., 2009. The No-Stats All-Star [online]. Available from: https://www.nytimes.com/2009/02/15/magazine/15Battier-t.html?pagewanted=all [Accessed 10 July 2021].

Liem, G., McInerney, D., and Yeung, A., 2015. Academic self-concepts in ability streams: Considering domain specificity and same-stream peers. *The Journal of Experimental Education*, 83 (1), 83–109.

Lleras, C., 2013. Ability grouping. *In:* J. Ainsworth ed. *Sociology of education: An A-to-Z guide, Vol 1*. Los Angeles: Sage, 1–3.

Malik, K., 2021. 'Race norming' is bigotry that began with good intentions [online]. Available from: https://www.theguardian.com/commentisfree/2021/jun/06/race-norming-good-intentions-bigotry [Accessed 10 July 2021].

Marklund, S., 1984. Mixed ability teaching versus streaming. *Scandinavian Journal of Educational Research*, 28, 101–110.

Michell, J., 2012. Alfred Binet and the concept of heterogeneous orders. *Frontiers in Psychology*, 3 (261), 1–8.

Morin, A., n.d. Flexible grouping: What you need to know [online]. Available from https://www.understood.org/articles/en/what-is-flexible-grouping [Accessed 10 July 2021].

One News, 2021. June 20. 1800hrs. Campaign to stop schools streaming students by perceived ability grows [online]. https://www.tvnz.co.nz/one-news/new-zealand/campaign-stop-schools-streaming-students-perceived-ability-grows

Pallas, A., *et al.*, 1994. Ability-group effects: Instructional, social, or institutional? *Sociology of Education*, 67 (1), 27–46.

Pine, S., 2018. Grouping students in mathematics … more than just mixed ability [online]. Available from: https://nzcurriculum.tki.org.nz/Curriculum-resources/NZC-Online-blog/Grouping-students-in-mathematics [Accessed 10 July 2021].

Reulecke, J., 1977. Population growth and urbanisation in Germany in the 19th century. *Urbanism Past & Present*, 4(21–28), 31–32.

Rubie-Davies, C., 2017. Raising the bar with flexible grouping [online]. Available from: https://nzcurriculum.tki.org.nz/Curriculum-resources/NZC-Online-blog/Raising-the-bar-with-flexible-grouping [Accessed 10 July 2021].

Sands, M. and Kerry, T. (Eds.). 1982/2020. *Mixed ability teaching*. London: Routledge.

Schullery, N. and Shullery, S., 2006. Are heterogeneous or homogeneous groups more beneficial to students? *Journal of Management Education*, 30 (4), 542–556.

Siegler, R., 1992. The other alfred binet. A centennial feature. *Developmental Psychology*, 28 (2), 179–190.

Silva, C., 2021. Meet UCLA gymnast Nia Dennis, who went viral after 'Black excellence' floor routine [online]. Available from: https://www.nbcnews.com/news/nbcblk/meet-ucla-gymnast-nia-dennis-who-went-viral-after-black-n1256191 [Accessed 10 July 2021].

Tait, S., 1999. Advertising, cultural criticism and mythologies of the male body. *In:* R. Law, H. Campbell, and J. Dolan, eds. *Masculinities in Aotearoa/New Zealand*. Auckland: Dunmore Press, 189–214.

Tereshchenko, A., *et al.*, 2019. Learners' attitudes to mixed-attainment grouping: Examining the views of students of high, middle and low attainment. *Research Papers in Education*, 34 (4), 425–444.

Tokona Te Raki, 2021. *End Streaming in Aotearoa* [online]. Available from: http://www.maorifutures.co.nz/wp-content/uploads/2021/03/TTR_Streaming_document.pdf) [Accessed 10 July 2021].

Turiel, E., 2020. Eugenics, prejudice, and psychological research. *Human Development*, 64, 103–107.

Witt, P. and Dangi, T., 2018. Why children/youth drop out of sports. *Journal of Park and Recreation Administration*, 36 (3), 191–199.

Wright, J. and Burrows, L., 2006. Re-conceiving ability in physical education: A social analysis. *Sport, Education and Society*, 11 (3), 275–291.

# 37

# SOCIAL JUSTICE ORGANISATIONS, COMMUNITY SPORT AND COACHING CHILDREN

*Matthew Atencio, E. Missy Wright, Duke Austin, Carl Stempel, and Christina Rodriguez*

## Introduction

Child and youth sport has historically been considered a vital life opportunity for many families and communities; Coakley (2011, p. 307) concomitantly reminds us that

> both public and private sector leaders fund policies and programs based on assumed developmental benefits of sports, and they are joined by others who believe that sport participation and consumption will create healthy, productive people; decrease deviance and disruptive actions; and alleviate boredom and alienation.

This view is widely held, and it is possible to see examples of how youth sport has been used for developmental purposes across the world (Coalter, 2010; Haudenhuyse *et al.*, 2012; Holt *et al.*, 2017).

Yet, Coakley as well as a growing number of policy bodies and scholars have raised increasing concerns about prevailing youth sport policy and practice, in relation to documented hierarchical and exclusionary aspects (see Côté and Hancock, 2016; Atencio *et al.*, 2018; The Aspen Institute: Project Play, n.d.). Simultaneously, given these concerns as well as broader social issues, an increasing number of grassroots programs have emerged and are explicitly attempting to refashion child and youth sport coaching provision, by addressing a range of social causes and promoting inclusion and civic engagement (Jones *et al.*, 2017; Atencio *et al.*, 2018; Whitley *et al.*, 2019a).

In this landscape, it seems vital to understand the global literature that examines programs and research regarding how various child and youth sport coaching organisations seek to improve the lives of marginalised youth based in underserved communities. This type of integrated practice seems to rely upon diverse public and private organisational stakeholders that facilitate relationship building and trust at the local level of youth sport coaching practice. Consequently, this chapter will outline global research and practices that incorporate this type of cross-sector organisational practice especially under neo-liberal conditions, followed by a more fine-grained examination of working organisations such as the San Francisco Bay Area's Center for Sport and Social Justice

DOI: 10.4324/9781003199359-42

(CSSJ) and its community partners. Finally, the chapter concludes with a discussion of this approach using field analysis (Fligstein and McAdam, 2011) in order to signal future directions in the international child and youth sport coaching field.

## Review of Current Research

### *Neo-Liberalism and Youth Sport Coaching Practices*

It has been suggested that neo-liberalism thrives in Western contemporary youth sport, often to provide purported positive developmental experiences, within contexts such as North America, Australia, New Zealand, and Europe (Darnell, 2010, 2012; Coakley, 2016). During the latter half of the 20th century, a time of rapid globalisation and industrialisation, the Western world, in particular, witnessed the rise of neo-liberal or 'post-Fordist' economic belief systems and policies. The ascendance of neo-liberalism augured new roles for state governments, private industries and markets- as well as individual citizens. Neo-liberalism functions as a pervasive socio-economic condition that has specific effects upon the organisation and valuation of human activities:

> Neoliberalism sees competition as the defining characteristic of human relations. It redefines citizens as consumers, whose democratic choices are best exercised by buying and selling, a process that rewards merit and punishes inefficiency.
>
> *(Monbiot, 2016, para. 4)*

Under the neo-liberal world view, then, it is clear that free market ideals including entrepreneurialism and 'personal responsibility' strongly govern the organisation and valuation of human activities, including "specific markers of appropriate citizenship linked with meritocracy and individualism" (Beal *et al.*, 2017, p. 12). Given this understanding of neo-liberalism and its social impacts, Andrews and Silk (2012, p. 10) go on to further suggest that more localised investigation into neo-liberalism's impacts upon sport are needed:

> A lacuna of work has explicitly centered on critical explication of how, in various guises and often in highly localised contexts, the tentacles of neoliberalism have been manifest, experienced, appropriated, and mobilised within multifarious iterations of sporting experiences, expressions, and structures.

In order to comprehend the local-level "tentacles of neo-liberalism" referred to by Andrews and Silk (2012), as this condition currently impacts upon youth sport provision, readers must first address how child and youth sport evolved – particularly during the late 20th Century. Youth sport scholars have indeed outlined the increasingly privatised conditions underpinning contemporary youth sport programming (Coakley, 2011; Skolnikoff and Engvall, 2013). It has been reported that under the neo-liberal ethos that emphasises a strong role for the private sector and less emphasis on state support, there has been a marked decrease in funding for child and youth sport on behalf of government entities. This can even be the case within historically socialist European nations such as France, where these types of privatised youth sport practices have been increasing with particular effects on community and family involvement (Schmitt *et al.*, 2020). Instead of the school, parks and recreation department or council solely leading youth sport provision, then, it is possible to observe that increasingly private sector groups have taken up a prominent role in operating child and youth sport in conjunction with public bodies.

Working hand in hand with public entities, it is often the case that both for-profit and non-profit private groups have created symbiotic working arrangements with public bodies to support youth sport provision in communities. This type of practice occurs globally, including within projects that are focused on Western nations. Scotland, for instance, hosts several projects affiliated with a 'Sport Social Enterprise Network (Sport SEN)' which "exists to create a supportive environment where sport social enterprises can be informed, inspired and connected to help each other and create strong and flourishing organisations" (Sportscotland, 2021, p. 9). Several public-private projects are thus explicitly using "grassroots sport and/or physical activity as a means of addressing a social or environmental problem" (Sportscotland, 2021, p. 2) found in a local area. This public-private model is also found in developing nations located in the Middle East, South America, Africa, and Asia, where extensive public-private work has been undertaken by organisations such as Skateistan (2021).

Simultaneously, the consequences of neo-liberalism as this underpins modern child and youth sport programming often relates to major social divides and inequities that have become increasingly prominent in our global cities. Indeed, the impact of neo-liberalism upon North American communities, for instance, arguably reflects "decades of financial restructuring and fiscal austerity measures," ultimately leading to "heightened levels of social polarisation and a growing gap between the rich and poor" (Scherer *et al.*, 2016, p. 187). Andrews and Silk (2012) therefore remark that neo-liberalism contours a shifting sporting landscape that is increasingly marked by various social inequalities. Given this current state of sport within the global child and youth sport landscape, it is consequently demonstrated below how at the global level there have been increasing 'social enterprise' projects that are aiming to serve youths in sport within these types of community contexts. In many cases, these working projects are particularly focused on serving the needs of society's 'in need' and marginalised youths.

## Social Enterprise Practice in Child and Youth Sport Coaching around the World

Given the neo-liberal contextualisation outlined above, child and youth sport coaching projects around the world often embrace what has been characterised as social enterprise partnership building in order to overcome systemic inequalities and challenges. Child and youth sport project are often confronted with complex social and economic issues, and particularly lack sufficient resources and capacities found in other types of sport organisations (Blom *et al.*, 2015; Misener and Misener, 2017; Svensson *et al.*, 2018). Svensson *et al.* (2018) indeed contend that under current socio-economic conditions, many sport programs rely heavily on 'interorganisational linkages'; they refer to the work of Welty Peachey *et al.* (2017, p. 298) who argue that "partnerships are the lifeblood of many organisations and are undertaken for multiple reasons, such as to secure funding, for assistance in program design, delivery, and implementation, and for monitor[ing] and evaluation". Svensson *et al.* (2018, p. 299) go on to further suggest that "Collaborative networks and coalitions provide an alternative strategy whereby non-profits gain access to shared expertise and pooled resources aligned with a shared common mission". Partnership development under social enterprise practice is thus critical to effective and sustainable programming and can greatly enhance sport coaching work (Blom *et al.*, 2015).

At the global level, then, particularly in light of prevalent neo-liberalism, there has been a move towards creating these forms of working hybridic public-private relationships to benefit child and youth sport provision. A systemic/collaborative strategy of child and youth sport coaching- involving researchers, organisations and participants- diverges from the prevailing isolationist, top-down approach (Whitley *et al.*, 2019a). This collaborative strategy instead prioritises equitable partnership building amongst a range of governmental, non-governmental, and private sector stakeholders to address local issues and solutions (Schinke *et al.*, 2019). Moreover, this type of partnership building frequently occurs amongst projects integrating diverse commercial, governmental, and non-profit interests and mechanisms, under what has been deemed social enterprise practice (Atencio *et al.*, 2018; Bjärsholm, 2019). This model involves networking patterns and mechanisms that blur the traditional divisions between non-profits, businesses, and state governments. 'Social enterprise,' which is also sometimes framed as 'social innovation' and 'social entrepreneurialism,' thus reflects a continuum of public and private interests and approaches that are used to address deficits in funding and capacity, as has been noted by various scholars working in the Scandinavian context (Bjärsholm, 2017; Tjønndal, 2018; Bjärsholm, 2019). In some cases, universities are teaming up with these projects, further adding another layer of complexity to this type of youth sport coaching provision.

This chapter discusses two U.S.-based social enterprise organisations, Soccer Without Borders and Skate Like A Girl, due to the authors' experiences with them. Soccer without Borders is a soccer/football-focused program that engages under-served youth (predominantly youth of colour, including refugees and new immigrants) in global communities located in the United States as well as nations in Africa, Central and South America, and Southeast Asia (Soccer Without Borders, n.d.).

Skate Like A Girl is an organisation that "empowers skaters, especially young women and or trans people, to grow into strong, confident leaders who promote and implement social equity." (Skate Like A Girl, n.d.). This group is headquartered in Seattle with chapters in places such as San Francisco. it is important to note that there are many similar types of programs that have rapidly expanded since the 1990s found in other parts of the world, within both Western and developing nations (Whitley *et al.*, 2018).

Despite the prevalence of social enterprise projects involving diverse public and private stakeholders as detailed above, it is often the case that the specific manner in which these networks come to exist and become facilitated by different stakeholders is not adequately articulated (Bjärsholm, 2019). Having outlined several cases of social enterprise above, the chapter then addresses below how partnership building to support holistic and youth-centred sport programming is a complex and perhaps uncertain endeavour; that is, many considerations must be taken into account to understand precisely how mutual benefits may actually accrue in terms of how organisations come together and work to increase their organisational capacity within increasingly difficult conditions to achieve their goals (Blom *et al.*, 2015; Jones *et al.*, 2017). Lyras (2012), working in the nation of Cyprus, has noted that further evidence and theorising is required to understand how sport programs may or may not actually provide certain personal and social benefits. Specifically, it has been suggested that further research is required to understand the capacity benefits as well as issues that arise from these types of partnerships. Therefore, "a more nuanced picture of collaborations and partnerships" is required in order to "determine when and under what circumstances such initiatives are productive or unproductive (perhaps even destructive) for an organisation's capacity endowment" (Svensson *et al.*, 2018, p. 309). It has thus been acknowledged that there is significant need for more detailed theorising and accounts that explain how social, cultural, and economic benefits, or capitals, are systematically generated through social enterprise organisational partnerships (Schulenkorf *et al.*, 2016; Atencio *et al.*, 2018). Within this type of environment, it is crucial for youth sport coaching organisations to participate in mutually beneficial social networking to sustain operational capacity through capital generation, while also providing marginalised children and youths with opportunities to obtain capital benefits through sport participation in their local communities.

Thus, while "collaborative networks and coalitions provide an alternative strategy whereby nonprofits gain access to shared expertise and pooled resources aligned with a shared common mission," (Svensson *et al.*, 2018, p. 299) further research into this practice is still required. There is a specific need for academic researchers to delve into the nature of hybridic public-private organisations that are operating in the Sport for Development and Peace (SDP) field (Svensson and Seifried, 2017). Moreover, according to Giles and Lynch (2012, p. 94), "partnerships between NGOs and academics are beginning to emerge in evaluating sport for development initiatives and thus building an apparently legitimate evidence base (e.g. Sport for Life and Johns Hopkins University)". It is therefore vital that university-based researchers increase the understanding of how various organisations – reflecting governmental, non-governmental, and private industry interests- developed key relationships and networks as part of sustaining SDP practice (Welty Peachey *et al.*, 2017; Bjärsholm, 2019; Schinke *et al.*, 2019). This type of understanding can inform the field, given that Whitley *et al.* remind us that there is a need to develop more systems-based and collaborative knowledge regarding SDP projects that have increasingly emerged across the globe in diverse developing contexts within India, Africa, and Asia, as well as North American and European nations; these scholars suggest that critical assessment of SDP provision is needed to ascertain the dynamic and complex ecologies involving individual and organisational stakeholders, which could subsequently lead to more enhanced and sustainable impact (Whitley *et al.*, 2018; Whitley *et al.*, 2019a).

This section has demonstrated that child and youth sport is often facilitated by community organisations reflecting public and private interests (Jones *et al.*, 2017). Organisational networking thus frequently relies upon the notion that local-level youth sport programs incorporate social enterprise networking practices, reflecting "blurred sector boundaries," that may lead to particular organisational capacity contributions as well as challenges in the domain of youth sport coaching provision (Misener and Misener, 2017, p. 125). Below, reflective analysis and concluding ideas are integrated with existing global research and theoretical discussion by conceptualising the overlapping yet distinctive social enterprise "fields" where organisations such as the Center for Sport and Social Justice (CSSJ) and affiliated SDP groups such as Skate Like A Girl and Soccer Without Borders seek to cooperate.

## Implications for Children's Sport Coaching

The discussion below will address certain issues faced in the social enterprise field, in a local context where the CSSJ operates as well as global contexts where public-private projects frequently underpin the delivery of child and youth sport coaching. Initially, the chapter outlined potential linkages and benefits that arise through social enterprise networking. Later in the chapter, critical concerns about this type of collaborative practice are consequently raised.

According to Fligstein and McAdam (2011), the formation of fields of strategic action are often triggered by external shocks (in our case the state defunding of sport and recreations services) that initiate processes of 'emergent mobilisation' by actors who recognise opportunities to pursue interests in new ways. Crucially, for this chapter, this type of field activity involves interaction with a 'complex web' of others, going beyond self-interest to generate forms of mutual support and a shared worldview, as reflected in various collaborative endeavours. This complex networking within what has been deemed as fields of action can be found in all public-private collaborations functioning in Western and developing nations where SDP groups operate to serve children and youth. In a local sense, the CSSJ supports an emerging field of action through its cultivation of relationships with allied SDP groups working in child and youth sport coaching. Stakeholders with different organisational profiles and backgrounds, such as the academic-based CSSJ and community-based partners such as Skate Like A Girl and Soccer Without Borders, can come together in order to achieve sustainability and enhanced outreach by sharing resources and expertise including those coming from academia and industry as well as facilitating mechanisms of mutual support and refining common aims, leading to further skill and capacity building to further the scope of collective action.

The collaborative endeavours undertaken by organisations such as those based in universities, including the CSSJ, and youth and child focused sport SDP groups, can serve to generate various capitals within their respective yet overlapping fields. For instance, frequent interaction between leaders of higher education and community organisation fields means that all groups gain access to new social networks as well as cultural codes and knowledge that would enable all parties to fulfil their missions better. Then, in terms of economic capacity building, university programs may compensate community SDP groups by paying for their expertise and supporting fundraiser events, while simultaneously promoting SDP work to a higher education audience via university-based media platforms. University-based programs and centres can also provide interested students studying within sport-related disciplines that will directly work with SDP projects in local communities. These university students doing volunteer or paid work on the ground so to speak will consequently develop cultural and social capital through their exposure to leaders and staff of the SDP field; students will obtain access to new networks, as well as knowledge and experiences that cannot be gained in the classroom.

At the same time, university-based organisations such as the CSSJ are considered academic entities that can provide program evaluation research expertise to these high-profile community programs. This is particularly vital given that Whitley *et al.* (2019a) have noted that there is a limited amount of effective intervention studies conducted on these programs. It is suggested here that longitudinal design and integrating philosophical, methodological, and theoretical perspectives are useful to improve program evaluation studies. Long-term partnerships can be strengthened by the implementation of longitudinal program evaluation studies utilising various theoretical and methodological approaches developed by program leaders and academics. In another sense, academic-based groups that rely upon both university and non-university funding increase their own visibility and credibility through prominent community connections. Collaborations including awareness events and public debates serve to increase the cultural and social impact that academic groups can have with campus-based administration, general student population, alumni, and faculty, as well as within local regions more broadly. Academic centres also generate further social and cultural benefits by leveraging work with SDP projects in ways that snowball with other associated prominent SDP groups that will provide further capital-building opportunities.

Yet these initial examples of mutual capital-building amongst academic and SDP groups still raise critical, complex issues that remain for the respective fields involved in global social enterprise networking. For instance, SDP projects have often conducted substantial work prior to the establishment of relations with university members. Academic groups will thus need to foster respectful, trusting, and supportive relationships with SDP groups, instead of working in top-down, dominant ways. Academics involved in this manner will need to deeply understand SDPs and their histories, needs, goals, and strategies in order to help support such organisations. A collective challenge that must be faced globally is thus to move from the initial interactions, acts of mutual support, and recognition of common interests to form more robust "organisational vehicles … sufficient to launch and sustain innovative collective action" (Fligstein and McAdam, 2011, p. 91). It therefore behoves academic-based members to explore ways to further advance and support an emergent network as a whole; collaborations involving academics and SDP leaders can turn to the tools of field analysis with its focus on the processes of forming shared identities, a consensus around goals and ideals, and mechanisms to take concerted action to advance those goals more profoundly. As discussed below, this also means paying close attention to how higher education institutions, NGO's, and other agencies might better value and incorporate local knowledge. An adaptive and open-ended approach is warranted here, in order to avoid re-inforcing dominant neo-liberal and neo-colonial beliefs and power relations (Darnell and Hayhurst, 2011; Welty Peachey *et al.*, 2018; Whitley *et al.*, 2019b).

As part of enhancing global partnerships that are emerging to support inclusive child and youth sport provision, field analysis also calls for clear-eyed recognition of the power relations within the fields each stakeholder operates in and the influence of external powers with different needs and motivations. Specifically, many SDP projects and their allies including those in universities focus on what can be defined as human capital development. Human capital developers look for ways that sport participation builds normative traits (e.g. discipline, self-control, leadership, assertiveness, controlled aggression, teamwork, will to win, perseverance) which seemingly translate into neo-liberal education and employment sectors. "Human capital" frames treat this as *individual* processes (the individual invests in his/her/their self) to develop traits or dispositions which are more or less *universally* valuable – they instil qualities that lead to success in other areas of life. The purported source of the value of these traits is the demands of modern workplaces and schools (even as these appear to be socially-neutral sites). Rather than using sport to promote social democratic values including solidarity and communal responsibility, recent policy trends advance the prioritisation of neoliberal conceptions of individualised citizenship, in terms of how citizens are held accountable for taking personal responsibility over their lives (Österlind and Wright, 2014).

## Summary, Future Directions, and Future Research

Under a critical view of human capital development, global youth sport coaching organisations, even those invested in promoting social justice in the communities they serve, should reflect upon how they may reinforce or ratify several negative neo-liberal tendencies which may reproduce racial and class inequality. Neo-liberalism arguably works to break up working class and minority solidarities (Bourdieu, 1998; Lamont *et al.*, 2016), so that each person faces the evaluating market as an individual. And increasingly, responses to social inequality and marginality are being individualised; this obscures both the structural impediments to sport participation for lower-income and minority youth and possibilities for making collective demands on the state. In many neighbourhoods, neoliberal governance is oriented more by a will to punish/discipline the undeserving poor minority youth than to provide support and resources needed to strengthen mutual support. Organisations invested in making social change for children, youth, and communities should reflect upon the history of sport as disciplinary and the current moral and ethical uses of sport in poor communities (Wacquant, 2004). This is especially crucial in the global contexts where state activity governing the dispossessed has arguably shifted from support and caring to punishment and discipline (Wacquant, 2009; Rios, 2011). The neo-liberal preoccupation with individual human capital building may be valuable for many sport programs in the world's low-income, underserved communities, but it may also foreclose collective responses which would better serve the community and the youth participants. There are instances of some SDP groups working at local and global levels that indeed have more thoughtful, nuanced ideas about the need for youths' safety, social justice, and organisational/community involvement. These include U.S.-based projects such as Soccer Without Borders and Skate Like A Girl, as well as others based in post-conflict and post-disaster zones where children and youth are considered valued agents and empowered leaders, and there is inclusion for all abilities and backgrounds, as well as emphasis on emotional well-being (see Thorpe, 2016; Marshall *et al.*, 2020).

Moreover, in respective yet intertwined child and youth sport coaching fields, stakeholders must consider the cultural and social capital relationships that emerge between dominant and dominated groups. For instance, cultural capital is constituted in processes where dominant groups possess and reproduce certain cultural dispositions and familiarity. Understanding these structures can animate efforts to provide information and experiences aimed at increasing this familiarity among excluded groups. This occurred, for instance, when Soccer Without Borders' immigrant and refugee youths were invited over several years to attend and interact with students, faculty, and administrators during campus events sponsored by the Center for Sport and Social Justice. Yet exposure to people and sites rich in cultural capital alone does not automatically build participants' 'capital' (Glass, 2015). Furthermore, given the debates surrounding social capital development and the need for more specificity into how this concept underpins SDP practice, field leaders need to find ways of measuring actual impact (Schulenkorf *et al.*, 2016; Adams *et al.*, 2018). Those involved in the SDP field, including program and academic leaders, should thus intentionally strive to observe and reflect upon what youth participants actually gain in terms of social and cultural capitals. This means taking into account which social networks are prioritised and considered most meaningful and advantageous for them to join. Furthermore, what resources and opportunities do these networks actually offer? Indeed, the private supporter model often used in SDP provision has been criticised for prioritising donor and funding agency needs rather than the participants' needs (Giles and Lynch, 2012). And within these social networks, whose knowledge and voice gets regularly prioritised? In essence, it is crucial to see whether academic and program leaders are imposing dominant class culture and schemes of evaluation on the local child and youth cultures they seek to serve; this view applies to both domestic programming with underserved communities as well as projects based in the West that have sites in developing nations. If so, what are the consequences of this in terms of access, power, and normative ideologies of youth participation and citizenship? Put simply, are inequalities faced by children and youth actually being reinforced or exacerbated despite good intentions?

Finally, in terms of economic capital reproduction, it is clear that social enterprise groups around the globe face resource deprivation and instability. Groups that are primarily made up of professors from a university often have access to limited funding for program infrastructure, research, and allocated time to consistently support community projects. This in turn compels program leaders to continually search for private donor funding, especially given the global condition of university defunding. The pressure to brand and market SDP child and youth serving projects, or to engage in knowledge transfer activities, will habituate academic members to the rules and strategies of a new field, involving private donors and industry sponsorship. However, this can augur tension with organisational aims to increase the opportunities for building community engagement and political representation that is indeed closer to the needs and interests of local children, youth, and their neighbourhoods. This goal can be obscured or brought into tension when corporate or private sponsor strings are attached. Concerns like these were mentioned by participants in Whitley *et al.* (2019b) study on SDP, with global strategies often resulting in money and resources not being allocated effectively at the local level. And, furthermore, despite the potential capital benefits of privatised support (e.g. industry and philanthropic) for child and youth sport projects, what happens when this type of support shifts in emphasis or scope? This can occur since the ideal of private sector freedom underpins neoliberalism, meaning that issues of children's and youths' social inclusion and civil rights may lose currency when compared to economic viability (Smith, 2017).

The shifting and complex fields involved in international child and youth sport provision require careful examination into power structures, dominant ideologies, and micro-level practices, in order to understand how academic and community program collaborations in global contexts actually benefit their intended stakeholders. Altogether, the critical questions raised in this final discussion regarding child and youth-serving collaborations under social enterprise set up future research questions that need to be advanced internationally.

## References


Adams, A., Harris, K., and Lindsey, I., 2018. Examining the capacity of a sport for development programme to create social capital. *Sport in Society*, 21 (3), 558–573.

Andrews, D.L. and Silk, M.L., 2012. *Sport and neoliberalism: Politics, consumption, and culture*. Philadelphia: Temple University Press.

Atencio, M., *et al.*, 2018. *Moving boarders: Skateboarding and the changing landscape of urban youth sports*. Fayetteville, AR: University of Arkansas Press.

Beal, B., *et al.*, 2017. Skateboarding, community and urban politics: Shifting practices and challenges. *International Journal of Sport Policy and Politics*, 9 (1), 11–23.

Bjärsholm, D., 2017. Sport and social entrepreneurship: A review of a concept in progress. *Journal of Sport Management*, 31 (2), 191–206.

Bjärsholm, D., 2019. Networking as a cornerstone within the practice of social entrepreneurship in sport. *European Sport Management Quarterly*, 19 (1), 120–137.

Blom, L., *et al.*, 2015. Sport for development and peace: Experiences conducting U.S. and international programs. *Journal of Sport Psychology in Action*, 6 (1), 1–16.

Bourdieu, P., 1998. *Acts of resistance: Against the tyranny of the market*. New York: New Press.

Coakley, J., 2011. Youth sports: What counts as "positive development?" *Journal of Sport and Social Issues*, 35 (3), 306–324.

Coakley, J., 2016. Positive youth development through sport: Myths, beliefs, and realities. *In:* N. Holt, ed. *Positive youth development through sport*. 2nd ed. New York: Routledge, 21–33.

Coalter, F., 2010. The politics of sport-for-development: Limited focus programmes and broad gauge problems? *International Review for the Sociology of Sport*, 45 (3), 295–314.

Côté, J. and Hancock, D.J., 2016. Evidence-based policies for youth sport programmes. *International Journal of Sport Policy and Politics*, 8 (1), 51–65.

Darnell, S., 2010. Power, politics and "sport for development and peace": Investigating the utility of sport for international development. *Sociology of Sport Journal*, 27 (1), 54–75.

Darnell, S., 2012. Global citizenship and the ethical challenges of 'sport for development and peace'. *Journal of Global Citizenship & Equity Education*, 2 (1) (Special Edition), 1–17.

Darnell, S. and Hayhurst, L., 2011. Sport for decolonisation: Exploring a new praxis of sport for development. *Progress in Development Studies*, 11 (3), 183–196.

Fligstein, N. and McAdam, D., 2011. *A theory of fields*. New York: Oxford University Press.

Giles, A.R. and Lynch, M., 2012. Postcolonial and feminist critiques of sport for development. *In*: R.J. Schinke and S.J. Hanrahan, eds. *Sport for development, peace and social justice*. Morgantown, WV: Fitness Information Technology, 89–104.

Glass, I., 2015. Three miles. *This American life* podcast [online], March 3. Available from: https://www.thisamericanlife.org/550/three-miles [Accessed 1 April 2021].

Haudenhuyse, R.P., Theeboom, M., and Coalter, F., 2012. The potential of sports-based social interventions for vulnerable youth: Implications for sport coaches and youth workers. *Journal of Youth Studies*, 15 (4), 437–454.

Holt, N., *et al.*, 2017. A grounded theory of positive youth development through sport based on results from a qualitative meta-study. *International Review of Sport and Exercise Psychology*, 10 (1), 1–49.

Jones, G.J., *et al.*, 2017. Leveraging community sport organisations to promote community capacity: Strategic outcomes, challenges, and theoretical considerations. *Journal of Sport Management*, 31 (2), 148–160.

Lamont, M., *et al.*, 2016. *Getting respect: Responding to stigma and discrimination in the United States, Brazil, and Israel*. Princeton, NJ: Princeton University Press.

Lyras, A., 2012. Olympism in practice: Psycho-social impacts of an educational sport initiative on Greek and Turkish Cypriot youth. *ICHPER-SD Journal of Research*, 7 (1), 46–54.

Marshall, J., *et al.*, 2020. "I feel happy when I surf because it takes stress from my mind": An initial exploration of program theory within waves for change surf therapy in post-conflict Liberia. *Journal of Sport for Development*, 1 (9), 1–17.

Misener, K.E. and Misener, L., 2017. Grey is the new black: Advancing understanding of new organisational forms and blurring sector boundaries in sport management. *Journal of Sport Management*, 31 (2), 125–132.

Monbiot, G., 2016. Neoliberalism – The ideology at the root of all our problems. *The Guardian* [online], April 15. Available from: https://www.theguardian.com/books/2016/apr/15/neoliberalism-ideology-problem-george-monbiot [Accessed 1 April 2021].

Österlind, M. and Wright, J., 2014. If sport's the solution then what's the problem? The social significance of sport in the moral governing of 'good' and 'healthy' citizens in Sweden, 1922–1998. *Sport, Education and Society*, 19 (8), 973–990.

Rios, V.M., 2011. *Punished: Policing the lives of Black and Latino boys*. New York: NYU Press.

Scherer, J., Koch, J., and Holt, N.L., 2016. The uses of an inner-city sport-for-development program: Dispatches from the (real) creative class. *Sociology of Sport Journal*, 33 (3), 185–198.

Schinke, R.J., *et al.*, 2019. Social justice in sport and exercise psychology: A position statement. *Quest*, 71 (2), 163–174.

Schmitt, A., Atencio, M., and Sempé, G., 2020. "You're sitting on a hot soccer field drinking Gatorade … I'm sitting in a yacht club just enjoying the view, enjoying the drinks": Parental reproduction of social class through school sport sailing. *European Physical Education Review*, 26 (4), 987–1005.

Schulenkorf, N., Sherry, E., and Rowe, K., 2016. Sport for development: An integrated literature review. *Journal of Sport Management*, 30 (1), 22–39.

Skate Like A Girl website, n.d. *About skate like a girl* [online], Available from: https://www.skatelikeagirl.com/about.html. [Accessed 8 January 2022].

Skateistan, 2021. *A new chapter* [online]. Available from https://www.skateistan.org/a-new-chapter. [Accessed 1 April 2021].

Skolnikoff, J. and Engvall, R., 2013. *Young athletes, couch potatoes, and helicopter parents: The productivity of play*. Lanham, MD: Rowman & Littlefield.

Smith, D., 2017. Betsy DeVos: Trump's illiberal ally seen as most dangerous education chief ever. *The Guardian* [online], July 26. Available from: https://www.theguardian.com/us-news/2017/jul/26/betsy-devos-education-secretary-trump [Accessed 1 April 2021].

Soccer without Borders website, n.d. Available from: https://www.soccerwithoutborders.org/ [Accessed 1 April 2021].

Sportscotland. 2021. *Social enterprise and sport in Scotland* [online]. Available from: https://sportscotland.org.uk/media/7209/social-enterprise-senscot.pdf [Accessed 1 April 2021].

Svensson, P.G., Andersson, F.O., and Faulk, L., 2018. A quantitative assessment of organisational capacity and organisational life stages in sport for development and peace. *Journal of Sport Management*, 32 (3), 295–313.

Svensson, P.G. and Seifried, C.S., 2017. Navigating plurality in hybrid organising: The case of sport for development and peace entrepreneurs. *Journal of Sport Management*, 31 (2), 176–190.

The Aspen Institute: Project Play, n.d. *What we do* [online]. Available from: https://www.aspenprojectplay.org/whatwedo/ [Accessed 1 April 2021].

Thorpe, H. 2016. "Look at what we can do with all the broken stuff!": Youth agency and sporting creativity in sites of war, conflict and disaster. *Qualitative Research in Sport, Exercise and Health*, 8 (5), 554–570.

Tjønndal, A., 2018. Sports innovation: Developing a typology. *European Journal for Sport and Society*, 15 (1), 1–17.

Wacquant, L., 2004. *Body and soul*. Oxford: Oxford University Press.

Wacquant, L., 2009. *Punishing the poor: The neoliberal government of social insecurity*. Durham, NC: Duke University Press.

Welty Peachey, J., *et al.*, 2017. Challenges and strategies of building and sustaining inter-organisational partnerships in sport for development and peace. *Sport Management Review*, 21 (2), 160–175.

Welty Peachey, J., *et al.*, 2018. Interrogating the motivations of sport for development and peace practitioners. *International Review for the Sociology of Sport*, 53 (7), 767–787.

Whitley, M.A., *et al.*, 2018. A systematic review of sport for youth development interventions across six global cities. *Sport Management Review*, 22 (2), 181–193.

Whitley, M.A., *et al.*, 2019a. Sport-based youth development interventions in the United States: A systematic review. *BMC Public Health* [online], 19 (89), 1–20.

Whitley, M.A., *et al.*, 2019b. Sport for development and peace: Surveying actors in the field. *Journal of Sport for Development*, 7 (12), 1–15.

# SECTION V

# Cultures and Context

## Introduction: Cultures and Context

*Martin Toms and Ruth Jeanes*

One of the things that is absolutely key in any research is the appropriate culture and context of the work being undertaken and the lived experiences of children playing sport within them. This doesn't just mean the political, geographical or physical context – but the broader impact of the 21st century on the environment in which they are in. Children's experiences of sport are changing considerably, and it is not just the choice of activity that is being researched, but the broader context of it and the wider implications that are clearly evident. As we move from the sport itself to explore the contexts and cultures that surround it, it is clear that since these factors envelop children's experiences this is an area that research will focus upon in even more detail in the future. Whilst it is not possible in this text to explore every culture or context in children's sport, the chapters in this section provide a broad framework of some of the research being undertaken to provide an account of some of the areas of study moving forwards. It is in that sense a selection of key topics from key researchers.

This section explores a number of areas that are pertinent to children's sport coaching and provides a broad range of topic areas. One of the key contexts of any children's coaching is around that of the coaches and volunteers that surround them, for at grassroots without these then there would be no sport. Hence the exploration of this resource is not just contextual to the socio-political and cultural environment, but also central to the understanding of children's sport involvement in the first place. Allied to this, the chapters in this section explore some of the key issues that relate to this vital resource as well as the policy that links to it.

The section delves into other key areas of children's lives, such as the impact of their engagement with social media, something that will continue to change as we all consume all areas of sport (including coaching) in new and different ways. In a related vein the consumption of individual and lifestyle sports appears to be on the increase so implications for such self-organised activities need consideration. Within this the physical environment and geography of participation is also important so that children can engage with activities in environments that are both appropriate and suitable, not to mention that are set up specifically for them. This physical and cultural context is important for participation and the need to understand this is central to policy.

The section considers other key elements of coaching children in context and whilst the issue of scaling sports is an important one (e.g. children being coached and playing on adult-sized

DOI: 10.4324/9781003199359-43

pitches), this is an area that is important to consider carefully around participation, success and also skill acquisition. An area related to this itself is also learning 'how' we coach children and the way that this occurs in different contexts and cultures across the world. The section provides food for thought, research contexts, and an appreciation of the complexity of the broader contexts in which children's sport participation occurs.

# 38

# COACHING CHILDREN AND YOUTH SPORT POLICY

*Anna-Maria Strittmatter, Iain Lindsey, Jimmy O'Gorman, and John Hayton*

## Introduction

Children and young people are one of the main target groups for sport policies developed by many national and international governments and by organisations that govern sport worldwide (Lindsey and Jeanes, 2011; Stylianou *et al.*, 2019). Policies directed to children and youth sport are also of interest due to their intersection with broader policy goals, sectors and institutions. Young people's engagement in sport is thus placed in diverse policy agendas such as those concerned with the welfare of citizens, healthy lifestyles, excellence and performance, educational attainment, crime reduction and youth unemployment (Houlihan and Green, 2006; Strittmatter and Skille, 2017; Hayton, 2018). Coaches often become the agents responsible for enacting these ambitious and diverse youth sport policy objectives.

The importance accorded to children and young people in sport policies is also represented in substantive academic research. This chapter is based on a comprehensive literature review examining research that has been published in leading sport policy, management, sociology, and education journals over twenty years on the content of youth sport policies and the decision-making processes through which they were created. Specifically, the analysis in this chapter seeks to identify the role of coaches in youth sport policy processes and how coaches are considered in the content of youth sport policies. By doing so, the chapter sheds light on the uneven extent of research on different aspects of youth sport policies, the expected role of coaches across different international and national policy contexts, and thus enables discussion of some of the challenges confronting youth sport coaches in responding to the ambitious aspirations expressed in youth sport policies. Children's sport is subsumed within the broader concept of youth sport, but the issues and points raised throughout the chapter are relevant for children and young people.

## Review of Current Research

Identification of relevant literature on youth sport policy for review in this chapter focused on research articles that:

> *specifically sought to contribute to understanding of the formation or content of policies that are directly orientated towards young people's engagement with sport and physical activity.*

DOI: 10.4324/9781003199359-44

The construction of this definition focused the review towards studies that analysed the creation or content of youth sport policies, rather than research that focused on the implementation of policies. It also enabled the review to consider studies that examined policies that were connected to sport and physical activity in schools, but not those that were exclusively focused on physical education.

This definition informed searching for articles published in 26 leading journals oriented towards sport policy, sport management, sport sociology, and sport and education. Through this search, a total of 81 articles were identified and categorised as being focused on the formation and content of youth sport policy. Of these, a subset of 41 articles included content specifically related to coaches or coaching.

The geographical scope of the full set of 81 research articles on youth sport policy is relatively narrow. Studies undertaking internationally orientated analysis of policies or cross-country comparisons are relatively rare, and collectively represented approximately 20% of all studies (eight articles in total). Of the remainder of articles, there was clustering towards research in a small set of individual countries. The 26 articles focusing on youth sport policy in the United Kingdom represented 32% of the total articles identified. The next most common countries in which youth sport policy was examined were some way behind with 15 studies undertaken in the United States of America and six specifically in Norway. Countries in Africa and Asia were the focus of only three and two studies respectively, although the latter may especially be a consequence of the Clarivate journal lists being predominantly focused on English-language journals.

The overall number and proportion of all included studies that examined different youth sport policy topics are presented in Table 38.1. Classification of topics was identified inductively through the process of identifying and reviewing articles, and the review classified some individual articles as having more than one focus topic.

Studies on policies associated with sport and physical activity in schools were most prevalent, with over a third of included articles focusing on such policies. At the very least, this can be taken as a focus that is oriented towards places in which all young people can potentially be engaged in sport and physical activity, and also a site that is often a prominent focus in youth sport policies. While there is less overlap with sport coaches specifically in this focus, the prevalence of this area of research can also be considered to be a consequence of it sitting at a point of overlap between studies of youth sport and those that are concerned with the broader field of physical education.

Just over a third of all studies also examined policies orientated towards further aspects of the traditional continuum of involvement in youth sport, namely community-based participation

*Table 38.1* Focus of youth sport policy research

| *Topic area* | *Number of articles* | *Proportion of all articles (%)* |
|---|---|---|
| **School sport and physical activity** | 30 | 37 |
| **Child welfare and safeguarding** | 15 | 19 |
| **Community-based participation** | 19 | 23 |
| **Elite sport and events** | 12 | 14 |
| **Other topic areas** | 13 | 16 |

(23%) and elite sport and events (14%). Alongside these proportions, the extent of research on specific child welfare and safeguarding policies represented what could be considered as a relatively high proportion of 19% of all studies. In this regard, it is notable that the interest in child welfare and safeguarding policies represents a particularly recent trend with all but one article with this focus being published from 2012 onwards.

Otherwise, the review identified a particular lack of research on more specific concerns in youth sport policy. No articles were classified as having a specific focus on youth sport coaching and only a single article, that was otherwise focused on safeguarding, included any of the terms 'coach', 'coaches' or 'coaching' in its title. Also, relatively few studies researched the orientation of youth sport policies towards particular target groups or social justice issues. Only three studies researched gender as a key policy issue, with another one focused on disability and one classified as addressing inclusion of young people more generally. While there may be few youth sport policies that specifically focus on inclusion or social justice, the lack of research considering the extent to which these issues may (or may not) be embedded within youth sport policies more broadly is an important limitation to address.

## *Coaches and Policies for School Sport and Physical Activity*

The most commonly identifiable theme in literature on policies associated with young people's engagement with sport in schools is the intersection of different policy issues, stakeholders and interests. As Houlihan (2000) characterised it, school sport is a 'crowded policy space'. Research across different country contexts gives recognition of different ways in which school sport may respond to or align with wider educational, health or other social policy goals and approaches (Houlihan, 2000; Fry and McNeill, 2011; Phillpots, 2013; Lund, 2014; Jung *et al.*, 2016). Studies also differentiate the relative policy priority given to different types of school-based provision and activities, one aspect of which is cross-country recognition of lower policy priority being given to Physical Education (PE) in comparison to school-based competitive sport (Houlihan, 2000; Fry and McNeill, 2011; Pope, 2011; Jung *et al.*, 2016). In terms of comparison between countries, Pot and van Hilvoorde (2013) also highlight differences between the Netherlands and United States of America in their respective focus on participatory and high-performance school sport, and the extent to which there is separation in policy approaches towards the two is also highlighted elsewhere by Houlihan (2000) and Lund (2014). Identification of specific aspects of policy related to coaches and coaching, however, is limited to links with specific policy initiatives for competitive school sport as a whole in England (Houlihan, 2000; Houlihan and Green, 2006; Phillpots, 2013; Jung *et al.*, 2016), bridging the 'gap' between schools and sports clubs in the Netherlands (Pot and van Hilvoorde, 2013) and training coaches to develop capacity to achieve policy goals for school sport (Fry and McNeill, 2011).

Neither are coaches commonly identified as a group with significant involvement in processes of policy-making for school sport. While the influence of particular individuals on policy development is highlighted in England in particular (Houlihan and Green, 2006; Phillpots, 2013), only Johnson *et al.*'s (2017) research on policies for competitive balance in school sport in the United States of America gives any recognition of specific representations made by coaches to influence school sport policies. Organisations that reflect the interests of coaches may, however, be involved in policy-making process, with different national sport organisations particularly mentioned in Sweden (Lund, 2014) and England (Houlihan, 2000; Phillpots, 2013). On the other hand, in the latter country, there is specific recognition that professional bodies representing PE Teachers have had a marginalised position in policy making for PE and school sport (Houlihan and Green, 2006; Phillpots, 2013). More broadly, while Houlihan and Green (2006) and Phillpots

(2013) recognise specific circumstances that have brought policy change in England, there is also identification of a range of wider cultural, economic and geographic conditions that may constrain possibilities for new policy developments for school sport (Houlihan, 2000; Pot and van Hilvoorde, 2013; Johnson *et al.*, 2017). Therefore, Pot and van Hilvoorde (2013) provide a note of caution regarding the limited potential for effective learning or transfer of school sport policies between countries, although this may be a possibility that is considered by school sport policy-makers across different states in the USA (Johnson *et al.*, 2017).

## Coaches and Policies for Community-Based Participation

There are relatively few examples of studies of how and where coaches are considered within youth sport policy content that is orientated towards community-based participation. The majority of these studies, and the youth sport policy concerns that they refer to, revolve around the nature and objectives of youth sport and its programming, with coaching practice and quality typically implicated (De Knop and De Martelaer, 2001; Skirstad *et al.*, 2012; Chalip and Hutchinson, 2017). Skirstad *et al.* (2012), for example, traced the attempts made by the highest decision-making body for sport in Norway to regulate youth sport to protect children from associated harms such as competitive pressures, early-specialisation, and burnout, until the point where such principles became recognised in children's rights policy in sport. The incremental regulation of children's sport in Norway has had implications for coaching practice, coach education, and the coach-participant relationship, each of which has been emphasised in policy iterations. Indeed, adult-orientated and achievement-focused approaches to community-based youth sport were commonly problematised in the literature as a policy concern in which coaches are implicated (De Knop and De Martelaer, 2001; Miah and Rich, 2006; Skirstad *et al.* 2012; Chalip and Hutchinson, 2017; Riehl *et al.*, 2019). Chalip and Hutchinson (2017) explained that national policy in the USA follows a demand-led discourse orientated towards sporting excellence, whereas local providers recognise the need for participatory youth sport programming – thus engendering implementation conflicts for coaches. The literature indicated that such discourses are reflected in and reinforced by the ethos' and practices prevalent across a largely amateur coaching workforce made up of volunteers and parents. De Knop and De Martelaer (2001) called for a more comprehensive and professionalised system that provides qualified youth coaches and implements evaluation measures as part of a quality control system that simultaneously inputs into the sport policy process. Elsewhere, Erwin *et al.* (2014) highlighted a policy gap in the USA that no national policies exist that require coaches to be trained to maximise physical activity opportunities for their participants.

Whilst coaches are rarely identified as a group with significant involvement in processes of policy making in the community-based participation literature, insights can be discerned as to how they are or should be implicated as stakeholders or policy actors. One theme evident in the literature is that coaches can undermine top-down policy goals if they are resistant to principles and programmes underpinning them (Støckel *et al.*, 2010; Skirstad *et al.*, 2012; Riehl *et al.*, 2019). When studying a provincial sport association in Canada, Riehl *et al.* (2019) identified coaches as an important resource for policy enactment. To this effect, Riehl *et al.*, (2019) advise that sport associations should work to engage, educate, socialise, and ultimately inculcate resistant stakeholders to share the values that the organisation is attempting to embed, otherwise policy change may need to be mandated. That said, Skirstad *et al.* (2012) and Støckel *et al.* (2010) have illustrated that knowledge of, or support for, centrally mandated regulations around the welfare and development of children were often weakly adhered to within sport clubs at the local level in Norway, and therefore not universally enacted within sport programming and coaching practice. Finally, the position of young and youth-aged coaches as policy actors was considered within the literature. Whilst the involvement of young coaches in decision-making processes represents a long-championed strategic objective in Norway (Strittmatter, 2016), White *et al.* (2019) reported that, in one of the largest national sport governing bodies in England, the voices of young and youth coaches were largely excluded from the decision-making processes which rule on complex policy issues that are of primary concern to young and youth participants.

## Coaches and Policies for Child Welfare and Safeguarding

The literature centred on child welfare policies in sport generally posits coaches as pernicious actors. Scholarly work on the formation and content of policies in this area has, for example, identified coaches as complicit in prevailing subcultures which have normalised psychological/emotional maltreatment of young athletes (Donnelly *et al.*, 2016), prioritised their athletic performance at the expense of educational development (Platts and Smith, 2009) and compromised their physical health such as playing with or ignoring injuries such as concussion (Susnara and Williams, 2019). Notwithstanding a lack of focus on other important welfare topics (e.g. mental health and wellbeing, eating disorders, and addiction), much scholarly work in this area has focused on child protection and safeguarding policies in sport and their relation to different forms of exploitation, and specifically sexual, physical (e.g. violence) and emotional abuse (e.g. shouting at, humiliating and belittling, Rhind *et al.*, 2017; Donnelly *et al.*, 2016), perpetrated by coaches. For example, on the back of high-profile cases of sexual abuse perpetrated by coaches in the 1990s, Brackenridge (2004) noted sexual, physical, and/or emotional exploitation of children by actors such as sports coaches, was historically facilitated by a symbolic separation of sport from social and legal regulation and the traditional autonomy of the voluntary sport sector. This and other research commonly reviews the policy and practice landscape in the context of children's human rights leading to recommendations for existing or future strategy and policy-making centred on prevention of abuse by, and training of coaches (and other youth sports stakeholders such as parents) to recognise, refrain from and report, abusive behaviours (Brackenridge, 2004; Parent and Hlimi, 2013; Vertommen *et al.*, 2016; Kerr and Kerr, 2020).

Scholarly work in this area has also tended to focus on the micro and meso-level development of policy tools and measures aimed at protecting and safeguarding children from actual and potential adverse impacts of coaching and unwanted coach behaviour. However, (Kerr and Kerr 2020) note that many of the raft of codes of conduct and educational programmes for coaches to address such topics as maltreatment, strategies for prevention, and responsibilities for intervention have not been theoretically informed or empirically evaluated, tend to have a predominant focus on sexual abuse and lack attention towards physical abuse, neglect, and the most common form of maltreatment by coaches, emotional abuse.

In this context, Garratt *et al.* (2013) examined the discursive formation of child protection policy with a focus on swimming in England. Their analysis of policy documents and some data excerpts from coaches highlighted increasing anxiety about safe coaching practice, specifically about 'touching' by coaches. This, it has been suggested, may be displacing coaching pedagogy with the fear of perceived professional malpractice (see also Vertommen *et al.*, 2016). Rhind *et al.* (2017) adopted a sport-specific focus on youth (ice) hockey in Canada, identifying sports coaches as the main perpetrators of abuse (particularly emotional abuse and encouraging peer violence). Among other things, Rhind *et al.* (2017) suggested a democratic approach to governance in sports organisations to dilute the power of overzealous coaches alongside a universal, independent monitoring tool for youth sport that captures coaches' behaviours. Also, in the Canadian context, Donnelly *et al.* (2016) tracked the development of NSO harassment policies. It was found that 86% of national and 71% of the provincial (Ontario) sport organisations sampled had accessible harassment policies. However, only 10% and 14%, respectively, had harassment officers of which none were of arm's length to the organisation. Many of the policies also lacked a detailed complaint process, or articulation of the rights of the complainant and respondent, and did not distinguish between children, adolescents, and adults.

## *Coaches and Policies for Elite Sport and Events*

The fourth most prominent topic in the literature on youth sport policies focuses on elite sport and associated events. Scholars have examined governments' priorities defined in state elite sport policies and how these policies are adopted and put into action in national and regional sport organisations (Velenczei and Gál, 2011; Houlihan and Chapman, 2017). The content of state elite sport policies addresses governmental support in the form of initiatives and funds that aim at improving talent identification, development and management in order to ensure elite sport success in the respective countries. In this respect, scholars have examined who and what is prioritised in these policies and found that state-funded programmes are mainly addressed towards athletes and coaches (Velenczei and Gál, 2011; Bjørndal *et al.*, 2017; Houlihan and Chapman, 2017). Studies that specifically related to coaches and that are reviewed in this section were located in England, Hungary and Norway.

The content of elite sport policies' focus on coaches and coaching that is identified in the literature includes a) investment in sport sciences and programmes that ensure the quality of coach education, and funds to keep youth sport coaches in their professions, as well as b) explanation of stakeholders' involvement in such programmes (Miah and Rich, 2006; Velenczei and Gál, 2011; Houlihan and Chapman, 2017). Youth sport policies connected to elite sport thus emphasise not only the quality of coaching programmes for producing gold medals, where coaches undergo training in order to be able to identify and coach potential elite athletes, but also that such policies stress the protection of the welfare of (young) athletes. Houlihan and Chapman (2017) stress that the welfare of athletes is especially important in the coaching of disabled athletes.

The literature review also shows that studies on youth sport policy with an elite sport focus are limited to meso- and macro-level policy and from a top-down perspective; hence, they mostly look at state and/or international governing bodies' sport policies imposed on national sport organisations. Bottom-up and individual policy perspectives on street-level are lacking. There is a lack of consideration in existing research as to whether and in what ways coaches are included in the policy making for elite sport.

Literature on youth sport policy with a focus on elite sport also includes youth elite sport events, more specifically the Youth Olympic Games (YOG). The introduction of the YOG by the International Olympic Committee in 2007 has had implications for National Olympic Committees and governmental focus on youth elite sport events. In Norway, one youth sport policy aim connected to the YOG was the intention that the YOG would lead to an increase in the recruitment of young coaches, but any mention of how this might be supported or facilitated was absent (Strittmatter, 2016). Further, researchers see potentially negative impacts of the Youth Olympic Games, such as overzealous coaching and overtraining that could put young athletes' health in danger, as well as increase cheating and dropout rates (Parent *et al.*, 2015). For elite youth athletes, parents often adopt the role of a coach, which, to youth elite sport event organisers, gives parents a similar degree of importance as coaches (Parent *et al.*, 2015).

## Implications for Children's Sport Coaching

The literature draws attention to the ideological tensions about the nature and objectives of youth sport that have long jarred between different types of sport provider, diverging on the basis of whether youth sport programming should be highly organised and focus on competition and winning, or alternatively, emphasise play and the holistic development of the child that is underpinned by age-appropriate pedagogical knowledge. As De Knop and De Martelar suggest, 'converting play into work can expose young athletes to stress' (2001, p. 42) and, as well as potentially affecting child wellbeing and development, this can lead to drop-out – a consequence which runs counter to many national sport policies that link to broader public health, physical activity, and social policy aims. These matters are not necessarily helped if there is a culturally dominant tendency for participants, often based on the desires of parents, to be engaged in programmes that reflect elite and professional sport practices and objectives. To this end, Chalip and Hutchinson (2017) espouse greater coordination of local and national efforts to formulate and implement policy to build the status of participatory youth programming – and by implication, re-orientate coaching practices.

The absence of coaches in the literature of youth sport making might provide important insights for policymakers and leaders of sport governing bodies. Youth sport policies all over the world aim at having as many young people as possible being physically active for as long as possible. Coaches are an important stakeholder to achieve ambitious policy goals for youth sport, both at grassroots and elite level. Therefore, it is important that their voices and opinions are taken into consideration in the formulation and agenda-setting of youth sport policies. The interests of coaches do not appear to be sufficiently represented in youth sport policy making processes. Coaches therefore should be encouraged to make their voices heard, supported to develop their understanding of policy making, and presented with legitimate channels through which to contribute to policy discussions the feed into its formulation, in order to aid coaches to better represent themselves in the policy process.

Other professionalisation processes within traditional voluntary-based sport systems have resulted in increased competency among coaches. More coaches are more qualified as a result of youth sport policies and state funds that focus on education programs for coaches. This has both advantages and disadvantages. On one hand, the welfare and safeguarding of youth athletes are being strengthened. On the other hand, increased pressure and time consumption might lead to a drop-out of volunteer coaches. Policymakers thus should consider the extent to which bureaucratic requirements are relevant features of welfare and safeguarding policies, and the extent to which such policies protect coaches' interests as well. Coaches seem to be key drivers in the professionalisation of the voluntary sport sector into a high-performance sector, and thus their expertise and the enactment of it is likely to go hand-in-hand with the future success of sport federations and clubs' pursuit of sporting success, and so their role in the policy process and how this is managed is of critical importance.

In existing literature on youth sport, (social) problems associated with coaches and coaching practices are reported in studies more often than considerations surrounding what could be done to further support coaches, engender coach confidence and enhance coaching practice. Indeed, the literature highlights the ways that safeguarding discourses can displace coaching pedagogy and engender a sense of anxiety which can interfere with coaching practice. While existing literature does offer consideration on the role of the coach (both positive and negative) in and for youth sport policies, there is a lack of focus focus on the perspectives of the coaches themselves. The welfare of coaches is an important issue as well, especially in regard to coach wellbeing, burnout and attrition. Indeed, Cronin *et al.* (2019) emphasise that sport clubs have a duty of care to their employees and volunteers, and that organisational leadership should take seriously how they care for their coaches, and this is especially pertinent in grassroots settings where coaches are less confident and in relation to young coaches employed within elite environments yet with limited professional experience. Such factors and facets of the sporting infrastructure will of course come to bear on the quality and complexion of how sport policy is enacted and experienced.

As a final point, several articles reviewed for the research from which this chapter stems reflect a broadening remit of sport policy to also include and promote physical activity, yet there was no exposition of the role of sport coaches in the promotion and delivery of physical activity, other than to highlight this policy gap. Such a focus should therefore be more explicitly attended to in policy formulation, and coaches who are or would be charged with delivering on such an agenda should be able to feed in their perspectives on this matter to this process.

## Summary and Future Directions

This chapter reviewed research on youth sport policies, and specifically addressed issues related to the role and representation of coaches in these policies. The review suggests that coaches have not had a significant role in youth sport policy-making nor are they mentioned to any great extent in the content of youth sport policies aligned with topics across school sport and physical activity, community-based participation, and elite sport and events especially. Given that the review examined only published research, there remains an open question as to whether the general absence of coaches in youth sport policy literature is representative of their lack of involvement and recognition in policy processes and/or whether it is a consequence of researchers not specifically focusing on coaches and youth sport policy.

Moreover, the focus of the review on policy-making stages means that further work to review literature on the implementation of youth sport policies is recommended. Coaches are likely to be accorded more significant roles through the course of youth sport policy implementation and may therefore be more active as policy actors through the implementation stage of the policy process. Further research in this regard aligns with Potrac *et al.*'s (2016) proposal that future studies should focus on the (micro)political nature of coaching, not only at grassroots level but also in elite sport and school sport.

## References

Bjørndal, C.T., Ronglan, L.T., and Andersen, S.S., 2017. Talent development as an ecology of games: A case study of Norwegian handball. *Sport, Education and Society*, 22 (7), 864–877.

Brackenridge, C., 2004. Women and children first? Child abuse and child protection in sport. *Sport in society*, 7 (3), 322–337.

Chalip, L. and Hutchinson, R., 2017. Reinventing youth sport: Formative findings from a state-level action research project. *Sport in Society*, 20 (1), 30–46.

Cronin, C., *et al.*, 2019. "The cost of caring". *In:* C. Cronin and K. Armour, eds. *Care in sport coaching*. New York: Routledge, 101–123.

Donnelly, P., *et al.*, 2016. Protecting youth in sport: An examination of harassment policies. *International Journal of Sport Policy and Politics*, 8 (1), 33–50.

De Knop, P. and De Martelaer, K., 2001. Quantitative and qualitative evaluation of youth sport in Flanders and the Netherlands: A case study. *Sport, Education and Society*, 6 (1), 35–51.

Erwin, H., *et al.*, 2014. Best practices and recommendations for increasing physical activity in youth. *Journal of Physical Education, Recreation and Dance*, 85 (7), 27–34.

Fry, J.M. and McNeill, M.C., 2011. 'In the nation's good' physical education and school sport in Singapore. *European Physical Education Review*, 17 (3), 287–300.
Garratt, D., Piper, H. and Taylor, B., 2013. 'Safeguarding' sports coaching: Foucault, genealogy and critique. *Sport, Education and Society*, 18 (5), 615–629.
Hayton, J., 2018. "They do treat us as a bit normal now": Students' experiences of liminality and communitas whilst volunteering on a sports-based outreach project. *International Review for the Sociology of Sport*, 53 (7), 869–889.
Houlihan, B., 2000. Sporting excellence, schools and sports development: The politics of crowded policy spaces. *European Physical Education Review*, 6 (2), 171–193.
Houlihan, B. and Chapman, P., 2017. Talent identification and development in elite youth disability sport. *Sport in Society*, 20 (1), 107–125.
Houlihan, B. and Green, M., 2006. The changing status of school sport and physical education: Explaining policy change. *Sport, Education and Society*, 11 (1), 73–92.
Johnson, J.E., Giannoulakis, C., and Scott, B.F., 2017. Interscholastic competitive balance: An examination of state athletic association administrators. *Journal of Sport Management*, 31 (3), 256–274.
Jung, H., Pope, S. and Kirk, D., 2016. Policy for physical education and school sport in England, 2003–2010: Vested interests and dominant discourses. *Physical Education and Sport Pedagogy*, 21 (5), 501–516.
Kerr, R. and Kerr, G., 2020. Promoting athlete welfare: A proposal for an international surveillance system. *Sport Management Review*, 23 (1), 95–103.
Lindsey, I. and Jeanes, R., 2011. "Youth sport policy". *In:* K. Armour and K. Harlow, eds. *Introduction to sport pedagogy for teachers and coaches*. New York: Pearson Education, 77–87.
Lund, S., 2014. Regulation and deregulation in education policy: New reforms and school sports in Swedish upper secondary education. *Sport, Education and Society*, 19 (3), 241–257.
Miah, A. and Rich, E., 2006. Genetic tests for ability?: Talent identification and the value of an open future. *Sport, Education and Society*, 11 (3), 259–273.
Parent, M.M., *et al.*, 2015. The sustainability of the Youth Olympic Games: Stakeholder networks and institutional perspectives. *International Review for the Sociology of Sport*, 50 (3), 326–348.
Parent, S. and Hlimi, K.E., 2013. Athlete protection in Quebec's sport system: Assessments, problems, and challenges. *Journal of Sport and Social Issues*, 37 (3), 284–296.
Phillpots, L., 2013. An analysis of the policy process for physical education and school sport: The rise and demise of school sport partnerships. *International Journal of Sport Policy and Politics*, 5 (2), 193–211.
Platts, C. and Smith, A., 2009. The education, rights and welfare of young people in professional football in England: Some implications of the white paper on sport. *International Journal of Sport Policy*, 1 (3), 323–339.
Pope, C.C., 2011. The physical education and sport interface: Models, maxims and maelstrom. *European Physical Education Review*, 17 (3), 273–285.
Pot, N. and van Hilvoorde, I., 2013. Generalising the effects of school sports: Comparing the cultural contexts of school sports in the Netherlands and the USA. *Sport in Society*, 16 (9), 1164–1175.
Potrac, P., Nelson, L. and O'Gorman, J., 2016. Exploring the everyday realities of grass-roots football coaching: Towards a relational perspective. *Soccer and Society*, 17 (6), 910–925.
Rhind, D.J., *et al.*, 2017. Building a system to safeguard children in sport: The eight CHILDREN pillars. *Journal of Sport and Social Issues*, 41 (2), 151–171.
Riehl, S., Snelgrove, R., and Edwards, J., 2019. Mechanisms of institutional maintenance in minor hockey. *Journal of Sport Management*, 33 (2), 93–105.
Skirstad, B., Waddington, I., and Säfvenbom, R., 2012. Issues and problems in the organisation of children's sport: A case study of Norway. *European Physical Education Review*. 18 (3), 309–321.
Støckel, J.T., *et al.*, 2010. Sport for children and youth in the Scandinavian countries. *Sport in Society*, 13 (4), 625–642.
Strittmatter, A.M., 2016. Defining a problem to fit the solution: A neo-institutional explanation for legitimising the bid for the 2016 lillehammer winter youth olympic games. *International Journal of Sport Policy and Politics*, 8 (3), 421–437.
Strittmatter, A.M. and Skille, E.Å., 2017. Boosting youth sport? Implementation of norwegian youth sport policy through the 2016 lillehammer winter youth olympic games. *Sport in society*, 20 (1), 144–160.
Stylianou, M., Hogan, A., and Enright, E., 2019. Youth sport policy: The enactment and possibilities of 'soft policy' in schools. *Sport, Education and Society*, 24 (2), 182–194.

Susnara, D. and Williams, D., 2019. An analysis of classroom accommodations and return to learn protocols for students with concussion symptoms. *International Journal of Sport Policy and Politics*, 11 (1), 119–132.

Velenczei, A. and Gál, A., 2011. New challenges, old answers in hungarian sport: The case of talent management. *European Journal for Sport and Society*, 8 (4), 281–297.

Vertommen, T., *et al.*, 2016. A green flag for the Flag System? Towards a child protection policy in Flemish sport. *International Journal of Sport Policy and Politics*, 8 (1), 15–31.

White, A.J., *et al.*, 2019. The lack of age representation in the governance of Rugby Union in England. *Sociology of Sport Journal*, 36 (4), 300–310.

# 39

# VOLUNTEERING IN CHILDREN'S SPORT: FROM MOTIVATION TO CHILD PROTECTION

*Matheus Galdino, Sebastian Gehrmann, and Pamela Wicker*

## Introduction

Volunteers represent a critical resource for the delivery of services, coaching, and community sport programmes, especially aiming at the provision of children's sport around grassroots and recreational settings (Busser and Carruthers, 2010; Nichols and Taylor, 2010; Breuer and Feiler, 2019, 2020). In Germany, for example, voluntary coaches in community sport clubs have reported that children represent the main target group of their coaching activities (Breuer and Feiler, 2020). While a plethora of studies exist on volunteerism in community sport in general (for reviews see Wicker, 2017, 2019), much less research has been conducted on volunteering in children's sport. The majority of these studies have focused on voluntary coaches.

The purpose of this chapter is to review this body of research through the lenses of coaching antecedents and child protection. This chapter recognises that within children's sport, the person performing the coaching role is of particular importance because of a lack of role identity between those who demand the service provision (i.e. typically parents) and those who effectively consume the service (i.e. children). This discrepancy opens the door for misinterpreting the needs, the interaction, and even the relationship between coaches and children, yielding increased importance to the roles of incentive, power, and trust around volunteering in children's sport.

This chapter progresses with the following structure: The second section presents a literature review on antecedents of voluntary coaching, including volunteer motivation and commitment as well as volunteer education and social components. The third section outlines issues of child protection and its meaning to voluntary coaches. The fourth section provides implications for children's sports, while the fifth section concludes this review and suggests avenues for future research.

## Review of Current Research

### *Antecedents of Voluntary Coaching in Children's Sports*

Volunteering in recreational or grassroots sports can be perceived as an entry-level step to gain practical experiences as a coach, while interacting with children may offer opportunities to nurture a constructive environment both from a social and sportive perspective that may last for

DOI: 10.4324/9781003199359-45

years ahead, especially for children themselves. In fact, when it comes to personal and professional development, many individuals start their coaching careers as volunteers, whereby they also collaborate to make a positive difference in the lives of youth sport participants. From the volunteer's side, learning experiences may be accumulated across different coaching environments, age groups, and background conditions. Likewise, youth sport clubs and amateur organisations benefit from the support of voluntary coaches who contribute to the successful delivery of services within community sport programmes.

In terms of participation, children and youngsters engage in sport whenever the activities are fun and stimulate friendship, skill development, and fitness (Busser and Carruthers, 2010). To foster such a positive environment, volunteers represent a key component within the youth sport's workforce (Kim *et al.*, 2010; Engelberg *et al.*, 2014; Harman and Doherty, 2014). However, since volunteering involves considerable time, effort, and no pay, the motivation behind volunteers should be acknowledged, comprehended, and valued both by the individuals themselves and the organisations delivering sport services for children, since it resonates with an intangible source of investment. The commitment demonstrated by individuals may also be recognised as a crucial element for continuous volunteering, as they tend to bond with the organisation and its youth sport programmes. Besides, a respectable set of interactions amongst children with coaches and parents must be encouraged, as any signs of misconduct may compromise the environment. Therefore, by better understanding what drives volunteering motivation and commitment, as well as how to incentivise the education and social components around volunteers, youth sport organisations may strengthen the recruitment, retention, and experience of volunteers at the recreational and grassroots levels, providing more opportunities for children and youngsters to engage in sport activities over time.

## Volunteer Motivation

Tracking the antecedents of voluntary coaching, Busser and Carruthers (2010) studied the motivations of youth sport coaches at the recreational level in the United States, exploring their potential and motivational differences based on gender and length of volunteer experience. Positive values were suggested as the primary functional motivation for volunteering as a coach since respondents reported their wish for a positive contribution to the lives of youngsters. Similar findings were reported by Kim *et al.* (2010), who revealed that values and understanding were the first and second highest motives, respectively, amongst individuals volunteering at international, national, local, and special-needs youth organisations. Additional motives of importance were associated with social, personal growth, and self-serving aspects (Busser and Carruthers, 2010). Amongst non-parents, a prior involvement in the sport represented the main reason to volunteer in Australia, whereas for parent volunteers having a child involved turned out to be the primary motive, followed by a feeling of obligation (Engelberg *et al.*, 2014). Moreover, Graham *et al.* (2016) stated how male volunteers have used youth sport to fulfill their fatherhood responsibilities. Specifically for female volunteers, values and understanding were appointed as their highest motivational factors (Kim *et al.*, 2010). Nonetheless, female coaches were significantly less likely than male coaches to believe themselves to be more knowledgeable about their sport than others (Busser and Carruthers, 2010). Kim *et al.* (2010) also identified that volunteers working at international and special-needs sport events displayed higher motivations in comparison to volunteers at national and local organisations, which could be signs of preferences towards particular opportunities to improve professional skills and personal experiences amongst distinct sociocultural backgrounds.

## *Volunteer Commitment*

While focusing on volunteering commitment, Engelberg *et al.* (2014) analysed the commitment of volunteers to their youth sport organisations, the relationships between commitment and volunteer motivations, as well as attitudes and perceptions of volunteering. A prevalent view about commitment was that it fluctuated depending on the volunteer experience, with participants reporting an increasing level of commitment over time, and temporary declines often resulting from negative experiences (Engelberg *et al.*, 2014). In German football and track and field clubs, for example, improved voluntary experiences have shown to be influenced by the organisational culture, the network capacity, and the frequency of hosting social events, which consequently combine to incentivise volunteering engagement and retention (Swierzy *et al.*, 2018). Interestingly, in a study about the experiences of working mother-coaches, spending time alongside children, developing life skills, and role modeling were appointed as the main reasons for sustaining their voluntary youth coaching (Leberman and LaVoi, 2011), providing signs to augment how commitment levels may also be associated with a higher sense of purpose and relational enrichment as part of the volunteering services. On the other hand, father-coaches have increased their involvement in volunteering in youth sport due to a higher pressure to provide and share caregiving responsibilities (Graham *et al.*, 2016), leading to positive outcomes for the children's lives.

## *Volunteer Education and Social Components*

Volunteering in youth sport settings can be a complex phenomenon due to the social interactions amongst volunteers, children, and parents. Parental behaviour emerges as a paramount aspect influencing the volunteering environment because parents are responsible for the decisions about where their children might participate and get involved with sports, while holding the option of terminating unsatisfactory relationships (Horne *et al.*, 2020). This scenario represents a typical example of the principal-agency problem, whereby in this case parents (the principal) require the services of coaches (the agent), even though the actual consumption of services will be experienced by their children and not by the parents themselves.

Considering this dynamic, Horne *et al.* (2020) examined the relationship between parents and coaches of youth tennis players, identifying how signs of limited communication, mistrust, and a lack of shared goals between parents and coaches can negatively influence their relationship while generating a suboptimal athletic development for children. Raising further awareness to the concerns and issues youth sport coaches present, Wiersma and Sherman (2005) also emphasised the pedagogical, psychological, and managerial aspects required for coaching and parental education. For example, learning how to make practices fun, promoting team building and developing mental skills, as well as understanding appropriate physical contact have been captured as important educational avenues to meet the needs of voluntary coaches. On the other hand, barriers and problems of coaching education have also been discussed, such as the time demands to attend courses and the lack of personnel to implement education programmes. With that in mind, coaches recommended less formal approaches for coaching preparation instead (i.e. mentoring, roundtable discussions, online tools), while pointing out how parental codes of conduct may help control parental behaviour at practices and games (Wiersma and Sherman, 2005).

Since voluntary coaches are not financially rewarded to conduct their services in children's sports, a conflicting view of expectations may appear as part of the parent-coach relationship, with parents potentially correlating their financial investment towards the sport organisation to reflect on a more frequent proximity between coaches and children even when lessons or practices are not underway. Within this rationale, Horne *et al.* (2020) pointed out how parents were often disillusioned with youth tennis coaches not attending their children's events, whereas coaches framed these situations as opportunity costs, requiring them to forgo income from paid coaching lessons during the same period of time. Overall, the assumptions of parents and coaches inevitably influence the effectiveness of voluntary services in children's sports. Therefore, expectations should be clearly aligned, trust should be established, and communication should be fostered to compensate for the lack of a monetary investment for coaching duties, as well as to stimulate a positive environment for the children involved.

## Child Protection through Voluntary Coaches

In sports, the coach-athlete relationship can be portrayed as an important experience for children due to the underlying social and fun interactions. It may resemble a relationship of trust, guidance, protection, affection, and admiration in competitive just as in grassroots sports. Consequently, a voluntary coach should provide the same skills as a full-time coach concerning the relationship with their athletes. Depending on the environment, a coach may act as a supporter who contributes to the development of social skills, especially in lower-level coaching such as recreational or grassroots sports where actively encouraging children and youngsters may serve as an incentive for continuous participation (Robinson, 2010). Nevertheless, although the relationship between an athlete and his/her voluntary coach may be perceived as a positive influence, there can also be problems of abuse, as coaches represent authority figures with power over athletes even outside of the sport setting (Stirling and Kerr, 2009; Robinson, 2010; Fasting, 2013). Hence, voluntary coaches in children's sports must be aware of their ethical and moral decisions, considering the potential short- and long-term effects that any abusive relationship could generate. Moreover, these coaches should also have a good understanding of their legal obligations in terms of negligence, duty of care, and child abuse.

Reporting on how a distant relationship between children and their parents suggests a risk factor for sexual abuse, especially in cases where the father is distant, Brackenridge (2000) identified that female athletes with low self-esteem can develop a close emotional attachment to coaches and fall prey to sexual exploitation. To avoid this, she argued that it is necessary that sport clubs place importance on systematic recruitment, screening, induction, and monitoring of voluntary coaches. This is hard to manage for many sport clubs, especially for the ones with fewer (human) resources as they rely mostly on volunteers (Brackenridge, 2000).

The obvious need to tackle child abuse and sexual harassment has pushed youth sport organisations to develop preventive and protective measures in policy development. By immediately acknowledging the risks of power asymmetries in the coach-athlete relationship, safeguarding initiatives should be drawn to support a healthy and positive environment for children participating in sport activities. This aspect applies to full-time coaches as well as to voluntary coaches. For example, as part of the UK Coaching's policy for safeguarding children and young athletes, its Code of Practice for Sports Coaches emphasises that "coaches must not engage in behaviour that constitutes any form of abuse (physical, sexual, emotional, neglect, bullying)" (UK Coaching, 2018).

Yet, discrepancies between requirements or policy guidelines and actual safeguarding practices still prevail. In Canada, where most sport clubs have a voluntary base and are autonomous, Donnelly *et al.* (2016) captured how maltreatment issues have been addressed, showcasing that not all youth sport organisations within the country were meeting national recommendations for abuse and harassment, failing to provide clear and detailed articulation of the rights of the parties, as well as the complaint and appeal procedures. An explanation of this problem is seen in the fact that many clubs indeed have a harassment officer, but they mostly work on a voluntary basis. A similar scenario has been witnessed in the voluntary sport club sector in England (Brackenridge, 2002), where the main child protection issues appeared to suffer from an extremely varied pattern of awareness given the lack of clarity and inconsistent support, suggesting that local authorities should monitor the developments in child protection policy. She also found that just 2% of sport clubs have issued written rules or expectations to volunteers. Altogether, 12% of clubs said that they always offer child protection training to their volunteers. On the other hand, 75% of clubs reported that they would be confident in handling child protection disclosures from volunteers (Brackenridge, 2002). In additional group interviews, club representatives also pointed at the uncomfortable situation for volunteers concerning false allegations (Brackenridge, 2002).

Although aimed at improving the protection of children by ensuring unsuitable people are prevented from working with them, the implementation of policies has also imposed burdens on volunteers and voluntary administrators in Scotland due to multiple disclosure check requirements and the difficulty for volunteering in a child protection officer role (Nichols and Taylor, 2010). In a survey, 15% of volunteers reported that these disclosure check requirements would represent a threat to continuing voluntary work. This percentage is lower than for other reasons that threaten the continuity of volunteering, such as the time availability or the demands of individuals' paid jobs. However, two-thirds of respondents felt that taking a disclosure check is discouraging for potential volunteers (Nichols and Taylor, 2010).

## Implications for Children's Sport Coaching

Voluntary coaches are an important element in youth sport settings, where they are driven by motivation, commitment, and educational and social opportunities in order to continue with their voluntary engagement as well as their coaching career development. While the motivation to volunteer has been associated with positive values, understanding, as well as social and personal growth, volunteer commitment tends to be triggered by positive experiences that sustain both a personal and a professional growth from the perspective of voluntary coaches involved in youth sport. Positive experiences for coaches occur when their working efforts are recognised, they are provided autonomy and support to undertake the role and a collaborative, supportive environment is established. To avoid a potential lack of appreciation, unusual turnovers, and even burnouts amongst volunteers, youth sport organisations should offer operational support and training opportunities that may stimulate individuals to remain involved in children's sports. A proper orientation programme, constant feedback sessions, mentoring from experienced personnel, open roundtable discussions amongst voluntary coaches, and the willingness to invest in certification courses can be avenues to improve the retention of volunteers while securing a positive social engagement beyond short-term benefits in service delivery.

Besides, recognising the importance of a safe, healthy, and protective environment not only enables children and youngsters to participate in sports and physical activity more freely but also stimulates proper coaching behaviour at the recreational and grassroots levels, increasing the possibilities for optimal outcomes amongst all parties involved. Additionally, safeguarding initiatives should be constantly fostered and reviewed to secure an effective implementation of child protection policies. These include, for example, nominating child safety officers who are trained and qualified to address confidential disclosures and complaints, promoting a gender-balanced volunteer base for coaching and managerial roles in order to decrease risks of abuse and harassment originated from excessive power and negligence, as well as incorporating formal rules and codes of conduct to place parameters around the coach-athlete relationship and guide ethics and behaviour amongst coaches and parents alike.

## Summary and Future Research Directions

This chapter focused on reviewing the antecedents of voluntary coaching and child protection in youth sport. Overall, volunteers have emphasised that positive values, personal growth, and relational enrichment are important outcomes in their involvement with children, through which they can contribute to support a positive youth development environment while also acknowledging the non-monetary benefits generated from such a genuine caregiving collaboration. On the other hand, the imbalance of power between coaches and athletes, and the need to monitor parental behaviour have been recognised as challenging scenarios that may potentially lead to uncomfortable relationships amongst the parties, with clear testimonials of long-term effects on children's lives.

Although the existing literature has uncovered volunteers' motivation to get involved and their commitment to remain engaged in youth sport coaching mostly through qualitative studies, future research may still benefit from integrating quantitative findings to better analyse the behaviour and retention of volunteers with longitudinal data. In terms of child protection, since the topic carries a high level of sensitivity and underreporting amongst victims, future research could concentrate on understanding the lack of reactivity amongst peers, family members, and community sport officials to potential incidents that seem to violate social and ethical norms in their surroundings. As any youth sport organisation relies on a positive environment to sustain its effective delivery of services, encouraging, monitoring, and safeguarding children should be a priority area, protecting them from their vulnerability to abuse and harassment even outside the sport setting.

## References

Brackenridge, C., 2000. Harassment, sexual abuse, and safety of the female athlete. *Clinics in Sports Medicine*, 19 (2), 187–198.

Brackenridge, C., 2002. ' … so what?' Attitudes of the voluntary sector towards child protection in sports clubs. *Managing Leisure*, 7 (2), 103–123.

Breuer, C. and Feiler, S., 2019. *Sportvereine in Deutschland: Organisationen und Personen. Sportentwicklungsberichte für Deutschland 2017/2018 – Teil 1.* Bonn: Bundesinstitut für Sportwissenschaft.

Breuer, C. and Feiler, S., 2020. *TrainerInnen und ÜbungsleiterInnen in Sportvereinen in Deutschland. Sportentwicklungsberichte für Deutschland 2017/2018 – Teil 2.* Bonn: Bundesinstitut für Sportwissenschaft.

Busser, J.A. and Carruthers, C.P., 2010. Youth sport volunteer coach motivation. *Managing Leisure*, 15 (1–2), 128–139.

Donnelly, P., *et al.*, 2016. Protecting youth in sport: An examination of harassment policies. *International Journal of Sport Policy and Politics*, 8 (1), 33–50.

Engelberg, T., Skinner, J., and Zakus, D., 2014. What does commitment mean to volunteers in youth sport organisations? *Sport in Society*, 17 (1), 52–67.

Fasting, K., 2013. Dangerous liaisons: Harassment and abuse in coaching. *In*: P. Potrac, W. Gilbert, and J. Denison, eds. *Routledge handbook of sports coaching*. London: Routledge, 333–344.

Graham, J.A., Dixon, M.A., and Hazen-Swann, N., 2016. Coaching dads: Understanding managerial implications of fathering through sport. *Journal of Sport Management*, 30 (1), 40–51.

Harman, A. and Doherty, A., 2014. The psychological contract of volunteer youth sport coaches. *Journal of Sport Management*, 28 (6), 687–699.

Horne, E., Woolf, J., and Green, C., 2022. Relationship dynamics between parents and coaches: Are they failing young athletes? *Managing Sport and Leisure*, 27 (3), 224–240.

Kim, M., Zhang, J.J., and Connaughton, D.P., 2010. Comparison of volunteer motivations in different youth sport organisations. *European Sport Management Quarterly*, 10 (3), 343–365.

Leberman, S.I. and LaVoi, N.M., 2011. Juggling balls and roles, working mother-coaches in youth sport: Beyond dualistic worker-mother identity. *Journal of Sport Management*, 25 (5), 474–488.

Nichols, G. and Taylor, P., 2010. The balance of benefit and burden? The impact of child protection legislation on volunteers in Scottish sports clubs. *European Sport Management Quarterly*, 10 (1), 31–47.

Robinson, P.E., 2010. *Foundations of sports coaching*. London: Routledge.

Stirling, A.E. and Kerr, G.A., 2009. Abused athletes' perceptions of the coach-athlete relationship. *Sport in Society: Cultures, Commerce, Media, Politics*, 12 (2), 227–239.

Swierzy, P., Wicker, P., and Breuer, C., 2018. The impact of organisational capacity on voluntary engagement in sports clubs: A multi-level analysis. *Sport Management Review*, 21 (3), 307–320.

UK Coaching, 2018. *Code of practice for sports coaches: rights, relationships and responsibilities* [online]. https://www.ukcoaching.org/resources/topics/guides/code-of-practice-for-sports-coaches [Accessed 10 June 2021].

Wicker, P., 2017. Volunteerism and volunteer management in sport. *Sport Management Review*, 20 (4) 325–337.

Wicker, P., 2019. Volunteering in sports clubs and its impacts. *In*: P. Downward, B. *et al.*, eds. *The SAGE Handbook of Sports Economics*. London: SAGE Publications, 92–101.

Wiersma, L.D. and Sherman, C.P., 2005. Volunteer youth sport coaches' perspectives of coaching education/certification and parental codes of conduct. *Research Quarterly for Exercise and Sport*, 76 (3), 324–338.

# 40
# RETAINING VOLUNTEER COACHES IN CHILD AND YOUTH SPORT

*Haley Baxter and Katie E. Misener*

## Introduction

Community sport organisations (CSOs) offer opportunities for organised sport participation in both recreational and competitive sport (Hoye *et al.*, 2020). While CSOs offer sport participation opportunities for individuals of all ages, there is a large emphasis on serving children due to the value placed on sport as a tool for positive youth development (Coakley, 2016). Children's sport coaches are tasked with responsibilities that include planning and leading practices and competitions, scheduling, and other administrative tasks (Hoye *et al.*, 2020). In addition, coaches often provide mentorship and guidance to youth athletes to support their personal and athletic development. In particular, research demonstrates that volunteer youth sport coaches who prioritise the psychological and social well-being of their athletes over winning can play an important mentorship role, support positive youth development, and encourage life-long involvement in sport and physical activity (e.g., Fraser-Thomas *et al.*, 2005). Coaches have an important social influence on children's enjoyment and effort in sport (e.g. Chan *et al.*, 2012). Considering the important role sport coaches can play in the lives of youth athletes, retaining skilled and dedicated coaches is of concern. Some sport cultures such as gymnastics and swimming have transitioned to an increasingly professionalised structure and often draw on the expertise of career coaches who are more typically paid for their services. The use of paid coaches can provide enhanced expertise and commitment to an organisation but often results in increased participant fees as coaching salaries add substantial financial expense to a club's budget. Traditionally, the non-profit structure of youth sport in countries such as Canada, Australia, New Zealand and much of Europe relies on the commitment and dedication of unpaid volunteers (e.g., administrators, board members, officials, coaches). Youth sport coaches represent a significant proportion of CSO volunteers and play a crucial role in the management and front-line delivery of sport services available for children (Harman and Doherty, 2014). Volunteer youth sport coaches are a unique group of individuals who have different motives, challenges, and needs. Yet, many volunteer youth sport coaches experience stress, lack of support from parents and sport administrators, and declining well-being which can contribute to a negative experience and impact their willingness to continue in coaching roles. Considerations for the well-being of volunteer coaches should evolve from research that suggests that coaches who experience psychological well-being are more likely to develop healthy relationships with youth

 DOI: 10.4324/9781003199359-46

athletes (Thelwell *et al.*, 2016). These findings highlight the importance of the fostering well-being amongst volunteers not only for retention but also to serve the best interests of youth participants.

In voluntary organisations such as non-profit children's sport organisations, staff and volunteers are distinct groups that face unique challenges. In contrast to the financial impact that losing a paid job may have on an individual (and their family), volunteers may have greater autonomy to leave at any time which can result in challenges for the organisation (Pearce, 1993). Thus, mechanisms for retaining this important group must be considered in order to continue to provide sport services for youth athletes. This chapter will outline the current profile of volunteer youth sport coaches, and discuss factors influencing turnover and burnout, as well as particular strategies for retaining this important group of volunteers.

## Review of Current Research

### *Current Profile of Volunteer Youth Sport Coaches*

Research and data on the current profile of youth sport coaches on a national and international scale is limited, however, common hegemonic traits have been identified in the limited findings within North American, European and Australian contexts. In Canada, findings show that the profile of youth sport volunteers is narrow, with roles being filled primarily by university- or college-educated males, ages 34–44, employed full-time, with a child involved in the sport (Doherty, 2005). This profile is consistent with research conducted across North America and Europe that has found that with the exception of some female-dominated sports (e.g., ringette, gymnastics) men are often involved in more highly visible coaching roles whereas women are more often involved in roles such as assistant coach or administrative functions (Baxter *et al.*, 2021). Children of parents who volunteer in sport and reside in Ontario Canada have even expressed a gendered importance of fathers in highly visible coaching roles in comparison to volunteer assistant coaching and administrative roles held by mothers that are often under-appreciated (Trussell, 2016). Recruitment of parents as coaches through word of mouth solicitation is a common and convenient method for non-profit youth sport organisations facing resource constraints and low volunteer numbers. Despite the ease of recruiting parent coaches and the benefits of their involvement (e.g., positive social interactions between parent and child), there are also feelings among youth athletes of increased pressure, expectation, and criticism for mistakes when a child is coached by their parent in addition to concerns about favouritism by the parent-coach towards their child (Weiss and Fretwell, 2005).

Turnover of parent coaches is high once their child is no longer participating in the sport. Findings from a municipal parks and recreation department's soccer program in the United States found that while parents initial desire to volunteer is because it directly benefited their child, coaches appeared to be motivated by the desire to help youth more generally (Busser and Carruthers, 2010). Busser and Carruthers (2010) encourage organisations to strategically retain volunteers and consider ways to support sense of volunteer identity amongst parent-youth coaches to encourage more prolonged volunteer involvement even as their child ages out of the youth sport system. Future research must also take into account contextual differences as a result of both location and sport as to how this impacts the necessity for volunteer involvement in youth sport. Traditionally, in the United States, the sport system is more closely tied to educational institutions, whereas in the United Kingdom and Europe, club systems are more deeply embedded in the community as separate organisations with looser ties to education-based organisations. Future research on these nuanced differences may bring insights into the impact, need, or effective use of volunteer coaches, the experience of volunteer coaches themselves, how volunteer coaches may influence the youth sport experience, the sustainability of sport systems, and youth access to sport.

The nature of volunteering in youth sport can differ based on the life stage (e.g., parenting young children) and motives of the volunteer, and the experience can vary based on how a club recruits and manages volunteers and from what sources. For example, while the majority of sport volunteers are parents (e.g., Doherty, 2005), North America's close ties between academic and sport institutions offer the opportunity to draw from students in high school and college/university. For instance, in Canada, it has become more commonplace for university sport management programs or athletic departments to partner with community sport organisations as a way to create volunteer opportunities for sport management students or varsity athletes, some of whom take on voluntary coaching roles. This can provide students with career-related benefits, opportunities to foster social relationships, skill/knowledge development, and satisfaction within the role. Organisations may benefit by having an ongoing relationship with a school and/or program in order to maintain a stream of incoming students. However, student turnover can also present an issue for sport organisations as volunteer certification processes for some sports are time-consuming. It can be expensive and investing in volunteers with particular skill sets requires an investment of these resources.

In addition to students, older adult volunteers can also be an important source of expertise to draw from to increase the pool of youth sport coaches (Hamm-Kerwin *et al.*, 2009). These individuals may have coached previously when they had children playing sport and may have taken a break for various reasons once their children left the sport. However, they are an important resource for clubs and can contribute without self-interest that often arises with parent volunteers (Hamm-Kerwin *et al.*, 2009). In addition, Coleman (2002) found that amongst volunteers in English county youth cricket, retirees contributed more hours and fulfilled multiple roles including and beyond coaching within the club. With an increasing aging population worldwide, this may be a more applicable source of volunteers for sport organisations that are structured within the club system versus an education-based system. This strategy may allow for individuals who are partially or fully retired to contribute increased free time no longer spent working, and expertise to foster community through intergenerational social connections.

## *Factors Influencing Turnover and Burnout*

There are a wide range of reasons that individuals discontinue coaching including burnout, lack of enjoyment, lack of challenge, time constraints, work-life balance, administrative problems, and lack of opportunity for development (Rundle-Thiele and Auld, 2009). As previously mentioned, many parent-coaches simply discontinue coaching after their child no longer participates in the sport or advances to levels beyond their coaching capabilities (Busser and Carruthers, 2010). However, some parents would continue to coach teams their child does not play on, as long as the commitment does not jeopardise their ability to see their own child play (Rundle-Thiele and Auld, 2009). The perceived lack of flexibility of volunteer coach expectations or inflexible sport schedules should be considered in order to accommodate for the challenges youth coaches face. Coaches tend to contribute more time to their volunteer pursuit than sport volunteers in other roles and are often required to commit to multiple sessions on both weekdays and weekends (Harman and Doherty, 2014).

Not only does the increase in weekly sport-specific training sessions have implications for burnout of youth sport coaches, but this may also have implications for youth athlete burnout. The burnout of youth athletes is negative for the overall influx of future youth sport coaches as former athletes who remain passionate and involved in the sport offer a pool of future volunteer coaches to draw from as many volunteer coaches are former players who have accumulated a passion and understanding of the game through participation. Cuskelly and O'Brien (2013) offer a transition extension framework to understand the impetus for former players choosing to transition to volunteers. Positive youth development (PYD) is also a popular framework for guiding research related to sport for development. Future research or interventions should consider the potential PYD outcomes that may result from looking to develop youth beyond their athletic abilities and intentionally focusing on harnessing the potential of youth athletes as future volunteer coaches themselves. In fact, in Portugal, the Instituto Português do Desporto e Juventude acts as a national governing body for sport federations and provides a holistic array of development resources including training and certification in sport and youth volunteering resources (IPDJ, n.d.). The centralisation of these resources is quite different than sport systems in North America that tend to remain insular to a specific sport.

In Hertting *et al.*'s (2020) study of Swedish junior soccer coaches found that other factors heighten perceptions of stress among youth sport coaches, including scheduling conflicts with family commitments, not having adequate time to develop coaching plans, feeling pressured when selecting the team, and demands to achieve high-performance results/winning. These stressors can impact the overall coaching experience and can lead to turnover and burnout among youth sport coaches.

Turnover and burnout are particularly high among female coaches who face unique challenges in the sport coaching role. Busser and Carruthers (2010) found that only 28% of females coaching within a municipal soccer program in the United States coached beyond their first year in comparison to 70% of males. Research suggests that female coaches discontinue in sport coaching based on their perceived lack of ability and success and the belief that they are less knowledgeable about the sport than others (Busser and Carruthers, 2010). Currently there remains a lack of research across a variety of countries and contexts on preventing burnout and turnover amongst female volunteer coaches, including volunteer coaches within the context of youth sport. Understanding how particular retention strategies can be effective for retaining female volunteer coaches at the youth sport level has important implications for challenging gender roles and increasing diversity amongst volunteer sport coaches within community sport (Baxter *et al.*, 2021).

## Retaining Youth Sport Coaches

Retention of volunteers is inextricably linked to issues related to motivation, satisfaction, morale, rewards, and recognition (Taylor *et al.*, 2008). Community sport volunteer managers can implement a variety of human resource management strategies to effectively retain youth sport coaches. This includes developing a set of expectations or coaching contract, providing coach education and training opportunities, implementing mentoring or social support programs, and putting in place a reward or recognition system (e.g. Harman and Doherty, 2017; Baxter *et al.*, 2021). This may prove to be a difficult task within voluntary clubs given the high demands already placed on volunteers' time and energy. However, sport governing bodies may consider innovative ways to encourage the implementation of these activities at a club level through engagement with key stakeholders and cross-sector partners.

## Setting Expectations

Volunteer coaches and community sport organisations alike have expectations that govern the relationship between the coach and the organisation. This set of expectations is referred to as a psychological contract and when expectations are not fulfilled, it can impact volunteer commitment, satisfaction, and retention. Harman and Doherty (2017) found that volunteer coaches expect relational support from clubs in the form of guidance to perform their role, autonomy in their role, and support for their decision-making. To a lesser extent, coaches also expressed expectations from club administrators to provide a positive coaching environment (Harman and Doherty, 2017). Other expectations include access to training opportunities, financial support, recognition, and social opportunities with other volunteers. In a similar vein, Rundle-Thiele and Auld (2009) suggest that rather than understanding retention by looking at factors that push coaches into leaving the role, it may be more helpful to understand the factors that pull individuals to coach. Youth sport coaches stay involved when team dynamics are positive, coaches are intrinsically motivated, there is clear and open club communication, and coaches feel they are supported (Rundle-Thiele and Auld, 2009). Club cultures that successfully manage the parent-coach relationship and emphasise camaraderie over winning sustain volunteer commitment (Toohey *et al.*, 2014). The qualities 67 youth sport coaches from Daejon Sport Council in South Korea felt were necessary to successfully fulfill their role included: enthusiasm, ability to motivate athletes, sports management, BA degree in exercise or sport, providing instruction without discrimination, establishing open and harmonious relationships with youth's parents, and risk management (Dae-Woo *et al.*, 2005). Understanding and fulfilling the expectations and desires volunteer coaches have towards their role are important to consider when looking to increase commitment amongst volunteer coaches.

## Coach Education and Training

Coaching education that is designed to meet the needs of volunteer coaches improves recruitment and retention rates (Wiersma and Sherman, 2005). However, despite numerous responsibilities placed on volunteer youth sport coaches, most are provided with little formal training (Busser and Carruthers, 2010). Training opportunities may help volunteer coaches develop skills such as people management (e.g., dispute resolution, player counselling/ mentoring, dealing with unrealistic expectations from parents) (Dawson *et al.*, 2013). Amongst a sample of 375 Australian Rugby Union clubs, the use of training and support practices has been shown to result in fewer perceived problems in the retention of volunteers (Cuskelly *et al.*, 2006). Training opportunities can also help to challenge coaches and develop their skills which may in turn influence their willingness to stay in the role.

The distinct difference between education and training needs for youth coaches in comparison to other coaching contexts has been highlighted over recent years to address past issues related to the health, safety, and protection of youth, as well as the increased emphasis on positive youth development through sport (Jones *et al.*, 2019). This is in part due to the recognition that proper training and education helps simultaneously retain both volunteers and youth athletes themselves, especially youth with traditionally lower sport participation rates. There are examples of sport organisations that provide youth-specific education and training opportunities and resources. For example, when USA hockey underwent a drastic transition to small area hockey format to make youth hockey more developmentally appropriate, new age specific modules were created on the USA Hockey e-Learning System in order to help volunteer coaches learn about coaching specific age groups (USA Hockey, 2020). Other organisations including Australian Rules Football (AFL) have developed junior coaching curriculum to support volunteer coaches (AFL, 2021).

Sport Organisations in Canada have also begun to offer specific certifications for coaches to better serve youth with lower sport participation rates (e g. aboriginal youth, girls). Examples include the National Coaching Certification Program (NCCP) Aboriginal Coaching Module

(Aboriginal Coaching Modules, 2022), and Canadian Women in Sport Keeping Girls In Sport module (Canadian Women in Sport, 2020). The United European Football Associations (UEFA) has also provided funding through their HatTrick programme to invest in football development projects that include coaching courses, grassroots and women's football, and social responsibility projects (UEFA, n.d.). Youth sport administrators should consider the delivery format and the added time required to complete any training programs so that the commitment required is not perceived to add burden for volunteers (Wiersma and Sherman, 2005).

## *Mentoring/Social Support Programs*

Youth sport coaches fulfill an important role for young athletes by mentoring and providing important support for sport and social development. Similarly, volunteer coaches also benefit from mentoring by others with coaching experience. This support can help coaches develop confidence, develop skill, and foster social connections amongst volunteer coaches. Inexperienced coaches have expressed that without mentoring, they often feel as though they are left on their own in regard to the tactical skills, institutional knowledge, and soft skills required for coaching (Wiersma and Sherman, 2005). Recognising the important role that mentors play, organisations such as Sport and Recreation New Zealand have developed a coaching mentor programme to provide guidance for effective mentoring (Sport and Recreation New Zealand). This document outlines the role of the coach and a mentor and mentee and provides suggestions for how to build mentoring relationships and how the mentorship process should unfold through guidance, encouragement, data, and feedback. The coaching mentorship programme also includes templates for formal observations and performance evaluations.

More recently, sport governing bodies and coaching associations have acknowledged the need to support coaches who are underrepresented within the current coaching system, including those with intersectional identities. For example, the Black Female Coach Mentorship Program offered by the Black Coaches Association of Canada provides mentorship support for individuals that identify as a Black, Biracial/Afro-mixed, or Indigenous Woman (Coaching Association of Canada, 2021). The Tucker Centre for Research on Women and Girls in Sport in the United States has also launched a broader scale initiative called #SheCanCoach that aims to create more widescale encouragement and representation of women coaches in efforts to increase the number of females in coaching. The centre also runs an annual Women Coaches Symposium for women coaches from youth, collegiate, to elite levels of sport. This blending of coaching backgrounds allows for female youth sport coaches to learn from high level coaches in an inclusive environment (Tucker Center, n.d.).

## *Reward/Recognition Systems*

Youth sport volunteering is a rewarding activity in itself, however, recognising volunteers in formal and informal ways can be a helpful retention strategy. Sport volunteers may seek diverse forms of rewards and recognition ranging from awards and public profile to financial support through covering the cost of professional development, to tangible items such as coaching apparel or new equipment. Some sport clubs designate awards such as 'years of service' or 'coach of the month' in order to profile those who have contributed in meaningful ways. In Dutch clubs, coaches in one-third of youth sport clubs were not reimbursed for expenses, although it is unknown as to whether some coaches are paid illegally under the guise of volunteering. Lack of proper human resource systems that help track and facilitate reimbursement may help to retain youth volunteer sport coaches and perhaps engage youth themselves in the coaching experience who may not have access to financial resources to obtain certifications needed to coach (De Knop *et al.*, 2004). Clubs can also recognise their coaches by coordinating end of season letters or videos for their coaches as a way for the club, parents, and athletes to thank coaches for their time and effort over the season. Small gifts and/or coaches' awards banquet are also used to cultivate a culture of appreciation within the club and can be useful for building club culture by rewarding those coaches who have demonstrated particular club values beyond winning. The ability to provide monetary gifts or tokens of appreciation may depend on the size of the club and their financial ability to do so, however regardless of the size or solvency of the club acts of gratitude can be meaningful to volunteer coaches who give their time and energy towards club activities.

There is no 'one size fits all' approach to rewarding coaches, however, the alignment between volunteer motivation and reward systems is critical for ensuring that coaches feel appreciated and supported in their role. While each sport setting may have unique features, common problems such as uneven distribution of work among volunteers, and complex organisational politics are often at play and can shape whether volunteers continue in their roles (Cuskelly, 2008). However, ensuring that volunteers are asked what types of support and rewards are most critical to them is one important step that should not be overlooked by volunteer managers and CSO boards. By doing this, organisations can focus their resources on reward/recognition systems that are truly valued within their unique context.

## Implications for Children's Sport Coaching

Fostering and retaining committed volunteers is of concern to the broader voluntary sector, but this has particularly heightened implications for children's sport that relies predominantly volunteers to offer sport experiences. The non-profit sector's concerns over a declining volunteer force has led to extensive research on the organisational commitment and retention of volunteers in many contexts, however not much of this research has taken place in the context of youth sport. Studies conducted in other voluntary contexts have primarily looked at commitment in relation to volunteer motives, positive relationships, and satisfaction (e.g. Aisbett and Hoye, 2015). The presence of positive relationships is powerful as it decreases volunteer dissatisfaction, turnover, and burnout (Kulik, 2007), and increases volunteer satisfaction and retention (Smith and Lockstone, 2009). Across voluntary contexts, satisfaction is influenced by recognition, interaction, role congruence (Stevens, 1991), quality supervision (Silverberg *et al.*, 2002), task and social cohesion (Doherty and Carron, 2003), empowerment (Kulik, 2007), having fun during volunteer tasks (Karl *et al.*, 2008), social contact with other volunteers (Osborn, 2008), rewarding experiences, and acknowledgement of the volunteer's contribution (Smith and Lockstone, 2009). In addition, affective commitment, defined as the emotional attachment or bond to an organisation, is the most salient form of commitment for volunteers (Cuskelly and Boag, 2001; MacLean and Hamm, 2007).

## Summary, Future Directions, Future Research

The more committed volunteers feel towards an organisation, the more likely they are to continue to volunteer for the organisation (Cuskelly and Boag, 2001; MacLean and Hamm, 2007). While future research needs to be conducted within the context of youth sport, the broader findings show potential mechanisms for retaining talented coaches who can provide children with meaningful developmental sport experiences. Future research should consider current and former youth sport coaches experiences to better understand factors that lead to turnover and eventual dropout to shed light on how they might better foster organisational commitment amongst youth sport coaches. Increasing rates of retention may play a crucial role for sport organisations seeking to develop a skilled group of coaches better able to provide positive and meaningful sport participation experiences for youth athletes and generate a feeder system of coaches who may wish to pursue higher levels of coaching. Considerations should also be made to conduct future research on youth sport coach retention across multiple countries, sport systems, and socio-demographics, to address the current lack of diversity amongst children's sport coaches and bring to light a more nuanced understanding of how the management of volunteer coaches impacts children's sport experience.

## References


Aboriginal Coaching Modules, 2022. [online]. Available from: https://coach.ca/indigenous-coaching [Accessed 10 January 2022].

AFL, 2021. *Junior coaching curriculum*. [online]. Available from: https://coach.afl/junior-coaching [Accessed 18 May 2021].

Aisbett, H. and Hoye, R., 2015. Human resource management practices to support sport event volunteers. *Asia Pacific Journal of Human Resources*, 53 (3), 351–369.

Baxter, H., Hoye, R., and Kappelides, P., 2021. Female volunteer coaches in community sport: A scoping review and research agenda. *Journal of Amateur Sport*, 7 (1), 64–94.

Busser, J.A. and Carruthers, C.P., 2010. Youth sport volunteer coach motivation. *Managing Leisure*, 15 (1), 128–139.

Canadian Women in Sport, 2020. *Keeping girls in sport* [online]. Available from: https://womenandsport.ca/learning-opportunities/e-learning/keeping-girls-in-sport-e-module/ [Accessed 18 May 2021].

Chan, D.K., Lonsdale, C., and Fung, H.H., 2012. Influences of coaches, parents, and peers on the motivational patterns of child and adolescent athletes. *Scandinavian Journal of Medicine and Science in Sports*, 22 (4), 558–568.

Coaching Association of Canada, 2021. *New mentorship program aims to empower black female coaches in Canada* [online]. Available from: https://coach.ca/new-mentorship-program-aims-empower-black-female-coaches-canada [Accessed 18 May 2021].

Coakley, J., 2016. Positive youth development through sport: Myths, beliefs, and realities. *In*: N.L. Holt, ed. *Positive youth development through sport*, 2nd ed. New York: Routledge. 21–33

Coleman, R., 2002. Characteristics of volunteering in UK sport: Lessons from cricket. *Managing Leisure*, 7 (4), 220–238.

Cuskelly, G., 2008. Volunteer retention in community sport organisations. *European Sport Management Quarterly*, 4 (2), 59–76.

Cuskelly, G. and Boag, A., 2001. Organisational commitment as a predictor of committee member turnover among volunteer sport administrators: Results of a time-lagged study. *Sport Management Review*, 4 (1), 64–86.

Cuskelly, G. and O'Brien, W., 2013. Changing roles: Applying continuity theory to understanding the transition from playing to volunteering in community sport. *European Sport Management Quarterly*, 13 (1), 54–75.

Cuskelly, G., *et al.*, 2006. Volunteer management practices and volunteer retention: A human resource management approach. *Sport Management Review*, 9 (2), 141–163.

Dae-Woo, C., Min-Haeng, C., and Young-Kum K., 2005. Youth sport coaches' qualities for successful coaching. *World Leisure Journal*, 47 (2), 14–22.

Dawson, A. and Phillips, P., 2013. Coach career development: Who is responsible? *Sport Management Review*, 16 (4), 477–487.

De Knop,P., Van Hoecke, J., and De Bosscher, V., 2004. Quality management in sports clubs. *Sport Management Review*, 7 (1), 57–77.

Doherty, A., 2005. *A profile of community sport volunteers*. Toronto: Parks and Recreation Ontario and Sport Alliance of Ontario.

Doherty, A.J. and Carron, A.V., 2003. Cohesion in volunteer sport executive committees. *Journal of Sport Management*, 17 (2), 116–141.

Fraser-Thomas, J.L., Côté, J., and Deakin, J., 2005. Youth sport programs: An avenue to foster positive youth development. *Physical Education and Sport Pedagogy*, 10 (1), 19–40.

Hamm-Kerwin, S., Misener, K., and Doherty, A., 2009. Getting in the game: An investigation of volunteering in sport among older adults. *Leisure/Loisir*, 33 (2), 659–685.

Harman, A. and Doherty, A., 2014. The psychological contract of volunteer youth sport coaches. *Journal of Sport Management*, 28 (6), 687–699.

Harman, A. and Doherty, A., 2017. Psychological contract fulfilment for volunteer youth sport coaches. *International Journal Sport Management and Marketing*, 17 (1/2), 94–120.

Hertting, K., Wagnsson, S., and Grahn, K., 2020. Perceptions of stress of Swedish volunteer soccer coaches. *Sports*, 8 (11), 146.

Hoye, R., *et al.*, 2020. *Sport volunteering*. New York: Routledge.

Instituto Português do Desporto e Juventude (IPDJ), n.d [online]. Available from: https://ipdj.gov.pt/ [Accessed 3 January 2022].

Jones, G. *et al.*, 2019. A community capacity building approach to sport-based youth development. *Sport Management Review*, 23 (4), 1441–3523.

Karl, K.A., Peluchette, J.V., and Hall, L.M., 2008. Give them something to smile about: A marketing strategy for recruiting and retaining volunteers. *Journal of Non-Profit and Public Sector Marketing*, 20 (1), 71–96.

Kulik, L., 2007. Explaining responses to volunteering: An ecological model. *Non-Profit and Voluntary Sector Quarterly*, 36 (2), 239–255.

MacLean, J. and Hamm, S., 2007. Motivation, commitment, and intentions of volunteers at a large Canadian sporting event. *Leisure/Loisir*, 31 (2), 523–556.

Osborn, J., 2008. Volunteer satisfaction and dissatisfaction: The impact on attrition. *Australian Journal on Volunteering*, 13 (1), 84–87.

Pearce, J., 1993. *Volunteers: The organisational behavior of unpaid workers*. London: Routledge.

Rundle-Thiele, S. and Auld, C., 2009. Should I stay or should I go? Retention of junior sport coaches, *Annals of Leisure Research*, 12 (1), 1–21.

Silverberg K.E., *et al.*, 2002. An 'effects-indicator' model of volunteer satisfaction: A functionalist theory approach. *Leisure/Loisir*, 27 (3), 283–304.

Smith, K.A. and Lockstone, L., 2009. Involving and keeping event volunteers: Management insights from cultural festivals. *In*: T. Baum, *et al.*, eds. *People and work in events and conventions: A research perspective*. Wallingford: CAB International, 154–167.

Sport and Recreation New Zealand, 2010. *Coach mentor programme* [online] https://sportnz.org.nz/media/3030/sport-nz-coach-mentor-programme.pdf [Accessed 18 May 2021].

Stevens E.S., 1991. Toward satisfaction and retention of senior volunteers. *Journal of Gerontological Social Work*, 16 (3/4), 33–41.

Taylor, T., Doherty, A., McGraw, P., 2008. *Managing people in sport organisations: A strategic human resource management perspective*. Boston: Elsevier.

Thelwell, R.C., *et al.*, 2016. Examining coaches' perceptions of how their stress influences the coach–athlete relationship. *Journal of Sports Science*, 35 (19), 1928 –1939.

Toohey, K., *et al.*, 2014. *Improving the identification and development of Australia's sporting talent: Overall findings*. Canberra: Australian Research Council.

Trussell, D., 2016. Young people's perspectives of parent volunteerism in community youth sport. *Sport Management Review*, 19 (3), 332–342.

Tucker Center for Research on Girls and Women in Sport #SHECANCOACH Project [online]. Available from: https://www.cehd.umn.edu/tuckercenter/projects/shecancoach.html [Accessed 18 May 2021].

Union of European Football Associations. *UEFA HatTrick development programme*. [online]. Available from: https://www.uefa.com/insideuefa/football-development/hattrick/ [Accessed 18 May 2021].

USA Hockey, 2020. *Age specific modules* [online]. Available from: https://www.usahockey.com/agespecificmodules [Accessed 18 May 2021].

Weiss, M.R. and Fretwell, S.D., 2005. The parent-coach/child-athlete relationship in youth sport: Cordial, contentious, or conundrum? *Research Quarterly for Exercise and Sport*, 76 (3), 286–305.

Wiersma, L.D. and Sherman, C.P., 2005. Volunteer youth sport coaches' perspectives of coaching education/certification and parental codes of conduct. *American Alliance for Health, Physical Education, Recreation and Dance*, 76 (3), 324–338.

# 41

# THE DIGITAL SIDELINE: WHAT COACHES NEED TO KNOW ABOUT CHILDREN'S ENGAGEMENT WITH SOCIAL MEDIA

*Victoria A. Goodyear, Mark Griffiths, Jonathon McKeever, and Gary Priest*

## Introduction

Social media is an integral aspect of many children's lives and accounts for the majority of their overall screen time (Rideout and Robb, 2019; Ofcom, 2021). In 2020, nearly all (97%) children in the U.K. aged 5–15 went online and just over half (55%) of 5–15-year-olds used social media, with rates of social media usage increasing to 87% for 12–15-year-olds (Ofcom, 2021). Similar usage rates have been reported across other nations (Third *et al.*, 2019). Although the average time reported being spent on social media per day is inconsistent and varies between children, samples in the U.K. and the U.S. estimate that the average time spent on social media is up to five hours per day (Rideout and Robb, 2019; Scott *et al.*, 2019; Ofcom, 2021). There can be little doubt therefore that contemporary children are avid consumers and producers in social media environments. While a child's phone and their engagement with social media may be left on the *sideline* during training or match play, children's lives can no longer be divided into digital and non-digital, or screen and non-screen time. The critical point to make here is that social media is a prominent characteristic of contemporary children. This characteristic presents new challenges to how coaches understand social media to support and enhance children's development through sport.

This chapter aims to increase awareness and understanding of social media's significance in coaching children in sport. This chapter is organised into three sections. Firstly, current research on the relevance of social media to sports coaching and the significance of social media in children's lives is reviewed, exploring key themes related to the development of sport-related behaviours, networks, and relationships, learning and vulnerability. Secondly, the implications of social media for coaching children in sport are discussed. Finally, we provide future practice and research directions.

DOI: 10.4324/9781003199359-47

## Review of Current Research

### *The Relevance of Social Media in Coaching*

Historically, the coach's role in practice has been significantly underplayed. Moving beyond passive descriptions of coaching as unproblematic and routine (Jones and Wallace, 2006), it is only in the last decade that researchers and coach developers have actively acknowledged the social and cultural processes that characterise any coaching interaction (Lyle and Cushion, 2016; Leeder and Sawiuk, 2020). The consensus is that coaching is not simply the delivery of sport-specific knowledge, but a process saturated with layers of social interaction, complexity, and meaning-making (Santos *et al.*, 2019). Coaching doesn't operate in a vacuum; hence, what coaches do in practice is continually shaped by their social and cultural conditions (Phelan and Griffiths, 2019). It is perhaps why Cushion *et al.* (2003, p.215) described the coaching process as "*structured improvisation*", intimating a much broader appreciation of coaching practices and the complexity of the coach's role is required

Contemporary research suggests that coaches significantly influence children's participation in sport (Duda and Appleton, 2016), particularly when their pedagogy draws from an evidence-informed position about what players know and can *do* (Côté and Gilbert, 2009). Indeed, coach behaviour is very much organised around coaches' understanding of their players' needs. The coach holds a degree of agency over their interactions and how they choose to coach (Camiré *et al.*, 2014). This understanding aligns with the physical education literature. Researchers have argued that effective teachers are driven by attending to their students' complex, diverse, individual learning needs (Goodyear and Dudley, 2015). Diagnosing the learning needs of children should drive the entire pedagogical process (Armour *et al.*, 2012). What might be concluded from this evidence is that effective coaches are driven by a need to attend to their players' learning requirements.

At the heart of effective practice is coaches' interpersonal knowledge. In creating meaningful relationships and positive interactions with players (Côté and Gilbert, 2009), interpersonal knowledge has been described as the capacity to connect appropriately and effectively with others (Jowett, 2017). Indeed, the levels of similarity and understanding between coaches and players substantially impact the quality of practice experienced by both (Jowett and Shanmugam, 2016). Where effective coaching is organised around coaches' empathy towards their players' needs, then diagnosing needs is clearly shaped by understanding their players' social and culturally constructed worlds (Daniels, 2012). In this context, understanding the role of social media in children's lives, and drawing on this knowledge to create appropriate learning practices, is a critical endeavour for coaches seeking quality interactions.

### *Social Media in Children's Lives*

There can be little doubt that understanding the role of social media in children's lives is highly complex and challenging to navigate. Children engage with diverse types of social media (e.g. Instagram, Snapchat, Tiktok, YouTube, WhatsApp) that include varied and multi-dimensional functionalities (e.g. photo/video sharing, live streaming, likes) (Ofcom, 2021). This medium is also in a constant flux of change, with new platforms, functions, and features frequently introduced, such as reels, stories, and disappearing content in recent years. The content shared on social media is also user-generated. Children access content from known or unknown individuals, commercial parties, government, community, or organisational groups (James *et al.*, 2014; Ito *et al.*, 2019).

In considering this further, a key attribute that separates social media from other forms of digital media is the ability to have a user profile where users can participate and produce content

(Ito *et al.*, 2019; Third *et al.*, 2019). Overall, this user-generated content disrupts the traditional flow of knowledge where, for example, the coach is no longer a primary source of knowledge of practice. Understanding the role of social media in children's lives is even more complex, given that children's engagement with social media often occurs in 'private' digital spaces and outside of the direct view of many adults (Ito *et al.*, 2019; Third *et al.*, 2019). While gaps between the world of children and adults have always existed, there are also significant gaps between how adults and children understand, engage with, and use social media (Goodyear and Armour, 2021). All of this suggests that coaches require access to the latest evidence on social media and children to make informed decisions about the role of social media in the lives of their players and the implications and opportunities for their coaching practices.

There is limited evidence on the influence and use of social media in coaching children in sport. The majority of research on children's engagement with social media has been mainly undertaken in the fields of anthropology, psychology, education, and sociology. The fields of public health and epidemiology also provide valuable insights into the role of social media in children's health and the types of social media interventions that influence health behaviour change. In this section we draw on this body of research to help coaches better understand the role of social media in children's lives and their coaching practices. The evidence presented in this section has also been informed by our consultations with children and professionals in sport, education, and coaching, and the authors' knowledge and awareness of coaching needs and professional practice. Accordingly, this section summarises evidence in four main areas: (i) sport-related behaviours, (ii) networks and relationships, (iii) learning, and (iv) vulnerabilities.

## *Sport-Related Behaviours*

In this section, sport-related behaviours refer to physical, cognitive, affective, and social dimensions of children's engagement with sport, such as physical activity, knowledge generation, mental health outcomes, and behaviours in social contexts. Evidence has highlighted the positive effects of social media interventions on sport-related behaviours. For example, systematic reviews have identified that social media interventions can positively influence positive changes in physical activity and dietary behaviours through increases in physical activity levels, healthy modifications to food intake and beneficial changes to body composition or body weight (Hamm *et al.*, 2014; Shaw *et al.*, 2015; Chau *et al.*, 2018; Hsu *et al.*, 2018; Goodyear *et al.*, 2021). Social media interventions can promote positive changes to sport-related behaviours through (i) interaction – social support, interactions between peers, or live counselling; (ii) information – the sharing of guidance, advice, and educative materials delivered through text, videos, tailored/unique content, detailed instructions, electronic newsletters, notifications or reminders; (iii) gamification – encouraging and motivating participants to engage in specific behaviours through competitions, challenges and rewards (Hamm *et al.*, 2014; Shaw *et al.*, 2015; Chau *et al.*, 2018; Hsu *et al.*, 2018; Goodyear *et al.*, 2021). This evidence suggests that social media can be used in specific and tailored ways to change children's sport-related behaviours. For example, coaches could consider how aspects of social media such as interaction, information, and gamification support the coaching process in their context. They may also consider how social media can support further learning aspirations related to training, physical activity, and diet.

## *Networks and Relationships*

Children's participation in social media occurs through their networks, which foregrounds opportunities to develop relationships with known or unknown and online or offline peers

(Ito *et al.*, 2019; Third *et al.*, 2019). Ito and colleagues (2019) argued that children participate in two main types of networks: (i) friendship-driven networks, which are spaces for social and emotional support, where children engage in self-expression and both evaluate and give feedback to one another; and (ii) interest-driven networks, that are more specialised and niche spaces centred on a common topic, where children interact with others who have greater expertise or where children mentor others. Accordingly, these networks provide valuable opportunities for children's development, such as socialisation, self-expression, leadership, and mentoring.

In a coaching context, social media networks allow clubs to connect with players, coaches, and parents, share information, promote club values, recruit players, and build community. It is well established that effective coaches consider optimising the parents' role in players development, as parent engagement can significantly impact psychological maturity (Harwood *et al.*, 2019; Furusa *et al.*, 2020). Given that parents and clubs play a significant role in the athletic triangle (i.e. parent, club, player) (Smoll *et al.*, 2011), social media networks have the potential to have a positive impact on player development. However, a rising issue related to children's engagement with social media is parents' unconsented sharing of their child's information through social media, sometimes referred to as sharenting (Blum-Ross and Livingstone, 2017). It has been reported that parents share an average of one hundred photos and videos of their children each year through social media (Nominet, 2018). Motivations for sharenting behaviours include receiving affirmation and social support, demonstrating the ability to care for their child, social participation, and documenting memories (Latipah *et al.*, 2020). While sharenting practices are often good-intentioned, it is notable that sharenting is not always viewed positively by children, particularly when it can threaten their social status and privacy (Barnes and Potter, 2021). A recent study showed that up to a third of children in European countries (an average of 14%) reported asking their parents to remove information they have shared about them online (Smahel *et al.*, 2020). Children have also described the contradictions between their online image and their parent's posts and explained how this operates as a source of public embarrassment (Ouvrein and Verswijvel, 2019).

The evidence concerning sharenting raises pertinent considerations regarding what, when and how adults share about children in a sporting context, extending across all stakeholders on the digital sideline. These concerns do not mean that coaches or parents should be prevented from sharing information about children on social media. Instead, it is essential for coaches and parents to consider the child's digital footprint through informed consent practices. Children should be given opportunities to decide what is shared about them online by parents and on club social media groups, pages, or accounts.

## *Learning*

Research has reported that children use social media for active and self-directed learning, largely separate from formal educational activities (e.g. school), and are often focused on developing their knowledge and interests and learning new skills (Greenhow *et al.*, 2019; Rutledge *et al.*, 2019). Research has shown that children increasingly turn to social media for health-related information in areas related to physical activity, diet and nutrition, lifestyle and body image (Camacho-Miñano *et al.*, 2019; Goodyear and Armour, 2019). The typical information children access to inform their behaviours is primarily related to body changes or transformations resulting from physical activity, the usage of diet supplements or a combination of both (Camacho-Miñano *et al.*, 2019, Goodyear and Armour, 2019). Accessing this type of content has apparent risks for children's development, particularly in areas related to mental wellbeing, body image, and self-esteem (Camacho-Miñano *et al.*, 2019; Goodyear and Armour, 2019).

At the same time, children have been reported to be critical users and generators of social media content, where they can recognise content that can positively inform their health-related behaviours and disregard content that has the potential to harm their bodies (Goodyear and Armour, 2019). The critical point is that social media fundamentally changes how children learn about physical activity, sport, and health. Engagement with these mediums allows children to develop new knowledge outside of coaching sessions.

Children have reported that social media could be used as a pedagogical tool by adults (including teachers and family members) to connect informal and formal learning contexts and support the development of their knowledge about health and sports topics (Goodyear and Armour, 2021). Furthermore, children have reported that accessing relevant advice and guidance from adults about social media content is essential for their well-being (Goodyear and Armour, 2021). However, a clear challenge for many adults is to move from risk-related approaches to children's social media use and be more empathetic and less judgemental on children's usage of social media. In this context, coaches need to recognise their levels of influence related to the type of content their players' access and be open-minded to social media and its potential role in the coaching process.

## *Vulnerabilities*

The dominant narratives surrounding social media usage are associated with risk in areas such as bullying, social isolation, reduced physical and psychological health, and obsessive or addictive behaviours. Although the risks for Internet-using children are relatively low and exposure to content does not necessarily lead to harm (Livingstone, 2018), some children can find themselves in a position of vulnerability either as a result of social media engagement or other issues that become magnified in a social media environment (Goodyear *et al.*, 2019). Specific experiences, cognitive approaches or environmental stimuli can heighten an individual's vulnerability to certain social media content (Orben, 2021), e.g. a child with low body satisfaction viewing idealised images of the body. Individual differences in how children engage with social media content may also vary by personality, life history, self-regulation ability and demographics, making them more sensitive to content than others (Orben, 2021). Overall, social media is a dynamic medium where children's physical, social and emotional needs can change rapidly where negative impacts can escalate quickly due to the power of the medium and its contents (Goodyear *et al.*, 2019).

For many sports organisations, addressing childhood vulnerability and directing coaches to child welfare policy, guidance, and procedures is organised under safeguarding. Broad definitions of safeguarding can be taken from the internationally ratified Convention of the Rights of the Child (United Nations, 1989), which ensures the equal protection of children from physical and mental harm, including, but not limited to, abuse, discrimination, bullying, and neglect (National Society for the Prevention of Cruelty to Children [NSPCC], 2021). Most coaching organisations are mandated by international recommendations, national law, and national governing bodies to adopt, implement, and review these child protection principles, where safeguarding is part of contemporary coach education (Lang and Hartill, 2016). However, there is limited guidance for clubs and coaches on safeguarding practices related to social media within current coach education programmes and coaching literature. For example, within the U.K., guidance from national organisations such as Sport England and The Football Association is beginning to direct practice. The aim of the Child Protection in Sport Unit (CPSU), a partnership between the NSPCC, Sport England, Sport Northern Ireland, and Sport Wales, aims to work with U.K. Sports Councils, National Governing Bodies, and County Sports

Organisations to help them minimise risk to children during sporting activities. The emerging resources from these partnerships will be helpful for coaches in directing their practice concerning social media, and children's vulnerability and online safety.

## Implications for Children's Sport Coaching

It is well established that coaching is more than the delivery of sport-specific knowledge. Instead, it is a process layered with social interaction, complexity, and meaning-making. The effective practice encompasses coaches' interpersonal knowledge that involves coaches connecting meaningfully with players, having a degree of empathy towards players' needs, and understanding players' social and cultural worlds. In this context, understanding the significance of social media in children's lives and how social media has the potential to support, inform or hinder engagement with and performance in sport is a critical endeavour for coaches.

The literature presented in this chapter illustrates how social media has the potential to inform and support children's sport-related behaviours, their networks and relationships with coaches, clubs, parents and other players, and children's knowledge about sport and sport-related topics. Coaches could take advantage of these affordances of social media to (a) design relevant pedagogical experiences that draw from an understanding of how children use social media in seeking to improve player development, and (b) frame how they design practices to enrich player's development and engage parents to support player wellbeing. For example, coaches could consider how videos shared on social media from professional matches could enhance players' situational decision-making. Another example concerns how coaches could use social media to build a community that effectively and appropriately engages parents in training and games. In doing so, coaches can aim to build connections with their players through the design of relatable practices and tactical scenarios and develop constructive player-coach-parent relationships.

Although there are many benefits to social media use, the literature presented in this chapter also identified that in using social media, some children could find themselves in a position of vulnerability where there is the potential for harm to their health and wellbeing. An important responsibility for coaches is to improve their understanding of how they can support children to help mitigate potential risks and embrace the opportunities presented by social media, even though social media may not be used specifically within their coaching sessions. At the same time, and while resources for coaches and clubs on social media use are emerging, coaching organisations (national and sport-specific) must do more to provide appropriate guidance and training for clubs and coaches on social media. Like educational contexts (Livingstone *et al.*, 2018; Ito *et al.*, 2019) coach education must help coaches better understand how to mitigate potential risks (e.g. safeguarding) while respecting children's digital rights and opportunities for learning and development. The notion of continuous training or continuous professional development (CPD) is vital in this context. The speed at which new technologies emerge and are used and adopted by children means that sporadic training is likely to be woefully inadequate and possibly even harmful (Goodyear and Armour, 2021). Hence, there is a convincing rationale for new research on designing and delivering effective and continuously updated CPD for coaches in a digital age.

## Summary, Future Directions, and Future Research

This chapter aimed to increase awareness and understanding of social media's significance in coaching children in sport. Through an analysis of existing literature, this chapter has explored: how social media could inform the design, organisation, and delivery of coaching children; the role of the coach in children's and parent's engagement with social media; and how coach education could be changed to support coaches to operate effectively in a digital age. From our review of the current literature, we make the following recommendations for future practice and research:

- Coaches should take advantage of social media attributes and use these to (a) design relevant pedagogical experiences that improve player development and (b) frame how they design practices to enrich players' development and engage parents to support player well-being.
- Coaches should critically evaluate evidence related to children's engagement with social media, inquire into their player's uses of social media and, in turn, develop appropriate practices to help mitigate potential risks of social media use and help their players to embrace the limitless opportunities presented by social media.
- The coaching profession should consider developing and evaluating a research programme focused on effective guidance and CPD for coaching in a digital age.

## References

Armour, K., Makopoulou, K., and Chambers, F., 2012. Progression in physical education teachers' career-long professional learning: Conceptual and practical concerns. *European Physical Education Review*, 18 (1), 62–67

Barnes, R. and Potter, A., 2021. Sharenting and parents' digital literacy: An agenda for future research. *Communication Research and Practice*, 7 (1), 6–20.

Blum-Ross, A. and Livingstone, S., 2017. "Sharenting," parent blogging, and the boundaries of the digital self. *Popular Communication*, 15 (2), 110–125.

Camacho-Miñano, M.J., MacIsaac, S., and Rich, E., 2019. Postfeminist biopedagogies of Instagram: Young women learning about bodies, health and fitness. *Sport, Education and Society*, 6, 651–664.

Camiré, M., Trudel, P., and Forneris, T., 2014. Examining how model youth sport coaches learn to facilitate positive youth development. *Physical Education and Sport Pedagogy*, 19 (1), 1–17.

Chau, M.M., Burgermaster, M., and Mamykina, L., 2018. The use of social media innutrition interventions for adolescents and young adults – A systematic review. *International Journal of Medical Informatics*, 120, 77–91.

Côté, J. and Gilbert, W., 2009. An integrative definition of coaching effectiveness and expertise. *International Journal of Sports Science and Coaching*, 4 (3), 307–323.

Cushion, C.J., Armour, K.M., and Jones, R.L., 2003. Coach education and continuing professional development: Experience and learning to coach. *Quest*, 55 (3), 215–230

Daniels, H., 2012. Institutional culture, social interaction and learning. *Learning, Culture and Social Interaction*, 1 (1), 2–11.

Duda, J.L. and Appleton, P.R., 2016. Empowering and disempowering coaching climates: Conceptualisation, measurement considerations, and intervention implications. *In*: M. Raab, *et al.*, eds. *Sport and exercise psychology research: From theory to practice*. Cambridge Massachusetts USA: Elsevier Academic Press, 373–388.

Furusa, M.G., Knight, C.J. and Hill, D.M., 2020. Parental involvement and children's enjoyment in sport. *Qualitative Research in Sport, Exercise and Health*, 13 (6), 936–954.

Goodyear, V.A. and Armour, K.M., 2019. *Young people, social media and health*. New York: Taylor and Francis.

Goodyear, V.A. and Armour, K.M., 2021. Young people's health-related learning through social media: What do teachers need to know?. *Teaching and Teacher Education*, 102, 103340.

Goodyear, V. and Dudley, D., 2015. "I'm a facilitator of learning!" Understanding what teachers and students do within student-centered physical education models. *Quest*, 67 (3), 274–289.

Goodyear, V.A., *et al.*, 2021. The effect of social media interventions on physical activity and dietary behaviors in young people and adults: A systematic review. *International Journal of Behavioral Nutrition and Physical Activity*, 18, 72.

Greenhow, C., *et al.*, 2019. Education and social media: Research directions to guide a growing field. *Teachers College Record*, 121 (14), 1–22.

Hamm, M.P., *et al.*, 2014. A systematic review of the use and effectiveness of social media in child health. *BMC Pediatr*, 14 (1), 138.

Harwood, C.G., *et al.*, 2019. Advancing the study of parental involvement to optimise the psychosocial development and experiences of young athletes. *Psychology of Sport and Exercise*, 42, 66–73.

Hsu, M.S.H., Rouf, A., and Allman-Farinelli, M., 2018. Effectiveness and behavioural mechanisms of social media interventions for positive nutrition behaviors in adolescents: A systematic review. *Journal of Adolescent Health*, 63 (5), 531–545.

Ito, M., *et al.*, 2019. *Hanging out, messing around, and geeking out, tenth anniversary edition: Kids living and learning with new media*. Massachusetts: Massachusetts Institute of Technology.

James, C., *et al.*, 2014. *Young people, ethics, and the new digital media*. London: MIT Press.

Jones, R.L. and Wallace, M., 2006. The coach as 'orchestrator': More realistically managing the complex coaching context. *In:* Jones, R.L. eds. *The sports coach as educator*. Routledge. 69–82.

Jowett, S., 2017. Coaching effectiveness: The coach–athlete relationship at its heart. *Current Opinion in Psychology*, 16, 154–158.

Jowett, S. and Shanmugam, V., 2016. Relational coaching in sport: Its psychological underpinnings and practical effectiveness. *In*: R. Schinke, K.R. McGannon, and B. Smith, eds. *Routledge international handbook of sport psychology*. London: Routledge, 501–514.

Lang, M. and Hartill, M., 2016. *Safeguarding, child protection and abuse in sport: International perspectives in research, policy and practice 2021*. London: Routledge.

Latipah, E., *et al.*, 2020. Elaborating motive and psychological impact of sharenting in millennial parents. *Universal Journal of Educational Research*, 8 (10), 4807–4817.

Leeder, T.M. and Sawiuk, R., 2020. Reviewing the sports coach mentoring literature: A look back to take a step forward. *Sports Coaching Review*, 10 (2), 129–152.

Livingstone, S., Mascheroni, G., and Staksrud, E., 2018. European research on children's internet use: Assessing the past and anticipating the future. *New Media and Society*, 20 (3), 1103–1122.

Lyle, J. and Cushion, C., 2016. *Sport coaching concepts: A framework for coaching practice*. Taylor and Francis.

Nominet, 2018. More than 2·7m parents share family photos with complete strangers online. Oxford, UK: Nominet.

NSPCC, 2021. *Child protection in sports: Child abuse in a sporting setting* [online]. Available from: https://thecpsu.org.uk/help-advice/introduction-to-safeguarding/child-abuse-in-a-sports-setting/ [Accessed 26 May 2021].

Ofcom, 2021. *Children and parents: Media use and attitudes report*. [online]. Available from: https://www.ofcom.org.uk/__data/assets/pdf_file/0025/217825/children-and-parents-media-use-and-attitudes-report-2020-21.pdf [ Accessed 26 May 2021].

Orben, A., 2021. Digital diet: A 21st century approach to understanding digital technologies and development. *Infant and Child Development: iFirst*, 31 (1).

Ouvrein, G. and Verswijvel, K., 2019. Sharenting: Parental adoration or public humiliation? A focus group study on adolescents' experiences with sharenting against the background of their own impression management. *Children and Youth Services Review*, 99, 319–327.

Phelan, S. and Griffiths, M., 2019. Reconceptualising professional learning through knowing-in-practice: A case study of a coaches high performance centre. *Sports Coaching Review*, 8 (2), 103–123.

Rideout, V. and Robb, M.B., 2019. *The common sense census: Media use by tween and teens. 2019*. San Francisco, CA: Common Sense Media.

Rutledge, S.A., Dennen, V.P., and Bagdy, L.M., 2019. Exploring adolescent socialmedia use in a high school: Tweeting teens in a bell schedule world. *Teachers College Record*, 121 (14), 1–30.

Santos, F., *et al.*, 2019. Coaching effectiveness within competitive youth football: Youth football coaches' and athletes' perceptions and practices. *Sports Coaching Review*, 8 (2), 172–193.

Scott, H., Biello, S.M., and Woods, H.C., 2019. Social media use and adolescent sleep patterns: Cross-sectional findings from the UK millennium cohort study. *BMJ Open*, 9 (9), 1–8.

Shaw, J.M., *et al.*, 2015. Social media used as a health intervention in adolescent health: A systematic review of the literature. *Digit Health*, 1, 1–10.

Smahel, D., *et al.*, 2020. *E.U. kids online 2020: Survey results from 19 countries*. E.U. Kids Online.

Smoll, F.L., Cumming, S.P., and Smith, R.E., 2011. Enhancing coach-parent relationships in youth sports: Increasing harmony and minimising hassle. *International Journal of Sports Science and Coaching*, 6, 13–26.

Third, A., *et al.*, 2019. *Young people in digital society: Control shift*. London: Palgrave Macmillan.

United Nations, 1889. *Convention on the rights of the child* (UNCRC) (adopted 20 November 1989, entered into force 2 September 1990) (online0 1577 UNTS 3. Available from: https://www.ohchr.org/en/ProfessionalInterest/Pages/CRC.aspx [ Accessed 26 May 2021].

# 42

# A SPACE TO PLAY: THE GEOGRAPHIES OF CHILDREN'S SPORT AND PHYSICAL ACTIVITIES

*Catherine Waite*

## Introduction

Children's geographies are recognised to have emerged as a distinctive subdiscipline in the latter years of the twentieth century (Holloway and Valentine, 2000). The key features of the discipline are a focus on the core geographical concepts of space and place, whilst placing the voices of children and young people at the forefront of research. Consideration of children's geographies has always been inter- and multi-disciplinary (Robson *et al.*, 2013), yet there is comparatively little work that brings together geography and sport in relation to young people. More broadly, the geographies of sport remains a niche topic (Wise and Kohe, 2020), so the additional focus on children is perhaps unsurprising.

Despite this, there are lots of passing references to sport in geographical research on children; typically it appears within wider discussions around play and the leisure activities of young people. Children's geographers have often focused on play (Woodyer *et al.*, 2016), rather than formal sports activities, although there are some blurred lines surrounding the terminology that is used. The literature that is reviewed in this chapter utilises a variety of terms including play, recreation, sport, and physical activity. But, it is fair to suggest that sport involves some form of formal moderation to reflect the rules of game (Evans and Horton, 2016) and can therefore be coached or taught. At the outset of this chapter it is important to note that the research cited has primarily been conducted in the global north. It is acknowledged (Smith, 2013; Holloway, 2014; Holt *et al.*, 2020) that whilst children's geographies research takes place across the world, the global south is still under-represented. When drawing on the learning from this, readers should appreciate and reflect on how this may need to be adapted to suit majority world contexts.

## Review of Current Research

### *Spaces of Children's Physical Activity*

Much geographical research is concerned with how activities are undertaken in space and this focus on the concept of space is evident in the published work on children's physical activity.

DOI: 10.4324/9781003199359-48

There is a significant body of work on the space of the school, which is to be expected given the importance of education in the everyday lives of young people, and of interest here is the research that has specifically focused on school playgrounds in a global north context.

Reviewing the literature on this topic highlights the importance of the design of space and the extent to which it can encourage/discourage physical activity. Typically, school play areas are designed to promote traditional physical activity, which can be understood as formal, competitive, and rule-bound sports, whilst this appeals to some young people, for many children this results in a lack of participatory desire (Dyment and Bell, 2007). The use of these traditional play spaces is dominated by physically competent boys (Dyment *et al.*, 2009) and reflects the cultural importance of masculine physicality (Newman *et al.*, 2006). Consequently, it is vital to ensure that these educational spaces are inclusive and encourage children to be physically active.

Several suggestions have been proposed to facilitate this, first, the creation of greenspace in school grounds has been shown to encourage physical activity in a way that goes beyond typical gender-segregated and stereotyped activities (Dyment and Bell, 2007; Pawlowski *et al.*, 2019). Second, designs for both greenspaces and other play-spaces should encourage a balance between cooperative and competitive play (Tranter and Malone, 2004). Finally, geographical research has highlighted the importance of ensuring that children's voices are incorporated into the evaluation and design of play-spaces. Gustafson (2009) noted that explicit sports spaces in school playgrounds are perceived by children as boys' spaces, with girls indicating that it is space that they actively avoid. It is important therefore to consult with a diverse range of children in the design process to ensure that the spaces motivate all young people to be physically active (Pawlowski *et al.*, 2019).

Continuing to think about the role that space plays on children's physical activity, there is a body of work which has explored understandings of what comprises play and play-spaces. In order to best understand what spaces young people need to be able to access in order to participate in physical activity, there needs to be a more child-centred understanding of what they perceive play, including active play, to be (Thomson and Philo, 2004). Once in those spaces children's voices continue to be important as research has shown that, for them, participating in physical activity is as much about the social experiences, such as the chance to make new friends, as it is the overall act of participation (Lee and Abbott, 2009). Further, contrasts have been identified between children's desires and the best intentions of adults in moderating the use of space for physical activity. In some cases, adults have a clear role in controlling the use of space, for example the strict moderation of the boundaries of a soccer pitch within a school playground. But it is evident, that despite adults' best intentions, non-compliance and alternative applications of activities are widespread with outdoor physical activities (Thomson, 2005). Whilst this is prevalent in play-based situations, it is important that the potential for children to subvert adult discourses is both acknowledged (Wake, 2008) and incorporated by coaches when delivering more formal physical activity sessions.

As would be expected, parents and guardians have a significant role in moderating children's use of space and their access to physical activity opportunities. It is widely recognised that across the global north there has been a shift from spontaneous and self-initiated play to planned, organised and adult-controlled activities (Skår and Krogh, 2009). This change can be partially attributed to the perception that organised sport is safer than the alternative of unsupervised play in neighbourhood spaces (Holt *et al.*, 2015; Russell and Stenning, 2020). Research has shown that parents facilitate participation in organised leisure activities as this is seen as learning time (Nordbakke, 2019) and an opportunity for children to acquire social and cultural capital that can be a valuable future asset (Pynn *et al.*, 2019). Free play can be considered to lack purpose by parents, so leisure activities need to be adult moderated in order to have educational value

(Parsons and Traunter, 2020); a finding drawn from research on the integration of Forest School into Primary Education in England. Forest school exemplifies how geographical research has typically focused on the distinction between (in)formal education (Pimlott-Wilson and Coates, 2019) and play, but still provides an opportunity for children to be physically active, so can be useful work for sports coaches to reflect upon. A key ethos of forest school is active learning through play in an environment where children do not need to suppress noise, movement, and energy levels. Consquently, it has been shown to be more memorable and children to be more receptive to learning than they would be in more formal and controlled educational settings (Harris, 2018). Despite these benefits, Parsons and Traunter (2020) found that parents lack confidence in moderating purposeful outdoor play, as facilitated at Forest School and they see equipment provision and dealing with dirty clothing challenging. Whereas, a further evaluation of Forest School, focusing on the views of children, indicated that their desire to play outdoors exceeded possible barriers, including the weather or muddy conditions (Ridgers *et al.*, 2012); highlighting the importance of empowering children and incorporating their voices rather than relying on an adult perspective.

The final aspect of spatial research undertaken by geographers on physical activity relates to observable generational shifts in the extent of children's independent mobility (Valentine and McKendrick, 1997). It is recognised that young people are spending an increasing amount of time at home, indoors, and participating in sedentary activities. There is generally felt to be a good understanding of the factors that discourage children from playing outdoors, but this is more limited when considering the factors that pull children indoors (Maitland *et al.,* 2019). In urban areas, there is a positive association between the presence of local public greenspace and participation in physical activity (Veitch *et al.*, 2007). Yet between generations of young people (Woolley and Griffin, 2015) outdoor space has been transformed from child-space to adult-space (Karsten, 2005) and perceptions of safety-risks mean that parents are increasingly limiting independent access to these spaces (Veitch *et al.*, 2007) and, consequently, the opportunity to be physically active in these spaces.

## *Socio-Economic Status and Access to Sport and Coaching*

Human geographers, and by extension, children's geographers, seek to understand social phenomena by considering how aspects of social identity can have an influence. This is evident in the literature on young people's participation in out-of-school enrichment activities, which includes formal sports coaching, where there is a large body of work on the impact of socio-economic status (SES) and ethnic background (Nordbakke, 2019). The declining participation in unstructured outdoor play has been mirrored by the increasing availability and formalisation of extra-curricular activities (Witten *et al.*, 2013). Such activities have overall become easier to access, although a range of barriers to participation exists.

Enrichment activities come at a cost to parents, and for some these costs can be restrictive (Trussell and Shaw, 2012). The costs include the direct cost of the activity, as well as the requirement to purchase equipment and the transport costs associated with participation (Holt *et al.*, 2015; Holloway and Pimlott-Wilson, 2018). Alongside these participation restrictions, geographical research has highlighted how children of lower SES have a smaller spatial range for activity participation because they are more likely to be reliant on walking/cycling or public transport to attend activities (Dyment, 2005). This potential lack of access to spaces for physical activity is problematic given those from lower SES backgrounds are also likely to have smaller home spaces where they can spend their leisure time (Stenning and Russell, 2020). This is a particular issue that has been exposed by the Coronavirus pandemic in the early 2020s as young people from lower SES backgrounds had limited space for play and physical activity at home, as well as restricted access to both private (domestic gardens) and public outdoor space (Russell and Stenning, 2020). In contrast, young people from middle-class backgrounds typically have larger home spaces so that even if they are spending more of their leisure time indoors, they are still able to bring traditional outdoor activities inside e.g. soccer or den building. However, children of this SES have been labelled the 'backseat generation' as they are constantly being taken to formal leisure activities, of which sports coaching is typically the most popular (Karsten, 2005). As noted previously this is believed to allow children to acquire social and cultural capital for their future development and so it becomes an integral part of what may be perceived as the ideals of good parenting (Pynn *et al.*, 2019). Consideration is therefore required about how access to activities such as formal sports coaching can be made more equitable so that all children have the opportunity to acquire social and cultural capital.

Yet the extent of this participation can cause issues to arise. Research on enrichment activities has exposed problems of time scarcity for both parents and children (Witten *et al.*, 2013) and over-scheduling (Karsten, 2015). Additionally, it has been demonstrated that sibling activity can be a barrier to the participation of other family members in leisure activities. Since adults are required to transport children to activities, it may be that compromises must be made, and parents become the gatekeepers of children's participation. This raises questions about the decision-making process that is involved here, what the consequences of these decisions are, and who experiences the impacts?

One solution that has been proposed to help overcome this, is the integration of extra-curricular activities into formal education provision, scheduling activities at lunchtime or after-school. There are multiple possible benefits of this, first, it means that schooling and additional activities are hosted in the same location, which reduces the need for children to be transported to activities. Second, since it has been shown that parents from all SES backgrounds recognise the benefits of enrichment activities, aligning them with school-based education provision may facilitate some state-subsidies to be made available to make activities more accessible (Holloway and Pimlott-Wilson, 2014). As well as addressing class-based barriers, this may also enable participation by those from other social backgrounds as, for example, it has been shown that migrant children are less active outdoors and are less likely to be members of sports clubs (Karsten, 2005). Third, it can be argued that the social and cultural capital acquired through enrichment activities improves educational attainment (Holloway and Pimlott-Wilson, 2014), thus current arrangements for participation in enrichment activities risk becoming a factor in the reproduction of social inequalities (Poveda *et al.*, 2007) so it is important that opportunities to address this are considered for implementation.

## Physical Education in School Settings

Schools are an important space in the lives of young people and therefore the learning and encounters that children have there are significant, particularly in terms of their experiences with physical education. One of the most widely cited studies on children's sports geographies investigates emotional geographies of sport, exercise, and active play in UK primary schools (Hemming, 2007). In this work Hemming reiterates the importance of including and valuing children's voices both in research and when overseeing the activities that they participate in. In a sport and exercise context, it is noted that adult, specifically political, discourses are centred on the benefits for physical health (Radkowska-Walkowicz, 2021), as well as increasingly the mental health and wellbeing benefits (Holloway and Pimlott-Wilson, 2018). Whilst young people were shown to recognise these benefits it was not their focus, with participation being more about fun and enjoyment (Hemming, 2007). It is important to acknowledge this in the design and implementation of the physical education curriculum in schools, as teaching typically conveys adult interpretations of ideal childhoods, as opposed to those desired by young people from diverse social backgrounds (Holloway *et al.*, 2010).

Geographical research has considered the delivery and consumption of physical education in schools and has exposed several important areas for consideration. In education settings there has been a shift towards more structured play to encourage physical activity. However, it is important to consider how this is moderated to ensure that it has a positive impact. For example, during research with 9–10-years-old children at a primary school in the English midlands Hemming (2007) observed how teachers moderated games, through a flexible interpretation of the rules, to encourage participation and inclusion. Conversely, the games played may require children to wait in line for a go or result in children being eliminated from the game which could result in the child being more sedentary than they would have been if they were simply given the option of participating in active free play (Snow *et al.*, 2019). But, it is possible for active free play and structured physical activity to co-exist. Further observations from Hemming (2007) noted the alternative use and repurposing of PE equipment, for example, using tennis balls for soccer, to initiate and enable enjoyment of physical activity when children are given free choice. Whilst this may already occur during recreational time in schools, this research would indicate that there are benefits to incorporating the chance of unstructured play into formal physical education teaching time.

This suggests that it is important to consider how physical education is framed in a formal school context, although the learning from this can be applied in other coaching contexts. Young people are more likely to be active when there is an intrinsic enjoyment of the activity, so it is necessary to understand what sports are considered boring or which activities are disliked, e.g. outdoor games when it is muddy (Hemming, 2007). Children also value the opportunity to play with, or make new, friends during physical activity (Lee and Abbott, 2009) so this should be incorporated into the pedagogical design of physical education programmes. Finally, the wider positioning of physical activity within formal education should be explored. Hemming (2007) reflects on his observation of physical activity being used as a disciplinary tool, with access to outdoor activities being enabled or withheld depending on behaviour during other classroom-based learning. This has the potential to be problematic when considered alongside the narrative of encouraging children to be more physically active overall.

## Children's Bodies, Gender, and (Dis)ability in Sport

As discussed previously one of the key concerns of geographers is how actions play out in particular spaces. Going beyond this, geographical research, notably from a feminist geography perspective, has considered how identities and aspects of social difference influence behaviour across space. Feminist thought recognises children as different and a marginal social group who benefit from dedicated study (Valentine, 2000). Consequently, much of the research conducted on children's geographies has feminist roots (Holloway and Pimlott-Wilson, 2011) and there is a small body of this work that relates to children and their participation in sport. Although there is scope for considerable additional work from a feminist sports geography perspective (Pavlidis, 2018).

The work of Judith Butler (1990) has inspired a significant volume of geographical research on the ways in which gender is performed, including the ways in which this plays out in a sport context (Spark *et al.*, 2019). Consideration has been given to the ways in which gender is performed in sports spaces, for example in school playgrounds (Holloway and Valentine, 2000).

Spark *et al.* (2019) have shown how the perceived inclusivity of sports spaces varies by gender; speaking to young people, aged 11–12, in Australia exposed how girls generally felt excluded from the spaces because "we're not very good at soccer" (p. 198) and they are spaces "that boys used that I don't" (p. 196). Whereas boys felt they were inclusive spaces as they were places that local boys, as well as newly arrived migrant boys, could play soccer together. Similar findings regarding gender-based migrant integration through sport have been demonstrated elsewhere including Germany (Burrmann *et al.*, 2017), Ireland (Ní Laoire 2011) and Spain (Lleixà and Nieva, 2020). Adults have also been shown to perceive sports spaces as gendered, with locations such as baseball fields seen as ideal sites to instil good citizenship values for boys (Gagen, 2000).

Gender differences have been exposed in geographical studies in relation to the activities in which young people participate. Arvidsen *et al.* (2020) have discussed how equipment can encourage physical activity as spaces, such as playgrounds or soccer fields that are considered traditional sports spaces are more likely to be places where children stand still. Conversely, the inclusion of a trampoline, which attracts children across genders and age, encourages mobility and activity participation. Asking young people to draw maps of particular areas is a commonly used research method in children's geographies and one such study, with secondary school students in Queensland, Australia, highlighted differential desires to participate in physical activities. Male participants included both formal sports and recreational physical activity spaces on their maps, whereas female references were less common and tended to be to recreational rather than organised sport spaces (Lee and Abbott, 2009). This raises questions about why these differences exist and what strategies can be used to address them.

Further geographical research has contributed some ideas about the causes of lower levels of sports participation among young girls. First, Evans (2006) has exposed a reluctance of girls to participate due to concerns about their bodies. Significantly, this was shown to occur in a range of settings: in co-educational settings girls fear the masculine gaze, but they are equally concerned about judgement from other females and the authoritative gaze that comes from staff about the quality of their participation. Second, Spark *et al.* (2019) highlight that girls feel that they lack the necessary experience to participate and that due to societal expectations throughout childhood they have become socialised into exclusion. There are gendered expectations of sports participation from an early age, for example primary school-aged boys feel that dance is 'girly' (Hemming, 2007), but girls felt that if they had been more widely exposed to playing and coaching in soccer and other sports from an early age then it would alleviate exclusionary issues when they are older (Spark *et al.*, 2019). It is therefore important that adults encourage inclusive participation from a young age to help enable a more level playing field for continued participation in sports and physical activity.

Children's geography research has investigated the experiences of disabled young people in relation to sport, leisure, and exercise. Although, despite a large volume of work about children's play spaces, and similarly about spaces used by those with disabilities, there is only limited work on disabled play spaces (Yantzi *et al.*, 2010). One potential explanation for this is because leisure and sports-based activities for disabled young people are often conflated with rehabilitation work rather than play (Hodge and Runswick-Cole, 2013). Participation in leisure activities is impacted by discourses that disabled children are perceived as dependent, vulnerable, and in need of protection (Holt, 2010). As such opportunities to participate may be limited to segregated leisure activities which is then further amplified by the requirement for accessible and affordable transport and/or equipment to enable participation (Hodge and Runswick-Cole, 2013). This research demonstrates some of the barriers that exist to participation by all those with physical disabilities, although it is likely to be children that are most adversely affected. Additional research is required to propose solutions as to how these barriers can be overcome to help enable equal opportunities to participation.

Alongside research on disabilities that impact on mobility, geographers have investigated how chronic conditions can impact on physical activity participation. Cardwell and Elliott's (2019) work on 11–18 years old asthma sufferers in youth sports teams in Canada exposes several important issues that sports coaches should be mindful of in their practice. First, it is necessary to reflect upon the spaces that are being used for sport, is there dust on the playing surface, or are they close to main roads where there is a risk of high levels of pollutants? Second, they highlight that in the case of asthma sufferers, as well as for those with other conditions or disabilities, coaches should ensure that every individual feels accepted in the leisure space even if the extent of their participation is limited. Children should not feel that they are to blame as this can create additional stigma from both peers and coaches which can contribute to other issues such as stress and bullying, within and beyond the sports context.

## Implications for Children's Sport Coaching

From the geographical research on children's sport and physical activity there are two areas of focus. First, what can be learned from the findings of research and second, how geographical approaches to research can be adapted for use as evaluation techniques for sports coaching.

It has been shown that geographical research has centred on active play and informal physical activity as opposed to formal sports participation. Despite this, some important questions are raised about how an effective balance can be achieved when trying to ensure maximum participation. The research evaluation in this chapter has shown that simply participating in formal sports activities may not always result in an increased level of physical activity. It should also be acknowledged that the extent of participation in organised sport is limiting the time that children have available for free-play (Holloway and Pimlott-Wilson, 2018) so coaches could consider whether more playful activities can be incorporated into organised sport, both within, and external to, school settings.

Studies in children's geographies have highlighted the importance of reflecting upon the spaces used for physical activity. Formal sports spaces are viewed by young people as a place for fitness (Chaudhury *et al.*, 2019), however since being active is now understood to be important for well-being and mental health, how can the narratives be adjusted, and the spaces be adapted, to encourage participation amongst those children who are less willing or able. It is often assumed that physical activity only equates to competitive sports, which is what traditional school grounds are designed to support (Dyment and Bell, 2007). Likewise, how can equipment be utilised effectively by young people under the guidance of coaches. The research has shown that both traditional and alternative equipment can influence participation in physical activity, and the manner in which participation occurs. Therefore, can spaces, and what is included in them, be redesigned, or alternative spaces used to maximise inclusive participation.

Finally, geographers have highlighted the importance of considering social difference in relation to the opportunity for children to access and participate in sport and physical activity. Ordinarily children want to participate and take pride in their sports successes (Holloway and Pimlott-Wilson, 2014) so it is necessary to give greater consideration to the barriers that prevent them from participating. In some instances, for example in relation to chronic conditions such as asthma (Cardwell and Elliott, 2019), additional coach education may enhance awareness of strategies that can be incorporated to enable participation. But in other cases, it may be that more extensive changes are required, beyond the capability of individual coaches, to overcome barriers to participation caused by socio-economic status, gender and disability for example.

Alongside these findings from children's geographies research, the research methods applied may have value for evaluating coaching practice. First, consideration of the techniques that can be used with young people when discussing issues relevant to coaching. For example, when discussing body image and health discourses, children are aware of the associated stigma so are hesitant to discuss them or incorporate them into visual methods activities such as drawing or taking photographs (Gunson *et al.*, 2016). Instead, more unobtrusive methods such as participant observation may be appropriate (Hemming, 2007). But, perhaps the most important take-away from children's geographies, is the importance of listening to and incorporating children's voices (Holloway, 2014) as opposed to relying on adults to convey their views for young people. This is an approach that could be easily and effectively utilised to evaluate and enhance coaching practice.

## Summary, Future Directions, and Future Research

Children's geographies can offer valuable learning points for sports coaching, particularly when reflecting on the spaces of sports coaching and ability of children to access formal coaching. At present there is only a small volume of geographical research on children's coaching activity, but this chapter has shown that there is potential to undertake more research in this area. It is likely that there is much to be learned from an explicitly geographical focus, when moving beyond play and informal physical activity to organised sports activities, both within and external to education settings.

With this in mind, future research could usefully investigate the spaces used for formal sport and who is able to access these spaces. This could be done at a global scale given that virtually all the existing research has been done in the global north and therefore little is known about the sport and coaching experiences of children in the majority world. Children's geographers have also made important contributions to work on gender and disability, amongst other aspects of social difference, and it would be valuable to see further research investigating the impacts of these in relation to sport and coaching. This is research that could be undertaken by geographers or sports coaches or researchers could come together and take an interdisciplinary approach. It is vital that any future research incorporates young people into the research process, this would empower the children as researchers and/or participants and provide them with the opportunity to use their voices to shape future practice.

## References

Arvidsen, J., *et al.*, 2020. 'It's fun in the legs': Children's dwelling in garden trampolines. *Children's Geographies*, 18 (3), 312–324.

Burrmann, U., *et al.*, 2017. Ethnic identities, sense of belonging and the significance of sport: Stories from immigrant youths in Germany. *European Journal for Sport and Society*, 14 (3), 186–204.

Butler, J., 1990. *Gender trouble: Feminism and the subversion of identity*. London: Routledge.

Cardwell, F.S. and Elliott, S.J., 2019. They say 'kids with asthma don't play sports': Geographies of asthma. *Children's Geographies*, 17 (6), 649–663.

Chaudhury, M., *et al.*, 2019. Children's independence and affordances experienced in the context of public open spaces: A study of diverse inner-city and suburban neighbourhoods in Auckland, New Zealand. *Children's Geographies*, 17 (1), 49–63.

Dyment, J.E., 2005. 'There's only so much money hot dog sales can bring in': The intersection of green school grounds and socio-economic status. *Children's Geographies*, 3 (3), 307–323.

Dyment, J.E. and Bell, A.C., 2007. Active by design: Promoting physical activity through school ground greening. *Children's Geographies*, 5 (4), 463–477.

Dyment, J.E., Bell, A.C., and Lucas, A.J., 2009. The relationship between school ground design and intensity of physical activity. *Children's Geographies*, 7 (3), 261–276.

Evans, B., 2006. 'I'd feel ashamed': Girls' bodies and sports participation. *Gender, place & culture*, 13 (5), 547–561.

Evans, B. and Horton, J., 2016. Introduction to play, recreation, health and wellbeing in geographies of children and young people. *In:* B. Evans and J. Horton, eds. *Play and recreation, health and wellbeing*. Singapore: Springer, 1–14.

Gagen, E.A., 2000. Playing the part: Performing gender in America's playgrounds. *In*: S.L. Holloway and G. Valentine, G. eds. *Children's geographies: Playing, living, learning*. London: Routledge, 184–198.

Gunson, J.S., *et al.*, 2016. Participant observation in obesity research with children: Striated and smooth spaces. *Children's Geographies*, 14 (1), 20–34.

Gustafson, K., 2009. Us and them–children's identity work and social geography in a Swedish school yard. *Ethnography and Education*, 4 (1), 1–16.

Harris, F., 2018. Outdoor learning spaces: The case of forest school. *Area*, 50, 222–231.

Hemming, P.J., 2007. Renegotiating the primary school: Children's emotional geographies of sport, exercise and active play. *Children's Geographies*, 5 (4), 353–371.

Hodge, N. and Runswick-Cole, K., 2013. 'They never pass me the ball': Exposing ableism through the leisure experiences of disabled children, young people and their families. *Children's Geographies*, 11 (3), 311–325.

Holloway, S.L., 2014. Changing children's geographies. *Children's Geographies*, 12 (4), 377–392.

Holloway, S.L. and Pimlott-Wilson, H. 2011. Geographies of children, youth and families: Defining achievements, debating the agenda. *In:* L. Holt, ed. *Geographies of children, youth and families: An international perspective*, London: Routledge, 9–24.

Holloway, S.L. and Pimlott-Wilson, H., 2014. Enriching children, institutionalising childhood? Geographies of play, extracurricular activities, and parenting in England. *Annals of the Association of American Geographers*, 104 (3), 613–627.

Holloway, S.L. and Pimlott-Wilson, H., 2018. Reconceptualising play: Balancing childcare, extra-curricular activities and free play in contemporary childhoods. *Transactions of the Institute of British Geographers*, 43 (3), 420–434.

Holloway, S.L. and Valentine, G. 2000. Children's geographies and the new social studies of childhood. *In:* S.L. Holloway and G. Valentine, eds. *Children's geographies: Playing, living, learning*. London: Routledge, 1–22.

Holloway, S.L., *et al.*, 2010. Geographies of education and the significance of children, youth and families. *Progress in Human Geography*, 34 (5), 583–600.

Holt, L., 2010. Young people's embodied social capital and performing disability. *Children's Geographies*, 8 (1), 25–37.

Holt, N.L., *et al.*, 2015. 'Eyes on where children play': A retrospective study of active free play. *Children's Geographies*, 13 (1), 73–88.

Holt, L., *et al.*, 2020. Editorial introduction to Children's Geographies Sponsored lecture section: Generational orderings and Geographies of Children and youth. *Children's Geographies*, 18 (2), 125–127.

Karsten, L., 2005. It all used to be better? Different generations on continuity and change in urban children's daily use of space. *Children's Geographies*, 3 (3), 275–290.

Karsten, L., 2015. Middle-class childhood and parenting culture in high-rise Hong Kong: On scheduled lives, the school trap and a new urban idyll. *Children's Geographies*, 13 (5), 556–570.

Lee, J. and Abbott, R., 2009. Physical activity and rural young people's sense of place. *Children's Geographies*, 7 (2), 191–208.

Lleixà, T. and Nieva, C., 2020. The social inclusion of immigrant girls in and through physical education. Perceptions and decisions of physical education teachers. *Sport, Education and Society*, 25 (2), 185–198.

Maitland, C., *et al.*, 2019. Capturing the geography of children's active and sedentary behaviours at home: The HomeSPACE measurement tool. *Children's Geographies*, 17 (3), 291–308.

Newman, M., Woodcock, A., and Dunham, P., 2006. 'Playtime in the borderlands': Children's representations of school, gender and bullying through photographs and interviews. *Children's geographies*, 4 (3), 289–302.

Ní Laoire, C., 2011. 'Girls just like to be friends with people': Gendered experiences of migration among children and youth in returning Irish migrant families. *Children's Geographies*, 9 (3-4), 303–318.
Nordbakke, S., 2019. Children's out-of-home leisure activities: Changes during the last decade in Norway. *Children's geographies*, 17 (3), 347–360.
Parsons, K.J. and Traunter, J., 2020. Muddy knees and muddy needs: Parents perceptions of outdoor learning. *Children's Geographies*, 18 (6), 699–711.
Pavlidis, A., 2018. Making "space" for women and girls in sport: An agenda for Australian geography. *Geographical Research*, 56 (4), 343–352.
Pawlowski, C.S., *et al.*, 2019. Changing recess geographies: Children's perceptions of a schoolyard renovation project promoting physical activity. *Children's Geographies*, 17 (6), 664–675.
Pimlott-Wilson, H. and Coates, J., 2019. Rethinking learning? Challenging and accommodating neoliberal educational agenda in the integration of Forest School in mainstream educational settings. *The Geographical Journal*, 185, 268–278.
Poveda, D., *et al.*, 2007. The after school routines of literature-devoted urban children. *Children's Geographies*, 5 (4), 423–441.
Pynn, S.R., *et al.*, 2019. An intergenerational qualitative study of the good parenting ideal and active free play during middle childhood. *Children's Geographies*, 17 (3), 266–277.
Radkowska-Walkowicz, M., 2021. Bad television, unhealthy computers? Children's mapping of health, fun and morality. *Children's Geographies*, 19 (6), 629–645.
Ridgers, N.D., Knowles, Z.R., and Sayers, J., 2012. Encouraging play in the natural environment: A child-focused case study of Forest School. *Children's Geographies*, 10(1), 49–65.
Robson, E., Horton, J., and Kraftl, P., 2013. Children's geographies: Reflecting on our first ten years. *Children's Geographies*, 11 (1), 1–6.
Russell, W. and Stenning, A. 2020. Beyond active travel: Children, play and community on streets during and after the coronavirus lockdown [online]. *Cities & Health*. Available from: https://www.tandfonline.com/doi/full/10.1080/23748834.2020.1795386 [Accessed 31 March 2022].
Skår, M. and Krogh, E., 2009. Changes in children's nature-based experiences near home: From spontaneous play to adult-controlled, planned and organised activities. *Children's Geographies*, 7 (3), 339–354.
Smith, T.A., 2013. The dominant/marginal lives of young Tanzanians: Spaces of knowing at the intersection of children's geographies and development geographies. *Geoforum*, 48, 10–23.
Snow, D., *et al.*, 2019. Girls' perspectives on the ideal school playground experience: An exploratory study of four Australian primary schools. *Children's Geographies*, 17 (2), 148–161.
Spark, C., Porter, L., and de Kleyn, L., 2019. 'We're not very good at soccer': gender, space and competence in a Victorian primary school. *Children's Geographies*, 17 (2), 190–203.
Stenning, A. and Russell, W., 2020. *Improving safe access to street space for children's play and physical activity* [online]. Available from: https://blogs.ncl.ac.uk/alisonstenning/improving-safe-access-to-street-space-for-childrens-play-and-physical-activity/ [Accessed 31 March 2022].
Thomson, S., 2005. 'Territorialising' the primary school playground: Deconstructing the geography of playtime. *Children's Geographies*, 3 (1), 63–78.
Thomson, J.L. and Philo, C., 2004. Playful spaces? A social geography of children's play in Livingston, Scotland. *Children's Geographies*, 2 (1), 111–130.
Tranter, P.J. and Malone, K., 2004. Geographies of environmental learning: An exploration of children's use of school grounds. *Children's Geographies*, 2 (1), 131–155.
Trussell, D.E. and Shaw, S.M., 2012. Organised youth sport and parenting in public and private spaces. *Leisure Sciences*, 34 (5), 377–394.
Valentine, G., 2000. Children, geography and. *In:* R.J. Johnston, *et al.*, eds. *The Dictionary of Human Geography, 4th Ed.* Oxford: Blackwell Publishing, 78–79.
Valentine, G. and McKendrick, J., 1997. Children's outdoor play: Exploring parental concerns about children's safety and the changing nature of childhood. *Geoforum*, 28 (2), 219–235.
Veitch, J., Salmon, J., and Ball, K., 2007. Children's perceptions of the use of public open spaces for active free-play. *Children's Geographies*, 5 (4), 409–422.
Wake, S.J., 2008. 'In the best interests of the child': Juggling the geography of children's gardens (between adult agendas and children's needs). *Children's Geographies*, 6 (4), 423–435.
Wise, N. and Kohe, G.Z., 2020. Sports geography: New approaches, perspectives and directions. *Sport in Society: Cultures, Commerce, Media, Politics*, 23 (1), 1–169.

Witten, K., *et al.*, 2013. New Zealand parents' understandings of the intergenerational decline in children's independent outdoor play and active travel. *Children's Geographies*, 11 (2), 215–229.

Woodyer, T., Martin, D., and Carter, S. 2016. Ludic geographies. *In:* B. Evans and J. Horton, eds. *Play and recreation, health and wellbeing*. Singapore: Springer, 17–34.

Woolley, H.E. and Griffin, E., 2015. Decreasing experiences of home range, outdoor spaces, activities and companions: Changes across three generations in Sheffield in north England. *Children's Geographies*, 13 (6), 677–691.

Yantzi, N.M., Young, N.L., and Mckeever, P., 2010. The suitability of school playgrounds for physically disabled children. *Children's Geographies*, 8 (1), 65–78.

# 43

# THE LEARNING CULTURES OF INFORMAL SELF-ORGANISED ACTION SPORTS: IMPLICATIONS FOR CHILD AND YOUTH COACHING

*Belinda Wheaton and Robert C. Townsend*

## Introduction

The global sporting landscape is undergoing some notable shifts in youth participation, particularly with respect to the largely unquestioned dominance of traditional sports. The increasingly popularity of action, lifestyle, and adventure sports such as skateboarding, parkour, BMX, mountain biking, and snowboarding, is an important trend in youth lifestyles noted in many countries around the world (Wheaton, 2013; Jeanes *et al.*, 2018). As a result, traditional sports must compete for attention against an "ever-increasing range of leisure activities and trends in the digital world, and in 'real' time and space" (Gilchrist and Wheaton, 2017, p. 6). As the decision to include surfing, skateboarding and sport climbing in the Tokyo 2020 Olympics clearly demonstrates, even the Olympic Movement is having to respond to new consumer interests to remain relevant to younger generations through the assimilation of youth-oriented action sports into the Olympic programme (Wheaton and Thorpe, 2021). Thus, while activities such as skateboarding were once seen by parents and youth sport providers as encouraging 'rebellious' and 'deviant' behaviour, they are increasingly being recognised as important sites for youth development (Bradley, 2010; Säfvenbom *et al.*, 2018) including in institutionalised settings and PE curricula (Wheaton and O'Loughlin 2017; Jeanes *et al.*, 2018; O'Connor and Penney, 2020).

As such, some action sports are quickly becoming integrated into 'mainstream' sporting culture, resulting in the increased visibility of informal, lifestyle sports in youth leisure and influencing the way action sports are practiced. For example, Thorpe and Wheaton illustrate the increasing professionalisation of some action sports through their inclusion in international competitions such as the Olympics (Thorpe and Wheaton, 2011; Wheaton and Thorpe, 2021). One way of examining how action sports are moving towards professionalisation is to consider their investment in, and importance attached to, coach and athlete development (Ellmer and Rynne, 2018). Typically, 'coaching' is largely invisible in action sports contexts with athlete learning largely informal and self-regulated, with peer-to-peer learning dominating and digital technologies playing a central role (Wheaton, 2013; Ellmer *et al.*, 2019; Ojala and Thorpe,

 DOI: 10.4324/9781003199359-49

2015). However, the level of professionalism and interest in action and lifestyle sports has resulted in increased recognition from organisations on the importance of coaching (Ojala and Thorpe, 2015). Furthermore, positioning action sports as an important trend in youth lifestyles necessitates a critical focus on developing high-quality coaches in these contexts to support equitable, quality experiences, reduce risk and ensure safeguarding. Therefore, the rapid institutionalisation of action sports provides a unique framework for examining the role, practice, and function of coaches in these unique sporting cultures.

This chapter will explore this changing landscape of action and lifestyle youth sports cultures, considering this shift from informal learning to formalised coaching and learning in more structured environments, as well as examining some of the challenges and opportunities for children and youth. First, the dominance of informal learning environments in lifestyle sports is discussed, including the use of digital technologies. Drawing on sociocultural views of learning (Lave and Wenger, 1991) the discussion shows how disrupting the 'adult as expert' – commonly observed in traditional coaching cultures – can create less hierarchical and more equitable learning environments. Second, the ways the professionalisation of some action sports is impacting on these informal learning environments and cultures is outlined, including engaging young athletes in structured training programmes, coaching, and high-performance pathways (Ojala and Thorpe, 2015). The ways that coaching often differs in ethos and approach to many traditional sporting cultures are highlighted, examining some of the challenges and opportunities for formalised coaching practices in action sports. Third, the chapter considers the potential implications for safety management and young athlete welfare in action sports, particularly where coaches are absent from learning environments. Lastly, it outlines future directions and considerations in coaching research and policy/practice.

## Review of Current Research

### *Action Sports and Informal Learning Cultures*

A defining feature of action and lifestyle sports is their self-organised and spontaneous nature, with participation in predominantly informal settings, often without external regulation or institutionalisation (Wheaton, 2013). While the reasons for the popularity of particular action sports vary, key aspects that appear to engage children and youth include their flexible formats often without competitive structures or leagues; their individualistic nature lacking rules and regulations, their anti-authoritarian, 'do-it-yourself' cultural values, and the ability for self-definition often without adult control (Gilchrist and Wheaton, 2017). Within these environments, attributes including physical prowess, creativity, and risk-taking are often highly valued.

Despite the proliferation of research on the changing cultures of action and lifestyle sports, research on the learning of action sport participants and how it takes place is limited (Ellmer *et al.*, 2019). Furthermore, as part of this learning process while coaches and coaching are acknowledged as becoming more prominent in these contexts (Ellmer *et al.*, 2019) it is evident that comparatively little about coaching in these sub-cultures compared to more 'traditional', established sports (e.g. soccer, rugby). Ojala and Thorpe (2015) suggested that for young athletes the lure of a highly profitable career in action sports has necessitated increased guidance from coaches in more organised training structures. Nevertheless, the cultural values of action sport cultures influence how some athletes perceive and approach working with coaches. For example, Wheaton (2004) has highlighted the importance of participant control, creativity, and 'do-it-yourself' ideologies. As such, the existing empirical work in action sports paints a picture of athlete learning as highly networked, largely informal, and, more recently, technology-assisted (Ojala and Thorpe, 2015; Enright and Gard, 2016). Rather than engaging in directed training programmes under the watchful gaze of coaches, many participants draw on a mixture of trial-and-error practices characterised by a high volume of self-directed repetition, observation of others, peer feedback and mentoring, and increasingly the use of technology and social media to learn the skills required to perform and, in some instances, compete (Ojala and Thorpe, 2015; Ellmer *et al.*, 2019).

In terms of skill development, research has illustrated the various ways that action sports athletes adopt a 'self-check' style through the use of images – from sequences of still images in magazines to moving imagery in films and videos (Gilchrist and Wheaton, 2013). Watching videos as a method to learn physical tricks has been identified across different action sports from longboard skateboarders (Enright and Gard, 2016) to surfers and parkour (Gilchrist and Wheaton, 2013). Increasingly, fuelled by advances in and greater access to technology many action sports participants film their own tricks to review and improve their performance. For example, Jones (2011) explored the role of digital media and creativity in the processes of learning that occur amongst urban skateboarders, showing that the production and consumption of DIY videos contributed to skaters' mastery of the techniques of the sport, to document the stages of their learning, as well as to their integration into the culture. This is typically achieved through establishing social media profiles and developing content with friends and the wider community. As such, athletes participate in the production, sharing, and acquisition of knowledge (termed prosumers, see Woermann, 2012) but also for feedback and critique from others.

A further line of inquiry into learning in action sport cultures has illustrated the value of sensory feedback and embodied knowledge (e.g. Bäckström, 2014). This perspective examines the ways in which the built and natural environment where the activities take place – from mountains and oceans to city streets – are central to the practice and learning of embodied knowledge. Participants have also been constructed as being in synergy with the space and their environment they engage (Kidder, 2012; Bäckström, 2014), which is also important for developing skills and cultural knowledge. For example, surfers need to acquire knowledge of the weather to be able to predict swells, and learn to read and respond to ocean currents and waveforms as part of their immersion in the culture and their training practices.

## *Implications for Learning and Coaching*

Together, this body of work highlights a unique landscape for the learning and acquisition of skills and knowledge in action sports. Despite being an individualistic activity, social engagement with others is a primary mechanism for learning for athletes in informal, action sports. In essence, learning is viewed as part of social practice, and participation in social (communities of) practice by definition will involve learning, as the process of becoming a member of a community allows learning to take place. Being 'situated' means that people learn as they participate (Cushion and Townsend, 2016). Importantly, while interaction does form the basis for learning in these cultures, unlike in traditional sports these interactions do not follow the typical hierarchical, 'expertise' driven model of instruction between coaches and athletes, where coaches engage in a 'top down' transmission of expert knowledge (Côté, 2006; see also Wheaton and O'Loughlin, 2017). Rather, the 'coaching' process is based on a distribution of power across networks that are intergenerational and interdependent, where knowledge is co-constructed between learners and mediated by the language and norms of the culture, the availability of and access to technology as well as the built or natural environment. This represents a distinct and important departure in coaching research, where a body of critical sociological scholarship has illustrated the power of coaches in directing the norms within a sporting subculture, where athletes are passive recipients of coaches' values and preferences (e.g. Cushion and Jones 2006, 2014) and are immersed in disciplinary training regimes based on body management, surveillance, and control (e.g. Williams and Manley, 2016).

Together, this complex assemblage provides a framework for learning in sporting subcultures that reflects a powerful form of enculturation, involving the construction of identities and the historical production, transformation, and change of persons (Lave and Wenger, 1991). The informal nature of lifestyle and action sports cultures, with an absence of coaches, means that athletes adopt the language (vocabulary), customs (values), and beliefs of the subculture to direct their learning. Importantly, in so doing athletes are engaged in a process of identity construction through participation and learning in a community through socially-situated activity (Holland and Lave, 2009). For participants within informal, action sports, central identity-generating activities take place *in* practice, in which learners participate, and *through* the digital spaces they also inhabit, further reinforcing the absence of adult mediation and instruction. As such, learning can be understood as a process of becoming, of forging identities in the world, with action sports providing a focused site for youth development (Thorpe, 2016). Therefore, the impact of large scale shifts in lifestyle and action sports characterised by formalisation, institutionalisation, and innovation linked to professionalism has important implications for individual and collective identities.

## Sportisation, Professionalism, and Coaching

'Sportisation' (Elias and Dunning, 1986; Maguire, 2007) is a useful concept to help illustrate the processes by which informal, play-like activities become more regulated, organised, and 'sports-like' (Wheaton and O'Loughlin, 2017). Sportisation, along with commercialisation and higher levels of media exposure has had a significant impact on the cultures and practices of most action and lifestyle sports over the past decades. With the proliferation of international competitions (e.g. X Games), the emergence of lucrative commercial sponsors (Smits, 2019) – even for some young children – and the increased use of social media technologies (Evers, 2019) the experiences of action sport athletes is rapidly changing with competitive success seen as increasingly legitimate, particularly by youth (Wheaton and Thorpe, 2021). This is further exemplified through the 'fast tracking' of youth athletes into elite sport environments, such as the teenage girls who dominated in skateboarding's debut Olympics in Tokyo (Jancetic, 2021).

The rapid professionalisation of action sports has clear implications for the development of coaching. Wheaton and Thorpe (2021) examined the impact of the Olympic inclusion on the sports of skateboarding, surfing and sport climbing between 2015 and 2020 in their preparation for inclusion in the Tokyo summer Olympic Games. Each sport has had a different development pattern; for example, in skateboarding, sportisation was less advanced than the other new Olympic action sports, and many countries did not have a sport governing body even by 2020. In sports including snowboarding, BMX, surfing, windsurfing, kite-surfing, and skateboarding, inclusion in future Olympic programmes has in some national contexts intensified the process of sportisation through the increased allocation of high-performance funding to coach and athlete development (Ellmer and Rynne, 2016; Strittmatter *et al.*, 2019; Wheaton and Thorpe, 2021). While the distribution of funds varies between countries and sports, there is a noticeable trend in national sports organisations and National Olympic Committees investing in their performance pathways, for example through allocating scholarships to talented athletes, developing elite training facilities, and providing athletes with access to full time coaching and sport science support (Ellmer and Rynne, 2018; Wheaton and Thorpe, 2021). For some of these sports, this has meant a radical shift in approaches to learning and training. As noted above unlike more traditional sporting cultures the use of coaches as a way to learn skills was considered antithetical to the value systems embedded in many action sport cultures. In skateboarding, for instance, coaching has long been considered a "taboo" subject, as one skateboarding journalist wrote:

> For many of us the idea of skateboarding as a competitive or team sport has long been a point of contention. And because the word "coach" automatically conjures up images of sweaty old jocks with whistles and exercise drills, it's sometimes not a very respected profession in the skateboarding world.
>
> *(Nieratko, 2014, para. 2 cited in Wheaton and Thorpe, 2021, p. 153)*

Despite a degree of hesitance in some action sports such as BMX racing, sport climbing, and snowboarding, elite athletes – many of whom are teenagers – are increasingly engaging in full-time, structured, and disciplined training regimes working with coaches, personal trainers, and sport scientists, to develop the skills and physical conditioning (i.e. strength, endurance and flexibility) necessary for international competition while minimising the potential for injury (Wheaton and Thorpe, 2021). While very little is known about the day-to-day practices of coaching in these contexts, nonetheless, as Ojala and Thorpe (2015) suggest athlete–coach relationships tend to differ from more traditional, hierarchical coach–athlete relationships observed in traditional sporting contexts. The suggestion is that the role of coaches in some action sports (e.g. snowboarding) is unique and evolving, and further research is needed to challenge and expand our understanding of the role, function, and practices of coaches in general.

So, despite some observable changes in the organisation of action sports there is considerable variation in the importance attached to formalised coaching structures. Indeed, arguably the nature of the role is yet to be fully realised in informal action and lifestyle sports (Lyons *et al.*, 2012) bearing in mind the extensive contribution of coaches to high-performance sport generally. Noticeably, in action sports such as snowboarding, surfing, and sport climbing the importance attached to coaches (in some national contexts) is reflected in the lack of clear developmental pathways for coaches and limited appetite for accreditation, credentials, and licensing (Ellmer and Rynne, 2018). As such, the extent to which sports organisations invest in coach development is indicative of an emerging and evolving position in relation to coaching and a sub-culture where coaches do not feature prominently (Wheaton and Thorpe, 2021). In many countries, the lack of funded national/regional development pathways for either elite or youth competitors means that even for those who wanted to access coaching it is not always available. Wheaton and Thorpe's research found that in 2018 most international surfing competitors in New Zealand (including the Olympic qualifiers) did not have a coach for their skill development, nor support for fitness and preparation. Most relied on local support, Instagram and video analysis; some occasionally paid for coaching including overseas. As a world top 16 competitor explained:

> I just try and coach myself a lot of the time, or I'll send the footage to a coach or I'll work with a coach maybe every couple of months and take something away from them and try and work on it.

The extent to which sportisation is likely to collectivise action sports coaches and situate them within a professional pathway is yet to be seen. However, there are some general trends across actions sports in the willingness to adopt aspects of high-performance sporting culture such as coaching. First, and a familiar situation in the broader coaching literature (e.g. Townsend and Cushion, 2017), action sport athletes traditionally place greater value on coaches with high levels of experience as athletes themselves, bringing with them a high level of cultural status and respect most often as a recently retired athlete (Ojala and Thorpe, 2015). Such individuals are perceived to bring important embodied understandings of the unique cultural dynamics and value systems within action sport cultures. Wheaton and Thorpe's (2021) interviews with those working in surfing's NSOs and preparing athletes for Olympic readiness highlighted almost all elite surfing coaches having previously been professional surfers themselves, often without formal coaching skills or qualifications. They explained that most surfers held the view that "if you don't surf, there's no way you can be a coach" (interview, 2017); athletes appeared to need to be 'managed' by individuals with understanding of their sport's ethos and culture values.

Second, as some action sports lacked national sporting bodies – and therefore formal athlete development pathways – coaches have typically been hired as independent contractors either by the athlete, their parents, or brand-based performance teams (e.g. Team Burton). This situation has created problems for NSOs to implement an integrated high-performance team structure as is common in most high-performance sports. For example, in Australia, although coaching was being more widely adopted in surfing than in many countries, the NSO found it was a complex area to develop effectively. As such, the NSO had to facilitate significant changes in cultural attitudes for the surfers and their support to recognise and accept more mainstream professional approaches to skill development and value other aspects of HP training:

> The idea is that we have integrated performance teams. That's very new to surfing. That's pretty standard [in] high-performance sport ... but surfing, that was foreign to our sport.
>
> *(interview Surfing Australia, 2018 cited in Wheaton and Thorpe, 2021, p. 245)*

Third, expertise in areas such as physical conditioning, applying psychological skills and nutrition was largely informal and self-directed or absent. For example, Surfing New Zealand (SNZ) held its first-ever high-performance workshop for national-level junior and senior athletes in 2017. Many of the surfers attending were unaware of areas such as mental skills, and did not have any input into their physical development or conditioning. As with skill coaching, the NSO found they had to "educate" the athletes, their parents, and surfing's "old-school skills coaches" about the role and benefits of such expertise, where sport-specific knowledge was valued over high-performance training or sports medicine principles:

> It's like no, "He doesn't know that, he's not a surfing coach", and yet they're a qualified doctor or strength and conditioning coach, and they deal with Olympic athletes in soccer and all these things.
>
> *(interview at SNZ event, 2017 cited in Wheaton and Thorpe, 2021, p. 238)*

Nonetheless, Wheaton and Thorpe (2021) found that the teenage athletes' who had attended these HP camps thought it was very effective, with many subsequently choosing to train regularly with these and other individuals for their physical development. As one 15-year-old surfer claimed:

> It's probably the best thing I've done for my surfing. It's really good because I just kind of – it's injury prevention. I use my body in the right way and it just means that I'll be at the top of my form when I go out and compete.
>
> *(interview, 2017 cited in Wheaton and Thorpe, 2021, p. 238)*

Despite this situation at the elite level, many parents are seeking out coaches and training camps (e.g. Camp Woodward, Windells for skateboarders) for their children who are entering action sports competitions and pursuing careers as action sport athletes from ever younger ages. Coaching is also becoming much more prevalent amongst more recreational participants, with the concept of youth residential 'camps' (e.g. in skateboarding and surfing) proliferating in some countries where – due to a lack of full-time contracts and roles in the sport – coaches look to supplement their income. Finally it is important to note that as action sport coaching is a relatively new development, the lack of coaches and of coach development opportunities remains an issue, as does the limitations of only involving those individuals with the levels of cultural capital in the sport to aid in this professionalisation process. Concurrently, there is a reluctance among some action sports coaches to engage in traditional coach education and professional development (Wheaton and Thorpe, 2021). Thus, while the opportunities for action sport coaches are increasing as these sports become more institutionalised, social networks and personal connections remain the main gatekeeper to access this unique labour market. Given the male-dominated cultures of most action sports, particularly at the elite level and within their industries, this appears to have impact on opportunities for female coaches; the majority of which are men (although the USA Skateboarding National Team hired long-time professional skateboarder, Mimi Knoop, as team manager for the 16 members). Reflecting many traditional sports, women are also critically underrepresented across formal leadership positions in action sports (Wheaton and Thorpe, 2018, 2021). The gender and racial politics in such leadership positions, both formal and informal (see Wheaton and Thorpe, 2021), and the implications for more professional opportunities for coaches, across action sports are deserving of further attention. Furthermore, as discussed in the following section, there are also several issues to consider in relation to equity and welfare of participants, especially children.

## Implications for Children's Sport Coaching

This section outlines two interrelated issues of particular relevance for coaching children and youth in action sports; child welfare, and risk and safety. It can be reasonably argued that all action sports do, to some extent, involve a degree of risk since they require specific and often complex skills, possess an element of physical challenge, and occur in either continually changing or dynamic environments (Collins and Collins, 2013). This may be part of the 'pull' for some participants, and thus is a major factor in participation (Salome and van Bottenburg, 2012; Wheaton, 2013). As action sports become increasingly institutionalised and professionalised, younger athletes are training and competing at the elite level which has provided lucrative sponsorships and advertising deals for some young action sport stars. For example, Tokyo Olympic medal-winning skateboarders Sky Brown and Rayssa Leal were just 13 years old and yet have multi-million-dollar corporate contracts including Nike, and digital followers in the millions. Such visibility brings with it a range of often competing expectations and pressures which must be navigated including from parents, coaches, corporate sponsors, national sporting bodies, and digital audiences. While some action sport athletes have employed agents and social media teams to manage their multiple roles and responsibilities, including competition schedules, training, and corporate and media interests, in most cases athletes are working alone, or with the help of their parents, often with little support for safety management and athlete welfare. In sport such as skateboarding and surfing, many of these athletes are teenage or younger girls, raising important questions about child welfare.

Some commentators have observed increasing parental pressure on younger athletes in recent years; for some, this is because the parents "grew up in a high pressure, high performance" sport culture, and "are really trying to apply that type of belief on behalf of their children" (interview, 2015 in Wheaton and Thorpe, 2021). This pressure, and the often-unacknowledged mental health issues that can come with such expectations, were brought to the fore with the tragic suicide of British professional snowboarder Ellie Soutter on her 18th birthday (in 2018). Soutter's father subsequently spoke publicly about mental health concerns, head injuries, and the excessive pressure on young athletes. In the lead up to the Tokyo Olympics the horrific life-threatening crash experienced by the then 12-year-old world number three skateboarding sensation, Sky Brown while 'training' with legend Tony Hawk on his private ramp, gained widespread international media attention. Although Brown was using a helmet, she had serious injuries including skull fractures, and it is reported that the hospital ICU team struggled to get her conscious and keep her alive (Morse, 2020a, 2020b). Such incidents, while rare, raise important questions about the normalisation of the high-risks being taken by increasingly young action sport athletes, and the responsibilities of adults (i.e. parents, agents, coaches) who are "supporting" these pre-teen action sport participants in their careers. While young athletes may wish to take calculated risks, they should only do so with the necessary skills and experience, underlining the need for coaches to ensure safe, effective, and enjoyable experiences for children. In the subsequent media coverage of Sky Brown's crash, her father claims that the pressure for Sky to continue preparing for the Olympics was his daughter's, and that he tried to dissuade her. The family also claims that her decision to represent the UK not Japan (she has dual nationality) was Team GB's more laid-back approach (Hayes, 2021); "Come be on our team, there's no pressure, just get out there and have fun'. Sky recounts that this approach "made my parents feel a little better" (Sky Brown cited in Hayes, 2021).

With coaches absent from many learning environments, the issues for athletes' protection and welfare – as well as equity issues more widely – in action sports are complex. Olympic inclusion has certainly nudged some action sport IFs and NSOs to develop policies and processes to better support athlete health and wellbeing, but these are largely underdeveloped (Wheaton and Thorpe, 2021). Issues of athlete welfare and protection, particularly for young girls, need to be at the forefront of developments facilitating ethical and responsible young athlete support and development (Smits, 2019).

## Risk, Safety, and Coaching

A range of responses to the concerns around risk has materialised. On one hand those who promote and practice the activities have pointed out that perceptions of high-risk are often unfounded (Bradley, 2010; Gilchrist and Wheaton, 2011). However, some have expressed disquiet about children's safety in these unregulated environments, and where the use of protective clothing (especially helmets) is not enforced, and cultures often glorify a 'no-pain no gain' attitude (Beal and Wilson, 2004; Dumas and Laforest, 2009). Furthermore, in activities like parkour and street skateboarding, participants use the city's streets and landscapes in ways that are seen as challenging their designated function (Borden, 2001). For example, public perceptions of parkour is that it is dangerous and participants are irresponsible (see Atkinson and Young, 2008, Gilchrist and Wheaton, 2011). These attitudes, along with conflicts around the use of space, have been prevalent in skateboarding and parkour (Borden, 2001; Thorpe, 2011; Wheaton and O'Loughlin, 2017), and have fuelled forms of regulation, and the emergence of more regulated, but mostly commercially-driven environments, particularly for children (Atencio *et al.*, 2018).

In relation to coaching, a key challenge however is how to formalise training for action sports athletes, ensuring a level of safety and risk management in these activities, without stripping them of the flexibility, informality, and opportunities for self-directed practices that have been central to their appeal. Part of this challenge is addressing the potential role of coaches. Collins and Collins (2013) argued that risk management is an essential element of a coach's skill set and is routinely embedded in the decision-making processes of action sports coaching. Furthermore, safety and risk management tends to occupy a small, but important, place in coach education programmes. The broad range of children's motivations for engaging in action sports requires a differentiated pedagogic skill set from coaches that is balanced with a considered understanding of the risks associated with training and performance. Yet, the absence of many formalised coach education pathways in action sports means that coaches may act on intuition and experience, which as Collins and Collins (2013) argue can be clouded by familiarity with the environment, adherence to 'fixed' coaching plans, a heightened sense of confidence in decision-making and minimisation of risk, which can increase the risks associated with action sports participation particularly in a youth sport context. Hence, the need to educate coaches and instructors, evaluating and certifying their expertise, is an issue of particular importance in lifestyle and action sports. However, as noted above in some sports there is a resistance to the perceived need for accreditation and the proliferation of coaching qualifications to support coaches professional judgement and decision-making.

The challenges for sports that are predominantly based on individual experiential learning and peer support is thus magnified when considering risk and safety. To illustrate, research on the ways in which parkour has been adapted for more formal and adult-led settings, including school physical education programmes, is informative. Shifts to assimilate Parkour into contemporary youth sport has resulted in increased focus on managing risk and safety (Wheaton, 2013; Sterchele and Ferrero Camoletto, 2017), which in turn has created calls for formalising safety standards and regulations, including the introduction of coaching qualifications (Gilchrist and Wheaton, 2011; Wheaton, 2013). The imposition of coaching standards is, for some, perceived as necessary for reassuring public opinion and legitimising the activity as safe (Sterchele and Ferrero Camoletto, 2017). However, the challenge of a professional and regulatory framework enacted through coach education is that it necessarily 'normalises' and standardises the practice of Parkour, positioning it as a 'set of skills', and reducing the number of interpretations and performance styles evident throughout the sport (Wheaton, 2013). Central to the teaching and learning of parkour is recognition that it is not a set of skills – as is often believed by those who are not practitioners (i.e. gymnasts) – but rather it represents a hidden curriculum into which athletes are socialised to value responsibility and self-mastery rather than overt competition, promoting coping with managed risks, fear, and working on problem-solving and decision-making (Fernández-Río and Suarez, 2014). Thus, creating coach education pathways is likely to continue to meet pockets of localised resistance from practitioners, notwithstanding broader governance issues about 'who' has the power to create and administer formal coaching qualifications (Sterchele and Ferrero Camoletto, 2017; Wheaton and O'Loughlin, 2017).

## Summary, Future Directions, and Future Research

This chapter has examined the changing landscape of action sports with a particular focus on the implications for youth sport coaching. Clearly, the ongoing professionalisation of action sports will impact on the extent to which coaching will establish itself as fundamental to the delivery of action sports in youth contexts. Against this background further research might wish to consider the unique context of action sports to explore the creation of coaching as a profession. Specifically, how coaching is implicated in protecting the shared cultural interests of action sports in the face of rapid professionalisation, exploring the hybridisation of the coaching role, and how action sports cultures respond to the corresponding need for educational pathways and credentials to support coaches all offer fruitful lines of inquiry.

Further questions might also examine the dynamic learning communities that exist in these youth contexts. In action sports, the processes, relationships, and experiences that constitute the participants' sense of identity and belonging underpin the nature of subsequent learning, providing a unique framework for the development of coaching knowledge. Furthermore, the shifting material-economic practices and power relations shaping action sports globally can create sites of "contentious local practice", where participants are "historically related, partially united, partially divided, and surely always in conflict and tension through different political stances and relations of power" (Holland and Lave, 2009, p. 3). As such, researchers may wish to consider exploring both the development of coaching knowledge and the ongoing struggles to develop coaching as a legitimate, knowledge-building activity and practice (see Wheaton and O'Loughlin, 2017). Finally, further research is required to shed light on the coaching processes evident in action sports, with particular focus on managing risk and the welfare of youth athletes.

## References


Atencio. M., *et al.*, 2018. *Moving boarders skateboarding and the changing landscape of urban youth sports.* Fayetteville, AR: University of Arkansas Press.

Atkinson, M., & Young, K. (2001). Flesh journeys: The radical body modification of neoprimatives. *Deviant Behavior*, 22 (2), 117–146.

Bäckström, A., 2014. Knowing and teaching kinaesthetic experience in skateboarding: An example of sensory emplacement. *Sport, Education and Society*, 19 (6), 752–772.

Beal, B. and Wilson, C., 2004. "Chicks dig scars": Commercialisation and the transformations of skateboarders' identities. *In*: B. Wheaton, ed. *Understanding lifestyle sport: Consumption, identity and difference.* London: Routledge, 31–54.

Borden, I., 2001. *Skateboarding, space and the city: Architecture and the body.* Oxford: Berg.

Bradley, G., 2010. Skate parks as a context for adolescent development. *Journal of Adolescent Research*, 25, 288–323.

Côté, J., 2006. The development of coaching knowledge. *International Journal of Sports Science and Coaching*, 1, 217–222.

Collins, L. and Collins, D., 2013. Decision making and risk management in adventure sports coaching, *Quest*, 65 (1), 72–82.

Cushion, C.J. and Jones, R.L., 2006. Power, discourse and symbolic violence in professional youth soccer: The case of Albion Football Club. *Sociology of Sport Journal*, 23, 142–161.

Cushion, C.J. and Jones, R.L., 2014. A bourdieusian analysis of cultural reproduction: Socialisation and the 'hidden curriculum' in professional football. *Sport, Education and Society*, 19 (3), 276–298.

Cushion, C. and Townsend, R., 2016. Jean lave: Learning in coaching as social praxis, *In*: R. Groom, L. Nelson, and P. Potrac, Eds. *Learning in sports coaching*. New York: Routledge.

Dumas, A. and Laforest, S., 2009. Skateparks as a health-resource: Are they as dangerous as they look? *Leisure Studies*, 28, 19–34.

Elias, N. and Dunning, E., 1986. *Quest for excitement: Sport and leisure in the civilizing process.* Oxford: Blackwell.

Ellmer, E. and Rynne, S., 2016. Learning in action and adventure sports. *Asia-Pacific Journal of Health, Sport and Physical Education*, 7 (2), 107–119.

Ellmer, E. and Rynne S., 2018. Professionalisation of action sports in Australia. *Sport in Society* 1–16. Epub ahead of print 13 March 2018.

Ellmer, E., Rynne, S., and Enright, E., 2019. Learning in action sports: A scoping review. *European Physical Education Review*, 26 (1), 263–283.

Enright, E. and Gard, M., 2016. Media, digital technology and learning in sport: A critical response to Hodkinson, Biesta and James. *Physical Education and Sport Pedagogy*, 21 (1), 40–54.

Evers, C. 2019. The gendered emotional labor of male professional 'freesurfers' digital media work. *Sport in Society*, 22 (10), 1691–1706.

Fernández-Río, J. and Suarez, C., 2014. Feasibility and students' preliminary views on parkour in a group of primary school children. *Physical Education and Sport Pedagogy*, 21, 281–294.

Gilchrist, P. and Wheaton, B., 2011. Lifestyle sport, public policy and youth engagement: Examining the emergence of parkour. *International Journal of Sport Policy and Politics*, 3, 109–131.

Gilchrist, P. and Wheaton, B., 2013. New media technologies in lifestyle sport. *In*: B. Hutchins and D. Rowe, eds. *Digital media sport: Technology and power in the network society*. New York: Routledge, 169–185.

Gilchrist, P. and Wheaton, B., 2017. The social benefits of informal and lifestyle sports: A research agenda. *International Journal of Sport Policy and Politics*, 9, 1–15.

Hayes, M., 2021. Teenage skateboard superstar Sky Brown: 'I begged my parents to let me go with Team GB' [online]. The Guardian, July 17. Available from: https://www.theguardian.com/lifeandstyle/2021/jul/17/skateboarding-sky-brown-begged-parents-to-let-me-go-olympics-team-gb

Holland, D. and Lave, J. 2009. Social practice theory and the historical production of persons. *Action: An International Journal of Human Activity Theory*, 2, 1–15.

Jancetic, S., 2021. Heartwarming scenes as girls aged 12 and 13 savour Olympic skateboard medals [online]. August 4. Available from: https://7news.com.au/sport/olympics/olsen-through-to-tokyo-park-final-c-3592061

Jeanes, R., *et al.*, 2018. Managing informal sport participation: Tensions and opportunities. International Journal of Sport Policy and Politics, 11 (1), 79–95.

Jones, R.H., 2011, Sport and re/creation: What skateboarders can teach us about learning. *Sport, Education and Society*, 16 (5), 593–611.

Kidder, J. 2012, Parkour, the affective appropriation of urban space, and the real/virtual dialectic. *City and Community*, 11 (3), 229–253.

Lave, J. and Wenger, E., 1991. *Situated Learning: Legitimate Peripheral Participation*. New York: Cambridge University Press.

Lyons, M., Rynne, S., and Mallett, C., 2012. Reflection and the art of coaching: Fostering high-performance in Olympic ski cross. *Reflective practice*, 13, 359–372.

Maguire, J. 2007. Sportisation. *In*: G. Ritzer, ed. *Blackwell encyclopaedia of sociology*. London: Blackwell, 4710–4711.

Morse, B. 2020a. Skateboarder Sky Brown, 11, hospitalised after horrific fall [online]. CNN. June 3. Available from: https://edition.cnn.com/2020/06/02/sport/sky-brown-injury-fall-skateboarding-spt-intl/index.html

Morse, B. 2020b. Skateboarding prodigy's father speaks of terror not knowing if daughter would 'make it through the night' after horror fall [online]. CNN. June 3. Available from: https://edition.cnn.com/2020/06/03/sport/sky-brown-father-stewart-fall-injury-spt-intl/index.html

O'Connor, J. and Penney, D., 2020. Informal sport and curriculum futures: An investigation of the knowledge, skills and understandings for participation and the possibilities for physical education. *European Physical Education Review*, 27 (1), 3–26.

Ojala, A.L. and Thorpe, H., 2015. The role of the coach in action sports. *International Sports Coaching Journal*, 2, 64–71.

Säfvenbom, R., Wheaton, B., and Agans J., 2018. 'How can you enjoy sports if you are under control by others?' Self-organised lifestyle sports and youth development. *Sport In Society*, 21, 1990–2009.

Salome, L. and van Bottenburg, M., 2012. Are they all daredevils? Introducing a participation typology for the consumption of lifestyle sports in different settings. *European Sport Management Quarterly*, 12, 19–42.

Smits, F., 2019. Young Dutch commercially sponsored kite surfers: Free as a bird? *Sport in Society*, 22 (10), 1707–1723.

Sterchele, D. and Ferrero Camoletto, R., 2017. Governing bodies or managing freedom? Subcultural struggles, national sport systems and the glocalised institutionalisation of parkour. *International Journal of Sport Policy and Politics*, 9 (1), 89–105.

Strittmatter, A-M., *et al.*, 2019. Dual governance structures in action sports: Institutionalisation processes of professional snowboarding revisited. *Sport In Society*, 22, 1655–1673.

Thorpe, H., 2016. Action sports for youth development: Critical insights for the SDP community. *International Journal of Sport Policy and Politics*, 8 (1), 91–116.

Thorpe, H. and Wheaton, B. 2011., 'Generation X Games', action sports and the Olympic movement: Understanding the cultural politics of incorporation. *Sociology*, 45, 830–847.

Townsend, R.C. and Cushion, C.J., 2017. Elite cricket coach education: A Bourdieusian analysis. *Sport, Education and Society*, 22 (4), 528–546.

Wheaton, B., 2004. *Understanding lifestyle sports: Consumption, identity and difference*. London: Routledge.

Wheaton, B., 2013. *The cultural politics of lifestyle sport*. London: Routledge.
Wheaton, B. and O'Loughlin, A., 2017. Informal sport, institutionalisation, and sport policy: Challenging the sportisation of parkour in England. *International Journal of Sport Policy and Politics*, 9, 71–88.
Wheaton, B. and Thorpe, H., 2018. Action sports, the olympic games, and the opportunities and challenges for gender equity: The cases of surfing and skateboarding. *Journal of Sport and Social Issues*, 42, 315–342.
Wheaton, B. and Thorpe, H., 2021. *Action sports and the Olympic Games: Past, present, future*. London: Routledge.
Williams, S. and Manley, A., 2016. Elite coaching and the technocratic engineer: Thanking the boys at Microsoft! *Sport, Education and Society*, 21 (6), 828–850.
Woermann, N., 2012. On the slope is on the screen: Prosumption, social media practices, and scopic systems in the freeskiing subculture. *American Behavioral Scientist*, 56, 618–640.

# 44

# SCALING CHILDREN'S SPORT TO AUGMENT MOTOR SKILL ACQUISITION

*Tim Buszard, Machar Reid, and Damian Farrow*

## Introduction

The concept of modifying children's sport so that the equipment and the task are more appropriately sized might seem common-sense. Junior sports coaches have been offering cut-down equipment and smaller play areas for decades, and more recently sports authorities have mandated new rules to force the adoption of scaled environments. For example, in 2010, the International Tennis Federation made a significant change to junior tennis by mandating the use of lower compression balls in tournaments for children aged 10 and under. Arguably there are few other matters in sport that can have such profound effects on children's on-going participation and development of skill (Reid *et al.*, 2018).

Given the significance of the topic, an important question that must be asked is: *when should children's sport replicate the same dimensions of adult sport?* Although this question cannot be answered with precision yet, the current approach adopted by many sports is to introduce adult-sized conditions by 10 years of age (Buszard *et al.*, 2016b). Indeed, the hypothesis of the current chapter is that this is too young, and the consequences of inappropriately sized games are diminished skill development and decreased participation.

The aim of this chapter is to take a closer look at studies published over the past five years that have focused on the scaling of junior sport. Indeed, there have been at least 24 articles published since the most recent systematic review on the topic (Buszard *et al.*, 2016b). These 24 studies include the reporting of empirical data (as outlined in Table 44.1), as well as review articles or articles describing simulations (e.g. Buszard *et al.*, 2020a; Harwood *et al.*, 2020; Buszard *et al.*, 2021). These contributions are addressed by summarising the results under the same sub-headings as the previous systematic review: (1) psychological factors, (2) skill performance and acquisition factors, (3) biomechanical factors, (4) cognitive factors. We then conclude the chapter by outlining the practical implications when coaching children, as well as summarising gaps in the field for future research to explore.

## Review of Current Research

### *Psychological Factors*

Previously the consensus was that appropriately modified equipment for children leads to greater engagement (Farrow and Reid, 2010), boosts self-efficacy (Chase *et al.*, 1994; Arias, 2012), and is


DOI: 10.4324/9781003199359-50

*Table 44.1* Studies examining the influence of equipment scaling on children's sport performance since Buszard *et al.* (2016b)

| *Sport* | *Reference* | *Modification* | *Population studied* | *Primary outcome: positive (Y/N)* | *Main finding* |
|---|---|---|---|---|---|
| Australian Football | Hadlow *et al.* (2017) | Ball size | 13 y experienced | N | Kicking performance did not differ between two ball size (size 4 and 5) during two types of skills tests: a decision-making test (i.e. dynamic) and a set shot test (i.e. stationary). Kinematic differences were apparent between ball types during the decision-making test. |
| Badminton | Nor Azmi *et al.* (2020) | Court size and racket size | 7–9 y beginners | Y | Following five weeks of practice, children who practiced using a modified racquet with the modified court (compared to children using any other combinations of racket and court) recorded the highest hitting opportunities and stroke effectiveness. However, no pre-test was performed so we cannot make comment on the effect of practice. |
| Basketball | Gorman *et al.* (2021) | Ball size | 11 y club | N | Following small-sided games with 4 ball sizes (size 3,4 ,5, and 6), children's preferred ball was either size 5 or 6. Experienced influenced preference, with the most experienced children preferring the size 6 ball. |
| | Arias-Estero *et al.* (2018) | Ball mass | 9–11 y club | Y | Matches played with a lighter ball (440 g), compared to a regulation ball (485 g) or a heavier ball (540 g), led to more one-on-one situations in the frontcourt, and more correct (but not incorrect) decisions. |
| Cricket | Dancy and Murphy (2020) | Bat mass and ball size | 4–7 y beginners | Y | Children hit the ball more accurately in a batting skills test when using a larger tennis ball compared to a regular tennis ball. A modified plastic bat (0.3 kg) also resulted in better performance than a regular children's bat (0.6 kg), but only when using the modified ball. |
| | Harwood *et al.* (2019) | Pitch length | 10 y club level | Y | Batsmen played more back foot shots to short-pitched deliveries when the pitch length was 14.6 m rather than 18.3 m. |

(*Continued*)

*Table 44.1* (Continued)

| *Sport* | *Reference* | *Modification* | *Population studied* | *Primary outcome: positive (Y/N)* | *Main finding* |
|---|---|---|---|---|---|
| | | | | | Comparatively, the longer pitch led to batsmen playing short-pitched deliveries off the front foot more often. |
| | Harwood *et al.* (2018a) | Pitch length | 10 y skilled | Y | Fast bowlers released the ball at an angle that more closely replicated a professional fast bowler when the pitch length was 14.6 m compared to 17.4 m). Ball speed and position at release changed negligibly between the two pitch lengths. |
| | Harwood *et al.* (2018b) | Pitch length | 9–10 y club level | Y | Playing cricket on a 14.6 m pitch rather than an 18.3 m pitch resulted in more running between the wickets but fewer boundaries, an increase in the number of playable deliveries which was due to a reduction in the ball bouncing twice, and fewer shots to the mid-wicket area, therein leading a more even distribution of fielding opportunities. |
| Field Hockey | Brocken *et al.* (2021) | Reverse bat | 9–12 y skilled | Y | Practicing with a reverse hockey stick for four sessions improved performance on a dribbling skills test when using a regular stick (measured by time to complete the course) compared to practicing with a regular stick. |
| | Brocken *et al.* (2020) | Irregular ball (changed weight distribution) | 7–10 y range of skill levels | Y | Two weeks of practice with a modified (off-balanced) ball led to greater performance improvement than two weeks of practice with a regular hockey ball. Performance improvement was not predicted by experience and/or initial skill (i.e. pre-test score). |
| Tennis | Buszard *et al.* (2020b)* | Racket and ball | 5–8 y beginners | Y | Children performed a forehand task with greater functional movement variability in the hitting arm when using a smaller racket and lower compression ball. When using full-sized equipment, children tended to freeze their upper arm, leading to a lack of co-variation between the upper arm and forearm. |

| | | | | |
|---|---|---|---|---|
| Buszard *et al.* (2020c)* | Racket and ball | 5–8 y beginners | Y | The distance between the shoulder and the racket was deemed a performance variable when performing a forehand hitting task, and children using a smaller racket and a lower compression were better able to control this variable, which was a product of greater contributions by the proximal segments (i.e. wrist-racket). |
| Gimenez-Egido *et al.* (2020b) | Court size and net height | 9–10 y club level | Y | Matches played on a smaller court (18×8 m compared to 24×8 m) and with a lower net (0.8 m compared to 0.91 m) led to greater service effectiveness and more situational and special strokes (i.e. creativity). |
| Gimenez-Egido *et al.* (2020a) | Court size and net height | 9–10 y club level | Y | Matches played on a smaller court (18×8 m compared to 24×8 m) and with a lower net (0.8 m compared to 0.91 m) led to greater first serve success, including more unreturned serves and more aces. |
| Limpens *et al.* (2018) | Net height | 9–10 y skilled | Y | Matches played with lower nets (0.65 m and 0.52 m), relative to higher nets (0.78 m and 0.91 m), resulted in more winners without a commensurate increase in errors, and more shots struck inside the baseline. Lower nets also led to a greater percentage of successful first serves. A downside of the lowest net (0.52 m), however, was shorter rallies and therefore fewer hitting opportunities. |
| Fitzpatrick *et al.* (2018) | Task constraints within a modified environment | 7 y beginners | Y | Manipulating task constraints within practice activities in a modified environment resulted in a greater percentage of backhand strokes and backhand winners during match play relative to the control group (note – the task constraints were manipulated with the intention of increasing backhands). The experimental group also improved forehand and backhand technical proficiency and the ability to maintain a rally with a coach more than the control group. |
| Fitzpatrick *et al.* (2017) | Ball compression & court size | 6–14 y (skill relative to stage) | Y | Matches played in modified environments led to a greater percentage of forehands than full-sized conditions, and this was amplified in the most modified conditions ("red stage"). Rally length was also longer in modified conditions ("red" |

(*Continued*)

*Table 44.1* (Continued)

| *Sport* | *Reference* | *Modification* | *Population studied* | *Primary outcome: positive (Y/N)* | *Main finding* |
|---|---|---|---|---|---|
| | | | | | and "orange" stages), whilst first serves-in percentage was greater for the "red" stage. |
| | Buszard *et al.* (2016a) | Racket | 6–8 y beginners | Y & N | The high child-to-coach ratio (22:2) seemingly led to a small number of practice opportunities for children. Children who practiced for five weeks with a smaller racket (48 cm) displayed greater improvements in forehand and backhand technique than children who practiced with a larger racket (72 cm). There were no differences between the two groups in hitting performance following practice. |
| Soccer | García-Angulo *et al.* (2021)# | Field size, goal size, player numbers | 11 y club level | N | Children's perceptions of cooperation did not change when playing matches with modified conditions (reduced field and goal size, and less players). |
| | García-Angulo *et al.* (2020b)# | Field size, goal size, player numbers | 11 y club level | Y | Matches played with modified conditions (reduced field and goal size, and less players) generated more individual and collective actions performed by players. Modified conditions also increased the use of lateral areas on the pitch. |
| | García-Angulo *et al.* (2020a)# | Field size, goal size, player numbers | 11 y club level | N | Children's self-efficacy (physical and football-specific) was no different after playing matches played with modified conditions (reduced field and goal size, and less players) compared to regular junior conditions. |

*Notes*
⋆ same participants
# same participants

preferred over full-sized equipment (Regimbal *et al.*, 1992; Buszard *et al.*, 2014a; Timmerman *et al.*, 2015). Since then, however, evidence supporting these statements is mixed. 4 to 7-year-old children who were beginners to cricket preferred batting with a modified bat and ball when performing a skills test (Dancy and Murphy, 2020). As children gain experience, however, their preference shifts towards full-sized equipment. 11-year-old's with less than one year of experience playing basketball shared mixed preference for ball size (size 5 or 6), whereas the more experienced players preferred the full-sized (size 6) ball (Gorman *et al.*, 2021). These results can be rationalised as follows: beginners want to use equipment that enables successful competition of the task, but with experience they are often exposed to full-sized equipment (particularly in basketball) and consequently they develop an attraction towards these conditions. Indeed, Gorman *et al.* (2021) hypothesised that children's preferences would not be so heavily geared towards full-sized conditions if they were exposed to modified environments from a younger age. Alternatively, motivation might play a role, and children (or their parents) might equate the use full-sized equipment as a sign of 'having made it', 'grown up', or 'now playing the real sport'.

Support for the claim that children's self-efficacy is heightened when playing in modified environments remains inconclusive. Eleven-year-old Spanish soccer players reported no change in self-efficacy as a consequence of playing a modified soccer match, but their efficacy did increase from simply playing more matches (i.e. following both modified and regular matches) (García-Angulo *et al.*, 2020a). Admittedly, however, this study only assessed the acute affect from a single match, which might have been insufficient exposure to boost self-efficacy.

## Skill Performance and Acquisition Factors

Underpinned by a constraints-approach to skill acquisition (Newell, 1986), the modification of task constraints, such as the equipment or play area, influences performance of a skill. Its effect, however, is determined by its relationship with other constraints, such as those within the performer (e.g. a person's height, fatigue, skill level, etc) and those within the environment (e.g. temperature, wind, etc). A young child, for instance, will respond differently than an adult when asked to use a heavy full-sized tennis racket. The consequence being that the young child will likely have a reduced repertoire of strokes available to perform given the difficulty in wielding the racket's inertia. This brings us to an important concept – *action capabilities*. Action capabilities refer to the range of actions that a person can perform in an environment. The modification of equipment and/or play area in children's sport can therefore either create or constrain opportunities to perform actions (referred to as affordances; Fajen *et al.*, 2008). Given the inherent link between constraints and skill, it is believed that children will be afforded opportunities to perform skills that better resemble the professional game when the task and equipment are scaled to match children's physical size.

Previously it was concluded that: "children (a) perform skills better when the equipment and play area are scaled, (b) are presented with increased opportunities to practice skills, and (c) are able to play matches in a style that more closely resembles an adult match" (Buszard *et al.*, 2016b: p. 837). This assertion has been replicated, either directly or indirectly, across several studies in recent years. Most notably, the general finding that children can perform skills with greater success is well supported – whether that be in a controlled skills test or in a match-play environment. For instance, Dancy and Murphy (2020) replicated the experimental design of Buszard *et al.* (2014a) but in a cricket setting. They found that hitting accuracy improved when 4-to-7-year-old children used a modified (larger) tennis ball rather than a standard tennis ball, with the rationale being that the larger surface area on the bigger ball simplified the task.

Indeed, much like in tennis (Buszard *et al.*, 2014a), the ball was found to have a greater influence on performance than modifying the hitting implement (i.e. the bat or racket).

A strength of many studies examining modified junior sport is the assessment of performance during competitive match-play. Indeed, these studies revealed desirable changes to tactical behaviour when conditions are modified, such as more aggressive intent by skilled junior tennis players (Kachel *et al.*, 2015; Timmerman *et al.*, 2015). In further support of these findings, lowering the net on a full-sized court for skilled 10-year-olds led to more first serves-in, more winners without an increase in errors, and more shots struck from inside the baseline (as opposed to behind the baseline) (Limpens *et al.*, 2018). The combination of a lower net and a smaller court for the same age group also improved serving success whilst simultaneously promoting situationally appropriate strokes (e.g. lob shots) (Gimenez-Egido *et al.*, 2020a; Gimenez-Egido *et al.*, 2020b).

A common finding from modified sport studies is that appropriate scaling increases the frequency of actions, which therefore increases opportunities to learn. This was demonstrated across a five-week learning intervention (Farrow and Reid, 2010), and recently this was replicated in a badminton setting (Nor Azmi *et al.*, 2020). In a similar vein, a study of junior basketball matches revealed more one-on-one situations for 9-to-11-year-old's when a lighter ball was used (Arias-Estero *et al.*, 2018). Significantly, the lighter ball also increased the proportion of correct decisions made by the player with the ball when faced with one-on-one encounters. A case was therefore made that a lighter ball augments the development of decision-making skill since children are exposed to more decisions during gameplay.

However, the increased frequency in actions does not necessarily equate to improved performance or learning. By way of example, playing tennis in modified environments increased the proportion of forehands played (and therefore reduces backhands), and this was amplified in the most modified conditions (i.e. the "red stage") (Fitzpatrick *et al.*, 2017). To highlight the disparity, the percentage of backhands played by 7-year-olds in the "red stage" was 31%, whereas for 13-year-olds in full-sized conditions it was 48%. Although this difference might have been due to differences in skill level, the flow on effect is that children in scaled environments might not be exposed to sufficient backhand opportunities. Fortunately, there is a solution to counter this – but it requires clever coaching. In a study spanning eight weeks focused on "red stage" tennis players (mean age = 7.4 years), the use of the backhand, including the ability to hit winners with the backhand, increased after being exposed to practice conditions whereby the coach purposefully altered constraints to create more backhand opportunities (Fitzpatrick *et al.*, 2018).

An opportunity that has presented researchers in recent years is the ability to assess the effect of task and equipment scaling across an entire junior season. This opportunity is a consequence of governing bodies mandating new rules in junior sport to create more appropriately sized environments. Indeed, an observational study investigating England's new junior cricket formats found that shorter pitches led to more opportunities for batters to hit the ball (due to fewer balls that bounced twice) and fewer shots being hit to mid-wicket (hence, shots were hit towards a greater variety of locations) (Harwood *et al.*, 2018b). Shorter pitches were also reported to foster perception-action couplings that better resemble the professional game, with children playing short-pitched deliveries off the back foot more frequently with the shorter pitch (Harwood *et al.*, 2019). Comparatively, on a longer pitch, children played more short-pitch deliveries off the front foot due to the ball's downward trajectory as it reached the batter. This finding resembles the central argument in favour of scaling junior sport; that being, that appropriate scaling preserves perception-action couplings that are integral to the game.

Finally, recent studies in field hockey have taken a different approach to understanding modified equipment. Rather than simplifying the skill, a field hockey ball with an off-centre weight distribution was used during practice for 7-to-9 year-old players (Brocken *et al.*, 2020). The weight distribution was moderately off-centre, meaning the ball's roll was only subtly different to normal. Nonetheless, the variable roll that resulted was hypothesised to promote *movement redundancy* – the ability to achieve the same task goal with multiple movement solutions. Although movement redundancy was not measured, performance – as assessed via time to complete a skills test – improved significantly more when using the irregular ball compared to a standard ball following two weeks of practice with each.

A separate study then investigated the effect of practicing field hockey with a modified (reversed) stick (i.e. left-handed) (Brocken *et al.*, 2021). The authors invoked the symmetry hypothesis which states that the development of a new coordinative structure via practice will also cause the emergence of another new coordinative structure – its symmetrical equivalent (Zanone and Kelso, 1997). This means that for skills involving both limbs, such as striking the ball in hockey, practicing on one side of the body will simultaneously improve performance for the other side. Results revealed that five sessions using the modified reverse stick (during a 20-minute pre-training activity only) improved performance more than when their regular stick was used during this time. Whilst these studies are not related to task and equipment scaling per se, they do speak to the modification of children's sports equipment to facilitate skill acquisition (e.g. similar questions are studied under the banner of nonlinear pedagogy; Lee *et al.*, 2014).

## Biomechanical Factors

The equipment used during sport has a profound impact on movement kinematics and the resulting technique adopted by any performer. In essence, equipment constraints the solution space – the space defining the range of possible movement solutions for a given task. Notwithstanding the efforts of Bruce Elliot who initiated the biomechanical analysis of modified equipment work (Elliott, 1981; Elliott *et al.*, 2005), there have only been a few attempts to measure the effect of modified sport on movement kinematics. These attempts have revealed desirable changes to movement patterns when the equipment and task are appropriately scaled. For instance, in continuing earlier cricket research (Elliott *et al.*, 2005), a study of 10-year-old cricket fast-bowlers showed that bowling on a 14.6 m pitch rather than a 17.4 m pitch led to deliveries being projected at angle (−4.2° below horizontal) that better represents professional fast bowlers (~ −7° below horizontal). Ultimately it allowed young fast bowlers to bowl "into the wicket" – a desirable (and necessary) trait for this skill in senior competition.

Studies in tennis have focused on the measurement of coordination. Seven-year-old children who were beginners to tennis displayed greater co-variation between the upper-arm and forearm when performing a forehand with scaled equipment (a smaller racket and a lower compression tennis ball) than full-sized equipment (adult racket and standard tennis ball) (Buszard *et al.*, 2020b). Co-variation amongst joints is often termed *functional movement variability* as it is an important ingredient in the coordination of movement (Bartlett *et al.*, 2007). More specifically, co-variation amongst body segments can help stabilise *performance variables* – the variables that influence task success (Scholz *et al.*, 2000). Indeed, the co-variation amongst the hitting arm segments when using scaled equipment shaped a more distal control of the shoulder-racket distance (a performance variable), whereas full-sized equipment constrained a more proximal control (Buszard *et al.*, 2020b; Buszard *et al.*, 2020c). In lay terms, the scaled equipment promoted a smoother swing as compared to the rigidness that often manifested with full-sized equipment. It was therefore suggested that appropriately sized equipment facilitates the *releasing of degrees of freedom*, whereas inappropriately sized equipment causes the *freezing of degrees of freedom*.

## *Cognitive Factors*

In the systematic review (Buszard *et al.*, 2016b), cognitive factors were discussed with respect to implicit motor learning. Only one study had assessed this hypothesis and the results implied that equipment scaling is more likely to facilitate implicit motor learning as a consequence of simplifying the skill, therein reducing cognitive demands (Buszard *et al.*, 2014b). Unfortunately, no more studies have addressed the link between scaling and implicit motor learning and, therefore, this aspect of the review cannot be expanded on.

Nonetheless, two recent publications have drawn connections between scaled environments and the development of anticipatory skill, which for the purpose of this chapter will be classified as a cognitive factor. Harwood and colleagues' analysis of cricket fast bowling was extended with the aim of identifying the pitch length that allows young fast bowlers to release the ball at the same angle as a professional fast bowler (Harwood *et al.*, 2020). The authors ran simulations based on the kinematic data available and identified that a 14.8 m pitch length would best allow U12 fast bowlers to replicate the release parameters of professional fast bowlers. The study was not performed with anticipatory skill in mind, but rather to preserve perception-action couplings from junior cricket into senior cricket. Nonetheless, the authors did speculate that such a shortened pitch might facilitate the development of anticipatory skill; defined as the ability to exploit advanced information (i.e. pre-ball flight) to guide the control of movement (this hypothesis has also been posed previously; Weissensteiner *et al.*, 2008; Farrow and Reid, 2012).

A similar analysis was performed across tennis, baseball and cricket, but this time with the specific goal of formalising a hypothesis for the development of anticipatory skill (Buszard *et al.*, 2021). It was hypothesised that temporal demands dictate the necessity to develop anticipatory skill and, therefore, children will only learn to anticipate once the game's speed increases beyond a certain threshold. Indeed, an analysis of temporal demands revealed that 10-year-old children replicate the speeds of professional sport by reducing the baseball pitching distance to 9.59 m, the cricket pitch length to 11.75 m, and the tennis court length to 13.51 m. Of course, increasing temporal demands also comes with a risk, and therefore care is warranted before making any changes. It must be acknowledged that up until a few years ago only baseball (of these three sports) had scaled the environment for 10-year-olds, with pitching distance for Little League Baseball being 14.02 m (rather than the 18.39 m on a full-sized field). Hence, it is possible that baseball was better at stressing the need for young players to couple their actions with advanced informational cues (e.g. kinematics of the pitcher) compared to tennis and cricket.

Two other interesting observations emerged from this simulation study. First, the 13.51 m tennis court length, which was deemed to recreate the temporal demands of professional tennis, is similar to the court length recommended by the International Tennis Federation for "red ball" players (i.e. beginners aged 5 to 8 years). This therefore raises the question of whether skilled 10-year-old children could also benefit from playing and practicing in this environment? Second, the cricket pitch deemed to best replicate the temporal demands of the professional game was also approximately equivalent to the pitch length in many Australian backyards, whereby *backyard cricket* has been a staple feature in the development of many cricket players. Hence, a strong case can be formed that these environments should be continually recreated in children's sport.

## Implications for Children's Sport Coaching

The study of scaling constraints in junior sport has strong links to coordination dynamics (Kelso, 2009) and the ecological approach to perception and action (Kugler *et al.*, 1980; Kugler *et al.*, 1982; Warren, 1990). The constraints impacting performance govern what can be perceived and subsequently acted on (i.e. perception-action coupling), and this in turn regulates the possible movement solutions that can be explored by the performer. A useful framework for understanding the influence of (scaled) constraints is the *coordination, control and skill* outlook (Newell, 1985). *Coordination* refers to the function defining various movement solutions; *control* refers to the parametrisation of the coordination function to particular values; and *skill* refers to the optimisation of the coordination function based on the confluence of constraints. Hence, when constraints are scaled in junior sport, the landscape of movement possibilities is altered, and this can influence the coordination function (and therefore control and skill).

Given this approach, we must then ask: *what perception-couplings should be present in junior sport?* To answer this question, consider that the transfer of skill from one environment to another – such as from the U10 age group to U12's – is based on symmetry in perception-action couplings (Pacheco and Newell, 2015, 2018). By extension, this implies that the aim in children's sport should be to create environments that best replicate perception-action couplings of the next age group (or setting) until eventually reaching professional tennis. The implicit assumption is that sufficient exposure to an appropriately scaled environment will augment the learning of the most salient perception-action couplings. Although this assumption remains to be tested and proven, we nonetheless argue that the scaling of children's sport offers a simple strategy to preserve (and therefore develop) the key ingredient of skill – perception-action couplings.

This viewpoint gives rise to simple (yet powerful) practical implications for coaches: to ensure the task and environment are appropriately scaled to children's physical capabilities; whether that be the equipment being used or the playing space available. A basketball coach, for instance, might lower the ring so that the children can experience success when shooting with a jump shot technique; a soccer coach might reduce the size of the goals so the likelihood of a goal-keeper saving a shot is equivalent to an adult goal-keeper with full-sized goals; and a tennis coach might lower the net and reduce the court's length to make it easier for children to pronate their arm when serving. In each of these examples, the aim for the coach is to shape the learning of desirable behaviour whilst maintaining a representative environment. On occasions coaches cannot adjust the most obvious constraint limiting a child's success. For example, basketball rings in many locations are fixed at an adult height. In these situations, its critical coaches consider the other constraints available that they can scale to create a more effective learning environment. In our basketball example, that might see the basketball coach utilising a smaller, lighter ball if the ring height cannot be adjusted.

## Summary, Future Directions, and Future Research

Given the impact that junior sport can have on a person's life – whether that be related to physical health or creating a career in sport – the question of *how to scale constraints to allow children to perform the relevant skills* should be of interest to all sports governing bodies. An important concept to acknowledge at this juncture is *critical fluctuations*. A critical fluctuation is when a constraint changes by a certain threshold which causes a qualitative change in behaviour (Kelso *et al.*, 1986). For instance, let's say a child was playing tennis and the racket's mass was sufficiently light to afford a one-handed backhand. Now let's say the racket's mass increased; there exists a particular threshold (the critical fluctuation) where mass increases by a margin that forces the child to swing the racket with two hands on the grip (obviously in reality this may be an unrealistically heavy racket!). The importance of critical fluctuations is evident when we consider: *how much does the task and equipment need to be scaled?* Indeed, it is apparent that constraints need to be scaled within certain boundaries to allow particular perception-action couplings to emerge (Broadbent *et al.*, 2021). Our understanding of the variables governing the boundaries, however, remains elusive.

The discussion of how to scale constraints brings attention to two key concepts when adapting constraints: *body-scale* and *action-scale* (Fajen *et al.*, 2008). Body-scale refers to the relationship between the environment and a person's physical size (e.g. stair height relative to leg length influences when a person can climb stairs; Warren, 1984), whereas action-scale refers to the relationship between the environment and a person's action capabilities (e.g. the leg power of a goalkeeper influences the timing of their jump when attempting to save a penalty kick; Wilson *et al.*, 2018). In the context of scaling junior sport, a body-scale approach might be used to scale the net height in tennis based on the height of the performer. Alternatively, an action-scale approach could be adopted whereby net height is scaled based on ball trajectory information which is a product of the performer's action capabilities. Whilst both scaling approaches could elicit similar results, our understanding of which approach to adopt given the constraint of interest is limited.

We must also recognise that there are many variables that could be scaled. For instance, given that a racket's moment of inertia is represented by the racket's length and mass ($I = mr^2$), these variables would need to be adjusted to allow a young child to swing a racket more easily. However, these are not the only variables to consider in the design of a racket; the size of the racket's head is also essential as this influences the ability to strike the ball. Quite simply, a larger racket head corresponds to a larger surface area for striking the ball, but a larger racket head also increases the racket's moment of inertia. The logical outcome is therefore to scale the racket's length or mass (or both) to allow a child to perform the necessary shots whilst maximising the size of the racket head to increase the likelihood of success.

To summarise, studies consistently reveal the benefits of appropriately scaled environments; that being, children can perform skills with more success, display improved coordination, and adopt match tactics that were otherwise not attempted. With this in mind, the next frontier in the science of scaling sport is to understand the dynamics of scaling as it relates to critical thresholds, including the application of body-scaling and action-scaling techniques for multiple interacting variables. In the meantime, coaches (and performers) can discover much of this information by purposively exploring a variety of different-sized constraints. Indeed, regardless of empirical evidence for guiding the scaling process, the pedagogical approach of tinkering with constraints to help performers search the landscape of movement possibilities is advantageous for skill acquisition.

## References

Arias, J., 2012. Influence of ball weight on shot accuracy and efficacy among 9-11-year-old male basketball players. *Kinesiology*, 44 (1), 52–59.

Arias-Estero, J.L., Argudo, F.M., and Alonso, J.I., 2018. One-on-one situation decision-making according to equipment in youth basketball. *International Journal of Sports Science & Coaching* 13 (1), 72–77.

Bartlett, R., Wheat, J., and Robins, M., 2007. Is movement variability important for sports biomechanists? *Sports Biomechanics* 6 (2), 224–243.

Broadbent, N., Buszard, T., Farrow, D., *et al.*, 2021. Scaling junior sport competition: A body-scaling approach? *Journal of Sports Sciences* 39 (23), 2746–2754.

Brocken, J.E.A., van der Kamp, J., Lenior, M., *et al.*, 2021. Using modified equipment in field hockey leads to positive transfer of learning effect. *Frontiers in Psychology* 12, 1–9.

Brocken, J.E.A., Van Der Kamp, J., Lenoir, M., *et al.*, 2020. Equipment modification can enhance skill learning in young field hockey players. *International Journal of Sports Science & Coaching* 15 (3), 382–389.

Buszard, T., Farrow, D., and Reid, M., 2020a. Designing junior sport to maximize potential: The knowns, unknowns, and paradoxes of scaling sport. *Frontiers in Psychology* 10, 1–5.

Buszard, T., Farrow, D., Reid, M., *et al.*, 2014a. Modifying equipment in early skill development: A tennis perspective. *Research Quarterly for Exercise and Sport* 85 (2), 218–225.

Buszard, T., Farrow, D., Reid, M., *et al.*, 2014b. Scaling sporting equipment for children promotes implicit processes during performance. *Consciousness and Cognition* 30 (1), 247–255.

Buszard, T., Garofolini, A., Reid, M., *et al.*, 2020b. Scaling sports equipment for children promotes functional movement variability. *Scientific Reports* 10 (1), 1–10.

Buszard, T., Garofolini, A., Whiteside, D., *et al.*, 2020c. Children's coordination of the "sweet spot" when striking a forehand is shaped by the equipment used. *Scientific Reports* 10 (1), 1–9.

Buszard, T., Reid, M., Masters, R.S.W., *et al.*, 2016a. Scaling tennis racquets during pe in primary school to enhance motor skill acquisition. *Research Quarterly for Exercise and Sport* 87 (4), 414–420.

Buszard, T., Reid, M., Masters, R.S.W., *et al.*, 2016b. Scaling the equipment and play area in children's sport to improve motor skill acquisition: A systematic review. *Sports Medicine* 46 (6), 829–843.

Buszard, T., Whiteside, D., Krause, L., *et al.*, 2021. Formalising a hypothesis for the development of anticipatory skill in time-constrained interceptive actions: Implications for the design of junior sport. *Psychology of Sport and Exercise* 55, 101933.

Chase, M.A., Ewing, M.E., Lirgg, C.D., *et al.*, 1994. The effects of equipment modification on children's self-i and basketball shooting performance. *Research Quarterly for Exercise and Sport* 65 (2), 159–168.

Dancy, P.A.J. and Murphy, C.P., 2020. The effect of equipment modification on the performance of novice junior cricket batters. *Journal of Sports Sciences* 38 (21), 2415–2422.

Elliott, B., 1981. Tennis racquet selection: A factor in early skill development. *Australian Journal of Sport Sciences* 1 (1), 23–25.

Elliott, B., Plunkett, D., and Alderson, J., 2005. The effect of altered pitch length on performance and technique in junior fast bowlers. *Journal of Sports Sciences* 23 (7), 661–667.

Fajen, B.R., Riley, M.A., and Turvey, M.T., 2008. Information, affordances, and the control of action in sport. *International Journal of Sport Psychology* 40 (1), 79–107.

Farrow, D. and Reid, M., 2010. The effect of equipment scaling on the skill acquisition of beginning tennis players. *Journal of Sports Sciences* 28 (7), 723–732.

Farrow, D. and Reid, M., 2012. The contribution of situational probability information to anticipatory skill. *Journal of Science and Medicine in Sport* 15 (4), 368–373.

Fitzpatrick, A., Davids, K., and Stone, J.A., 2017. Effects of Lawn Tennis Association mini tennis as task constraints on children's match-play characteristics. *Journal of Sports Sciences* 35 (22), 2204–2210.

Fitzpatrick, A., Davids, K., and Stone, J.A., 2018. Effects of scaling task constraints on emergent behaviours in children's racquet sports performance. *Human Movement Science* 58, 80–87.

García-Angulo, A., Ortega-Toro, E., Giménez-Egido, J.M., *et al.*, 2020a. Short-term effect of competition rule changes on collective effectiveness and self-efficacy in youth football players. *Psychology of Sport and Exercise* 49, 1–6.

García-Angulo, A., Ortega-Toro, E., Giménez-Egido, J.M., *et al.*, 2021. Does youth soccer players' group cooperation improve when pitch, goal, and team size are reduced? *Journal of Human Kinetics* 78 (1), 151–160.

García-Angulo, A., Palao, J.M., Giménez-Egido, J.M., *et al.*, 2020b. Effect of the modification of the number of players, the size of the goal, and the size of the field in competition on the play actions in U-12 male football. *International Journal of Environmental Research and Public Health* 17 (2), 518–530.

Gimenez-Egido, J.M., Ortega-Toro, E., Palao, J.M., *et al.*, 2020a. Effect of scaling equipment on U-10 players tennis serve during match-play: A nonlinear pedagogical approach. *Chaos, Solitons & Fractals* 139, 1–9.

Gimenez-Egido, J.M., Ortega-Toro, E., Palao, J.M., *et al.*, 2020b. Effect of modification rules in competition on technical–tactical action in young tennis players (Under-10). *Frontiers in Psychology* 10, 1–15.

Gorman, A., Headrick, J., Renshaw, I., *et al.*, 2021. A principled approach to equipment scaling for children's sport: A case study in basketball. *International Journal of Sports Science & Coaching* 16 (1), 158–165.

Hadlow, S.M., Pinder, R.A., and Sayers, M.G., 2017. Influence of football size on kicking performance in youth Australian rules footballers. *Journal of Sports Sciences* 35 (18), 1808–1816.

Harwood, M.J., Yeadon, M.R., and King, M.A., 2018a. Does shortening the pitch make junior cricketers bowl better? *Journal of Sports Sciences* 36 (17), 1972–1978.

Harwood, M.J., Yeadon, M.R., and King, M.A., 2018b. Reducing the pitch length: Effects on junior cricket. *International Journal of Sports Science & Coaching* 13 (6), 1031–1039.

Harwood, M.J., Yeadon, M.R., and King, M.A., 2019. A shorter cricket pitch improves decision-making by junior batters. *Journal of Sports Sciences* 37 (17), 1934–1941.

Harwood, M.J., Yeadon, M.R., and King, M.A., 2020. Scaling the cricket pitch to fit junior players. *Journal of Sports Sciences* 39 (1), 31–37.

Kachel, K., Buszard, T., and Reid, M., 2015. The effect of ball compression on the match-play characteristics of elite junior tennis players. *Journal of Sports Sciences* 33 (3), 320–326.

Kelso, J.S., 2009. Coordination dynamics. In R.A. Meyers ed., *Encyclopedia of complexity and systems science*. New York: Springer, 1537–1564.

Kelso, J.S., Scholz, J.P., and Schöner, G., 1986. Nonequilibrium phase transitions in coordinated biological motion: Critical fluctuations. *Physics Letters A* 118 (6), 279–284.

Kugler, P.N., Kelso, J.S., and Turvey, M., 1980. 1 On the concept of coordinative structures as dissipative structures: I. Theoretical lines of convergence. *Advances in Psychology* 1, 3–47.

Kugler, P.N., Kelso, J.S., and Turvey, M., 1982. On the control and coordination of naturally developing systems. In J.S. Kelso and J.E. Clark, eds., *The development of movement control and coordination*. Vol. 5. New York: Wiley, 1–78.

Lee, M.C.Y., Chow, J.Y., Komar, J., *et al.*, 2014. Nonlinear pedagogy: An effective approach to cater for individual differences in learning a sports skill. *PloS one* 9 (8), e104744.

Limpens, V., Buszard, T., Shoemaker, E., *et al.*, 2018. Scaling constraints in junior tennis: The influence of net height on skilled players' match-play performance. *Research Quarterly for Exercise and Sport* 89 (1), 1–10.

Newell, K.M., 1985. Coordination, control and skill. *Advances in Psychology* 27 (1), 295–317.

Newell, K.M., 1986. Constraints on the development of coordination. In M.G. Wade and H.T.A. Whiting, eds., *Motor development in children: Aspects of coordination and control*. Dordrecht: Spinger, 341–360.

Nor Azmi, A.M.K. Suppiah, P., Low Fook Lee, J., *et al.*, 2020. The influence of modified equipment in developing skills in badminton. *Malaysian Journal of Movement, Health & Exercise* 9 (1), 67–76.

Pacheco, M.M. and Newell, K.M., 2015. Transfer as a function of exploration and stabilization in original practice. *Human Movement Science* 44, 258–269.

Pacheco, M.M. and Newell, K.M., 2018. Transfer of a learned coordination function: Specific, individual and generalizable. *Human Movement Science* 59, 66–80.

Regimbal, C., Deller, J., and Plimpton, C., 1992. Basketball size as related to children's preference, rated skill, and scoring. *Perceptual and Motor Skills* 75 (3), 867–872.

Reid, M., Buszard, T., and Farrow, D., 2018. Learning, activity … and injury? Caring for young athletes through appropriately designed modified (developmental) sport. *British Journal of Sports Medicine* 52, 1285–1286.

Scholz, J.P., Schöner, G., and Latash, M.L., 2000. Identifying the control structure of multijoint coordination during pistol shooting. *Experimental Brain Research* 135 (3), 382–404.

Timmerman, E., De Water, J., Kachel, K., *et al.*, 2015. The effect of equipment scaling on children's sport performance: The case for tennis. *Journal of Sports Sciences* 33 (10), 1093–1100.

Warren, W.H., 1984. Perceiving affordances: Visual guidance of stair climbing. *Journal of Experimental Psychology: Human Perception and Performance* 10 (5), 683–703.

Warren, W.H., 1990. The perception-action coupling. In H. Bioch and B.I. Bertenthal, eds., *Sensory-motor organizations and development in infancy and early childhood*. Vol. 56. Dordrecht: Springer, 23–37.

Weissensteiner, J., Abernethy, B., Farrow, D., *et al.*, 2008. The development of anticipation: A cross-sectional examination of the practice experiences contributing to skill in cricket batting. *Journal of Sport and Exercise Psychology* 30 (6), 663–684.

Wilson, R., Dicks, M., Milligan, G., *et al.*, 2018. An examination of action capabilities and movement time during a soccer anticipation task. *Movement & Sport Sciences – Science & Motricité* 102, 61–70.

Zanone, P.G. and Kelso, J.S., 1997. Coordination dynamics of learning and transfer: Collective and component levels. *Journal of Experimental Psychology: Human Perception and Performance* 23 (5), 1454–1480.

# 45

# LEARNING TO COACH CHILDREN IN SPORT

*Brian Gearity and Clayton Kuklick*

## Introduction

The purpose of this chapter is to review research on children and youth sport coaches learning to coach and to contextualise this learning in our current time with respect to coach development, to provide implications for coach development programs, and to offer recommendations for high-impact research on coaching children and youth in sport. Empirical research shows that children in sport (i.e. athletes) can benefit physically, psychologically, socially, and in other ways by engaging in sport, and that outcomes are usually enhanced when a higher-quality sport coach is coaching (MacDonald *et al.*, 2010). Quality coaches of children are socialised into coaching and deliberately learn to coach through a number of learning situations, such as communities of practice, self-reflection, and coach development programs. Compared to less skilled coaches, higher quality coaches of children deliver positive sporting experiences that result in greater retention, self-esteem, and skill development. Unfortunately, in addition to there being less skilled or under-prepared coaches of children, there are also abusive coaches operating within systems that fail to adequately safeguard children. Therefore, to address the global need and crisis to provide safe and positive experiences to children through sport, this chapter recommends compulsory sport coach education, regulation, and accountability, alongside the creation of local, national, and culturally fitting systems to systematically develop, implement, evaluate, and improve coach preparation, which would include transformational investments in research on sport coaching children.

## Review of Current Research

In order to understand and apply evidence-informed research, the reader is reminded that the requirements to become a sport coach of children vary by country and context and that all research on coach learning has its strengths and limitations. While much of the research to date on sport coaches learning to coach children has focused on North American contexts by US and Canadian researchers, similarities and differences exist globally and additional cross-cultural and culturally-sensitive research is needed to better understand these nuances. Although this chapter is focused on how sport coaches of children learn to coach, research designs and real-life experiences are not so easily categorised. For example, Wright *et al.* (2007) studied youth

DOI: 10.4324/9781003199359-51 

coaches, but the ice hockey league they studied organised participants aged 8–20. The league's midget category was 16–17 year-olds and junior was 17–20. However, their research findings were aggregated across the large swath of coaches interviewed. Furthermore, it is commonplace for coaches to coach children and adolescents of varying age groups, which means the same coach may work with 6–8 year-olds, 12–14 year-olds, and 16–18 year-olds. In summary, and with this caveat in mind, the reader is wise to keep in mind this messy reality of how coaches learn to coach children.

The review of the research section of this chapter is organised under three subheadings that categorise sport coaches of children learning to coach. Section one is focused on deliberately structured education and researchers' interventions or programmes designed to facilitate coaches' learning. Section two is about what practicing sport coaches of children think, feel, and do while coaching, often in naturalistic settings or the coaches' reflections on their experiences. Section three is on coaches' perceptions, preferences, and attitudes towards an issue or topic, in which researchers often used surveys and qualitative or quantitative interviews as methods for data collection.

## *Structured Education and Researchers' Programs on, for, and with Sport Coaches of Children*

Some of the first studies specifically in coach education focused on developing coaches of children and youth. In this regard, the quasi-experimental research of Smith and Smoll, and their colleagues, led the way in showing how coaches who received their coach effectiveness training program (later updated and expanded to mastery approach to coaching) on how to create a mastery motivational climate and provide instruction and encouragement (Smith *et al.*, 2007) towards athletes' efforts and skill enhancement led to greater outcomes, such as reduction in athletes' anxiety (Smith *et al.*, 1995), increased self-esteem (Smoll *et al.*, 1993; Coastworth and Conroy, 2006), and desire to continue to sport participation (Barnett *et al.*, 1992). Coach development organisations, including the Canadian National Coaching Certification Program (NCCP), have also evaluated their own coach education programs. In one of the first of these studies, Gilbert and Trudel (1999) evaluated the strategy of the NCCP's Level 2 coaching certification program through the Canadian Amateur Hockey Association. They collected data on one male coach of a boy's 13–14 year-olds competitive ice hockey team in Canada. The findings of the study are somewhat mixed in that the coach's knowledge gain and knowledge use did not improve across all areas or applications. The researchers concluded that the overall strategy of the coach education program was not realised, likely due to course delivery maligned with its design and the coach's existing knowledge leading to reinforcement or remembering, rather than new knowledge gained.

Noting that team building is often an essential part of coaching children and the paucity of research on how coaches understand and implement this into practice, Newin *et al.* (2008) examined eight Canadian Peewee-level (11–13 year-olds) ice hockey coaches' perceptions of a team-building workshop. The researchers collected data via interviews, observations, and pre- and post-intervention forms. They categorised the findings into four main areas: coach, team, and athletes' outcomes, and program involvement and assessment. For coach outcomes, coaches reported learning how to communicate, break down complex tasks and explain instructions more succinctly, give quality feedback, and communicate more positively rather than negatively in relation to team building applications. The coaches reported the youth learned to work together for success and bonded and developed friendships and that athletes enjoyed the team-building activities and enhanced their perseverance, abilities to reflect and problem solve, and focus. Regarding program involvement and assessment, the coaches planned team building like they would plan practices, some coaches were anxious or lacked confidence in delivering the sessions whereas some were relaxed, and the coaches thought debriefing the activities with athletes was crucial. Finally, while some were skeptical about the value of the sessions, at the end of the season, all the coaches believed in the efficacy of the activities. Related to athlete life skills transference, some of the coaches thought transfer occurred, others did not, and still some thought that the transference may only be temporary.

Several studies have looked at values-based approaches to coach education and developmental models of child development such as long-term athlete development (LTAD) or positive youth development (PYD). In what is believed to be the first study focused on coaches of children aged 0–6 years-old, Banack *et al.* (2012) conducted a qualitative study with a convenience sample of seven cross-country ski coaches in an urban city of Canada. The researchers concluded that the coaches gained knowledge of LTAD and were able to integrate its concepts into practices, and that the coaches' growth likely occurred due to their minimal existing understanding of LTAD.

Delivering a multistage coach education workshop to six recreational and competitive level (12–13 year-olds) coaches in soccer and basketball in an urban Canadian city, Falcão *et al.* (2012) integrated PYD, life skills, and athlete development. The coaches reported the training increased their knowledge and understanding of their players, promoted cohesion and communication, and the 5Cs (e.g. competence, confidence, connection, character, and caring/compassion) of PYD. In a similar study, Falcão *et al.* (2017) designed and delivered a humanistic coaching workshop to 12 Canadian youth sport basketball coaches. The average age of the ten male and two female coaches was 25.16 years and they had an average of 3.62-year coaching experience. Six of the coaches had a national coaching certification and eight had university degrees, five of the eight in Physical Education. The two-hour workshop was delivered prior to the beginning of the season and the coaches were interviewed several weeks later and kept a biweekly journal. The researchers concluded that the workshop was effective at teaching the coaches humanistic coaching, but time and added effort to implement humanistic practices were reported by the coaches as challenges. The coaches reported the effectiveness of the workshop in teaching them humanistic practices, such as how to make team decisions, build relationships with athletes, focusing on athletes' needs, and facilitating athlete independence, autonomy, critical thinking, and problem-solving. The coaches also reported their intent to continue humanistic coaching because of its perceived greater positive impact on athletes on and off the court.

In a similar study designed to promote youth sport coaches' knowledge and practice of youth development, Falcão *et al.* (2012) drew upon frameworks from PYD, life skills development, and athlete development for their 4-stage workshop. The first 3-stages of the two-hour workshop introduced the coaches to the program and then provided conceptual and practical youth development strategies. Subsequently, the coaches practiced the intervention stage of the workshop via 4 × 45 minute activities about every four weeks throughout their season. Six youth sport coaches (one in soccer, five in basketball) working within lower-income areas of a city in Canada participated in the program. After collecting data from interviews, pre- and post-intervention forms, field notes, and a reflective journal, the researchers concluded that the coaches reported the training increased their knowledge and understanding of the players, and helped to promote cohesion and communication, as well as the 5Cs of PYD. The researchers also concluded that the active learning approach used throughout the study likely contributed to the desirable outcomes and efficacy of the program.

Drawing upon research on transformational leadership theory (TFL), Lawrason *et al.* (2019) delivered a three-hour Transformational Coaching Workshop underpinned with behaviour change theory to eight male head coaches of competitive children's soccer teams in Ontario, Canada. The researchers collected observational data pre- and post-workshop to validate behaviour change. Their results showed that coaches' use of TFL behaviours increased across all categories (i.e. idealised influence, inspirational motivation, intellectual stimulation, individualised consideration), however, while some of the changes were statistically insignificant, many were practically significant (i.e. according to effect size). Improving upon existing research in this area, the researchers reported that non-TFL behaviours for neutral and laissez-faire leadership went down. Finally, as some of the behaviours were unchanged, the researchers suggested that social norms and culture need to be examined further to enhance behaviour change.

As reviewed already, a variety of research designs and methods have been used to understand how coaches learn to coach. Pulido *et al.* (2021) recently conducted a quasi-experimental study in Spain examining coaches who received a coaching effectiveness intervention to coaches in a control group. Coaches in the experimental group received a 12-hour training program based on broad topics, such as the social foundations of soccer, technical training, motivational and leadership theory, and positive communication, and based on multiple self-reported questionnaires, the coaches in the experimental group showed greater perceived competency as reported by the athletes. The researchers concluded that the intervention was effective at enhancing the trained coaches use of motivation, technical and tactical error correction, and character development. In one of the few randomised control trials focused on coach learning and behaviour change, Eather *et al.* (2021) randomly assigned 16 Australian girls (aged 8–16) community/club netball coaches (mean age = 45) to an experimental group that received the researchers' MASTER coaching intervention or a control group. The experimental group received a six-hour master coach development workshop face-to-face, eight-weeks of mentoring that included coaches implementing what they learned, support via a Facebook group, discussions, and problem-based learning, and a one-hour training mid-way through the intervention. The MASTER framework was designed with a game-based coaching approach to develop athletes' skills, engagement, motivation, enjoyment, and relationships amongst coaches-athletes and athletes-athletes. Results showed significant and meaningful effects for the experimental group. The trained coaches reported greater confidence and competence and their athletes' skills, engagement was much higher than in the control group, and the coaches gave high ratings for the training. However, there were non-significant differences in some of the athletes' measures including enjoyment and motivation.

The aforementioned study by Eather *et al.* (2021) was a more extensive study developed from their pilot MASTER study (Eather *et al.*, 2020) with six youth football (soccer) coaches at one club in Australia. This sample included five male and one female coach aged 18–40+ with a range of qualifications. The single sample study showed significant improvements of the coaches' ability to give less total feedback to athletes, but more correction feedback. The coaches also improved their use of active practice engagement with the athletes and use of questioning to prompt athletes' learning. The intervention with the coaches included three-phases, with the first being a two-hour engaging workshop (i.e. lecture, discussion, group work, opportunity to plan sessions) on positive and game-based coaching. Phase two involved mentoring by the research team to the coaches, a Facebook discussion, and feedback and dialogue on the coaches' sessions. Phase three consisted of coach assessment and reflection that featured a two-hour training, MASTER checklist used for group discussions and coach observations, and multiple rounds of collaborative feedback, observation, and dialogue. The researchers concluded that the coaches' improvements in coaching practices, specifically game-based coaching and motivational environment, was likely due to the duration, mentoring, and multiple engagement opportunities throughout the coach education intervention.

## Children's Sport Coaches' Cognitions, Emotions, behaviours, and Reflections

Literature on what, why, and how coaches of children behave, think, and feel during and after coaching has been researched through a variety of naturalistic methods, such as observations, interviews, and coaches' reflections of their experiences. In many ways, this literature has been used to inform coach education programs on what knowledge is needed by coaches of children and how to guide their own learning out there in the coaching world. Research has shown how coaches of children in action make decisions in their respective sports, communicate with their team, engage parental interactions, and address athlete's individualised personal characteristics (Gilbert *et al.*, 2001a, 2001b; O'Connor *et al.*, 2017). Child coaches learn on the fly by solving problems associated with having fun, developing mastery of sport skills and techniques, athletes' attitudes, team dynamics and management (e.g. coordinating athletes before, during, and after practice and competitions), parental issues with coaches, athletes, and officials, and personal challenges reflective of coaches' abilities to influence athletes (Gilbert and Trudel, 2001). As highlighted early in this chapter, many contexts within children in sport exist, seemingly child coaches at the elite level or those considered to be model coaches also engage in similar thoughts, behaviours, and reflections (Gilbert and Trudel, 2001; Preston and Fraser-Thomas, 2018). To solve practical problems and develop their expertise, child coaches learn on their own through a variety of sources spanning books, the internet, other coaches, along with reflection and learning by trial and error in experience (Lemyre *et al.*, 2007; Wright *et al.*, 2007). Informing many of these explorations, child coaches are socialised on how to coach and solve problems in certain ways based on other child coaches and/or coaches from other levels, age groups, and contexts, which can potentially limit what child coaches learn or contributes to child coaches implementing practices that may be inappropriate for the child context (Sage, 1989; O'Connor *et al.*, 2017). This research provides support for the need for deliberate learning and how coach education can expand child coaches' knowledge towards marginalised areas and topics directly relevant to children in sport.

A few studies, all conducted in Canada, exemplify this cluster of research and merit elaboration. Gilbert and Trudel (2001) studied how six (three in competitive soccer and three in competitive ice hockey) model Canadian youth team sport coaches learned to coach through experience and reflecting on that experience. Five of the coaches were male, all competed as youth or adult recreational athletes, and all had a level I or II certification through the NCCP. Drawing upon Schön's (1983) work on reflective practice, they collected data via interviews, observations, and documents from the coaches over an entire season. They concluded that six components of reflection captured how the youth coaches reflected on their experience: issue setting, strategy generation, experimentation, and evaluation captured the coaches' active problem solving, which was triggered by coaching issues and bound within the coaches' role frame. The issues or problems the coaches described were vast, with 136 unique issues reported. The researchers categorised these issues into five types: athlete behaviour, athlete performance, personal characteristics, parental influence, and team organisation (Gilbert *et al.*, 2001a, 2001b). After identifying these problems, coaches would reflect on them to generate problem-solving strategies.

Retrospective research has also been conducted where 36 Canadian children and youth head sport coaches across three sports (ice hockey, soccer, and baseball) recalled their perceptions of learning to coach (Lemyre *et al.*, 2007). The coaches, 12 from each sport, coached children aged 7–16 at a recreational or developmental-performance level. Twenty-nine coaches had no professional teaching certificates or degrees, whereas two had physical education degrees, and five were students in Human-Kinetics programs. It was overwhelmingly common for the ice hockey and baseball coaches to have played the sport, while for soccer only 58% of the coaches played it prior to coaching. The researchers reported key learning situations included training courses, resource materials, internet, and interactions, which consisted of interactions with numerous stakeholders, such as assistant coaches, managers, league supervisor, players, parents, friends and family members, and rival coaches. As they became head coaches, they reported needing to learn things like the rules of the game, strategy and tactics, technical skills, and motivation, nutrition, and stress management.

An interview-based qualitative study involved 35 volunteer ice hockey coaches in Canada recalling their learning situations (Wright *et al.*, 2007). All the coaches interviewed were male, aged 33–65, coached a range of youth teams, and were NCCP certified. The seven learning situations reported were categorised as: large scale coach education programs, coaching clinics or seminars, formal mentoring, books or videotapes, personal experiences related to sport, family, and work, face-to-face interactions with other coaches, and the internet. Within the large-scale coach education program, at level 1, coaches reported learning about fundamental aspects of youth sport and child development, and level 2 and 3 progressed to strategy, skill development, and advanced techniques and tactics. Coaches also reported learning basic skills and drills from books and videotapes and that competition with other coaches inhibited sharing of knowledge. Experience, reflecting on experience, and mentoring or collaborative problem-solving were also reported within the learning situations. Coaches also used the internet to learn so-called advanced topics such as sport psychology, nutrition, and physical training.

In a unique autoethnography on learning to coach children, doctoral student and coach Preston (Preston and Fraser-Thomas, 2018) chronicled his own learning experiences as a first-year head coach of seventeen 10-year-olds in a Canadian youth hockey league. Preston focused his season-long journaling and reflections on juggling performance (i.e. winning) and PYD (i.e. 5Cs of competence, confidence, character, connection, caring) demands. Drawing upon his extensive hockey playing experience and assistant coaching experience, as well as his formal education in sport psychology, specifically achievement goal theory and self-determination theory, Preston journaled after every practice or game (about 4 × week total) throughout the six-month season. He reported three themes that captured his major learning experiences: pursuing personal development and performance success, creating a task-oriented environment, and implementing autonomy-supportive behaviours. Throughout the findings, Preston noted his thoughts, emotions, and behaviours on how he considered pertinent issues, such as playing time, metrics of success, and developing a deeper understanding of motivational praxis. Of note for this chapter is also that Preston reported reaching out to one of his former coaches to help problem solve autonomy-supportive vs coach-controlled behaviours.

## *Children's Sport Coaches' Perceptions, Preferences, and Attitudes*

Finally, a third body of literature examines coaches' perceptions, preferences, and attitudes about coaching. For example, as a precursor to today's interest in established frameworks, such as PYD and life skill development, researchers studied children coaches' perceptions of their coaching philosophies and values (McCallister *et al.*, 2000). McCallister *et al.* (2000) interviewed male and female softball and baseball coaches who coached 7–12 year-olds in the state of Illinois, United States (U.S.), about values and life skills they deemed important to teach. Sportsmanship, teamwork, learning skills, and having fun were identified as important, but despite coaches thinking they were effective at teaching these skills, they also struggled at articulating how they or sport specifically did this. Another contradiction was that coaches' had an attitude that de-emphasised winning, but they also acknowledged that you have fun by winning, and so winning and fun were inextricably connected. Also interesting was that all coaches were volunteers, but felt adequately prepared to coach based on their playing experience, watching the sport, and limited knowledge base.

Different from the existing research on coaches' actual learning sources, Vargas-Tonsings' (2007) examined the learning preferences of US youth sport coaches. Three hundred and sixty-six coaches (i.e. 281 males, 45 females, 40 unidentified) that possessed from 0–10 years of experience in baseball, basketball, football, soccer, softball, and volleyball completed a 45-item questionnaire that was used to determine the coaches' educational content preferences, the reasons affecting coaches' decisions to pursue coaching educating, and their perceptions of coaching education. The coaches' main preferred topics for coach education spanned communication with parents and athletes, advanced instructional drills, motivational approaches, character building, conditioning drills, visualisation, and goal setting, while gender differences, addictive behaviours, drugs in sport, and stress management were lesser desirable topics. Highly impactful factors implicating coaches' decisions on engaging in coaching education were dependent on whether the league required it, the topics were relevant and desirable, the online accessibility of the material, and the desire to coach at higher levels. Monetary payment, course costs, and time requirements were less important factors influencing coaches to take up coaching education. Despite the coaches acknowledging the importance of coaching education and the need for coaching certifications and coaching education mandates, they were a bit reluctant to commit to pursuing coaching education on their own; only 46% of the participants planned to pursue coaching education. However, relevant online topics that increase accessibility and availability to materials were found to be a critical factor in coaches' engagement and preference for coaching education. The findings were limited to mostly male coaches and the questionnaire potentially limited the topics from which coaches chose their preferences. While these hot topic areas (i.e. parent communication, motivation, character building) can be considered important and positive, they have shown to be absent in coaching education and connected to power relations and social norms that change over time. Therefore, coach education and coach developers are challenged by engaging coaches' desires and needs of relevant topics, yet with consideration for addressing marginalised areas to address a diverse coaching knowledge repertoire.

The nuances and differences between coaches' perceptions, preferences, and actual thoughts or behaviours continue to be of interest to researchers. One study determined coaches preferred to learn through guided learning and less so from self-directed learning, but their actual learning was led by learning by doing (experiential learning), interaction with coach peers, and formal coach education. Having conducted 44 quantitative interviews with Canadian developmental coaches, Erickson *et al.* (2008) concluded that the largest discrepancies between actual and preferred knowledge were learning by doing (preferred less), the NCCP (preferred more), and a mentor (preferred more). In yet another study based in Canada, Misener and Danylchuk (2009) surveyed 251 coaches who had taken a NCCP course and 34 who had not to examine their awareness of the program and its perceived value. Specific to coach learning, in general, participants thought the courses had value, and 79.8% reported to themselves as likely to take another NCCP course. Outcomes or topics that were noted to be especially helpful were early career coach knowledge, networking and learning from others', coaches' decision making, and increasing athlete safety.

A PYD framework has also been utilised to advance an understanding of how youth sport coaches believe they specifically integrate PYD in the messy reality of coaching practice. In what appears to be the first PYD study specific to an Australian context, Vella *et al.* (2011) conducted interviews with 22 youth participation coaches in a metropolitan area of Sydney. The coaches represented five sports (soccer, netball, softball, cricket, basketball), coached athletes aged 11–19, and an equal number coached male and female teams. Twenty of the coaches had received minimal relevant accreditation from a national sporting body, seven had a step-up accreditation but not the highest, and eight coaches were also teachers. The researchers categorised the coaches' responses into eight major PYD outcomes: competence, confidence, connection, character, life skills, climate, positive affect, and positive psychological capacities. The researchers argued that unique findings existed when the coaches reported attempting to develop sport-specific self-efficacy; the PYD literature usually refers to confidence as a global outcome. They also stated that climate, positive affect, and positive psychological capacities were underappreciated in the PYD and life skills literature. Particularly relevant to coach learning, participants rarely identified winning as a desired outcome or measure of success. One of the limitations of the study could have been the presence of socially desirable responses, which may have occurred from the coaches being socialised into believing that sport can and should produce PYD.

PYD is an approach to organised activities, like sport, music, and the arts, that lead to positive developmental outcomes for children and youth participants. Sport is therefore a space for PYD (i.e. competence, competence, character, connection, care) where life skills, values, leadership, goal setting, and other interpersonal and intrapersonal skills can be developed. Camiré *et al.*'s (2014) research explored how youth sport coaches learned how to implement and use PYD into their coaching. Sixteen coaches (i.e. basketball, volleyball, soccer, wrestling, and ice hockey) were purposefully selected based on being considered a 'model' coach, had an average of 12 years of coaching experience, and received coaching awards from the Quebec and Ontario (Canada) Federation of School Athletic Associations. The coaches cited drawing upon a variety of formal, non-formal, and informal learning sources to inform their use of PYD in their coaching. Formal sources included learning various aspects of PYD from professional development courses and university education coursework. Non-formal sources of learning included various conferences and seminars that presented PYD content. Within informal learning scenarios, the coaches developed their PYD repertoire by way of previous experiences, experiential learning situations, peer coaches, books, and the internet. Non-formal and informal learning scenarios were most appreciated by the coaches because they were able to make connections to the learning materials that were relevant to PYD and their coaching. Formal education situations were considered not as important and suggest the need for formal education to address relevant and learner-centered approaches to learning. A key finding from this research was that these model coaches were constantly searching and exploring learning opportunities to gain more knowledge on PYD.

While PYD is a deliberately structured approach to positive biopsychosocial outcomes for youth, researchers in the U.S. note that youth coach education is haphazard, mostly non-compulsory, and materials often fail to adequately reach the wide range of youth sport leaders (YSL). Newman *et al.*'s (2016) exploration of YSL' (coaches, administrators, camp counselors, etc. that fulfill the role of facilitating PYD through sport) 'pressing issues' provides some indication for the hot topics that implicate PYD outcomes. One hundred and nineteen YSLs completed a questionnaire to identify relevant topics, issues, and concerns experienced by them, their team, or communities. From a list of 25 issues or topics, the coaches were asked to identify the top five most pressing issues. Subsequent analysis found the top four issues were team building/teamwork, parental influence/involvement, sportsmanship, and teaching life skills. Years of experience (i.e. 1–5; 6–10; 11–20; 21–45), type of sport coach, (i.e. contact vs. non-contact), gender, team gender, and whether YSLs had coaching education experience were also analysed across the top four pressing issues. Parental issues were mainly addressed by male coaches, while female coaches were more concerned with teamwork and communication.

Teaching life skills, egos, and goal setting were more prominent in coaches with less experience. The factor of coaching education experience did not change what YSLs considered a 'hot-topic' issue. The four lowest rated issues were race/ethnicity/diversity, crisis intervention, disabilities, and LGBT. Newman *et al.* noted that despite these low rankings, issues of diversity, inclusion, and equity have been argued of central importance in coaching children and calls exist for this to be a focus in youth coach education.

## Implications for Children's Sport Coaching

Implications for organising and administering sport for children and preparing and qualifying children's sport coaches are underpinned by social issues and researchable problems identified in this chapter's review. Key issues appear to be how to effectively and efficiently prepare coaches to coach children and preventing unethical or abusive coach behaviour (Raakman *et al.*, 2010; Jacobs *et al.*, 2017). Unfortunately, much of the coach learning literature does not specifically focus on how coaches of children learn to be unethical or abusive, as the research foci have been on coaches' acquisition of positive behaviours, such as effective instruction and motivation. As youth sport has become more rationalised, commercialised, and directed by managers and coaches for their benefit (e.g. winning, profit, fame) over children's (Farrey, 2009; Jacobs *et al.*, 2017), and that there is a lack of strong qualifications to become a coach of children and engage in continuous education, researchers have focused on understanding why, what, and how coaches come to coach the way they do and how education can facilitate coach improvements in processes and children's outcomes. Based on the available research, this chapter concludes that children's sport coaches can learn to be better coaches and demonstrate more desirable actions and outcomes than lesser prepared coaches.

Quality children's sport coaches develop a philosophy based on children's enjoyment and safeguarding, mastery and task-oriented motivation, the development of fundamental movement skills and life skills, and inclusivity, while being able to problem solve and think critically about their own coaching, its effects, and how to improve all aspects of the coaching process to create a better sport experience. To develop their own self-awareness and developmental plan, children's sport coaches can appreciate and problematise how socialisation and deliberate learning affect what they think, feel, and do. Coaches should realise that their preferences for learning may not align with available opportunities and that preferences are different from actual learning. Newcomers to children's sport coach should seek out high-impact learning opportunities that include issues of philosophy (particularly axiology and ethics), safety, and legal issues, and highly essential biopsychosocial knowledge and skills (e.g. pedagogy, holistic youth development, critical thinking). Coaches should continue to engage in professional development and could become more focused in their learning by deepening and broadening their understanding of subject matter on children's mental health, strength and conditioning and nutrition, and social justice.

Because coach learning research has focused on individual or groups of coaches' acquisition of knowledge and skills or changes in cognition or behaviour, the preceding implications also focus on the individual coach as learner. However, governments, communities, and organisations should likely do more to create the structural conditions for quality children's sport coaching. Without widespread legal and regulatory processes to raise the standard of quality coaching, organisations and individuals will be left to prepare themselves. A bold and socially impactful strategy would be to develop standards for children's and youth sport coaches and use the available evidence on coach learning to design onboarding and ongoing educational requirements. Legislation and policies for systematic social improvement of children's coaches would necessitate a shift in research from 'Can coaches learn?' and 'What do coaches prefer to learn?' to 'How do newly passed laws affect coaches' learning?' and comparisons pre- and post-change across a range of biopsychosocial approaches.

## Summary, Future Directions and Future Research

Research has tended to focus on how children's sport coaches learn to coach, what these coaches' think, feel, and do while coaching, and their perceptions, preferences, and attitudes about coaching and coach education. Some countries (e.g. Canada) have legal or institutionalised requirements to coach children or youth that subsequently affects how coaches learn to coach (e.g. NCCP), whereas other countries lack or have widely variable legal requirements to coach, but social norms may induce coaches to obtain some sort of rather minimal qualification to coach. While some research argues that the efficacy or desirability of coach education programming is lacking or less than ideal, other research shows coaches support minimal educational requirements to coach (Vargas-Tonsing, 2007; Misener and Danylchuk, 2009). Several studies show how and why coaches learn in a variety of contexts, although sometimes this research also shows a lack of change in aspects of coaches' cognitions, emotions, or behaviours. Researchers have pointed to personal characteristics, culture, the timing of data collection within the scope of the season, and floor and ceiling effects to explain that lack of change (Sage 1989, Smith *et al.*, 1995; Pulido *et al.*, 2021). In today's evidence-based, accountability, neoliberal culture, there are a growing number of studies attempting to validate their learning efficacy (Eather *et al.*, 2020; Eather *et al.*, 2021). There are also a growing number of theoretically complex and longer programs to promote coach learning (Preston and Fraser-Thomas, 2018; Camiré *et al.*, 2021; Eather *et al.*, 2021). Consequently, and perhaps undesirably, the research field is saturated with learning terminologies, such as mediated, unmediated, internal, informal, non-formal, formal, structured, organic, natural, and community, amongst a backdrop of many learning theories and epistemologies. A weakness of existing research has been the focus on technical-rational instruction, generic coach reflection, and positive psychological approaches, to which there is a lack of focus on abuses of power and how this intersects with coach learning. Unpinned by the belief that youth sport participation should be safe, inclusive, and widely accessible, additional research is warranted on preventing violence towards youth (Jacobs *et al.*, 2017) and enhancing justice, equity, and diversity, with the coach's role front and center (Camiré *et al.*, 2021; Gearity and Szedlak, 2022).

## References

Banack, H.R., Bloom, G.A., and Falcão, W.R., 2012. Promoting long term athlete development in cross country skiing through competency-based coach education: A qualitative study. *International Journal of Sports Science and Coaching*, 7 (2), 301–316.

Barnett, N.P., Smoll, F.L., and Smith, R.E., 1992. Effects of enhancing coach-athlete relationships on youth sport attrition. *The Sport Psychologist*, 6 (2), 111–127.

Camiré, M., Trudel, P., and Forneris, T., 2014. Examining how model youth sport coaches learn to facilitate positive youth development. *Physical Education and Sport Pedagogy*, 19 (1), 1–17.

Camiré, M., *et al.*, 2021. Reimagining positive youth development and life skills in sport through a social justice lens. *Journal of Applied Sport Psychology*, 2 (2), 92–99.

Coatsworth, J.D., & Conroy, D.E. (2006). Enhancing the self-esteem of youth swimmers through coach training: Gender and age effects. *Psychology of Sport and Exercise*, 7 (2), 173–192.

Eather, N., *et al.*, 2020. Evaluating the impact of a coach development intervention for improving coaching practices in junior football (soccer): The "MASTER" pilot study. *Journal of Sports Sciences*, 38 (11–12), 1441–1453.

Eather, N., *et al.*, 2021. Evaluating the impact of a coach development intervention for improving coaching practices and player outcomes in netball: The MASTER coaching randomised control trial. *International Journal of Sports Science and Coaching*, 16 (3), 439–455.

Erickson, K., *et al.*, 2008. Gaining insight into actual and preferred sources of coaching knowledge. *International Journal of Sports Science and Coaching*, 3 (4), 527–538.

Falcão, W.R., Bloom, G.A., and Bennie, A., 2017. Coaches' experiences learning and applying the content of a humanistic coaching workshop in youth sport settings. *International Sport Coaching Journal*, 4 (3), 279–290.

Falcão, W.R., Bloom, G.A., and Gilbert, W.D., 2012. Coaches' perceptions of a coach training program designed to promote youth developmental outcomes. *Journal of Applied Sport Psychology*, 24 (4), 429–444.

Farrey, T., 2009. *Game on: How the pressure to win at all costs endangers youth sports, and what parents can do about it*. USA: ESPN.

Gearity, B.T. and Szedlak, C., 2022. Developing as a coach: Leadership, culture, and purpose. In: A. Turner and P. Comfort, eds. *Advanced strength and conditioning: An evidenced based approach* 2nd ed. London: Routledge, 396–408.

Gilbert, W.D., Gilbert, J.N., and Trudel, P., 2001a. Coaching strategies for youth sports part 1: Athlete behavior and athlete performance. *Journal of Physical Education, Recreation and Dance*, 72 (4), 29–33.

Gilbert, W.D., Gilbert, J.N., and Trudel, P., 2001b. Coaching strategies for youth sports part 2: Personal characteristics, parental influence, and team organisation. *Journal of Physical Education, Recreation and Dance*, 72 (5), 41–46.

Gilbert, W. and Trudel, P., 1999. An evaluation strategy for coach education programs. *Journal of Sport Behavior*, 22 (2), 234–250.

Gilbert, W.D. and Trudel, P., 2001. Learning to coach through experience: Reflection in model youth sport coaches. *Journal of Teaching in Physical Education*, 21 (1), 16–34.

Jacobs, F., Smits, F., and Knoppers, A., 2017. 'You don't realise what you see!': The institutional context of emotional abuse in elite youth sport. *Sport in Society*, 20 (1), 126–143.

Lawrason, S., *et al.*, 2019. A transformational coaching workshop for changing youth sport coaches' behaviors: A pilot intervention study. *The Sport Psychologist*, 33 (4), 304–312.

Lemyre, F., Trudel, P., and Durand-Bush, N., 2007. How youth-sport coaches learn to coach. *The Sport Psychologist*, 21 (2), 191–209.

MacDonald, D.J., Côté, J., and Deakin, J., 2010. The impact of informal coach training on the personal development of youth sport athletes. *International Journal of Sports Science and Coaching*, 5 (3), 363–372.

McCallister, S.G., Blinde, E.M. and Weiss, W.M., 2000. Teaching values and implementing philosophies: Dilemmas of the youth sport coach. *Physical Educator*, 57 (1), 35–45.

Misener, K.E. and Danylchuk, K.E., 2009. Coaches' perceptions of Canada's national coaching certification program (NCCP): Awareness and value. *International Journal of Sports Science and Coaching*, 4 (2), 233–243.

Newin, J., Bloom, G.A., and Loughead, T.M., 2008. Youth ice hockey coaches' perceptions of a team-building intervention program. *The Sport Psychologist*, 22 (1), 54–72.

Newman, T.J., *et al.*, 2016. Informing priorities for coaching education: Perspectives from youth sport leaders. *International Journal of Sports Science and Coaching*, 11 (3), 436–445.

O'Connor, D., Larkin, P., and Williams, A.M., 2017. What learning environments help improve decision-making? *Physical Education and Sport Pedagogy*, 22 (6), 647–660.

Preston, C. and Fraser-Thomas, J. 2018. Problematising the pursuit of personal development and performance success: An autoethnography of a Canadian elite youth ice hockey coach. *The Sport Psychologist*, 32 (2), 102–113.

Pulido, J.J., *et al.*, 2021. Methodological intervention with soccer coaches to improve athlete-perceived coaching competency, satisfaction with the coach, enjoyment and intention to persist. *International Journal of Sports Science and Coaching*, 16 (1), 16–26.

Raakman, E., *et al.*, 2010. The development of a typology of abusive coaching behaviours within youth sport. *International Journal of Sports Science and Coaching*, 5 (4), 503–515.

Sage, G.H., 1989. Becoming a high school coach: From playing sports to coaching. *Research Quarterly for Exercise and Sport*, 60 (1), 81–92.

Schön, D.A., 1983. *The reflective practitioner: How professionals think in action*. New York: Basic Books.

Smith, R.E., Smoll, F.L., and Barnett, N.P., 1995. Reduction of children's sport performance anxiety through social support and stress-reduction training for coaches. *Journal of Applied Developmental Psychology*, 16 (1), 125–142.

Smith, R.E., Smoll, F.L. and Cumming, S.P. 2007. Effects of a motivational climate intervention for coaches on young athletes' sport performance anxiety. *Journal of Sport and Exercise Psychology*, 29 (1), 39–59.
Smoll, F.L., *et al.*, 1993. Enhancement of children's self-esteem through social support training for youth sport coaches. *Journal of Applied Psychology*, 78 (4), 602–610.
Vargas-Tonsing, T.M., 2007. Coaches' preferences for continuing coaching education. *International Journal of Sports Science and Coaching*, 2 (1), 25–35.
Vella, S., Oades, L., and Crowe, T., 2011. The role of the coach in facilitating positive youth development: Moving from theory to practice. *Journal of Applied Sport Psychology*, 23 (1), 33–48.
Wright, T., Trudel, P., and Culver, D., 2007. Learning how to coach: The different learning situations reported by youth ice hockey coaches. *Physical Education and Sport Pedagogy*, 12 (2), 127–144.

# INDEX

Note: **Bold** page numbers refer to tables and *italic* page numbers refer to figures.